MAFIA KINGPIN

Dear Reader,

I am *not* an informant. The things you are about to read are not meant to praise my past. At one time, I was a vicious animal, consumed by greed, obsessed with power. The events in *Mafia Kingpin* may shock, anger, and repulse you. . . . My story pulls no punches, but it was not written to be sensationalistic or exploitative. The whole truth must be told for you to see the full impact of my transformation. Today I am a man who believes peace and love are stronger than violence and hate. I sincerely hope this book will be able to show the world that no matter how bad a person is now, or has been, anyone can change.

Sonny Gibson

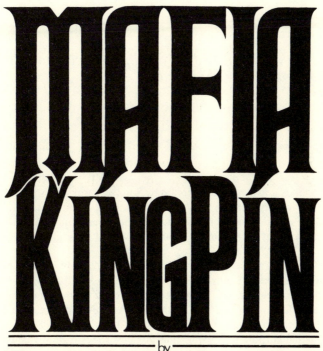

MAFIA KINGPIN

by
Reparata Mazzola & Sonny Gibson

GROSSET & DUNLAP
A FILMWAYS COMPANY
Publishers • New York

This book is dedicated to youth, convicts, and prison clergymen around the world.

This book is a first-hand description by Sonny Gibson of his life. However, most of the names of persons who participated in the events described and the institutions involved have been changed, and fictitious names have been used. Any resemblance of such names to names of actual persons is purely coincidental.

The Transcontinental Casualty Co., Ltd. and the Bank of Sark were two key entities involved in Sonny's "Big Scam." However, all names of the other corporations, companies, and businesses mentioned in this book have been changed, and fictitious names have been used. Any resemblance of such names or the name Transcontinental Casualty Co., Ltd. and the Bank of Sark to the names of actual corporations, companies, or businesses is purely coincidental.

1
Streetwise

Johnny's hand reaches over and clicks on the car radio. It crackles with static until he finally tunes in a local D.J. drawling, "It's nine-fifteen P.M., ninety-two degrees, the hottest night yet in Indianapolis for 1954. This is your Country Cousin Chickie bringin' you the best of down-home country music. Now, neighbors, lazy back and get ready for a Hank Williams tune, 'Your Cheatin' Heart.' " Just as the steel guitars begin to twang, Sonny reaches over and clicks off the radio angrily. "What the hell's wrong with you, Johnny? We're pullin' a goddam armed robbery and you're listenin' to Country Cousin Chickie!"

"I like country music!"

"Listen to it when I can't get my ass shot at. . . . Pay attention, will ya, Johnny."

"Awright, awright."

Johnny's souped up '49 Ford circles the block for the third time, headlights piercing the inky darkness. It stops across the street from Winston's Jewelers in the deserted downtown section. Johnny taps the steering wheel nervously. "Are you sure your contact's right? You sure the stuff's in there?"

His partner says coolly, "It's there. Those fences aren't meetin' to play pinochle . . . they'll be out soon." Both pairs of eyes are glued to the door of the jewelry shop. When it opens, the teenagers slide down in their seat.

Johnny peeks out the window and sees two men pull away in a car. "There's two of 'em . . . let's go in and get it now."

Sonny sits up. "Just hold on a minute. Somethin's funny. It's nine-twenty and there's been no cop car by yet . . . drive around the block."

Johnny argues hotly. "Hell no, those other guys might leave."

Sonny stares at him steadily. "It's better they leave than we get caught, I'm not takin' no chances . . . drive, Johnny."

Johnny starts the car and puts it in first. He resents being told what to do by a boy three years his junior, but he has to admit Sonny's instincts have always been right. Sure enough, as they turn the corner, a black-and-white squad car is cruising toward them. The bright lights illuminate the interior of their Ford as the cops drive on. Johnny wipes his sweaty forehead with his sleeve. "Whew, that was close . . . how in the hell'd you know they'd be there?"

"I told ya . . . I don't take no chances. I cased this neighborhood for a week. They always make their round at nine. Turn right on Capital and head back to Sixteenth." The driver follows his directions. Sonny hadn't particularly liked teaming up with Johnny . . . he was too thick. But Sonny was too young to get a license, and he needed a car. Now they park in the same spot across from the jeweler's. Two shadowy figures are still seated in the window behind the drawn shades.

Johnny is apprehensive. "Whaddya say we hit this place tomorrow night?"

Sonny snaps, "Don't be stupid! When the hell you gonna get this much stuff again in this town?"

"What's takin' so long . . . they've been in there an hour . . . old man Winston must be buyin' a ton of stuff. How'd ya know about it?"

"Some whore."

"Damn, we're smart, aren't we?"

"Shut up, Johnny . . . we gotta get ready." Sonny reaches into a brown paper bag on the seat between them and hands Johnny a can of black shoe polish. As they smear it on their faces, Johnny complains, "I hate puttin' this stuff on. Why can't we just wear the masks?"

" 'Cause it's safer this way. Put it on, Johnny. . . . And for Chrissake don't forget to talk nigger talk, will ya? Last time ya forgot."

"So what? Nobody knew it was us."

"That don't matter . . . they gotta really think we're niggers. Just do it!"

"O.K., O.K."

The jewelry shop door opens again, and the third fence comes out, leaving just a solitary silhouette in the store window. Sonny takes two Lone Ranger masks from the bag, hands one to his partner, then reaches behind him to grab a sawed-off shotgun from under a blanket in the back seat. He puts the gun under his coat. Johnny goes for the ignition key, but Sonny says sharply, "Leave it runnin'."

"Hell, no, somebody might steal my car!"

"We don't have a driver. It's too dangerous to shut the motor."

"What if the car's gone when we come out . . . where we gonna be then?"

Sonny doesn't have time to argue. He gives in reluctantly. "Awright, I still don't like it . . . but come on."

They get out of the car, and Sonny scans the street for cops while Johnny knocks on the jeweler's door. George Winston thinks one of the fences must have forgotten something, and when he opens the door a crack, Johnny kicks it open. The force knocks the frail man down to the floor. Johnny shuts the door, and Sonny puts the sawed-off shotgun in the jeweler's face. "Where's the shit, motherfucka. Don't make me blow your head off."

The terrified man trembles, but protests, "I don't know what you're talkin' about . . ." Sonny kicks him in the ribs, hard. Blood gurgles from the old man's mouth as he doubles over in pain, moaning.

Johnny panics. "Hold on . . . you'll kill him before we find out where the stuff's at." He rushes behind the counter. "It's gotta be over here someplace." The robber ransacks the shelves but finds nothing.

Sonny grabs Winston by the throat menacingly. "Guess I'm gonna have to kill your white ass, motherfucka . . ."

The old man grovels. "Wait . . . wait. Don't kill me." His shaking finger points across the room. "The jewelry is in a black cloth bag under the table."

Sonny barks, "Go git it, Amos." He squeezes the jeweler's neck until Johnny calls, "It's here," then throws the man back down to the floor.

Winston begs, "Please don't take all of 'em . . . you'll wipe me out."

"Shut up, peckerwood." Sonny picks up the sniveling man and tosses him over the display case. When Winston lands, Sonny smashes the butt of the shotgun repeatedly across the old man's face.

Johnny leaps over the counter. "What the hell you doin'? He's out—you're gonna kill him! We got the stuff . . . let's go."

Sonny turns on him maniacally, "You're not talkin' nigger talk, motherfucka! I told you to talk nigger talk!"

"O.K., O.K., man, but let's get outta here. We got the shit."

The pair rush out. As soon as they're in the car, they pull off the Lone Ranger masks. Johnny turns the ignition key but hears only the sickening grind of a dying battery. *"Shit!"* Sonny goes crazy. "You dumb son of a bitch . . . I told ya not to shut off the goddam car!" Johnny pumps the accelerator frantically, trying to get the engine to turn over. Sonny looks in the rear-view mirror. "Holy shit . . . duck!"

"What?"

"Duck!"

He pulls Johnny into the well of the front seat just as the jargon of a police radio crackles from across the street. They hear two doors slam, and in a few seconds a shout: "Call an ambulance. Old man Winston's hurt bad . . . looks like a robbery."

Johnny's shirt is soaked with perspiration. "What're we gonna do now?"

Sonny says calmly, "We only got two choices, Johnny. We're either gonna start this car or we gonna blow those cops away . . . maybe both." He takes the shotgun and wraps it in his coat, then aims it up over the back seat. "Start the car, Johnny."

"Are you crazy? I'm not gettin' up . . .."

Sonny aims the gun at him. "I said start the car." He would blow his partner's head off in a minute just for his stupidity, but he needed him right now.

Johnny is still in a panic. "O.K., I'll start it." He sits up and turns the key.

The cop snaps his head around. "Hey, you . . . what're you doin'?"

Johnny panics again. "Shit . . . they spotted us. What now?"

Sonny shouts from beneath the seat, "I'm havin' a little car trouble, officer." He warns his partner through gritted teeth, "Keep tryin' to start it."

The battery's shrill death whine jangles Johnny's nerves. "Shit . . . it's still not workin'!" He sees the cop coming toward them and whispers fiercely, "What the hell we gonna do now?"

Sonny is still cool. "Kill him." Just as he cocks the shotgun, the engine kicks over. Johnny revs it and jerks the car into first. They peel away as the officer screams, "Hey, come on . . . we got 'em!"

The policemen jump into the squad car and make a sliding U-turn to take off after the robbers. Sonny turns around and sees the red light whirling behind them. "Shut the lights!"

"What! How the hell am I supposed to drive?"

"Shut the goddam lights so they can't see the plates!" Johnny hits the switch, and the road ahead goes black. Now a piercing siren wails as the cops follow in hot pursuit. "Step on it, Johnny."

"I can't, I'm goin' sixty now." Sonny reaches over and puts his foot on the accelerator. The car takes off like a shot. Johnny screams, "Jesus Christ . . . we must be doin' eighty!" He tries to hang onto the wheel as Sonny barks, "Make a right and a left!" The Ford screeches around two corners, losing the squad car momentarily. Sonny turns. "Good . . . now pull in here. We're gettin' out." The car grinds to a halt in the pool hall parking lot. They jump out, run into the alley, and press themselves against the wall as the police car races by. Johnny holds back his head, panting. "Shit . . . that was close."

"You're an asshole, Johnny. Next time we leave the goddam car runnin', and I don't wanna hear shit outta you." Sonny starts back to the car. "Come on. Let's wipe this crap off our faces and get somethin' to eat."

They remove the shoe polish with mechanic's grease as they head over to Foster's Drive-In. In the daytime a cacophony of fifties rock and roll blasts from the parking lot of the local hangout, where teenagers strut beside their jalopies. But when Sonny and Johnny arrive, the restaurant is nearly empty. A perky carhop comes over to take their order. "Do you know what you want?"

Johnny looks her over. "You bet I do."

She says coolly, "Just stick to the menu, O.K.?"

Sonny says, "I'll have a cheeseburger, fries, and a cherry Coke."

Johnny nods. "Yeah . . . me too." By this time he has calmed down. "How much ya think we got back there?"

"I dunno, there's a coupla gold necklaces, some rings, a few bracelets—it's a big haul, probably three hundred bucks' worth."

"You got Red lined up, right?"

"Yeah, we're meetin' him downtown at nine-thirty tomorrow mornin'."

Johnny rubs his hands together. "Man, I can't wait to get my hands on the bread." He frowns. "Hey . . . maybe we better get a driver now, huh?"

Sonny nods reluctantly. "Yeah . . . I don't like splittin' the take, but it's better'n what we hadda go through tonight. I gotta find one we can trust, though."

The waitress comes over with their order. "Anything else I can get ya?"

Johnny winks. "No, but I'd sure like to get you, baby. What're ya doin' after work?"

She says frostily, "I'm goin' home, and even if I weren't, I wouldn't be out with you." The carhop holds out her hand. "That'll be $1.50."

Johnny pulls out two dollar bills with a smile. "Keep the change."

"Thanks."

Johnny watches her go as he unwraps the burger. "She's sure got a cute ass, huh, Sonny?"

"My mind's not on broads right now."

Grease from Johnny's cheeseburger dribbles down his chin. He wipes it away with his hand. "Ya know somethin', Sonny . . . you're tough for fourteen. Why'd ya have to beat up that old man so bad?"

Sonny takes a sip of his Coke. "Why not, Johnny? Some nigger'll take the rap."

"Hey, I never thought of that." Johnny smiles. "I remember when ya saved my ass in here a coupla months ago."

"Yep . . . if I hadn't taken a pipe and busted those guys in the head, you'd a got your face cut up bad."

"What made ya pull your first job, Sonny?"

"Money . . . I wanted to buy my mother a dress."

"Your mother! How old were ya?"

"Eight."

"Man, that's young. What the hell'd you do at eight years old?"

Sonny pours a mountain of salt on his fries. "In October I'd go around in a Boy Scout jacket sellin' Christmas cards at fifty cents a box. In December I told everybody the company lost their orders." He laughs. "Mosta those suckers gave me a quarter tip for bein' so honest."

"Where was this . . . not your neighborhood?"

"Hell, no . . . I did it on the rich side of the river."

"Your folks still live over in Rivertown?"

Sonny's face hardens. "Yeah . . . but I'm gonna get 'em outta that shithole someday."

Johnny dips a potato in a big glob of ketchup. It runs down his fingers while he eats. "When'd ya get into robbin'?"

Sonny looks at him. "With you, Johnny . . . when we hit that first junkyard."

"Yeah . . . I remember that." Johnny smacks the dashboard, grinning. "Damn, I never would've thought of using that bitch dog to get the watchdogs away from the fence."

"That's 'cause you didn't grow up on a farm . . . any hick knows that trick. When'd you get into crime, Johnny?"

"A while back . . . I've been pullin' armed robberies for two years. My old partner just went to the pen."

Sonny crumples his burger wrappings into a tight ball. "That's the difference between him and me, Johnny. I ain't never goin' to prison . . . I'm too smart." He tosses the garbage out the window. "Come on . . . drive me over to Old Lady Thompson's."

The older boy is surprised. "You're goin' over there again? That's the third time this week. What the hell's she see in a kid like you?"

Sonny reminds him harshly, "Ya didn't think I was such a kid with that shotgun in my hand."

"No . . . but Mrs. Thompson's thirty-three . . . she's old." Sonny grins, "Yep . . . old enough to know when she's gettin' screwed good. She pays me ten dollars."

"Aw, come on . . . she doesn't either."

"Yeah, she does."

"I don't believe it. Why would she give you ten dollars for screwin' . . . you should pay her."

Sonny smiles. "She has her reasons."

"Man, that's a real racket."

Johnny starts the car. "Three times a week, you could live pretty high doin' that alone, huh?"

Sonny answers seriously, "It takes two thousand down for a new house. I told ya I was gonna get my folks outta Rivertown someday, Johnny . . . I meant it." He stretches. "Let's go. I wanna get this over with. We got an early date with a fence."

"What time should I pick ya up?"

"Toot the horn around nine . . . I'll be ready."

The next morning Johnny's honk comes at a most inconvenient time. Sonny looks up without missing a beat. "Shit, what lousy timing." Mrs. Thompson, however, is completely oblivious of the horn . . . she's on the brink of climaxing. Sonny gives her a few more hard, fast thrusts, and she finally comes to a screaming orgasm.

When Sonny jumps off her, the woman looks up in a daze. "Where are you going in such a hurry?"

He's dressing hurriedly. "That's my ride . . . I gotta get downtown."

"The money's on the dresser, Sonny . . . my husband will be out of town on Thursday . . . can you make it?"

"Sure."

She sits up, pulling the sheet around her. "I love him, but I just wish he could make love better."

Sonny has no time for idle chatter. He picks up the ten-dollar bill and his black cloth bag. "So long . . . I'll see ya Thursday." He bounds down the steps, out of the house to the waiting car.

Johnny grins. "You don't look like ya got much sleep last night."

Sonny waves the money. "Nope, I got somethin' a lot better!" He stuffs the bill in his shirt. "Let's go. We're meetin' Red at the White Castle on Union Street."

The squatty, middle-aged fence is already in the restaurant when they arrive. Sonny apologizes. "Sorry we're late, Red."

The hard man looks up. "It's O.K. Ya got somethin' for me?" Sonny hands him the bag. "This is it . . . it's worth three hundred bucks."

The fence looks inside, then looks up. "I'll give you a hundred and twenty."

Johnny protests, "A hundred and twenty?" He looks at Sonny. "What should we do?"

Sonny is mad, but he's in a bind. "Sell . . . we can't eat it and we can't wear it." He turns to Red. "Awright, you got a deal."

The boys exchange the bag for cash and head over to Arnie's, another local hamburger joint. After they order a couple of Cokes, two sexy regulars, Carolyn and Brenda, saunter up to their table. Carolyn leans over and puts her full breasts an inch from Sonny's face. "Why don't cha introduce me to your friend, Johnny? He's cute."

"Sonny, this is my friend Carolyn. I'd watch it if I were you, partner . . . those things are deadly."

"Nothin' I can't handle, Johnny." However, Sonny is already feeling the deadly effects of Carolyn's femininity—his pants are bulging.

Johnny takes an ice cube from his glass and rubs it on his face.

"Man, it is hot! Country Cousin Chickie says it's gonna be a hundred and eight today . . . why don't we go to the swimmin' hole?" He turns to the girls. "You'd like to do that, wouldn't ya, dolls?"

Brenda protests coyly. "But we don't have any suits."

Johnny winks. "Hey, fish don't gotta wear suits . . . you two beautiful fish don't gotta wear 'em either." He takes Brenda's hand. "Come on, honey." Then he stops and looks at Sonny, who is balking at the idea. "Let's go!"

"Nah . . . I'm not goin'. I got a lotta plannin' to do for tomorrow." Sonny knows that if he stands up now, everyone will see his erection. But Johnny pulls him up from the chair. "Come on, we're celebratin' for last night." Sonny grabs a menu from a passing waitress to hold in front of him as they head out the door.

When they get to the waterhole, Johnny and the girls race down to see who makes it in the cool water first. Sonny lags behind, too hot to run, so the other three are already splashing playfully when he gets to the edge of the hole. Johnny grabs Brenda and kisses her—a promise of better things to come. Sonny is on the sidelines watching, still fully clothed. Johnny teases him. "What's the matter . . . you shy or somethin'?"

Brenda taunts, "Maybe he's afraid of the water. You some kinda chicken?"

Carolyn exposes her dripping naked breasts to coax him. "I'm waitin' for ya, Sonny. What'sa matter, don't ya wanna 'swim' with me?"

That makes Sonny give in. He takes off his shirt. "Sure I do . . . I'll make ya splash good, baby." He unzips his fly, and when he pulls down his pants, both girls gasp simultaneously. Even Johnny's mouth is agape, amazed that a fourteen year old could be so well endowed. "Shit, Sonny, when you were born, God musta thought he was passin' out socks insteada cocks . . . you got plenty for two!" A gland problem has caused Sonny's sex organ to overdevelop, making him the butt of many a cruel joke in the gym showers. Now Johnny cracks crassly, "No wonder Old Lady Thompson's payin' ya . . . hell she oughta give you a twenty!"

Sonny crooks his finger, calling Carolyn out of the water. He takes her by the hand and leads her toward the woods.

Johnny calls after them, "Hey, where are you two goin'?"

"Not far, Johnny . . . Carolyn and me are gonna take a nice long nature walk." The brunette giggles as they sink down behind the bushes.

An hour later Johnny and Brenda are sitting on the grass next to the car. Their lovemaking finished forty minutes ago. Johnny scratches his head. "How the hell can they keep that goin' so long?"

Brenda says coolly, "I don't know, but I'd like to find out. I'd love to make it with your friend."

Johnny says, annoyed, "It'll cost ya twenty bucks."

Brenda answers quickly, "I'd pay that if I had it."

"O.K. how'd ya like to make a fast twenty bucks? I know some guys at the drive-in who'd pay you to screw in the cars, and if you do it, you can have my friend for nothin'."

She looks at him suspiciously. "Oh, yeah . . . what makes you so sure?"

Johnny assures her, "He'll bang ya if I tell him . . . he needs my car. We'll go to a movie tonight, O.K.?"

"O.K."

"What about the drive-in idea?" Brenda smiles. "I could use the money . . . I'll do it."

Carolyn turned out to be such an avid nature enthusiast that Sonny decided to ask her to the drive-in movie that night. Johnny picked up Brenda, and the four of them got on the long line waiting to see the biggest smash of 1954, *On the Waterfront.*

Brenda sighs, "I can't wait to see Marlon Brando . . . he's so sexy. Don't you think so, Carrie?"

Carolyn looks over at Sonny. "Oh, I dunno. There's a guy in Indianapolis I like a lot better than him."

The car inches toward the box office window. Finally they get their tickets and pull into a space in front of the huge white screen. When the movie starts, Brenda is mesmerized by Brando. Johnny tries to get her to kiss him, but she pushes him away, saying "I wanna see Marlon . . . he's my idol."

Sonny is bored and stares out the window. The sky is particularly clear for a humid Indiana evening. Sweltering, he leans his head back, lost in thought. There's no relief from the scorching summer nights in the big city, but on the farm where he grew up, Sonny would lie out on the cool grass in their orchard when it was too hot to sleep indoors. Often his mother would join him, and together they would watch the stars twinkle, making wishes on them. Sonny spent many happy hours playing in that arbor . . . his imagination turned it into a magical forest where anything could happen. He really hated losing the farm.

Now he recalls bitterly having to leave his dog, his pony, and his freedom behind him to move to the crowded city. The first day in Indianapolis is particularly vivid in his memory. Instead of the soft chirping of birds, it was the insistent clank of machinery that was his alarm clock. Mentally he is dragging himself from his hard cot in the Gibsons' two-room shack when Carolyn nudges him. "Sonny, you're not watching the movie. Don't you like it?"

He turns, confused. "What?"

"The movie . . . you're missing it." Sonny looks through the windshield. "Oh . . . oh, yeah."

The picture on the screen is a poor waterfront section. Johnny calls back to him, "Hey, Sonny . . . that looks just like Rivertown, don't it?"

Sonny says dully, "Yeah."

Brenda comments, "I'm glad this is only a movie, cause if that was really Rivertown, it'd stink to high heaven." Carolyn says, "Anyplace would stink if it had a slaughterhouse and a bait factory."

Sonny's mind wanders again, this time to his first day at school when the kids laughed and called him "Stinky" because he reeked from the stench of those two factories on the polluted river next to his house. He remembers that his mother washed his clothes every night so they wouldn't smell. The sparsely decorated tree at Christmas was the only thing that ever obliterated the view of the huge smokestacks outside. That first Christmas Sonny gave his mother a beautiful chiffon dress. She had wanted an oven, but the dress was all he could afford with his Christmas-card money.

Carolyn puts a hand on his knee. Johnny and Brenda have just disappeared in the front seat. Sonny's date whispers, "Come on, let's have some fun, too."

Sonny complains, "I can't stand this goddam movie."

Carolyn rubs his thigh. "Well, we don't have to watch it." She puts her arms around Sonny's neck and they kiss, just as a whistle from one of the celluloid smokestacks blasts.

Sonny jumps. It sounds like the factory at Rivertown. He opens the door. "I'm gettin' outta here."

Carolyn follows him anxiously all the way to the edge of the large field at the end of the drive-in. Sonny sits on a log, sulking. She sits down too. "Did I do something wrong? Are ya mad at me? You were staring out the window so long . . . "

Sonny looks straight ahead. "Nah . . . ya didn't do nothin' wrong."

She asks quietly, "Do you like me, Sonny?"

He's still disconnected. "Yeah, I like ya."

"You know, making love was really wonderful today. Jimmy never made me feel like that in the whole year I went with him." Carolyn asks softly, "Could we go steady?"

Sonny turns. "Huh?"

"Could we go steady?"

"Oh . . . yeah, yeah, sure . . . sometime maybe we could do that."

There is a pause. "You really hate Rivertown, don't you, Sonny ."

"Wouldn't you? It stinks, it's ugly, and it's loud . . . those goddam factories never stop."

"One of the girls told me today everyone used to call you 'Stinky'."

Sonny's expression turns to ice. "Nobody calls me that anymore, Carolyn . . . nobody."

"Oh, I don't think you stink . . . I think you're nice." She says tentatively, "I'm not the first one for you, like I was for Jimmy, am I?"

"Nope."

"Who was your first girl?"

"Mrs. Arnold."

Carolyn is stunned. "You mean Tubby Arnold's mother?"

"Yeah."

"She was your girlfriend?"

"Hell, no . . . I was at her house for a Boy Scout meetin' and I hadda go to the bathroom. Old Lady Arnold saw me. She came in and locked the door behind her. I've been screwin' her ever since. I screw a lotta the kids' mothers . . . they pay me to mow their grass." He smiles. "But not the kind on the lawn."

Carolyn confesses, "I can see why they'd pay you . . . you're bigger than both my uncles put together."

He looks at her. "You're big for your age too, Carolyn, and I'm not talkin' about your height."

She blushes. "I know, that's what Jimmy told me . . . I think that's why he left. We make a good pair, you and me."

The country boy looks at this city girl. "Were you born here, Carolyn?"

She nods. "Ya got any brothers and sisters?"

"Yes, I have three sisters and three brothers. How 'bout you, Sonny . . . you have a big family?"

"Kinda . . . I have a half-brother and a half-sister, but they're a lot older'n me."

She slips her arm in his. "Are you from Indianapolis?"

"Nope . . . I grew up on a farm in Noblesville."

"That musta been nice."

He says wistfully, "Yeah, it was."

"Why'd ya move here?"

"A greedy farmer foreclosed on us cause my Pops couldn't pay the mortgage . . . there was a bad drought for two years . . . Your folks alive, Carolyn?"

"My father's dead . . . Mom takes in washing and I have to work in the five-and-dime to help feed everybody." She sighs. "It's not easy bein' poor."

Sonny smirks. "Tell me about it." He turns to her with resolve. "I'll tell ya one thing, Carolyn—if it's the last thing I do, I'm never gonna have to live in a place like Rivertown again . . . and I'm not ever gonna be poor no more."

"How are ya gonna make money?"

Sonny smiles. "Oh, I got a few ideas." He grabs her hand. "Come on, let's take a nature walk . . . in the back seat of Johnny's car."

After the movie, when Sonny sees Carolyn to her door, Johnny gets out of the car, waiting to talk to him. "I got somethin' to ask ya."

"What is it, Johnny?"

"Can ya screw Brenda for me?"

"What? What the hell you talkin' about?"

His partner hesitates. "Well . . . I told her you'd lay her if she works the drive-in and make some money for me. We'll split it, of course."

Sonny considers this a second. "Yeah, O.K., maybe we could get one of her girlfriends and start workin' her, too."

"Hey, how 'bout Carolyn?"

Sonny says quickly, "Nah . . . you don't wanna use her." He wouldn't admit that he liked this girl.

"What'sa matter with her, Sonny?"

"She's too goddam big to screw anybody."

Johnny grins. "Except you, huh?"

"Knock it off, Johnny. Where we gonna work the other girl at? Can't do 'em both at the drive-in."

"We could use my apartment."

"Don't be stupid . . . you live with your mother."

"Aaaa, my old lady's always sleepin' off a binge. Besides, she ain't gonna say nothin'—I pay the rent. When do ya wanna bang Brenda?"

Sonny smiles. "Right now . . . we'll go to your place."

A few nights later Sonny and Johnny take the girls to a carnival that's come to town. As they detour off the main drag and drive on the dirt road toward the entrance, Johnny points to a Ferris wheel making colorful neon circles in the sky. "Hey, man, look at that . . . I haven't been on one of them things since I was little."

Brenda is excited. "Me either. Can you win a stuffed teddy bear for me, Johnny?"

"Sure, Brenda."

Carolyn is excited, too. "I've always wanted one of those big stuffed tigers. Do you think you could win that, Sonny?"

He smiles confidently. "I don't see why not."

When they get to the midway, it is teeming with people. Loudmouthed men hawk games and sideshows to the customers. While Johnny stops to try and win Brenda a teddy bear, Sonny leaves for the bathroom. Using the urinal next to him is a sleazy, fat, carny con man. Eyeing Sonny's crotch, he says coolly, "You could make yourself a couple a hundred a week with that thing . . . ya interested?"

Sonny is skeptical. "How?"

"Just stick with Blackie . . . I'll show ya."

Sonny zips up his fly hastily. "You queer or somethin'?"

Blackie keeps his cool. "Nah."

"Then how do I make the money? Whadda I have to do?"

The con man's smile is oddly crooked. "Just be yourself, kid . . . Just be yourself."

Sonny is leery of this fat conniver. "That don't tell me nothin'. Whadda I have to do?"

"Just take down your pants."

"That's all? Who'd pay to see that?"

Blackie smiles. "Kid, you have two and a half times what the average man's got. I been around carnies all my life. We're gonna make money, don't worry."

Sonny agrees. "O.K., I'll do it if ya gimme twenty-five dollars now."

Blackie pats his shoulder. "You're a smart kid, but I've been livin' a lot longer than you. You'll get your money when we start workin'."

"When's that?"

Blackie thinks. "Tomorrow. The first place we'll go is the county meeting hall in Evansville."

"Ya mean we're gonna travel around?"

"Yeah . . . we can pull this off all over the country. Meet me here at five tomorrow night."

"O.K., Blackie . . . I'll see ya then."

When Sonny gets back out to the midway, Johnny is alone. "Where's the girls?"

"In the bathroom."

"Hey . . . you'll never believe what just happened to me in there. Some guy just offered to pay me two hundred a week just for showing my cock.

Johnny is amazed. "Holy shit! He's payin' ya that much just to see your cock?"

"He's takin' me around to meeting halls . . . we're goin' to Evansville tomorrow.

"What about me?"

"You can come if ya want . . . I could use a car, and we could make some money on the side pickin' pockets. I'll go with the guy by myself tomorrow to see if he's on the level." Sonny sees Brenda and Carolyn making their way through the crowd. "Here come the girls . . . let's get outta here."

Johnny kids him. "Takin' another nature walk?"

"That's right."

"Ya know, Carolyn really likes you . . . Brenda wouldn't tell her you two screwed last night."

"It don't matter what she says, as long as Brenda's ready for me when I drop Carolyn off tonight."

Johnny shakes his head. "Man, I never seen a guy that hadda have it all the time like you do."

Carolyn comes over and gives Sonny a peck on the cheek. "Are you gonna win my tiger for me?"

"Nope . . . we're goin' now. You're gonna have a real live tiger tonight, baby." He winks. "In the back seat of Johnny's car."

At midnight, when Sonny has finished with Carolyn and dropped her off at home, he walks to his partner's house a few blocks away to make love to Brenda. She's already been with Johnny, which has only whetted her sexual appetite. Brenda jumps on Sonny passionately as soon as he comes in the door, but after two hours of torrid sex she falls out, sore and exhausted. Brenda is still asleep when Sonny and Johnny leave at nine o'clock to get an early start on the day.

While most teenage boys are cruising the city in their hot rods looking for girls, these two are looking for action. They stake out places for potential hits, but either the stores are too crowded or the police are visible nearby. Eventually the pair drive over to Foster's, where they hang out until it's time for Sonny to meet Blackie.

At five o'clock Johnny drops Sonny off at the carnival entrance, where Blackie is waiting. He seems even sleazier in the daylight. "Well, kid, you about ready to start work?"

"Yeah, but this better be everything you said it is . . . and I'm expectin' to get paid tonight."

Blackie opens the door of his beige '51 Chevy coupé. "You'll make a mint, kid. People are gonna pay to see this sideshow."

The drive to Evansville takes about an hour and a half, and on the way Blackie tells Sonny what he has to do. When they arrive at the large meeting hall, it is already jammed with men. Blackie heads straight to the back and sets up a card table to begin the con game. He starts his pitch. "Awright, you guys, before we bring on the girlie show, I got somethin' extra special for ya."

A voice in the back calls out, "Come on, Blackie . . . we don't wanna see nothin'. Bring on the broads."

The carny man chews his fat cigar butt in the corner of his mouth. "You'll wanna see this. I'm gonna give you two-to-one odds that this fourteen-year-old kid standing next to me has a bigger dick than anyone in this whole county."

A voice scoffs, "Aw shit . . . he's not even a man yet." Sonny would like to throttle the overalls off that farmer, but he keeps his head.

George Peabody, president of the Evansville lodge, is interested. "Now hold on, Goober. This here could be some easy cash. Take your pickup and go get Wilbur." He turns to Blackie. "I don't know what your boy is like, but sure as shootin', he's no match for young Wilbur." George lays fifty dollars in front of Blackie. "Put this on our boy."

The con man takes the money and smiles. "Any more bets? I'll take any bet up to fifty dollars."

A line of lodge members forms, and Sonny wanders off. The two black hookers who will supply the evening's entertainment come over to him. Candy is a thin, hard-faced whore, but Ruby, the older of the pair, still has the look of an easygoing schoolgirl despite her fifteen years in the business. Ruby is the personification of a "hooker with a heart of gold."

Sonny has just found out the girls are from Chicago when Blackie calls to him, "Awright, kid. Time for the unveiling." The men have brought in their local talent, a pimply twenty-year-old, and the Legionnaires form a circle around him and Sonny. As they both unzip their flies, the farmers stare expectantly at the two crotches. Wilbur shifts uncomfortably as he drops his pants, but Sonny does it with ease. Being gawked at is nothing new for him. Since he was ten, Sonny has known he is different. He hasn't been able to wear a regular bathing suit at the public pool but needs special cutoffs to go swimming because his privates stick out. People have been staring at him ever since . . . now he is finally getting paid for it.

George Peabody had been rubbing his hands in greedy anticipation until Sonny exposes himself. He and the rest of the men can hardly believe their eyes. Sonny has a good five inches on Wilbur. No contest . . . Blackie wins hands down. Peabody shakes his head. "That's just not human . . . no sir, that's a freak there. I want my money back!"

Blackie grins as Sonny pulls up his pants. "No freak, gentlemen, just a farm boy from Noblesville whose mother fed him the right foods."

Goober shouts, "Hot damn, I wish my mother fed me them vittles!" The crowd breaks into bawdy laughter, and the two hookers move in to begin their portion of the program.

After all the men have had their fun and gone home, Ruby comes over to Sonny. "Chile, if you wanna make some real money with that thing you got, you come to Chicago with me, hear?"

Sonny's reply is quick. "Yeah? What's there? I don't need another Blackie."

"Uh-uh, honey . . . there's somethin' fine waitin' for ya. A buncha sex-starved whores who'd love the shit outta you, sugar . . . and pay top dollar for it, too!" She hands him a slip of paper. "Look up Miss Ruby when you ready to make it in the big time." She gives his crotch a pat in parting. "I'd treat that beautiful thing a whole lot better'n fat ol' Blackie."

A minute later the con man comes over counting the night's take— about $500. He peels off $50 and hands it to Sonny. "Here's an advance on your salary, kid," Blackie says as he pockets the rest of the money. "I knew it, kid. We're really gonna clean up on this circuit. People love seein' a freak . . . don't matter if it's a bearded lady or a big cock."

Sonny is unsettled by this remark but replies coolly, "For two hundred bucks a week, I'll show it to whoever ya want. I'll even stand on my head for 'em."

"You don't gotta do that, kid." Blackie smiles his crooked smile. "Just keep pullin' down your pants."

The next day, while the carnival is setting up, Sonny calls Johnny from a pay booth in a gas station nearby. "Hey, Johnny, this guy's on the level, man. I got fifty bucks last night just for showin' my cock to a buncha asshole farmers."

"Shit, that's a lotta money."

"Yeah . . . listen. The midway won't be up for a few days. I want ya to come down and get me . . . there's somethin' I gotta do in town."

Johnny hesitates. "I dunno . . . I need a new tire. I might make it there, but we'd never make it back."

Sonny says confidently, "I'll buy ya a new tire when ya get here, O.K.?"

"O.K. Hey, whaddya gotta do that's so important?"

"Don't waste time talkin', huh, Johnny . . . just get down here."

The first money Sonny got selling himself on the carny circuit went to buy his mother a new stove. He and Johnny drive all the way from downtown Indianapolis to Rivertown with the appliance in the trunk of the car. Mrs. Gibson is out when they get to the two-room shack, so the boys install it as a surprise. When she comes through the door, however, the first thing she sees is her son. Mrs. Gibson, proud of him as any mother would be, kisses him and fusses with his hair. "You really ought to get a haircut this week."

Sonny fidgets. "Aw, come on, Mom." Then he blurts out, "Hey, how about a cup of coffee?"

She looks at him questioningly. "You don't drink coffee."

"Uh . . . no, but"—Sonny shoots a look to his partner—"Johnny wants one, don't ya, Johnny?"

"Oh . . . yeah. I'm dyin' for some coffee, Mrs. Gibson."

She turns. "Well, all ri—" She stops short at the sight of the gleaming white stove. "What's this?"

Sonny puts an arm around her. "It's a present, Mom. Now you can bake."

"Where did you get money to buy this?"

He says proudly, "I earned it, Mom. Johnny and I got jobs travelin' the carny circuit workin' games on the midway. I got my first paycheck last week and bought this stove. You like it?"

She says with a break in her voice, "I love it . . . but you should be saving your money."

"Mom, I remember how you couldn't bake no cookies for me when I was little . . . I wanted you to have it."

Mrs. Gibson points to the timer on top. "Look at that!" She runs her fingers over the clock. "I've always wanted one of these new things. This has all the modern conveniences." Then she turns to him, teary-eyed. "You used your first paycheck to get me this?"

"Yep . . ."

She hugs him. "You didn't have to do that."

"Yeah, I did, Mom." He smiles. "This is nothin' compared to all the things you did for me."

"Your father will be happy to hear you boys are occupied. It's so easy at your age to get into trouble."

Sonny assures her, "Don't worry, Mom . . . I can't get into trouble this summer. I'm workin'."

Sonny and Johnny both went back to Evansville. In just two weeks Sonny became an equal partner in the con game. Blackie agreed readily to the fifty-fifty deal—he was not about to lose his star attraction. So Sonny stuck with Blackie the rest of the summer, working smokers all over the country. He called home once a week, and when he got to Mooresville, about twenty minutes outside Indianapolis proper, he paid a visit to his maternal grandmother. He was looking forward to seeing his "Mamma Rose." The sweet Sicilian woman had been his friend as a child . . . now he would make her his ally.

It is about five-thirty when Sonny rings the doorbell. Mamma Rose comes to the door in her apron and when she sees her grandson showers him with kisses, then exclaims in broken English, "Santino, my Santino. Why you no calla before you come?"

Sonny hugs her. "I wanted to surprise you, Mamma Rose." He turns to his friend. "This is Johnny."

The old lady smiles graciously. "Ah, Giovanni. I'ma happy to know you. Coma inside. You two stay for supper, eh?"

The aroma of spaghetti sauce lures him inside. "No, Mamma Rose, we can only stay a few minutes."

She stops. "Ma whatsa matter you? How long it taka to *mange* a nicea plate a shells? I no see you in such a long time, Santino."

Sonny smiles. "O.K., Mamma Rose . . . we'll stay."

"Bene, bene."

The boys follow her to the kitchen of the tiny cottage, the only place that isn't littered with laundry bags. When her husband died ten years before, Mamma Rose had insisted on living alone, supporting herself by taking in washing. When they get to the kitchen, the teenagers sit at a big table covered by a plastic flowered cloth. Mamma Rose fills a huge pot with water for the macaroni. While they wait for it to boil, she says, "You two wanna cup a coffee?"

Johnny accepts eagerly. "Yeah, that'd be great."

Sonny says, "Yeah, Mamma Rose. I only drink yours . . . it's so good."

In a few minutes she brings over two cups. When Johnny is handed his, he says, "You got any milk, ma'am?"

Mamma Rose cocks her head. "You sure you wanna milk?"

"Yeah . . . I never drink black coffee." As she walks to the refrigerator, she says to herself, "*Questi Americani sono pazzi.*" Rose takes out a small creamer and places it in front of Johnny, then turns away to check her sauce. He pours some milk into his coffee.

When he takes his first sip, Johnny gags. "What the hell kinda coffee is this?"

Sonny says sharply, "Don't use that kinda language in here. What's a matter with you? You never had espresso before?"

"Where the hell would I have it . . . Foster's? Shit, the niggers got things that taste better'n this stuff."

Sonny holds up his cup. "Hey, this is good for ya, Johnny . . . it makes ya strong."

His grandmother returns to the table, oblivious to the incident. "Santino, you mamma she's a tell me you work inna circus. Whadda you do inna circus?"

Sonny lies, "I'm an assistant there, but ya know what?" He leans in to her. "I got lucky playin' a coupla games a pool." He takes an envelope from his pocket. "I want you to give this to Mom and Pops so they can buy a new house. I wanna get 'em outta Rivertown."

Mamma Rose looks inside, then up at Sonny in concern. "*Che cosa e Santino?* How much isa inna here? Is a lotta money . . ."

"About two thousand dollars. That's how much it costs for a down payment on a house in Broadripple. Pops would be too proud to take that much money from me, but he'd take it from you."

She closes the envelope and sighs. "Ma, how I'ma gonna explain to Pops about this?"

Sonny thinks a second. "Tell him you made extra money doin' your sewin'. You coulda been sellin' that stuff for six years." His grandmother's home is filled with exquisite embroidery.

She nods. "*Si*, Santino. that'sa smart. I shoulda charge all these years insteada give away my work."

"Will you tell Mom and Pops that's where you got the money?"

Rosa smiles. "*Si*, I tella them. You such a good boy to do this for you mamma and pappa." She frowns. "But donna you gamble no more, *capisce*? You Uncle Pietro, he gambled." Her face softens. "My son was a gooda boy, too. He always bringa me nice tings. In the old country people no makea two t'ousand dollars ina ten years."

Johnny breaks in. "Where's the old country? . . . it must be pretty poor."

"Sicily, Giovanni. It is poor but it is very beautiful." Mamma Rose says wistfully, "I was very beautiful, too, when I was a young girl there.

Now"—she pats her belly— "I'ma too fat. The *doctore,* he say I gotta losea weight, Santino. Is no gooda for my heart."

Sonny jokes, "Mamma Rose, when you get skinny, then you gotta fight the men off."

She laughs. "I'ma too old for that, Santino. Besides, you grandfather isa watchin' me. He's a very jealous man." The steam rising from the big pot on the stove gets her up. "Attsa good. I putta the shells ina now. We eat soon." Sonny grabs her hand.

"Thanks, Mamma Rose, for doin' this for me."

The old lady smiles down at him." You were always my besta grandson. I givea you money to you father tomorrow."

That was the last time Sonny ever saw Mamma Rose. Two weeks later, when he called Indianapolis, his mother told him that she had died of a heart attack. Sonny tried to comfort his mother on the phone, though he knew there were no words to express the loss both of them were feeling. So he tried instead to cheer her by telling her Dayton was the last stop on the carny circuit and he would be home in time for school. He was anxious to start Cathedral High.

Sonny couldn't have cared less about getting an education, he wanted to play football . . . and play he did. As a brawny freshman he made the varsity team his first time out, winning Cathedral a trophy for the most touchdowns in the state that year. In spite of the athletic activities Johnny was still a prominent part of Sonny's life. They continued to pull armed robberies, but it was only the younger boy's methodical planning that kept them far away from the arm of the law. Sonny devised a checklist for their safety. Each jewelry shop they hit had to be in a lightly trafficked area and have a rich clientele. Any store run by a family was considered too dangerous because they'd stick together if there was trouble. Elderly owners were ideal targets. Sonny checked out the police in the area by making phony emergency calls about a man being shot. This way he could see how fast a squad car would get to the scene of the crime. It usually took about ten minutes, so Sonny planned each job to take half that time . . . his insurance against getting caught. That year the pair successfully robbed twenty stores.

When summer rolled around again, Sonny went back to work for Blackie on the carny circuit. Johnny went along, too, this time to scout pretty farm girls to bring back to pimp out in Indianapolis . . . he had three working for him already. The carnival's first stop was Akron, Ohio. A new attraction had joined the troupe . . . Madam Zoreh. Sonny's interest was immediately piqued by this pretty, dark-haired woman who told fortunes on the midway. He watched her puttering around her curtained booth while Blackie set up his Hit the Bottle game.

"Hey, Blackie, maybe you can fix it so I drop my pants for the fortune-teller, huh?"

The con man scoffs. "Forget it, kid. I worked with that one a coupla years back. No one can get under those gypsy skirts. I wouldn't mess with her anyway, if I were you. She's got some kinda powers."

Sonny grins. "Shit, Blackie . . . I got a special power of my own that gets me into any broad's pants. I'm gonna bang that one good."

"Good luck, kid."

The next afternoon Sonny hangs around the midway, watching Madam Zoreh at work. He is impressed to see only satisfied customers leave her tent. One middle-aged farmer emerges, scratching his head in amazement. "Land sake's, Addie, I don't know how she knew all them things. Let's go git Earl . . . he's been wantin' to know about his hemorrhoid condition."

The couple brush past Sonny just as he parts the beads of the fortune-teller's doorway. He grins. "Hey, Zoreh, see anything in that crystal ball a yours about you an' me makin' it?"

She gives him an icy stare. "You'd have to cross my palm with a lot of silver to find out."

"Come on, Zoreh, cut the hocus-pocus shit and meet me later . . . you won't be sorry."

Her bangle bracelets clatter as she waves him away. "Run along, kid. You're not man enough for me. Come back when you're grown up."

At that moment a tanned bricklayer taps Sonny's shoulder. "Hey, you in line or not?"

The teenager whirls around. "Hell, no! I don't believe in this shit." He crosses the midway angrily, then stops to buy a hot dog. Sonny is chomping on it, still furious, when Baghdad, the carnival midget, catches his eye. The tiny man is picking the pockets of some men, putting wallets back into the back pockets of others. Sonny finds this odd until he sees the midget going into Madam Zoreh's tent. He must supply the fortune-teller with information about her marks—Baghdad is her "magic power." Sonny has a very good use for this revelation.

That night, when Zoreh gets to her trailer, Sonny is waiting for her outside. He blocks her path, smiling lecherously. "Hey, Zoreh, why don't cha cross my lips with a kiss, huh?"

She puts her hands on her hips defiantly. "I thought I told you to grow up, kid."

Sonny toys with one of her large hoop earrings. "Ya know I'm old enough to tell everyone you're a phony. Now, you wouldn't want that out, would you?"

Zoreh's dark eyes flash. "My powers are real. They were handed down to me by my grandmother." She tosses her dark ringlets proudly.

"She was a gypsy queen."

Blackmail is surprisingly easy for Sonny, "Is that right? She hand Baghdad down to ya, too?"

I don't know what you're talking about."

Sonny moves closer, untying the string of her lacy peasant blouse. "I won't tell anyone about this, Zoreh"—he gives her bare breasts a firm squeeze—"if you're nice to me."

Zoreh is helpless as Sonny lifts her skirts and slides his hand into her panties. The gypsy heaves a sigh of surrender. "All right, all right." She pushes him back. "But not here . . . let's go into the trailer."

Sonny pinches her as they climb the steps. "We'll see who's man enough for ya now . . . won't we, bitch?"

The fortune-teller enjoyed her blackmailer so much that she invited Sonny into the trailer every night, but he tired of Zoreh soon after his conquest. He was also tired of being exhibited as a freak by Blackie, so he decided to take Ruby up on her offer to come to Chicago. Sonny and Johnny were now into prostitution. Ruby, Candy, and another black hooker made enough to keep them living comfortably. But the big money was in Sonny. Ruby sold him to whores in convention hotels and sometimes staged live sex shows for conventioneers, with Sonny as the star. Even though he enjoyed this cushy life, the sixteen-year-old was impatient to get back to school. Ruby tried hard to persuade him to stay, reasoning, "You'll make more money with your dick than your diploma," but Sonny was adamant—he wanted to play football, a passion that Ruby couldn't understand. Johnny didn't understand it either, and as badly as Sonny wanted to play ball, it was important to keep his crime partner happy, too . . . he couldn't afford to lose that second pair of eyes so critical in armed robberies. Sonny convinced Johnny that they could set up a better whorehouse in Indianapolis, and he made it home just in time for the fall semester.

A sophomore now, Sonny still couldn't read or write. In spite of this obvious shortcoming he got straight A's. Brother Reilly, Cathedral's principal, was an avid football fan and had plans for Sonny to carry the school banner on to greater glory at Notre Dame. Unfortunately, Brother Reilly died. His successor, Brother Gaudio, was a scholar, and Sonny's average took a desperate plunge.

One day in class, during a true-false history exam, Nick Loganno, who is sitting next to Sonny, slips him a sheet with the answers. After the test, Sonny stops Nick in the hall. His curiosity is aroused. "Why'd you save my ass in there?"

Nick looks up with admiration at the football star towering over him. "I like seeing Cathedral win, and they can't do that without you."

"Yeah, well they're gonna have to try . . . Brother Reilly croaked last month. He let me slide by, but this new guy . . ."

Nick shakes his head understandingly. "Yeah, Gaudio's a real ball-buster."

Sonny is surprised at Nick's crude vocabulary. This kid is small but gutsy. "You're smart. How come you don't talk like a brain? Where you from?"

"Brooklyn."

"Brooklyn? Where the hell is Brooklyn?"

Nick laughs. "New York."

"Yeah, so what're ya doin' here?"

"My grandfather sent my father here to run a big produce business for him." Nick sighs. "I sure hope we can go home soon."

"Don't cha like Indianapolis?"

The New Yorker buttons his expensive sport jacket. "Yeah, it's O.K. I just miss my grandfather." A bell rings for the next period. Nick looks at Sonny's pale complexion and light eyes. "Somebody said you were Italian. Is that right?"

"I'm half . . . my mother's Sicilian."

Nick smiles. "I'm Sicilian. Sit next to me and you'll be gettin' straight A's from now on."

The Loganno boy was right. Sonny's grades improved, and one month later he was still on the varsity team, practicing for the "big game" against the school's archrival, South Bend High.

During practice Sonny makes what appears to be an unnecessarily rough tackle. It does not go unnoticed. When a whistle ends the scrimmage, the injured player yells angrily, "What are you tryin' to prove, Gibson . . . you're some kinda animal?"

Larry Barton, the quarterback, defends Sonny. "He's provin' we can beat the pants off South Bend, and remember, we're in the finals 'cause a him . . . so lay off." The team disperses, grumbling, and Nick, who has been watching, walks over to Sonny. Before they can start talking, Coach O'Malley, a one-time all-America fullback, approaches, his face stern. "I watched you in practice today, Gibson. You just wanna crack skulls and break bones. You don't care about winning . . . I do." O'Malley's face turns scarlet as he continues his tirade. "Remember, Gibson, you've got to pass those finals tomorrow or I'll be forced to kick you off the team . . . You'd better go after those exams like you was bustin' through defensive lines. I have no pull with Gaudio." The coach shoots Nick a sharp look. "Sonny's gotta pass tomorrow, understand, Nick? We're gonna beat those bastards . . ." O'Malley stalks off.

It is the night of the championship game. The score is tied and sixteen seconds are left in the final quarter. Even the cheerleaders have put down their pom-poms, breathlessly awaiting the outcome. A touchdown will give Cathedral the team trophy they desperately want. Their quarterback has called time out. In the huddle he's bombarded with suggestions until he finally explodes, "Shut up . . . everybody! I decide the plays." He looks over at Sonny. "How 'bout it, Forty-three, got enough wind to run this one?"

Number 52 protests strongly. "Gibson's been carryin' the ball all night . . . they'll be waiting for him."

Sonny is panting hard. "Yeah . . . but they'll be expectin' us to play the ends. I'll go straight up the middle."

Number 52 is incensed. "That's plain crazy. A Sherman tank couldn't get through those guys."

Barton looks at Sonny. "Maybe a tank can't, but I think Gibson can." The quarterback buckles his helmet. "All right . . . it's Forty-three through the number-two hole on two. . . . Let's break."

The huddle dissolves into formation, and as soon as the play is called, Sonny gets the ball. He plows down the defensive line with the strength of a steamroller, exhilarated by the brute force he exerts, elbowing everyone out of his path. Sonny scores the winning touchdown, and Cathedral fans jump to their feet, roaring approval. Nick races over with the rest of the mob to congratulate the hero. When the bedlam subsides, Sonny takes off his helmet and plops it on Nick's head.

"Wow! . . . Can I keep this, Sonny?"

"It's yours, Nick. You deserve it . . . after all, you carried the ball in the classroom for me." The friends walk to the locker room, arms over each other's shoulders, proud of their achievement.

Only a few weeks after Sonny's triumphant night, however, his football career came to an untimely end. One afternoon Nick is accosted in the schoolyard by five members of the Union Street gang. He had refused to lend them money for a neighborhood crap game, and now the ruffians hurl insults at him. "Hey, wop, you tied to your mother's purse strings?"

The delinquents circle Nick as they taunt him. "Hey, wop, go home."

"Yeah, we don't want no greaseballs with golden spoons here."

"Guineas got no guts."

In spite of his slight build the Italian boy lashes out furiously at them. Instantly all five converge on him in a vicious attack. Sonny, on his way to his car, hears the commotion, and when he sees his friend in trouble, gets a baseball bat from the trunk. With a loud whoosh Sonny enters the fray, swinging his club. With one pass he cracks the skull of the bruiser who has Nick pinned to the ground, then snaps around, and with a quick left-right, sends two others reeling. The rest of the gang quickly retreats. When they are all gone, Sonny carries his wounded friend to the car and takes him to the nearest hospital.

The battle is over, but Sonny's troubles have just begun. Both he and Nick are called into the principal's office the next morning. After half an hour of questioning Brother Gaudio is fuming. His attempt to find out anything about the fight has been fruitless. Now the principal leans forward, eyes blazing, elbows spread on the desk, his tone severe. "Gibson, I'm asking you for the last time—who was involved in that fight?"

Sonny sticks to his story. "I told ya . . . it was personal. Those guys been after me for a long time."

Gaudio continues to probe for the truth. "You still maintain Nick had nothing to do with it . . . even though he's the one with his arm in a cast?"

Sonny looks directly at his interrogator. "Nick fell down some stairs. You gotta see his house, man . . . that winding staircase is a killer."

Nick remains silent throughout the exchange. The principal clasps his hands in front of him. "All right. . . . Nick, you're an A student and you have a good record here . . . you may go. But I advise you to stop associating with Gibson. He's a bad influence."

Nick starts to speak, but he's silenced by a glare from Sonny. "He said you could go, Nick . . . go, man."

Reluctantly, Nick leaves, and as soon as the glass door to the principal's office is closed, Gaudio starts to shout. "Gibson, if you want to stay in school and play ball next year, I want to know who's in that gang so I can turn them over to the police! Captain Sandler knows how to deal with hoodlums."

Sonny stares at Gaudio. "And those guys go to jail 'cause a me? Forget it. I don't know 'em."

Gaudio explodes, "You're lying, Gibson! Get out of my office. Get out of this school. Get off these grounds. If I ever see you here again, Captain Sandler will haul you off to jail personally!"

Sonny smiles slyly, provoking him further. "Does that mean I'm expelled?" Blood rushes to Gaudio's face, popping out the veins in his neck, straining his collar. He stammers in exasperation, "Gibson, you're . . . you . . . get outta my sight—just get out, get out, *get out!*"

A few minutes later Nick meets Sonny in the hall and asks him excitedly, "Why didn't you tell him? You know you had nothing to do with it . . . those guys started it. Why didn't you save yourself?"

Sonny stops abruptly and turns to him. "Nick, your grandfather wouldn't've done that. If you don't believe me, ask him someday. No way I'm tellin' 'em nothin'. I'm no stoolie." He looks his friend straight in the eyes. "And you keep your mouth shut, too, Nick . . . rats don't live long."

The next day, instead of driving to school, Sonny drove to Johnny's apartment. The older boy had four hookers working for him at the time, but when Sonny arrived back on the scene, they doubled their stable in two weeks. The pair teamed up again for armed robberies too, still using their unconventional Lone Ranger style. Often they made their exit by jumping into Johnny's car and shouting, "Hi-yo, Silver . . . away!"

The two colorful holdup men became the talk of the state. It wasn't long before they asked Nick to join them as a lookout. Sonny had finally found someone he could trust. The rich boy eagerly agreed to the job, not only because he was indebted to Sonny for saving his life and his education, but because crime gave him an excitement all his wealth couldn't provide. A few months later, however, the trio was forced to split up when Nick's family moved back to New York. Sonny and Johnny had to continue their robbery spree without him. Sonny enjoyed this work tremendously. To him, pulling off a successful job was as titillating as a night of passionate sex. He got plenty of that, too. In addition to selling himself to women and picking them up, Sonny was now going steady with Carolyn.

One night at the drive-in the usually buoyant girl is depressed. Sonny puts an arm around her. "What'sa matter, Carolyn?"

The brunette teenager looks up at him, her brown eyes filled with tears. "I went to the doctor today."

"What for? You look healthy to me."

She lowers her head, ashamed. "Sonny, I'm pregnant."

This news startles him. For some reason he's never even thought of the consequence of screwing around. "Are you sure it's my kid?"

Carolyn looks up, hurt by his implication. "Of course I'm sure. I haven't been with anybody else . . . you're my boyfriend."

"Well, how come ya never got knocked up when Jimmy was your boyfriend?"

"He had some kind of medical problem. He could never have kids."

Tentatively she says, "I found out about an abortion. It costs four hundred dollars."

This gets Sonny's attention. "Four hundred bucks! That's a lotta money."

Carolyn suggests shyly, "Maybe we should just get married."

Sonny panics. "Oh, no . . . I'm not doin' anything that stupid."

She starts to cry. "What am I gonna do if you don't marry me? I don't wanna have an abortion . . . it's a mortal sin."

Sonny holds her. He should do the right thing. It might be nice to have a son . . . but he wants to have enough money so they can all live comfortably. Sonny does have some plans to make big money soon, so he finally agrees. "O.K., Carolyn, we'll get married."

Now she shakes her head. "I don't know. Maybe I should just have an abortion."

He grabs her face. "What'sa matter with you? I said we'd get married."

"I know, but you'd be runnin' around the country with Johnny all the time, pickin' fights or whatever you two do when you're out. It wouldn't be good for the baby. You wouldn't be any kind of a father for our child."

Sonny hesitates. How could he give up working with his crime partner? "Hey, Carolyn, what am I gonna do without Johnny, huh? I mean, we work together, ya know?"

"You could get a regular job." She looks at him pleadingly. "Don't you love me?"

Sonny takes her hand. "Yeah, I love ya." He sighs. "O.K., I'll tell Johnny I'm goin' straight. We'll get the blood tests tomorrow for us to get married."

A look of combined shock and joy crosses the young girl's face as she throws her arms around his neck. "I love you, I love you . . . I'll make you happy, Sonny . . . I promise."

The next day at Foster's Sonny breaks the news of his impending marriage to Johnny, who tries hard to talk him out of it. Sonny really intends to go straight, but before he gives up crime for good, he has an idea for his biggest job yet. At sixteen Sonny is a budding criminal Einstein. He has made contact with a doctor who knows the payroll schedule of a large drugstore chain around the state. In exchange for this information he wants the boys to steal morphine jugs from the stores for him. Sonny tells Johnny about his ambitious plan over their third cherry Coke. "We're gonna hit five cities in twenty-four hours. It'll be amazin'."

His partner is incredulous. "What? Now, how we gonna do that? It takes too much time to drive, especially in these rainstorms we been havin'."

"We won't be drivin', Johnny."

"How the hell we gonna get there, then?"

Sonny grins. "We're gonna be like Superman . . . we're gonna fly."

"What the hell you talkin' about? You think you're from Krypton or somethin'." He adds snidely, "Yeah, maybe your dick is from there, come to think of it."

"Cut the crap, Johnny. Remember when we got stopped at that roadblock a couple a months ago?"

Johnny whistles. "Do I. It's a damn good thing we was comin' home from a date and not a job. We woulda gotten our asses caught for sure."

"Right . . . well, there's no roadblocks in the sky, Johnny. I been takin' flyin' lessons ever since."

The older boy chokes on his Coke. "Wha—you . . . you're gonna be a pilot?"

"Yeah, that's how we get to five cities so fast."

Johnny waves his hand negatively. "Oh, no . . . no, no. You're not flyin' me anywhere."

Sonny looks at him seriously. "I know. I made a deal with my instructor to fly us for a cut. He used to be a pilot in the air force. . . . It's all set. We're meetin' him tomorrow at a small strip outside the city."

Johnny looks at him skeptically. "Are you sure we can trust this pilot you got?" Sonny smiles.

"Johnny, I trust him like I trust myself."

The next evening at dusk the pair board a small Air Coupe parked on the deserted airfield. As Sonny closes the door, Johnny asks, "Hey, what time's the pilot gettin' here?"

"Soon."

Sonny starts the engine. His partner demands nervously, "What the hell're ya doin'? Where's the pilot?"

"Don't worry, he'll be here. Frankie said I should warm up the plane for him." They start to taxi to the runway. Johnny's head darts around, looking for the instructor, when suddenly he can feel the plane lifting off the ground. He is hysterical as the plane climbs steadily. "What the fuck you doin'!"

Sonny pats his shoulder. "Relax, Johnny, I've had sixteen hours of lessons."

This makes the older boy even more frantic.

"But you can't even read . . . how the hell can you do this?"

Sonny smiles at him. "Hey, Johnny, who says you have to read to fly?" He banks the plane right and heads for their first destination.

In one twenty-four-hour period the pair hit five cities, according to Sonny's plan. Landing at a small airport in each place, they take a cab into town, then check the local movie listings, picking only box office hits. Any couple, especially one without kids whining to go home, would be occupied inside the theater for at least four hours. Using a master ignition key, they "borrow" the couple's car, rob the drugstore, returning the car to its original location. A quick cab ride back to the airport leaves no stolen car, no evidence, no perpetrators. . . . Each operation takes forty minutes.

On the way back to Indianapolis Johnny is fairly relaxed until it starts to storm. Thunder cracks threateningly as clouds engulf the small plane. Only a skilled pilot relying on his instruments could navigate in such heavy weather. Sonny can't read those instruments, so he must fly dangerously low in order to see the railroad tracks he is following back to Indianapolis. The landscape looms up beneath them as he descends ever farther. Johnny begins screaming, "You're a fuckin' maniac! What are——"

Sonny tries to calm him. "I have to fly this low to save fuel. You wanna run out of gas? There's no gas stations up here, Johnny." The lie works, but despite his aplomb, Sonny is concerned. They have reached a complex network of tracks at a switching yard. A wrong turn could take them anywhere. He chooses the right, then, without warning, banks steeply to the left. Johnny screams, "Jesus Christ!" as Sonny just misses a water tower whose large letters spell out INDIANAPOLIS.

"Well, that's my landmark. I knew it was here someplace." Sonny points straight ahead. "There's the airport." Johnny, the color completely drained from his face, raises his eyes to heaven in thanks when they finally touch down.

All told Sonny and Johnny made $7,000 from the scheme. Sonny's half of the take gave him a substantial nest egg to start his new life. He and Carolyn got married one month later in a small Catholic church. The wedding was attended by his beaming parents and a handful of friends. Johnny was the best man. When the nuptial mass was over, well-wishers showered the couple with fistfuls of rice as they came down the church steps. Johnny did not participate in this tradition, nor did he offer any congratulations to the newlyweds. After a few snapshots were taken by Pops Gibson, Sonny escorted Carolyn to their waiting "limo," his '55 T-Bird, now garishly adorned with ribbons and streamers. When Sonny started the engine, he stuck his head out the window. "Hey, Johnny . . . Hi-yo, Silver."

There was only a sad acknowledgment. "Yeah . . . Hi-yo, Silver, Sonny." As the bridal car pulled away, tin cans rattling behind it, Johnny stood there, stonefaced. He knew he had just lost the best crime partner he'd ever have.

The honeymoon was over for Sonny almost as soon as it began. It took only one month for the novelty of married life to wear off, and the thrill of being a father wore off even more quickly. With the baby came a lot of expenses. Sonny had to hold down two jobs: carrying cement at a construction site by day and pumping gas at night. He'd lost most of the money he'd made with Johnny when a shady developer sold him a plot of land in the summer that was completely under water in the winter. Now Sonny couldn't even get the government loan he had been counting on for his house because the FHA had ruled his land unfit to build on. He and Carolyn were forced to live in a cramped one-room apartment. After the carefree life he had led with Johnny, Sonny was like a wild animal in a cage.

All these problems were compounded by his wife's constant complaining. The only time she really saw him was at dinner between his jobs, so Carolyn usually started in as soon as Sonny sat down at the table.

One night she is particularly shrewish, dropping his hamburger in front of him with a nasty remark: "I don't know what the hell happened to you. You and that horse dick a yours were excitin' before we got married, but now all you wanna do is fuck me 'til I can't walk, then go to sleep. You never take me nowhere no more."

Sonny has finally reached the boiling point. He pounds his hand on the table. "You goddam fuckin' bitch!" He takes the radio and hurls it against the wall, waking the baby . . . whose crying only aggravates his father's frustration. *"Shut up! Shut the fuck up!"* He shakes a warning fist at his cowering wife. "I've had it with that brat and your goddam harpin'. I sunk all a my money into that fuckin' lake 'cause *you* wanted a house. Shit, I had enough to start my own business. Now I gotta hold down two half-ass jobs."

Carolyn starts in again. "Well, if you hadn't a been so——"

Sonny cuts her off sharply. "Fuck you . . . fuck the kid . . . fuck everything. I gotta get to work." He storms out of the house, slamming the door on the life that has become so miserable for him.

That night is an especially hot and humid one in Indianapolis, and Country Cousin Chickie predicts the heat wave will continue. Sonny is still out of sorts from Carolyn's nagging when an old, beat-up station wagon pulls into the gas station. A boisterous, bald man gets out. "Fill her up with ethyl, kid." Sonny takes the hose and starts pumping gas into the tank. The man comes over to him. "Hey, kid, where's Leroy?"

Sonny's answer is curt. "He got fired."

"Why'd he get fired? He did a good job." There is no response this time. A minute passes, and the man is on Sonny again. "You gonna wash my windows and sweep out my car?"

Sonny grits his teeth. "I'll get to the windows in a minute."

The man persists. "You're not gonna sweep out my car? Leroy *always* swept out my car."

Sonny turns to him, trying hard to keep his head. "Look . . . I'm not your fuckin' nigger, mister. I said I'd clean your windows when I'm finished."

The crank quiets down. "Awright, awright . . . but I want my oil and air checked. You have to do that."

At this moment Johnny screeches his brand-new, bright-red Cadillac into the station. There is only one hooker with him. Johnny needs his partner back, desperately. Sonny kept the girls happy; when he left, most of them did, too. He yells to Sonny, "Hey, how 'bout goin' for a ride, huh?"

Sonny says evenly, "I can't, Johnny."

"Shit, I forgot . . . you got more important things to do."

The owner shouts across from the office. "Hey, Gibson, your old lady's on the phone again."

"Tell her I'll get back to her."

Johnny sees his opening. "Aren't you tired a goin' straight?"

Sonny looks at him evenly. "Get lost, Johnny. Can't ya see I'm workin'?"

Sonny jerks the nozzle from the gas tank, and the customer goes crazy. "Hey, stupid, watch how ya handle that hose. You're scratchin' up my fender." This is the last straw. Sonny pushes the trigger, spraying the car with gas. The man starts to shout excitedly.

"What the hell do you think you're doin', idiot!"

Sonny grabs the customer by his collar and throws him across the hood. He wraps the hose around the petrified man's neck, leaving him half-strangled.

Johnny leaps out of his car when he sees Sonny is about to toss a match at the car. He jerks back his partner's arm. "Be cool, man, you don't wanna go to the chair for that asshole."

Sonny looks down in disgust at the choking man. "You're right. This piece a shit's not worth it . . . neither is this fuckin' job." He jumps over the door of the car into the back seat.

Johnny runs around to the driver's side, whooping, "Hot damn! We're back in business."

Just then the owner comes out of the back office. At the sight of his station in chaos, he bolts over to Sonny. "Gibson, what the hell's goin' on here?"

"I just quit . . . find yourself another sucker."

Johnny revs the engine and roars out of the station, with Sonny sitting on top of the convertible's back seat.

The owner runs after them and waves an angry fist in the air. "Gibson, I'll find you . . . I'll call the police, I'll . . ."

Sonny gives him the finger. The irate man keeps on yelling long after they're gone.

That night Sonny left Carolyn, his baby, and everything he owned behind him. In the next six months he and Johnny pulled off over forty armed robberies, mostly jewelry stores in hick towns . . . but Sonny was scoring more than just money. Because of his "extra-added attraction," females flocked to him like bitches in heat. He laid at least two a night, leaving a trail of exhausted women in small burgs all over the country.

Sonny had *all* the luck in Hawkins Junction, Kentucky. The town doesn't even have a jewelry store, and since they haven't hit one in a few days, Johnny wants to get an early start. He heads for Sonny's room at eight A.M. and is about to knock on the door when he hears a woman exclaim, "Oh, Sonny, don't stop . . . ooo, it's so good. Oh . . . oh . . . oh!" At her high-pitched climax Johnny smiles—his partner is at it again. When things are finally quiet inside, he knocks on the door. It opens a few minutes later, and Johnny observes, "Shit,

Sonny, your hit-and-run average is better than Babe Ruth's."

Sonny grins, tucking in his shirt. "Man, that bitch kept me up all night. This Cora Lee sure is a hot little broad."

"Forget her. We gotta get on the road now. Come on, let's check out."

The pair have never skipped out on a motel bill—it would bring too much heat. When they get to the office, a pretty, nubile blonde is on duty. She looks up at Sonny and exclaims, "Why, Joe Johnson, I never thought I'd see you again in all my born days!" Sonny and Johnny both turn around, searching the lobby for Joe. The clerk continues, to Sonny, "You know, I've been looking all over for you." He stares at her blankly until she says impatiently, "I used to work at the Dairy Doll over in Harmonyville. Don't tell me you don't remember me after the night we had together."

Sonny stammers, "I . . . I . . . of course I remember you."

"I called that number you gave me in Indianapolis, but they said they never heard of any Joe Johnson." The clerk comes out from behind the desk. "That night at the Moonlight Motel was fun." Then she pulls him aside and tells him in an urgent whisper, "But, Joe, I'm pregnant. I need five hundred dollars for an abortion."

He says firmly, "I'm not givin' you no money. I don't even know if it's my kid!"

She starts weeping hysterically. "It's yours! I ain't been with a man since." The blonde looks up. "Here come my daddy and brother. I'm gonna tell them you don't wanna take care of me."

Sonny and Johnny turn and look across the road. A scowling older man and an enormous hulk with a shotgun are walking toward them.

Johnny pulls his partner aside. "What the hell we gonna do? The piece is in the car!"

Sonny thinks a second. "I'm gonna marry her, Johnny."

"What! Are you fuckin' crazy? Remember what happened the last time you tried to go straight. You'd go nuts in this one-horse town."

Sonny snaps, "Shut up. I know what I'm doin', Johnny. A two-dollar license is a lot cheaper than a five-hundred-dollar abortion." He adds, "That's a down payment on a car. Hell, she can have that kid for all I care."

Sonny walks back to the girl and puts his arm around her. "Honey, I love ya. I wanna get married and have that baby. I want you to give him my name, too . . . Joe, Jr." He picks a rose from the flower arrangement on the desk and presents it to her gallantly. "To the future Mrs. Johnson."

She gushes, "Oh, Joe, this is the happiest moment of my life," and rushes to the men who are now coming through the door. "Daddy, Bubber . . . I'm gonna get married." She links arms with Sonny. "This is Joe Johnson. Daddy, you will marry us, won't ya?"

Her father is the justice of the peace. He looks at Sonny suspiciously. "You love my baby, fellar?"

"Oh, I do. I can't wait to marry her."

"Good, 'cause you're gettin' married right now."

Bubber pumps Sonny's hand roughly. "You treat my sister good, and you'll like workin' with me on the farm."

The couple get married and spend a passionate honeymoon night at the familiar Moonlight Motel. As soon as the blonde falls asleep, Sonny climbs out the window to Johnny's waiting car, and they leave Hawkins Junction, Kentucky, as fast as four wheels can take them.

The pair continue to hit small towns for the next two months with excellent luck. Sonny had devised a scheme to keep the police occupied while he and Johnny rob the local jewelry store: They start a brushfire at one end of the town, and while the (usually) lone squad car goes to investigate, the Lone Ranger bandits stick up a shop at the other end.

They are using this diversion to hit George's Jewelry in Croger's Creek, Iowa. It's closing time as they burst into the store. Johnny holds the gun on the owner and his customers while Sonny empties the safe. At the sound of glass breaking Sonny whirls around to see his partner smashing a display case filled with wedding rings. As Johnny is picking them out of the fragments, Sonny barks, "Forget that cheap shit. Let's get outta here."

"Hell, no, we *need* these, man. You've been married seventeen times already!"

As the holdup men argue back and forth, the customers watch them like spectators at a tennis match. A police siren wailing in the distance settles their disagreement. Sonny rushes past Johnny. "Forget that shit . . . we'll talk about it later." At that moment the only pressing need is for a quick exit, and the pair escape out the back door.

Since Christmas is the next week, Sonny goes back to Indianapolis to see his Mom and Pops. While in town, he gets a phone call from a girl. He is used to these calls by now—and is cautious. Most of the girls who call are pregnant. He doesn't give out his number anymore, but an army of women still have it. The voice on the phone sounds slightly familiar. "Hi, Joey. Remember me from Hawkins Junction?"

Sonny panics. How did that blonde desk clerk get this number? He stammers, "Uh . . . you must have the wrong——"

She cuts in. "Oh come on, Joe. It's me—Cora Lee Atkins."

Sonny grins. She was the "hot little broad" he had the night before his shotgun wedding. "Oh yeah, yeah. Where are ya?"

"I left Kentucky and moved to Williamsville, Illinois. It's not too far from you. I work in a supermarket in this brand-new shoppin' mall.

This town is a lot bigger than Hawkins Junction. They even got a movie and a jewelry shop here."

Now Sonny is interested, but he's still wary. "Hey, you wouldn't be knocked up, would ya, Cora?"

She laughs. "Land sake's, no. My doctor says I can never get pregnant. I've been thinkin' about you a lot . . . I really wanna see you, Joe."

Sonny's mind begins to scheme. He could get laid and hit that shop in Williamsville, the same night. "I wanna see you, too, honey. I'll be up there after the first of the year."

When the crime partners arrive in Williamsville, they find Cora Lee Atkins six months pregnant. Sonny knows he's been conned, but his solution is simple: that night he gets married again. An aging country minister dressed in a frayed black gown, collar white with wear, officiates at the ceremony. Johnny, the perpetual best man, stands next to Sonny. The frail cleric bleats pompously to the empty room, "Friends and neighbors, we are gathered together in the presence of Almighty God on this sacred day to join these two young people in holy matrimony. Before we proceed, I'd like to share one of my favorite quotes about marriage from the Good Book—the King James Version, Genesis, chapter three, verse twenty-four: 'Therefore, shall a man leave his father and his mother, and shall cling unto his wife . . . and they shall be one flesh.' Now, brothers and sisters, this is——"

Sonny interrupts him loudly. "Excuse me, Reverend. That's Genesis, chapter two, verse twenty-four . . . isn't it?"

The old preacher peers over his spectacles, amazed at the correction. "Why, you're absolutely right, son. What a fantastic knowledge of the Scriptures!"

Sonny winks at Johnny, and the ceremony continues. Finally it's time for Sonny to take the marriage vows.

"Do you, Joe Johnson, take Cora Lee Atkins to be your lawfully wedded wife until death do you part?"

Sonny grins. "Sure I do."

"I now pronounce you man and wife."

Sonny lifts the bride's veil and gives her an indecent, passionate kiss. Johnny just sighs. In the vestibule of the chapel he pulls his partner aside, pretending to wish him good luck. He whispers, "Same getaway?"

"Yeah, we'll meet in the lobby after I fuck her to sleep. Be there at twelve."

At midnight exactly Sonny meets Johnny as planned. Before they leave the area, however, they hit a jewelry store in neighboring Fiona Falls. The Lone Ranger bandits speed away in a cloud of exhaust and a hearty 'Hi-yo, Silver.' A few miles down the road Sonny opens the bag of loot and finds some gold bands mixed in with the diamond rings.

"Shit, Johnny, I told ya not to bother with this cheap crap."

Johnny defends himself. "Hey, buyin' wedding rings is takin' up a lotta my time. Haven't you been married enough? Even I know it's Genesis, chapter *two*!"

Sonny reasons, "Pancho Villa did it . . . so can I."

"Yeah, but he's dead. All those naggin' wives musta killed him."

"That wasn't it, stupid. Don't you know nothin', Johnny?"

"Yeah, I know you're not gonna be so lucky someday. Cora could've had a brother with a shotgun like that broad in Hawkins Junction."

"I'll never get caught, Johnny . . . I'm too smart." A few minutes pass. Then Sonny says, "Ya know what, Johnny? I don't think I will marry these broads no more."

His partner sniggers. "I'll believe it when I see it."

Sonny rolls down the window. "It's true, Johnny. I'm tired a being a nice guy." He tosses the wedding rings out as the car roars over a hill.

There are no more marriages after that, and only a few more robberies. The risks of being killed in a holdup outweigh the profits, so Sonny devises a safer scheme that could bring them a lot of fast money. He knows every small town has a pool hall with a poker game going on in the back room; most of the players are wealthy farmers. Robbing from them would be sweet revenge for Sonny, who still remembers bitterly the rich farmer who foreclosed on his folks' farm in Indiana. Sonny's scheme is to pose as a rich kid and set up the men by losing badly. Then, allegedly to recoup his losses, he tells them he knows a "real big sucker" he can bring into the game. But the farmers must have $15,000 in cash to make the game interesting. In exchange, Sonny gets a piece of the action.

Greed prevails, as usual, and arrangements are made for a big game at Homer's Pool Hall in Maple Creek, Iowa. Because of the number of marks, Sonny and Johnny pick up two black partners for the job. The air is already thick with cigar smoke when Sonny arrives at the back room of Homer's to make sure that everything is in order. Ollie Peters, the unofficial spokesman for the group, drawls, "Well, boy, when's the ol' pigeon gonna fly into our coop?"

"Soon as I call him."

A hefty farmer of about fifty named Buford lisps through his missing front teeth, "Sooner the better. We're fixin' to give that city slicker a lickin' he'll never forget." The others mumble in agreement.

Sonny grins. "Good, I got a whole list of 'em . . . we can make a fortune. You got the cash?"

Peters throws an envelope on the table. "Right here."

"Mind if I see it?"

"Go ahead."

Sonny dumps out the money and counts it. When he's satisfied it's all there, he turns to the farmers. "You guys got any pieces on ya? This city slicker could get pretty mad . . . no tellin' what he'll do."

Peters leans in to Sonny, pats his pocket, and says in a low voice, "I got mine right here . . . that way no one's the wiser."

Buford volunteers, "I always keep mine in muh belt." He whips out his .38 proudly. "Easy to git it."

Another farmer opens an oak cabinet by the door. "This is where we store the shotguns. That fella ain't got a snowball's chance in hell against them."

Sonny smiles. "Good . . . real good."

Ollie then pulls out a wallet from his back pocket. There is a badge pinned to it. "And no need to worry 'bout the law, boy—I'm it."

Sonny gives them all a verbal pat on the back. "Well, I guess you guys got it covered. I'll call the sucker." He walks to a pay phone and dials. "Mr. Sullivan, this is Charlie. The poker game's waitin'. . . . O.K., see you in five minutes."

Exactly five minutes later two black men and Johnny (with brown shoe polish on his face) burst into the room wearing masks and carrying sawed-off shotguns. The two blacks hold their weapons on everyone as Sonny collects their pieces. "Get those guns in the cabinet, too." When he's finished, Sonny shouts abusively, "Awright, hicks, get your clothes off and toss 'em in the corner." Johnny goes through the pockets for money while Sonny puts the $15,000 cash into a sack.

When he sees this, Peters gets testy. "You tricked us, boy. You can't get away with this . . . you're messin' with the law."

Sonny whacks the rich sheriff across the face with the butt of his own gun. "Shut the fuck up, you greedy son of a bitch."

Johnny asks, "Got everything?"

Sonny nods, and his partner leaves with one of the blacks. A toot from the horn signals the other two men that everything is ready for the getaway. On the way out Sonny stops at the door to spit out his hate at the nude farmers. "It's a pleasure takin' your stinkin' money . . . stealin' is something you guys really understand."

In the months that followed, Sonny and Johnny continued pulling these cons. The mode of operation was basically the same, with one exception: their black partners were different each time. Before every hit Sonny would spread all the gun shells out on a table, insisting that each man load his own piece, for added safety. As an extra precaution he supplied the men with guns whose serial numbers had been filed off to make them untraceable.

Sonny warned Johnny strongly that you couldn't trust anybody, and he was right. One night the blacks wanted more than their fair share of the take. They wanted it all.

After a successful job at a pool hall in Boswell, Ohio, Johnny is driving with Sonny next to him, counting the money from the game they just hit. Sonny turns to Rufus and Andy, the two blacks in the back seat. "Man, we really did good tonight. This is our biggest take so far . . . $18,400."

Johnny laughs. "Yeah, I can remember the days robbin' junkyards and gettin' chicken feed."

Suddenly Sonny and Johnny feel cold steel pressing firmly against their temples. The blacks reach over and pull the pieces from the white men's shoulder holsters. Rufus grabs the shotgun on the front seat and orders Johnny, "Take the next turnoff." Johnny drives a little farther and pulls off the main road. About a mile into the woods he's told, "Stop here."

When the car rolls to a halt, Johnny is sweating; he looks over at Sonny. "You know what's happenin', man . . . we're dead."

Sonny is expressionless. Andy snarls, "Get out, honkies," then snaps at Rufus, who's holding his gun on the white men, "Walk 'em into the woods."

"Fuck, no . . . I'm killin' 'em right here." He fires his gun point-blank at Sonny, who doubles over. Johnny is petrified, convinced his partner is dead, when, without warning, Sonny straightens up, holding a .25 he had hidden in his boot. He shoots his assailant, and the wounded black man's eyes widen in amazement.

Meanwhile, Andy has turned his sawed-off shotgun on Sonny, its repeated fire reverberating through the forest like a sonic boom. Sonny fires back, and Andy falls. Johnny goes for the shotgun, takes the butt, and bashes in the black man's skull, splattering it like a melon. To finish them off Sonny puts his gun into each black's mouth and fires twice, then angrily orders Johnny, "Take this nigger shit into the woods." Numbly Johnny drags the bodies behind some trees. Sonny has made his first kill.

A half-hour later they cross the state line back into Indiana. Johnny is still visibly shaken by what has happened. Mystified, he asks, "I don't get it, man . . . how'd both those guys miss you at such close range?"

Coolly, Sonny replies, "They didn't miss me, Johnny. Empty one of those chambers." Puzzled, Johnny complies. Sonny takes a bullet and places it in Johnny's hands. He cracks it hard with the butt of his gun, and the bullet crumbles.

Johnny is stunned. "What the hell is that?"

"A plaster-of-paris bullet mixed with a little gunpowder. I painted it to look real. I did the same with the shotgun shells."

"What'd you do that for?"

Sonny turns to Johnny. "I never trust no one . . . that's why we always loaded our own guns before each job."

"So that's why you used to throw shells on the table."

They continue driving for a few more minutes before it dawns on Johnny.

"Hey . . . wait a minute! I got my gun from the same table." He starts to rant. "You mean I . . . I . . . I never had any real bullets in my gun? I could've been killed!"

Sonny narrows his eyes. "Ya would've been, Johnny, if those bullets were real."

"And that explains your ugly cowboy boots—you had the only real piece. I still can't believe it . . . all those fuckin' jobs . . . and I had an empty gun."

Sonny spots a roadside greasy spoon. "Hey, man, quit worryin' about it. . . . Come on, let's get something to eat. I'm starvin'."

He pulls the car into a gravel parking lot, lit intermittently by a flashing neon sign inviting people to "Eat at Flo's" . . . it has drawn just a few seamy patrons inside. Sonny stops at the jukebox before they sit down, and after the waitress has taken their order, his selection, "Blue Suede Shoes," comes on. He taps his fingers on the table in time to the driving beat. Johnny, upset by the murders, asks, "How can you listen to music? Don't you feel anything?"

Sonny says callously, "Pass the ketchup."

Johnny thinks Sonny is the coldest man he's ever met, then gets an idea on how to use that quality to his advantage. "You know, Sonny, you'd be a good hit man . . . we could make a lotta money doin' that. I know where to get the jobs."

Sonny looks across the table icily. "No way, Johnny . . . you just don't kill a man for nothin'. You gotta have a good reason. What I did tonight was for survival. Pass the mustard."

Johnny hands his partner the jar and changes the subject. "Man, I'll sure be glad when we get back to Indianapolis."

Sonny takes a messy bite out of his hamburger. "We're not goin' to Indianapolis, Johnny."

"What? Why not?"

"We're not goin' back till I know it's safe."

"Hey, man, it's safe now . . . those guys are dead. No one knew we was with 'em. Even if they did, they didn't know our right names."

Sonny wipes his mouth with a greasy paper napkin. "How do ya know they didn't point us out to somebody? We're not goin' back."

Johnny takes a sip of his Coke. "Well, where we goin'?"

"Florida. We can get the Indianapolis papers down there. If there's no heat, we'll go back home."

Johnny argues, "I still think it'd be safe to go back now."

Sonny points a warning finger at his partner. "I don't give a damn what you think, Johnny, I'm not takin' no chances."

Soon after their arrival in Miami, Sonny and Johnny meet a blonde hooker named Jennifer, who is the jewelry connection for high-class call girls all over the town. Sonny is using her to pick up some new prostitutes for his expanding Indianapolis operation. One day at a fancy hotel bar the three of them run into her contact, Ira Feinstein, a fiftyish, bespectacled, balding miser. Ira is flushed with excitement. "Hey, Jenny, I just got a shipment of hot diamonds from Cuba. Oy, what a deal I made." Since Ira thinks Sonny and Johnny are good friends of Jennifer's, he lets his guard down. "Wait till you see them."

They go to a secluded table in the back of the lounge, where the jeweler unlocks his attaché case and removes a black felt bag. He shakes a few of the diamonds into his palm, boasting, "They're absolutely flawless . . . perfect . . . worth about a quarter of a million on the street."

The gleam in Sonny's eyes is almost as bright as the sparkling stones. He senses Ira is an easy mark. "I know someone who'd buy this ice from you. How much you want?"

Ira blusters pompously, "I could get a hundred grand from a fence . . . no problem, but I don't want to take time to haggle. For you, since you know Jenny, seventy-five thousand cash."

"Sounds good. Come with me, I'll call my guy right now."

Sonny makes a bogus phone call to his fictitious buyer in front of Ira. Before hanging up he asks Ira, "Can you meet him in about an hour? It'll take him that long to get the money together." Ira nods eagerly, anxious to unload his haul. After a few more drinks at the bar he goes with Sonny and Johnny to make the deal.

Instead of driving to the Doral Country Club, where the buyer is allegedly staying, they head out toward the Everglades. Ira jokes to Johnny, who's at the wheel, "I forgot you boys don't know Miami. You just missed your turn."

Sonny pulls out his gun and holds it against Ira's head. "We didn't miss nothin'." He grabs the attaché case from the lap of the quaking man, who swallows hard, frozen in fear.

There is no resistance from the jeweler, only concern: "Don't hurt me, please."

"You won't get hurt if you do what you're told. Gimme the key."

Feinstein's hand shakes as he reaches into his breast pocket. "You'd better not hurt me. Jenny knows we're together."

"Fuck Jenny."

He hands Sonny the key. "I'll go to the police."

Johnny laughs. "Oh, yeah. What're ya gonna tell them—we took your stolen diamonds?"

This remark and Sonny's warning, "Open your mouth one more time and I'll blow your brains out," silence the frightened jeweler.

When they get to a deserted section of swamp, Sonny orders Feinstein out of the car and ties him to a tree. Ira starts to beg, "Please . . . don't kill me. Why are you doing this? I've got a family . . . have mercy."

The pleading irritates Sonny. He backhands Ira savagely across the face with his gun. Johnny screams, "Cool it, man. You'll kill him . . . he's old."

"So I kill him . . . that's one less rich Jew bastard." Sonny looks at the sniveling man. "Besides, I'd rather kill him than listen to him." He gives the terrified jeweler a vicious kick in the shins with the sharp point of his cowboy boot. The man yowls in pain, and Sonny shoves the barrel of his gun into Feinstein. "I thought I told you to shut up. Looks like I'm gonna have to shut you up, Jew."

But Johnny grabs his arm excitedly as Sonny cocks the gun. "Hey, man . . . he's no threat to us. Just knock him out. We'll be outta state before he comes to." Sonny hesitates a second, then whacks Ira on the back of the head; the jeweler's body drops limply forward on the tree. Sonny and Johnny get back in the car and drive north to find a fence for the hot diamonds.

They travel through the night and most of the next day, finally stopping in a sleepy little Georgia town. They crash for a few hours at a seedy motel, then get up to look for a place to eat. They find that and more at Ma Hooper's Skillet.

Instead of the usual hamburgers and fries, the teenagers order a special dinner to celebrate. Johnny polishes off the remains of a huge T-bone steak, still smacking his lips with relish. He is ecstatic about their windfall. "What a score, huh, Sonny? A hundred fuckin' diamonds." He wipes his finger across the plate, scraping up the last of his mashed potatoes, "How long ya think it'll take us to find a fence?"

Sonny leans against the back of the booth and unbuckles his belt, stuffed from the meal. "I dunno. Friendly Fred in Detroit should be right for us, but if I don't like his deal, we'll go to Chicago. We can always unload the stuff with Wachovsky." He pats the attaché case at his side. "We shouldn't have this ice more than a few days."

Johnny hasn't really been listening to Sonny. He's been watching a stacked redhead, the center of attention of a crowd near the jukebox. "Man, get a load of those knockers . . . mmmm-mmmm." The redhead's been looking them over, too, and finally she saunters over to their table. The barefoot girl's tits spill out of her halter top at Johnny's eye level.

She smiles seductively. "Hello, boys. My name's Mable."

Sonny winks at Johnny. "Looks like Mable's able . . . huh?"

"Looks that way . . ." Johnny slides over to make room in the booth. "You want somethin' to eat, honey?"

"Sure do." She bends over and rubs his thigh suggestively. "But it ain't on the menu." Mable sits down. "What's your names?"

Johnny introduces Sonny, "That's my brother Tom. I'm Bill." He whispers in her ear, "Tom's got a mental disorder . . . I'm takin' him to a hospital up north. Mosta the time he's fine, but when he's not . . ." Johnny says grimly, "we hadda chain him up at home." The girl looks across the table at Sonny, horrified. Johnny is making sure he has no competition.

Sonny ignores the talk. All he can think about is getting to the fence. He lays three dollars on the table and motions to Johnny. "Come on, we gotta get goin' "

"Nope, I'm goin' back to the motel." He looks at Mable. "I'm gonna get some sleep tonight."

She giggles and tousles his hair. "I'll tuck you in real good, curly."

Sonny tries to argue. "Man, it's a long drive."

Johnny's mad now. "Goddam it, a few hours ain't gonna make no difference. You've had plenty of good nights' sleep . . . it's my turn."

Against his better judgment Sonny gives in. "O.K., O.K. But I wanna be on the road by five."

At three A.M. Sonny jumps out of bed with a start. There is an angry rapping, and a deep, loud, southern voice booms, "I know you're in there with my baby girl. You'd better come out with your hands up . . . or I'm comin' in to git ya." Sonny grabs his gun and cracks the slats of his venetian blinds. The red light of a police car blinds him. When his eyes adjust, he sees a beer-bellied sheriff pointing his gun at Johnny's door.

Inside Mable is hollering at the top of her lungs, "Daddy, Daddy . . . help me! He's rapin' me . . . oh, he's rapin' me."

Johnny reaches over her, scrambling for his gun on the night table. In the rush he puts his foot through the blinds on the window near the bed. Just then Mable's father breaks down the door. His daughter runs to his arms, crying, "He made me do such *terrible* things, Daddy."

The sheriff aims his shotgun at Johnny's head. "You're gonnna wish your mamma never had you, boy. I'll horsewhip your Yankee hide, then make ya dig your grave 'fore I kill ya."

Sonny has been watching the drama through the keyhole of his adjoining room; he can see by the man's eyes that he means to kill Johnny. "Awright, Yankee, you're comin' with me." The teenager has been trying desperately to untangle himself from the blind, and when the sheriff yanks him off the bed, the metal slats slice Johnny's ankle. Mable starts screaming at the sight of blood. In the confusion Sonny sneaks into the room. He smashes his gun down on the sheriff's head, sending the fat man sprawling.

Johnny grabs his clothes, but Mable tugs at his arm. "Take me with you, please . . . take me with you! I hate him . . . he beats me!" She is hysterical. "I gotta get outta this one-horse town . . . kill him!"

Johnny smacks her hard across the mouth. "Fuckin' bitch!" Mable flies back against the vanity mirror, shattering it with a loud crash.

By this time the other guests in the motel have begun to stir. Sonny yells to Johnny, "Take care of his car," and runs around to the motel office. He rips the pay phone off the wall while Johnny shoots up the engine and radio of the sheriff's car. They speed away, then, sure their shots woke the whole county.

Sonny blasts his partner. "You and that barefoot bitch could've blown this whole deal!"

Johnny shouts back, "Hey . . . I never say nothin' when you're out chasin' pussy—which is a lot of the time!"

"There's more at stake now than a piece of ass, Johnny. Business and broads don't make it."

"Fuck you!"

Sonny's voice is flat and steady.

"Johnny, you ever say that to me again . . . I'll kill ya."

For twenty minutes there is a stony silence. Johnny finally breaks it. "Sonny, you're right. I don't know what I saw in that cunt."

"Yeah, she smelled worse than a French whorehouse." His tone gets more serious. "There's gonna be no more fuckin' around till we get our money . . . understand, Johnny?"

"Yeah, yeah, O.K. . . ." For the rest of the ride they talk about the killing they're going to make. When they get to Detroit, Sonny makes a call and they go directly over to Friendly Fred's.

The pawnshop is closed when Sonny and Johnny arrive at six P.M. They knock anxiously until Friendly Fred, the 350-pound owner, pulls the shade aside cautiously to check his visitors, then opens the door. "Good, you guys are on time. Louie's here already. He's all set up to look at the ice."

They follow Fred to the back room and are introduced to the fence, who's less than cordial. "Let's see the stuff."

Sonny takes the black felt bag from his attaché case and hands it to him. "No way we're takin' less than a hundred grand for this."

The gaunt man doesn't react to this cocky statement, but brings the jewels over to a table equipped with a box illuminated by high-intensity light. He then puts on special high-powered glasses to examine the stones, which are two to five carats each. Sonny stands behind him, scrutinizing his every move. When Louie finishes looking at the first diamond, he makes a notation in a small black notebook.

Sonny challenges him. "What the hell you doin'?"

The fence looks straight at him. "I'm checkin' an insurance hot list. I gotta be sure these stones aren't on it."

Satisfied with his answer, Sonny allows Louie to continue. When the appraiser is through, he hands the black felt bag of gems back to Sonny. "I'll need to check these one more time. Be back here at one A.M."

"What for? Ya just checked 'em."

"I told you, I gotta check 'em again—this time for quality. I don't have time to do that now."

Sonny doesn't like it but agrees. "All right, we'll be back at one."

When Sonny and Johnny return to the pawnshop, the street, busy as a carnival midway by day, is eerily still. Louie reexamines their stones. As Fred and Johnny look on expectantly, Sonny once again scrutinizes Louie's movements, counting each stone as it is returned to the jeweler's bag. Finally the fence removes his glasses and rubs the bridge of his nose. "They're worth the hundred grand . . . like you said."

Sonny retorts, "Bet your ass they are."

Louie stands and puts on his coat. "Meet me back here at ten tomorrow morning. Fred'll have the money."

"What the hell you talkin' about? We been here twice already."

The fence holds up a skinny hand to stop Sonny's anger. "Relax . . . relax. Fred's gotta go to the bank. He doesn't keep that kinda cash around here."

Sonny looks at the fat man. "That right, Fred?"

"That's right, kid."

"O.K., we'll be here at ten."

The next day, spirits high, Sonny and Johnny leave the hotel to make their big score. They arrive at the pawnshop just as the fire engines are leaving. A harried policeman is trying to break up a crowd of curiosity seekers. Sonny rolls down the window and shouts, "Hey, what's goin' on here?"

A short, round man answers, "Three shops burnt up . . . some guy died."

The afternoon-paper headlines identify the dead man: "LOCAL PAWNSHOP DEALER KILLED IN MYSTERIOUS FIRE: *Police hunt five in the homicide.*"

Johnny scans the story. "Holy shit, they found him tied to a chair. Louie must've killed Fred for the cash."

Sonny's jaw tightens. "We're gettin' outta here."

"No, man, let's find that fence . . . we know he's got our money."

Sonny warns, "If he killed Fred for the hundred grand, sure as hell he'd kill us for the stones."

"But there's two of us."

"Don't matter. Besides . . . we've been seen in that neighborhood . . . we're suspects. We don't need that heat." The pair split to Chicago to look up Wachovsky.

Two days later Wachovsky, a wiry pawnshop owner, is hunched over the stones intently, examining them with his jeweler's loupe. The change in Johnny's coat pocket jingles as he turns it, over and over, waiting for some word. He finally looks up at Sonny. "You said you wanted a hundred grand for these?"

"Yeah, that's what they're worth."

"You guys must be kidding. I'll give you twenty-five hundred for the lot"—he puts his jeweler's loupe away—"and that's only 'cause they're cut so well."

Sonny explodes. He jumps over the counter and throttles Wachovsky. "Motherfucker! You think we're some kinda hicks! I'm gonna choke ya till ya can't see."

The man's eyes bulge. With Sonny's hands around his throat, he can barely whisper: "They're glass . . . those stones are glass." He gasps for air. "If you don't believe me, take one and smash it . . . you can't do that to a diamond."

Sonny releases the man roughly and grabs the largest stone to perform the crucial test. Instantly the "diamond" shatters.

Johnny is aghast. "Holy shit, how can that be?"

Sonny balls up his fist in anger. "That fuckin' fence."

"Louie?"

"Louie. He pulled the old switch game on us. Remember we came back that second time?"

"Yeah . . . "

"The first time he wasn't checkin' no insurance list . . ."

Johnny is getting upset. "Whaddaya mean . . . I saw him myself."

"You're stupid, Johnny." Sonny pounds his fist on the counter. "That son of a bitch! He was sizing our stones to cut the glass ones! Louie's got our diamonds."

"No wonder he killed Fred—he's got the cash *and* the stones."

"It doesn't take a genius to figure that out, Johnny. And we could've taken the rap for that murder."

"We'd better split fast."

Before they go, Sonny looks down hatefully at Wachovsky, cowering in the corner, still gasping for air. "They're all the same, Johnny. Don't ever trust a fuckin' fence."

The best deal they could get on their glass jewels was $3,000, but

Sonny was determined to get the real diamonds back. He called the one person in Chicago he knew he could trust—his old friend Ruby. She put him in touch with Bennie, a local bookie, who told Sonny the only man powerful enough to help him recover the stones was Sam Scorzelli. Sonny recognized Scorzelli's name as the boss of the numbers rackets in Chicago. Bennie made a few phone calls, and two days later a meeting with Sam was arranged.

On the appointed day a shiny black limousine arrives with two burly men—Sonny's "escorts." His gun is taken away from him before he gets into the car. Then the bodyguards draw the window curtains and sit in jump seats opposite Sonny, their muscles tensed for action. Thirty minutes later the car passes through a pair of elaborately laced wrought-iron gates and stops in front of an imposing mansion. Sonny is told to wait in the lofty, domed foyer. A few minutes later he is summoned to meet Sam.

The bodyguards show Sonny into a spacious two-story library. The gold cherubs, lamps, and Italian statues on their pedestals seem oddly out of place among the antiques in the dark oak-paneled room. Sam Scorzelli sits in front of a wall of leatherbound books, the large wing chair almost overpowering him. A slight paunch and white hair give the fifty-five-year-old man a grandfatherly aura, but cold, penetrating dark eyes belie his benevolence. "Sit down, kid." Sonny takes a seat in a stiff, ladder-back chair opposite him. Sam continues, "I know why you're here. Since you saw Bennie, I did a lotta checkin' on you. I'm not gonna lie to you, kid. Sam Scorzelli never lies. There's no way to get the diamonds back. Forget it. It's more trouble than it's worth." Sam lights up a cigar. "I wanted to meet you, though, kid. I hear you're tough." He takes a long puff. "How'd you like to work for me?"

Sonny is guarded. "Doin' what?"

"Well, I hear you're an expert at handlin' niggers and broads. I want you to handle my niggers—my numbers runners and my broads in the whorehouses. I know you can keep 'em all in line . . . it's worth a grand a week."

Sonny studies the boss's face. "A thousand a week to bust nigger heads and watch broads?"

"Sounds easy, kid, but believe me, you're gonna earn that money. What do ya say?" Sonny hesitates, and Sam picks up on it. "If ya do good, kid, you could maybe work your way up to be a chief bodyguard someday, like Danny or Joe here." He points at one of the burly men. "Danny was about your age when he started workin' for me."

The bodyguard says proudly, "That's right, Sam. I started out as an enforcer for you in Local 441."

Sam turns back to Sonny. "See, kid, if you're good, you can move up in my organization."

A few seconds pass; then, Sonny offers Sam his hand. "You got yourself a deal. When do I start?"

"Right away. My guys'll show you around."

"Can I have my piece back now?"

"Sure. Joe . . ."

The bodyguard takes the bullets out of the gun and hands it to Sonny. "Here, kid, you're gonna need this, the neighborhood you're workin' in."

After the meeting the bodyguards escort Sonny back to the limo. On the ride into town Sonny asks, "Joe, I understand the broads and the prostitution—that's been part of my life. But what about this numbers racket? How's the game played?"

Joe explains: "Every day the niggers buy the newspaper and check the Dow Jones average on the stock page. There's five lines of numbers. They run down the last one on each line and check it against their tickets. If they're holding a three-way ticket—like a four-five-six—and that number shows up, they win. The same thing for a four-way."

"Why do you use the Dow Jones report?"

Danny supplies this information. "It's the only authentic number the bookie's got. The New York Stock Exchange isn't gonna fix their report for somebody to win a numbers bet."

"What do they win?"

Danny says, "On a three-way ticket, five hundred to one. A four-way pays twenty-two hundred to one."

"Isn't that a lot?"

Joe assures him, "No, the odds on a three-way comin' in are about one in ten thousand. On a four-way it's one in fifty thousand."

"Anybody ever hit?"

Danny smiles. "We have shills who win . . . then everybody gets excited and keeps on playin'."

Joe says seriously, "The real problem we have isn't losers, it's the cops. We gotta pay 'em off."

"Why?"

" 'Cause they can pick up our guys with their book—"

"What's that?"

"The receipts—they have to turn them in with the cash every day—that's evidence."

Sonny is amazed. "That's a big operation."

"Yeah. Sam probably makes half a million a month."

Sonny settles back comfortably. "Well, it's not any different from any other kinda gambling. You got the bookmaker, the player, and you got me—the enforcer."

Sonny was enthusiastic about his new high-paying line of work but now had the unpleasant task of splitting from Johnny. Even though they'd been together five years, it was still easy for Sonny to con him. One night, after they'd been out whoring together, they went to a diner for some coffee. Over the second cup Sonny told his partner, "You know, Johnny, I think you'd be better off without me. I can see it . . . you're a lot sharper. I'm just slowin' ya down."

Johnny agrees. "Yeah, you made a lotta stupid mistakes with that fence."

Sonny wanted to flatten him for that remark, but instead he shook Johnny's hand and said sadly, "Well, Hi-yo Silver, Johnny . . . and remember what I told you—don't ever trust a fence."

As soon as Johnny left for Indianapolis, Sonny began working his territory for Sam—a small area on Chicago's South Side. Except for the streetlights, Sonny was the only white thing in the neighborhood. Well suited to the violent life of an enforcer, he adapted quickly, even inventing a special piece of equipment to break arms and legs more efficiently. The limb of the offender was placed in a large steel loop with a handle on it; a sharp upward jerk snapped the limb like a toothpick. Another piece of equipment, the one between Sonny's legs, was equally efficient in keeping Sam's hookers in line. If a girl was suspected of holding back money, Sonny would threaten to rape her with a gigantic prophylactic coated with sandpaper. Any woman's insides would be torn to pieces. The guilty whores usually handed him the cash before he even unzipped his fly.

Sam was pleased with the resourcefulness his new recruit had shown and took full advantage of that ingenuity. Two months after Sonny started work, Sam called him in for a second meeting.

When Sonny enters the oak-paneled library of the Scorzelli mansion, Sam is seated in an overstuffed armchair. He rises and gives Sonny a hug; Sonny takes a seat in the matching armchair opposite him. Sam points to a tray on the coffee table between them. "You want some wine, kid?"

"No, thanks, Sam . . . I don't drink. It rots your brains."

Sam smiles. "You will someday. As you get older, you'll indulge . . . and this is what you should drink." He pours a burgundy stream from the cut-glass decanter into a goblet, "It's from the old country . . . it's from Sicily." Sam settles back in his chair. "I only drink one glass myself . . . too much of anything is no good, Sonny. That's what happened to my runners . . . I've been too nice. The niggers are takin' that niceness for weakness . . . So we're gonna get tough with them now." Sam circles the rim of the silver cup with his finger. "I'm losin' ten grand a month on each route . . . a hundred grand on your ten routes alone."

Sonny is impassive but is amazed to hear that this much money was being stolen. He tries to reason. "Maybe business is just off . . ."

Sam laughs, "Hell, no . . . the only time the numbers drops is the week before Christmas when everybody's buyin' kiddie cars and dolls." He says positively, "I know my niggers are stealin' . . . I want you to find out who."

Sonny then looks up. "I got an idea who it is. Five of these guys work with your hookers, pimpin' 'em on the side, and all their routes are down."

Sam goes crazy. "What! You mean my carriers are workin' with my girls?"

"That's right, Sam."

He shouts to his bodyguards angrily, "You guys know about that?"

The men shift uncomfortably. "Well, uh . . . no, Sam."

Sonny comes to their rescue. "How could those guys know that? They're white. Niggers ain't gonna tell them nothin' ." He leans forward. "I got a way to find out who's stealin', though."

"Must be all five of those guys."

"Not necessarily, Sam . . . just because they all turn their money into the main pickup point doesn't mean they're all involved."

Sam slams his glass down impatiently. "Just find out who's stealin' . . . I don't care what it takes. There's ten grand when you do."

Sonny stands. "O.K., Sam . . . but you gotta give me a free hand."

Sam nods. "I'm puttin' you in charge." The enforcer turns to go, but Sam has one final word for him. "I don't want my niggers hurt too bad." He holds up a warning finger. ". . . but I want them to learn a lesson. They can't steal from Sam Scorzelli."

As soon as Sonny hits the streets, he starts the wheels turning to find the thieves. He knows the 98th Street whorehouse is the main pickup point for the daily take and figures the runners must be in collusion with the hookers there, so he pays a visit to some of the girls. His way of getting the truth out of them is sheer genius.

Sonny waits in an upstairs bedroom for Danny, who's been sent to the docks to pick up some special equipment ordered from South America. When the bodyguard arrives, he hands the package gingerly to Sonny. "Here it is. What the hell you gonna do with this thing?"

"I'm gonna make these fuckin' broads talk. When's the doc gettin' here?" Before Danny answers, Joe and the doctor walk through the door. Sonny greets him, "Ya got the serum, Doc?"

"Right here . . ." The doctor takes a small vial of amber liquid from his bag. "It has to be administered in two minutes for it to work . . ."

Sonny turns to the bodyguards. "O.K., go get 'em."

Danny and Joe bring in three hardened whores in handcuffs. Sonny is pleasant to them at first. "Now look, girls, I know ya been stealin' money for your old men . . . I know they put ya up to it. It's best ya tell us right now who they are . . ."

The girls protest vigorously, "Somebody told you wrong sugar . . . This is a bad rap, baby."

"We ain't stealin' nothin', honey, we loves Sam."

Sonny says flatly, "O.K., you don't wanna talk . . . but you're gonna talk. *Strip!*" The girls are forced to undress. Sonny nods to the bodyguards, who strap them onto a special board he had made to restrain them. Sonny snaps, "All right, cover 'em up," and Joe sprinkles their bodies from breasts to toes with dead flies. Then Sonny unwraps his equipment . . . a glass box with a deadly tarantula crawling inside. The whites of the hookers' eyes expand wildly when Sonny removes the lid and puts the open box at their feet. Two of the girls scream and squirm as the hungry spider slowly makes his way toward them. Sonny is slicing some salami and cheese. He stuffs a big hunk of meat into his mouth. "You're gonna die, girls, unless ya tell me who's been stealin' from Sam." The end girls shout simultaneously, "It's Wanda . . . she the one. It's her . . . you tell him, Wanda."

"Tell him, Wanda. I ain't dyin' for you and your old man . . ."

The girl in the middle shouts back, "I'm gonna cut your black tits off, you goddam niggers."

Sonny turns to the men. "All right, the bitches that talked can go . . ." Danny and Joe untie the trembling hookers, who flee from the room.

Sonny stands over Wanda threateningly. "If ya don't talk, bitch, I'm gonna let the spider eat ya alive. After ya get bit, in two minutes ya die . . ."

Wanda glowers at him. "I ain't tellin' you nothin', honky."

He bends down close to her face. "First you feel a burning, then a tingling, like somebody's stickin' needles in ya. Then your stomach starts aching like it's been cut up with a bunch of razor blades. By that time you'll be beggin' me to shoot ya. . . . But I'm gonna finish my salami and watch ya die." In the meantime the tarantula has eaten the flies off her leg and is crawling up her thigh. She watches expressionlessly as the poisonous insect approaches her groin. "I guess you're gonna die, bitch." Wanda remains motionless. Sonny heads toward the door. "He's not worth it. He's just gonna be with some other cunt tomorrow night."

Outside Joe asks anxiously, "What happens now?"

"Now she's gonna die . . ."

"Maybe you'd better not do that . . ."

Sonny laughs coldly. "No . . . why not? The two other broads will tell the rest of 'em, and those nigger whores will be afraid to shit. It'll straighten everyone out."

He's interrupted by a horrifying yell. They rush inside. Wanda's face is three shades lighter. "I got bit . . . I'm bit . . . *HELP ME!*"

Sonny says dully, "Doc here can give ya a shot to save ya . . . otherwise ya got two minutes to live. Tell me who's stealin' ."

"Gimme the shot and I'll tell ya . . . I promise. Save me!"

"Nah . . . I'd rather your black ass die." He turns his back on her, "Come on, Doc, let's go."

"O.K., O.K. . . . I'll tell . . . It's Otis and Washington . . . they've been makin' me and Iris hold back on Sam . . . I didn't wanna do it. He said he'd kill me." She begs, "Don't tell him I told ya. He'll kill me . . . he'll kill me."

"Otis and Washington, huh? Thanks, Wanda." Sonny starts to go.

She panics. "My shot . . . hey, what about my shot?"

Sonny takes a beat, then says, "Oh, yeah, I forgot. Doc . . . save the fuckin' bitch."

The next day Sonny calls a meeting with his runners. He tells them they're all getting a raise, and he is throwing a party to celebrate. On that festive night fifty blacks crowd into a warehouse near a steel mill, consuming gallons of a favorite drink, Thunderbird wine and Coke. As soon as the carriers are relaxed, Sonny and the bodyguards arrive, pieces drawn, locking the doors behind them. The men sober up fast as they're being frisked.

"Hey, what's happenin', man?"

"What you doin'?"

"What's goin' on?"

A shot reverberates through the concrete building and ends the tumult. It is quiet enough to hear ice melting when Sonny starts to speak. "A couple of you niggers been stealin' from Sam. You come forward now, we'll be easy on ya . . . he don't want me to do no hurtin'. But if ya don't talk now, I'm gonna fuck ya up bad." He walks to the first man. "I'm gonna ask ya one atta time. Don't lie to me 'cause I'll know . . . I read minds."

Sonny questions each one, but every runner denies that he has cheated Sam, including Washington and Otis. Sonny stares directly at the two guilty men. "I told you fuckers I could read minds . . . I know who's stealin'. Now I'm gonna break their legs." The terrified blacks are dragged from the group and start yelling even before they're pinned to the ground. Washington points accusingly. "It was Otis, man . . . it was his idea. I was just goin' along with him."

Sonny looks down coldly. "Then I'm gonna break *your* legs for bein' so stupid." Four bodyguards hold down their ankles while Sonny uses his special tool to snap their limbs. With the crippled men lying in pain at his feet, Sonny warns the others, "From now on I'm gonna be whippin' asses . . . There's gonna be no more cheatin' on Sam."

Every night after that Sonny picked one runner at random and worked him over; twice a week he beat a hooker or two, reminding them their old man had better stay honest. Sonny's vicious reputation grew, and, because they thought he could read minds, the blacks christened him "The White Devil." Sonny's fear tactics worked well; Sam's losses decreased substantially. And Sonny was called in for a third meeting.

The Chicago boss is seated behind a massive mahogany desk as his enforcer stands before him. Sam half-smiles. "You did a good job, kid . . . my niggers are scared to death of you." The smile vanishes, "I can see why. You have eyes like ice. I know you've killed." Sonny's face is immobile. Sam gets up and crosses to a lead-paned window with a vista of his rolling estate. He surveys the land for a moment, then turns. "How'd you like to go to Cuba, kid? You like Cubans?"

"Do you?"

Sam's reply is firm. "No."

"If you don't like 'em, Sam, then they're just niggers to me."

Sam paces, his enormous pinkie ring catching the light from a nearby cherub. "You're loyal, Sonny . . . that's good." He stops. "I have a special job for you . . . a contract to kill two generals in Batista's army."

The assignment surprises Sonny. "Why am I hittin' two Cuban generals?"

Sam looks at Sonny. "You're young, kid. I'm gonna tell ya . . . but never ask again why you're makin' a hit . . . understand?" Sonny nods, and Sam starts to pace once more, collecting his thoughts as he explains. "These men stole millions from the Mafia. You see, Sonny, we helped the Cuban government—we put up hotels and casinos and brought a lot of American tourists into the country. Now Batista is cutting us out. He's afraid of Castro."

"Castro? Who's that?"

Sam smiles at his ignorance. "He's a hoodlum from the hills who's trying to overthrow Batista . . . and a lotta the Cuban people like him." Sam continues. "Now . . . these two generals were working for us. . . . Suddenly they claim they don't know anything about Batista pulling our money out of the casinos and putting it into Switzerland. . . . But we know the generals are lying . . . they're Batista's carriers." He stops and looks at Sonny. "So we have to kill 'em . . . to scare Batista back to workin' with us." He heaves a sigh. "It's my responsibility . . . I got the Mafia involved in Cuba . . ."

Sonny looks at Sam questioningly. "Does that mean I'm Mafia, too, if I make this hit?"

Sam laughs. "No . . . Sonny . . . it takes more than a hit to be Mafia. You know nothing of the Sicilian ways." He says solemnly, "But the guys around the country will respect you for this hit. It'll open the door . . . if you wanna be in someday."

Sonny files that idea away for the future and gets down to brass tacks for the present. "O.K. . . . so I hit these guys. What's in it for me?"

"More territory."

"How much?"

"Three times as much."

This promise gets him more interested, "O.K. What do I do?"

"You'll have two partners in the hit . . . a Brownsville torpedo and a Sicilian. They'll tell you everything." He puts a fatherly arm around Sonny. "You're smart, kid, but do me a favor. I want you to trust these men completely. They're soldiers for the Mafia, and you'll learn a lot from them . . . they're professionals." Without hesitation Sonny replies, "Whatever you say, Sam."

The two professionals were an odd couple of organized crime. Eddie, from Brownsville, Illinois, a slovenly six-foot-four bruiser, could not have been more a diametric opposite of Franco, a diminutive Sicilian with distinguished good looks and impeccable taste, but their common denominator was soon obvious . . . both were consummate craftsmen. The trio rehearsed the minute details of their hits for ten days. The first general would be killed on his way home from his routine visit to a Cuban whorehouse. The men studied films of him walking down the dark street to be certain of their positions. The three would come from different directions but fire from the same angle, guaranteeing a hit. The second general would be invited to their hotel suite and presented with a gift. While he opened it, Sonny would shoot his bodyguard, then Eddie and Franco would take care of the mark. Sonny, the last to leave, would put three final slugs through the general's head as insurance. The team pored over blueprints of the hotel's escape routes and practiced the hit for hours so that no one would be caught in the crossfire. Sonny was getting a comprehensive crash course in assassination. They showed him how to use silencers. Franco even taught him how to kill so that the victim couldn't yell even if a bullet was fired directly into his heart. With 80 percent of your palm over the mouth and your index finger crushing the nostrils down to prevent snorting, it is impossible for a victim to make any kind of sound that might attract a guard outside . . . a dead man has enough wind to sputter and choke for at least ten seconds. By the tenth day, their final runthroughs were letter perfect. The professionals were satisfied that the novice was ready for the kill.

Castro's guerrillas and Batista's army were fighting fiercely in the hills when the three arrived. American travel to Cuba was highly restricted, but customs officials believed the threesome to be steel executives in the country to discuss new oil refineries. The marked generals also believed the men were there to discuss "business." Eddie had some papers that were supposed to help Batista get his money out of the country. The morning after their arrival the first hit was made, exactly according to plan. The second was scheduled for the following afternoon. The two professionals wanted to keep a close watch on Sonny that night, but the raging sexual bull was looking for action. He went with Franco and Eddie to the hotel bar, hoping he'd find some.

The ceiling fan turning lazily above hardly stirs the air of the dimly lit lounge as the two hit men sip their wine. Sonny and a blonde in the corner have been giving each other the eye, but her boisterous husband, returning from the bathroom, puts an end to their visual seduction. Sonny turns back to his partners, who are speaking in Sicilian. "Hey . . . what're you guys talkin' about?"

Eddie answers, "Broads . . ."

Sonny nods to a woman coming through the door. "Here comes one right now I'd like to ram."

"That's Juanita, Cuba's most valuable whore. She's our contact."

The sinewy, dark-haired beauty sits down at their table, her Latin face telegraphing urgency. She looks questioningly at Sonny. Eddie assures her, "It's O.K., he's one of us."

She speaks quickly, "Batista is trying to get a shipment of gold to Switzerland . . . it's being loaded on the *Mare Donna* tomorrow, but the freighter will be in the harbor for a week. It's heavily guarded. Felipe has the plans of the ship and the schedule of sentry watches for you. He's waiting in the *cantina* across the street." Juanita says with concern, "I hope you can stop that shipment. Castro needs the money for the cause."

Eddie tosses twenty pesos on the table. "We've gotta go talk to Felipe. . . . See you tomorrow afternoon, like we planned, Sonny." The hit men hurry out, and Juanita gets up to leave, too. Sonny stops her, "What's the cause?"

She looks down at him fiercely. "Saving the Cuban people from Batista. You Italians kill for money, you wouldn't understand."

"I understand one thing, these hits aren't costing you a dime."

This infuriates her. "Nothing's free . . . Castro's paying plenty for your services."

Sonny says casually, "After he gets in power, he'll be as bad as Batista."

Her eyes narrow. "Never . . . Castro is one of us."

She glares at Sonny, who tries to smooth things over. "Hey, you're a beautiful woman . . . why are we talkin' about politics? Why don't ya have a drink? My name's Larry." Juanita hesitates. "Come on, honey. What's one drink?"

She stares at his a second, then sits. The huge rattan fan chair makes her looks regal, queen of more than a local whorehouse. The waiter appears, and Juanita orders a bourbon. She looks curiously at Sonny. "You look very young to be in your line of work."

Sonny sips his orange juice. "Ya don't look worn out enough to be in yours."

She smiles and raises her glass. "Touché."

Sonny doesn't understand her remark. "You talk kinda funny for a prostitute, and you speak good English for a Cuban."

Juanita's smile fades. "I didn't always sell myself for a living. I'm a doctor . . . a gynecologist."

"You're a doctor? How'd you end up running a whorehouse?"

"I lost my job as a professor at the university for speaking out against Batista."

"Ya got kicked out just cause ya said something bad about him?"

She motions to the waiter for a refill. "No, they warned me first . . . the soldiers told me not to demonstrate with Castro sympathizers. They raped me to make sure I understood." She drains her glass. "I was fired the next day for engaging in immoral acts on campus. So . . . I decided to live up to my sinful reputation. It was the only way I could make a living." A waiter brings her another bourbon. "Now I help the whores . . . I keep them free from VD and give them abortions." She downs the glass in one gulp and looks straight at Sonny. "I love women now."

"You're a lesbian?"

Juanita nods. "I hate men. I only fuck for the cause."

Sonny's surprised. "You shouldn't hate all men 'cause a few guys raped ya."

She laughs cynically. "Why not? They're all the same, and none of them knows how to make love."

Sonny moves his chair closer to hers. He takes her hand and puts it on his bulge. "That's not even hard yet . . . I think it might change your mind."

The Cuban's eyes widen slightly but still reflect doubt. "I don't think so, but you could try." She smiles. "Wouldn't you like to try?"

Sonny grins. "Fuck, yeah."

After a night of incredible sex Juanita concedes that Sonny is a man who's an exception to her rule . . . no one has made her feel such passion. They make arrangements to meet that evening, and Sonny takes the morning off to play tourist. Arriving back at the hotel, he is greeted by Juanita. Her nonchalant walk cannot conceal the alarm in her eyes. She kisses him and whispers urgently, "Don't ask any questions . . . get in my car *quickly*."

During the ride to her place she reveals that the second hit has already been made. Through her contacts Juanita has learned that Batista's police are after Sonny. "Why are they after me?"

"They got an anonymous phone call informing them that you were paid by the Chicago Mafia."

"Mafia! I'm no Mafia."

Juanita continues, "The caller said you were staying at the Hotel Americana. The gun next to the body had your fingerprints on it. Your passport was there, too."

"*My* prints?" Sonny thinks for a second, then pounds his hand on the dashboard. "Damn . . . so that's why Eddie handed me his gun last night. There was nothing wrong with the chamber. That's how they got my prints. Those bastards! I trust 'em like a fence."

Juanita is puzzled. "Like a fence?"

"Never mind, I'll tell you later."

For the next few days Sonny is obsessed with killing Eddie and Franco. Juanita helps him plan his revenge, knowing he could not survive if he went out searching for them alone. It was hard enough for an American to be inconspicuous in Havana, but a police sketch of Sonny was being circulated all over the city. Juanita tracks the hit men down through her hooker friends. Eddie is hiding out in a shack on the beach. Sonny pays him a surprise visit one night and blows his brains out . . . he never did care much for Eddie. It was harder with Franco. Sonny had become close to the amiable older man, who told glowing tales of life in Sicily and the time-honored loyalties of Mafia tradition.

Juanita sets up Franco for Sonny by arranging a tryst at the Hotel Havana with one of her hookers. At the climax of the Sicilian's passion Sonny bursts into the room, his gun drawn. Franco leaps from the bed, straight into the barrel of Sonny's gun. "Don't move a fuckin' muscle." Franco's face registers the astonishment of a man who's seen a ghost. Surely Batista's notorious kangaroo courts would have made Sonny a firing squad victim by now. Sonny goes for Franco's piece hidden under the pillow and orders the shaking, naked man into a corner. A nod from Sonny dismisses the hooker.

The Sicilian pleadingly explains, "Look, Sonny . . . believe me . . . I had nothing to do with setting you up."

Sonny cocks his gun. "Who ordered it?" Franco is silent. "If ya don't tell me, I'll kill ya. If ya do, I'll let ya go. I'm gonna count to five."

Before Sonny reaches three, Franco blurts out, "Sam!"

Sonny says, in stunned disbelief, "You're dead. Why would Sam wanna kill me?"

Franco explains in a rush, "Sam thinks you're too rough on his niggers—he's losin' too many of his runners."

Sonny is convinced Franco is telling the truth. The Sicilian hit man could not know about Sonny's violent methods as an enforcer unless he had been told by Eddie . . . or by Sam himself. Beads of sweat crown Franco's forehead. To relax him Sonny slowly lowers his gun. "Everything's all right, man. I believe ya . . . go ahead and sit down." Franco, swept with relief, turns to sit on the edge of the bed. At that moment Sonny raises his gun with the swiftness of a cheetah and shoots Franco in the face. The impact throws Franco's body across the room. Sonny looks down at the once-distinguished features, now a bloody mass, without remorse. "Shit, and Sam said you were a professional."

Cuba is now equally split between Castro sympathizers and Batista loyalists. The police are still after Sonny, so he hides out at Juanita's until it's safe to leave the country. During his stay, Juanita's house is busier than Grand Central Station. Her twenty-five hookers are in awe of Sonny, not only for his magnificent manhood but also for his skill in using it. For all his sexual prowess, however, Juanita is the one who teaches Sonny the things he needs to know about pleasing a woman.

His introduction to her course comes one night while Sonny and Juanita are taking a break from a marathon of making love. He is sitting up in bed, eating grapes; she is lying next to him, deep in thought. Outside gunfire of the guerrilla war still rings out in the night. Sonny nudges his lover. "That go on all the time? Don't they ever quit?"

Juanita doesn't respond . . . sex, not politics, is on her mind. After a few moments she sits up and turns to Sonny. "Santino, you are the best lover I've ever had." He smiles confidently as she goes on. ". . . but you know nothing about making love."

Sonny puffs up indignantly. "What do you mean? I've been fuckin' since I was thirteen . . . I know *everything* about making love!"

She tells him softly, "There is more to sex than just mounting a woman. What about stimulation?"

Sonny looks at her, bewildered. "What the hell is that?"

"Teasing a woman, playing around, arousing her . . ."

Sonny is impatient. "Playing around? What for? Women wanna fuck . . . we fuck. You must like it . . . you saved my life."

She tries to reason. "Some women can't take you. Wouldn't you like to relax them enough so you wouldn't have such a hard time?"

Sonny is uncompromising. "Nah, I just pass on those broads."

Juanita is determined to get her point across. "I want you to go down on me."

Sonny looks at her blankly. When Juanita gives a graphic description, he jumps out of bed, outraged. "I certainly won't do that . . . Nobody does that in the Midwest . . . it's perverted. I'd rather fuck a cow!"

Juanita laughs as he declares emphatically, "No way I'm doin' what you said . . . you get diseases that way. I won't even drink out of somebody's cup." Juanita is persistent. Suddenly Sonny realizes he has to keep her happy; she is his ticket out of Cuba. "O.K., I'll try it." He grabs her thighs roughly and dives into her crotch. She wiggles away from him. Sonny looks up. "What'sa matter? I'm doin' just like you said . . ."

"You must be gentle with a woman, Santino . . . it's more excit-ing." She pulls him up on top of her. "Now kiss me . . . we'll go on from there." Under Juanita's expert guidance, Sonny's lips slowly work their way down her voluptuous body, past her nipples and belly to her most sensitive erogenous zone. His tongue is clumsy in his attempts to please her. Finally she taps him on the head. "No, no, Santino . . . it's not right. I must teach you." That night she does.

As the weeks pass, Sonny's erotic education continues. Juanita is a patient teacher, Sonny an eager student, and the hookers more than willing experimental subjects. Every day a long line of them is outside Juanita's classroom door, waiting for Sonny to start his gynecology lesson. They sit in wet anticipation as the screams of pleasure come from within. Now it is Carolina's turn with Sonny. "That's it, that's it . . . don't stop . . . oh, yes, yes . . . OMIGOD . . . I'M COMING!!!" The girl's body shakes for thirty seconds before it finally goes limp. Sonny looks over to Juanita for approval. She nods to him. "Very good, Santino . . . much better." Then to the girl, still in the aftershock of her orgasm, "You can go now, Carolina . . ."

As soon as she's gone, Sonny asks, "Why'd she come faster than the last one, Juanita?"

The doctor launches into her lecture. "This time you did exactly what I taught you . . . you used your finger to stimulate her spinal nerve. Remember I told you there are four main nerves that come from the clitoris and pass through the vagina to the spine? With practice you'll be able to identify each one and see which is the most sensitive for the woman you're with." She fixes his hair affectionately. "You're also much gentler . . . you've learned how to apply pressure at just the right time. You're keeping a steadier rhythm now, too." She smiles. "In a few weeks you'll be able to make a woman climax in two minutes from the time your tongue touches her."

Sonny pulls a towel around his waist. "That'll be great. The faster they come, the sooner I can fuck 'em, right?"

"That's right, Santino. When a woman has a clitoral orgasm, her vagina muscles relax. She opens up, and that makes it easier for you to penetrate her."

Sonny grins. "What are we waitin' for, then? Bring in the next one . . . let's keep practicin'."

Juanita shakes her head. "Not yet, Santino . . . there is one more thing I want to tell you now."

Sonny sighs impatiently. "What the fuck else is there to know?"

"You should know about a woman's fantasies."

"Fantasies . . . what kind of fantasies? You mean like 'Alice in Wonderland'? That stuff?"

The Cuban laughs. "Not exactly, Santino, but not too far off. A fantasy is what a woman's thinking."

Sonny dismisses this. "How can anybody know what a broad's thinkin'?"

"You can read her stimulation . . . feel this." She puts his hand on her belly. "There's a muscle that goes from the clitoris to the navel . . . it tells you a lot. Ask her questions. If you talk about making love to three men, nothing may happen, but mention something else to her, like making love to someone your size, and she could respond."

Sonny can feel Juanita's stomach muscle tighten. "That's really somethin'."

She continues. "Breasts are another indicator. Nipples will get hard if you're talking about something exciting. Some women might like you to be someone else, too . . . the milkman, a lion tamer, another woman . . ."

Sonny reacts strongly. "What! You mean I'm gonna have to put on a fuckin' show for these broads?"

"You might, but don't forget . . . you have a selfish motive. It makes it easier for you." She takes off his towel and lies back on the bed. "Now, let's see how much you've learned today, Santino."

One month later Sonny graduated from Juanita's course . . . sexually, a Phi Beta Kappa. She wanted him to stay on permanently but knew it would be too dangerous. Batista's men were still looking for Sonny. She was afraid one of her hookers, jealous because she didn't get enough sex time with Sonny, might expose his hideout. Through another Castro sympathizer, a ship's captain, Juanita arranged for Sonny's transportation to the States.

The trip on the stinking fishing trawler was no pleasure cruise, but it was a safe way home. Without a passport or other identification Sonny couldn't go through U.S. Customs; the captain agreed to drop him two miles off the coast of the Florida Keys. Night fell, and Sonny, his money taped tightly to his body in a plastic bag, plunged into the shark-infested waters. A full moon lit the way as he swam for shore, each stroke bringing him closer to his betrayer—Sam Scorzelli.

At midnight a shoeless, bedraggled Sonny finally reached the beach. From a nearby nightclub strains of "The Twist" echoed across the deserted dunes. Exhausted, Sonny checked into a motel; he'd need a long, hard sleep to prepare him for his planned retribution. The next morning

Sonny called Sam. His boss was glad to hear from him. He said he knew
the other men were dead and was anxious to know what went wrong.
Sonny was deliberately evasive. "I'll tell you when I see you . . . I'll
be in Chicago tomorrow. I'll call you when I know my flight number."
Sonny arranged for Sam to meet him at the airport . . . he planned to
kill him right there. The confusion of the teeming rush hour crowd
would effectively cover his escape.

The following evening Sonny's plane taxis to the gate at exactly
five-thirty. Sonny's body is tense with anticipation as he searches the
busy terminal for Sam. Looking up, he sees the old man motioning to
him from the observation deck. For Sonny it is the final confrontation.
A quick check in his pocket assures him his gun is concealed; gripping
it firmly, he climbs the spiral staircase to the deck.

Sonny has insisted that the two talk in private. When he opens the
steel door and scans the area, there is no sign of the bodyguards . . . they
are alone. Sam comes over to Sonny and hugs him warmly. "We were
worried about you, kid, you were lucky to escape . . . I guess Batista's
men got to Eddie and Franco."

Sonny answers flatly: "No, Sam . . . I hit 'em."

Sam feigns surprise. "You hit them. . . . Why?"

"They changed procedure. I was afraid they were gonna set me
up." Sonny searches Sam's face for a hint of guilt.

Sam replies, without missing a beat, "Then good—they deserved
to die." Sam believes this will convince Sonny of his sincerity. The old
man does not suspect that Sonny knows of his involvement, nor does
he imagine the naive boy is his executioner. "You did a fine job, Santino.
I'm gonna reward ya, just like I promised . . . Sam Scorzelli always
keeps his promises."

"Yeah . . . what territory do I get, Sam?"

"I'm takin' ya off the streets, kid. You're too violent, but you're
valuable to me. You're gonna be my chief carrier. I need someone
tough to pick up my money . . . nobody's gonna mess with you." By
this time Sonny realizes he can't hit Sam on the open observation deck
with no means of escape—but Sam's offer has changed Sonny's plans
to try again. A carrier makes a lot of money . . . Sonny was not about
to kill his golden goose.

"Sounds good, Sam . . . let's talk about it on the ride into town."

Sam puts his arm around Sonny. "That's great, kid."

Sonny sidles away from him and looks back coldly. "Sam . . . don't
call me 'kid' no more."

Sonny's new job would have shattered the nerves of a weaker man.
In the numbers rackets it is the carrier's responsibility to see that the
day's cash and receipts are safely returned to the main office. Each day
the runners deliver their packages to flower shops, antique stores, bars,

and other inconspicuous drop-off points. Even though poor blacks usually bet ten or twenty-five cents, every station had a daily take between $15 and $30 thousand. If anything happened to that money, Sonny would be summoned before the gambling syndicate's judgment council for interrogation, just as a bank teller might be called in by his superiors to account for his losses. There was, however, one major difference. The most the bank teller had to lose was his job . . . Sonny could lose his life.

For the first few weeks Sonny was skeptical of Sam's good intentions. He still believed the cunning old man might try to hit him. Sonny protected himself by carrying three guns, one cocked in constant anticipation. Recalling his earlier experience with the two blacks in the car, he never allowed his drivers to sit or walk behind him.

One month passed. Now Sonny was fairly certain Sam was on the level, but his cautious procedure did not change. One day a former runner approaches Sonny with a chance to buy a load of stolen portable radios at a very good price. He makes the deal, and his two drivers take Sonny and the man to pick up the hot merchandise at an abandoned warehouse. Inspection shows that the boxes contain tape recorders, not radios. Sonny is angry. "What am I supposed to do with this shit?" He offers the confused black man $50 for the entire haul, and the frightened runner, an eyewitness to his ex-enforcer's violence, quickly accepts the offer.

It doesn't take Sonny very long to figure out a good use for the recording devices. He goes to Sam with an idea. Sonny explains that he has devised a system that could revolutionize the numbers rackets. "It would stop the niggers from stealing . . . and you could stop paying off the cops."

Sam, who has been listening with his chin resting on clenched hands, looks up with interest. "How is that possible? Greasing the palms of Chicago cops is an old, expensive necessity."

Sonny paces as he goes on. "Very simple . . . We put the numbers and amounts on tape. There are no receipts to grab, so there's no evidence. A runner can't steal 'cause his own voice is on that tape . . . it's a permanent record. It'd be almost impossible to cheat with this new method." The old man finally agrees to try it out on his lowest route.

In a short time the experimental route became one of Sam's most profitable. It really was obvious then just how much the runners had been stealing. Sam stopped paying the cops, and Sonny received half of the money saved. As the new system spread throughout Sam's operation, he couldn't afford to give Sonny the same deal, so he offered his carrier a raise that was hardly commensurate with the increased earnings. Sonny had an alternate proposal. If Sam could open syndicate doors in other cities, Sonny thought he could sell them his idea, with him and Sam equal partners. Sam explained gravely that the Mafia families would be hard to reach at this time because they were engaged in an all-out war. Coincidentally, a temporary truce was declared that week, and a summit conference to discuss peace was scheduled in up-state New York. This was a perfect opportunity for Sam. He would look good if the families bought Sonny's lucrative idea, and he'd be in a position to ask them for a favor later.

The powerful Chicago boss takes Sonny with him to Buffalo. As Sonny boards Sam's private plane, he is excited about the enormous financial potential of the trip, but he is totally unaware of its true significance.

When they land, a limousine is waiting on the field to take the Chicago representatives to the meeting. After a short drive they arrive at the steel gates of a walled property. A security guard calls the main house and clears them to enter. Their car passes a long, black snake of nearly sixty limos parked along the winding road, each with an attendant driver. These are no ordinary chauffeurs. Their gruff, muscular exteriors are a sharp contrast to the popular image of "James," the obsequious uniformed man in his peaked hat. To Sonny these hardened men look incongruous in the tranquil, rural setting.

Crossing an ornately turreted bridge, Sam's car pulls up in front of a stately Tudor-style mansion overlooking a lake. They enter the house, and Sonny is told to wait in the portrait gallery; Sam disappears with two men down the hallway. Under the watchful eye of three armed bodyguards Sonny surveys his opulent surroundings. After an hour he is escorted down the long hallway, then thoroughly frisked before they allow him to join the meeting. At last the large double doors swing open to admit him.

Over forty men wait for Sonny in the spacious, elegantly furnished drawing room. Most of them are Sam's age or older—only a handful are in their thirties. When Sonny enters, Sam greets him with a hug and introduces him to the others. "This is Sonny Gibson, a very close friend. His blood is not pure, but he is loyal . . . all my soldiers should be as loyal to me as he is. Sonny has devised a system for the numbers that increased Chicago's route sales nearly thirty percent." Then with another hug Sam turns the floor over to Sonny, who gives a brief, effective demonstration of his recording method. When he is finished, questions are fired at him rapidly.

His answers seem to satisfy everyone until an old man stands, his heavily scarred face clouded with doubt. "If this was Sam's idea, it'd be O.K., but I don't think we should get involved with anyone outside the family . . . we can't trust 'em."

At that point a soft voice from the back of the room speaks. Everyone turns to listen respectfully. "This man once saved my life. His blood isn't pure, but his heart is . . . We can trust him." His surprise bene- factor steps forward and hugs Sonny. It is Nick Loganno, his boyhood friend. Sonny is amazed. Why would Nick be at this important meet- ing . . . and why does he command such respect? Nick addresses him. "Sonny, you're going to have to leave the room for a while. We'll call you back in when we're done."

Sonny looks over at Sam. "Do I leave?"

"Yeah, I'll take ya out." Sam looks at the group. "I apologize for Sonny. I told ya . . . he's very loyal to me.

Sonny follows Sam out, and as they are walking back to the portrait gallery, pumps him for information, "What's Nick doin' here?"

Sam is genuinely surprised. "Don't you know anything, Sonny? Nick's grandfather is the boss of bosses. The old man never leaves New York. Nick is his representative. When he speaks, it is the don's word."

A flood of questions races through Sonny's head. "But why is . . ."

Sam cuts him off. "I gotta get back in there . . . they'll call ya."

While he waits, Sonny has time to think. He's slightly confused. Why didn't they go for the idea right away? It was a guaranteed moneymaker . . . Sam had already told them how much he'd made. There had to be something else at work besides greed; Sonny realizes he is dealing with men of principle.

Thirty minutes later Sam sticks his head out the door, "Hey, Sonny . . . they accepted your idea . . . but it looks like we're gonna be in here a long time. Go to the kitchen at the other end of the hall and help yourself to some pasta. There's a guy there . . . Alfredo . . . ya can't miss him, he's three hundred pounds . . . he's the cook. Tell him to bring the stuff down here . . . we're starvin'. Everybody's ready to *mange.*"

When Sonny gets to the enormous kitchen, he spots Alfredo im- mediately. The obese man is rolling out noodles on one end of the twelve-foot service island in the center of the room. Fifteen chief bodyguards sit around it, eating. They watch closely as Sonny goes up to Alfredo. "Sam said you should bring everything in to them . . . he said they'd be there a long time."

Mario, a slim, well-groomed Italian, holds his shoulder holster in place as he reaches for a bottle of wine. "I wonder what's takin' 'em so long . . . this was supposed to be a short one."

Danny, Sam's bodyguard, holds out his glass for Mario to fill. "Well, if it's anything like it was eight years ago, they'll be in there two days."

Sonny exclaims, "Two days! You mean they could be in that room for two days?" The clink of knives and forks stops suddenly. The men look at the intruder, but no one answers him. Sonny breaks the awkward silence. "Alfredo . . . Sam said I could get something to eat."

The fat man points to a large pot of spaghetti on the table. "Help yourself." Sonny sits down on the only empty stool and serves himself some steaming linguine with clam sauce. He hunches over his plate, listening while the bodyguards continue their meal and their conversation. Pete, a husky man with the vestiges of adolescent acne, says to the others, "I remember the war in '52. What a bitch . . . I never thought that one'd be over."

Mario recalls, "It started over Antonelli, didn't it?"

Pete says, "Yeah, he was carrier for the Cassano brothers."

Sonny's fork stops twirling pasta at this remark. Sonny is a carrier . . . what could he possibly do that would start a Mafia war?

Pete calls to a round-faced man at the other end of the table, "Hey, Mattie, you and me was shootin' at each other across Canal Street in '52 . . . remember? You were a lieutenant for the Bonacci family then."

Matie grabs a fistful of olives from a dish in front of him. "Yeah . . ."

Sonny intrudes. "Were you guys in the army together?"

The men stare at him. Pete smiles. "You could say that, kid . . . but it wasn't Uncle Sam's." They all laugh, pointing up the fact that Sonny is an obvious outsider in the group. After this he asks no more questions . . . he will have to be content to get his answers by listening.

Pete picks up the conversation again. "Mattie, who was your driver in '52? Shit, he was great . . . he could turn a car around in the Battery Tunnel."

Mattie taps his fork on his temple, trying to remember. "Uh . . . let's see . . . that was Freddie the Fingers. Man, that guy couldn't tie his shoes, he scared us all shitless when he got his hands on a gun . . . but with his hands on the steering wheel that son of a bitch was like a brain surgeon."

Mario asks, "Wasn't he killed in this last beef?"

Pete replies, "Nah, his old lady killed him. Caught him in bed with his head between some broad's legs. She shot both of 'em."

Mattie spits an olive pit onto his plate. "What a waste . . . that guy could *drive*."

Sonny sops up the remains of his clam sauce with a piece of bread. As he wipes his plate, he wonders what kind of men could shoot at each other one day and eat together the next. Joe, Sam's other bodyguard, asks Mattie, "How's it workin' for the Castino family?"

The hard-boiled lieutenant says stonily, "How's it workin' for anybody? You guys know how it is . . . you do your job. You keep your eyes open and your mouth shut."

As soon as he's finished eating, Sonny returns to wait outside the meeting room. Nine hours later the huge double doors swing open. As the men file out, Nick tells Sam, "Sonny is coming with me . . . for good." Without hesitation Sam agrees. Sonny is shocked—he has never seen anyone tell Sam what to do.

The limousine ride back to New York City helps to reacquaint the two old friends and fills in some of the blanks for Sonny. Nick explains, "My grandfather is a don. A don is the head of his family and territory. According to the ancient Sicilian customs he's also the power . . . the judge, jury, and executioner for all. It is a position men envy."

"Why was your family in Indianapolis, Nick?"

"In the fifties there was a Mafia war in New York for control. My grandfather shipped us to Indiana for protection. When the power struggle was over, Don Giuseppe was declared the boss of bosses . . . and we moved back to New York."

"That explains why you talked about your grandfather so much . . . he's a powerful man . . ."

"But a just one, Sonny. By the way, he knows all about you. I talked to him on the phone in front of the council and told him I thought we should use your system for the whole territory. He wants to do it."

"He knows a moneymaker . . ."

"Yes, but it's more than that. You'll see when you meet him. Your things are still in Chicago, right?"

"Yeah."

"We'll send you there to pick them up. You'll have two bodyguards with you."

Sonny is puzzled. "Why do I need bodyguards?"

"The don wants to make sure nothing happens to you."

"Nothin's gonna happen to me . . . I was the best enforcer Sam had."

Nick says firmly, "That's the way we do things. When you start working for the Loganno family, you'll be assigned two of your own bodyguards."

Sonny agrees, "It's O.K. with me, as long as they don't interfere when I'm chasin' broads."

Nick smiles. "Don't worry, Sonny. You'll find out soon enough that bodyguards aren't paid to chase broads."

When Sonny arrives back in New York two days later, he is set up in a beautiful hotel suite overlooking Central Park. For the next two weeks he is kept busy teaching his method to the East Coast organization. Finally he receives a call from Nick. "My grandfather wants to see you."

That evening a driver and a bodyguard are Sonny's companions for the forty-minute ride to Nick's grandfather's home on Long Island. The country boy from Indiana has been exposed several times to the trappings of power, but he is not prepared for the grandeur of the Loganno estate . . . Sam's mansion would be a guesthouse on this property. The car passes some manicured formal gardens and pulls around the circular drive to the front entrance. Nick is there to meet them. Sonny is awed by the splendor of the large entrance hall. In the center of the foyer Neptune sits majestically atop a deep-blue, mosaic fountain; small, delicately sculpted sea nymphs ring the pool below him, as a waterfall from his trident cascades gently over them. Nick tells Sonny the fountain is from the villa of the Roman Emperor Caracalla. Hand-painted murals of Mediterranean vistas decorate the walls of the hall, and statues of the purest Carrara marble stand in each corner.

A bodyguard leads Sonny and Nick through a living room with the dimensions and decor of a small cathedral. Shrines of various saints accent the room. The three continue down a hall until the bodyguard stops at the door of the don's study. He knocks, and a deep voice instructs them to enter.

Nick's grandfather is sitting in an antique rocker, an open book on his lap. Traces of jet black pepper the old man's gray hair. He wears thick reading glasses, but they do not conceal the dark, piercing eyes of the powerful don. Unlike Sonny's former boss, who believed flashy clothes and jewelry a symbol of rank, Don Giuseppe is casually dressed in a burgundy silk smoking jacket. His nails are highly polished, but his fingers are unadorned. He rises and greets Sonny with a hug. When the don speaks, it is with the assurance of a man who knows his power. "Santino, your name has echoed through these halls many times . . . have a seat."

Nick and Sonny sit in two chairs in front of a battered teakwood desk with a badly ink-stained marble top. While the don is returning his book to the shelf, Sonny whispers, "What's that old desk doing in this beautiful room?"

Nick whispers back, urgently, "Shh . . . that's gran'pappa's proudest possession!"

The old man takes his seat behind the desk. Sonny says, "I like your desk, Don Giuseppe . . . was it expensive?"

The senior Loganno smiles. "This desk is worth more than anything in the whole house." He rubs a corner of the faded marble top. "You know, Santino, some things are worth more than money. One thing worth more is loyalty to the family. This desk has been a loyal servant in my family for generations. It was given to me by my godfather . . . as well as this gold stallion." He picks up a small, shiny horse from the desk and hands it to Sonny. "What does this stallion mean to you, Santino?"

Sonny says quickly, "Speed, boldness . . . freedom."

"You are very fast with your answers, Santino." Sonny hands the stallion back to the don, who says wistfully, "I brought these things from Sicily when I was just about your age."

His eyes penetrate Sonny's. "What do you know about Sicily, Santino?"

"Don Giuseppe, I know . . . it is a beautiful country."

The don's face softens. "Yes, it is . . . very beautiful."

A knock on the door interrupts his nostalgic reverie. "Dinner is served, Don Giuseppe."

According to Italian custom, business is never discussed at dinner—real conversation begins when the traditional Sicilian meal is over. Don Giuseppe sits at the head of a long table in the sumptuous baroque dining room; Nick is on his right, Sonny on his left. His chief lieutenant, Mario, refills the don's wineglass. The old man takes a sip of wine, then turns to Sonny. "I want to thank you for what you taught Nick."

"I taught Nick somethin', Don Giuseppe?"

"Yes, Santino. He learned from you the most important part of being a man . . . the code of silence. Because of you Nick was able to stay in school without disgracing himself or the Loganno name. Last year my grandson got a college degree in economics. His knowledge is very valuable to the organization. I'm very proud of him." He beams at Nick, then continues to Sonny. "I like the economics of your numbers system, but there is something else I like about it even more . . . it doesn't tempt the runner to cheat. Why open a door for a man to steal if you can lock it first?" Sonny is surprised by the philosophical wisdom of the powerful leader. The don straightens up in his chair. "I also believe in our custom that a man should always repay a favor. What can I do for you . . . for helping Nick?"

The offer startles Sonny. He deliberates a few seconds. "Don Giuseppe, I wanna be in. Give me this chance."

The don studies him closely. "Why?"

"I wanna make money, Don Giuseppe. There's more opportunity here than Sam ever offered. I could grow with your organization."

The don questions him solemnly, "Santino, if you were a soldier and were given a command, would you follow it without asking any questions?"

Sonny replies hastily, "Yes, I would."

"Would you kill your own mother?"

"Hell, no, I wouldn't kill my mother!"

The old man's eyes blaze. "Then you don't even know what loyalty of command means . . . you must be taught that. Are you willing to learn, Santino?"

"Yes, Don Giuseppe."

Leaning over, he grabs Sonny's hand. "Then I will grant you your request." His dark eyes narrow. "There is no turning back,

Santino . . . you *will* learn our ways."

One week later a second meeting with the don is scheduled. Again Sonny is picked up by limousine, but this time two bodyguards accompany him. A drive through deserted Brooklyn streets finally brings them to Pier 53. An Italian freighter is almost ready to set sail. The don is sitting in his limousine on the dock, and Sonny is escorted to it. Before he is allowed in, he is routinely frisked. Now he must surrender not only his gun, but also his identification. Sonny climbs into the car, and the old man hands him a passport. The name is Joe Lee Miller, the picture is Sonny's. Don Giuseppe says, "You are going to Sicily to learn our ways. When you get there, you will have a sponsor who will teach you everything . . . his name is Alfonso Lambretti."

"How will I recognize Alfonso?"

The don peers over his thick glasses. "You won't have to . . . he knows you *very* well." A kiss from the don signals the end of the conversation. *"Buona fortuna centianni,* Santino."

A few minutes later Sonny's luggage arrives. As it is being loaded on board, Sonny asks the bodyguard to return his gun. Mario tells him, "It won't be returned . . . the don said you won't need it where you're going." Being unarmed for the first time in his crime career worries Sonny, but he knows he cannot contradict the orders of the don. A whistle blasts loudly from the freighter's smokestack as he hurries up the gangplank.

The trip to Sicily was more pleasant and more promising than the one from Cuba. It was also more mysterious. This time Sonny knew nothing at all about his destination. The fourteen-day passage relaxed him, but when the coast of Sicily came into view, his pulse quickened. The once-distant future was about to become a reality.

2
Sicily

As the boat pulls into the slip at Palermo and drops anchor, Sonny anxiously scans the crowd of men on the dock, trying to guess which of them is Alfonso Lambretti. A closer look tells him it would be unlikely for his sponsor to be among the shirtless, bandannaed workers who are waiting to unload the ship's cargo. Bags in hand, Sonny descends the gangplank to the dock, but no one comes forward to meet him. A whistle blows, and the men disperse; he stops one of them, "Hey, you seen a guy called Alfonso Lambretti around here today?"

The rugged Sicilian holds out his hands and shrugs his shoulders. *"Non capisco . . . America . . . non parlo . . ."*

Sonny can see he's getting nowhere. "Never mind . . . never mind." The man hurries off, and the newcomer is now alone on the dock. He puts down his suitcases, feeling very vulnerable. He is 6,000 miles from home in a country where he can't speak the language . . . with no gun. Sonny has never before been in a situation where he hadn't left himself alternatives. This time he has none . . . so he waits. Even though he hasn't known Don Giuseppe that long, for some strange reason Sonny trusts him. He swivels his head slowly, looking for any sign of his sponsor. Then, as if by magic, three men appear in the distance. Two tall, refined-looking Europeans carrying shotguns flank a short, flabby man in his sixties. When they reach Sonny, the older man steps forward. "I am Alfonso Lambretti. Welcome to Sicily, Santino . . . " He embraces Sonny warmly. Sonny tries to conceal his surprise. He had imagined his teacher would be a dignified scholar, the antithesis of the coarse man who stands before him. The odor of cigar and sweat cling to Alfonso's wrinkled, cream-colored suit: his jacket is open, revealing a pasta belly that hangs over his low-slung trousers. He has thinning brown hair under a soiled, white straw hat, which he removes several times to mop his head with a large handkerchief. His black eyes are prominent even under thick, dark eyebrows. His age, and a long scar across his throat, suggest that Alfonso Lambretti is a survivor.

As they walk to the car, Alfonso introduces Sonny to the others. "This is Gino and Carlo, Santino . . . two of my men." The amenities are acknowledged with a nod from the bodyguards. Sonny points to the shotguns at their sides; the small handle and long barrel are unusual. "What kind of guns are those? I never seen nothin' like that before."

"They're *schipettas,* Santino. In your country they're called shot-guns . . . used as weapons to hunt and kill. Here, according to our tradition, we use them for much more."

"What do you mean, Alfonso . . . they're used for more."

"They are the weapon of vendetta, Santino . . . You'll soon know."

By this time they have reached the end of the long dock. Sonny looks around. "Where's the limousine?"

"Right there, Santino . . ." Alfonso points to a small white Fiat.

"That little thing . . . that's it?" Sonny is used to the big black Cadillacs of the American dons.

"Yes, Santino . . . it's not like it is in America. Your big auto-mobiles would never get down our narrow streets . . . and gas here is too expensive . . . in your money over a dollar a gallon." This is way above the twenty-four cents it costs in Indiana.

"A dollar! What's in it . . . gold?"

"You'll find out, Santino, many, many things are different in this country." Alfonso smiles. "But that's what you're here to learn, isn't it?" He sees that Gino and Carlo have finished loading Sonny's bags into the trunk. "Let's go, Santino . . . it's a long ride." As Sonny gets into the back seat, he asks, "Where are we going, Alfonso?"

"To Catania."

Sonny has never heard of Catania, but that's not surprising. His grandmother had only mentioned Sicily a few times.

"Is it far?"

"Almost four hours away . . ."

The trip to Catania is as cramped and as bumpy as a New York cab ride, but Sonny watches the metamorphosis from city to countryside with interest. As they get farther away from Palermo, the villages get poorer. Most of the two-story buildings along the way are in disrepair, except for the churches, and the same flag waves everywhere—clothes on long lines stretched across the streets. About an hour out of town a deep pothole bounces Sonny to the top of the car. "Man, these roads are bad . . . don't they ever fix 'em?"

Alfonso mops his brow. "They only repair them near Palermo, where the traffic is . . . they don't bother out here." It seems to be hotter in the country, and the tiny car is like an oven. The smell of sweat is strong even with the windows down.

Alfonso lights up a cigar, and his first puff hits Sonny directly in the face; he starts to cough. "That smoke . . . I'm not used to that."

Gino turns around from the front seat. "No one gets used to those things, but we all smoke 'em."

Carlo adds, "They're called guinea stinkers . . . Our wine is better." The Sicilians laugh.

Sonny asks, "Why do they stink like that?"

Alfonso explains, "Years ago . . . before I was born even . . . the men used to work in cheese factories. When they came home at night, their clothes would smell, so they smoked these to kill the odor."

Sonny recalls the days when he reeked of the slaughterhouse in his neighborhood. "Yeah, I know how bad it is when your clothes stink. Man, that'd kill anything."

Alfonso holds up the butt. "It's not as good as a Cuban cigar, but it's what I've been smoking all my life."

Just then Carlo swerves the car to avoid hitting a donkey cart. Sonny turns to get a better look at its vividly painted intricate designs. "What's that cart . . . is it decorated like that for something special?"

Gino answers, "That's a Sicilian cart . . . every family has one. I used to help my father mix his paints when I was little. You know, it takes six months just to carve one of those wheels."

Sonny faces front again. "Why bother makin' 'em so fancy just to ride on these lousy dirt roads?"

Alfonso looks at Sonny. "The Sicilian people take pride in whatever they do. They are craftsmen, Santino. That is one of the things you will come to know."

The car winds through another tiny village, and the men drinking *vino* at the outdoor *cantina* raise their glasses, toasting the Fiat as it drives by. "What do the men do in a place like that, Alfonso?"

"They work in the vineyards or the straw nurseries. Many of them are fishermen . . . away for most of the year."

Sonny has noticed some beautiful girls in the villages they've passed through. He smiles. "That must make for a lotta lonely broads"—he pokes the old man in the ribs—"huh, Alfonso?"

Alfonso doesn't reply. A few seconds later he says something in Sicilian to his men, and the car stops abruptly. "Get out, Santino . . . "

"What?"

Gino turns with his shotgun in the crook of his arm and aims it at Sonny. Alfonso repeats quietly, "I said, get out of the car."

Sonny starts to sweat; he's unarmed. His mind races. Is this a setup? Is he the victim of a vendetta against Don Giuseppe? Is this the real Alfonso Lambretti? As soon as he's outside, Alfonso removes his hat and calls from the window, "Take down your pants, Santino."

Sonny hesitates. "What the hell's goin' on here?"

The bodyguards raise their shotguns to shoulder height. Alfonso's voice is steady. "I don't want to tell you again, Santino . . . " Perplexed, Sonny drops his pants to his ankles.

Carlo looks at Gino. *"Mamma mia . . . come grosso."*

Alfonso snaps, "That's enough . . ." and says something else in Sicilian. The bodyguards then aim their schipettas at Sonny's naked crotch. The old man warns sternly, "In this country you will keep that in your pants at all times. There are no broads here, they are Sicilian women. If you violate them, you'll get that cut off, and you could get me killed. There won't be thirty marriages for you here, Santino." Sonny is amazed. How did Alfonso, living in the hills of Sicily, know what he had done in the Midwest? "Is that clear, Santino?"

Sonny replies gravely, "Yes, Alfonso."

"All right, get back in the car." Sonny pulls up his pants thinking Don Giuseppe was right . . . Alfonso knows his charge very well.

A few minutes after they're on the road again, Alfonso puts a hand on Sonny's arm. "You know, Santino . . . I was young once myself. I know you must have women, so every six weeks Gino and Carlo will take you to a whorehouse in Rome. For two days you can have all the *puttanas* you want . . . but you must never approach any of our women. I hope I've made that clear."

"Yes, Alfonso . . ."

The old man wipes his forehead. "Good . . . you've just had your first lesson in our ways." Sonny buckles his belt and sits back. For the rest of the ride he stares out the window, wondering how he'll survive six weeks without sex and what other lessons he'll be learning from Alfonso Lambretti.

An hour later the Fiat stops in front of a white stucco wall. Gino gets out and opens the high wooden gate for them to enter. The front of the brick house beyond is almost the length of a football field. Small balconies with curlicued wrought-iron railings and multipaned French doors dot the second story. As Carlo pulls the car around back, Sonny sees several men climbing ropes strung on fifty-foot poles. "What are they doin', Alfonso?"

"They're trainees like yourself, Santino."

One of the men falls ten feet and struggles back up again. "Man, I'd never be able to do anything like that . . . that's a lotta work . . ."

Alfonso says seriously, "You will be doing that . . . and harder exercises, Santino." He turns to Sonny. "And Santino, 'never' is a word we do not use here."

The car rolls to a halt at the back of the house. The vista past the yard is breathtaking. The villa sits in the shadow of beautiful Mount

Etna, its pearly peak clearly visible against the seamless blue sky. They pile out of the car. "Alfonso, is this where I'm gonna live?"

"Yes, Santino." The bodyguards walk ahead of them to the house.

"Where do you stay . . . you live close by?"

Alfonso smiles. "This is my home, Santino . . . the men who are training live here, too."

"What are they training for?"

"Special missions."

They enter the spacious parlor of the villa. The furnishings inside are more modest than those in Sam's mansion or Don Giuseppe's. There are a few overstuffed couches covered in damask, several heavy wooden tables stained walnut, and sheer cotton curtains on the windows. Fat red candles, two and three feet high, stand in holders around the room. Sonny thinks this looks more like an old hotel than a home. The man who'd been rope-climbing comes into the parlor and sits down. Sonny whispers to Alfonso, "What's his mission . . . is it important?"

"It is only important for you to know your own mission . . . not his."

"What is my mission?"

"It's much too early to tell you, Santino. Only the Cosa Nostra and I know what you will be doing."

"The Cosa Nostra? . . . I've heard of it. What is that?"

"The ruling body for all the Mafia. The Catania family is the black hand for the Cosa Nostra . . . our soldiers are respected by the families throughout the world. That is another thing you will come to understand, Santino."

One thing Sonny understands perfectly right now . . . to have a house like this takes a lot of cash to operate. Alfonso must be worth a fortune. They must pay big money in Sicily. "Alfonso, how much does a soldier——"

The old man cuts him off. "That's enough questions for today, Santino. Get a good night's rest . . . you have a big day tomorrow. Gino will take you upstairs."

Sonny's quarters, on the second floor, are a nine-by-twelve-foot room outfitted like a monk's cell, including the crucifix. A chair and an oak dresser are the only furniture. The bed is small and hard, but as soon as his head hits the thin feather pillow, Sonny is fast asleep. The next morning he is allowed to get up late. It is the familiar sound of shots that wakes him. Instinctively Sonny reaches for his gun, usually tied on a string to his wrist, but then remembers . . . he has no gun. Looking outside, he sees the source of the shooting—a rifle range about 500 yards from the house, where three men are practicing. Directly below his window a calisthenics instructor is putting two other trainees through their physical paces. That's one part of his indoctrination Sonny wishes he could skip. His exercise for the past eight years has been making love—sexual workouts are a lot more enjoyable. The new recruit walks to the old sink in his room and turns on the water to shave. He throws the blade away reluctantly, knowing there are no modern drug-stores in town where he can buy replacements. From now on he'll have to use the straight razor and the strop Gino left for him.

By the time he finishes, it's noon. Alfonso comes to get him for lunch, a meal of many courses, much heavier than the sandwiches and hamburgers Sonny is used to. The dining room is divided into sections. The six instructors sit at one table; the trainees with their sponsors sit at the other. Before they begin eating, Alfonso stands. "We have a new man who is joining us here. This is Santino . . . from America."

Sonny nods to the others. When Alfonso sits, a heavy man with badly scarred hands starts serving the antipasto. Sonny whispers, "What happened to that man, Alfonso?"

"He was persecuted because he would not betray the family."

"Who persecuted him?"

"There are many things to know before you can understand what happened to Pepino . . . Hand me the bread basket, Santino."

Sonny passes the bread but watches the fat man until he disappears through the double doors to the kitchen. Sonny thinks Pepino must be quite a man to have undergone that torture and lived. The newcomer then turns his attention to the other men at his table and studies their faces. All of them have swarthy complexions and dark features. There is only one man in the room with sandy hair—Sonny.

"Where are these guys from, Alfonso?"

"Different towns and villages in Sicily. You have a lot to learn about our country that they already know, Santino . . . we have a lot of work to do."

Sonny cuts off a wedge of cheese from a wheel that is passed to him. "Why did Don Giuseppe pick me to come here?"

"You must be very special, Santino. The Loganno family has never sent anyone here before. This is the first time he has ever called on me for a favor." The old man's face softens. "In the early twenties, when Don Giuseppe and I were young men . . . about your age . . . we trained together in this house. Things were different in those days, Santino." Alfonso laughs. "Once we felt the stings of the lash on our backs for talking to each other."

Sonny hands the cheese to the man next to him. "Whaddya mean? You couldn't talk then?"

His sponsor's tone gets serious. "The men are only allowed to speak to their instructors or their sponsors. This is still a very strict rule. But we don't need the lash anymore, Santino. Today the men are too busy to talk to each other. When Don Giuseppe and I were here, they didn't have all the electronic devices you have to learn about."

Sonny shakes his head. "I still think it's a crazy rule . . . I don't see what's wrong with gettin' to know another guy."

"You were not sent here to make friends, Santino"—he looks straight at Sonny—"and you might be commanded to make a hit on one of these men in this room someday." Sonny remembers how the body-guards laughed about shooting at each other across Canal Street. A dish of pasta is placed in front of him. *"Mange, mange.* As soon as you finish eating, we're gonna go to work, Santino."

After lunch Gino brings Sonny to a sparsely furnished sitting room, which is to be his classroom. Seated at a mahogany table, he watches the waning afternoon sun shine through a pair of net curtains, throwing lacy patterns across the polished hardwood floor. What will his first lesson be? Sonny is hoping it will be on the rifle range, not on the ropes. A few minutes later Alfonso comes in with Carlo. *"Buona sera,* Santino. That means 'good afternoon' . . . you'll be learning Sicilian as we go on." The old man sits down on a high-backed wooden chair across from his pupil. He challenges Sonny, "How bright are you, Santino?"

The answer is quick and flip. "I'm pretty smart . . ."

"Good." Gino brings over a reel-to-reel tape recorder, and Alfonso pulls a tape from his pocket. "Then you should have no trouble learning what's on this tape." He threads it into the recorder's spools and starts the machine. "I'll see you in the morning, Santino."

Alfonso leaves, and Sonny watches the wheels of the recorder turn. A gruff male voice tells Sonny about the habits of Ronald Benson, an American furniture manufacturer. After a few minutes of listening Sonny's mind wanders. A sensuous, raven-haired young woman passing in front of the window is a painful reminder of his forced celibacy. When the girl is out of sight, Sonny focuses his attention on the tape once more. Now he's being told about the hobbies of Benson—stamp col-lecting, bird watching, and cribbage. Sonny stretches his arms over his head and yawns. "What the fuck does this have to do with the Mafia?" He pulls out his wallet to look at the calendar, then circles the date, six weeks away, when he'll be taken to the whorehouse in Rome. A few minutes later he falls asleep, dreaming of more passionate nights as the voice on the tape drones on.

The following morning Sonny returns to his classroom. Gino and Carlo, ever-present sentinels, stand in the doorway. Alfonso enters. *"Buon giorno,* Santino. Today we are going to have a test. Please tell me everything you know about the habits of Signor Ronald Benson."

Sonny is dumbfounded. "Are you crazy? . . What the hell are you talkin' about?"

Alfonso slaps him hard across the face for his insolence. Sonny is enraged and goes for his sponsor's throat. The bodyguards, their schipettas aimed at Sonny, quickly step between him and Alfonso, but the old man waves them away. He says sternly, "Sit down, Santino."

Sonny, his face still flushed with anger, takes a seat. "What the fuck did you hit me for? I don't go for that shit . . ."

"That is the first and last time I will ever hit you, Santino. But from now on, when I give you a tape and tell you to learn it . . . you will learn it." Alfonso's voice is harsh, but his eyes mirror the love of a father for a son. He walks around the table and kisses Sonny on the forehead. "It's for your own good, Santino. You must learn discipline." He pulls out another tape. "That was just a test—now you will really start your education."

Sonny looks up at him, mystified by the incident. "Yes, Alfonso."

For the next month Sonny worked intensely, memorizing tapes and pictures of subjects, mostly insurance executives. Sonny learned their habits, assuming they were targets for future hits. Each day around midafternoon Alfonso would come in with a bottle of wine. He was always friendly, but when the break was over, he resumed his role as teacher, drilling Sonny rigorously on his tapes. The old man sat stiffly, arms folded. "All right, Santino . . . tell me what you know about Albert Carstairs."

Sonny usually paced as he rattled off the information. "Let's see . . . he's thirty-seven years old, five-ten, one hundred fifty-nine pounds. Married, wife's name is Ann . . . thirty-six. Has two kids, Geraldine and Jerome. They're Protestant and go to church on Third Street and Maple every Sunday. He works for Prudential, wrote seven million in insurance last year. He plays tennis every Thursday, he——"

Alfonso interrupts. "Who does he play tennis with?"

Sonny squints his eyes in thought. "Uh . . . Jerry . . . Jerry . . . shit, I can't remember . . . he was only mentioned once."

"Jerry Stone could be the key to the success of that assignment, Santino. . . . Now, which route does Ann Carstairs take to her Tuesday-night bridge game?"

"Who knows? Why is that important . . . she's not even the subject."

Alfonso reminds him, "There are no unimportant details, Santino . . . remember that." Alfonso stands. "On the whole I am pleased with your progress. You are learning how to listen . . . that will be your most valuable tool. But you have a lot more to learn, Santino, a lot more."

Two weeks later, as promised, Sonny was sent with Gino and Carlo on his sexual excursion to Rome, just when he thought he would burst out of his skin from pent-up passion. The old madam of the whorehouse greets them. Her flowing black peignoir billowing behind her, she shows Sonny to a small room with an iron-frame bed. Periodically girls are sent in to him, often two at a time. The bodyguards outside his door are a virgin experience for Sonny, but they do not inhibit him in his carnal recreation.

Saturday night, at the change of shift, Gino says to his partner, "That American is like a bull . . . they never stop screaming, those *puttanas.*" Carlo sandwiches a hunk of cheese between some bread. "You saw him . . . *madonna,* no wonder they yell."

Gino sits. "But there are so many women . . . I would be out after three." He tips his chair back. "He's had thirteen already . . . with no sleep."

Carlo yawns. "Well, I gotta get some sleep . . . I can't keep up with him."

Just then another girl starts hollering. Gino shakes his head. *"Dio mio . . . Buona notte,* Carlo."

A total of two dozen hookers visited Sonny's room that weekend. On Monday morning he is beaming and ready to go back to work again, but instead of returning to the villa, he is taken to a rustic inn fifty miles outside of Catania. His sponsor is there, waiting for him. "We are going on a little trip, Santino." For the first time he dismisses the bodyguards, and Alfonso and Sonny get in the car alone.

"Where are we going, Alfonso?"

"To some of the neighboring towns. A country is a product of its people, Santino. To understand our ways, you must understand the people . . . their culture and their history. That is what you will learn on this trip."

Forty-five minutes later they pull off the road. Alfonso unloads a straw case from the trunk and leads Sonny over to a grove of olive trees. It is a hot summer day; Alfonso takes off his hat and fans his face with it, shaking sweat from the brim. The old man leans his schipetta against a tree, hangs his jacket on the lowest branch, and opens his case. He takes out a red-checked tablecloth and carefully spreads it on the grass, then lays out the contents of the satchel: a long salami, various cheeses, and freshly baked bread, still warm to the touch. Two wine-glasses and a bottle of Chianti complete the trimmings of the picnic. While they eat, Alfonso explains how cheese is kept in underground caves in the summer months to keep from spoiling. Wood planks covered with stucco are a primitive but effective form of refrigeration, and the only one found in the villages. Wine is kept cool the same way—the caves, usually ten feet wide and ten feet high, double as wine cellars.

Sonny slices some salami. "That's all very interesting, Alfonso . . . but, uh . . . one thing's been botherin' me since I got to Sicily . . ."

"What's that, Santino?"

"Why can't I go out with Sicilian women . . . is it because I'm

American . . . because I'm only half Sicilian?"

"That's only part of it, Santino. The others are not allowed to see them, either . . . there's no time."

Sonny jams a few slices of meat in his mouth. "But we have our nights free." Alfonso explains patiently, "We have a very strict courtship here. You don't have time to be courting, Santino . . . to spend time with the girl's family so they can get to know you."

"Hey . . . I'm not goin' out with the girl's family."

"No, but they expect when you go out . . . you'd want to marry her, go to bed, and have children with her. They have to accept you." He motions Sonny to start packing the remains of their lunch. "That is why, Santino, in this country there is no divorce. We don't change wives like you Americans change cars." Sonny snaps the satchel closed. Alfonso smiles. "Don't worry about going out, Santino. You are not ready to be tamed by one woman . . ." They walk back to the car and put the case in the trunk. "Come, Santino . . . let's talk." As the two stroll leisurely on the verdant, rolling hills, Alfonso begins the lesson. "I want you to remember this well, Santino. Sicilians are a proud people. We have a great love for our country. We have fought valiantly to defend our homeland against many ruthless oppressors. Once there were two Sicilies; they included all of Italy as we know it today. In 415 B.C. the Greeks were our conquerors. Theirs was a benevolent rule, and their culture made a valuable contribution to ours, but for thousands of years after that Sicily was the spoils for a succession of fierce barbarians. In the next fifteen centuries the flags of the victors changed many times, but the poverty and persecution of the people remained the same . . . until 1282. A cruel French leader, Charles of Anjou, had been king for nearly twenty years when the people rose up against him. The bloody massacre in Palermo that ended his power is called 'The Sicilian Vespers.' The Mafia was responsible for the victorious revolution."

Sonny, who has been listening halfheartedly to his compulsory history lesson, is suddenly interested. "I thought there was no Mafia before 1900. You mean it goes back *hundreds* of years?" Alfonso smiles at his pupil's ignorance, "The history of the Mafia is an old and noble one. In 1282 the landlords of the large estates in Palermo banded together for one purpose: *Morta alla Francia Italia adesso* . . . death to all the French in Italy." Sonny could tell by the quaver in the old man's voice that this is an emotional subject for him. These were more than facts from a dusty volume in a library . . . Alfonso was reliving this history. "Mafia vigilantes trained secretly for months before the uprising. When they were finally ready, these men were warriors, determined to end the centuries of oppression. After the French were driven out, the Mafia spread throughout Sicily, fighting invaders . . . they were champions of the people. The landlords became dons—rulers and judges over all. These men had courage, discipline, and loyalty. If an injustice was done to their family, it was a duty to avenge it. Today a man still has that same duty . . . even more, he has that right." Alfonso kisses Sonny on both cheeks, "Once I feel you have become such a man, Santino, I will be your godfather, and you will have a family." Alfonso motions for Sonny to sit next to him on a large tree stump. The old man's face hardens as he speaks. "Santino, I have told you about the oppression by the barbarians, but the worst oppressor we have had was one of our own."

This surprises Sonny. "An Italian? Who was it?"

Alfonso's eyes narrow. "Mussolini. He not only betrayed the Italian people to Hitler, he tortured our men and killed innocent women and children. He murdered young students in Rome who refused to become his informants. Until the day I die I will try to avenge their deaths."

"Mussolini, wasn't he the one that died a really gruesome death?"

Alfonso says, clenching his fist, "Hanging him upside down, slicing him up the middle with his balls stuffed in his mouth, wasn't good enough for him . . . I know . . . I know."

Sonny is curious about what Alfonso knows that could fill him with so much hate, but the old man comes out of the past, back to the present. "We must leave now, Santino. We'll be staying the night with a good friend of mine . . . Vincenzo . . . a lieutenant for Don Lo Manzo."

"Does he live far from here?"

"No, just a short drive . . ."

On the way to their lodging Alfonso continues the lesson. "You see, Santino, the Mafia here is different than in America. There they control the law . . . here the Mafia is the law."

"That villa I'm stayin' in . . . it's as big as a hotel . . . did the Mafia give you that house? Are you a don?"

"No, Santino, I'm a servant . . ."

Sonny laughs. "I never seen a servant live like that . . . that villa costs a lotta money. You must be rich, Alfonso."

Alfonso raises his finger in admonishment, "Don't be fooled, Santino . . . a parish with a big church isn't always prosperous. Often they give their money away to less fortunate parishes around them. My home is one of the Mafia's cathedrals. I share it with other men because I believe in what I teach . . . and my return is great." He says with conviction, "I am rich, Santino . . . in loyalty. Tonight you will meet a very loyal and a very powerful man. You will see how a Mafia lieutenant really lives."

"Alfonso, I know from being with Don Giuseppe, some of the guys are lieutenants. How do you get to be a lieutenant?"

"You have to earn it, Santino. You don't become one just because you want to . . ."

"Who decides you deserve it?"

"The men are picked by the dons . . . it is an honor, Santino."

"Are Gino and Carlo lieutenants?"

"No . . ."

Sonny now has the chance to bring up the question that's been on his mind ever since that day with the bodyguards in the kitchen. "Is the Mafia run like the American army?"

"In some ways . . . our soldiers have military discipline and follow the orders of their superiors without question." His grip tightens on the wheel. "But that is where the similarity ends. I'm glad you brought this up, Santino. Vincenzo can tell you some things about your American army that they don't teach in your schools."

Half an hour later, at dusk, they pull up in front of a modest building of brick and mortar. "Why are we stopping, Alfonso?"

"We're here, Santino . . . this is Vincenzo's house." Sonny looks at the lieutenant's house with surprise. He was expecting to see a villa even bigger than Alfonso's. There is no high stucco wall surrounding this small plot, just an unpainted wooden fence with a rusty metal gate. In the front yard a few chickens peck at their food while a rooster struts the perimeter of his territory.

Inside, the entire family is waiting. Vincenzo greets his visitors warmly, hugging Alfonso, who introduces Sonny, "This is Santino from America."

The host says in heavily accented but good English, "Ah, America . . . I have cousins in New York and Boston." He hugs the new arrival. "Welcome to Sicily . . . Santino, this is Angelina, my wife." The peasant woman nods shyly, then her husband calls their five children over; they have been standing quietly in a corner of the tiny parlor. "This is a friend of Uncle Al's from America." The three boys shake Sonny's hand, and the two girls curtsy. The American is struck by their politeness. When he was a child, his companions barely showed respect for their own parents, let alone a stranger. Angelina disappears into the kitchen, and Vincenzo orders the children to take their places at the supper table. When the adults are seated, Angelina reappears with an antipasto tray of olives, provolone, and mortadella, a type of bologna with large circles of fat. Sonny has never seen anything like that or the pasta with whole fish heads laid out across the top of it. When Angelina sits, all heads bow as Vincenzo says grace. *Padre nostro benedici il nostro cibo. Amen.*

While they pray, Sonny sneaks a look at the family gathered around the table. They are ordinary . . . with one exception: The father has committed murder. When he's finished praying, Vincenzo makes the sign of the cross. He raises his head, then his wineglass. "Angelina, some *vino,* eh? Santino . . . Alfonso, *mange, mange.*"

Sonny takes some of the antipasto from the large platter Vincenzo hands him. The American likes the taste of mortadella but is squeamish about the fish heads . . . he has never had food look back at him. Once he gets past the esthetics, however, Sonny finds the spaghetti dish delicious. Since there is very little meat in Sicily, fish is also the main course: *arringa.* For dessert Angelina serves Sicilian zabaglione with grapes from their vineyard. Alfonso compliments her, "Everything was *molto bene, molto bene,* Angelina."

The plump woman blushes; her husband points, "This woman . . . my wife . . . she is the greatest cook in all Sicily." He pats his protruding gut to emphasize his point. "I eat too much . . . but you only live once, eh?" Angelina sets out cups of espresso before the men, and Vincenzo excuses the children from the table. Each one gives Alfonso, Sonny, and their pappa a kiss good night.

When they leave, Sonny says, "I like your kids, Vincenzo. They're real polite." The lieutenant's face softens, "They have respect, Santino . . . that is more important." The host opens up a box on the table and passes out cigars to his guests. Sonny lights up his, choking on the raw taste. Vincenzo laughs. "That is something you must get used to slowly, Santino. It is not as smooth as our fine wine." Vincenzo holds his head back to drain the last drop in his glass. "Some of the best wine in the world comes from Sicily. Would you like to see our vineyard, Santino?"

Sonny is enthusiastic. "Yeah, they don't have nothin' like that where I come from."

Vincenzo rises, and they go out through the parlor again. He stops to light a candle in front of a statue of the Madonna. Most Sicilian homes, no matter how poor, have a crucifix and a shrine to the Blessed Mother. Sonny whispers to his sponsor, "What's he doin'?"

Vincenzo hears the question and turns. "I'm lighting a candle for all the souls who died protecting our country."

"The men in World War II?"

Alfonso replies gravely, "And the women and children, Santino."

Vincenzo puts on his cap. "Come, let's go. It is a beautiful night." They walk through the mouth of a valley and up the side of a small hill.

When they reach the vineyard, Vincenzo stoops to pick a large grape. He squeezes it between his fingers, "Juicy, eh, Santino?"

"Your vineyard's big, Vincenzo."

Vincenzo corrects him. "This is not mine, Santino . . . it belongs to Don Lo Manzo. It is my job to see that the wine gets to Palermo safely." His chest expands proudly. "There has not been a hijacking or any trouble from another family since I was put in charge seven years ago.''

Alfonso puts an affectionate arm around Vincenzo's shoulder. "That is because you are one of his best soldiers, my friend.''

The men continue their walk through the vineyard, passing under a white latticed arch, finally coming to a bench. Alfonso sits. "Vincenzo, Santino thinks that Mafia soldiers are like American soldiers.''

Vincenzo spits on the ground. "That is what I think of your American army.'' He looks at Sonny. "No disrespect to you, Santino.''

"Why do you hate the Americans so much . . . what'd they do?''

Vincenzo says, "Come. I will show you.'' They climb to the top of the small hill. "Past these mountains is Messina, Santino, where the army came through during the war. The Mafia helped them get in and kick out Mussolini. In return the Americans raped our land . . . and our women.''

Sonny had no idea the GIs were so cruel. "Was it any better when Mussolini was handling things with the Germans?''

Alfonso answers, "No, Santino, Vincenzo wanted to make a point . . . to show you that the Americans were no saints. But at their worst they never came near what Mussolini did to the Sicilian people.''

Vincenzo spits again. *"Morta, morta, morta . . .* that's all Hitler and Mussolini knew. Mussolini gave the Germans a free hand in Sicily . . . he knew the Mafia was working against him. The Nazis persecuted the families of Mafia men.''

Alfonso says solemnly, "Mussolini wanted Vincenzo's boss, so they went to Vincenzo's house . . .''

Vincenzo remembers bitterly, tears in his eyes. "They raped my mother and tortured my father in front of her. The SS soldiers sliced off pieces of flesh until he bled to death . . . but he wouldn't talk. Many families hid out in the wine and cheese cellars in those days. That was seventeen years ago, but it seems like it was yesterday.''

Sonny is startled to hear about the brutality the Sicilian people suffered at the hands of their allies. "Did any of the Mafia men get caught?''

Alfonso's voice is steady. "Yes, Santino . . . they were sent to a prison on the island of Ponza . . . off the coast. This was Mussolini's hell, run by the devil himself: a Nazi named Krueger.''

Vincenzo's voice breaks with emotion. "They tortured my brother there. They tore out his fingernails one by one and poured alcohol on the raw skin. Then they rubbed sand into the wound.'' Sonny is speechless as Vincenzo continues. "Each SS officer had a specialty. I'll never forget Krueger. He had a moustache like Hitler . . . he had a special wall built with a hole in it. He made a man put his *ucazza* through the hole, then stuck a long, thin needle into it. That bastard left his prisoner pinned against the wall till he talked. After a few days without sleep a man would fall, ripping his *ucazza* off. Then they just let him bleed . . . they were animals. There wasn't a moment at Ponza when you couldn't hear the screams of pain." He straightens up proudly. "But very few of the Mafia soldiers gave away the secret hiding places of the dons." For the next minute all that can be heard is the wind in the palm trees high above them.

Alfonso says quietly, "Vincenzo wouldn't tell you . . . but he was a victim of that torture, too." He picks up Vincenzo's hand to show the mangled fingers. Sonny stares at them. He'd seen those scars before . . . the fat man serving at the villa had them, too.

"My God . . . how the hell did you take that?"

Alfonso says gravely, "Before you leave Sicily, Santino, you will be able to withstand the same kind of torture." Sonny looks back at the mutilated fingers. What could he possibly learn that would help him bear up under such pain? Alfonso continues, "Vincenzo escaped. When he got to Sicily, he told the dons who was giving information. Then he and an American marine . . . one of the good ones . . . made a daring raid on Ponza and rescued all of the men."

Sonny looks at Vincenzo. "When you got to the compound, what'd you do to Krueger?"

Vincenzo's eyes glow with hate. "I was just with all the evil men there, Santino . . . I blew their heads off. The rats . . . they were something else."

"What happened to them?"

"When we got back home, they were executed Sicilian style . . . sliced up the middle, their heart ripped out, and their balls stuffed in their mouth . . ."

Sonny recalls, "Just like Mussolini . . ."

"Yes, Santino," Alfonso tells Sonny, "Because of his bravery Vincenzo became a lieutenant. You see, Santino . . . he earned it."

Vincenzo breaks in. "Alfonso wouldn't say, because he's modest, Santino. There are many lieutenants in Mafia ranks, but there is only one chief lieutenant chosen to be over all of us and spokesman to the dons. . . . In Catania . . . Alfonso is our chief lieutenant. His reward for his devotion to the vendetta."

Sonny asks innocently, "Which vendetta?"

Vincenzo looks over at Alfonso. "I can see now he hasn't been here too long." He turns back to Sonny. "It's the vendetta of all the Mafia . . . to kill communists." Alfonso puts a hand on Sonny's arm. "When we kill, we kill for a reason . . . we kill to protect our own. You see, Santino . . . the Mafia is much different from the American army."

The three are silent again. Now the barking of a sheepdog in the valley below is the only sound. Vincenzo shivers. *"Madonna . . .* the night air gave me a chill. Come, let's go back to the house for some espresso." He pats Sonny on the back, "This time we'll put in some anisette."

"What's that?"

Vincenzo smiles. "It's like . . . *come* . . . how do you say in English?"

Alfonso helps him. "Licorice."

"Yes, that's it! Like licorice candy, only for the grown-ups . . . not the kids, eh, Alfonso?"

The old man laughs. *Si, si* . . . Vincenzo." The two friends put their arms around each other's shoulders and start back to the house. The visitor hangs back, looking at the hills toward Messina, remembering Vincenzo's stories. Alfonso was right . . . they would be too shocking to put in the annals of American history.

The following morning Angelina laid out a special breakfast of eggs and cheese for the visitors, a change from the semolina she usually served her family. After they left Vincenzo's family, Sonny and Alfonso traveled around the country for three days, meeting the peasants who are Sicily's lifeblood. Sonny enjoyed seeing the women hang long strands of spaghetti on clotheslines to dry, and he watched attentively while craftsmen blew delicate glass figures and made baskets. Despite the language barrier, everywhere Sonny went, he was welcomed as a son. For the first time in his life he felt he was meeting people who truly had love in their hearts.

The student was also seeing another side of his teacher . . . one that bounced babies on his knee and roughhoused playfully with young boys; one that respected women and sat in *cantinas* with men in small villages reminiscing about Sicily before the war. In those three days, alone with Alfonso, Sonny was learning a very important lesson . . . how to temper heartlessness with humanity.

When their trip was finally over, Sonny returned to his strict life at the villa. Every morning he studied Sicilian; his afternoon classes were diverse. Several hours a day were spent on awareness training. In one exercise Sonny was placed in the center of the room, a bandanna over his eyes, while a circle of men around him dropped safety pins on the wood floor. Sonny had to identify the exact direction the sound came from each time. Alfonso was always present during his drills. When Sonny missed, he was scolded. "You're not paying attention, Santino . . . try it again." The pupil also spent hours memorizing the aromas of perfumes, aftershave lotions, and dry cleaning fluids. Sonny resisted this test; he thought it was silly.

"Why am I smellin' all this shit . . . what's it for?"

Alfonso was patient. "If you're in a closed place, like a bar or an airport, and you smell the same perfume or aftershave twice, nine times out of ten someone is following you. Your senses have to be sharper than a blind man's, Santino."

Sonny's sense of balance was perfected by riding a wheelchair around the room on its back two wheels and by walking on a one-and-a-half-inch-wide piece of metal, carrying a man on his shoulders. The narrow plank was only a few feet off the ground at first, but eventually Sonny had to perform this test at a height of thirty feet. His reflexes were honed another way. He had to catch a pencil in midair as it was dropped . . . a command of "right" or "left" told him which hand to use. Alfonso insisted he do this 100 times without missing before the teacher was satisfied with the student's acuity.

As time went on, Sonny grew bored with these tests. He was anxious to get on the rifle range with the others who were being trained to shoot. Alfonso constrained him. "Santino, you will be an expert with weapons more deadly than a rifle."

Sonny did learn some handgun techniques that were vital to his profession. Alfonso would throw a gun across the room. The student would have to get it and hit his target before he was shot with a Ping-Pong ball from Gino's air gun. Because he would make a wild lunge wherever the gun fell, Sonny was always badly bruised during this exercise, but soon he was getting bull's-eyes every time.

In this phase of his instruction he was also trained to identify the type of gun a man was carrying by the shape of it under his jacket. Before long Sonny was able to tell at a glance the bulge of a .38 from that of a Luger.

Sonny learned self-defense and attack from Roberto, a middle-aged lieutenant who had survived the atrocities of Ponza. The first thing the veteran soldier taught the rookie was how to protect himself without a gun. "There are four spots on the body which will disarm or kill a man, Santino . . . the eyes, the throat, the nose, and the groin. If you push your thumbs into a man's eyes, you hit a nerve. It'll take him an hour to get his sight back . . . if his eyeball doesn't pop out. That will give you enough time to escape or kill him. Another spot is the Adam's apple . . . punch it with two knuckles and it's gonna knock his wind out. Even a woman can do this . . . it doesn't take a lot of strength. One thing that will kill a man . . . take the palm of your hand, break the bridge of the nose, then push the ligaments up into the brain. It's instant death." Roberto pulled out a knife to illustrate his next lesson. "There are several things to remember when using this . . . first of all, the height of your target. If he's short, stand sideways, protect your groin . . . and go right for his ear . . . a hit there will go straight to the brain. If he's tall . . . go for the groin and twist—that is sure to do damage. Forget aiming for the heart . . . it is not in the same place on every person. Another thing . . . the chest is the hardest part of the body. It takes more force to push through all that bone and muscle. Your knife could get stuck, and a man can run after you with it in him . . . at least for a couple of minutes.''

Every day for the next six months (except Sundays) Sonny went through the same rigorous routine. His only break from the daily monotony was an hour spent with Gino and Carlo in town. They were his constant shadow. One night Sonny decided to sneak away, just to be alone. He climbed down an olive tree outside his window and went for a solitary walk along the old Moorish ruins on the beach.

The crescent moon is casting eerie shadows across the ancient ruins as Sonny closes his eyes and luxuriates in the warm evening breeze. When he opens them again, he thinks he is seeing a mirage. A stunning young woman stands before him . . . she is taking off her clothes in a ballet of sensuous movements. One graceful motion unties a ribbon, and a mane of chestnut hair tumbles loosely down her back. The waves caress her shapely legs as she takes a step into the ocean. Sonny moves closer, aroused. Her finely chiseled features are an artist's dream, but even Michelangelo could not capture the fire in her coal-black eyes. In spite of Alfonso's ominous warning Sonny feels free to speak, assuming she only knows Sicilian. "God, you're beautiful. I'm so horny I could lay ya right here.''

The girl, though startled by his presence on the usually deserted beach, doesn't reach for her clothes. Instead she replies, "You're not the only one who's horny.'' Her fluent English catches Sonny off guard. He looks around, scanning the beach cautiously. She assures him, "It's safe . . . I've been coming here for years, and you're the first person I've ever seen. I know who you are. It's no secret.'' He looks at her quizzically. "Trust me. Come.'' The alluring beauty takes his hand and leads him over to a grassy knoll. Exchanging feverish kisses, they sink slowly to the ground while she undresses him. Her eyes burn with longing at the sight of Sonny's naked manhood. From the first touch their lovemaking is an explosion of desire. Looking at the beautiful woman beneath him Sonny knows, as Shakespeare did, the incomparable feeling of "the first penetration of love.'' For an hour they explore each other with a lustful thirst, quenched only by the nectar of their satiated bodies. When their passion is spent, the new lovers sit quietly under the stars, discovering each other.

The girl sits next to Sonny, sifting the warm sand through her fingers. Bathed in moonlight, she is exquisite. "What's your name?''

"Laura . . . I know yours . . . Santino.''

"How do you know me, Laura? You said it was no secret who I was.''

She smiles. "I noticed you in town one day with Signor Lambretti.''

"You know Alfonso? How do you know him?"

She shrugs. "Everyone knows Alfonso Lambretti."

Sonny pauses a second. "Tell me somethin' . . . are you a Sicilian? I can't believe it . . . you speak better English than I do."

Laura brushes the sand from her hands. "I'm very much a Sicilian, but I speak seven languages. I just got a degree in languages from the University of Rome." She sighs. "I didn't want to come home, but my father insisted. I'm not like other women around here." Laura says in a mocking whisper, "My father still thinks I'm a virgin." Laura presses against Sonny seductively. He holds her close, still thinking this is part of a lovely dream.

"Where did you learn to make love? You're fantastic."

"I'm that way with you, Santino . . . we were made for each other. With other men I never feel anything."

Sonny smiles. "Well, you're all woman . . . some helluva woman."

He moves to kiss her, but her expression suddenly changes to concern. "You know, Santino, what we are doing is very dangerous for you. We must be careful."

Alfonso's words echo in his mind. "I was warned about this very thing. We must be very careful, Laura."

For the next two months Sonny meets Laura twice a week at the ruins. At first he walks the mile and a half to the beach, but he soon finds an old bike in a shed behind the villa. With this speedier form of transportation he is able to spend a few more precious hours with Laura before he has to be back at dawn. Nothing could have kept the two apart . . . Sonny is finally in love. He wants to stand atop Mount Etna and shout his feelings for Laura to the world. Time and Cupid have made him impervious to the danger of their affair, but an incident in town makes him an eyewitness to its consequences.

One day, instead of taking their usual break in the villa, Alfonso and Sonny take an afternoon off. They sit outside the cafe, drinking wine, watching the sleepy town come alive after its siesta. An angelic-looking young woman on crutches passes . . . she has only one leg. The package she is carrying drops to the ground. Balancing precariously on one limb, the girl crouches to retrieve her parcel; she falls in the attempt. Sonny feels sorry for the girl and goes to her aid, but Alfonso pulls him back roughly. "Leave her be, Santino."

Sonny fights him. "But Alfonso, look at her . . . she's handicapped."

The old man's grip tightens. "I *said,* leave her be."

Sonny hears the earnestness in his tone and watches helplessly as the girl struggles to get back on her crutches, arms full. Their eyes meet for a second. He sees in hers the pain of a dying animal caught in a trap, begging to be put out of its misery. Finally she stands, embarrassed by the episode, and limps away with her head down. Sonny demands hotly, "What did ya do that for? I thought you loved these people?"

"I do love them, Santino"—Alfonso's eyes are cold—"but she is no good. Her father had her leg cut off."

Sonny is flabbergasted. "Her father did that! Why?"

Alfonso shoots him a stern look. "Her father is a don . . . she insulted him."

Sonny cannot conceive of any insult with such severe repercussions. "What did she do, Alfonso?"

His teacher turns with foreboding. "She gave herself to a man."

Sonny is wide-eyed. "That's all she did? . . . make love? She lost her leg 'cause she got fucked?"

Alfonso reminds him, "That is our way, Santino."

That night the pathetic image of the crippled girl still haunts him as he makes love to Laura . . . he is impotent.

"What's wrong, Santino?"

Sonny lies back with his wrist on his forehead, staring at the sky, "I saw a girl in town today . . . her father had cut off her leg."

"Yes, that is Anna Bastini. We've got to be more careful, Santino . . . that could happen to me. My father is a don, too."

Sonny sits bolt upright. "What! Your father's a don? Shit, Laura . . . you could lose your leg."

"You could lose more than that. My father would kill you if he ever found out."

Sonny gathers up his blanket and puts it into the basket of his bike. "We can't see each other anymore, Laura. It's too dangerous." He gets on the bike to go. "It's not just me I'm thinking about, Laura. I don't wanna know that I made you a cripple the rest of your life. I'm gonna leave Catania sometime, but you gotta stay here and live your life with that disgrace."

Sonny starts to pedal away, and she runs after him. "Wait . . . wait! Santino, wait!" He stops. Laura reaches him, panting. "I have an idea, Santino . . . there is a cave about a mile from here. No one else knows about it . . . we could meet there."

"No, Laura . . . it's too risky."

She looks at him with large, pleading eyes. "Please, Santino . . . let's try it. Nothing can hurt our love . . . please." She kisses him.

Sonny cannot refuse her; he finally concedes, "All right, Laura . . . we'll try it."

The next week their assignations are moved to the cave, which Laura has cleverly camouflaged with thick bushes to ensure their safety. Sonny alone knows that behind them a candle, a bottle of wine, and his love wait. Laura has fixed up the cave with a crucifix and a Madonna statue; a rug over the damp, dirt floor is their bed. Sonny feels more secure here than he did in the open ruins on the beach, but when he first sets foot in the hideout, a peculiar sensation sweeps over him. His instincts tell him this place holds the secrets of souls who suffered the iniquities of the war. After they make love the first night, Sonny tells Laura, "There was a lot of pain here once. . . . Something bad happened . . . I can feel it."

She looks at him steadily. "Yes, Santino . . . but how did you know?"

Sonny rubs his throbbing temples. "I don't know how . . . I just know certain things . . . I always have, ever since I was a kid."

Laura sits up and holds their thin wool blanket around her. "This cave was a hiding place for our family during the war."

Sonny sits up now, too. He remembers Vincenzo telling him how women and children hid out in the wine cellars. "Your family?"

"Yes, Santino. The SS was looking for my father. My mother made this cave our hideout . . . nobody knew about it except my sister and me." Her lower lip trembles as she speaks. "One day, while my mother was asleep, my sister Carlotta left the cave . . . our dog had gotten out, and she went looking for him. When she didn't find him, Carlotta came back here, but a German officer had followed her. When he came in, I was playing behind the water keg. He didn't see me . . . my mother warned me in Sicilian not to move." Laura stares glassy-eyed, almost in a trance, as she goes on. "He shook my mother, trying to find out where my father was. When she wouldn't tell him, he tied her to a chair and tortured her. He burned her nipples and breasts with his cigarette . . . I can still hear her crying. Then she started begging . . . begging him not to rape Carlotta, but he just laughed. He did it right in front of her . . . that bastard. When he had his fun, he dragged my mother and sister from the cave. Two days later they found the bodies. Carlotta's throat had been slit. He had burned my mother alive . . . all that was left of her was a charred skeleton. One day later they found me . . . wandering in the hills." She looks at Sonny. "I couldn't speak . . . I didn't say a word for years after that. I know that's why I majored in languages . . . I had to overcome it."

"Your father . . . then he knows about this cave?"

"No, Santino . . . he was in the hills for over a year. He never knew where it happened. Yesterday I came back here for the first time. I stood outside for almost an hour. It took all of my courage to go inside, but I knew I had to. I cleaned all day . . . I thought maybe the memories could be cleared out with the cobwebs." Her eyes brim with tears. "But I could still see those Nazi boots and hear my mother's and sister's cries. It's something I can never forget, Santino."

"How could you come back here, Laura, after what happened?"

"Because of my love for you, Santino . . . I know this is the only place in the world we can be together. It sounds funny . . . but I feel secure here, in a way. This cave kept me safe once . . . and it will keep us safe from now on."

Sonny thinks of the agonies suffered by Laura and her family. He clenches his fist in anger. "Vincenzo said it . . . The Nazis were animals." For a long time Sonny and Laura are silent. He holds the Sicilian girl close, as though trying to hug the pain from her.

Finally she looks up at him. "Let's offer a prayer for their souls, Santino."

This snaps Sonny out of the past. "I don't do that shit, Laura. I feel bad, but I'd rather get my hands on that German asshole so I could cut his dick off. That would be better than prayin'." Laura goes over to the Madonna. She kneels by herself and bows her head.

It takes a few hours before Sonny is able to shake off the uncomfortable feelings he has in the cave, but when he does, the star-crossed lovers are then able to carry on their dangerous romance in peace.

It was now six months since Sonny had left New York for Sicily. In that time he'd made great strides in his education, but a lot of questions remained unanswered. How much longer would he be in Catania? What was his assignment? Where would he be sent? It was clear that each of the men was being trained for a special job, though they saw very little of each other except at dinnertime . . . the rule of noncommunication was strictly adhered to. Only by accident did a fellow trainee divulge some startling information.

One morning Sonny was hurrying down the hallway, panicked because he'd overslept. Too many nights this week had been spent making love to Laura until dawn. Knowing Alfonso did not condone lateness, Sonny rounded the corner fast and crashed into another trainee, Giorgio, who was just coming out of his room. A folder flew from his hand, and its contents were scattered on the floor. "Giorgio, I'm sorry, man . . . I didn't see ya." Sonny stoops to gather some of the papers and is astonished by what he sees . . . pictures of Marilyn Monroe. All kinds of shots, from every conceivable angle, some nude ones in explicit detail. There are photographs of her activities at home, with her friends, in her car, even shots of her in her bedroom with a prominent American politician. Sonny hands Giorgio the pile he'd collected . . . then spots something else that's rolled into a corner . . . a rifle scope. He picks it up and looks through it. Suddenly the dim hallway is brightly illuminated. "What kind of scope is this?"

"It's specially coated with fluorescent glass for night shooting. You can see an African move in the dark with that thing."

Sonny hands it back to him. "I seen you shootin' on the

range . . . you're an expert with a rifle."

"Just like you are, climbing up and down with those guys on your shoulders. I don't know what they're training you for . . . but that's tough."

"I dunno what they got in mind for me . . . but they must got an important hit planned for you if rifles are your specialty."

Giorgio cleans a speck of dirt from the lens. "Rifles aren't my specialty."

"What is?"

"Drugs and chemicals." He pockets the scope. "We've talked too much already." Giorgio starts to go, then remembers something. "Santino, you're from America . . . what is it like in Hollywood, California?"

"I dunno . . . I never been there . . . I'm from another part of the country."

Giorgio is disappointed. "Oh . . . well, I'm going to be out there for a long time." He pats the folder. "I got a job to do."

Sonny pieces the amazing puzzle together. "Man, that's sure a heavy job."

"You'll know soon enough, Santino, everything done around here is heavy . . . you're with the best." At the sound of approaching footsteps Giorgio rushes down the hall, and Sonny hurries off to class. On the way he tries to imagine why anyone would want Marilyn Monroe dead. He knows she is linked to that important political figure in the states. Maybe she's putting some kind of pressure on him that could cause a scandal and destroy his career. What would the Mafia get in return for the hit? Why would they get involved . . . and why wouldn't the American Mafia take care of it? The answer suddenly hits him. No one would suspect the Sicilians. If the CIA were involved or the military, they could supply the Mafia with information about communist leaders. It was a good deal for both sides. The politician gets rid of his problem, and the Mafia is helped in their vendetta. Sonny is still absorbed in this intrigue when he gets to his martial arts class.

Alfonso is waiting at the door for him. "I'm sorry I'm late, Alfonso."

"Being late is a dangerous habit, Santino . . . it could get you killed." Alfonso takes a seat, and Sonny changes into his workout pants. "I know you're excited about leaving for Rome tomorrow, Santino, but you're not there yet!"

Rome . . . Sonny had forgotten all about this trip. He was only going to the whorehouse now so that Alfonso wouldn't get suspicious . . . the only woman he wanted was Laura. "Stop daydreaming, Santino. We've wasted enough time already." Alfonso claps his hands, "Get to work. There won't be any warm-up today."

By the time Sonny marked his first anniversary at the villa, he was fluent in Sicilian, and had also learned the Mafia's secret code language. This hybrid of church Latin and Sicilian had been used by the dons and their soldiers since the 1940s to protect them from bugging by law-enforcement agencies. Sonny's memory had been considerably sharpened in that year. He could repeat, verbatim, any tape Alfonso gave him to learn in just a few hours.

Sonny was to continue his classroom work for six more months until finally, in December, he would be ready to move on to his specialty—demolitions.

The American trainee was anxious to start his instruction, but Alfonso's plans delayed him for a while. "Santino, you are going to spend this Christmas in Indianapolis."

"What? Why do I have to go back home?"

"To convince your family that you're working in the States."

"They already think that . . . I've been callin' 'em every six weeks from the whorehouse. They think I'm a truck driver."

"Well, from now on you are an aluminum siding salesman."

"Alfonso, I don't know anything about that."

"You will." The old man hands Sonny a packet. "Inside there's a tape on the complete line of Manhattan Siding Company. Learn it. . . . Santino, you must become an expert on aluminum siding."

"Why?"

"Because we want your parents to be convinced that is what you do."

"O.K., Alfonso." Sonny looks inside the package. "What else is in here?"

"A payroll check from Manhattan. Have your mother open up a savings account for you in Indianapolis. . . . She'll get one of those checks every few months. When you call her from now on, tell her you're on the road for the company. If she wants to call you, give her the number of your main office in Des Moines."

"My main office?"

"Yes, Santino . . . Manhattan Siding works with the Mafia. They'll relay your messages here."

"Why go to all this trouble? Why don't you just have Gino write letters for me and have them mailed from the States?"

Alfonso raises a warning finger. "Mothers are the most skeptical people in the world, Santino . . . she'll never believe anything until she sees you in the flesh." Sonny sighs. He doesn't want to be away from Laura, and he wants to start his training. "Santino . . . you'll only be gone three days . . . just enough to convince them. When you come back, you'll meet your new instructor." Alfonso hands him his ticket. "Have a nice trip, Santino."

Gino and Carlo take Sonny to the airport. At the gate Gino hands Sonny an envelope. "Santino, this is a Christmas card to my cousin Richie . . . mail it when you get to America, eh? The mail is so bad here."

Sonny looks at the address. "Chicago, huh? What does your cousin do?"

"He is a policeman."

"Your cousin's a cop?"

"Yes, Santino . . . but he is a loyal soldier first. He works for the Mafia." Sonny nods. "Then he must work for Sam Scorzelli."

"He works for all the families. He is our undercover man in the States."

Sonny slips the card in his pocket. "I'll mail this as soon as I get through customs."

Christmas in Indianapolis went off exactly as planned. Mr. and Mrs. Gibson were pleased to see that their son finally had a good job with a steady income. His mother thought this would be a perfect time for her son to settle down, but Sonny told her since the aluminum siding business took him all over the world, he couldn't think of marriage. Sonny was happy to see that his parents were in good health and happy. His father, a TV repairman now, enjoyed his work. His half-brother was a junior bank executive, and his half-sister was married. When it was time for Sonny to leave, he gave his mother his main office number in Des Moines. "I call in for my messages there, Mom . . . Call me if you need me."

The day after Sonny got back to Sicily, he met his new instructor. Forty-seven-year-old ex-Marine Sergeant Robert Sanders was one of the best demolitions experts and commercial divers in the world. The lines of his face were a badge of his experience; the icy blue eyes, a warning of it. The Mafia had used his expertise many times in the past; they respected him. During Patton's invasion of Sicily Sanders was decorated for commanding a special raid on Ponza. The dons never forgot his bravery in that daring rescue.

The marine's arrogance caused Sonny to dislike him immediately, but this was not a personality contest for Sanders. His job was to educate Sonny.

Sonny sees Laura the night before he begins his training with Sanders. When he arrives at the cave, she is waiting for him under their blanket . . . naked. She looks so beautiful, he hates to give her his bad news. "I'm starting some new kind of trainin', Laura. I don't know what I'm gonna be doin', but Alfonso says I gotta get a lotta rest."

"Does that mean you have to go home earlier, Santino?"

He unties his shoes. "No . . . I can't see you for six weeks, Laura."

Because of her upbringing Laura knows she can't ask him any questions about this. "I will miss you Santino . . . be careful. I would die if anything happened to you."

Sonny takes off his shirt and pants. "Don't worry, nothin's gonna happen to me. Let's not spend the whole night thinkin' about it, O.K.?" He crawls under the blanket and kisses her gently, but she doesn't respond. "What's the matter?"

She says tentatively, "When you finish your training in six weeks, I guess you'll be going to Rome, won't you . . ."

He picks up her chin and turns her face to his. "Is that what's botherin' you? You know I only go so Alfonso won't suspect us. He'd never believe it if I told him I didn't want to go." Her eyes are still sad. "I told you, Laura, those girls don't mean anything to me . . . No one could ever take me away from you . . . I love you."

"I love you too, Santino." She sits up and hugs her knees. "I still wish you didn't have to go."

"Yeah . . . I just wish you could come with me." He sits up. "Wait a minute . . . why don't you meet me there? The girls would sneak you into my room. They'll do anything I ask them to."

"I can understand why, Santino . . ."

"They could come in and pretend I was making love to them. Gino and Carlo wouldn't even know . . . they'd still see a lot of girls going in and out." She gives him a jealous glance. "Don't worry, Laura, I'll only make love to you. I'll be finished with my trainin' the second week in February. You go to Rome and wait for me . . . If I'm late, you can spend a few days there, right?"

"I think so."

"O.K., stay at the Hotel Veneto, and one of the girls will come and get you."

"Do you think it will work, Santino?"

"I'll make sure it does. He lays her back down on the rug. "I only want you, Laura." The lovers have an especially passionate night, and the next day at dawn Sonny reports to Sanders for his first lesson. It is an appropriate start for the two fiery personalities . . . explosives.

Academically they are an unbeatable team: an excellent teacher and an exceptionally bright student. In just three weeks Sonny could rig a set charge to cut a rock in half with an edge smoother than glass, quarter it, or blow it to smithereens. When the uncompromising teacher is satisfied with Sonny's expertise in demolitions, they move on to the next phase . . . underwater diving. In the weeks Sonny spends with Sanders there is a noticeable change in his feelings toward him. His former dislike for the tough ex-marine has now turned to hatred, which intensifies when Sonny and Sanders enter the icy water for Sonny's first diving lesson. The instructor is outfitted in a full wet suit and light scuba gear, the student is dressed only in a tee shirt and shorts. "Watch carefully, Sonny . . . pay close attention." Sanders takes a beach ball underwater with him. A few minutes later it pops up, and the Marine surfaces.

Sonny is unimpressed by the demonstration. "So what's the big deal about that? That's a kids' game."

"No, Sonny. It's to show you how strong the pressure is down there. Normally your regulator will equalize that pressure for you . . . but if anything happens to it and you have to surface . . . you gotta open your mouth and breathe out as you go up. Don't hold your breath. Whatever air is left in your lungs will expand and bust 'em wide open. Ya got that, Sonny?" Sonny nods apathetically, and Sanders continues. "Now . . . I'm gonna teach you to control your breathing so that in case something happens, you'll have enough air to surface. Here, put this on and take a deep breath." He hands Sonny a plastic bag to put over his head, then tapes it tightly closed around his neck. Sanders forces him to submerge. Sonny thrashes wildly as he struggles for air, but the marine holds his head down firmly. When Sonny finally is allowed to surface, he tears the bag off and lunges violently at his tormentor. With one hand covering Sanders' face, Sonny pushes him backward, pinning his instructor down as the waves crash over him. "I'm gonna kill ya . . . I'm gonna drown your fuckin' ass." Suddenly the marine gives him a karate chop that sends Sonny reeling back to the beach. Coughing and sputtering, Sanders tries to regain his balance. Sonny rushes at him again, but Gino and Carlo restrain him. Sanders, still gasping, warns, "You don't wanna fuck with me, kid. I know too many tricks." He points a finger at his hot-headed pupil. "What I'm teaching you now will save your life . . . one day you'll thank me."

Sonny is still seething. Gino pats him on the shoulder. "Relax, Santino. I don't like the *baccola* either, but Alfonso says you have to do this."

Sonny dries himself, rubbing his skin red, using the towel to dissipate his anger. He stares hatefully at Sanders. "I'm gonna get your motherfuckin' ass someday!"

The ex-marine just grins. "Could be . . . if you make it through my training . . ."

For the next month Sanders pushed his pupil hard. Every morning on his bike the marine clocked Sonny's five-mile run, increasing the distance if his time was off, even by seconds. An hour of calisthenics on the beach was followed by a mile swim out to the diving boat, with Sanders, Gino, and Johno riding in a launch alongside Sonny. Once on board the exhausted pupil was allowed only five minutes before the lessons began. At this point Sonny was learning far more than sport scuba. Sanders was teaching him the sophisticated methods commercial divers use in their deep ocean dives. At 199 feet compressed air is toxic, and a special mixture of gases must be mixed with the air in the tanks. Sonny coupled this new information with his knowledge of demolition and eventually was able to rig a set charge at depths down to 400 feet. The instructor was pleased with his pupil's progress, but their personal relationship worsened daily. Sonny resented being a pack horse for the heavy gear they used on the ocean floor, while the marine descended empty-handed.

One day Sonny rebelled. He told Alfonso, "I'm not goin' down with that son of a bitch anymore . . . in fact, I'm gonna kill him."

Alfonso replied calmly, "That's O.K., Santino . . . you don't have to go out if you don't want to. Besides, I'm taking you to a party tomorrow afternoon." Sonny puffed up proudly . . . he had won his first argument with Alfonso. It seemed a double victory: the odious diver disappeared from his life, and at last Sonny able to mingle with townspeople at a local celebration. That night, he tossed and turned in restless anticipation of the festivities.

The next day the sound of Sicilian folk songs fills the air of the Catania countryside as Sonny and Alfonso join the party. Benito, a slim, gray-haired man in a starched, collarless shirt approaches them. He is the host of the celebration and an important don. Benito welcomes the new arrivals warmly. "*Buona sera,* Alfonso . . . my loyal friend."

They hug. "Benito, this is Santino."

"Ah, Santino . . . *si* . . . we have heard many good things about you." The host embraces his guest. "Alfonso, he is strong . . . like a bull."

The sponsor laughs. "You should have seen him when he first came to me . . . all that boyish fat from greasy American food. Now he has the body of a man."

"*Si, si* . . . he is a fine young man . . . just like my sons"—Benito's face darkens—"except for one." The sound of an accordion lightens his mood. Benito puts an arm around Sonny's shoulder and escorts the new arrivals to a clearing in the woods where a long table of food and wine is lavishly laid out. "Enjoy, my friends . . . enjoy." Then Benito leaves with Alfonso to talk to two of the men. Sonny pours himself a glass of wine. He has only recently begun to find the taste pleasing, even though he indulges infrequently. The American is assimilating many of the Sicilian ways, but there are a multitude of them left to discover. Today Sonny watches in fascination as the men dance the traditional Campagnola, with their arms linked high in the air. He finds that they are much freer with themselves than most men. Here they hug, kiss, and dance with each other openly. They are not afraid to show their emotions—an apparent inconsistency, considering that their profession is one of the most dispassionate in the world.

The American finds it odd that there are no women present, but thinks it is just another unusual custom. As the drinking and laughter continue into the night, Sonny begins to feel less of a foreigner among the men. He is really enjoying himself.

After everyone has eaten and the food is removed rom the table, Benito makes a toast: "To Giovanni." Everyone turns to acknowledge a handsome, strapping youth of about twenty. They drink to his health, then each man kisses him on the cheek. Suddenly two men grab the unsuspecting boy and pin him down on the table. Benito steps forward, a large butcher knife in his hand. *"No, Pappa!* PLEASE!"* are Giovanni's last words before a clamp is placed in his mouth. With one swift movement Benito cuts out the terrified boy's tongue. Sonny is horrified by the maiming, but he does not react openly. The bleeding, mutilated boy is given a shot to sedate him, then is carried to the car. The other men in the room murmur approvals as the "party" breaks up. Alfonso and Sonny drive away in silence.

On the way home Sonny finally asks, "Alfonso, what did that guy do to deserve that? That's the coldest thing I've ever seen."

Alfonso looks at the road ahead. "He talked to the wrong people, Santino."

"Man, I feel sorry for him . . . "

Alfonso says coldly, "It is better to lose your tongue than your life. The other families would have killed Giovanni; Benito knew what he had to do to save him and to set an example for his other sons." Alfonso continues unemotionally, "If the boy had discipline, it would not have happened." Sonny is silent. As the lights of Catania twinkle in the distance, he thinks about his own rebellion against discipline and wonders about its consequences.

The following morning Alfonso knocks loudly on Sonny's door. "Are you ready to go diving today, Santino?"

Sonny opens it immediately. "I'm ready, Alfonso."

The old man replies with a knowing smile, "I'm happy to hear that." Alfonso is certain he has made a strong point to his charge. On the way to the beach Alfonso says, "Do you understand what the lesson was yesterday, Santino?"

"I think so, Alfonso . . . Giovanni shouldn't have talked . . . but what he said didn't get him in trouble . . . it's the fact that he said it at all, right?"

"Yes, Santino . . . Mafia rules are strict, but they are well-founded. If one brick is loose, the rest of our house can fall. The Sicilian Mafia replaces the bad brick before it does any real damage. . . . That is our way, Santino."

Alfonso lets Sonny off at the dock, and Sanders is already in the launch. He's mad. "Let's move it . . . you're late . . . I don't like to be kept waiting by a kid.''

Sonny looks at Alfonso. "You see what I gotta take? That's not part of my training.''

The old man wags his finger at him. "What you put up with today will reap many rewards for you tomorrow, Santino.''

Sanders starts the motor. "Come on, kid . . . I don't wanna say it again.''

Sonny and the bodyguards get out of the car. Gino grumbles to Carlo, "That guy . . . sometimes he goes too far.'' Sonny overhears the remark but says nothing.

The ride out to the diving boat is tense that day. The hatred Sonny feels for Sanders is now mutual. With great relish the instructor tells Sonny, "Wait till you see this maneuver I got planned. Everything else was child's play.'' He smiles. "This one could really cost you your life.''

As soon as they board the boat, Sanders and Sonny gear up on the deck for the exercise, an old military maneuver used in sabotage. Sonny is to blow up four poles on the ocean floor—all must explode simultaneously. When both divers are suited up, they begin their descent. Sunlight shafting through the crystal blue water creates a backdrop of heavenly rays as they follow the anchor line to the bottom.

Once they reach the target, Sanders hands Sonny a pack of explosives. Sonny wraps the pack around a pole, then rigs the primer cord, which sends electrical current to ignite the blasting cap he finally puts into the charge. When all four poles are set, the divers surface. Back on deck Sonny pushes the starter mechanism . . . Nothing happens. Sanders sits on the rail. "Go down and check the misfire, Sonny.''

"Why me?''

The marine smiles. " 'Cause you set it, and I said so.'' Annoyed, Sonny starts overboard, but Sanders jerks him back by his weight belt. "Now I'll save your life, Sonny. What's the first rule?''

Sonny controls his temper and grudgingly recites, "To be totally safe, you gotta wait an hour before checking a misfire. If an ocean current has caused a problem, the current could correct it, and the charge will explode.''

"O.K., Sonny, now sit down and wait.''

An hour passes, and Sonny enters the water again. This time he breaks into a cold sweat as he makes his descent. One wrong move will ignite enough explosives to blow up a city block. Time drags on interminably as he checks the connections and sets new blasting caps. When thoroughly satisfied that everything is in order, he ascends, positive that the set charges will fire.

Sanders is waiting for his pupil on the deck. When Sonny pushes the starter mechanism, nothing happens. Sonny presses the button furiously. "There must be somethin' wrong with this fuckin' starter.''

The marine says provokingly, "There's nothing wrong with it . . . but you're still gonna misfire."

"Whaddya mean? I double-checked everything . . . it's perfect."

Sanders replies smugly, "Not quite, Sonny, I didn't put any live explosives in those packs." He holds up the charges and laughs.

Sonny is irate. He grabs Gino's gun from its holster to shoot the irksome marine. Sanders doesn't even flinch, but sits down casually on the edge of the boat, smiling. Carlo steps between Sonny and Sanders. "Get outta here, Carlo, I'm gonna kill this son of a bitch right now."

Gino tries to reason, "Hey, Santino, Sanders is a good friend of the family . . . he did a lot for our kind during the war. He's trying to teach you things to save your life. Besides, you take orders from Alfonso, and Alfonso didn't tell you to kill him. Give me my gun, Santino."

Sonny hesitates, then reluctantly hands Gino his gun. Sonny's eyes blaze. "Look at that son of a bitch grinning, just look at him . . . I'm still gonna kill him."

Sanders says coolly, "I've saved your life again, Sonny. Remember, never let anybody pack your explosives. Don't trust another diver."

At that moment Sonny is not listening to the advice; he is making a mental vow. By this time tomorrow Robert Sanders will be dead.

Sonny's plan was to kill Sanders during his lesson the next day, but Alfonso tells him diving instruction is over. "You've done a good job, Santino . . . you deserve a trip to Rome." This time Sonny was looking forward to going to the whorehouse. He knows Laura is meeting him there.

The girls sneak her into his room as planned and cover for them. The bodyguards still see a parade of women pass through Sonny's door, but each hooker sits quietly in the bathroom while the young lovers rediscover each other. The creaky, flat-mattressed cot feels as luxurious as a feather bed after the cold, hard floor of their cave. This procedure becomes a routine for each rendezvous. Everyone involved knows that if the deception is exposed, they will all be killed, but even the hardened prostitutes are willing co-conspirators for such deep love.

The day after Sonny returns from Rome, Alfonso invites him to another party. Sonny asks warily, "Am I gonna see another person get his tongue cut out?"

Alfonso says coolly, "Santino . . . I wouldn't take you to anything like that again. This will be good for you." Sonny's eyes reflect doubt, but he can only take his sponsor at his word.

The next afternoon, when they arrive at the large assembly hall in town, the revelry is well under way. Sonny is relieved to see women and children present at this affair. A plump, ruddy-cheeked accordionist provides lively music as jovial men whirl their portly wives around the room. Small boys chase each other across the floor, darting through the dancers. In one corner a circle has formed, and a crowd claps spiritedly around a young couple performing the traditional tarantella. Swept away by their enthusiasm, Sonny joins the group; he is thoroughly at home. Soon it is time to eat. In the adjoining room snow-white cloths cover a banquet table with elaborate antipasto trays laid out every few feet. Every person takes a seat at random with the exception of the don, whose place is reserved at the head of the table. Before the meal begins, he rises and taps his wineglass steadily until there is silence. The elderly man then raises his glass and speaks solemnly. "We are gathered here this afternoon to salute Luigi Manzone." He indicates a jowly, middle-aged man. "Luigi, we are happy to have you back safely in Catania." The don then addresses a heavy-set peasant woman. "And to you, Maria Manzone, and to your children, may God always watch over you . . . *Salute,* Luigi." The men stand, their glasses in hand. As a chorus of *Salute!* fills the room, Luigi acknowledges the toast. The don sits, signaling the women to bring in the first course—large, over-flowing platters of pasta. Conversation and wine flow freely throughout the meal.

"Where was Luigi, Alfonso?"

The old man methodically peels an apple. "He was out of the country, Santino, but he was away much too long." He hands Sonny a slice of the fruit.

Sonny looks over at Luigi, who is eating with gusto. "I can see why everybody likes him so much . . . he seems like a real nice guy."

Alfonso turns to Sonny. "That may be, but you must never say whether you think a person is good or bad, Santino. Keep it to yourself. Things are not always as they seem . . . one day your feelings could be used against you."

As soon as the extravagant feast is over, the don taps his glass again and announces, "It is time for the women and children to leave." When they've gone, the men continue the festivities, drinking, singing, and dancing. Later on in the evening each man, in turn, goes up to kiss Luigi, who is still seated at his place; Sonny follows suit. He looks over at Alfonso, happy to see this time there will be no violence. But Alfonso looks away. Suddenly two men pull Luigi to his feet, and the elderly don aims a schipetta at his face. With the cold steel barrel of the shotgun between his eyes, the marked man makes a rapid sign of the cross. Before he can finish, a single blast blows his head completely off his shoulders, showering the table with blood and brains. Sonny does not react visibly, but inside he is shaken. As the body is removed, the men turn their backs and walk away coldly. Sonny follows them in a daze. Just a few minutes ago they were all drinking to Luigi's health . . . now he was dead.

When they leave, he asks Alfonso, "What was that all about?"

"Luigi had the kiss of death."

"Why, Alfonso? What did he do?"

The old man stops at the door and turns to face Sonny. "He betrayed his own blood for money."

Betrayal . . . this was something Sonny knew well. He'd been betrayed by the blacks, by the fence, and by Eddie and Franco. He felt death was the only just punishment for betrayal. They leave the large hall and walk to the car. Before they get in, Alfonso asks, "What did you learn from this, Santino?"

Sonny thinks for a moment, then gravely says, "You must never betray the family."

Alfonso's eyes penetrate his. "And how do you feel? Do you feel sorry for Luigi?"

"No, Alfonso." Sonny looks at him stonily. "He had to die."

Sonny has now been in Sicily two and a half years. He continued to practice diving and demolitions twice a week and to work out every day, but the major portion of his physical training was completed. Alfonso felt he was finally ready to start another phase of his training. "For the next few weeks, Santino, you will learn how to defeat the communists in the games they play with a man's mind. Remember when you asked Vincenzo how he could take that torture at Ponza?"

"Yeah . . . I remember."

"Now, Santino . . . you will learn."

"Learn what, Alfonso?"

"The secrets of mental discipline, Santino."

On the first day of class Roberto comes into the room carrying a black leather case. He opens it like a book and lays it out on a table next to Sonny's chair. The long, thin needles inside look a lot more menacing than the ones women use for sewing. Sonny's skin bristles at the sight of the gleaming points. Alfonso enters with the bodyguards, and Gino sets up a tape recorder near the window. The old man smiles. *"Buon giorno,* Santino . . . today you are going to learn a lesson you must remember your whole life . . . how to control your mind." Alfonso pulls up a chair next to him. "The human mind can absorb a tremendous amount of pain, far more than the human body."

While Alfonso lectures, Roberto says casually, "Let me have your hand, Santino."

Sonny extends his left hand as Alfonso goes on. "Listen closely to what I am telling you now . . . it is the most important thing in our lesson. Pain is a simple case of mind over matter. Now——"

Just then Sonny lets out a yell. "What the fuck are you doin'? That hurts." There is a long needle under his thumbnail.

Roberto looks over at Alfonso. "That was about three seconds."

Alfonso nods. "Santino, that needle was stuck in you for three seconds before you yelled. . . . you see, you didn't feel the pain until you saw the needle."

"The fuck I didn't . . . I felt it right away."

Roberto shakes his head, "No, Santino . . . I put the needle in when you were listening to Alfonso."

Sonny calls to Gino, "Hey, Gino . . . is that right? Were you watchin'?"

"Roberto's right, Santino . . . you didn't yell at first."

The old man nods to Roberto, and another needle is stuck into Sonny—this time under his arm. "Shit . . . that hurts . . . goddam it."

Alfonso prompts him. "Mind over matter, Santino . . . think of something else. Think of the girls at the whorehouse . . . when you see them naked. Think of how you feel when they spread their legs, Santino." He tries those images, but the excruciating pain overpowers any other thoughts. Alfonso keeps suggesting, "Think about money, Santino . . . millions of dollars . . . what you can do with it."

Sonny continues to howl in pain as Roberto now sticks the needles under each of his toenails. Alfonso tries a different angle. "Think of Sanders, Santino . . . how much you hate him. It's mind over matter . . . you can do it." By this time Sonny is in agony. Even thinking of Sanders would be better than his reality, but he can't seem to keep his mind off the pain. Roberto sticks several needles in the tender skin in the crook of Sonny's arm. When he screams this time, Alfonso leans over and starts shouting right in his face, "You're a man, Santino, stop yelling . . . you're a man." Sonny listens for the first time. "Count backward in your head, Santino." Sonny braces himself and begins the mental countdown from 100. By forty-five the pain lessens. When he gets down to one, Sonny looks at his bleeding fingernails and toes. How did Vincenzo ever last through his torture?

Alfonso brings over the recorder. "Now we'll see how well you did, Santino." When the tape rolls, Sonny flinches at the sound of his yells. He notices, however, that on the last part, when he was counting, his screams were not as loud, even though there were more needles in him. "When your mind was occupied, Santino . . . you were not able to think about what hurt. People who lose an arm, they complain about a tingling in their fingers . . . or a person who loses a leg sometimes thinks he's sprained his ankle. The mind remembers the feeling of pain and then feels it. You are training your mind to forget pain, Santino. Once you learn this, you will be able to withstand anything. It will be impossible for you to betray the Mafia under torture."

As Sonny progressed, the volume of his screams diminished, and in just a few weeks he was able to hold all of them inside. The third week Roberto subjected Sonny to torture by fire, lighting the ends of his fingers. But Sonny was able to control the pain so well, even with his burns, there was never any swelling. "You are learning the secrets of sword-swallowers and fire-eaters, Santino . . . they are ordinary men like you and me, except they know how to control their sensibility."

The fourth week of this training Sonny was not allowed to eat. For five days he was given nothing but fruit juice, and on the sixth day he was half-crazy with starvation. "Alfonso, when am I gonna get some food? I'm so hungry I could eat a fuckin' horse . . ."

"Today you will eat, Santino . . . Roberto is going to blindfold you first."

"I don't give a shit if he hangs me upside down, just give me some goddam food . . ." When Sonny's eyes were covered, the first forkful was fed to him. After a few chews he spit it out, "This shit's not even cooked. What the hell . . . I can't eat this."

Alfonso calms him. "You don't have to eat it, Santino . . . but someday it may be all you can get." Sonny assumes this exercise is for outdoor survival, where you might not be able to cook your food, but he still could not eat for two days. Finally, on the eighth day of his compulsive fast, Sonny breaks down, devouring anything put in front of him. Most of it tasted like raw meat and cold spaghetti. Later Alfonso showed him the pictures of his meals. Sonny was revolted. Nausea churned in his stomach as he saw himself eating beetles, raw birds, and worms.

"Man, I never would've eaten this shit if I knew what it was."

"Someday you might have to eat these kind of things to stay alive. When the communists get hold of you, the first thing they do is starve you to tear down your strength. You must keep yourself physically strong . . . you might be in a position to get information out. Roaches and beetles are the most common insects you'll find in most prisons . . . but if there aren't any, your own fingernails can keep you alive."

"My fingernails?"

"Yes, Santino . . . they contain calcium . . . and you can eat your skin. There is a lot of protein in your flesh . . . you can survive for days by scraping off pieces from parts of the body where the skin is thick . . . like the bottom of the foot or the palms of the hand."

"I don't know if I could do that."

Alfonso raises a finger. "Mind over matter again, Santino . . . let your mind do the work. Just like pain, it remembers taste and smell . . . you can train your mind to believe you're eating lasagna, and you will be eating it."

Immediately after this phase of his education Sonny returned to the classroom. He had to familiarize himself with the heads of families all over the world, memorizing pictures of international Mafia figures.

He also studied their hit men (known as button men) and chief lieutenants so that he would be able to spot potential enemies. The only
family excluded from this examination was that of his American sponsor,
Don Giuseppe. The don was protecting himself. If Sonny went to work
for another family someday, Don Giuseppe didn't want him bringing
secrets of the Loganno family with him.

One day Alfonso presents him with a thick folder. "This family will
be most influential for you, Santino . . . it is extremely important that
you know everything about them." The file is labeled "Genetti Family
History."

Sonny looks at the pictures inside while the tape reveals an unusual
story. In 1940 an American soldier was working with the Mafia in Sicily
for military intelligence. During his stay he had gotten the daughter of
Don Genetti pregnant, a crime punishable by death. Because of the
officer's connection with Washington, Genetti, the most powerful don
in Sicily, allowed him to live. The couple married, and a beautiful son,
Santino Gino, was born. Ten years later, in Dayton, Ohio, the don
finally took his revenge. After killing his daughter and her husband the
old man stole his grandson. Neither Don Genetti nor Santino Gino were
ever seen again. The don's estate at that time was valued at $40 million,
and he and his only heir had disappeared. The incident puzzled the
entire Mafia world. When Sonny had memorized the information, he
is quizzed on it by two men and Alfonso. Later Sonny asks why he
needs to know so much about this particular family. Alfonso answers
mysteriously, "You will know in time, Santino."

The next day he is finally given his first real assignment. Sonny
would be making hits on thirteen communist leaders all over the world.
He's surprised to hear his targets will be communists. After all those
years of preparation he thought he would be hitting business executives.
"Alfonso, what about all those guys in insurance? Why'd I have to know
about them?"

"You will be told later on, Santino . . ."

"You know, you guys should be going after that rat Valachi . . . he's
spillin' his guts out right now."

Alfonso assures him, "The families in America have already been
assigned to take care of that problem."

Sonny balls up his fist. "Boy, I'd sure like to go after him . . . I
know I could get him."

The old man says sternly, "You must not concern yourself with
Valachi, Santino . . . your first job is to wipe out these filthy communist
pigs." He hands Sonny a thick portfolio of pictures and three tapes.
"You have ninety days to memorize this material, Santino." Sonny
studies his tapes diligently. When he meets these men, there would be
more at stake than a quiz.

Three months later, when Alfonso grills him on his subjects mercilessly, Sonny answers perfectly. "You know your facts cold, but stay sharp, Santino. Eat, think, and drink these people. Within the next few weeks you'll be drilled again. The next time it will be by two men who know these subjects better than their own mothers. You must satisfy them before you start your mission." He puts an arm around Sonny's shoulder. "You've done well, Santino . . . I have a surprise for you tomorrow. Get a good night's rest."

The next morning Alfonso knocks on Sonny's door at seven o'clock. When he gets no response, the old man goes in and shakes Sonny by the foot. "Come on, Santino . . . get up." Sonny groans sleepily. "Santino . . . let's go."

Sonny opens one eye. "I thought I had the day off." Assuming he could sleep late, Sonny hadn't left Laura until five o'clock that morning.

Alfonso opens the curtains. "I have a surprise for you. . . . Look, it's a beautiful morning." Alfonso goes to the dresser. He takes out some clothes and throws them on the bed. "Here, wear your white shirt and new pants."

Sonny yawns. "Why?"

"Don't ask questions, Santino . . . just hurry up." He watches Sonny drag himself out of bed. "What have you been doing all night, Santino?" Before Sonny answers, Alfonso is halfway out the door. "I'll be waiting downstairs."

Fifteen minutes later, clean-shaven and more awake, Sonny meets his sponsor in the parlor. "Where are we going, Alfonso?"

The old man grabs his hat from a rack on the wall. "Into town . . . and we're late." They take their usual route, but this time Alfonso stops at the parish church they've passed so many times on the way to the cafe. Alfonso climbs the steps.

Sonny asks as he follows him, "What are we doin' here . . . what's here?" Alfonso turns at the door and puts a hand on Sonny's shoulder. "Three years ago I said when you were a man of courage, discipline, and loyalty, I would be your godfather . . . The time has come for that sacred tradition . . . you are going to be baptized, Santino."

"But I was already baptized in Indiana . . . I didn't think they let ya do that twice."

"You've forgotten what I told you . . . over here we are the law . . . even when it comes to the Church. The priest who is going to perform the ceremony is a priest first, but he also has family who are Mafia. . . . Father Basanti is Pepino's brother." Alfonso opens the door and goes inside. The old man removes his hat and genuflects before the tabernacle behind the front altar. He looks up at Sonny. "Show some respect, Santino."

"I don't believe in this stuff, Alfonso."

His sponsor points a warning finger. "You are in the house of God . . . do what I tell you."

Sonny bends one knee slightly, then follows Alfonso to the back of the church, where Father Basanti is waiting. As they walk to the silver baptismal font, Sonny looks around. The rich appointments of the small parish church surprise him. The altar rails and crucifix are gold. The floors are marble, and the statues are jeweled. On the right side of the altar the crown of the blessed Virgin is inlaid with sapphires. Sonny lets out a mental whistle. He has never seen precious gems like these in any Indiana church. If he had, he would have robbed it in a minute. Here, however, the statues are safe . . . the Mafia protects its own. Sonny's eyes are still roaming when the sacred ceremony begins. An elbow nudges him, and Alfonso whispers sternly, "Pay attention, Santino."

Father Basanti addresses Alfonso. "What is the name of this man?"

"Santino Gino, Father . . ."

"What do you ask of God's church for him?"

"Baptism."

"Alfonso Lambretti, are you ready to fulfill your duties to Christ as godfather and sponsor of Santino Gino?"

"Yes, Father."

Basanti then prays over Sonny. "May Almighty God send His only son to pray for this man and help him fight the devil in all its cunning. Bring Santino out of darkness in Christ's light for his life's journey . . ." The priest turns back to Alfonso and says gravely, "Do you reject sin?"

"Yes."

"Do you reject the glamour of evil and refuse to be mastered by sin?"

"I do."

"Do you reject Satan, the father of sin and Prince of Darkness?"

"I do."

"Let us now profess our faith together."

Alfonso says with the priest, "I believe in God, the Father Almighty, Creator of Heaven and earth; in Jesus Christ His only Son, Our Lord, who was crucified, died and was buried. He rose again from the dead and is now seated at the right hand of the Father." Sonny watches Alfonso recite the prayer from memory. He has never seen Alfonso go to church or even talk about it . . . until today.

The priest continues. "Do you believe in the Holy Spirit, the Holy Catholic Church, the communion of saints, the forgiveness of sins, the resurrection of the dead, and life everlasting?"

Alfonso says, "I do."

Father Basanti turns to Sonny. "Is it your will, Santino, that you should be baptized in the faith of Christ we have professed?"

Sonny hesitates. When Alfonso shoots him a sharp look and a nod, he answers, "Yes."

The priest blesses him and sprinkles holy water. "I baptize you in the name of the Father and of the Son and of the Holy Spirit." The priest dips his finger in some salt on the tray next to him and places it on Sonny's tongue, "You are the salt of the earth . . . this is the salt of wisdom." Father Basanti dips his thumb in the oil, making a tiny sign of the cross on Sonny's forehead and eyes. "This is the chrism of salvation. I annoint you in the name of God the Father who has freed you from sin." The priest wets his thumb with saliva and makes two more tiny crosses: one on Sonny's ear and one on his mouth. "May you always hear God's name and proclaim the glory of his word."

The priest then blesses both men and walks them to the doors of the church. He shakes Sonny's hand. "You are lucky to have Alfonso as your godfather." Father Basanti turns to the old man. "Maybe we'll see you at Mass more often now . . . ."

Alfonso shakes the priest's hand. "God bless you, Father." He puts on his hat. "Come on, Santino, let's go."

The day after the sacred ceremony his godfather invited Sonny to dinner. At seven P.M. sharp Alfonso raps urgently on his door. "Hurry up, Santino, we don't want to be late."

Sonny can't imagine why Alfonso is so impatient, but he rushes out, knowing by now never to question his godfather. Sonny stops in his tracks. He has never seen his sponsor in a pressed suit and tie. "What are ya all dressed up for, Alfonso? Ya look really nice . . . ya look twenty-five years younger."

Alfonso grins. "I feel twenty-five years younger, Santino. This is a very special night."

A few minutes later the two men get in the car. As they drive through the narrow streets, Sonny tries to imagine what could be so special that he hasn't already seen. He and Alfonso have been to most of the places in town. They've been to parties and weddings, but the old man had never gotten this spruced up before. After a fifteen-minute drive across town they arrive at an elaborate home surrounded by a high, white-brick wall. Alfonso opens a heavily scrolled iron gate and walks Sonny through a beautifully landscaped patio to the front door.

An elderly man answers their knock. Sonny recognizes him as the don who executed Luigi at the party. Alfonso introduces them. "Santino, I would like you to meet Don Belfiore." Sonny's heart pounds wildly—this man is Laura's father. Was this party his execution. . . . How had the don found out about him and Laura? Laura . . . had she been punished? He hadn't seen her for a few days. Perhaps she was already a cripple. Skillfully concealing his astonishment and his concern, Sonny accepts a kiss from the don, who then escorts them into the parlor. It is filled with men, both young and old, some of whom Sonny has seen at other parties. There is one comforting face in the crowd, Mario, Don Giuseppe's chief lieutenant. Why is he here?

Mario hugs Sonny warmly. "Don Giuseppe and Nick send their regards, Santino."

Sonny answers earnestly, "I can't wait to see 'em again, and please tell Don Giuseppe I'm anxious to get home. But what are you doing here?"

Mario is about to reply when Don Belfiore calls for silence. The men take their seats, and Don Belfiore begins. "We all know what we are here for tonight. We are sorry that Don Giuseppe cannot be with us, but we welcome his chief lieutenant, Mario, who represents the Loganno family."

Don Belfiore then turns ceremoniously to Alfonso and nods. Alfonso addresses the group solemnly. "It is my honor to present to you Santino Gibson. I know that we have never before allowed anyone outside the Sicilian blood to enter the family, but Santino has learned our ways. He has been under my supervision for three years . . . I am his godfather. I give you my word that he will make a respected and loyal soldier . . . He is ready." Alfonso turns to his student, who is slightly bewildered. "Santino, are you ready to take your vows to become a soldier?"

At that moment Sonny realizes this is his initiation into the Mafia. He answers respectfully, "Yes, I am ready."

Alfonso speaks formally in Sicilian. "Death to me if Santino betrays any of the family that is gathered here. If he does, may my soul, the souls of my children and their children, never enter heaven, and may the souls of my dead loved ones never rest until the debt has been paid."

Don Belfiore hands him a large sheet of paper, which Alfonso shreds. He asks Sonny to cup his hands and places the pieces in his palms. "These are the signatures of the men who witness your vows tonight. If you betray these vows, they have committed themselves and their families to hunt you down like a wild dog. Do you understand what I am saying, Santino?"

Sonny answers gravely as the men watch him closely. "Yes, I understand."

His sponsor and godfather then burns the paper in Sonny's hands. "These ashes will surround the air where you walk so that these men can find you and hunt you down. Repeat after me, Santino: I swear on my soul, the souls of my children and their children, and on the souls of my dead loved ones that I will never betray any of the family. I swear to these men and Almighty God that I will obey every command given to me as a soldier of the Sicilian Mafia."

Sonny repeats the vows in Sicilian and English. When he is through, Don Belfiore gives him a kiss on the mouth, then one on the cheek, the reverse of the kiss of death with which he marked Luigi. Each man in the room comes up to give Sonny the ritual kiss—Mario is last. He says to Sonny, "I have a question for you from Don Giuseppe. If you were given the command to kill your mother, would you do it without asking questions?"

Now Sonny replies quickly, "Yes."

"Then you are truly a soldier. Don Giuseppe knew that you would learn well from Alfonso. The man that taught you has been one of the Mafia's most feared soldiers for over twenty years. That scar on his throat is just a small token of his loyal service. It was his hero's hand that killed the pig Mussolini. Mussolini had his two sons murdered on the steps of Rome University."

Sonny looks over in awe at the short, fat man across the room. Alfonso had covered the dictator's execution in his history lesson but never mentioned that he was the assassin. By this time the crowd has dispersed, and Alfonso turns to Sonny. "The Mafia is the most loyal group of men in the world, but I will tell you one more thing, Santino. I survived because I never trusted anyone." He puts his hand on Sonny's shoulder. "Do you trust me, Santino?"

Sonny looks directly at the only man who has ever given him such love, and he lies, "No, I don't trust you, Alfonso."

The old man's eyes mist over as he kisses Sonny. "I am proud of you, Santino. You have learned well."

For two days following his vows Alfonso and two other men cross-examine Sonny on the details of the thirteen hits he is to make. His godfather is particularly relentless with him, but Sonny understands why and is glad to be able to help Alfonso with his vendetta; he answers every question flawlessly. The other two interrogators congratulate Alfonso on Sonny's sterling performance, and the old man beams with the pride of a father on his son's graduation day. Giorgio, the severest of the pair, still has some reservations though. "Alfonso, how can you be so sure this kid will be able to pull off these hits?"

Alfonso smiles. "Look at him . . . no one will ever suspect he's a hit man. They'll think he's an American tourist."

Freddo, the second man, marvels. "He's got the best memory I've ever seen for a man who can't read or write English."

Alfonso reminds him, "That's why his memory is so good. Santino knows tapes will keep him alive, Freddo."

When they leave, Sonny asks Alfonso, "Am I working for you or Don Giuseppe?"

"You work for the Sicilian Mafia, you'll always be working for us. But after you've finished your mission, you'll be taking orders from Don

Giuseppe."

"Can I go after Valachi if he's still alive when I get back to the States?"

"I don't see why Don Giuseppe wouldn't let you. After you do this job for us, you'll be the best hit man in the country. You'll have the respect of all the Mafia." The old man smiles. "I'm very proud of you, Santino. Tomorrow night we are going to give you a party."

Sonny throws him a suspicious glance. "A party . . . for me?" He teases his teacher. "Well, I hope I have a better time than I did at those other ones."

A broad smile spreads across the wise man's chubby face. "Don't worry, Santino, this party will be different . . . You are going to be the guest of *honor*."

As the two men hug, Sonny feels a special closeness to Alfonso and to all the people he has met in Sicily. They have embraced him as one of their own; Sonny now has a family.

The next evening Sonny and Alfonso meet outside the villa to go to the party. The old man kisses him, "*Buona fortuna centianni. Tu sei i fio mio.*" ("Good luck for a hundred years. You are my true son."). He hands Sonny a small, gift-wrapped box. "Open this when you get to your party. Gino and Carlo will drive you . . . I'll see you later." He gives Sonny an especially long, firm hug. As they pull away, Alfonso stands at the gate, waving slowly, until the car is out of sight.

About a half-hour out of town Sonny asks how much longer it will take to get there. He's anxious to get back to Catania that night; Laura would be waiting for him. "Hey, where the hell's this party . . . Rome? What's takin' so long?"

Gino says, "You're not going to a party."

"Whaddya mean, no party? Where are we goin'?"

"I can't tell you, Santino . . . Alfonso's orders." Sonny can only wait to find out what's happening, but by now he has become a loyal soldier. He knows whatever lies ahead is for the good of the family. A few hours later they arrive in Palermo; a Spanish passenger ship is ready to set sail. Sonny now sees that his departure from Sicily is reminiscent of the way he left New York. He's concerned about saying good-bye to Laura but knows that there is nothing he can do. Johno unloads his luggage as Gino hands him a ticket and a passport with a new identity: David Stevenson. Carlo gives Sonny a thick portfolio of tapes and files. "Here are your instructions. There is a tape recorder packed in your bag. In each city you will make a new contact. You won't know who he is . . . he'll find you. He might be a native of the country you're working in, but all of your contacts will have Sicilian blood."

"I know, Alfonso told me that."

"One more thing, Santino. Alfonso said he doesn't want you to open your present until you get to Majorca."

Sonny shrugs. "O.K., if that's what Alfonso wants." A signal blasts from the ship. Sonny puts a hand on each of the bodyguard's shoulders. "I wanna thank you guys for puttin' up with me all these years . . . I guess it was pretty bad sometimes."

Carlo says, "It was nothing, Santino . . . part of our job."

"I gotta ask you guys one more thing. That first day I got here . . . I hadda drop my pants, remember?"

Gino lets out a low whistle. "*Madonna,* how could we forget it . . . eh, Carlo?"

"Yeah, well . . . I just wanna know . . . would you guys really have shot me?"

The bodyguards look at each other, then at Sonny. Gino says more seriously, "If Alfonso had put on his hat, we would've blown you in half."

Carlo adds, "It would've been your first and last lesson."

Another boarding signal blasts. They hug each other for the last time. Then Sonny hurries up the gangplank. When he's halfway up, he turns and shouts, "Hey Gino . . . Carlo . . . I'm countin' on you guys to get Sanders some day."

The bodyguards watch him melt into the crowd. Gino says, "Remember the first day he arrived, Carlo? I never would have figured that Santino would learn our ways . . . but you know what, I'd hate to be his enemy now."

"Yeah, I fear him even more than I fear Alfonso."

3
Mafia Soldier

Every night during the three-day trip Sonny looks at Alfonso's present sitting on his dresser. He is burning with curiosity and knows he could open the present anytime, but Alfonso has him so well disciplined, the box remains sealed for the entire trip. After they arrive in port, Sonny goes through customs with the other passengers. When he gets to the head of the line, the bored official on duty looks at his passport. He takes out a large book to check if the passport has been stolen, if Mr. Stevenson is a fugitive, or if he's been marked for deportation by another country. When everything clears, he stamps the passport routinely. "Enjoy your stay in Spain, *señor*."

Outside on the pier Sonny hails a cab to take him to the Hotel Majorca. As soon as he's in the taxi, he tears off the wrappings of Alfonso's mysterious present. He lifts the lid from the box and pushes the tissue paper away. Inside there is a note from Alfonso. "Santino, I'll let Laura know you won't be able to see her tonight." Sonny lowers the note to his lap in amazement. All those years Alfonso had known; he had saved Sonny's life and risked his own, the ultimate act of love. He stares out the window of the cab but doesn't see the skyline of the city come into view. A flood of memories washes over him as he thinks of his years in Sicily and the wise old man who gave so much so selflessly.

"Hotel Majorca . . . *cincuenta pesos, señor . . . señor?*" The insistent voice of the cab driver jars Sonny from his thoughts. *"Cincuenta . . .* feefty pesos, meester." The driver turns with his palm out.

Sonny peels off six ten-peso notes from his wallet. "Here, man . . . keep the change." The cabbie deposits Sonny's luggage on the sidewalk. The bellman of the hotel grabs the bags and escorts the American to the front desk.

"Do you have a reservation for David Stevenson?"

The clerk on duty checks his list. "Stevenson, Stevenson, *sí* . . ." The man hands him a registration card. "Please fill this out."

Sonny hands it back, knowing he can't write. "I'm with the Valencia Agency, they got all my information. Can I have my room . . . I just got in, and I'm beat."

The clerk gives a key to the bellman. "Take Señor Stevenson to 416, Pedro." The Spaniard shows Sonny to his room, and as soon as he leaves, Sonny starts his check for bugging equipment. The first places he looks are behind the curtains and picture frames. Next he turns the mattress over; if a mike were hidden in there, it wouldn't be able to pick up on the reverse side. He looks under the tables and chairs, in the corners of the rug; he presses the rims, tops, and bottoms of all the lampshades in the room. Outside he shakes the plants and runs his fingers under the edges of the balcony railing. When he knows it's safe, he settles down to listen a few more times to the tapes the Mafia has prepared for him. Sonny's cover is a job as a tour guide with a local travel agency. Their tour buses were bugged for a week and the information condensed for Sonny to learn. He was now as well versed about the island of Majorca as any veteran guide.

The day after his arrival Sonny receives a visit from his contact, José Valdés, a government employee. He supplies the hit man with an updated portfolio on his target, Port Commissioner Tomaso Morales, an important financier of the communist party. Like the Mafia, José is determined to sever the wealthy arteries that keep the blood of communism flowing. Sonny orders tequila with lemon and salt on the side for José and as soon as the room service waiter is gone, they go out on the balcony to talk. Before they do, Sonny turns on the radio in the room. José asks, "Why did you turn it up so loud?"

"In case I missed a monitoring device somehow."

"Oh." José sits down. "How much detail did they give you on the Valencia agency, David?"

"You want me to give you my tour guide routine?"

"No, I assume they taught you that . . . I want to know if you know how they operate."

"They have twenty-six guides, eight buses, and three tours a day. I'll be working the morning and afternoon shifts. My route hits four museums, Valldemosa Monastery, the caves of Artá and Drach, and Lover's Leap, a scenic spot. Most people I'll be handling come from the United States or Canada. The most common complaints from tourists are no ice cubes, hating the food, and getting the runs from it." José nods, "You've done your homework . . . but I should have known you'd be well prepared. This Morales . . . he has to die. He is a threat to the whole government of Spain. We don't want the communists to have a stronghold here like they do in France or Italy. Are you briefed on his activities, David?''

"Yeah." Sonny puts his feet up on the glass of the wrought-iron table in front of him. "I'm not gonna tell you where I'm gonna make the hit, but I know his schedule."

"O.K. Do you know about his girlfriend?"

"Yep . . . she's a newspaper reporter. They meet every night at El Chico Bar."

"That's right . . . is that where you think you might hit him?"

Sonny plants his feet on the floor again and leans forward. "That's not your business, José . . . it's mine."

"Sí, David . . . *sí.*"

The next morning David Stevenson reports to work and takes his first group of twenty-five sightseers on their tour of the town. For ten days David puts on a terrific show for the budget crowd. He is congenial, witty, and easygoing . . . an average kid who could be any mother's son. The Americans love David because the Indiana boy gives them just the right touch of home. On the eleventh day the bus makes its usual stop at Lover's Leap, a hill with a picturesque view of Majorca. In his best camp counselor's voice Sonny announces, "O.K., you have fifteen minutes to look around. There's a small restaurant down there on your left where you can go to the bathroom and buy souvenirs." He looks at his watch. "Meet me back here at one-thirty . . . Please be on time." He dismisses the group with a winning smile, and when they are gone, he gets down to business. Now there is only one other visitor at this scenic spot—his target. In a shady glade 1,000 feet from the parking lot a handsome older man is sitting at a cloth-covered picnic table having lunch. Sonny knows Tomaso Morales comes here three times a week to escape from his hectic job for a few hours. Morales' chauffeur always waits for him next to the long Mercedes limousine. Somehow Sonny must distract the driver so that he can set a pack of plastic explosives on the rear wheel of that car. With a camera in hand Sonny walks over to the limo innocently. Using sign language he indicates he'd like the driver to take a picture of him with the view in the background. The amiable Spaniard agrees. Sonny shows him where to press the button, then positions himself by the left front fender, one car length away. When the picture is snapped, he walks around the front bumper toward the back, then stops to tie his shoe. While he is crouching, he removes the explosives pack from his jacket and sticks it to the top of the rear wheel; when the car rolls over this, the whole frame will blow. He is on the ground less than five seconds. The chauffeur returns the camera to Sonny, who makes the "O.K." sign. *"Gracias, señor."*

Sonny returns to the bus just as his group is filtering back. A teenage girl who still has all of her baby fat approaches. She has an enormous crush on Sonny. "Mr. Stevenson . . . this is such a romantic place. Do you know how many people have jumped off Lover's Leap?"

"I dunno. There's usually nobody around when they do it."

He says with mock seriousness, "But I heard one guy threw a girl off 'cause she asked too many questions . . . not too long ago."

Both of the girl's chins drop as her mouth opens in horror. "Oh . . . that's awful."

"Erma . . . Erma." The girl's mother grabs her by the elbow. "I told you not to bother Mr. Stevenson."

Sonny smiles ingenuously. "It's O.K. . . . part of the job, ma'am. Now watch your step gettin' on." He climbs aboard after them, does a quick head count, then tells the bus driver to move out.

As the bus snakes down the hill back to town, a blue-haired old lady from Wisconsin asks Sonny about the crime rate in Majorca. "Isn't it dangerous at night?"

His microphone crackles as he speaks. "Why, these are the most peace-loving people in the world. The most violent thing they do is fight bulls. You're as safe here as you are in your own living room." As he continues his discourse on the tranquility of Spain, the rumble of an explosion is heard in the distance. The crowd murmurs excitedly; he says calmly, "That's just a construction crew blasting another scenic lookout, folks . . . nothin' to worry about." Everyone settles down. Through the rear window of the bus Sonny sees a column of heavy black smoke spiral toward the sky. He hangs up his microphone and, with a great sense of accomplishment, sits back to relax. Sonny has carried out his first command as a soldier for the Sicilian Mafia.

Two days later, when Sonny is taking his lunch break with a tour, an emaciated old geezer approaches his table. The guide tries to busy himself stirring coffee to avoid catching the man's eye, but the tourist sits down right next to him. Sonny waits for another ice cube question. "David . . . could we talk outside for a minute? I'm not feeling too well." The man holds his stomach.

Sonny helps him up, grabbing a sick bag. "Are you gonna throw up, mister?"

"I don't think so . . . I just need some air." Sonny maneuvers the old man around the tables to the door. When they are in the parking lot, Rosado doubles over and says quietly, "I'm your contact. Your new instructions will be under my seat cushion when we get off the bus at the next stop." Sonny looks at the skinny old man in amazement. Who'd ever think he'd be a Mafia contact? Rosado straightens up. "I think I'll be O.K. now . . . that fresh air did it. The food is so spicy here." The men walk back to the restaurant, and the tour resumes. Sonny finds his package exactly where Rosado said it would be.

In the coming months Sonny's thick portfolio of hits dwindles slowly. Each job is meticulously planned and executed with the skill of a seasoned professional. The former farm boy finds his looks a tremendous asset, just as Alfonso predicted; none of the victims ever suspect this innocent-looking kid is a cold-blooded hit man for the Sicilian Mafia.

The last target on his list is the owner of a diamond mine in South Africa who smuggles stones for the communists. After Sonny has blown him up in one of the shafts, he occupies himself with some local beauties while he waits for new orders from Alfonso. It should be time for him to go to New York to work for Don Giuseppe . . . and maybe get Valachi, who's still alive. The call from his contact comes at a most inconvenient time, but Sonny would leave any woman's bed for this news. He gets dressed immediately and meets his contact in the hotel bar downstairs. The blond South African tells Sonny, "I just got word you're supposed to meet one of Alfonso Lambretti's men, Gino, in Honolulu."

"Hawaii? Are you sure he said Honolulu?"

The contact nods. "You've got a reservation tonight at five on TWA. Check into the Hotel Mahi and wait for him to get in touch with you."

The long flight to Honolulu gives Sonny plenty of time to think. He stares down at the deep-blue water thousands of feet below him and wonders what it feels like to die. He recalls his victims, not because he has any pity for them . . . the hit man wants to be certain that they were killed in the quickest, most efficient way possible. Sonny goes over the details of each assassination in his head. Then his thoughts turn to the future, to his meeting with Gino. What would be his new assignment? Would he be going to New York to work for Don Giuseppe, or would Alfonso consider him so valuable that he'd be ordered back to Sicily? Perhaps Alfonso would make him a lieutenant. Sonny felt sure he had earned that rank. Maybe he'd be given his own territory, and even become a don himself someday. His rewards now were not simply geared toward money; he wanted power, too. A stewardess's voice brings him back from the daydream. "Fasten your seat belt, sir . . . we're landing in Honolulu."

When Sonny arrives at the Hotel Mahi, he finds a message from Gino to meet at his room. The two reunite as warmly as long-lost friends; it's been a year since they've seen each other.

"Santino . . . you're looking very well." The Sicilian slaps Sonny's back. "Alfonso is proud of you . . . he said to tell you you're doing a good job."

Sonny pours them both some wine. "I made my reputation . . . now I can go after Valachi, right?"

Gino takes his glass. "No, Santino . . . someone more important than Valachi."

"Who? Who could be more important? That rat is talkin' more every day . . . why don't they let me go back and get him? I'm the best. I'm the best . . . I've proven I'm the best."

Gino shakes his head. "I don't know . . . but this hit Alfonso himself wants you to take care of . . . it's a direct order."

Sonny sits on the couch. "O.K." Gino hands him a tape and an envelope of pictures. "If you have any questions, you ask me at breakfast."

He gets up to go. "I'll see you tomorrow morning at eight-thirty, Santino."

Sonny listens to the tapes and studies the pictures all night. The next morning at breakfast he has only one comment to Gino. "I feel it's an honor Alfonso wants me to do this."

"Yeah, Santino . . . I don't know why he didn't give the job to me or Carlo, but he knows what he's doing . . . you must be the only one who can do it."

"Gino, this guy . . . he don't deserve to walk the face of the earth. Tell Alfonso I'm happy to do this for him." Sonny puts three heaping teaspoons of sugar into his black coffee. "How is Alfonso?"

Gino smiles. "You know . . . he is the same . . . still eating too much pasta and smoking too many guinea stinkers . . . but he feels O.K."

"And Carlo?"

"One *bella ragazza* he found in Naples . . . he tries to see her a lot, but you know . . . it's hard. Me . . . I'm not looking to be tied down yet."

Sonny looks straight at Gino. "And Laura . . . how's she doin'?"

"Her father just took over a new shipping line. She stays with him a lot now and doesn't talk to too many people . . . Laura misses you, Santino."

"How did Alfonso find out about us? How did he know?"

Gino spears a large piece of papaya from his fruit cup. "Come on, Santino . . . don't think it was just Alfonso's life at stake. We kept a close watch on you. Didn't you ever think it was strange when you were out late at night only one of us was around the next day?"

"Yeah, but I thought that was procedure."

Gino laughs. "That was us, catching up on our sleep. . . . I don't know how you did it, Santino."

Sonny's cup stops in midair. "Then you knew about the cave?"

"We stood outside with our schipettas. Sometimes Laura screamed so loud, we figured the whole village would come out."

Sonny puts his cup back down on the saucer. "Shit . . . and I thought I was so sharp. All those nights I climbed down that olive tree, scratching my ass on the fuckin' branches. I could've gone out the front door."

Gino says more seriously, "No, Santino . . . that would have been going too far . . . it would have been disrespectful. Alfonso may be old, but he's no fool."

Vancouver, Canada, six weeks later. Light snow flurries fall outside the hotel room window as Sonny studies the picture of his special mark, a contractor named Jeremy Thompson. The face, with its snow-white hair and severe eyes, is that of a benevolent, kindly uncle. The voice on the tape that goes with the picture has the very faintest trace of an accent . . . the origin is difficult to pinpoint. Sonny clicks off the tape, "You did a helluva good job, Bobby. That connection's so clear, when he goes to the bathroom I can hear him pee."

Bobby is the Mafia's number-one electronics man. "All in a day's work, Santino."

Sonny grabs a handful of cashews from a dish on the coffee table opposite him. "How come you wired up Jeremy's crapper? Is that normal?"

"Not usually. In a businessman's house we monitor the den, library, bar, and kitchen. We keep the mikes away from any appliances, radios, TV's, and hi-fi's. At work we'd put three devices in the conference room and two in his private office . . . and of course mikes on all the phones."

Sonny tosses a bad nut into a wastepaper basket across the room. "So why the crapper?"

"Jeremy spends a lotta time there."

"How the hell ya figure that out?"

Bobby rifles through the pile of tapes on the coffee table. "Very simple, Santino . . . listen to this." He puts on a reel that has a voice in the distance. "That picked up from the bedroom. I had an idea where it was comin' from."

"Why didn't ya just put another monitor in the bathroom right off the bat?"

Bobby stops the tape. "Too expensive . . . those babies cost five hundred bucks apiece, and we don't send a man back in to get 'em when we're through. Jeremy spends a lotta time in the bathtub dictating tapes to his secretary, so we needed one there."

"Yeah, the tape from his car wasn't too good."

Bobby nods. "Cars are tough. Puttin' it in the ceiling's no problem, but there's too much noise from the motor, the horn, the radio. . . . We're lucky Thompson doesn't have any friends he drives around. We really didn't need a car mike."

Sonny does some quick calculating in his head. "You musta lost eleven, twelve monitors on this guy in six weeks."

"Plus the phone taps."

"You usually lose that many on a mark?"

"Nah, you'll never use hardly any on a woman . . . she tells everything on the telephone. Only other place you mike is her closet."

Sonny puts his feet up on the coffee table. "What dingy broad's gonna talk in a closet?"

"The ones you'll be wirin' . . . they're wealthy. They got closets bigger than this room. We put a monitor there and the maid's room . . . they love to talk. Forget about cars . . . broads always play the radio." Bobby looks at the hit man. "You got enough on him, Santino?"

"Yeah . . . just one thing's been botherin' me, but I'll figure it out."

"I'm sure you will. Word's out you're one of the best. You're the youngest I ever worked with, but you sure had good training." Bobby puts on his gloves and pulls a black knit cap over his ears. "I gotta get goin'. You know where I'm stayin' . . . .Call if you need me."

When Bobby leaves, Sonny listens to the original briefing tape on Jeremy. What still bothers him is the fact that there are no dental records in the otherwise comprehensive file. This is unusual, especially since Jeremy had a bad tooth last week. It's odd that he didn't take care of it. Thompson is health conscious otherwise. Sonny closes the file and picks up the phone. After a few seconds he says, "Mr. Thompson please." An operator puts him through. "Hello, this is Mr. Murphy . . . I'm calling to confirm my five-o'clock appointment tomorrow. . . . Good . . . has he had a chance to look at the artist's conception? . . . I'm glad he did . . . yes, I do. I'll see him tomorrow at five."

Sonny arrives at the luxurious offices of Thompson Construction at 4:59. The secretary, Miss Winters, a Katharine Gibbs graduate, class of '25, greets him. "Have a seat, Mr. Murphy. Mr. Thompson is just finishing up an overseas call." She gets up from the desk to help Sonny off with his overcoat. He stops her. "I think I'm gonna keep this on . . ." Miss Winters says maternally, "Now that's just how you get pneumonia. You shouldn't do that. Last year I got so sick because I sat——" A buzz cuts off her medical history. She runs to the intercom. "Yes, Mr. Thompson."

"Show Mr. Murphy in, Aggie."

"Yes, sir." She looks at Sonny. "Right this way, Mr. Murphy . . . would you like some coffee? I'm just about to leave, but I can get it before I go."

Sonny smiles. "Thanks, but I don't think I want anything." She opens the door to her boss's office. Sonny closes it behind him. As he approaches Thompson's desk, his footsteps are barely audible on the thick carpet of the plush executive suite.

When the contractor looks up from his paperwork, Sonny is standing in front of him. Thompson extends his hand mechanically. "Won't you have a seat, Mr. Murphy?"

"Thanks."

Sonny sits in a leather contour chair at Thompson's right. "I hear you like the complex."

Jeremy raises an eyebrow, "Aggie talks too much . . . but yes, I think the idea of putting shops in the apartment complex is a good one. Do you have the plans?"

Sonny nods and takes them from a long tube. "Say . . . you think I could get some coffee?"

"Certainly . . ." Jeremy buzzes the intercom a few times. No answer. "I guess my secretary's gone for the day. I could get you some if you like."

Sonny hands the plans to the contractor. "No, no . . . don't bother . . . it's O.K."

Jeremy unrolls the papers in front of him. While he is studying them, Sonny gets up. He takes out his gun and puts it to the contractor's head, then quickly grabs his bony shoulder and pushes Thompson's chair back against the picture window. It is obvious now that Sonny is no client, but Jeremy remains cool. The hit man frisks him, checks his desk for panic buttons, and empties the drawers looking for weapons. When he's finished, Sonny levels the .357 magnum as he speaks, his tone flat. "I've been ordered to kill you."

Strangely enough the slender, white-haired contractor is not frightened. A look of resignation crosses his face. "Are you going to kill me here?"

Sonny is taken aback by his composure. "No, and before I blow your head off, I've been ordered to make sure ya know why."

Thompson replies calmly, "I already know why." The man's steel-blue eyes are chilling, even to Sonny. "I know I didn't make my plans fast enough. By this time tomorrow I would've disappeared off the face of the earth. I was leaving the country with all my cash . . . but there's no use telling you about it now."

"Ya don't have to . . . I know everything ya did for the last month." The money, however, intrigues Sonny. It was never mentioned by Thompson on any of his tapes. "How much cash is that?"

"Two million dollars."

This unforeseen windfall gives Sonny an idea. "I'll tell ya what. I'm gonna make it look like you're dead and ya can go on your trip . . . but it'll cost ya two hundred grand." Sonny cocks his gun. "You interested?"

The contractor studies his executioner. "Of course."

"A couple of weeks ago you had a bad tooth. You or your secretary never made an appointment with the dentist. Why didn't ya take care of that? It was killin' ya."

"I know how to take care of my pain. Why is my health so important to you?"

"It's not." Sonny starts planning. "You ever had any dental X-rays done?"

"No."

"That's just what Sonny wanted to hear, but he stops for a minute. "How come? You never been to a dentist?"

"No," Thompson says coldly, "I hate dentists."

Sonny can feel the loathing in his voice, but the answer is good enough. "O.K. . . . how long will it take to get your cash?"

"Not very long . . . it's over there." Thompson points to a bubble aquarium with a vicious magnified pirhana swimming restlessly inside. He pushes a button on his desk, and the fishtank swings aside to reveal a wall safe.

Sonny asks cautiously, "You keep that kinda cash here?"

Jeremy smiles slyly. "I told you . . . I was leaving the country tomorrow."

"Open it."

Jeremy clicks in the numbers of the combination and presses down on the steel handle. The door swings open; inside is a shelf stacked with money. Below it are two large metal cases, obviously receptacles for the cash. With his gun Sonny motions Thompson inside. "Start packing." As Jeremy puts the money into two large suitcases, a small, round object falls to the floor. The old man scrambles to retrieve the piece, but Sonny steps on it. He picks up a solid gold swastika with an inscription engraved on the back. Sonny can't read the inscription—translated, it read: "To Colonel Helmut Glutman. For loyal service in the SS. Adolf Hitler"—but Sonny knows he has his man.

Thompson snaps angrily, "That's mine. That's not part of the deal." Sonny glares at the old man. For a moment their eyes mirror mutual hate.

Sonny slips the medallion in his pocket. "Shut up and take off your jacket."

"Why?"

"Just do what I tell ya." As the contractor removes his coat, Sonny backs up to his attaché case. He reaches in and pulls out a bulging vest, which he hands to Jeremy. "Put this on backward." When the old man has the vest on, Sonny zips it up and turns him around roughly; he shows Thompson something resembling a small, slim flashlight. "If I see ya more than ten feet away from me, I'm gonna push this button. There's enough dynamite on ya to blow up your whole building. If I lose ya, I'm dead anyway . . . and so are you. Understand?" The man nods as Sonny pockets the detonator. "Grab those cases." Sonny puts his gun away and his hand back in his pocket. "O.K., let's go." When they get to the door, Sonny takes one last look around; he grabs the contractor by the collar. "Hold on." They back into the office together, and the hit man scoops up his plans from the desk.He stuffs them into his attaché case, then nudges Jeremy forward. "Remember . . . don't get any funny ideas."

From the office building Sonny and Jeremy drive to a mental hospital outside Vancouver. Through a Mafia contact there Sonny buys an unclaimed body that is physically close to that of Jeremy Thompson. Through another contact he has X-rays made of the dead man's teeth. They return to the office and put these prints in Jeremy's medical file. Around two A.M. Sonny drives the contractor in his Rolls Royce to an isolated area of a city park. There he dresses the cadaver in Jeremy's clothes and props the body up in the driver's seat. He asks for the contractor's ring, watch, and wallet and places them on the corpse. Sonny sets his charges on a timer to blow at three A.M. As an extra precaution he also rigs the doors. If anyone opens them, they'll be blown sky high. From the park the pair take a cab to a Hertz office nearby. Sonny plans to drive Jeremy to San Francisco so he can catch a plane out of the country. On the way to the States a news bulletin informs them that wealthy contractor Jeremy Thompson was killed when his car exploded in a park in Vancouver. Positive identification of the victim has been made. Sonny clicks off the radio and looks over at Jeremy with satisfaction. The plan worked.

Ten hours later, in a pay phone at a roadside diner, Jeremy overhears Sonny's conversation. "Whaddya mean, I didn't kill him? It's all over the fuckin' news. . . . What? They're after me? Shit." Sonny hangs up and turns to his prisoner. "They know you're not dead. They're sending somebody to kill you and me. I'm your life insurance, mister. I know every button man on the street." Sonny hustles Thompson out of the diner.

The old man starts to worry. "What are we going to do?"

"We can hide out in Mexico. I know some people in Guaymas. Later we can both get new identities and go to Rio." At the car door Sonny confronts the contractor coolly. "Listen, Thompson, you need me more than I need you. I'm taking half your cash."

Thompson is hardly in a bargaining position. "O.K., O.K. . . . but let's get away from here before someone sees me." They get back in the car and drive to a local airport. That night Sonny charters a plane to head south.

In Guaymas Sonny decides he'd have more control over the contractor on a boat than in a hotel, so he buys a seventy-five-foot cabin cruiser for them to live on. He also purchases some scuba gear, planning to anchor the cash down on the ocean floor. On the first day out Sonny puts the two million dollars in plastic bags in a waterproof case, then lays explosives carefully across them.

Thompson watches closely. "What are you doing now?"

Sonny is absorbed and doesn't look up, "I'm settin' a timer. If anybody pulls this case off the anchor, it'll blow up."

"What'll happen to my money?"

"It'll be gone . . . same as if somebody gets to it."

"Who's gonna get to it? Nobody will know where it is except you."

Sonny makes his final solder. "I'm not takin' no chances . . . I trust you and everybody else like a fence. Ya never know, some treasure hunter might find it . . . but if they do, no one knows where the safety valve is in these explosives 'cept me. Push the wrong valve and boom."

"I don't feel safe putting explosives in the money."

Sonny locks the case and stands. "You don't have to . . . it's my insurance, Thompson. Now drive . . . head straight, southeast." Jeremy starts the engine, and they take off. About a mile out Sonny cuts one of the anchors and marks the spot in his head. A little farther out he drops the second one . . . farther still, he drops the third, then has Jeremy stop. "Shut her off . . . I'm goin' down." He puts on his scuba gear and plunges overboard with the money. Remembering the compass marking for the second anchor, he swims toward it. Thompson might be able to figure out where the boat was moored at that moment, but until he looked for it, would never know the money wasn't there. When Sonny gets to the right spot, he wraps a chain through the handle, around the case, and fastens it securely to the anchor.

The job takes forty-five minutes. When he surfaces, Thompson asks, "What took you so long?"

"I had trouble with one of the charges." Sonny removes his mask. "It's O.K. now." He puts an arm around Thompson's shoulder. "This will keep us friendly, Jeremy . . . now I don't have to worry about you killin' me and tryin' to take the money." He takes off his wetsuit. "We got a lotta time to spend together. Whaddya say we go fishin'?"

During their time on the boat the contractor begins to feel more relaxed around Sonny. He's convinced the hit man's life is also in danger and feels that they are allies against a common adversary. Each day, for two weeks, Jeremy enjoys a few hours of fishing in the peaceful waters off Guaymas. One particularly fruitless morning, while Sonny trawls the boat, Thompson sits in the fishing chair, his rod motionless. Suddenly he leaps up and shouts to Sonny, "Come here quick . . . bring your gun!" Sonny stops the motor and jumps down from the bridge. The contractor points nervously to an enormous fin circling the boat. Sonny aims and fires several shots at a twenty-foot blue-white shark. Water splashes turbulently over the deck as the giant animal thrashes wildly, blood spurting from a gaping hole in its side. Almost instantly a school of ravenous sharks appears alongside the boat. They attack the dead fish in an agitated feeding frenzy. Thompson backs away, panicked. Sonny seizes this unique opportunity. He grabs a cord and wraps it around the unsuspecting contractor's throat. Hoisting the strangling man over the rail, Sonny dangles him precipitously above the starving sharks. Thompson's eyes bulge as he looks back at Sonny. The old man squirms, clutching at Sonny's wrists and struggling to speak. "Are you crazy? You've got half my money."

Sonny yells back contemptuously, "No, I got it all. This is an execution for the Sicilian Mafia." He tightens the garrote.

The old man grimaces with pain, choking out, "I never hurt any Mafia . . . I only murdered Jews. Aren't you an assassin for the Jews?"

Sonny lowers the German closer to the sharp teeth snapping perilously at his heels. Thompson's feet kick desperately. "You know you murdered more than Jews, you Nazi bastard. You were an SS officer in Rome. You executed students for Mussolini during the war." Glutman's mind flashes back to 1943: two teenage boys are carrying schoolbooks and laughing as they climb the university stairs. A young Helmut Glutman dressed in a Nazi uniform calls to them. When they turn, he cuts them down ruthlessly with a machine gun, leaving their limp, bloodied bodies on the steps. Sonny interrupts Glutman's flashback. "Ya did a good job changing identities, Colonel Glutman, but no one can hide from Alfonso Lambretti. . . . You killed his sons." At that moment a crazed shark jumps up and chews off Glutman's right foot. A bloodcurdling shriek pierces the air as a red spray gushes from the stump. The writhing man howls in agony at the top of his lungs. Glutman flashes back again, this time to Auschwitz. Colonel Glutman inspects the last naked Jew, an old woman, being herded into the showers. Before she enters, he opens her mouth and yanks out two gold teeth with a pair of pliers. A guard pushes the nearly unconscious woman through the door. When it's bolted, Glutman signals, and the poisonous gas is released into the chamber. Inside, hundreds of Jews moan with pain. This horrifying sound parallels Glutman's screams as the Nazi murderer wails in excruciating agony, but his death cries can never atone for the massacre of the thousands of innocent souls who died by his satanic hand.

Sonny shouts vindictively over the deafening screams, "This is for Alfonso Lambretti," and drops the petrified man into the open jaws below. He is ripped apart viciously. Within seconds all that remains of Colonel Helmut Glutman is a bloody pool. Sonny looks down at the red circle in the water. . . . Alfonso's vendetta is complete.

A few hours later Sonny recovers the two cases filled with cash, sells the boat in Guaymas, and checks into a hotel. In his room Sonny takes out the present Alfonso gave him when he left Sicily and removes the note. The cherished slip of paper is placed in a special pocket in Sonny's attaché case. He then puts Glutman's gold swastika inside and rewraps the box. Later Sonny buys a car and drives to New York; when he arrives, he calls Don Giuseppe. A meeting is scheduled that afternoon.

When Sonny gets to the Loganno estate, he is surprised to see three guards stop him at the gate. He sticks his head out the window. "I'm Santino Gibson . . . Don Giuseppe's expecting me."

One of the men says, "I've seen your picture many times . . . welcome home, Santino." But this is not enough to admit him. One of the other men calls to the main house for clearance. A few minutes later the gates swing open, and the guard waves him through. Sonny wonders about this heavy security. Maybe there has been a Mafia war in his absence. The car passes the formal gardens to the circular drive . . . Nick and Mario are there to meet him. They both give him warm hugs.

"Hey, Sonny," Nick says, "you look good . . . that Sicilian pasta didn't put any pounds on you."

"You look pretty good yourself, Nick. We got a lot to talk about, huh?

"Yeah . . . it's been a long time, but the don's waiting for you. He wants to see you right away."

"O.K. I gotta get somethin' from the trunk first." Sonny takes out the metal case, which Mario carries.

"What the hell's in this, Sonny . . . man, it's heavy."

"It's a present for Alfonso Lambretti." As they walk through the house to the library, Sonny asks, "Hey, what's with the three guys at the gate?"

Nick answers, "It's a long story. I'll tell you later at dinner, after your meeting."

When they get to the door of the don's study, Mario knocks, but this time Don Giuseppe opens the door himself. He greets Sonny with open arms. "Welcome home, Santino." The don gives him a long hug, then turns to his grandson. "Nick, we'll see you later, eh? Santino and I have many things to discuss."

Don Giuseppe takes a seat behind his old Sicilian desk. He is full of questions. "What took you so long to get here, Santino? We heard you blew that guy up two weeks ago."

Sonny sits down in front of him. "He didn't die that way, Don Giuseppe. Alfonso ordered a special execution."

The old man nods understandingly. "You killed him Sicilian style?"

Sonny's jaw tightens before he speaks. "No, Don Giuseppe, cutting his balls off and ripping out his heart would have been too good for the Nazi pig."

The don leans forward. "How did he die, Santino?"

"Alfonso wanted him fed to the sharks, so I took him down to Guaymas, Mexico."

The don is puzzled. "But why go all the way to Mexico? Aren't there sharks on the West Coast?"

"Yes, Don Giuseppe, but the waters of Guaymas are the most shark-infested in the world."

"Good job, Santino, that man was Satan himself . . . He killed many innocent Italians." The don's eyes burn with envy. "I only wish I could have been the one to feed him to the sharks."

Sonny picks up the metal case at his side and places it carefully on the don's desk. Unlocking it he says, "This is two million dollars the pig had. I conned him out of it."

The don smiles when he sees the money. "Santino, you're something else. I bet you could con the devil into buying a Bible."

"I have a request, Don Giuseppe."

The old man nods. "What is it, Santino?"

"I would like the money to be given to Alfonso."

The don looks at the two million dollars, then rises to give Sonny a hug. "You are very loyal, Santino. Not too many men would have brought this money back. I know Alfonso will be happy to have it. . . . There are still many families over there who bear the scars of Mussolini's executions."

Sonny takes out the small wrapped package from his pocket, "In this box is a trophy for Alfonso. I know it will mean a lot to him."

Don Giuseppe takes it. "I will see that he gets it, Santino." He spreads his arms open wide, "Come, let's have dinner. We'll celebrate your return . . . Nick is anxious to talk."

Nick is waiting for them in the dining room. As soon as they sit down, Don Giuseppe pours each of them a glass of wine, then raises his. "To a fine soldier . . . to Santino." Sonny raises his glass and adds, "Death to the rat, Valachi." They all clink and take a sip. Nick passes Sonny the antipasto. As Sonny piles Italian delicacies on his plate, he asks, "Nick . . . so why the guys? Why are there three men on the gate now?"

Nick takes the platter from him. "Things have changed since you left four years ago. Grandpa has become more powerful. He's head of the council now."

Sonny looks over at the don, who explains, "That means I am advisor to all the dons, Santino. There are more than three men at the gate . . . I've doubled my security."

"Why, Don Giuseppe?"

"I'm making decisions for families all over the country. You can't satisfy everybody, Santino . . . that can cause jealousy and make enemies. I give one guy more territory for gambling, I gotta give another guy more in narcotics. If I give one of them more control with the stocks, I gotta give another more union locals. Some of these men act like children . . . they lack respect. They forget, we must all share the same well." The old man slices off a piece of salami and changes the subject. "Did Nick tell you he was a lieutenant now?"

Sonny stares in disbelief at his well-educated friend. "Whaddya mean, a lieutenant? Nick never killed nobody."

"The lieutenants you're familiar with are the enforcers, and they're very important, but we also need men like Nick. Nick is my financial advisor. Since he's been handling things, we've made thirty percent more on our money."

Sonny raises his glass to Nick. *"Salute."* His friend does the same, then says excitedly, "Hey, Santino . . . I almost forgot. I got engaged last month. I want you to meet my girl."

"That's great, Nick . . . who is she?"

"Her name is Erminia . . . her father runs a shoe repair in Queens."

"That's good, Nick. If you ever go broke, at least your kids won't have to wear shoes with holes in 'em." This is a painful memory from Sonny's own childhood. "Where'd ya meet her?"

"At a party one of the guys had." Nick laughs. "She thinks I look like Rudolph Valentino."

"You're kiddin'. She must be blind!"

The don nods. "Most women are blind, Santino."

Nick protests. "Hey . . . she's not blind, she's beautiful. You judge for yourself. Maybe after dinner tonight we can take a ride over there."

The don interrupts. "Nick, I think Santino needs his rest, and so do you . . . you've got to be at his hotel early in the morning." The don continues sternly. "And from now on, when you go out, you take a driver."

Nick groans. "Aw, come on, Grandpa."

The old man holds up a finger, "Nick . . . I don't want to tell you again."

"O.K. . . . O.K." During this conversation Sonny's mind has been far away. He is anxious to find out what the future holds for him with the Loganno family, and he is anxious to go after Valachi.

When the meal is finished, Don Giuseppe lights up a cigar and leans back in his chair. "I have an assignment for you, Santino." Sonny sits up expectantly. He can't wait to hear what exciting plans are in store for him. "Santino, what do you know about the insurance business?"

Sonny is slightly baffled, "Uh . . . I don't know too much, Don Giuseppe."

The don puffs on his cigar. "Well, you're going to know a lot. This coming year you'll be one of the top insurance agents in the country. You'll be writing industrial policies for the unions.''

Sonny protests. "But Don Giuseppe, I can't even read or write!"

His negative attitude irritates the don. "You won't have to, Santino, your office staff will do that. In two days you'll be in Oklahoma working for one of the biggest insurance companies in the country. You keep the commissions you make, and you'll be paid additional money to be our contact.''

Sonny has the look of a man who's just been sentenced to Siberia. "But why insurance, Don Giuseppe?"

The old man stubs out his cigar. "The Mafia wants to get into legitimate business . . . insurance and banking are perfect for us. Everyone buys insurance, everyone puts money in a bank. We can turn our millions into billions.'' The don rises and paces slowly as he continues, his face flushed with enthusiasm. "With legitimate sources we can control politicians. Today they're scared of the Mafia, tomorrow they'll love us. Any candidate in the world would take a campaign contribution from a bank or an insurance company . . . but very few would take money from Giuseppe Loganno. Eventually we won't have button men on the streets . . . we'll have an army of attorneys, congressmen, and senators to fight our battles.'' He puts a hand on Sonny's shoulder. "Santino, politicians are easier to handle than hookers or dope addicts." The don shakes his head sadly. "Things have changed, Santino. Loyalty and respect don't mean as much anymore . . . especially after that rat Valachi got diarrhea of the mouth.'' The don sits again. "We have to go into legitimate business to survive. It's the best thing for the families.''

Throughout the don's speech Sonny has been listening patiently, but his tone is troubled as he speaks. "Don Giuseppe, I'm from the streets. I'm the best hit man there is . . . I'm the only guy who could get Valachi. I can't work in an office!"

The don gives him a stern look. "I thought you took vows."

Sonny replies quietly, "Yes, Don Giuseppe . . . I'm sorry. I'm a soldier."

The old man leans forward and puts his hand on Sonny's arm. "By the way, Santino, Mario told me he spoke to you after you took your vows . . . don't worry, I won't ask you to kill your mother''—he sits back again—"but I will ask you to become an insurance agent in Oklahoma. Nick will brief you at the hotel tomorrow.''

"I'll be waiting for him, Don Giuseppe.''

The next day Sonny finally vents his frustration to Nick. "Shit! It's been over a year. The best button men in the country couldn't get Valacchi. I can." He grabs Nick by the shoulder. "I know I could get him, but you guys got me goin' to Oklahoma. What am I gonna do there? I'm not a fuckin' cowboy!"

Nick says calmly, "Sonny, the family needs you there. You're the only one qualified to get what we want."

Sonny is still agitated. "What the hell's that, Nick?"

"Sonny, for the Mafia to start their own legitimate business, they need people to invest in them. There's an insurance company based in Oklahoma that underwrites for over eighty other insurance companies. Each week they release a computer list of new stockholders . . . over 20,000 names . . . all potential investors for us. You have to get us those lists."

Sonny is still contrary. "I don't know nothin' about computers."

Nick smiles. "Maybe not . . . but you know about women. If you can con nigger whores our of their money, you should be able to con this broad out of a simple list." He hands Sonny a picture of a plain-looking woman around thirty-five, with stringy brown hair, glasses, and buck teeth.

"What am I supposed to do with this? This broad looks like she was hatched out of an alligator's egg."

"Whatever it takes to get the information . . . you're gonna do . . . you might even have to fuck her."

Sonny slaps the picture hard. "Man, I'd rather kill this broad than look at her, let alone fuck her."

"Maybe so, Sonny, but she's the executive secretary to the president of the insurance company and one of the few authorized to take the computer lists out of the building." He sees Sonny needs more convincing. "Sonny, at the end of the year the Mafia will have over a million names of wealthy people who buy bank and insurance stock. That means within the next five years, with their investments in our companies, the Mafia can control major financial institutions in the real estate and commercial fields. By having this monetary power we'll be able to push up the prime rate." Sonny demands impatiently, "Prime rate, shit . . . what's that worth, huh?"

Nick gives Sonny a steady look. "By my estimates the Mafia can make over three billion dollars in one year from those lists."

This figure finally gets through to Sonny—large dollar signs have always appealed to him. He looks at the picture again. "With that kind of money involved, this broad's gettin' better looking by the minute."

Nick puts his attaché case on the desk. "Don Giuseppe said to ask you what you know about religion."

Sonny sighs. "Now what? . . . I don't know nothin' about it. Why should I?"

Nick crosses to Sonny. "Well, it's important for you to know now. Cora Pitkin is a Sunday school teacher. If you think looking at her is something, you should hear her voice." He hands Sonny a bulging manila envelope, "We taped her last six months of Bible lessons for you to learn." Sonny sits down on the bed in disgust. Nick continues, "I have one more thing for you from Don Giuseppe." He holds up a small white envelope. "Twenty thousand dollars. Don Giuseppe says at the end of the year, it's yours . . . you've got your open contract to go after the rat." Sonny jumps up excitedly, a clenched fist in his palm punctuating his hate. "Valachi . . . "

Nick nods. "If you hit him, you get another hundred grand." He puts the envelope inside his coat pocket. "But for the time being, you'll have to forget about Valachi."

For the next several days, Sonny listened to insurance briefing tapes to familiarize himself with industry jargon. When he finally went to work, he did his job better than anyone else ever had; at the same time, he learned all of the company's trade secrets. His conquest of Cora Pitkin did not come as easily, but after a month of dinners and Bible classes, Sonny finally got her to succumb to his charms. She saw to it that her lover had everything he wanted. Every Friday afternoon like clockwork, Don Giuseppe received the list of stockholders.

Within a short time, Sonny knew enough about insurance to see how some standard ind stry practices could be used to con other businessmen on a scale no one would have dreamed possible. At the end of his stay in Oklahoma, Sonny was awarded the company's highest honor, Agent of the Year. Soon after that, Don Giuseppe gave him permission to leave. Sonny took the first plane out of town—not to New York, not yet, but to Indianapolis to see his parents. Before he left Oklahoma, Sonny made a deal with the company president to give him all his renewal commissions if he'd hire Pops Gibson as the chief agent for the state of Indiana. His father made only seventy-five dollars a week as a TV repairman. This plan would get him out of overalls and into a suit . . . he'd be the boss of an office instead of an employee in a sweatshop. When he arrives in town, Sonny goes directly to Stouffer's Inn, where his parents are waiting. Since Sonny will only be in town one night, he's taking them out to dinner.

As the lights of Indianapolis sparkle through the panoramic windows of the penthouse restaurant, the Gibson family studies their menus. After they've ordered, they catch up on Sonny's life since his last visit. Sonny notices a new network of lines on his mother's face and knows he has probably been the cause of at least a few of them. His older brother, Don, a bank manager at a small local branch now, asks Sonny, "So . . . you like selling insurance better than aluminum siding?"

Sonny breaks his roll open and spreads a ball of butter on it. "Yeah, you can make more money in the insurance business . . . you can move up a lot faster, too."

His mother beams. "Yes, we saw the articles in the paper—'Hoos-IER BOY MAKES GOOD'—we were so proud. I mailed the articles to Carolyn, but I don't know if she got them. . . . They won't let me see little Jimmy anymore since she got married again."

"You shouldn'ta sent 'em to her, Mom . . ."

"Why not? Don't you want Jimmy to know about what you're doing?"

Sonny takes a healthy bite of his roll. "It don't matter." Mr. Gibson speaks up, "I think it would be nice for your son——"

Sonny counterattacks. "Hey, I told ya . . . I don't care . . . that was eight years ago. That shit's way down the river now."

The waitress brings their food, and the family eats to avoid speaking to each other. After a few minutes Sonny turns to his father, changing the subject. "Listen, Pops, I wanna talk to you about something. How'd ya like to get away from that sweaty workbench ya sit behind all day?" His father looks at him quizzically. "It's all set . . . you're gonna be the Indiana state insurance agent for our pet company."

Pops is skeptical. "Me? Oh . . . no . . . I don't know anything about insurance."

The son can see the father's enthusiasm has been eroded by hard times and too many false starts. Sonny encourages him. "Believe me, Pops, you don't have to know anything about it. Hell, what'd I know? I learned everything in one year. Besides, you'll have a whole office staff to help ya out." He pulls his trump card. "You can make over five hundred dollars a week."

This figure gets his father's and his brother's attention. Don chimes in. "Hey, maybe I could get involved, too . . . through the bank."

Sonny now sees an opportunity to help both of them. "Yeah, you could. I'll tell you what, I'll send some insurance-policy manuals so you can read up on the business. I'll have it all set up in a few days . . . O.K.?"

Pops concedes, "O.K., if you really think I can do it."

Sonny says, "I know you can."

Mrs. Gibson starts to cry. "Sonny, what a good boy you are."

Don jumps in quickly. "Yeah, it's good you stopped hanging around with your buddy Johnny." Hearing his old crime partner's name jolts Sonny back into the past. He feels sorry for Johnny but knows splitting from him was the first of many smart moves Sonny's made. Pops adds, "You know he's in Michigan City State Penitentiary now. Got accused of white slavery . . . . some women testified against him. He never was any good." He looks at his wife for confirmation. "You know it's true, Nina."

Mrs. Gibson has been noticeably silent during this exchange. She says gently, "Now, Pops, we shouldn't judge the boy. He never had the love Sonny did. Without that our son wouldn't be as successful as he is today."

Sonny says affectionately, "I remember how you used to wash my clothes out every night, Mom . . . . Johnny's mother would never've done that for him."

Don asks, "Are you gonna go up and visit Johnny?"

"Hell, no. It's his own damn fault for gettin' himself in there in the first place . . . he's stupid." Sonny calls for the check. "Besides, I'm too busy with my own business. In fact, I gotta go to my room right now . . . I got an early flight tomorrow."

Sonny pays the check, and his family walks him to the elevator. On the ride down to the lobby, Mrs. Gibson says, "When will we see you again?"

"I dunno, but I'll be here whenever I'm anywhere near Indianapolis."

"Where are you living now? Don't you have a home?"

Sonny writes down the number of his hotel in New York. The Loganno family owns it, and he knows they'll cover for him at the switchboard. "This is my place . . . call if ya need me."

"Do you have a special girl back there?"

"No, Mom, you know . . . I'm still traveling . . . it's hard to meet anybody on the run."

She touches his cheek. "Whoever gets you is going to be a lucky girl."

"Yeah, well she'd have to be as good as you . . . I dunno where I'd find that . . ." Sonny kisses her forehead. The elevator opens at his floor, and Don holds the door open. Sonny hugs his mother, then shakes his father's hand. "I'll be sending those books to you. I know you're gonna do great." He gets off the elevator, and his mother waves as the doors close; Sonny waves back. "I'll call ya . . ."

The next morning Sonny flies to New York for his meeting with Don Giuseppe. When he arrives at the Loganno estate late that afternoon, Mario takes him straight to the study where Nick and his grandfather are waiting. All three exchange hugs and kisses, then sit, the don at his usual place behind the cherished old Sicilian desk. Sonny smiles. "Well, Nick, when's the big day? I'm lookin' forward to it myself . . . I never been a best man before."

Nick waves his hand in disgust. "It's off . . . it didn't work. She turned out to be a royal bitch. But my new girl, Maria"—he fashions her curves in the air—"mamma mia, now there's a woman. She's an Italian from Brooklyn."

Don Giuseppe breaks in, "And the other one was an Italian from Queens. The trouble with young people is not enough courting. No one gets to know anybody. When I went out with your grandmother, women were chaperoned. That's why in the old country—"

Nick interrupts him impatiently. "Grandpa, that was forty years ago. We're not in the old country now . . . we're in America. Courting like that is so old-fashioned."

The don shakes his head sadly. "Young people . . . they have no respect for tradition today. That is the root of many of our problems already."

Sonny defends the don, "Your grandfather's right, Nick . . . tradition is important."

His friend looks over at him, annoyed. "You think he's so right, you be his grandson."

"It would be an honor to be Don Giuseppe's grandson, but I'm not. You have that honor, and you should respect what your grandfather is saying."

Nick throws his hands up in surrender. "All right, I don't wanna hear it from both of you guys. I'll be more traditional. Sonny, how about you chaperoning me and Maria tonight?"

The old man's eyes gleam devilishly. "But who will chaperone Santino? He's been in Oklahoma a long time, eh?"

"Yeah, and if Nick gets out of hand, you can send him there, Don Giuseppe. I got the perfect girl for him . . . she's real traditional. You've seen her picture, Nick."

"Oh, no, I'd rather be on death row."

The three laugh, and when things quiet down, the don speaks proudly, "Santino, you did an excellent job in Oklahoma. Because of those lists you got for us our legitimate businesses are off to a very profitable start. I called you back to New York for two reasons. First, I want you to go into securities now. Second, I made a promise to you when you left for Oklahoma . . . Nick." Nick hands the don an envelope, which he puts on the desk in front of Sonny. "I said if you stayed in insurance for one year, you could go after Valachi. Here is your twenty thousand. If you hit him, you get a hundred grand."

Sonny looks at the money, then back at the don, and weighs his words carefully as he speaks. "Don Giuseppe, for the past year I have been part of a very sophisticated financial circle. I not only learned the intricate operations of the insurance business, but also the securities and mortgage-lending fields." Both Nick and his grandfather look at Sonny in surprise. This is not a hit man talking now. Sonny continues, "Don Giuseppe, I'm not the same person who left New York a year ago. If you're giving me a command to go into securities and a command to hit Valachi, of course I'll obey them. But I have something more valuable to the Mafia than selling a couple of stocks and killing one rat." Sonny stands, his energy too high to be confined to a chair. He walks around the room as he continues. "Thanks to you, Don Giuseppe, I have learned how to take thousands of dollars and turn 'em into millions . . . without any heat on the Mafia. I have an idea which I'd like to present the council and their *consigliores.*"

Don Giuseppe questions the unusual request. "Why can't you just tell me? If I think it's a good idea, I'll tell the council."

Sonny says carefully, "With all due respect, Don Giuseppe, I don't think you'd understand it if I told you now . . . it takes time. Besides, I have tapes which explain all the details of my plan. I'd like a council meeting because I need money from the families to start the operation. I guarantee they'll get back a hundred times their investments in the first year."

Nick interrupts him, slightly defiant. "Sonny, what makes you think you can handle such a big operation? You've only been in the business world one year; I've studied economics for eight years. I have a degree . . . you can't even read or write. You'll be talking to a lot of educated men."

Sonny answers the challenge patiently. "I'm aware of my limitations, Nick, but I still want the chance to explain my whole program to the council. Let them make the decision."

The don rises and looks into Sonny's eyes. "Santino, are you sure you don't want to go after Valachi?"

Sonny says respectfully, "I'm sure, Don Giuseppe. In the past year I've done some research on the rat . . . no one will ever get him. We'll never know where the real Valachi is. The government has him too well protected. Besides, I'm offering much more to the Mafia than Valachi."

"You may have something more valuable, but Valachi is important. Remember, when a man gets bitten by a snake, sometimes he has to cut off a limb to save a life." He puts a hand on Sonny's shoulder. "But you're right, Santino . . . Valachi is hard to get, and I do see a different man standing in front of me now. I will set up one council meeting for you, but if you don't sell your idea, you'll forget the whole operation and continue to work for us."

"O.K., Don Giuseppe. I'll keep my word to go after Valachi then, even though we both know it's a suicide hit." He pauses. "Don Giuseppe . . . I'd like to request one more thing." The don nods for him to go on. "I'd like to have Alfonso at the council meeting."

Nick jumps in hotly. "I don't see why we should bring in any of those people over there. They're not interested in what we do."

Don Giuseppe snaps back quickly, "Nick, you don't know what you're talking about. You must have respect for them, there is a reason for what they do . . . . you remember that!"

Sonny breaks the uncomfortable silence that follows. "Don Giuseppe, I took my vows in Sicily . . . that's why I want Alfonso there."

The don ends the discussion: "I understand, Santino . . . your godfather will be there. I'll schedule the meeting for one week from today."

"Thank you, Don Giuseppe. Is there any way I can get my tapes transcribed?"

"Give them to Nick's secretary in the morning. By the way, I'm assigning you a driver, one of Mario's men . . . Angelo Colucci."

Nick enters the conversation again. "Have you ever met Angelo, Sonny?"

"No. I don't think so."

Nick laughs. "Wait till you see him, he's really somethin'."

"Whaddya mean, somethin'? Is there somethin' wrong with him?"

"No, no . . . on the contrary, he's one of Mario's best men. But he's kinda unique . . . like you."

Later that night ten of Don Giuseppe's hookers are sent to Sonny's room to welcome him back from Oklahoma. The next morning, after just a few hours sleep, he gets a call. "Uh, Santino? Is this Santino Gibson?"

"Yeah . . . who the hell's this?"

The voice on the other end has the rasp of a punch-drunk fighter's. "Uh . . . this is Angelo Colucci. I'm your driver . . . your personal bodyguard. I just wanted to let you know I was waitin' downstairs."

"Oh, yeah . . . Angelo. Good . . . I gotta go over to Nick's office. I'm gonna take a quick shower first. How will I recognize ya?"

Angelo looks down at his body. "Well, uh . . . I have on a blue plaid jacket."

"O.K., I'll be down in about a half-hour."

Thirty minutes later Sonny finds the plaid jacket and is stunned by the size of the man in it. Angelo is six foot eight and almost as wide as he is tall. The bodyguard spots Sonny immediately and strides over to him energetically. "You ready to go, Santino? Mario says I should take you wherever you want." He points to the street. "The car's this way."

Sonny looks up at him, still amazed as he follows the bodyguard. "Angelo, you ever play football?"

"No . . . uh, I was too mean to play . . . that's what they said, but I was good."

"How much do you weigh?"

"After a plate of spaghetti about 410 . . ." Outside, Sonny doesn't see the limousine until Angelo steps aside and opens the door. "Nick's first, right?"

"Yeah . . ."

While they drive across town, he asks Sonny, "Where you wanna go after Nick's?"

"Take me someplace to get laid. I wore out all ten a those girls they sent me last night . . . not one was worth a shit. They pop two, three times and they're out."

"I know one broad who can go all night. They call her 'Hot

Pasta' . . . I could fix you up with her . . ."

Sonny is interested. "Can you get her for me now?"

"No, she's workin' . . ."

"Big deal . . . Don Giuseppe said any broad in the city's mine."

"She doesn't work for Don Giuseppe . . . she's a stock clerk at Gimbel's."

"What!"

"Pasta's not a hooker, but she'll outfuck any of 'em." Angelo's face reddens. "Uh, I don't know myself, but I know she'll love you, Santino . . . everybody knows about your salami."

Sonny laughs. "O.K., Angelo . . . make a date with this broad for eight o'clock. After we drop this stuff at Nick's, I gotta get some new clothes. I'm tired of fuckin' cowboy outfits."

Angelo smiles at him through the rear-view mirror. "Uh . . . you do look a little funny . . . like a tourist. I'll take you to Nick's tailor." The clever observation does not go unnoticed. Sonny wants to find out more about this man. "Angelo . . . how fast are you with a gun?"

Almost before Sonny has gotten the words out, Angelo has his .357 magnum drawn. "I got a zip holster . . . I never use an automatic, a guy could get his dick blown off."

"You're right, Angelo, an automatic can jam."

"You know, when you came down in the lobby, there was a guy there . . . he had an automatic. Probably he was the hotel dick. Could be the FBI, though, they're so obvious."

Sonny is impressed. Of all Don Giuseppe's men, Mario excepted, Angelo is the sharpest he's met so far. This giant would make a great security man for Sonny someday. The car stops in front of an elegant brownstone. "This is Nick's office . . ." They both get out, and when Sonny is finished with his business, they go to get his clothes.

That night, as promised, Angelo gets him "Hot Pasta." Her real name is Carla Pastarone, and she lives up to her reputation. As soon as she gets into the limo, the sexy Italian girl goes after Sonny. He's been playing it so straight with Cora for a year, Carla's boldness is surprising, but it only takes seconds for him to dive headfirst into the passionate waters again. Angelo drives them around Central Park for an hour. When they finally come up for air, Carla says, "You really like to play, don't you? I know a coupla groovy girls who love to play, too . . ."

"Oh, yeah? . . . these girls friends of yours?"

Carla smoothes the wrinkles of her skirt.

"Uh-huh . . . and there's plenty of you to go around. If I call, I'm sure we can go there right now . . . they live just over on West 75th Street." She giggles. "I mean . . . what are good friends for?"

Sonny shouts to Angelo, "Hey, stop at the first phone

booth . . . we're gonna make a call. We're goin' to a party on the West Side."

When they get to the apartment, Gina and Joya, gorgeous twin brunettes, come to the door dressed only in their robes. "Come on in . . ."

Joya looks up at Angelo and squeals to Carla, "O-o-o, you didn't tell us about this one . . . he's cute."

Carla looks at Sonny. "Can he play, too?"

Angelo says quickly, "Uh . . . I can't . . . I'm workin'. Santino, I'll stay out here in case you need anything."

"O.K., Angelo."

Gina takes Sonny's hand and leads him through the apartment to the bedroom. "Carla told us so much about you . . ." Her dark eyes tease his. She unbuttons his shirt; the other twin unbuckles his belt, while Carla kisses him. She gets her intended result, and the twins' eyes widen when they see Sonny's size. Joya pushes him on the bed to climb on top, and Gina positions herself over Sonny's face. After a year of the missionary position in Oklahoma he climaxes six times in ten minutes. Meanwhile, thanks to Juanita's expert training, Sonny's tongue works steadily—soon Gina is having an orgasm, too. His hips pump Joya furiously, and not wanting to neglect Carla, Sonny reaches over to bring her to the peak of pleasure with his finger. He gets the girls to come simultaneously. The quartet continues to experiment wildly, but just forty-five minutes later the twins are exhausted . . . Sonny goes at it alone with Carla until dawn. When he finally gets back to the hotel, he falls asleep, satisfied and happy to be out of the Bible Belt and back in the big city.

Sonny spends most of his time with Carla that week. He's not nervous about his meeting with the families . . . a year in the business world has prepared him well for that moment. The night before his presentation Alfonso arrives in town, and Sonny explains the whole plan to him; his godfather thinks the idea is a sound one. The following morning at ten the Mafia council convenes in an office on a high floor of the RCA building in Rockefeller Center. The czars of the underworld slowly filter into the large conference room, each accompanied by an Ivy League attorney. The conservative lawyers are a striking contrast to the earthy dons. Sonny, the image of a Wall Street tycoon in his pinstriped suit, stands at the door next to Don Giuseppe, who is greeting the men as they enter the room. Sonny recognizes each from the council meeting in Buffalo, but only one remembers him. Sam Scorzelli stops to say hello. A cigar butt hangs from his mouth as he speaks. "Santino, it's good to see you. Ya know, it seems like yesterday you were workin' for me, bustin' nigger heads!"

Sonny smiles. "Yeah, Sam, it's been a long time . . . I'll talk to ya later." He watches Sam take his place at the rectangular conference table. The last time they were together Sonny worked for him. Now the Chicago boss, who's been in the Mafia all his life, would have to listen to what a twenty-four-year-old, who came in just four years ago, has to say.

At ten-fifteen Don Giuseppe claps his hands and calls the meeting to order. "All right, everybody, listen up." There is immediate silence in the room from the fifteen dons and their attorneys. "I've called the council together today for an important reason. I want to introduce you to the man who is responsible for bringing us over three billion dollars in investments for our legitimate operations. He has some other ideas he wants us to hear today. . . . But before I turn the floor over to him, I'd like to introduce the *consigliores* of the dons who could not be with us today. Our fine family member, Frank Castino from New Orleans, couldn't be here, so he's sent his *consigliore,* Mario Lambazzo. Tony Tedesco, the head of the St. Louis family, couldn't be with us—he's in the hospital, and we all wish him a speedy recovery. Tony has sent Larry Magiollo to represent him. We're also honored by a man whose presence is always warmly welcomed at any of our council meetings. He has our deepest respect, and we certainly hope that we in America will always be able to keep the peace with our family from Sicily. Here today, representing the Sicilian Mafia, Alfonso Lambretti." All eyes turn toward the powerful soldier from Catania, sitting on Don Giuseppe's right. Most of the dons know Alfonso and his fierce reputation. The New York don continues, "Now I would like to introduce Santino Gibson . . . he's a true soldier. This man has already proven his loyalty to the family in many ways. Sonny has an operation he wants to present which he says will benefit all of us. Listen to him closely . . . he's a remarkable young man. Santino, you can have the floor now."

"Thank you, Don Giuseppe."

Sonny stands confidently as he addresses the powerful men, who watch him expectantly. "Before I begin my presentation, I'd like to thank you all for taking the time from your busy schedules to be here. I'd also like to thank Alfonso Lambretti for coming all the way from Sicily to hear what I have to say. Gentlemen, I'm gonna offer each of you the chance to share in an operation that will make over two hundred fifty million for the Mafia in the first year. I have come up with the perfect crime." This statement gets everyone's full attention. "I know it sounds impossible, but it's a fact . . . I have a way of taking the major insurance companies, corporations, and investment conglomerates in this country without putting any heat at all on the Mafia. For the past year I've been in Oklahoma working in the insurance industry. In the time I spent there, I received a very comprehensive financial education and got involved in international investments. I discovered something unique . . . it's called an offshore corporation, or in technical terms, a shell corporation. These corporations aren't subject to regulation by any United States agency under financial laws 'cause they're out of U.S. jurisdiction. There are no tax restrictions on money made from a shell corporation as long as the money doesn't come back into the states for eighteen months. This is called a tax shelter. All of the major companies are starting to use them. The shell corporations can do whatever they want right now because the Justice Department doesn't even know about 'em, and by the time Washington finds out and imposes tax laws, we'll have made three or four billion dollars." Sonny picks up his folder. "In front of you is a portfolio of my research. If you turn to page three, you'll see a list of shell corporations in existence already. I've found several licensed to do business in the Bahamas, and they're ripe for the picking. We can get 'em for peanuts. These corporations are owned by legitimate businessmen who have one thing in common . . . they're all greedy men. For our own protection the corporations I've picked for us to purchase don't have any Italians working for them and don't have any connections with Italians anywhere. That means there's no visible link to the Mafia. Only one of us will deal with these people— me . . . and who'd ever expect an Indiana country boy like me, an insurance executive, to be with the Mafia. . . . Hell, I don't even look Italian."

This remark gets a few smiles from the group. One don calls out, "Yeah—hey, Don Giuseppe, the kid don't look Italian."

Another voice says, "Come on . . . quiet down. I wanna hear what the kid has to say."

When there is silence again, Sonny continues, his tone more serious. "I want you all to know, if something goes wrong at any time during this operation, I'll take the full responsibility to make sure no one in this room or any of his family is involved. Now, for this operation to go into effect, I need two things . . . an insurance company and a bank. I have two in mind." Sonny pulls down a map of the world from a hook behind him and picks up a pointer to indicate. "Both are outside the United States. Transcontinental Casualty Company is in Nassau in the Bahamas. The Bahamas, gentlemen, is becoming a tax haven for major U.S. companies." He points northeast of that on the map. "The Bank of Sark is here in St. Petersport, the Guernsey Islands. This bank has never done any international business with the banks in Italy or Sicily. Again . . . no link with the Mafia." Sonny calls for the lights to dim, then pulls down a screen. "Why do we need the Bank of Sark? Because it already has international clearance with the Bank of England and a credit line with Lloyds of London." A slide of a small two-story building on the corner of a narrow, cobblestoned street appears. Sonny points to the top floor office over a beauty shop. "This is the Bank of Sark.

It will be the front bank for our money transfers. That way we'll have no leaks." Sonny continues speaking in the dim glow of the slide. "Why do we need an insurance company? To write loan commitments. Gentlemen, we can make millions of dollars with a ten-cent piece of paper. How? By charging developers ten to fifteen points up front for our commitment letters to the bank saying that we'll pick up his long-term financing. . . . It's legitimate . . . all the big insurance companies are doing it. However, we'll never have to honor any of our commitments unless we want to. Why not? Because we'll have loopholes. Our average commitment letter will have around fifteen loopholes, but I'll explain the major ones we'll be using." A slide of a thirty-story building comes on the screen. "Prudential gave the developer a loan commitment of twenty million dollars to build this apartment house. When it came time for Prudential to honor their commitment, they refused because the contractor used inferior materials for the molding around the windows. In other words, the contractor didn't build to specifications. Insurance records show and I know that ninety-one percent of the contractors in this country cut corners. All we have to do is bug the contractor's telephone and wire his offices to find out where he's cutting corners; then we can use the information as a loophole in his commitment." The slide changes. "This is a motel in Muncie, Indiana. Metropolitan Life gave a long-term loan commitment to build it. In the original feasibility study, the projected income of the property was listed at eight hundred sixty thousand dollars a year. However, when it came time to honor their commitment, Metropolitan refused to take out the loan. . . . the motel was only grossing about six hundred twenty grand a year. The insurance company didn't have to pick up the loan until the cash flow reached the eight hundred sixty grand stated in the original agreement. Last year seventy-seven percent of loan applications that came into our Oklahoma insurance company had inflated cash flow figures. The greedy developer will overestimate his cash flow just to get his commitment—with this rope, gentlemen, they hang themselves. This is another loophole for us."

The lights come up on Sonny again. "The third major loophole involves appraised value. Ninety-seven percent of loans submitted to the insurance company last year had inflated appraised values of thirty percent more than what the property was actually worth. Most major insurance companies have a clause in their loan commitment stating that they don't have to honor the commitment until they receive their own appraiser's report. For example, if our appraiser says a building isn't worth the twenty million estimated in the original agreement, then we have no obligation to pick up our commitment . . . we can't lose." Sonny studies the audience. They seem to understand what he's saying, so he goes on. "Remember, I said we would get front money from the developers? How? By sending in Brownsville torpedoes? Muscle? No, gentlemen—the developer's bank and the bank escrow officer there are gonna collect our money for us. How can we be sure of that? Well, in the escrow agreement, it will state that the insurance company backing the loan, that's us, must have a financial statement of two hundred ninety million dollars. Once the statement is delivered to the escrow officer, then the money is released to Transcontinental Casualty in the Bahamas or one of our designated agents. O.K. . . . so where is our company going to get a two hundred ninety million-dollar statement? Simple . . . we're gonna get it by buying other shell corporations to inflate our financial statement. Gentlemen . . . I need a million dollars from each one of you. With fifteen million dollars I can buy these offshore companies." A slide with the names comes on: "These corporations will be the vehicle to inflate our financial statement to two hundred ninety million—remember this figure, I'm gonna come back to it. I worked for them for one year and never saw any cash. I'm not sayin' the insurance companies don't have money, I'm just sayin' they don't use it . . . they use paper. I saw a lot of securities and real estate put up as collateral but never any real money. What I'm talking about, gentlemen, is sellin' nothin' but a ten-cent piece of paper and makin' millions. We'll do the same thing. After your initial investment we can make millions without puttin' up any more cash. Gettin' back to shell corporations . . . the ones we're buyin' are licensed under international law to do business in the Bahamas. We have a license to steal there, as long as we don't take any Bahamian people or corporations. Here's why. . ." The lights dim again, and a slide of a stocky black man in uniform is projected. "This is a high-ranking Bahamian official. Last year he bought South American stocks as a personal investment using government funds. I'm not sayin' he's crooked, ya understand . . . but"— Sonny pulls a reel of tape from his attaché case and tosses it on the table—"I'm sure this will get me anything I want in the Bahamas." The screen is blank again. "The men you're gonna see now will be my executives in this operation. None of them are Italian, none have criminal records, and not one knows anything at all about the Mafia. But I know a lot about them. I've had 'em under surveillance for months. They're all outstanding members of the community. However, my tapes tell a different story."

A slide of a smiling full-faced man in his thirties comes up. "This is Jeffrey Wolfman. He's a Jew from Kansas, a good family man, and one of the best insurance underwriters in the country. So good that he gets kickbacks from his clients, mostly major insurance companies. To look authentic we need Jeff to underwrite our high-risk insurance. Of course we'll never pay on any of these claims." Next is a slide of a man whose image is definitely "Father Knows Best." "This is Allen Collins, vice-president of a top casualty company in Chicago. He gets his kickbacks from a theft ring that steals everything from fleets of cars to farm equipment and transports 'em across the border. Allen gets another kickback from the insurance company later when the stolen goods are found. We need him for our casualty department and to be our customs contact." The third picture is of a benign, grandfatherly man. "This is Dr. Benjamin Swanson, a physician and one of the top CPAs in the country. He was the staff doctor at a big insurance company before he became chief accountant. If the money was right, Dr. Swanson could get a dying man to pass his physical. As an accountant Swanson got his kickbacks by inflating certified financial statements for developers. Naturally he'll be doing financial statements for us . . . Remember, we need a two hundred ninety million-dollar statement to get our front money." The last slide is of a particularly handsome older man. "This gentleman is president of a major bank in Southern California. Gregory Stanford will be our puppet; he's scared of his own shadow, and he should be. With my tapes the government would have enough to put Gregory and his whole bank board away for years for misappropriation of funds. But Gregory's unblemished record with his bank will be our most valuable asset. . . . He'll be able to negotiate our escrow agreements so we can get our front money."

The lights come up on Sonny again. "There will be many other men working for us. A majority will be top stockbrokers and insurance salesmen. They all have something in common . . . they're greedy and they're crooked. Gentlemen, that's what makes good salesmen." Sonny grins. "I should know, I was a top agent myself last year." He pauses to take a sip of water. The smile vanishes as he gets back down to business. "Now you heard me talk earlier about the Bank of Sark. How would you gentlemen like to be able to buy anything you wanted without ever having to pay for it? Through our bank and our shell corporations, we can do just that. We can purchase land, boats, houses, buildings— and never spend a penny. How are we gonna do that? Through my manipulations, the Bank of Sark will have an inflated balance sheet showing deposits of over seventy-two and a half million. With that I can write international bank drafts, up to seven hundred twenty thousand dollars, the bait to attract the developers to get involved with us. Suppose your hotel is worth four hundred thousand dollars. I offer you seven hundred thousand for it with one stipulation . . . you have to keep my Bank of Sark cashier's check in escrow for two years. You agree to sell under those terms, and I get immediate ownership of your property. In two years I drain the cash flow from the hotel, then sell it for three hundred thousand dollars. At the end of two years, when your escrow officer deposits the cashier's check for collection, it'll never reach the Bank of Sark. Our man working in the clearing house in

England will destroy all Bank of Sark checks that come through. In order for the government to prosecute us they gotta have the original check . . . photocopies are not admissible evidence. It's the most clean and legal scam ever to be pulled in this world." There is a low murmur in the room as the dons and their attorneys react to this. The talking stops when Sonny pulls another chart from the wall. "Now let me show you how your million-dollar investment is protected, gentlemen, and also assure ya I'm not gonna disappear with your money. Each man will deposit his million in the bank in Zurich with a ten-year pledge. At the end of the term, with a compound interest rate of ten percent, you'll get back two million nine hundred nine-five dollars—more than double your money. This protects each family and gives me the money I need to buy the Lucky Ace, a hotel and casino in the Bahamas which will be the center of our operation. I guarantee that you'll have my complete cooperation for any type of money transactions ya wanna carry on there. Also, I guarantee I'll be a carrier for the families, provided I'm not carryin' nickels and dimes . . ."

Don Giuseppe interrupts. "You mean you'll be a carrier for all the families?"

Sonny says, "Yes, Don Giuseppe. Because every man here will be my partner. Who can they trust more than me? I'm not affected by their differences." Sonny looks at each man as he speaks. "Some of you have heard of me. I am feared by a lot of men . . . with good reason. I'm a loyal soldier to the Sicilian Mafia and the only one without pure blood who's taken the vows." He walks over to Alfonso and puts his hand on his shoulder. "Alfonso Lambretti was my sponsor, and today he's my godfather." Sonny returns to the head of the table and leans over. "Gentlemen, I think I've made it very clear in this meeting that the return on your investment is millions. I'm prepared to answer any questions you have at this time."

A short, stocky man chewing a cigar stands. He is head of the Boston family, Frank Manadeli. "Hey, Santino—what happens to our money if something happens to you, God forbid . . ."

Sonny answers, "A good question. You'll see on page twenty-six I'm requesting fifteen bodyguards to make sure nothing happens to me. Every family has to furnish me with a top soldier. From each million dollars, fifty thousand will be given to the Sicilian Mafia for a prepaid contract on each man. If I die, even by natural causes, all my bodyguards get hit. It'll keep 'em loyal."

A voice from the back of the room shouts approval. "That's a hell of an idea. If Anastasia had thought of it, he'd be here today."

Another voice agrees. "Goddam good idea. It's too late for him, but not for me. Hell, I'm gonna do the same thing myself when I get back to Philly."

Sonny continues. "These prepaid contracts will keep the families from usin' me to settle any personal vendettas . . . but with my reputation as a hit man and a soldier and my loyalty, I don't anticipate any problems. I know every man here understands what I'm saying."

An attorney for the St. Louis family breaks the tense moment. "What about records? How are we protected from subpoena?"

Sonny says, "A good point. Our records will be on a computer memory bank with a high-speed erase system. Only four of my employees will have access to the controls, and they'll rotate on twenty-four-hour shifts. One call from me and they can erase all the information in our files in five seconds. What's important to us is the cash, not the records. By the way, none of your accountants will be allowed to check my records . . . it could get me indicted. I'll only go to jail for my own mistakes . . . not for someone else's. Well, gentlemen, you've heard my plan for the perfect crime . . . believe me, it will work."

At this point the silence in the room is broken by animated discussion of the presentation. Don Giuseppe taps his glass for order. "Thank you, Santino. The council will now review the portfolio and vote on the proposal. Can you please step outside, Santino, until we come to a decision?"

Sonny leaves and waits in the outer reception area, knowing he gave a good, clear presentation to the dons. In two hours he is called back into the conference room. Don Giuseppe gives him the decision, "I'm sorry, Santino, you've been outvoted. Many of the men feel you're too young to handle a fifteen-million-dollar investment. Personally, I'm behind you. I think it would be a good thing for the families."

Sonny is crestfallen. He was sure he had delivered a convincing argument for his plan. "O.K., Don Giuseppe, I made a commitment to you."

He packs up his attaché case and heads for the door, but just as he reaches for the knob, a familiar voice says, "Wait a minute, Santino." A hush falls over the room. Alfonso stands and speaks for the first time. "You're right, Don Giuseppe, it would be a good thing for all of us." He crosses the room and puts his hand on Sonny's shoulder. "This man was under my guidance in Sicily for three years. Two years ago, when he left, he was a loyal soldier, dedicated to the service of the Mafia. Today he has proven that he is that and much more by bringing you one of the most sophisticated moneymaking ideas I've ever heard of . . . he is a financial genius. The Sicilian Mafia is behind Sonny and this operation . . . more than we are behind some of you here today. We gave a simple command: get Valachi. You failed. Since Valachi four more rats have crawled out of their holes and gone to the Justice Department." He pauses to let this sink in, then continues. "In Sonny's operation we don't have to worry about that—there's no link to the

Mafia. We are requesting that you get involved." Alfonso's face hardens. "No, it is not a request. Santino, will you please leave the room." Sonny steps out once again. This time only five minutes pass before he is called back in again. Now, he is greeted with hugs from all the men. The dons and their attorneys congratulate him on his brilliant scheme. In the midst of all this Sonny shoots Alfonso a puzzled look; the old man just smiles. Whatever he said in that room was strong enough to scare the fifteen most powerful dons in the United States . . . Sonny will get his money.

Sam comes over to him. "You did a helluva job, Sonny. How soon will you need the money?"

"In thirty days . . . you'll be notified where to send it."

Sonny's been waiting for this moment a long time. "By the way, Sam, I wanna talk to you for a minute." They move away from the crowd into a corner. Sonny says flatly, "I wanted ya to know somethin' Sam . . . all these years . . . I knew it was you who tried to hit me in Cuba." The butt drops from Sam's mouth as he protests, "Oh . . . no . . . no . . . it was . . ."

"Save it, Sam, I'm not a green kid bustin' nigger heads no more. I know it was you. Franco told me before I blew him away."

Sam lights up a fresh cigar and puffs while he makes his excuses. "Well . . . I figured if you came back, you'd have to be better than the two professionals. I'd keep ya . . . I didn't want any losers on my team."

Sonny nods. "I understand. I'd do the same thing myself today . . . with one difference." His eyes bore into Sam's, "If it was me, I'd've made sure I finished it."

Alfonso comes over at the tail end of Sonny's remark. "Finish what, Santino?"

Sam brushes it off. "Nothin', Lambretti, just an old joke between Sonny and I."

"Yeah, Alfonso," Sonny concurs, "an old, private joke."

The Sicilian puts an arm around Sonny. "You did a good job up there today. I didn't get a chance to congratulate you. . . . Tonight we celebrate . . . your godfather is taking you out to dinner."

Sam, obviously uncomfortable, pats Sonny's shoulder. "Sonny, I'll see ya. Keep me posted on this thing. I know we're gonna all make a bundle." He shakes Alfonso's hand. "It was good seeing you again, Lambretti."

Alfonso watches as Sam leaves. "What was between you and Sam was no joke, was it, Santino?"

"No, Alfonso."

"Did you learn from what happened?"

"Bet your ass, I did."

"Then that's all that matters. Sam is a good man, but even good men make mistakes."

Before Sonny takes the reins of power, he is looking forward to spending a quiet evening with his mentor. Angelo drives him to meet Alfonso at a family restaurant on the West Side. The bodyguard stations himself near them at a table facing the door while Sonny and Alfonso give the waiter their order. To ensure complete privacy the two men speak the Mafia's code language whenever he is around. "Santino, I was impressed by your presentation this morning. How much will your operation cost to set up?"

Sonny smiles. "About a million and a half. I'm giving Don Giuseppe's money back as soon as I get it."

"But why did you ask for so much money from the dons?"

"Side investments." Sonny adds quickly, "Of course, I'm gonna split everything with the Sicilian Mafia."

"No, no, no . . . forget it. We just want half of you, Santino. By the way, that idea you have for your bodyguards is very good. Prepaid contracts will keep them alert."

"Yeah, and just to be sure there's no pressure from anybody, I'm takin' contracts out on their families, too."

"Great . . . Santino . . . great. Gino has a cousin in Chicago who'd be a good man for you. His name is Richie. He was kicked off the police force last year, but he was Sam's inside contact with the cops for years."

"I know . . . Gino told me about Richie. I can't wait to meet him."

"I'll tell Sam to send him down to the Bahamas to meet you." The waiter appears with their antipasto; after he leaves, Alfonso changes the subject. "Santino, remember when you were in Sicily, I gave you tapes on the Genetti family?"

"Yeah . . . the old man killed his daughter and son-in-law in Ohio, then disappeared with his grandson, right?" Alfonso nods and pulls some tapes from his case. "I want you to learn these and refresh your memory. From now on, you'll have a dual identity . . . You'll still be known as Sonny Gibson, but the families will think it's a front. When they check, they'll find out you were born in Sicily and your real name is Santino Gino Genetti."

Sonny is amazed. "What? How'd ya do that?"

"Remember what I told you in that little church in Catania? The Mafia controls everything. We duplicated your birth records. We left the originals in Indiana, then took the copies to Sicily and had them stamped by the Church. That took some doing, but it makes proof of your birth look official. Only you and I and your natural family know where you were really born. Everyone else will think the Indiana records are false, not the Sicilian ones. We've been looking for someone like you for over ten years, Santino . . . you're perfect."

"Perfect for what?"

The old man's eyes narrow. "To avenge the Sicilian Mafia. Long before Valachi spilled his guts, we lost respect for the families over here. Everyone started to go their own way. They didn't want to share the same well anymore. That goes against everything the Mafia stands for . . . we've always looked out for our own. Many American dons refused to listen to the voice of the Cosa Nostra. Now it's too late; they have to pay the price."

"Why don't you just get rid of the families that caused the trouble?"

Alfonso tells him bitterly, "In the old days we would have. I wanted to put the hit on them, but I was outvoted. . . . If we'd done it then, there would be no *baccalas* like Valachi. Today the Sicilian dons feel there's too much money at stake in America . . . killing would start a Mafia war here; many innocent families would get hurt. We don't want loyal men like Don Giuseppe to suffer." Alfonso says firmly, "So, Santino, you will take care of business for us."

"What can I do that the Cosa Nostra can't?"

Alfonso smiles. "You are going to hit them where it hurts . . . in the pocket. This morning you had those men convinced they're going to make millions of dollars. Well, you're going to see to it that some of them lose millions."

"Let me understand this . . . instead of sending a soldier to kill them, you want me to con these men out of their money?"

"Yes, the kind of money we're talking about will certainly kill their operations. They must be punished for being disloyal to us and to each other."

Sonny considers his assignment thoughtfully. "Alfonso, you know I'll do whatever you ask, but I don't wanna hurt Don Giuseppe."

"He is a good man, Santino. So are Sam, and Frank from New Orleans, and a lot of other men. You won't touch them."

This relieves him, but Sonny is thinking ahead. "Alfonso, you're talking about taking the top Mafia families in the country. There's gotta be a Brownsville torpedo around the corner when they find out how I conned 'em."

Alfonso takes a sip of wine. "Normally, yes . . . but everyone knows the power of the Genetti family—they're more scared of that than the devil himself."

"Why was everyone so afraid of Don Genetti?"

"He was the most feared head La Cosa Nostra ever had. His power was so widespread, he caused Anastasia to get killed in the barber chair and got Capone sent to prison."

"Did you know the don personally?"

"He made me a lieutenant. We were very close. I was Santino Gino's godfather."

". . . and that's why you wanted to be my godfather. Don't lie to me . . . that's why, isn't it?"

"Only partly . . ." Alfonso pats Sonny's hand. "I wanted to be your godfather because I was proud of you, but it's good, Santino, that the dons all know I'm your godfather, too." The waiter places their entrees in front of them, and they switch back to Sicilian. "What do you think happened to the don and his grandson?"

Alfonso shrugs. "No one knows . . . it could be that he was just tired of making decisions and wanted to live in peace somewhere." The old soldier points at Sonny. "Don't ever forget . . . you are Santino Gino Genetti. When I was training you, I knew you'd be the perfect one to pull this off—half Sicilian, half American. The dons you're conning . . . they'll never suspect a thing." Alfonso takes out another tape. "When you bring these men to the Bahamas to tell them they've been conned, instead of reading their death warrants, recite this to them." He hands Sonny the reel. "This lists the charges against them. Once you have done this, the Sicilian Mafia will be avenged. In the meantime we'll be sending you surveillance tapes on them."

Sonny says proudly, "It will be my honor as a soldier to do this, Alfonso."

After dinner the waiter brings them two espressos. Alfonso pours a shot of anisette in his. "There is one other thing we want you to do."

"Yes, Alfonso?"

"When you set up the Lucky Ace, you will become a very highly paid prostitute for the Mafia."

This irritates Sonny. "Come on, Alfonso, I finished with that . . . years ago."

Alfonso says firmly, "Not quite. Believe me, we have our reasons, Santino. No one can handle women like you. It is important that you do this for us." This drives the point home.

Sonny agrees. "O.K., Alfonso, you must have a good reason."

The Catania soldier continues, "You'll also be running one of the top prostitution rackets in the world from the Lucky Ace. We want the casino to be a success. A broad can bring in a man faster than anything else . . . and she can make him spend every lira he has on the crap table. How soon can you get whores down there?"

Sonny thinks. "Pretty soon. I'll call Maxi in Miami, he supplies all the call girls to the big hotels there."

Alfonso leans back in his chair and lights up one of his pungent guinea stinkers. "Good. Do you have any questions?"

"No. The operation is clear to me . . ." Sonny drains his espresso. "Alfonso, after I get your money from the families, I'd like something for myself."

A large smoke ring drifts toward the ceiling as Alfonso answers.

"What is it, Santino?"

Sonny's voice is steady. "I wanna be a don."

The old man almost swallows his cigar in surprise at this request. "Santino, you're too young. Besides, what territory would you want?"

Sonny says simply, "The whole world. Of course, I don't mean the United States, Europe, or Canada."

Alfonso laughs. "You know, I think you could handle it, too." He puts out his cigar and says seriously, "Santino, I can't talk them into letting you become a don . . . you don't have pure blood." This is an obstacle Sonny didn't expect. All this time he thought he could earn the rank of don. He rethinks his position quickly. "Then I wanna be a free soldier. I don't wanna report to any more dons, here or in Sicily. . . . Of course the Sicilian Mafia will still get half of whatever I make."

Alfonso says, "That has never been done before, Santino, but I will make the request for you and bring the answer down to the Bahamas." Alfonso pauses, studying Sonny. He's noticed a change in attitude that is disturbing. His godfather finally says, "Santino, you know, since I've been in New York, you haven't even asked me about Laura."

His statement disconcerts Sonny. Could it be that he hasn't thought of Laura once since Alfonso arrived? It was hard to admit, but it was true . . . this meeting meant more to him right now than Laura. "Alfonso, I been so wrapped up in things . . . there's so much goin' on."

"Loved ones are as important as things, Santino."

Sonny taps his spoon on the table. "Yeah . . . well, how is she?"

"She's fine. I think I could probably talk Don Belfiore into letting her come to the Bahamas with me."

"That's good, Alfonso." In spite of his apparent apathy Sonny still has a deep feeling for Laura. "Is she married yet?"

"No. She'll never marry . . . she only wants you, Santino."

Sonny says quietly, "You know, Alfonso, I never had the chance to thank you for keeping silent so we could be together all those nights."

The old man snaps his fingers and calls for the check, abruptly ending the conversation. "It is time to go now, Santino. You've gotta get a good night's rest. Tomorrow Don Giuseppe is taking you someplace he's never taken any of his soldiers."

"Where's that?"

"He's taking you to play bocce ball."

"Don Giuseppe plays bocce?"

"Of course, all the old-timers do."

"Where do they play at?"

"In a restaurant in Brooklyn . . . in the back."

"No shit . . . does Nick play, too?"

"No. Don Giuseppe says Nick likes to play tennis . . . bocce is too slow for him." Alfonso puts on his coat. "Tomorrow you knock on my door at ten . . . I'm right across the hall. We'll have breakfast in my suite."

The next morning, after they eat, Angelo drives them to Bay Ridge. As they go through the Battery Tunnel, the bodyguard says proudly, "As soon as we get outta this tunnel, we'll be in Brooklyn. I come from Brooklyn, Mr. Lambretti . . . Uh . . . most people when they come to New York never go there, but we got a lotta things in Brooklyn, too." Sonny asks, "Yeah . . . what's in Brooklyn, Angelo?" "Well . . . we got the most famous bridge in the world. And . . . uh . . . did you know we got more people in Brooklyn than they got in all of Kansas? And some of the most beautiful women come from here? Barbra Streisand's from Brooklyn . . ."

Sonny can hear the pride in the big man's voice. "You really love this place, huh, Angelo?"

"Yes, Santino . . . this is my home."

"You think you could live in a place like the Bahamas?"

"Uh . . . well, if Don Giuseppe said to, I could live there O.K., I guess."

Sonny lowers his voice to Alfonso. "I want this guy. Ya know, he's really smart. He just talks that way 'cause he has a voice defect."

"I know that, Santino, but Don Giuseppe wouldn't let him go. He loves Angelo like a son. Years ago Angelo's father was one of Don Giuseppe's chief bodyguards. He died protecting the don when Angelo was five. Don Giuseppe promised Colucci he'd take care of his son."

"Yeah . . . yeah . . . but how do I get him, Alfonso?"

"Santino, you heard nothing. I said they're very close. Why do you want this guy so bad?"

"He'd be perfect for one of my chief bodyguards."

Alfonso mops his brow, more out of habit than necessity in the cold New York weather. After a few minutes he says, "Santino, why not try and win Angelo? Make him the stakes in the bocce game today."

Sonny considers the possibilities. "I get him if I win, but what do I give Don Giuseppe if I lose?"

"You didn't tell him what you told me in the restaurant last night, did you?"

"No . . ."

"Well, tell him you won't take his million if you lose." Alfonso folds his handkerchief and puts it back in his breast pocket. ". . . but you're gonna win, Santino. Don Giuseppe can't beat you. You're too good."

"You think the don'll go for it?"

"He will. Giuseppe loves a good bet, and he'd love to beat you in front of the old guys."

"Who're the old guys?"

"The men from the neighborhood . . . most of them are poor retired guineas. When Don Giuseppe plays with them, it's a big deal. They'll go crazy when they find out about this game today."

The limo finally stops in front of a small Italian restaurant under elevated train tracks. The owner, Tony, comes out to greet them. "Ah, Signor Lambretti . . . *come sta*? It's been a long time."

"*Va bene,* Tony. It's good to see you. This is Santino."

"Santino . . . *si*. Don Giuseppe is waiting in the back. Come in. Come in. I bring you some special wine from my cellar."

The men follow Tony through the empty place, which is closed on Sunday afternoons for his friends. The smell of the wine and cigars filters through the restaurant from the back room. Inside, the old men sit on benches in front of a long wooden table cluttered with bowls of fruit and empty bottles. Most of the old-timers are in their sixties and wear nearly identical outfits—caps, pants with suspenders, and white shirts. They suck on oranges or peel apples as they watch one of their cronies shell out $10 to Don Giuseppe, who's just won a game. "*Madonna,* what luck today, Loganno. I can't wait till you get beat."

"It's not luck, Umberto, it's not luck. It's skill." Don Giuseppe sees his guests. "Ay . . . Santino . . . Alfonso . . . you're here. Hey, everybody . . . this is a good friend, Santino Gibson. You all know Alfonso Lambretti . . . he's lost more than a few games of bocce here." The old men all laugh, and the don says to Sonny, "You ready to take me on?"

One of the others calls out, "Be careful, Santino. He beat everybody today."

Sonny smiles. "That's good. Then the odds are with me."

"Ah . . . the young lion thinks the odds are in his favor. He's gonna need the odds . . . he's gonna need everything." Don Giuseppe hands Sonny four green game balls and keeps four gold ones for himself. "We play for a dollar a point, ten dollars a game. You think you can handle those stakes?" He turns to his friends. "Maybe these young guys wanna play for broads, eh?"

Umberto shouts, "Yeah . . . and when he gets to be our age, he'll wish he had the money."

The laughter that follows turns to shouts of approval as Tony wheels in another case of wine. Don Giuseppe grabs a bottle for him and Sonny to share. As he fills their glasses, Sonny whispers to him, "This game, Don Giuseppe . . . I wanna play for one guy to come to the Bahamas with me against the million dollars you're puttin' up." The don stops pouring. "One guy? Who in the hell's worth that much money, Santino?"

"Angelo."

"Does he want to go? Have you asked him?"

"In the car he said if it was O.K. with you, he'd go."

The don puts down the wine bottle. "O.K., Santino . . . we play for Angelo."

One of the men yells, "Hey, when you gonna start this game, Loganno? I'm gettin' old waitin' here."

The don jokes back at him, "Impossible . . . you're already old, Roberto." They all laugh, and Don Giuseppe rubs his palms together. "All right . . . let's see how much you really learned in Sicily, Santino. Since you're my guest, you can roll the *pallina*." Sonny takes the billiard-size ball and throws it down the sixty-foot alley. The dirt lane has been raked, watered, and dried until it's as smooth as a putting green. The *pallina* is the point ball. The object of bocce is to get the game balls to stop near it. The closer you get, the more points you score . . . twenty-one wins. Don Giuseppe's first gold ball rolls five inches from the *pallina*. The old men stomp their feet and whistle. *"Bene . . . molto bene . . ."*

The don straightens up. "It's your turn, Santino . . . let's see you beat that." Sonny takes aim and throws his green ball. It stops three inches from the mark. "A lucky shot, Santino, but I'm gonna put a hit on that one. I'll knock it clear out of the box." The don gets ready to throw again, and Sonny says, "With all due respect, Don Giuseppe, don't give yourself a hernia throwing the bocce ball."

Loganno points to Sonny. "See what the young lion is doing? You see? He's trying to get my mind off the game . . . but I'll show him." His roll hits Sonny's ball and spins it away from the point ball. The old man glows with satisfaction. His friends cheer vigorously on the side-lines . . . rooting for Don Giuseppe makes them all act like teenagers. He seems to give them life.

Forty minutes later Sonny is ahead by three points. They both have one ball left. The old-timers crowd around the court, waiting for the don's roll. They even stop puffing their cigars for fear it will break his concentration. Giuseppe throws. He walks down the side of the alley, stooping over, coaxing the ball along. "To the left . . . more, more . . . No . . . whoa . . . *basta, basta.*" Then, *"Mamma mia!"* There is a groan of disappointment as his ball passes the *pallina* by a foot. It looks like Sonny is a cinch to win. He rolls and Alfonso can't believe it when his green ball hits the point ball, knocking it over to the corner next to three of Don Giuseppe's. Sonny threw too hard.

The men whoop excitedly, patting Don Giuseppe's back in triumph. "Hey, Loganno, we won."

"That'll show these kids, eh?"

The don goads Sonny. "Well, Santino, it looks like the old lion beat the young lion."

Sonny concedes, "You beat me, Don Giuseppe. I'll keep my word . . . you don't have to pay the million."

Roberto calls to Sonny, "Hey, how about a game with me now?"

Sonny looks at the don, "Go ahead, Santino . . . Roberto's one of the best. I can never beat him."

"O.K., Roberto, we'll play for five broads."

Don Giuseppe takes a seat on the bench next to Alfonso. They watch Sonny play brilliantly. Soon he is way ahead of Roberto. "Look at that shot, Alfonso. I couldn't make that myself."

"You should have seen the way he played in Sicily. He was a champion."

The don looks at Alfonso suspiciously. "Did he let me win? He let me win, didn't he?"

"Giuseppe, you know a blind man could have finished that game and won."

"Why did he do that if he wants Angelo so bad?"

"Out of respect. He saw how the other men idolize you. How you represent the old country to them. Winning this match was like winning a victory for Sicily . . . Santino knew that."

"Alfonso, respect is one thing . . . but he lost a million dollars."

"No . . . it was never Santino's intention to take your money."

"What! Why not?"

"He doesn't need your million, Giuseppe, he needs your support."

The two old friends turn and watch Sonny enjoying himself with the others, smoking a big cigar and guzzling wine from a bottle. "You know, Alfonso, it's too bad that one isn't pure. I love him as much as my own blood."

"His is pure, Giuseppe . . . who of our own young men would have gone through the training he had? How many of them would play with the old-timers, eh?" His godfather says with pride, "I love Santino, too . . . and he is my blood now."

Roberto throws his cigar down when he loses. "Eh, Santino . . . where am I gonna get five broads?"

"That's your problem, not mine. Just make sure they're pretty and they're not over thirty."

The loser bargains, "Would you settle for one hot pizza waitress? Put a sack on her head . . . she looks good."

"For you Roberto, fine." Sonny goes over to Don Giuseppe, "That guy was easy to beat . . . you feel like playing again, Don Giuseppe?"

"No, Santino . . . once you get the goods, you keep the goods. Besides, we're gonna go now. Tell Mario to get all the cars lined up." The don stands and shouts, "All right everybody . . . listen up. At eight we eat at Vito's place. Everyone's invited . . . it's on me."

In Little Italy that night the Cadillacs stretch from one end of

Mulberry Street to the other. The bodyguards stand watch outside while the old-timers have their victory party. The next day Don Giuseppe rides to the airport with Sonny and Alfonso. The flights to Sicily and the Bahamas are just half an hour apart. Sonny gets dropped off at his terminal first. Before he gets out, he says to Don Giuseppe, "Which one of your men are you sendin' with me?"

"Well, Santino . . . I made that decision last night. I'm gonna give you Angelo."

"But you won the bocce game."

The don shakes his head. "Santino . . . we both win this way. You get Angelo and I get peace of mind knowing you'll be safe. This is good for Angelo, too. He can grow with you."

The huge bodyguard opens the door and bends his head down to look inside. "I got our tickets. Where's your suitcase, Boss?"

Sonny says, still surprised, "In the back, Angelo."

"Oh, O.K., Boss. I'll get it."

Alfonso hugs Sonny.

"I'll be down to the Bahamas soon with your friend . . . *buona fortuna,* Santino." Don Giuseppe hugs him, "Let me know if you need anything, Santino."

"Thanks, Don Giuseppe . . . for everything."

4
The Bahamas

The flight down to the Bahamas is smooth, and as soon as Sonny and Angelo get off the plane, a hefty black man comes up to them. "Mr. Gibson . . ." Angelo is instantly on the alert. He looks down at the man. "Who wants to know?"

The Bahamian's voice lilts musically, "I'm Louis. I was sent by Mr. Benton to pick you up."

"It's O.K., Angelo. Benton's the banker."

"Uh . . . before we go, Boss, I'd better call the banker and make sure they sent this guy."

"Good idea, Angelo."

He comes back in five minutes. "O.K., Boss. They sent him."

"Where's the car?"

The black points. "Just out here."

Sonny and the bodyguard follow the chauffeur through the tiny terminal to the street. "Gee, Boss, this don't even look like an airport . . . it's so small."

"Ya ever been out of Brooklyn, Angelo?"

"I have some cousins in New Jersey."

Angelo's geographical naiveté really shows on the drive to the hotel. "Boss, what kind of tree is that? It's all trunk."

Sonny looks out the window. "It's a palm tree. They got 'em in Florida."

"That sure is useless lookin'. It don't give you no shade to sit in."

"No, but see up there?" Sonny points to a cluster. "Those are coconuts."

"Who'd be crazy enough to climb up there to pick 'em?"

Sonny laughs. "Nobody—they shoot 'em down, Angelo."

Twenty minutes later they pull up in front of the Lucky Ace. Henry Benton is standing in the center of the lobby, waiting for them. The

153

six-foot banker is dwarfed by an enormous fountain next to him. On top three gilt nudes pour water from their pitchers to a pool, where bronze urchins urinate, creating a waterfall to another larger pool below them. Angelo circles the fountain in awe. "I never seen nothin' like that, even at the Plaza. You own this place, Boss?"

Mr. Benton smiles, "As of nine o'clock tomorrow morning he does. The attorneys have worked out the extra conditions. The papers are all ready for you to sign, Mr. Gibson. But first I'll show you around if you like."

"Yeah, let's do that. I wanna make sure those guys left all the pictures on the walls."

Benton takes them on a tour. There are three sections to the Lucky Ace, a main building of five floors and two wings of two floors each. The casino is a large room, 50 by 100 feet, with two roulette wheels, five crap tables, eight twenty-one games, and one baccarat table. Crystal chandeliers and red flocked wallpaper highlight the Las Vegas-inspired decor found throughout the hotel. The stuffy banker says as they walk, "I understand you've let the staff go."

"Yep. I'm closin' everything down for ten days to get settled in."

"Your good friend in the government wanted me to remind you that by law you must hire ninety percent Bahamians in the hotel . . . the casino staff is your own prerogative."

Sonny snaps, "Look, Benton, I know the fuckin' law, but I'm gonna hire the niggers myself—that way I know who I'm gettin'. There's not a nigger around that can run a casino. I hired the best guys in the world." The tour ends in front of the lobby fountain. "You tell my 'good friend' I don't want any of my men stopped coming through customs this afternoon . . . and tell him I want three-year work permits for 'em. Angelo will get a list of names and passport numbers."

"Would you like me to arrange for the sale of the fishing boats?"

Angelo says excitedly, "You got boats too, Boss?"

"Yeah, five of 'em. Forget it, Benton. I've decided to keep 'em for hotel guests to use."

"Very well, Mr. Gibson. If you need anything, feel free to call on me."

"Don't worry, Benton, if anything goes wrong, you'll hear about it."

The next morning at nine Sonny starts to organize his operation. He assembles his fifteen bodyguards in the hotel showroom. They sit at tables beneath Sonny, while he paces onstage, a king before his court. "I wanna welcome everybody to the Bahamas. You'll like it here and we'll all get along as long as you follow the rules. Some of them you guys should know already. First, there'll be no drinkin' or eatin' on the job. If we're in the hotel room and I'm not talkin' business, you guys can eat with me. When we go out, there'll be four guys inside and a man on each entrance. The rest of ya will be outside lookin' for trouble or cops. Only one of ya is gonna know what I order, and you're gonna have to eat some of it in front of me. You'll be with the chef when he makes it. Have him eat some of it in front of you, if you're smart. I got another strict rule. The call girls in the casino are off limits. You guys can't be watchin' me if you're lookin' up some broad's ass. What you do on your time is your own business. You'll work three weeks on and get ten days off. You'll be workin' in pairs on twenty-four-hour shifts. Some of you guys know each other, so you can team up together if you want. Now, you're gettin' paid double what you made with your other families for one reason . . . this is a high-risk job. You all know about the prepaid contracts. If ya don't like those terms, you can leave." No one objects, so Sonny goes on. "You guys are gonna be more than bodyguards. You're gonna be my eyes and ears. You'll be wearin' a walkie-talkie at all times . . . take it to the shitter with ya, you're on call twenty-four hours. Angelo's in charge of my personal security. He's gonna assign a couple of ya to be with me today. Richie's head of overall security and he'll give the rest of ya your assignments." A clean-cut man in his thirties comes into the showroom. Sonny welcomes him. "Hey, Frankie, great . . . you're here." He introduces the new arrival to the bodyguards.

"This is Frankie. He's my hotel manager. You guys who been to New York a lot all know Frankie. He managed our operation there. Frankie's gonna take you around and show you the layout of the hotel. O.K., let's go, Angelo. Some guys are waitin'."

Angelo picks two men to go with them, and Sonny heads to the casino to meet his new staff, the most skilled mechanics from the gambling capitals of the world. They are an assortment of looks and personalities—from smooth, continental types to poker-faced thugs. Mechanics keep the odds in favor of the house. These men can stack a deck of cards to show an ace or face card any time in a twenty-one game or throw a pair of cold dice in a winning crap table and turn the winner's luck around. Sonny scans the group. "Who's Joe Bartow?" The toughest-looking man raises his hand. "The boys have packed your bags. You're goin' back to the States tonight. Gentlemen, Joe's an agent put in here by the IRS. This is an example for all of you. I know everything that goes on." He turns to his chief bodyguard. "Angelo, send one of the guys with Joe. Make sure he gets on the plane all right. We don't want any trouble from the government."

A Vegas mechanic blurts out, "Man, I just told that son of a bitch how much I scammed last year."

Sonny glares at him, "What's your name?"

"Andy Paine."

"You're fired."

The boss warns the others. "He's the second example, gentlemen. It'll teach all of you not to talk to nobody. Angelo, get Andy's shit together."

The bodyguard grabs the blabbermouth by the shoulder. "Come on, Andy. You're gonna be Joe's travelin' companion tonight."

The two men are escorted out. When they're gone, Sonny concludes, "I got one other thing to say. I'm payin' you guys top dollar so you won't cheat, but if you put your hand in the cookie jar, it won't be like Vegas or Monte Carlo. There you get fired . . . here you get fed to the fish. Now, you all know Vito Lomuscio." Sonny indicates a man with the weathered face of an Old West gunslinger. "He's the casino boss. Vito knows my procedures and will be givin' you the rundown. He knows your talents, so he'll be assignin' you to certain tables. We open next Friday night. I expect you all to be sharp. This operation's gonna be the best on the island."

To maintain order in the casino a separate plain-clothes security force has been flown in from the States. Through Richie's access to police records they are supplied with mug shots of known cheaters on the gambling circuit and their specialties. This information protects Sonny from any one of them coming in to take the Lucky Ace for a bundle. In addition three rotating, closed-circuit TV cameras in the ceiling above the casino, monitored by four men in a security room, keep the operation under constant surveillance. This also guarantees that the dealers stay honest. Sonny himself has devised two electronic systems for his security which he wants Bobby to install for him. He meets the electronics man in his office to go over the setup. Bobby pulls out some plans to lay on the coffee table in front of them. He unrolls one. "This is the security system for the hotel safe." He points to a half-moon in the drawing. "This section is your weightless floor . . . it's glass. Anything over eight ounces you drop on it will set off a silent alarm to the police. The thief gets caught before he even makes it to the door. If he should happen to make it somehow, this other system will stop him." He hands Sonny a paper. "Those are the times when the tumblers of the lock click into position. They're the only times you can open it, and you got exactly sixty-eight seconds to push the right buttons. Now, if the door is forced open, it will release a nerve gas that'll blind the guy. If he's smart enough to be wearing a gas mask, it won't matter. The safe's wired up to blow in thirty seconds. That was a real good move, Santino."

Sonny smiles. "Yeah, I'm out the money if he gets it, so why not kill the bastard? I won't keep more than a week's cash there anyway. Did ya wire the alarm into customs, too?"

"Yep . . . if they make it through all this, they'll never make it out of the country . . . and they know about the reward."

"Good . . . what about hotel and casino systems?"

Bobby pulls out another set of plans. "There are six hundred twenty hidden panic buttons all together. In the hallways you got 'em every fifty feet. They'll always be on the left-hand side, under the light fixtures. I put 'em a foot off the floor so no one can lean on 'em accidentally. There are five panic buttons in your office, four in the conference room, and one on each side of your bed. Central control will know where you are if you hit one. It'll light up on their board, but only you, Richie, and Angelo will know the locations . . . and of course me and Paulie."

"I wanna talk to ya about him in a minute."

Richie leans over, looking at the blueprint. "What happens if the power fails? These buttons won't work."

Bobby answers, "Yeah, they will. The security system runs off a separate transformer in an emergency."

Sonny pats Bobby on the back. "It's good, Bobby." He gets up and sits behind his desk. ". . . but why'd ya need this Paulie with ya?"

"I couldn't set this up alone. I needed him. This was a big job, Santino."

"Ya shoulda checked with me first. I don't like it. The guy's not Italian."

Bobby rolls up the papers. "Don't worry, this guy's all right. He worked with the unions a long time."

This is not comforting news to Sonny. A lot of dons had pull with the unions and could easily get information out of Bobby's partner. Something had to be done. "Bobby, there's one other thing. I want you to bug my fishing boats."

"Hmm . . . that's gonna be rough, with the engine noise and all."

"What about the fishin' chairs? Those guys always talk when nothin's bitin'."

"Yeah . . . it's pretty quiet in the stern. We could put some equipment there."

Sonny stands to walk Bobby to the door. "O.K., get on it then. Angelo will take you out to the boats. Gigo, the captain, will give you whatever you need. And Bobby . . . make sure Paulie's with ya. I don't want him runnin' around here."

Bobby hesitates. "I need somebody on shore to check the system."

"Tell one of my guys what to do, and he'll do it. I want your guy on the boats. If somethin' don't work, he's gotta be with you to fix it anyway."

"Whatever you say, Santino."

Sonny calls in Angelo. "You're gonna take Bobby and his guy out on the boats this afternoon. They're gonna be puttin' in some bugs."

"Uh, O.K., Boss. We'll take the big one out first." The bodyguard says to Bobby, "I'll meet you at the pier at three."

"Right. See ya later, Santino."

When the electronics man leaves, Angelo walks Sonny down to the casino. "That's a good idea . . . buggin' the boats."

"Yeah, after they get the equipment in and it checks out, don't bring 'em back."

"You want me to kick 'em off the boat, Boss?"

"Yeah . . . and Angelo"—Sonny stops—"I don't know how you are at makin' hits, so to be safe, put three slugs in their heads. The captain'll know what to do with 'em after that."

"Who should I take with me on this? Maybe Eddie, huh?"

"Nobody . . . this Bobby's been around. If he sees more than one guy, he's gonna be concerned. You can do this yourself."

"I'll just tear their heads off, Boss."

Sonny points his finger. "Angelo . . ."

"Uh . . . O.K., Boss . . . three slugs apiece."

On Thursday Maxi's hookers arrive . . . fifty of the top call girls around the country, all with a rich clientele who can spread the word about the Lucky Ace. Sonny auditions each one personally before she is hired, with the exception of the one he picks to be in charge . . . Donna Dawson. The beautiful twenty-five-year-old blonde was a legal secretary who grew tired of long hours with low pay. She left the nine-to-five world to become a Las Vegas showgirl, but she soon found the only glamorous thing about that job was the costume . . . so Donna ended up in prostitution. Maxi met her in a lounge and asked her to come to Miami to be his head call girl. Donna always had a weakness for a man with a better offer . . . that's what enticed her down to the Bahamas. Sonny liked Donna's style. Outfitted exclusively in designer clothes, she gave the term "high-class call girl" a whole new interpretation.

In their first meeting he outlines her duties, which are basic enough: keep the girls clean and keep them out of trouble. Any fighting among them would be settled by Donna, not Sonny. She would make girls available to him at a moment's notice. Then he explains some new plans he has in the works. "Donna, we're gonna be startin' to fly some businessmen down here, and I need a dozen girls to work each flight. The broads on these planes gotta be sharp. I don't want 'em actin' like whores. Naturally, they gotta suck and fuck, do whatever the guys want, but they also gotta do somethin' important for me . . . get information. I wanna know who's got the big bank accounts. We're gonna be makin' movies of those guys screwin', then you're gonna give their wives a private screening."

The call girl takes a cigarette from a diamond-studded case. "Isn't that sort of backward for blackmail? Shouldn't you go to the tricks with the film first?''

"Nope . . . 'cause we're not blackmailin' them . . . we're sellin' me to the women."

Donna takes a good look at Sonny. He's gained quite a bit of weight since he left Sicily. "You? How?"

"After ya show the film, ya tell each of 'em how much money her husband spent on broads in the Bahamas . . . and how they can get even. Tell 'em there's a stud down there who's got more dick than their old man's got dollars. Then show 'em these." He hands Donna an envelope. "They were taken a couple a days ago."

Donna looks at the pictures and hands them back. "That's bullshit. Nobody's that big. They have to be phony." Sonny stands. He comes out from behind the desk and exposes himself to Donna. She is dumbfounded. "My god . . . you must hold the Olympic record with that thing."

Sonny zips up his pants. "Ya gotta understand somethin', Donna . . . we're not just sellin' cock. When these broads get down here, I got plans to use 'em."

"How?"

"That's for me to know. I'm goin' back up to my suite now. Get Dolores and Marsha up there. I'm so fuckin' horny I could screw this table."

Donna raises her skirt suggestively. "Why don't you forget them . . . you and I could get it on. I should test out the product, after all, before I sell it."

Sonny walks to the door. "That's out, Donna. I never mix business and broads . . . with you and me it's strictly business."

In the elevator, on the way up to the penthouse, Richie says, "How you gonna get money out of those rich broads? Most of them are stuck up."

"Easy, Richie, I'm gonna make 'em fall in love with me."

"But their old men have millions . . . they're not gonna fall in love so fast."

"Nope, they're not. That's why I'm gonna bug 'em."

The elevator stops at the penthouse. Richie opens the door with the special key. "What's buggin' 'em gonna do?"

"Richie, every woman has fantasies when it comes to sex. By the time they get here, I'll know every one of 'em."

"Oh, I get it . . . with your cock to fulfill their fantasies . . . they're bound to fall in love."

"You're gettin' smart, Richie."

When Sonny gets to his bedroom, Dolores and Marsha are already undressed and in his bed. Before he goes in, his bodyguard gets some final instructions. "Call Gino in Sicily. Tell him I need the electronics man here right away. And tell Angelo to pick up Linda, my new secretary."

"The congressman's assistant? I'm glad you hired her . . . she was the prettiest one."

"I didn't hire Linda for her looks, Richie. I hired her for her abilities and 'cause she knows how politicians think."

As he closes the door, he says, "I'm gonna be busy for a couple of hours . . . don't bother me unless it's important."

Two weeks later the junket flights to the Bahamas begin. Sonny uses Gregory Stanford's banking connections to get lists of depositors with a balance of $10,000 or more. These men receive a promotional brochure offering them an all-expense-paid, three-day trip to the Lucky Ace. Five chartered jets fly shuttles twice a week from every major city east of St. Louis to transport the gamblers. The hookers on the junket make it very clear that this is a pleasure trip and it's part of their job to see that everyone has a good time. The men are also assured that this is a safe place to swing . . . even a minister could let his hair down at the Lucky Ace. Of course booze flows freely on the flight, and liquor loosens tongues. By the time the plane touches down, the girls know all about their passengers and which men have seven-figure bank accounts. Once they check out as bona fide millionaires, the compromising movies of their sexual activities are made and used against them.

According to plan, Donna, posing as a mistress cruelly cast aside by the woman's husband, visits the wife. To prove she's telling the truth, she shows the damning film. Donna then offers the furious women her chance to retaliate. "Your husband screws around. Why not play the same game? There's a man in the Bahamas who can really take good care of you." Jealous rage is usually enough to get the women to agree, but the naked pictures of Sonny always close the deal. Half of the women approached by Donna fly down to the Lucky Ace to be with him. Prior to their arrival he is well briefed on their sexual preferences— every woman he makes love to leaves the island smiling. Sonny's fee for one night is $5,000. His average weekly take from this side operation is $30,000, but it is worth more than that in the long run. Some rich matrons, the ones in love, are romanced out of as much as half a million dollars to invest in his newly established companies. Sex had become a job to Sonny; his mind, above all, was on his shell corporations, the Bank of Sark, and his insurance scheme. His only loves now are money and power.

Within three months the Lucky Ace is the most successful hotel and casino on the island; it is turning over a half-million a week. Over 300 hookers now work in this swinger's paradise; the ratio of girls to customers is nearly one to one. Business at the Lucky Ace is booming, and his insurance company, Transcontinental Casualty Co., Ltd., is in full swing. The executives Sonny has hired are now writing loan commitments for developers all over the country. Gregory Stanford is working on getting control of the Bank of Sark. In the meantime, Sonny himself conjures up scams for the future. Figuring out the details of his con games presents as much of a challenge to him as a complex theorem does to a mathematician. Sonny's answers, however, are never abstract and always six figures or more.

Five months after the Lucky Ace's grand opening he decides it's time to start his mission for Alfonso. Sonny contacts eight American dons. Each one is told he's been picked to participate in a special deal Sonny has going and is flown down to the Bahamas by chartered jet. The night after they arrive Sonny outlines his plan to the men. Before dinner he introduces them to his influential government contact. There is no mention of the deal until the end of the Italian meal. After waiters pass out Cuban cigars to the men, Sonny gets up in front of the group in the small hospitality suite. He says affably, "I hope everybody liked the food tonight. Jocco, my cook, is from Messina, but we all know nothin's ever as good as family cookin'. Sorry I couldn't spend more time with you guys today. I heard a couple of ya went fishin'. Ya should know we got a great golf course here, too. Some of ya already found my bocce court. I understand there's a bet ridin' on the game between Vinnie and Mike." He grins, "You're better off throwin' your money away in the casino, gentlemen . . . at least there you'll see some action." His advice gets a hearty laugh from the dons. Then Sonny clasps his hands in front of him. "Now . . . down to business. I'm planning a development for the Bahamas that'll make this island bigger than Miami Beach in just five years. Angelo, have the guys bring in the picture." Two bodyguards carry an easel from the back of the room and put it next to Sonny. He pulls off a drape to uncover an artist's rendering, in cool pastels, of the complex he intends to build. The sketch shows highrise apartments, office buildings, and parks. "This operation is gonna bring in new industry. The Bahamian government is behind us because my good friend here is behind us . . . but his support has nothin' to do with friendship. He knows the more we develop this island, the more money he can get from the United States to build new airports and better public facilities. Naturally, he can't be involved with us publicly, but he will be one of our chief officers. At this time I'd like him to say a few words."

The black official, in his white suit, gets up on stage with Sonny. Soft, refined, British speech is a surprise coming from the stocky man. "I'm very excited indeed about Sonny's program . . . the Bahamas need this. As he said, the more we grow, the more money we can get from Washington. I want to make it clear that Sonny has free reign in his own operations here because of the deposits he's bringing into the country. I guarantee all of you that any money you bring in will be put in numbered accounts, and under no circumstances will we turn over information to the United States government, even under subpoena. You already know this is a tax haven for American corporations. That can work for your advantage, too. Now, I believe Sonny would like to give you a presentation of his idea."

He sits, and Sonny stands again. "Richie's passing out promotional packets to you. There's also a feasibility study and some other important documents with it. You can look at them later." Another bodyguard brings in a slide screen. "If you're all ready, gentlemen, I'll begin. Hit the lights, Angelo."

An hour and a half later Sonny finishes the presentation. He turns to the Bahamian. "If you don't mind, you'll have to leave now. We gotta discuss this in private."

"Of course, Mr. Gibson." The black says graciously, "I hope you gentlemen enjoy your stay in the Bahamas." He shakes Sonny's hand officiously and exits.

Sonny calls to Richie, "You guys can step out of the room, too." When they go, Sonny looks at the dons. "Anybody got any questions?"

Frank Manadeli, the don from Boston, has one strong objection. "I don't like workin' with niggers."

This incites the others. "That's right . . . we never worked with no niggers before."

Louie from Detroit agrees. "Yeah . . . and down here you gotta beg those bastards to bring you a fuckin' cup of coffee . . . the service is lousy."

Sonny stops them. "Wait a minute. We're not talkin' about waiters . . . we're talkin' about makin' millions of dollars. So the niggers down here are jungle people. We need my guy to pull this off." The dons continue grumbling about this until Sonny stops them again. "You see how much money I'm makin' down here . . . I'm givin' you a chance to get in on the ground floor. When we get finished, we'll own the Bahamas . . . it'll be our own private country." Manadeli asks dubiously, "Santino . . . how come there's only eight of us here? Where are the other families from the council?"

Sonny smiles. "The other families got old-fashioned ways. They're not progressive. I need men like you guys who are fast . . . ready to take chances"

He adds slyly, "Besides, they listen to the Sicilians too much."

Vinnie from Philly asks, "What do you want, Sonny?"

"Three million dollars a family."

This figure gets a reaction from Manadeli. "That's a lotta money. I'm not gonna go for that."

Louie agrees. "Me either. It's too risky, especially being tied up with niggers."

Sonny sees that to win this game he'll have to use his curve ball. He winds up for the pitch, "There's something you guys should know. I'm not who you think I am. I'm not Sonny Gibson from Indiana." He throws. "I'm Santino Gino Genetti from Sicily."

There is an excited murmur in the room. Vinnie points with his cigar. "Lemme get this straight . . . you say you're Santino Gino Genetti? That can't be. He's been outta the picture for twenty years." He turns to the others. "I don't know if you guys know the story . . ."

Manadeli flares, "We don't need you to tell us the story. We know our history."

Louie interjects, "Yeah . . . everybody knows the Sicilian Mafia took care of Genetti *and* the kid."

Sonny corrects him. "They didn't, but I'll tell ya what. I'm gonna give ya ten days to check me out"—he stares at the group icily— "but on the eleventh day I want your asses back here with the money."

Vinnie shouts abrasively, "Who in the fuck does this kid think he is?" He starts to stand, but Sonny pushes him back down . . . hard.

"Listen, guinea, I told ya who the fuck I was. Your money better be here in eleven days or I'm comin' after your ass myself."

Well before the deadline the dons' money is deposited in Sonny's numbered account in the Bank of the Bahamas. Alfonso had done his job perfectly. Birth and baptismal certificates in Sicily have proved without question that Sonny is Santino Gino Genetti. He would now have a powerful bargaining tool in all future negotiations with the Mafia.

Soon after the coup Alfonso calls to say he's coming to the Bahamas. As promised, he is bringing Laura with him. Sonny is looking forward to seeing her. Even though it's been over two and a half years since they've been together, the memories of their romantic nights in Sicily are etched in his heart.

On the morning of the day they arrive Sonny issues special instructions to his staff . . . he's not to be disturbed for any reason when he's with Laura. At eight o'clock Sonny is paged in the casino. Angelo answers it and comes back with the long-awaited news, "Your guests are here, Boss. Richie's gonna bring them to your suite. He says Laura's dynamite. I'll bet you can't wait to see her."

Sonny wants everything to be just right. "Did they order the special wine for Alfonso?"

"Yeah, Boss."

"You sure those yellow roses are in Laura's room?"

"I checked on it personally."

When Sonny gets up to the penthouse, Gino and Carlo are at the door. There are warm hugs all around. Sonny says, "You guys look great. How was your trip?''

Carlo gestures in disgust. "Aaa, I hate to fly . . . Naples once a week is plenty for me.''

Gino chides him. "Carlo, that's for Rosalie . . . you should be able to do anything for love. Remember what Santino went through?''

"How could I forget . . . we went through it too, eh, Gino?'' The men laugh, and Angelo's look of puzzlement at their joke reminds Sonny to introduce him.

"Carlo, Gino . . . this here's Angelo.''

The bodyguard says shyly, "Uh, nice meetin' ya.''

Carlo looks up at him. "Santino, you should have had Angelo around when you were going after Sanders.''

Sonny recalls his hated instructor. "Is he still alive?''

"Yeah, he just made it out of the explosion on that French oil rig last week.''

Sonny says sincerely, "Too bad.'' He looks at Angelo, "Stay out here with Gino and Carlo. You can call Eddie and Mike to relieve you.'' Sonny enters the suite. Inside Alfonso is in front of the TV, glued to a rerun of "I Love Lucy.'' He clicks it off as soon as Sonny comes in. They hug, and his godfather points to the television. "That thing . . . sometimes I wish we had it over there, but I know the women would sit around and watch all day. Nothing would get done.''

"Yeah, just like here . . . they piss on themselves to see the soap operas.''

"What's that, Santino?''

"Like the shit you were watchin'.'' He glances around the room. "I thought Laura was here?''

"You know women, Santino . . . she went to freshen up . . . she looked all right to me. I was just waiting to see you before I went to my room, too.''

"You're not havin' dinner with me and Laura?''

"No. Traveling takes a lot of strength from me now, Santino. Besides, a lover's reunion is no place for an old man.''

"Ya know I would forget the romance to talk to you, Alfonso.'' Sonny is anxious to hear how the families voted on his request to be a free soldier. "What's the word from the dons, Alfonso?''

"I'm just too tired to go into it now.''

Just then Laura says softly, "Hello, Santino.''

Sonny's head snaps around at the sound of her voice. She is radiant in a wine-colored dress scooped sexily down her back. Laura has remained as sensuous and beautiful as he remembered her. Alfonso slips out of the room quietly while the lovers embrace. When they break, Sonny looks around for his godfather. "Where'd Alfonso go?''

"He left, Santino . . . it was his way of telling us to enjoy ourselves."

Sonny grins. "Then let's get started." He begins undressing her, but she stops him.

"Santino . . . I want to go for a walk on the beach first . . . there's a full moon tonight."

"We haven't been together for two and a half years, and you wanna go for a walk?"

She looks at him with eyes he can never resist. "Please, Santino?"

"O.K., O.K. . . . Angelo!"

The bodyguard opens the door. "Yeah, Boss?"

"Tell the guys we're goin' for a walk on the beach."

Angelo closes the door and calls security on the walkie-talkie. "Eddie, I need four more guys. Meet at the beach. Uh . . . the boss is gonna go for a walk."

The tropical night winds flutter Laura's skirt as the lovers stroll hand in hand in the moonlight. "Remember when we met, Santino? You were so surprised that I spoke English."

"Yeah . . . but I was so fuckin' horny, I could care less if you were talkin' Chinese."

Laura picks up a pink seashell. "Look . . . it's so beautiful"—she looks up at him—"but not as beautiful as our love." She pockets the shell, and after a few minutes asks quietly, "Are you happy, Santino?"

Sonny laughs. "What kinda stupid question is that, Laura?" He opens his arms. "Just look around . . . I got money, power, the most successful place on the island. Of course I'm happy . . . what else could anybody want?"

"Love."

He turns to look at her. "Well, I've got that, too . . . you're here." They kiss, and Laura tries to pull him down on the sand. "What the hell you doin', Laura?"

"Let's make love here."

"On the fuckin' sand? Are you kiddin?"

She looks up at him, hurt. "That's why I wanted to come here . . . it would be like our first night."

"Laura . . . I got a million-dollar hotel to make love in."

"But it's more romantic here."

He says, irritated, "A bed's more romantic to me now . . . I've grown up. Besides, what am I gonna tell the guys . . . we're gonna fuck?" Just a few hundred feet in front of them, and a hundred feet behind, the four bodyguards wait for his next move.

Laura gets up, annoyed. "You really need those men with you? And why that big one?"

"I need 'em, Laura . . . I'm very powerful."

"My father is very powerful and he travels all over Catania alone."

"That's Sicily, Laura, but that's not even it . . . I'm more powerful than your father." He adds coldly, "Soon I'll be more powerful than any don in the Mafia." Sonny bends to brush off his pants cuffs. "Shit . . . now I got fuckin' sand all over me." He turns to leave, "I'm goin' back . . . I'm starved." Laura follows him to the suite. Sonny still wants to make love to her, so he smooths things over during dinner and that night in bed, they rekindle the glowing embers of their youthful love into a roaring blaze of passion. They finally fall asleep at five A.M.

The phone starts ringing at seven. Mrs. Anderson from Pittsburgh is demanding to know the whereabouts of her $5,000 companion. Sonny dresses quickly and nudges Laura gently. "Baby . . . I'm sorry, but we can't have breakfast."

She opens one eye. "Why not?"

"Somethin' came up. A couple a guys'll take ya around the island today. Buy whatever ya want. I'll see ya tonight." He kisses Laura good-bye, then leaves her bed for the wealthy matron's. She is the wife of the president of a large corporation. Mr. Anderson is a frequent visitor to the Lucky Ace, and since Donna's private screening, his wife has become a regular, too. Sonny has been trying to get money from the attractive forty-year-old blonde to build up his assets. He's done it successfully with many of his wealthy tricks, but so far he hasn't gotten any bonuses from Mrs. Anderson. As they walk down the hall, Angelo hands him a pair of thin white cotton gloves. "You want the mouthpiece today, too, Boss?"

"No, this broad's not a biter, but last time she scratched the shit outta me."

"Gee, Boss, this is a dangerous business, huh?"

Sonny replies less literally, "Anything to do with broads is dangerous, Angelo."

When they get to her room, Sonny finds the shrew on the phone, much tamer in person. She pouts, putting her arms around him. "Where were you? I've been waiting for hours."

Sonny lies. "I had an early business meeting, but you got me now, baby." She lies down on the bed while he takes off his clothes. "I can only be with you a couple a hours today."

She sits up. "Why? Last time you were here for four."

"I know, baby, but I'm workin' on a big deal gettin' money for my new casino. Don't worry, we'll still have fun." He hands her the gloves. "Ya gotta wear these from now on, though."

"What for?"

"Last time, when you were comin', you went crazy . . . my back got all cut up."

She giggles as she puts the gloves on. "It's your own fault, you know. You make me crazy."

He gently pushes her down on the bed. "I know. I want to." Sonny opens her peignoir and squeezes her breasts, "Mmm, you feel so good." Then he puts her hand on his crotch. "See what you do to me, you sexy bitch?" For the next hour he teases his trick, kissing the blonde from her little finger to her big toe and every point in between. She writhes wildly until she's almost near orgasm, then finally he climbs on top of her. There's a deep groan at his first penetration. Sonny pumps her hard, but at the first quivers of her climax, he rolls off. Mrs. Anderson gets hysterical. "What's the matter, what are you doing? Fuck me! FUCK ME!"

Sonny sits on the edge of the bed with his back to her. "I can't . . . I dunno . . . I guess I got too much on my mind."

She sits up, frustrated, "What is it, Sonny?"

He says sullenly, "This deal . . . I need another hundred grand to close it."

She rubs his shoulders. "Your hotel must be making millions of dollars . . . what's a hundred thousand?"

"Yeah . . . it's not as much of a moneymaker as you think. I got a big overhead here."

Mrs. Anderson nibbles his ear. "My five thousand should help . . . come on back to bed . . ."

He sighs, "O.K." They begin making love again, and just when she's ready to come, Sonny pulls out. "I can't do it . . . you can have your lousy five grand back."

Mrs. Anderson is still panting on the bed, "What if I give you ten? Could you fuck me then?"

Sonny wraps a sheet around him and paces around the room. "Nah . . . I gotta be honest . . . somethin' else is botherin' me. I'm leavin' today cause I'm gonna be with somebody else. I'd rather be with you, but she's givin' me the hundred grand I need." He stops and looks into her eyes, "You could keep me from havin' to be with this bitch."

"How can I do that?"

"Well, if you gave me the hundred grand, I could be with you."

His offer is tempting, but this blonde is not so dumb. "What do I get for the money?"

"Part of the action of my new casino."

"How much?"

"How about five percent?"—he drops the sheet—"plus me." That closes the deal.

Mrs. Anderson says, "All right, I'll get the hundred thousand for you."

"How soon?"

"How soon do you want it?"

"Now . . . my secretary Linda will call and give you the name of my bank."

She gets upset when Sonny starts dressing. "Where are you going? I thought we could be together if I gave you the money."

"Oh, no, honey, not till I get it. Anyway, I have a meeting."

"You're not going to see that other woman . . ."

Sonny pulls her close to him. "Uh-uh, baby . . . we're gonna be together all night." He pats her cheek, "Just be sure the money's down here today."

Sonny leaves Mrs. Anderson and rushes to his nine o'clock appointment with Alfonso. When Sonny gets to his Mediterranean-style office, his godfather is standing behind the heavy, carved oak desk, looking at a twelve-foot sailfish mounted on the wall. "That's quite a big fish, Santino."

Sonny grins. "It's a guppy compared to the ones I caught a couple of weeks ago . . . I'll tell ya about that in a minute." He says anxiously, "What'd the dons decide, Alfonso?"

The old man sits on the leather sofa. "I brought your request to the families, Santino. I had to fight hard for you, but I knew they'd listen to me now because they know they didn't listen to me twenty years ago. . . . We wouldn't have our problems today if they had." He leans back. "The dons have given their O.K. for you to be a free soldier. They said whatever you do in the Bahamas is fine with them as long as the Sicilian Mafia gets half the money. You'll have no interference from anyone . . . your decisions will be final."

This is exactly what Sonny has been waiting to hear. "Please thank the families for me . . . tell 'em they've given me the freedom I need to make a fortune for all of us." Sonny knows that without ties he can begin planning his own Big Scam for the future . . . one that will set him up for the rest of his life. "Now, Alfonso, I'll show ya my big catch. He pushes a hidden button under his desk, and the bookcase on the opposite wall slides away to reveal a walk-in safe. Sonny motions for Alfonso to join him inside. His hands sweep past two shelves stacked with money. "Twenty-nine million dollars, Alfonso . . . that's how much I got from those mackerel."

Alfonso nods his approval. "Did you have any trouble with them, Santino?"

Sonny laughs. "Nah, once they found out I was Genetti, their bankbooks opened up faster than the legs of a two-dollar whore. You should've seen those greedy bastards trying to cheat each other. Manadeli wanted to put more in so he could have control over the other dons. I told him, 'Yeah, I'll do that and took eight million from him. That's all the cash he had."

"Very good, Santino . . . you're hitting them where it hurts." Alfonso notices a small file cabinet inside the safe. "Why is this in here?"

He stoops down to read the labels on the drawers—" 'Operation BS.' What does that stand for . . . bullshit?"

Sonny laughs. "No . . . it stands for 'Big Scam.' It's too early to tell ya anything about it now. That deal's a few years down the road, but you'll be involved when it happens." When they leave the vault, the bookcase slides into place again. Sonny pours them both a glass of wine, and they sit on the couch.

"Don't forget, Santino, for the Sicilian Mafia to be avenged, you must read the dons their crimes. They must know why they're being punished."

Sonny savors his words. "I'm gonna really enjoy that . . ." Alfonso reaches for his bag and pulls out a package of tapes. He hands it to Sonny. "Are these my surveillance tapes on the dons?"

"Yes. They're up-to-date on every don."

Just then Angelo and Richie come into the room. Angelo asks, "Is it O.K. to talk, Boss?"

"Yeah."

"Benton's on the line. He said to tell ya he just got a wire for a hundred grand from Mrs. Anderson."

"Tell Benton to put the money in my numbered account."

"O.K."

Richie cracks, "Gee, that broad turned out to be a real golden goose for you."

Angelo says, "Uh . . . the boss don't need a golden goose, he's got a golden dick."

Sonny stands. "All right, cut the crap, you guys . . . is everything ready on the boat?"

Richie answers, "That's what I came in here for. Gigo wants to know which boat to take out."

"The big one, unless you guys wanna stand. There's gonna be eight of us."

Taking the afternoon off is a luxury Sonny has not allowed himself since he arrived in the Bahamas. He spends the day relaxing on the boat with Alfonso, who catches a 300-pound tuna and insists on having it stuffed to send back to Sicily. Back at the hotel Sonny gets ready to spend the night with Mrs. Anderson. He calls Laura to say their date is off . . . he's tied up with an important client. Between his assignations and the burden of being an executive with a staff of 260, Sonny sees very little of Laura over the next few days. When she calls him, he is often curt, but Laura is always patient and understanding. She sees that running this huge operation is an enormous responsibility that's extremely taxing on him. One afternoon, however, on her return from a shopping spree in town, Laura receives a devastating shock that tries her good nature. From her window she can see Sonny at poolside surrounded by a bevy of curvaceous, bikinied women. He is particularly responsive to one striking brunette who is playing with his chest and kissing him. In a few minutes they leave together; Laura does not have to guess where they are going. A sickening sensation sweeps the Sicilian girl as she turns away. The convulsive sobs that shake her body soon subside, replaced by the anger of wounded pride. Laura fumes until eight o'clock, when Sonny has promised to be with her. The designated time for their rendezvous passes, however, without a sign of her lover. She calls all over the hotel, but no one will give her any answers. Three hours later the wandering casanova arrives, a dozen yellow roses in hand. Sonny lets himself into Laura's suite quietly. She's standing on the balcony, and he surprises her with a kiss on the back of the neck. When she turns, he bows gallantly, presenting the roses to her . . . his peace offering. "For the most beautiful flower of all, my love . . . you."

Laura takes the roses and throws them on the floor angrily. "Where have you been, Santino?"

Sonny moves to hold her in his arms, "I've been busy all day, but nothing can take me away from you now."

She squirms out of his embrace, seething with Sicilian jealousy. "Don't give me that shit . . . you've been fucking all day, haven't you?"

Sonny's smile vanishes. "You know better than to ask questions Laura . . . you're the daughter of a don. What I do is none of your goddam business."

Laura's rage intensifies. "It is my business when I see you kissing some cheap *puttana* in plain sight where everyone can see. How can you humiliate me like that, Santino? I thought you loved me . . . I thought you wanted to marry me . . . after all we've been through."

Sonny is becoming increasingly uncomfortable. He's used to being the boss no one dares to challenge . . . especially not a woman. He points an angry finger at her. "Now you listen, bitch. I have to keep three hundred women happy down here, and I have to go to bed with some of them . . . and ya know what? I like makin' love to them." Tears well up in Laura's wounded eyes. "Look, Laura, I didn't ask ya to come down here, you invited yourself. If ya don't like the way things are, leave . . . get the hell home. You're a spoiled brat. Let Daddy take care of you."

This last remark sends a large porcelain vase flying toward his head. Sonny ducks just before it shatters against the wall. Laura is in a frenzy. She unleashes a tirade of insults as she hurls each object at her unfaithful lover. "Monster . . . pig . . . sex maniac."

By this time Sonny has lost his temper, too, and decides to brave the shower of ashtrays, glasses, and vases raining down on him. When he reaches the eye of the storm, he grabs Laura roughly by the hair, pulls her head back, and raises his hand threateningly. "Listen you stupid fuckin' little guinea . . . I love you." Angelo and Richie suddenly break into the room, aware that there is some kind of trouble. Sonny shouts, "Get the hell out . . . I didn't call you in here." They apologize profusely as they leave. Sonny looks back at Laura. Her fury has turned to fright as she covers her face, waiting for Sonny's blows. Instead, he cradles her in his arms. He lifts her head and kisses her lips gently. "I do love you, Laura." Her wounded expression touches Sonny, but he still says coldly, "But things can never be the same. I'm a different man now."

She searches his face for a hint of the boy she once loved. . . he is gone. Even so, she says, "I will always love you, Santino . . . always." Sonny sweeps Laura up in his arms and carries her to the bedroom. For that night they are transported back to their cave in Sicily . . . a time long gone but not quite forgotten.

Sonny keeps Laura waiting almost every night after that . . . except for the nights he doesn't show up at all. The magnitude of Sonny's personality change is now evident to Laura, but she is willing to accept him as he is. When they are together, she is submissive to him, even though he is often arrogant and short-tempered with her. One night he mercilessly fires a waiter for failing to put a rose on Laura's room service cart. When she tries to intervene in the innocent man's behalf, Sonny rudely informs her, "Mind your own fuckin' business." The nights he does see her, Laura finds Sonny distracted, and even during sex he is preoccupied. Sometimes a phone call in the middle of the night ends their lovemaking session abruptly. Laura's romantic dream of life in the Bahamas with her love rapidly becomes a nightmare. Eventually Laura finds herself a prisoner in the hotel. Sonny tells her he doesn't want her "running around the island." Once she had encountered him with a rich matron on his arm and created a scene that had almost cost him a good customer . . . a scene Sonny could not afford to repeat. Laura tries to discuss her unhappy situation with Alfonso, but he wants no part of it. He knows there isn't a woman in the world who could compete with Sonny's passionate love for money and power.

Sonny doesn't see Laura the night before she leaves, but he does ride with her and Alfonso to the airport the next morning. All of Sonny's bodyguards follow in a caravan of limousines behind them carrying the $29 million Sonny took from the dons. At the airfield Sonny gets out of the limousine first to give some last-minute instructions to his pilot. The former Alitalia captain now works exclusively for the Mafia and flies any jet Sonny hires. "When you stop to refuel, I don't want any of the guys gettin' off the plane. We got too much cash on board."

"You want us to turn right around and come back?"

"Yeah . . . I might need you."

The bodyguards start loading the money on board, and Sonny goes over to say good-bye to Alfonso at the steps of the plane. His godfather has a few parting words for him: "Remember, Santino, read them their crimes. And make sure they're all together . . it will be more effective that way." He hugs Sonny. "You are a true soldier, the best I've ever known. *Buona fortuna*, Santino."

At that moment Laura approaches them. Sonny shouts harshly, "Wait over there, can't ya see I'm busy talking to Alfonso?" She stops short and walks to the front of the plane as Sonny indicated.

He turns to his godfather, who is looking at him sharply. "Be careful, Santino. Power is nothing without wisdom and understanding. Don't let your loved ones get crushed in its path."

Sonny looks back at the pathetic figure of Laura waiting for him and then hugs Alfonso. *"Ciao . . . Buona fortuna centianni.* I'll be talkin' to ya soon." The old man climbs the steps. Halfway up he turns to wave. When he's safely on board, Sonny goes over to Laura in an attempt to pacify her. "I'm sorry I didn't get to spend more time with you, Laura."

She replies sadly, "That's all right, Santino . . . you were busy." A look of concern crosses her face. "Santino, there's something I've been wanting to ask you since I got here."

"What is it, Laura?"

The Sicilian girl frowns. "They say in Sicily you're a vicious killer . . . that you fed a man to the sharks . . . . is that true?"

Sonny smiles and opens his arms. "Baby . . . look at me . . . do you really believe I could be that cold?"

She throws her arms around his neck, relieved, "No, Santino . . . I knew it was a lie." He takes her chin gently in his hands. She looks up at him plaintively, "But you're not going to marry me, are you?"

Sonny's smile fades slowly. "How can I, Laura? I'm no good for you now . . . They taught me too well. I'd only hurt you."

A tear drops on his hand. "Santino, I'll be back . . . I still love you. I'll always love you." She kisses him good-bye and hugs him fervently. Sonny holds her tightly, facing the realization that some things, no matter how dear, must be sacrificed for ambition. Laura breaks the embrace and runs up the steps. He tries to catch a glimpse of her before takeoff, but she doesn't come to the window. As the plane vanishes in the clouds, a chill shoots through him. He has the strange feeling he'll never see Laura again.

On the way back to the hotel Sonny has some remorse about the cruel way he treated her. The ocean breeze blowing across his face through the open window of the limo reminds him of the beautiful long walks he took with his love along the beach in Catania; he wishes now he had made time for them here. He closes his eyes to dream of Laura but is rudely interrupted by the insistent buzz of the limousine phone.

Gregory Stanford is on the line from Los Angeles. There is a problem getting control of the Bank of Sark. Sonny explodes furiously, "What! I need that fuckin' bank. I don't care what you have to do to get it . . . I want everyone down in the Bahamas tomorrow afternoon . . . and I want answers!" He slams the receiver down. The Bank of Sark is becoming a thorn in his side.

By five P.M. the next day Sonny's top executives are seated around the circular conference table in his office: Gregory Stanford, Jeff Wolfman, Allen Collins, and Dr. Benjamin Swanson. Sonny stands behind his chair and addresses the men firmly. "I thought I made it plain enough to you guys before . . . we need the Bank of Sark to complete our operation. We're losing a lot of developers because we haven't got a bank to back our loan commitments . . . and I wanna start writing those cashier's checks. This is costin' me a lotta money, gentlemen, and I don't like it." He turns to the man seated next to him. "Gregory, lemme see those money transfers you got."

The distinguished man says haltingly, "Uh . . . Sonny, I wasn't able to get them. It's impossible to smuggle anything out of that building."

His answer sends Sonny into a murderous rage. He grabs Gregory by the collar and screams, *"Nothing is impossible!"* as he backhands the banker hard enough to send his glasses flying. He goes after the cowering man again, but Angelo restrains him.

"Boss, that's my job . . . let me take care of him."

Sonny lowers his fists as he comes out of his insane outburst. "Forget it. Just get him somethin' to wipe his mouth." The bodyguard brings Gregory a washcloth to wipe the blood from his split lip. The other men in the room sit rigidly in their chairs, frightened by the incident. Their eyes widen further when Sonny grabs Richie's .45 magnum, the most powerful handgun in the world. With the glint of a madman he points it at each man as he speaks, "I made it very clear to all of you . . . when I want something done"—he cocks the gun—"I want it done. Is that clear?" There is a silent chorus of meek nods and gulps in the room. Sonny returns the gun to Richie, then walks over to Gregory and puts a hand on his shoulder, "You're not workin' for a bank now, Gregory. That's the last time you'll ever tell me somethin's impossible . . . Right?" The banker nods. Sonny gives Gregory a few pats on his arm. "Good. Now gimme the details about where to get those money transfers . . . I'll take care of this myself." Gregory hands him a portfolio. His boss assures him. "I know just who to call."

Ten days later, through Alfonso's banking contacts in London, Sonny gets the exact information which he needs. Gregory and Jeff fly back down to the Bahamas to examine the papers. They're looking for evidence that the Bank of Sark has been doing business with "red-flag" banks—those involved in illegal money transactions. Most foreign banks place restrictions on the amount of money a person or company is allowed to take out of the country; in England that amount is only 500 pounds. However, with an accommodating banker like Larry Sark to forge your bank drafts, there is no limit. Gregory finds proof that the Bank of Sark has negotiated illegal money transfers with six international red-flag banks based in the United Kingdom. He presents the evidence to Sonny like a schoolboy giving a shiny red apple to the teacher. This is just what they need to blackmail Sark into cooperating. Sonny congratulates him. "Good work, Gregory. Now I want you to fly to Guernsey and invite Larry to be my guest in the Bahamas . . . and make sure he accepts."

"What if he doesn't want to come?"

"Goddam it, Gregory . . . do I have to educate you? Sell him. We got a fuckin' paradise here. He'll be runnin' to a plane to get away from that dinky little island . . . but I'm gonna send hookers with you. If you can't convince him to come down here, Dolores and Marsha will."

A week later Lawrence Sark arrived at the Lucky Ace. Sonny treats his guest royally, hoping he'll gain control of the Bank of Sark through normal channels. Larry takes full advantage of all the hotel's facilities. The staff is polite to him; he is pushy with them. They grumble privately about his demands for extra services, like heating his plates at dinner and having a maid draw his bath to a temperature of 101 degrees exactly, but no one dares complain, because Sark's red carpet has been rolled out by the boss himself. Even Sonny's personal secretary is a victim of the Englishman's abuse. He's seen Linda around the hotel and has decided that his attraction for the shapely brunette should be mutual. The obnoxious lecher has been pursuing her daily. On the third day of his stay Sonny finally calls Sark into his office for a meeting. The banker arrives half an hour late for his appointment . . . one black mark on the slate of British punctuality. Linda cringes when she sees the thin, pasty-faced man coming through the door.

Sark bows low and kisses her hand. "Ah, my lovely little queen . . . your king has arrived."

Linda gets up hastily, pulling away from him. "I'll tell Mr. Gibson you're here."

Linda goes into Sonny's office and slams the door. He looks up, surprised; she is usually even-tempered. "What the hell's wrong with you?"

She hands him the papers. "It's that Sark. He's the most detestable man I ever met." She shudders. "He's so slimy. Sark reminds me of all the politicians I know . . . they think they own you after they win one election."

"If you want me to, I'll put Willie out there."

"I would prefer to have someone out there whenever Sark's around."

Sonny calls to Eddie, "Tell Willie to get down to Linda's office right now."

"Will do, Boss." Eddie makes contact with the bodyguard on his walkie-talkie, then says, "He'll be down in a minute."

Linda continues her assessment of Sark. "You know, he's such a creep . . . he uses your name an awful lot around here, and he's really nasty to the cocktail waitresses."

Sonny is anxious to get Sark in his office. "I don't give a shit about their feelings. I'm only concerned that they keep Sark happy . . . but I don't want him fuckin' with you. That's why Willie's comin' down. Now, tell Larry he can come on in now."

Linda goes back to her desk, relieved to see Willie there already. "You can go in now, Mr. Sark."

"Pity. I was hoping I could stay here and chat some more."

Inside, Sonny greets him cordially, "Well, Larry, you enjoyin' yourself here?"

Sark props his walking cane next to him on the sofa. "Oh, yes, it's really splendid."

"Would you like a drink?"

Sark says pompously, "Oh, no . . . I never drink before noon . . . but if you insist, I'll have a gin on the rocks with a twist."

Sonny prepares the drink and hands it to his guest. "I have a proposition for you, Larry. I know it's gonna interest you."

The banker stirs the ice with his pinkie. "Do tell . . . what is it?" Sonny calls to his bodyguards to bring over the sketch of the bogus-land development complex. (Whenever Sonny is with a stranger, there are never fewer than two men with him.) "Eddie, Mike, show Mr. Sark that drawing." As the pair carry the easel over, Sark thinks to himself that these gargantuan men are odd-looking business associates. The men place the picture in front of Larry and uncover it. Sonny boasts, "This is somethin' I'm building down here . . . construction's already started. In five years it's gonna make this place more popular than the French Riviera."

"I dare say it should. The weather here is superb." He adds lecherously, "So are the women." Sonny has been supplying Sark with hookers on the house.

"Larry, you're one of the sharpest men I've ever met. I want you to come down here and run this whole development for me." Sonny leans back in his chair. "I'll pay you a half a million dollars a year. To show you how serious I am, I'm gonna have the contract drawn up right now." He buzzes Linda.

"Yes, Sonny?"

"I want you to call R.B. Agnew. Have him draft an agreement stating Larry's gonna be in charge of my new complex at a starting salary of a half a million a year. Tell him to put in all the benefits my other top executives have." He clicks off the box. "Agnew's my attorney." Sonny confides, "He's the Vice-President's nephew."

Sark raises his brow, impressed. "Really . . ."

"Yep . . . drawing up this contract is just an example of my good faith, Larry. I'll tell you what else I'm gonna do . . . I'm gonna get that bank of yours off your back. I know what a headache runnin' it's been to ya. I'll give ya a million dollars for it."

Sark laughs condescendingly. "My good man, your entire offer is tempting, I must admit, but if I were to sell my bank, it wouldn't be for less than five million dollars."

Sonny never thought he'd have to jump over this hurdle. He'd have to find a way to lower it. There was no way on earth Sonny would every pay that much cash for the Bank of Sark. "Gee, Larry, that's a little outta my league. I couldn't go for more than a million." He gets up and pats Sark's shoulder. "Why don't you sleep on it? You can let me know tomorrow." He hands Sark his cane.

The banker puts down his empty glass. "Very well, Mr. Gibson."

Sonny walks him to the door. "I want you to have a thousand dollars' credit in the casino tonight. You can have some fun gamblin'. Maybe you'll get lucky."

Sark taps his cane on the floor. "That's awfully decent of you, old chap. I played those infernal slot machines yesterday, but now I think I'll try the twenty-one game."

"How's eleven in the morning sound for our meeting? Is that a good time for ya?"

"A jolly good time. I'll see you then, Mr. Gibson."

At 11:15 the next morning Sark returns for the eleven-o'clock meeting. Sonny hands him a gin. "Well, did ya make up your mind, Larry?"

Sark sips his gin. "I'm afraid I have. It would be impossible for me to come work for you down here. I have a lot of obligations at home, and it would be difficult to leave Mummy by herself."

"Sure, I understand, but you could still sell the bank."

"True, but my price would still be five million dollars."

Sonny was expecting to hear this. He had never known a banker who wasn't greedy. "Is that decision final?"

"I'm afraid it is."

"That's too bad, Larry. I was hopin' I wouldn't have to do this." It's time to play his trump card. Sonny hands the foppish banker a portfolio containing the illegal money transfers. "I think you'll deal after you take a look at these."

Larry takes a few minutes to go through them, then hands the file back to Sonny. "I'm sorry, old chap, but these don't mean anything to me at all. The worst that can possibly happen is that they pull my charter. That isn't too convenient for me"—he snickers—"but it doesn't do you any good either." Sonny is speechless as Sark goes on, "Besides, I can be back in business in no time . . . I have connections in the House of Commons. I'll sell my bank to you for five million dollars . . . not a penny less."

Sonny is infuriated by this impasse and Sark's snobbish airs. When the Englishman leaves, Gregory is summoned. Sonny is frustrated— he's not used to failure. He rants at the executive maniacally. "Goddam it! Why in the hell didn't you tell me Sark had pull in Parliament?"

Gregory defends himself meekly. "I didn't know, Sonny."

"You're an idiot, Gregory. What the hell do you think I'm paying you for? You're supposed to know." Sonny knocks Gregory's golf cap off his head. "I thought I told you to wear a suit and tie around the hotel."

"I was out on the golf course with some clients."

Sonny shouts, "Well, you're in the office now. Carry a tie in the golf cart and put it on when you come in here."

He warns him, "I want that Bank of Sark. . . . Get it for me, Gregory . . . understand?"

"Yes, Sonny."

Gregory goes back to his clients, and Sonny buzzes Linda. "Call Donna. Tell her I want four broads up in my suite now."

"*Four* girls?"

"That's right. What'sa matter? Ya got wax in your ears today? If I want more, I'll tell ya. I need a couple hours of fuckin'." Sonny clicks off and heads up to his penthouse. He's hoping a good sex session will relieve some of his tension. It does that and more.

After they make love, Dolores says, "Boy, it's sure good to be with you, Sonny." She rolls her eyes, "That banker from England . . . he's a real weirdo."

Sonny's interested. "You mean Larry Sark?"

"Yeah, that guy you sent me to pick up. . . . Before he fucks, he likes to stick a feather up his ass and dance around the room like a chicken. I never seen nothin' like it." Sonny smiles to himself, imagining how foolish Sark must look. He came up there to forget about the banker, however, and the image is erased from his mind. Dolores gets dressed. "I hope we get together again soon, Sonny. I love fucking with you."

"Yeah, you and the three hundred other broads. Send Sandy in."

On Thursday Gregory reports that he's making no progress getting Larry Sark to budge from his five-million-dollar asking price. "There's no way, Sonny. I just can't get him to come down. I know you're pissed off . . .''

Sonny paces. "Nah . . . I'm not pissed off." He shakes his fist angrily. "There's gotta be a way to swing this guy."

Gregory's at a loss. "I don't know how . . . if he's got as much pull with the government as he says, it'll be hard to blackmail him."

Sonny pounds the desk. "There must be some way to get this chicken-feather-fuckin' guy."

Gregory raises his eyebrows in surprise. "That's a new one. I never heard you call anybody that before."

"What else do ya call a guy who fucks with a chicken feather?"

"What the hell are you talking about?"

Sonny explains mockingly, "Sark . . . before he fucks, this guy likes to dance around with a chicken feather up his ass."

Gregory blurts out, 'That's it!''

Sonny is impatient. "What's *it*?"

Gregory continues excitedly, "Our way to get him. The English are scared to death of sex scandals. You can screw the whole government out of a fortune, but screw one broad and it's all over . . . especially if your family has an important name . . . like Sark."

"You mean this might be what I'm looking for to get him?"

Gregory announces emphatically, "I know it is . . . you can get that whole island."

Sonny buzzes Linda. "Tell Richie to come in here." When the bodyguard arrives, Sonny gives him his orders. "Make sure the camera equipment's workin' in the Hollywood Suite. Then have Frankie move Sark in there."

"How soon, Boss?"

"Right away." Sonny smiles. "Tonight we're gonna make Larry Sark a movie star."

The next morning the skinny Englishman comes into Sonny's office to say good-bye. He breaks into a wide grin, revealing a set of crooked yellow teeth. "Mr. Gibson, I've had a frightfully jolly time here at your hotel and I am sorry that I had to disappoint you. I couldn't sell my bank . . . it just means too much to me and Mummy."

Sonny taps his pencil on the edge of the desk. "I'm sorry to hear that, Larry, especially for Mummy. I'd like to show you something that might change your mind." At the touch of a button an ornate panel disappears, uncovering a movie screen underneath it. "Hit the lights, Richie, then roll it." The room darkens, and the men are bathed in an eerie glow. From the first frame it is obvious that this film would never get a prize at Cannes, but it is an award-winner for Sonny. The Englishman gasps in alarm as he watches himself dancing naked around the room, squawking and flapping his arms like a chicken.

"I've seen enough . . . stop it . . . stop." Sonny keeps the camera rolling. When a large close-up of the feather in his ass fills the screen, Sark starts begging, "Please . . . in the name of all decency stop this . . . please ; . ."

Sonny says, "O.K., Richie, that's enough."

The projector whirs to a halt, and the lights come back on again. The banker slumps in his seat, his cheeks ruddy with embarrassment. He speaks quietly. "That's playing dirty, Mr. Gibson."

Sonny grins. "I never said I play by the rules, Larry . . . and I always play to win." He winks at Gregory and mimics Sark's British accent, "Gregory, old chap, I do believe we've got ourselves a bank." He looks straight at the humiliated Sark. "And it didn't cost me a shilling."

When he gets control of the Bank of Sark, Sonny goes on a spending spree. Now an accomplished pilot, he buys two turboprops, a Falcon and a Lear jet. A mansion in Bel-Air, California, is his West Coast home, and a house in Boca Raton, Florida, becomes his headquarters away from the Bahamas. A ski lodge in Michigan and a hotel on Hollywood's Sunset Strip are the first of many commercial properties he'll acquire in the coming months . . . all with worthless Bank of Sark cashier's checks that won't come in for collection for three to five years. When they do, they'll be destroyed, as planned, by Sonny's contact in England. Sonny also purchases a 110-foot motor sailer which he christens *The Lucky Dolphin*. He intends to use the boat for wining and dining developers out of their front money.

Sonny is showing Gregory around the luxurious yacht, which sleeps ten. There is an elegant dining room and a richly furnished living room on board. Sonny stops at the bar to pour Gregory a Scotch on the rocks and takes his own usual libation, a glass of wine. He sinks into the plush red velvet couch. "Yeah, between the broads and the booze on the high seas, those guys will be ready to sign anything. . . . That reminds me, Gregory, you know those TV monitors they use in banks to show balances on their depositors? . . . Stockbrokers use 'em, too, to show what their stocks are doing. . . . Get me one of those things."

"What are you planning to do with that?"

"I'm gonna put it on board. Then we'll program phony printouts to show our company's makin' millions of dollars. This way a developer can check us out and see how well we're doing."

Gregory congratulates him. "That's a great idea, Sonny . . . but why not install the system where it really counts?"

"What do you mean?"

"Well, you pick these men up in your private jet, right?"

Sonny snaps his fingers. "Of course . . . we'll put it on the plane. They'll have more time to look at it there. Once they get on the boat, they'll be too busy chasin' broads to bother. Good thinkin', Gregory."

The banker has a second plan that will be even more lucrative. "I have an another idea for the boat. What if I told you there was a way to get the developer's front money without using Bank of Sark checks to back your commitments?"

"That's a hell of an idea . . . it'd save me millions . . . I wouldn't have to pay any middle men. How do we do it?"

Gregory explains. "We can ask the developer to have his bank send a Telex to one of the major banks to verify that Transcontinental has enough cash to back the commitment."

"Where are we gonna get these banks?"

"We really don't even need a bank, Sonny. We'll install our own Telex machines on *The Lucky Dolphin;* that way we can intercept the developers' inquiries about us and send back only positive replies. It'll close deals a lot faster and keep you from wasting your cashier's checks."

Sonny gets up and pours himself another glass of wine. "What are the chances of gettin' caught?"

Gregory thinks for a minute. "Well, they'd have to run a high-frequency check. . . . If the boat keeps moving, it would be pretty hard to find us. Chances are about a hundred to one . . . Unless you have radar . . . then they'd never find you."

"Those odds aren't so good . . . but I like the idea." Sonny bangs his glass down on the bar, "How soon can we get these machines on board?"

"They can be ready to go by this time next week."

"Gregory, I think you've just earned your week's salary."

Within six days three Telex machines are in operation; one to send, one to receive, and an extra as backup. Through Gregory's contacts Sonny gets the Telex codes of four major U.S. banks. Whenever a deal is pending, a special code is sent to the ship: "*The Lucky Dolphin* will have a joker at one today." This alerts the Telex operator and the electronics man on board to stand by for an inquiry after the code time, in this case one o'clock. The line to the real bank is jammed, and the Telex is intercepted. Just as Gregory had guaranteed, every check run by the developer's bank comes back with an authorization number putting a hold on funds that do not exist. This system works so well that all of Sonny's companies receive the highest possible credit rating . . . a triple A.

Later that month, through Don Giuseppe's military connections, Sonny has satellite radar equipment installed that makes tracking a ship virtually impossible. Once *The Lucky Dolphin* was invisible at sea, he began operating his Telex scam all over the world. The Loganno family also put the boat to good use. Mario comes down to the Bahamas to tell Sonny that Don Giuseppe is planning to smuggle 1,800 pounds of gold and platinum out of Mexico (it's against the law to take even an ounce of precious metal out of that country). Sonny has some reservations. "Mario, it wouldn't be too smart for *The Lucky Dolphin* to get spotted in a port."

"That's all taken care of, Santino. The don's arranged for a tanker to take the shipment out to you in the Gulf. You'll have to figure out a way to get it into the States after that."

"O.K., but tell Don Giuseppe I gotta work on it . . . it'll probably be a couple a weeks before I can get the stuff to him."

Sonny comes up with a brilliant plan to smuggle the goods, but it has one serious flaw. His 110-foot motor sailer would never make it through customs without officials coming on board. He has to find a way to circumvent them, and he does. One of his smaller boats from the Lucky Ace is piloted to Florida and checked through customs as a sportfishing charter; eight of the bodyguards pose as the eager anglers. Since the trip is not for commercial purposes, the boat will not have to go through a check again when it docks. Seven miles out to sea the charter meets up with *The Lucky Dolphin* to transfer the valuable cargo. The gleaming bars of gold and platinum are then stuffed down the mouth of a 250-pound marlin. The extra 300 pounds of precious metals in its belly go unnoticed because the normally heavy fish is hoisted out of the boat on a block and tackle. An ice truck, allegedly from a taxidermist, takes the catch to a farmhouse in Pallaca, Florida where Richie is waiting to take the shipment to Don Giuseppe. Two weeks and five fish later all of the gold and platinum is in New York. Sonny's fee for smuggling the $3 million cargo is $300,000, but he earns far more than money. He now has the respect of every family as an international carrier for the Mafia.

Three months later Alfonso calls Sonny to Sicily. Two Turks had contacted the Sicilian Mafia about bringing heroin into the United States. His godfather had told the dons in Catania that Sonny was the best man to help them do the job. Since *The Lucky Dolphin* had already been used successfully in smuggling the precious metals, Alfonso was confident Sonny could find a way to get the narcotics in safely. He fills Sonny in on the details of the transaction on the ride from Palermo airport. The afternoon Sonny arrives a meeting is set up at Don Belfiore's to discuss the deal. The don greets Sonny with a hug at the gate of his villa.

"Santino . . . it's so good to have you back. . . . Come in, everyone's here." As they walk through the patio to the house, Belfiore congratulates him, "You did an excellent job with the American dons, Santino . . . it will be a long time before their pockets are full again."

Sonny answers in Sicilian, "It was a pleasure takin' 'em, Don Belfiore.

"I'll bet it was. I wish I could have been there to see it. When are you going to read them their crimes?"

"When you men tell me to."

Alfonso says, "It won't be too much longer now, Santino. We're getting some reports back already on their financial situations. You've pumped their wells almost dry."

They walk up a step to the front door. The don opens it and stops in the foyer. "It's a shame Laura is not here to see you." Sonny is disappointed. He was hoping his feelings about not ever seeing her again would be proven wrong on this trip.

"Where is Laura, Don Belfiore?"

"She went on a cruise of the Mediterranean with her cousin. She'll be back next week."

"I'm sorry I missed her. I can't be gone from the Lucky Ace that long—in fact, I'm leavin' tomorrow to meet some people."

"That's too bad, Santino. I know she would want to repay your hospitality. Laura told me what a good time she had in the Bahamas." Sonny does a mental flinch at this remark. It reminds him how much he mistreated his love. Don Belfiore adds, "I appreciate the respect you showed my daughter. A lot of men would have taken advantage of a young girl far away from her father."

Sonny continues Laura's obvious cover. "I would never disrespect her or you, Don Belfiore."

"I know that, Santino . . . come, let's go in now."

When they get to the parlor, five men are waiting. The last time Sonny was in this room, the night of his initiation ceremony, over sixty people were present. A lot more than time has passed since then. Sonny is now here speaking to these powerful dons, not as a neophyte, but as an equal. After the bodyguards pour the men some wine, everyone takes a seat and Sonny begins, saying with concern, "I don't understand why you guys are dealin' with these Turks . . . they're outsiders."

Don Lo Manzo, who made the initial contact with the foreigners, replies, "They're giving us the best price . . . we could never buy heroin that cheap anywhere else."

"If that's the case, I'll give you whatever help I can . . ." Sonny adds candidly, "I'll do it because I'm a loyal soldier, but I don't like it. So I'll be takin' some extra precautions."

Don Belfiore answers for the others, "Of course, Santino . . . we expect you to . . . that's why you're here."

"All right, then, this is what's gonna be . . . I don't want these Turks bringin' the stuff down to the Bahamas. Gino and Carlo can get it to me down there."

Lo Manzo objects strongly, "But Santino, it's their shipment. They're gonna insist on bringing it in themselves."

"It don't matter. I'm not dealin' directly with these people . . . I trust 'em like a fence. You deal with 'em."

The don challenges Sonny. "Santino, when we turn over ten kilos of pure heroin, we're talking about a million a kilo . . . that's ten million dollars. We should know how you're going to bring the stuff in." This is a clever ruse. Once the don finds out how to smuggle the narcotics in, he can cut Sonny out.

"Don Lo Manzo, I won't even tell my godfather how I'm doin' it . . . I'm sure as hell not tellin' you."

Alfonso interrupts, "Santino, for being the carrier you'll be getting five percent of the shipment."

Lo Manzo flares up. "Five percent of ten million! This guy will be making half a million on every trip."

Alfonso says plainly, "If you don't like it, you can pick somebody else to do the job. I know that with Santino our stuff will get there."

Sonny brings up another point. "By the way, I'm taking another five percent from the American families, which I'll split with the Sicilian Mafia. I'm not havin' anybody pick up the stuff. My men will deliver it."

Don Lo Manzo objects again. "How can we be sure all of it will get to New York? We don't know your men."

Sonny puts an end to these comments. "You'll just have to trust me . . . I'll get it to Don Giuseppe."

The arrogant don sees that Sonny is resolute and cannot be swayed. "All right, Santino, but how soon can we go? Can we go next week?"

"Nope, I need ninety days to set up my operation."

The greedy don argues, ". . . but the Turks might not want to deal with us then."

"Look . . . you guys buy the stuff from 'em now and keep it in this country . . . you're the law here. I'll let Alfonso know when I'm ready for it."

His godfather supports him. "If Santino needs the time, we'll give it to him. Whatever he's planning, I'm sure it's the best way for all of us."

On the way back to the airport Sonny asks his godfather, "Alfonso, do me a favor. I don't wanna leave a note for Laura, but would you get a message to her to have her give me a call?"

"Of course, Santino. When she gets back, she's leaving for Paris on business for her father, but I'll see she gets your message." After a few minutes he says, "You still love her, don't you?"

"Alfonso, you know that . . . I don't wanna talk about it."

"Why not?"

"I'm afraid I'm gonna hurt Laura."

"Santino, I've trained you not to be afraid. It's a waste of energy." His godfather says wisely, "You know, sometimes we bring on what we fear the most." Then, mopping his brow, "Besides, it's better for Laura to get hurt than you." This remark has to stem from some private bitterness. Sonny realizes at that moment how little he knows about his godfather's personal life.

"What happened to your wife, Alfonso?"

The mention of her takes Alfonso's breath for a second. "She died during the war . . ."

"The Nazis kill her?"

"No, she was killed when Patton's army invaded. There were more fireworks in Sicily than your American Fourth of July. She was caught in the fighting."

"Why didn't you get married again, Alfonso?"

The soldier turns and says absolutely, "I am married, Santino. The Mafia is my wife, my woman, my blood . . ."

Sonny devises a clever scheme for smuggling the heroin. He runs beauty contests in the Virgin Islands, Puerto Rico, and Bermuda, with the prize a ten-day, all-expense-paid vacation in Florida. Hundreds of girls, mostly impoverished, clamor to enter in every city, town, and village. Four winners are selected from each island and flown to the Bahamas to make a connection with *The Lucky Dolphin,* their transportation to the Key West. Two of the girls in the first group decide to stay at the Lucky Ace, convinced by Donna that they can make good money working as hookers for Sonny. Many of them have large families to support. The others eagerly board the boat looking forward to their first trip to America but unaware of the role they are about to play in Sonny's narcotics scheme. Richie and ten bodyguards accompany them to make sure the goods are delivered. A debonair Sicilian doctor also goes along. He is the key figure in the scheme.

The trip to the Florida Keys from the Bahamas takes five hours. Three hours out at sea the doctor has a conference with Richie on the bridge. "When will you be bringing in the champagne?"

Richie checks with the captain. "Hey, Gigo, how soon before we're forty miles from the coast?"

Gigo checks his charts. "We'll be there in another ten minutes."

"Good." Richie turns back to the doctor. "I'll tell the girls to come into the living room for their little celebration."

The doctor asks, "How soon before we dock?"

Gigo calculates, "About two hours at this speed."

The doctor nods, pleased. "That's more than enough time."

Excited anticipation is the feeling in the air as the girls giggle and chatter with each other, exchanging stories about their individual good fortunes. When the bodyguards carry in a huge crystal bowl filled with punch, the doctor claps his hands for attention. His Sicilian accent seems to make him even more handsome when he speaks. "We are almost in

America . . . now we celebrate . . ." There is unanimous approval of his suggestion. The beauties gather around the bowl, and when every girl has a glass in hand, the doctor says, "To the most beautiful women in the world." Naturally all of the girls drink to that, downing their champagne to the last drop. Ten minutes later they're fast asleep. The punch was laced with tranquilizers.

Richie snaps, "Hurry up, Doc, we've got to work fast."

The doctor grabs his black bag and begins working on one of the drugged girls. A tube about two feet long is forced through her nostril. Then, the narcotics, in eight flexible rubber balloons, each about the size of a Lifesaver, are pumped through the tube into her stomach. Instantly these paupers become walking treasure chests. Every girl is carrying inside of her half a million dollars of pure, uncut heroin, worth ten times that on the street.

Just as the doctor is finishing up, Willie rushes in. "Hey . . . there's a girl on the deck reading. I offered her a drink, but she won't touch the stuff . . . says she's religious. What should I do? Should I kill her?"

Richie says roughly, "No, knock her on the head and bring her in . . . and make it quick. When she wakes up, tell her she fell."

The bodyguard rushes out. A few minutes later the unconscious girl is carried in and the last of the heroin balloons is pumped into her. Suddenly she starts to convulse violently. Richie panics. "What the hell's happening, Doc?" The doctor, who has been leaning over, trying to help the sick girl, straightens up.

He says gravely, "One of the balloons broke . . . she's dead."

Richie goes berserk. "Shit, I'd better call the boss. We'll have to turn back. He's not gonna like this . . . goddam!"

A few minutes later, in the casino, Angelo comes over to Sonny, who is entertaining an Italian prince. "You got an emergency call on *The Lucky Dolphin* intercept line, Boss . . . it's Richie."

This smells like trouble to Sonny, but he smiles at his guest. "I gotta leave for a few minutes. I'll have someone take you to my penthouse. We'll meet back up there."

The Italian flashes Sonny a grin. "Please, take your time, Santino."

Sonny heads to Control to take the call. When he had his radar equipment installed, a special phone was also put in. The intercept line works on its own separate frequency, similar to those used by the military. Unlike regular ship-to-shore messages, transmissions from *The Lucky Dolphin* could not be picked up by the Coast Guard or any other source. Sonny listens as Richie explains the unexpected turn of events, then yells furiously, "Hell, no, you won't turn back! I got people in New York waitin' for that shipment . . . How many more balloons did she have in her? . . . Tell the doc to rip her open and get the other four out . . . I don't care. Throw her overboard. Weight her down with the extra anchors I had Gigo put on board. She'll be bleedin' like a stuck pig. By the time she hits bottom, the sharks will have her eaten up . . . What about the other girls? . . . When they come to, tell 'em the bitch fell overboard. Call the Coast Guard in front of everybody and report her missing. It'll keep the rest from askin' questions." Sonny throws the mike on the console and turns to Angelo. "When they get back, kill the bastard that filled those balloons . . . . He just cost the Mafia a hundred grand, he coulda cost us a twenty-million-dollar smuggling job."

Richie disposes of the body according to Sonny's instructions. About an hour later the beauty queens come to. Concita, one of the winners from Puerto Rico, looks around and asks, "Where's Estrellita?"

Willie says truthfully, "The last time I saw her, she was up on the deck reading."

Richie scolds the girls. "I told you all that was a slippery area . . . it's no place to be walking. I hope she didn't fall."

The girls get excited. He calms them. "All right, all right. Fan out, let's see if we can find her."

A massive search is conducted for the missing girl. After forty minutes everyone reassembles in the living room. Richie says solemnly, "I'm afraid Estrellita must have fallen off the boat."

Concita gets hysterical. "Turn around . . . maybe she's still alive. We have to go back. We have to try and save her!"

Richie puts a comforting arm around the excited girl's shoulder. "We'll call the Coast Guard. They'll find her a lot faster with their helicopters." Richie makes the phone call as planned to report the girl overboard. A pall is cast over the group because of the incident, but twenty minutes later, when the Florida coastline comes into view, spirits start to rise again . . . except Concita's.

The boat docks at Key West at last, and the second phase of the scheme is launched. The girls pass through customs undetected, unwitting accomplices to the smuggling. At the hotel they are checked into a reserved section and confined to this area by their "chaperones" for seventy-two hours. Laxatives are slipped into their first meal, and when the girls get diarrhea, the doctor tells them the condition comes from a change in drinking water. The plumbing in their suites empties into the boiler room. There a man wearing a gas mask and rubber gloves sifts through their waste material to extract the balloons as soon as they're eliminated. Keeping the girls close by guarantees that they won't flush the valuable heroin down another toilet. Once they get the narcotics, Richie and the other bodyguards take the drugs to New York on a private jet. Mario and his men meet them in a secluded hangar at La Guardia airport to take the heroin to Don Giuseppe. A chemist is with them to test the purity of the drugs. He melts a small chunk and puts that in a closed, calibrated test tube. An acid gas mixture is then injected inside. If the heroin is pure, the liquid will rise to the first notch; each line above that will tell how many times the drugs have been cut. The test shows all of this heroin is pure.

Sonny estimates ten more shipments like this one will be sent over a twelve-month period. At the end of that year, Sonny will have picked up five million dollars for his part in the scheme.

Two weeks later, Sonny is still basking in the success of his heroin scheme when Linda buzzes him in his office. "There's a call coming in from Catania, Sonny. The overseas operator said it'll be through in a few minutes."

"O.K., Linda . . . buzz me." What could Alfonso want? Everything had gone off perfectly. . . . Maybe the Turks were giving him trouble about sending the next shipment down with Gino and Johno. Sonny's mind created a myriad of problems that his godfather could be calling about. Linda buzzes, and he picks up the phone, ready to start solving them. He is pleasantly surprised. It's Laura. She is cool to him at first. "Hello, Santino . . . I got your message. Alfonso said you wanted me to call you." Her voice, even miles away, is like silk.

"Laura . . . where are you?"

"I'm home. I just got back from Paris. My father has a private jet now. I travel all over the world."

"That's nice, Laura." There is an awkward pause. Sonny doesn't know how to be humble, but he makes a stab at it. "Well, would you consider quittin' the jet set and comin' down to the Bahamas to stay with me for a while?"

Her reply is firm. "Not if it's like the last time, Santino . . . no . . ."

"It wouldn't be . . . I'd be with you . . . I need you, Laura." He adds quickly, "I'm not askin' you to come down here and get married, you understand . . . you know how I am. Would you wanna accept me with that kind of a life?"

There are a few seconds of silence. She finally says, softly, "I love you, Santino. Being with you is better than being without you . . . I'll come."

Sonny is excited. "I love you, too, Laura. How soon do ya think you can get down here?"

"I'd have to get permission from my father."

Sonny says with confidence, "He'll let ya come . . . he respects me. Uh . . . thanks to you, Laura. Tell him I want ya to work for me at the hotel. You speak seven languages, you're beautiful . . . you could be my head of public relations."

"I'd have to find someone to replace me first. I'm doing a lot for my father now. It won't be easy to find someone he can trust."

"Just get down here as fast as ya can, Laura . . . I miss you. Let me know when you're coming . . . I'll send my jet for you . . . I love you, Laura."

"I love you, too, Santino . . . *ciao.*"

After Sonny hangs up, he stares at the receiver for a long time. The feeling is back that he'll never see Laura again. It hovers over his happiness like a black cloud. Linda buzzes him out of it. "Sonny, Sheik Ali is waiting for you in the penthouse to talk about the oil deal."

"Tell him I'll be up in a few minutes . . . order him some Dom Perignon."

Sonny's organization has been growing steadily. Royalty from all over the world visits the Lucky Ace regularly. His Bank of Sark purchases have increased his assets by millions, and his companies are multiplying daily. He now has over one hundred corporations and eighty bodyguards on the payroll. His men have dubbed his mansion in Bel Air the "West Castle"; Sonny keeps eight to ten women in residence there and at his estate in Florida. This is Sonny's private stock . . . a very special group of females. Sonny has deals with insurance company gynecologists all over the country to provide him with a list of patients who have large vaginas. The women are then offered $2000 plus room and board to live with him. The attractive ones who accept are assigned to Boca Raton or the West Castle. He has no need for any at the Lucky Ace since there are plenty of hookers and wealthy matrons to keep him busy.

In spite of his hectic work schedule Sonny finds time for frequent sex sessions with all of his partners. Often he's called from the bedroom to take an important call, and no matter how much he's enjoying satisfying his lust, business always takes precedence over broads. One day, while Sonny is making love to a voluptuous Mexican girl, Angelo has to interrupt him. The bodyguard's knock cannot compete with the girl's moans inside the bedroom. Angelo starts pounding. Sonny stops midthrust. "What the fuck . . . who is it?"

"It's me, Boss."

"Goddam it, Angelo, you know I'm busy."

"Uh . . . Boss, you said you wanted to know when Mr. Monahan called . . . he's on the phone now." This makes Sonny leap out of bed and pick up the receiver. He's expecting the Las Vegas developer to tell him that Sid Dillman, Monahan's banker in Vegas, has approved Transcontinental's loan commitment. "J. R., when do we close the deal?"

"Well, Sonny, Dillman won't approve anything 'til he gets a two-and-a-half-million-dollar check from a major U.S. bank . . . he said he won't accept anything from the Bank of Sark."

With his Telex setup this is no problem for Sonny, "Tell him a New York bank's gonna issue the check, but Dillman's gotta give me a check for a million plus half a million cash before I hand it over." Sonny has some more instructions for J. R. "Tell Dillman we'll close the deal on my jet. I never conduct my business in a bank." He adds, "And J. R. . . . if you want that money to buy the land for your fancy hotel and casino, you'd better tell Dillman to get off his ass. He's had two days to check us out. Better remind him who he's dealin' with. If he's not at the airport at ten A.M. the deal's off." Sonny hangs up and buzzes Richie. "Tell John to get the Falcon ready. We're pickin' up a banker in Vegas tomorrow."

At that moment Sonny Gibson's activities are the topic of conversation in Sid Dillman's office in Las Vegas.

Sid Dillman leans back in his desk chair. He'd rather be out playing golf than listening to Mike Willis, his assistant, give him a report on Transcontinental Casualty, but Sid listens intently. "Mr. Dillman, Transcontinental shows assets of two hundred ninety million dollars and has done business with several major banks. Their credit rating is triple A, but there's something funny about them. I checked last year's ratings. Transcontinental wasn't even in existence then. I don't think we should take a chance with them."

The banker dismisses Mike's concern. "Don't believe everything you read. Those reports aren't worth the paper they're printed on."

"I think you should be aware of something else, Mr. Dillman. Sonny Gibson has heavy underworld connections. He's a known carrier for the Mafia. I don't think that kind of heat would be too good for the bank."

This confirms Dillman's suspicions, but he snaps, "I'll decide what's good for this bank. As long as Gibson has the two-point-five-million-dollar cashier's check, he can't hurt us. He's pledging it against his commitment."

Mike reminds Sid, "You'll have half a million in cash. Can't you insist on doing the deal here in your office?"

Sid argues, "Why? It'll be safe in the plane . . . Gibson always has a lot of security men around him. Besides, if he is connected with the Mafia, I can understand why he does his business there. I like the idea myself . . . It's discreet."

Mike can see his protests are futile. "O.K., but be careful, the man is vicious. There are rumors that even the Mafia is afraid of him."

Sid says smugly, "Don't worry, I've dealt with thugs all over the country and never gotten hurt. Vegas is *my* backyard . . . I call the shots here. Besides, I don't think Gibson is a very smart businessman . . . he can't even hold a decent conversation."

"Maybe not, but he has muscle." Mike warns, "Just remember,

Sid, those guys play for keeps."

The next day at ten A.M. sharp Sid Dillman boards Sonny's ten-seater Falcon jet at McCarran International Airport in Las Vegas. Sonny is waiting for him in his office on board. The banker clutches his metal case with the cash even as they shake hands. "Glad to see ya again, Sid." Sonny points to a velvet swivel chair. "Make yourself comfortable." Sid sits, then accepts a glass of wine from Sonny, who takes a seat opposite him. "We have to pick up some people in Phoenix. That's all right with you, isn't it, Sid?"

The banker nods amiably. "Sure, as long as I can be back by five this afternoon."

"No problem. We'll only be gone a few hours." Sonny leans back casually. "How's the banking business?"

"Frankly Mr. Gibson, if people knew the shaky situation most banks are in, it would cause a panic worse than the one in '29."

Sonny sympathizes. "The banks aren't the only ones in trouble, Sid. A lot of insurance companies don't have the reserve they should. . . . But you don't have that worry with Transcontinental. After we take off, you can turn the computer on and check out our assets." He indicates a small TV monitor near the bulkhead. "I'll be gone for a while. I like to do the takeoffs and landings myself." This fact surprises Sid. "I didn't know you were a pilot . . . that's quite a skill."

Sonny grins. "Yep . . . been flyin' ever since I was sixteen." He points to Sid's lap. "Better fasten your seatbelt now. We'll be in the air in a few minutes."

When they have been in the air fifteen minutes, Sonny returns to the cabin. Sid is studying the computer printout. "Very impressive, Mr. Gibson. No wonder your rating is so good."

Sonny boasts, "I'm probably one of the smartest men in the country in marketing, stock, real estate, and just plain makin' money."

"I can see that from your financial statement."

Sonny sits next to him. "And Sid, I'm really happy we're gonna be makin' some really big money together."

Sid smiles back. "I am, too, Mr. Gibson, that's why I'm here. By the way, do you have your cashier's check for me?"

"Yes, I do." Sonny takes a $2.5-million check from his briefcase and lays it on the table.

Sid is impressed. "Hmm . . . big bank, one of the biggest in New York."

"We're doin' a lotta business with them now."

Sid says, "I know J. R. will be pleased."

Sonny reminds him, "He's not the only one. You're gonna pick up a million yourself on this deal in two years."

"Not quite . . . remember, it's costing me half a million cash up front."

"By the way, Sid, I'd like to see that cash and your cashier's check now, too."

The banker turns the money over to Sonny, who hands it to Richie. "Make sure it's all there." Sonny makes small talk about the banking business while the bodyguard counts the money. In fifteen minutes Angelo comes over.

"Uh . . . Richie says it's all there, Boss."

Sid is offended. "Of course it is, my word is my bond . . . that's the way you have to be in this business."

Sonny assures him, "I couldn't agree more."

He studies the banker's million-dollar cashier's draft, then frowns. "Your signature is missing from the check, Sid. How come?"

"I wanted to wait until I saw your check."

"O.K., you've seen it . . . now sign."

Dillman explains, "I hope you understand Mr. Gibson, it's no reflection on you . . . I have to protect myself. Transcontinental is an offshore company. We have no way of forcing you to pay us two years from now."

Sonny nods. "I understand, Sid, but I'm givin' you a cashier's check to back my commitment. I'm certainly entitled to my fee."

"There's no question that you are . . ."

"O.K., then you shouldn't have any qualms about signin' the check. You can sign this release clause, too." Sonny hands him some papers. "It says you accept our commitment and approve all the terms."

Sid looks over the document. "No problem, as soon as we get back to Vegas and your check clears for collection, I'll be happy to sign both."

Sonny is peeved. "Sid, you yourself said that it's drawn on one of the biggest banks in New York . . . it's gonna clear."

Sid shakes his finger at Sonny. "Yes, but with your connections the check could be a fraud. When I verify your check, I'll sign mine . . . not before."

"I'm sorry to hear you say that, Sid."

"You just found out, Mr. Gibson, how I got my reputation as the toughest banker in Las Vegas." Sid looks out the window, "By the way, how soon do you think we'll get to Phoenix?"

Sonny folds his arms over his chest. "We aren't going to Phoenix. In fact, you might not be going anywhere, Sid."

With a look Sonny calls his four bodyguards over. They encircle the apprehensive banker. Angelo says, "O.K., Boss. John will depressurize the cabin at fifteen thousand feet. He wants to know what altitude he should fly at."

"Tell him ten thousand feet."

Sid panics. "What's happening? Will somebody tell me what's happening?"

Sonny says expressionlessly, "I'll tell you what's happening. You haven't kept your word. You won't sign the release or the check, and I'm upset . . . that's not good, Sid."

The banker protests. "What are you talking about? I told you . . . I have to wait until that check clears . . . I'm the head of a bank, I . . . ."

Before he can finish, Sonny grabs Sid by his tie and starts to choke him. "You son of a bitch . . . You're gonna sign those fuckin' papers, NOW!"

The banker struggles. "Just who do you think you're touching, Gibson . . ."

Sonny picks Dillman up by the throat. "Tell him who's touchin' him, Angelo."

"Uh, the boss is touchin' you . . . you fat-ass Jew." Angelo cocks his .357 magnum and holds it to the banker's head. Dillman's eyes nearly pop out of his head. Sonny shouts in his ear, "Sign the fuckin' papers, Sid."

Defiance burns in the banker's eyes. "You'll have to pull that trigger, Gibson . . . I know your type . . . I'm not afraid of hoodlums like you."

Angelo says eagerly, "Should I blow his brains out, Boss?"

Sonny drops the banker back to his seat. "Not yet, Angelo." He sits down again, his voice calm. "I'll tell you why I'm not gonna have Angelo blow your brains out, Sid. They'd splatter all over and that'd mess up my plane. I just had this cabin redecorated; hell, you're not worth the trouble." Sid massages his throat as Sonny continues. "You're smart, all right. You know I need your signature on this check." His tongue clicks disapprovingly, "Giving up your life for the bank's money . . . I thought you were smarter than that." Sonny leans forward. "I don't wanna kill you, Sid . . . really . . . but you're not givin' me any choice."

Richie informs him, "John says we're at ten thousand feet and cruising at a hundred ten knots right now."

Sonny smiles. "Good . . . crack the door, Richie."

Dillman demands, "What does that mean, 'crack the door'?"

Sonny turns to Angelo. "Tell Mr. Dillman what that means, Angelo."

The bodyguard obliges gladly. "Uh . . . it means Richie is gonna open the door, and me and the boys are gonna kick your ass out." At a signal from Sonny the door opens. A gale-force wind whips through the cabin. A waterfall of sweat pours down the banker's face as the bodyguards lift him up, kicking and screaming. "What the hell's going on here, Gibson?"

Sonny says flatly, "Good-bye, Dillman. When you hit that hot sand, you'll shatter like a piece a glass."

The banker tries to reason. "But the people at the bank know I'm with you . . ." Sonny shrugs. "You got off in Phoenix and took a commercial flight . . . I have witnesses to prove it. You're crazy to die for a bank, Sid . . . you could've made a lot of money if you'd played it my way." Sonny turns his back coldly. "Get rid of him . . ."

Angelo's blunt fingers dig into the banker's shoulders. "Come on, Dillman, you're clutterin' up the Boss's plane."

The banker has lost all of his bravura now. He starts to shake when the bodyguards lift him up in the air. "Hey . . . what the hell are you doing? . . . Put me down . . . help . . . put me down!" When Dillman sees his feet near the door and feels the force of the breeze up his pants, he is so petrified he pees all over himself. The banker screams hysterically, "Don't do it. I don't wanna die. Wait! I'll sign! I'LL SIGN!!"

Sonny holds up the check and the release papers. Still airborne, Sid signs. "O.K. boys, let him go . . ."

Angelo is disappointed. "Uh, Boss, can't we throw him out anyway?"

Sonny thinks a second. "Nah, he did what he was supposed to. I may need him again." Reluctantly the bodyguards drop Sid to the floor and close the door.

Dillman crawls to the nearest chair. He asks nervously, "What guarantee do I have that you won't kill me later?"

Sonny smiles. "No guarantee, Dillman . . . none at all."

Then he turns to Richie. "Tell Allen he can head for Chicago now."

The banker can't believe it. "You mean we're not going to Phoenix?"

"Nope. We're goin' to your correspondent bank in Chicago to cash your check."

Dillman is stunned. "You mean you've got my five hundred thousand and you're gonna cash in the million, too?"

Sonny grins. "Congratulations, Sid, you just put two and two together. I don't know what you're cryin' about . . . you've got Transcontinental's commitment. You'll make a million on this deal . . ." He pats Sid's cheek. "Don't forget . . . we're partners." Sonny pours him a glass of wine. "Ya look like you need a drink, Sid." He hands it to Dillman, then turns toward the cockpit. When he reaches the door, he stops. "Oh . . . and Sid . . . in case you're thinking of going to the police . . . I have a little tape on you I'm sure the FDIC commissioners would love to get their hands on. If anything happens to me . . . they'll get that tape . . . and there'll be a hundred-thousand-dollar contract out on your ass." His thumb indicates the bodyguards hovering like vultures. "The boys here would kill their own mother for a grand." The banker nods submissively. "I'm goin' up front, boys. Make sure Mr. Dillman has a pleasant flight."

Gregory Stanford meets the jet at a private hangar at O'Hare in Chicago. Sonny hands him Dillman's check. "I'm sendin' Richie and Willie with you to cash this. Richie has a Brink's truck waitin' to bring the money back."

"O.K., Sonny. We shouldn't be too long. My friend is the vice-president at First National . . . he's expecting us." Stanford compares the check to a signature card. "This is Dillman's signature, all right." He puts both in his leather attaché case. "Well, at least we have two years before our check comes in for collection." Sonny pulls out the bank draft. Gregory is floored. "You got his million without giving him your money? How the hell'd you do that, Sonny?"

Angelo answers, "Uh . . . the boss took Dillman for a plane ride, Mr. Stanford."

Gregory blanches. "What do you mean . . . took him for a plane ride? Where's Dillman now?"

Sonny smiles. "Sid's on the plane, resting . . . it was a rough flight. Flyin' doesn't agree with him."

Sonny starts tearing up the check. Gregory watches in amazement. "Why are you doing that?"

"Come on, Gregory, don't be so stupid."

The executive catches on. "It's a fake, isn't it. You don't have to pledge the two and a half million, and you got his million and a half."

"That's right, Gregory." Sonny says with foreboding, "One day you'll learn . . . no one can outsmart me."

As soon as Sonny gets his million from the bank in Chicago, he drops Dillman off in Las Vegas and heads straight back to the Bahamas. He has urgent business there. It is time to call in the dons he's conned for Alfonso. A year has passed since he made the phony deal with them, and they are coming to the Lucky Ace to get a full report on the status of their investments.

The first two days after the eight family heads and their bodyguards arrive, Sonny makes himself scarce but sees to it that they all enjoy themselves. A few of the dons have expressed concern over the delay; they're anxious to find out how much money they've made.

The second night Sonny comes down to the casino to be sure that Andrew Delacroix, his personal politician in the Virgin Islands, and his guest are having a good time. Frank Manadeli corners Sonny. "Hey, Santino . . . where you been?"

"I've been tied up all week with contractors."

"What's goin' on? How come we don't see any construction on the development yet?"

Sonny sidesteps the question, "I'll tell ya everything in the meeting tomorrow . . . all I can tell you now is it's workin' out just like I planned."

Manadeli grins. The greedy don assumes this means he's made ten times his $8 million. "That's a relief to hear . . . I'm a little short of cash. All the guys are." He laments, "I'm not havin' any luck on your crap tables either. This is not lucky for me like Vegas. Can you give me some credit?"

Sonny puts a friendly arm around Manadeli. "Sure, Frank. I'm gonna give you fifty grand. I know you're good for it."

"Thanks a lot, Santino," Manadeli laughs. "If I lose, you can take it outta my money from the investment."

"It's my pleasure . . . I'll go to the cashier's cage right now to arrange it." On the way across the casino to the cage Sonny tells Angelo, "Watch what table Manadeli plays . . . tell Vito I want a mechanic on it."

On the third night of their stay Sonny finally invites the eight deceitful dons to a special dinner. Sonny's bodyguards are stationed at the doors to the banquet room, where the smell of espresso and cigar smoke mingles with the low buzz of after-dinner conversation. It has been a relaxing three days for the dons, but now there is a sense of urgency in the air. They want to get down to business. When Sonny stands to tap his glass for order, he gets everyone's full attention. All eyes in the room are on Sonny as he raises his glass and speaks. *"Buona fortuna centianno . . .* good luck to the Sicilian Mafia for a hundred years." The men stand and acknowledge the toast. Sonny makes another. "To the power of the Genetti family." The dons nervously drink to that, then put their glasses down. Sonny walks around the table. He hugs each of the eight men and gives him a kiss on the mouth. When Sonny returns to his place, he says, "I have a little surprise for you gentlemen." Suddenly the double doors on both sides of the banquet room are thrown open, and bodyguards carrying machine guns pour into the room. Each don gets two weapons aimed at him. Sonny's men disarm the dons' soldiers and frisk the dons themselves roughly.

Simultaneously the eight demand, "What's going on here?" "What do you think you're doing?" "Get your hands off me." "Don't you know who the fuck I am? I run Cleveland."

Sonny snaps gruffly: "Sit down and keep your mouths shut." The dons can't argue with machine guns. They take their seats and sweat as if they were in a steambath. Sonny motions for Richie to come over, and the bodyguard hands him a sheet of paper. Sonny addresses the dons gravely: "At the request of Alfonso Lambretti I just gave you the kiss of death. If it were up to him, you would've been executed a long time ago. If it were up to me, I'd blow ya away right now. I'm not speaking as Sonny Gibson . . . but as someone with true blood . . . Santino Gino Genetti." He holds up the paper. "This lists your crimes against the Sicilian Mafia. I know them as well as you do. When Anastasia was murdered in the barber chair, a war of wars broke out among the families. The Sicilian Mafia, sanctioned by La Cosa Nostra, called a council meeting to end that war. They took a vote: peace or vendetta? They chose peace. They came up with a way to restore harmony by showing the families how to make money together. Their idea was presented to the fifteen American dons, and a vote was taken . . . you eight men here today voted against the Sicilian Mafia . . . you were warned not to. You were given a second chance, but you still didn't wanna share. In the past ten years your greed has been the cause of bickering and fighting among you. A lot of blood was shed and tongues loosened." Sonny's eyes shoot daggers at them. "The Sicilian Mafia has more respect for a pig wallowing in slime than for you." The dons shift uncomfortably in their chairs as Sonny allows this to sink in.

Detroit Louie finally shouts, "Fuck who they respect . . ."

Sonny reprimands them. "That's the trouble . . . you have no respect for anything. You don't even respect yourselves."

Vinnie complains, "All the Sicilians are interested in is keeping us under their control."

Manadeli asks impatiently, "So a lot of us have run-ins with La Cosa Nostra . . . what the hell does that have to do with our money?"

"Everything." Sonny drops the bomb. "I was called in by the Sicilian Mafia to take you men. Ya won't be going home with ten times your investment . . . you won't be takin' home nothin' at all." This elicits an excited reaction from the dons. The ominous click of machine guns restores order to the room.

Pete Manzini jumps up angrily. "Look, you goddam punk. You're not takin' *my* fuckin' money."

Sonny walks over to Manzini and slaps him hard, knocking the cigar out of the startled man's mouth. "Shut up, pig . . . you have no power here." None of the other men come to the don's aid. They can see the legendary viciousness of the Genetti family surfacing in Sonny. Tension mounts as Sonny returns to his seat and says contemptuously, "There is one thing you'll all be bringin' back to your ratholes . . . your worthless lives. But before you leave, I wanna show you men just how much you can trust each other." He pulls out a pile of cassette tapes from his briefcase and lays them on the table. He addresses a fat man with the face of a bulldog. "Vinnie, on your tape you'll hear how Big Louie made a side deal with your banker, Mike. Mike told Louie your account number in Geneva and all of your deposits there."

Vinnie leaps up. "You goddam fuckin' guinea . . . you're a dead man!" He tackles the 250-pound head of the Detroit family. Within seconds the bodyguards are there to break it up.

Sonny warns, "The next one who gets outta line, Angelo . . . break his neck."

The giant puts his gun down, takes off his jacket, and rolls up his sleeves. "I'm ready, Boss."

The rival dons glare at each other as Sonny continues, "Now here's a tape for you, Louie. Vinnie offered your legal staff money to draw up papers giving him control of the seven shopping centers you're going into."

The fat man shakes a fist at Vinnie across the table. "You dumb wop. I'm gonna murder you."

Sonny yells, "That's enough, Louie . . . I told you I'm talking." But the ruckus continues until Angelo looms over the pair, ready to attack. They both see the mammoth hulk and quiet down immediately.

Angelo looks at Sonny. "I'm gonna crush 'em, Boss."

"No . . . that's O.K., Angelo." Sonny turns to Manadeli. "Now, Frank, you gave me more money than anybody . . . you're the greediest bastard of them all. You wanted to get control over these other puppets . . . then you would've robbed them. Here's a tape of Freddie Pescara and Jimmy Manatello plannin' a hit on you. They were gonna take over your new territory as soon as you got your narcotics traffic going." Frank stares at Fred and Jimmy in disbelief. Sonny throws the tape at him. "It's all there, Frank." Sonny now turns his attention to three dons sitting in a row. "Pete Manzini, Jack the Knuckles, and Albert Franco . . . You all bought property together to go into the casino business in Vegas. Frank Manadeli convinced Jack to cut Pete and Albert out. Once the casino was built, you both would have a contract on you. But Frank also talked to you, Pete. Here's a tape where he's plannin' to hit Jack and Albert. Now Albert, you know you and Frank had the same deal. I can see why Manadeli has the most money of all you idots. He's smart. He don't even do his own dirty work. He lets you guys bump each other off." The room is uncannily silent. The dons cannot argue with the tapes in their hands, concrete proof that they've double-crossed each other. Sonny looks at them contemptuously. "I still don't understand why the Mafia doesn't kill you. You're scum. You've brought shame and dishonor to the Mafia. You'd rape your own mother and flush her down the toilet for a dollar." Sonny stands. "The vendetta for the Sicilian Mafia is paid . . . for now. Richie, take 'em to the plane . . . I never want to see this scum again." He shoots the dons one last scornful look. "You're lucky you're goin' back with your asses. If one of ya ever mentions my name to anyone, you won't live to see 1967. I'll personally tear all your hearts out and stuff 'em down your lousy throats." Sonny turns to leave, and the bodyguards start hustling the men out of the room.

As Frank Manadeli passes him, he grabs Sonny's arm. "What about——" In the middle of a word Angelo picks him up by the shirt and pins him against the wall. Manadeli's feet dangle three feet off the ground. "Should I crush his chest, Boss?"

"Don't bother, Angelo. It's better keepin' him alive. These scum got somethin' worse than death facin' them. They can never walk the street again without looking for that bullet around every corner." Angelo drops Manadeli. Sonny strides briskly out of the room. He has an important call to make to Alfonso.

Sonny instructs Linda to place an overseas call to Catania. Six hours later, at four in the morning, he is speaking to Alfonso. His godfather says, "*Come sta,* Santino?"

Sonny answers in Sicilian, "*Menza, menza* . . . you don't sound too good, Alfonso."

"I have a cold, Santino."

"Well, lemme cheer you up. I read the crimes to the dons tonight."

"Oh . . . I feel better already."

Sonny continues, "I also gave 'em the tapes where they were cheatin' each other."

Alfonso beams over the phone. "Oh . . . I'm completely well. I can't wait to tell the other dons. Don Belfiore will be especially pleased to hear it. I'm really happy about this, Santino."

"Yeah . . . and it looks like they're almost broke. They're gonna have to fight among themselves."

"Good . . . that's what they deserve."

Sonny asks Alfonso a question about Laura's imminent arrival. "How does Don Belfiore feel about his daughter workin' in my operation?"

"He has a lot of respect for you, Santino . . . he feels it's a good opportunity for her. Laura's been buying all kinds of clothes for the trip. I tried to tell her not to buy too many sexy things . . . her father will know then she's not going over there to work."

Sonny laughs. "Thanks, Alfonso . . . you're truly my godfather."

Alfonso warns, "You may have trouble with her, Santino . . . you know Sicilian women are jealous."

"Don't worry . . . Laura's not comin' down here with her eyes closed . . . she she knows how I am."

"By the way, Laura's going on a little farewell trip with her father before she leaves . . . she'll be gone for the next ten days, Santino."

"Oh, that's great . . . tell her to give me a day's notice, and my jet will pick her up."

"I'll do that, Santino."

"Stay well, Alfonso. *Ciao.*"

"*Ciao*, Santino." Alfonso hangs up. In the back of Sonny's mind that gnawing sense of doom still lingers, but he's relieved his feelings were wrong. He will see Laura again.

Sonny begins making preparations for her arrival. He has his penthouse bedroom painted yellow, Laura's favorite color, and even has Richie get a small statue of the Madonna for her. Sonny himself supervises the decoration of her office, which adjoins his suite. The room is turned into a minigallery of Michelangelo's works. Reproductions of Laura's favorite artist hang in elaborate antique gilt frames, and his most famous sculptures stand on pedestals in the corners. The focal point of the room is a life-size statue of David, which stands in front of a huge picture window overlooking the ocean. Within a week everything is completed, and the Lucky Ace is ready to receive its first lady.

At five-thirty one morning Sonny is awakened by a phone call from Alfonso. His godfather's voice quakes . . . it is the first time Sonny has ever heard him grope for words. "Santino . . . I . . . It's such a terrible thing."

"What? What is it, Alfonso?"

"It's Laura."

A million awful things race through Sonny's head. "Laura? What's the matter with her . . . is she sick?"

There is a pause on the other end. "No, Santino . . . she's dead. So are her father and brother."

The news paralyzes him. "Dead? Laura's dead? . . . No . . . How? Was it an accident?"

"We don't know, Santino. We got a report that her father's plane crashed over the Alps. There are rumors that it exploded."

Sonny clenches his fists. "That was no accident. It had to be a hit. Who'd want to kill Don Belfiore?"

"I don't know, Santino. We'll talk about it when you get to Catania."

"When is the funeral, Alfonso?"

"I don't know yet . . . it will be a few days before they find what's left of the bodies."

Sonny tries not to think about this—he'd rather have a living memory of Laura. "I'll be there for the funeral."

"Is there anything I can do, Santino?"

"No, Alfonso . . . there's nothing anyone can do now."

Sonny hangs up and puts his head in his hands. Retrospect plays havoc with his emotions. He blames himself for Laura's death. If he'd kept her in the Bahamas, she'd still be alive. If he hadn't asked her to live with him, she wouldn't have gone on that farewell trip. If only he hadn't felt so strongly he'd never see her again, he might have . . . Maybe Alfonso was right . . . maybe you can create what you fear most. Sonny dresses in the faint glow of dawn. In the open door to Laura's room David's snowy, marble loins are illuminated by the early morning light. He walks inside. As he looks around at the other things in her special room, anguish gives way to anger. Sonny takes the enormous statue and hurls it through the picture window to the rocks below. The crash sets off a loud alarm in the headboard of each chief bodyguard's bed. Angelo and Richie grab their clothes and rush down the hall into the room, guns drawn. The men stationed outside are already in Laura's room.

"What happened? What's goin' on?"

Willie tells them, "I don't know. He's goin' crazy." Sonny is in a rage, ripping the pictures off the walls, smashing the statues, bent on destroying everything.

Angelo tries to restrain him. "Hey, Boss . . . what're ya doin' to Laura's room?"

Sonny holds a picture high above his head to crash it down, but instead flings it aside. He says dully, "There's no Laura, Angelo . . . she's dead . . . she got blown up in a plane."

The bodyguard slumps. "Aw, no, Boss . . ." Sonny rushes past him. "I gotta get outta here."

Angelo struggles into his pants. "Wait a minute . . ."

"Fuck, no . . . I'm leavin'."

Richie yells to the other two men, "Keep an eye on him, but don't get too close."

In a few minutes Angelo and Richie join the others, keeping a respectful distance as Sonny walks along the beach where he and Laura once strolled hand in hand in the moonlight. An aching knot fills the pit of his stomach. Never before has this Mafia king felt so helpless . . . he knows how to take life, but with all of his money and power Sonny doesn't know how to bring life back. Thinking of Laura's gruesome end, his sorrow becomes resolve. He makes a vow to avenge the death of his only love. Sonny turns around and walks purposefully toward the bodyguards. "I'm goin' on *The Lucky Dolphin*. I'm stayin' on the boat until everything is outta that fuckin' room . . . And Angelo . . . tell Frankie I want it painted . . . any color but yellow."

A heavy thunderstorm greets Sonny when he arrives in Catania five days later on the day of Laura's funeral. The winds outside the tiny parish church howl in mourning as Father Basanti celebrates the Solemn Requiem Mass within. On the altar the don's casket is flanked by his son's and daughter's; just a few pieces of their bodies rest inside. Alfonso delivers a moving eulogy for his old friend, Don Belfiore. Sonny is numb during the church ceremonies; his grief at the graveside is exceeded only by that of the family, who weep and wail as the three coffins are lowered into the ground. He follows Sicilian custom and throws a handful of earth in Laura's grave. Her untimely death has made a deep chink in Sonny's emotional suit of armor.

A low solitary bell tolls as the mourners leave the cemetery. The thunderstorm has finally broken, and its angry clouds part to let the first rays of the sun shine through. Sonny stands motionless, still staring down at the dirt that barely covers the top of Laura's white coffin. A shadow from the cross on the church steeple falls across the open hole. Sonny looks at the symbol of God, then up at the invisible force it represents. "How in the hell could you take her? Why would you take her? For what reason?" He raises his voice bitterly. "Laura never did nothin' to you or nobody else. She was innocent . . . she even prayed to you every day." Now Sonny starts his battle with God. His volume is louder than that of a politician addressing a rally. "For thousands of years you been connin' men . . makin' 'em believe in your power. You have no power." His face contorts with fury. He shouts at the top of his lungs, "I'm gonna get even with you, God. I'll get even, you phony bastard." He shakes an angry fist at the sky, bellowing, *"I'll get even if it's the last thing I do."* The bodyguards on the perimeter of the tiny graveyard are at a loss during this emotional outburst. They've never seen their boss lose control before.

Angelo starts over to Sonny, but Alfonso pulls him back. "No . . . I'll go." When Alfonso reaches him, Sonny is in a trance. He doesn't feel the touch of his godfather's arm on his sleeve; Alfonso's voice sounds far away. "Santino, you can't get even with something you can't see. Come, let's go."

Sonny turns slowly, shaking. "I will get even, Alfonso . . . I will."

"O.K., Santino, but get even with the real people . . . the ones who killed Laura. Come on." Alfonso leads Sonny from the grave.

As they walk to the car, Sonny realizes that he got carried away. He stops. "I meant what I said back there, Alfonso. I'm gonna get even . . . even if it takes the rest of my life."

The old man says gently, "I understand, Santino. I've been waiting to get even with one man for twenty-five years." This time Sonny is too absorbed in his own vendetta to ask Alfonso about his. Before they get into the Fiat, Alfonso says, "Are you O.K. now, Santino?"

Sonny takes a deep breath. "Yeah . . . I'm O.K."

"You feel like talking to the dons tonight?"

"Bet your ass . . . I gotta find out who did this, Alfonso."

His godfather pats his arm. "Good . . . because you are going to avenge the death of Don Belfiore for us. We're all too close to it. We may make a mistake. The dons will be at the villa at eight."

His godfather sits at the head of the dining room table where the men are gathered to solve the riddle of the deaths. Sonny notices that

Alfonso has aged. The tragic loss of his close friend has taken its toll on him. Sonny now asks the question that has obsessed him since the moment he first learned of Laura's death. "Who do you think ordered the hit, Alfonso?"

The old man shakes his head wearily. "We don't know, but we are certain it has something to do with the communists." He hands Sonny a tape and some pictures. "Those are the hit men for the communist party."

As Sonny studies the names and faces, one thing disturbs him. "Some of these guys are Italian . . ."

Alfonso nods sadly. "Yes, Santino, it is possible we have been betrayed by one of our own blood. Since you left, the communist party has gotten stronger in Italy."

"That's nothin' new, Alfonso. They're gettin' strong everywhere . . . South America, Viet Nam, Europe." Sonny begins to explore the enigmatic fatality. "Alfonso, how many people knew where Don Belfiore was that day?"

Don Lo Manzo says quickly, "Nobody . . . we never knew he was taking his family on that holiday."

Don Salino, a wizened old man with angular features, confirms that. "Don Belfiore was shrewd. He was always careful not to let anyone know where he was going."

Sonny looks straight at him. "He wasn't too careful, Don Salino . . . he's dead." Sonny continues frankly, "Only someone close to him would have known he was in Switzerland that day." This statement heightens the tension in the room. Sonny leans forward and looks down the line of dons on either side of the table. His eyes search the eyes of each man.

Don Lo Manzo speaks up, "Well, whoever it is, the murderers must pay for this. An example must be made so that the communists know what a grave offense it is to kill a don." He adds emphatically, "Santino, you must avenge the death of Don Belfiore and his family."

"I've already accepted that command, Don Lo Manzo." Sonny's jaw tightens firmly. "It will be an honor for me, and I want every man here to know the deaths will be avenged if I have to sell everything I have to do it."

When the dons have gone and Sonny is alone with his godfather he says, "I got a strong feeling one of those guys betrayed Don Belfiore."

Alfonso is shocked. "You mean one of the dons?"

"I dunno, could be a bodyguard."

Alfonso says skeptically, "I have learned to respect your psychic powers, but . . ."

Sonny insists. "I'm gettin' my headache right now. . . . My feelings are never wrong, Alfonso . . . sometimes I wish they were. I just know that whoever pulled the strings to blow up that plane was with us in that room today." Sonny starts looking for clues to the riddle. "Alfonso, Don Belfiore was very powerful. Who took over his operation?"

"Well, there were three different operations . . . three different dons took over."

"What are they?"

Alfonso thinks. "Let's see . . . Don Respeni took over the international deals."

"How much was that worth?"

"Oh . . . fifteen million. Then there's the narcotics traffic, that's worth probably twenty-five or thirty million."

"Who got that?"

"Don Salino."

"What else, Alfonso?"

"Just the shipping lines. Don Lo Manzo got them. They're only making two million a year. It was one of Belfiore's newest businesses." It looked like Don Salino was the most obvious candidate. He had the best motive for the hit so far. Alfonso throws up his hands. "Look, Santino . . . not one of these men would have done it . . . we fought side by side against Mussolini. Don't waste your time . . . it couldn't be one of these men."

"What if it was, Alfonso?"

The old man stops, his face rigid with determination, "If I ever found out it was one of them, I would execute him personally. I'd even let you watch, Santino . . . and you've never seen me lift a finger to anyone." He dismisses the hypothesis. "Forget it . . . there's no way . . . a communist made that hit."

Sonny now gives Alfonso some of his own philosophy. "I've seen greed do strange things to men . . . some will do anything for money." He reiterates firmly, "I know the betrayer was here today. I'm gonna get him if it takes the rest of my life."

Gino and Carlo fly back to the Bahamas to help Sonny in his search for the betrayer. They are aware that this is a double vendetta for him. He is avenging the deaths out of respect for Don Belfiore and love for Laura. The Sicilian bodyguards are instrumental in locating some of the communists who were involved in the hit. One by one the suspects are kidnapped and brought to the Lucky Ace. All are thrown in a basement room at the Lucky Ace as soon as they arrive. Each day they are taken out and interrogated separately. Alfonso has sent Ivan Diotov, a former Russian agent now working with the Italian police, to help question the communists. Sonny doesn't want to torture the men. He only wants them to tell him who the assassins are. The suspects are wired to a polygraph to determine whether or not they were connected with the hit in any way.

Sonny and Ivan work the communists over for two weeks, finally piecing together information that leads to two more suspects, Guido Di Luca and Salvatore Cavale, a pair of Italian hit men. Guido is cross-examined first. The standard set of questions is asked, establishing a pattern; the graphs show nothing irregular. Sonny studies the beady-eyed man wired to the machine. He has a strange feeling about this one. When Ivan gets to the crucial question, "Did you have anything to do with blowing up Don Belfiore's plane?" Guido answers, "NO!" but the needle jumps erratically on the paper.

Sonny takes over. "Who were your partners in the hit?"

Guido protests, "Hey, I wasn't involved."

The needle jumps again. Sonny walks around the hit man's chair. "Ya know, Guido, I could use a man like you in my organization. If ya tell me who did it, I'll let you live and you can come work for me."

The Italian protests again, "I told ya. I had nothing to do with this killing."

Sonny motions Ivan to remove the man from the room. As soon as he's gone, the bodyguards descend on Sonny. Richie says heatedly, "He's the one, Boss. . . The needle went crazy, I saw it . . . let's kill him."

Angelo agrees, "Yeah, let's knock him off right here."

Sonny says calmly, "In the first place I'll do the knockin' off, but it's not time. If I kill him now, I'll never find out who ordered it . . . that's the one I really want. Bring in the other scum." Angelo gets Salvatore. After Ivan wires him up to the machine and the pattern is established, Sonny asks the crucial question. The needle goes wild when the man answers that he was not involved in the hit. Sonny asks, "Do you know Guido Di Luca?"

"No." The needle jumps again.

Sonny leans over him. "Come on, Salvatore, Guido told us that you and him were involved in the bombing."

Salvatore goes crazy. "That son of a bitch lied. I wasn't involved."

Sonny knocks him in the head and sends the hit man's chair flying backward. He picks Salvatore up by the hair and bangs his head repeatedly against the tabletop. "You're a fuckin' liar. Guido told us you did the killing."

Salvatore gasps the words out, sticking to his story. "No, no . . . I didn't do it . . . I didn't do it."

Sonny flings him to the floor. "Throw this scum back in jail."

Sonny knows these men are Laura's executioners, but to confirm his findings, the next day, he calls in the other communists. While they are wired to the lie detector, Sonny asks each one to look through a two-way glass and identify the two hit men in a lineup. All the men claim they don't know Guido and Salvatore, but only three out of fifteen are telling the truth. Sonny has positive proof that he has found the men who killed his beloved Laura.

Even though he now knows who performed the actual hit, Sonny still is unable to find out who ordered it. Despite harassment and beatings from Sonny and his bodyguards, the two guilty men refuse to divulge the information. They were trained well, too. Sonny knows that if a communist did not give the command, then the order must have come from within the family. He comes up with a surefire way of getting the men to talk. One afternoon he has all of his prisoners loaded on the Lucky Ace's four-engine prop plane and takes them on a little trip. They land at dusk on a small unsettled island in the Bahamas. The full moon shines brightly overhead, illuminating the abandoned military airstrip Sonny uses to make pickups for his smuggling operation. The bodyguards hold their machine guns on the handcuffed communists as Gino and Carlo remove the men's blindfolds.

Sonny roughly pulls the two accused hit men out of the group. He shouts above the engine's deafening roar, "If you tell me who ordered the hit, I'll spare your life until I can check it out." There is no response. "If you're telling the truth, you can go free." Still no answer. Sonny grabs Guido violently and holds his head inches from the nine-foot steel propeller spinning at 2500 rpm's. Sonny growls, "Who ordered the hit?"

The frightened man screams, "I don't know . . . I swear it . . . I never knew who gave the order . . ." Sonny can see the truth in the man's eyes and releases him. Terrified, the man slumps to the ground in a heap.

Sonny walks over to the second assassin, who informs him with a cocky smile, "If you kill me, you'll never find out who did it." His attitude frustrates Sonny; he knows Salvatore is right, but has a foolproof way of getting at the information. He turns and grabs Guido again and with one swift movement throws him backward into the spinning propeller. The horrified communists watch their comrade's body disappear with a loud poof as the blades chew up his flesh and bones. Three seconds later all that is left of Guido is some blood splattered on the front of the plane. Sonny grabs the second murderer by the hair, jerks his head back, and pulls out a knife menacingly. "I'm gonna cut your nuts off and rip out your heart . . . tell me who ordered the hit!"

Salvatore is not so cocky now. He sinks to his knees in fear. "Don Lo Manzo ordered it."

Sonny slaps him. "You're lyin'. Why would Don Lo Manzo do this?" Sonny feels greed could not be his motive for the hit. Don Lo Manzo took over the least profitable of Don Belfiore's businesses, the shipping line.

The trembling man looks up fearfully. "Don Belfiore . . . he wouldn't work with the communists. Don Lo Manzo would . . ."

Sonny brings his knife up to the man's throat. "You're lyin' . . . no don would help the communists."

The man pleads, "Wait! Don't kill me. I'll tell you why. They wanted the shipping lines to transport arms for the Red Brigade. They were willing to pay Don Belfiore ten million. He told them to get out of Europe and stay out, so the communists went to Don Lo Manzo . . . he accepted the money."

Sonny sees now why Don Lo Manzo didn't mind taking over such a small operation . . . it had big potential. Sonny presses his blade against Salvatore's protruding Adam's apple. "How did you know where the don was?"

"Don Lo Manzo set him up for us. He was running the shipping line while Don Belfiore was away . . . he trusted Don Lo Manzo . . . they were friends. That's how we knew when the plane was leaving Switzerland."

Sonny orders Salvatore to stand up. He comforts him. "Stop cryin', I'm not gonna have you shot." He turns toward the other communists and spits at them. "You scum . . . you're not powerful enough to challenge the Sicilian Mafia." His eyes burn with hate. " An innocent girl died on that plane. Here is what happens when you kill for no reason. This is for Laura." He swings around, grabs the guilty hit man, and hurls him into the prop. Instantly Salvatore's body disappears. Sonny shouts his warning to the others. "When you go back to Europe . . . we want it spread all over the world . . . You don't fuck with the Sicilian Mafia . . . or Santino Gino Genetti."

As soon as he gets back from the island, he holds the men at the Lucky Ace, telling them he has to clear their passports before they can leave. Sonny doesn't want any one of them alerting Don Lo Manzo that he's been discovered. He calls Alfonso to let him know that it was Don Lo Manzo who betrayed them. At first Alfonso refuses to believe him, but one week later he calls Sonny back to Sicily. On the ride from the airport to Catania, Alfonso tells him they have gotten tapes of wiretaps which prove that Don Lo Manzo was working with the communists. Sonny also learns that the dons are gathering later that afternoon to celebrate Don Lo Manzo's new position.

When they get to the hillside where the party is being held, Sonny spots the treacherous don. "There he is, that son of a bitch. Angelo, gimme your piece." The bodyguard hands him the gun, but Alfonso grabs Sonny's arm.

"You have been a good soldier, Santino, but your part in the vendetta is finished." Sonny nods in understanding; he is aware of the full meaning of Alfonso's instructions and gives Angelo his piece back.

Peals of spirited laughter and strains of Sicilian music highlight the joyous festivities of the men who are there to honor Don Lo Manzo. After the traditional meal is over wine continues to flow as they congratulate the don and embrace him warmly. Sonny has been watching Alfonso closely during the celebration. The old man appears to be enjoying himself and even gets in line to hug Don Lo Manzo, but when he finally reaches the don, Alfonso spits in his face. "Communist pig!" Gino and Carlo rush forward to grab the traitor and pin him down on the table; two other bodyguards aim their schipettas at him.

There is an outburst of protest from Don Lo Manzo and the others. "What are you doing?" "He's gone crazy." "Have you lost your mind?"

Alfonso yells, *"SILENZIO."* His cold, dark eyes speak as strongly as his words. "This man has betrayed us to the Italian communist party. Here are the tapes to prove it. He murdered Don Belfiore."

Don Lo Manzo defends himself desperately. "I had to kill him . . . he was a fool. You're all fools if you don't work with the communists . . . they're more powerful than we are."

Vincenzo steps forward. "Don Lo Manzo, have you forgotten how the communists brutally murdered your own brother? I was there the day they pinned him in the wall. You have brought dishonor to him and to all of us." The lieutenant spits in Lo Manzo's face.

At this point Alfonso takes a long knife from his coat and holds it before the treacherous don. "The time has come for you to pay for your crimes." He nods, and four men hold the squirming man while Gino and Carlo pull down his pants. As the sharp blade glints in the setting sun, Alfonso grabs the don's balls and makes his first cut. Lo Manzo squeals in horrifying pain as blood gushes from his groin. Alfonso warns, "Let this be a lesson to all who are disloyal to the Sicilian Mafia."

The perfidious man yells in agony as Alfonso finishes the castration. The fierce old soldier coldly takes the bloody genitals and stuffs them in Lo Manzo's mouth. Then with a sharp, quick stab, he rips open the dying man's chest. Alfonso reaches into the bleeding gash and rips out the heart. Holding it up for all to see, he shouts his proclamation over the hills of Catania: "This is what happens when a man betrays his vows and becomes a soldier of satan." Then he flings the heart back at the body and asks for a towel. "I want to wipe the pig's blood from my hands." Alfonso removes his bloodstained shirt and throws it on the table. "Burn this with the pig." Gino and his bodyguards pour gasoline over the body, then ignite it. As the roaring flames consume Lo Manzo's corpse, the other dons file past and spit contemptuously on their betrayer. When the last one leaves, Alfonso says, "We can go now, Santino." Sonny does not answer. He puts a hand on Sonny's shoulder. "I said we can go now, Santino, it's over. Don Belfiore can rest in his grave."

Sonny says bitterly, "Laura never did anything to deserve that grave, Alfonso . . . it will never be over for me . . ."

Alfonso agrees. "I know how you feel, Santino . . . my vendetta will never be over until I find that one man."

Now Sonny finally asks, "Who is that man, Alfonso?"

The old man's eyes grow hard. "Adolf Hitler."

"Hitler?"

"A vendetta is against someone who's hurt you directly. Did Hitler do something to you personally, Alfonso?"

The old man nods solemnly. "He gave a direct order to his friend Glutman to kill my sons."

"How do you know?"

"The Allies confiscated Nazi documents . . . the order was there, Santino. I saw it with my own eyes."

One thing doesn't make sense to Sonny. "Alfonso . . . Hitler's dead. He burned up."

"They never found the body." He looks at Sonny. "I have feelings like you, Santino . . . I feel it inside . . . Adolf Hitler's alive, and I will find him."

At the airport Alfonso boards Sonny's jet to say good-bye. "Santino, why don't you sell everything and stay here? All the men love and respect you. We are your family . . . you belong with us." There is a strain in the old man's voice as he speaks. "You can only be young and brave so long, Santino. I won't be here much longer . . . I would feel better if I knew you were here to take my place. You are my son, Santino."

Sonny is moved by his godfather's speech "I haven't made my mark yet, Alfonso. I'm planning a big scheme." He thinks a second. "But you know . . . you know, I would stay here if I could be a don."

"There would be none better . . . but I cannot change the code of the centuries. . . . Even with my influence I cannot do that for you, Santino."

Sonny looks in the old man's tired eyes. "I respect that code, Alfonso, but I hope you understand that when this plane takes off, I am a don . . . I'm the don of many . . . I am the boss of my operations . . . I can't give all that up."

Alfonso nods slowly. "I understand, Santino . . . *Buona fortuna centianni.*" The two men hug firmly. Sonny looks out the window as the old man walks laboriously down the steps of the plane. As the jet takes off, Sonny and his godfather watch each other until they are both out of sight.

The first thing Sonny does when he gets back to the Bahamas is to call a board meeting with his executive staff and his attorneys. When he gets to the conference room, Gregory hands him a file. The operation's financial statement is on top. Sonny hunches over the sheet of paper, staring at the figures, tapping his pencil in a crescendo of frustration. When the point finally breaks, he shouts angrily at Richie, "What the fuck's wrong with you . . . can't you do anything right?" He hurls the pencil at him. "These pencils aren't worth a shit. . . . Get me some pens."

Richie hands Sonny some ballpoints and returns to his post by the door. He whispers to Angelo, "Boy, the boss sure is jumpy these days."

Angelo whispers back, "Uh . . . yeah, he's been that way ever since Laura died. Yesterday he got mad at me 'cause the limo's white walls were dirty. He made *me* clean 'em. That's not *my* fuckin' job!" They both look at "the boss" sprawled out in his armchair. Sonny now weighs over 250 pounds, but this fat man's disposition is far from jolly. He points to a word. "What's this?"

Gregory looks over his shoulder. "That's capital return."

"What the hell is that thirty million?"

"Well, Sonny, that means . . . over a period of years that'll be our capital return. It's . . . "

Sonny throws the papers down. "What the hell you talkin' about, 'years' . . . how many fuckin' years? I might be dead next year."

Gregory says calmly, "Well, we're depreciating the equipment and—"

"Fuck the depreciaton of the equipment. I don't pay taxes down here . . . You're stupid, Gregory."

Sonny looks up from his papers at the men in the room. "I can't read or write but I know figures . . . and I don't like the ones I see here. You guys are jackin' off on my time. I told ya over a month ago to get off your asses and get these scams going." He addresses his top CPA. "Swanson, what's happenin' with our hotel chains?"

Dr. Benjamin Swanson rises and walks over to a movie screen. Sonny insists on seeing slides of everything they talk about. The first one projected shows a portion of a freeway in Kearney, Nebraska. Swanson points to land on either side of the highway. "We can buy this right now for five hundred dollars and sell it in three months for twenty thousand."

Sonny is skeptical. "How's it gonna go up that much in three months?"

An identical slide comes up with one addition—Swanson puts an X on the freeway. "The state has approved this location for a new on-and-off ramp. Every hotel chain in the country will be bidding on these four corners when it's made public. If we buy that land now, we're sure of getting back forty times our money." Sonny demands impatiently, "If ya know that, why the hell haven't we bought it already?"

"You told us we had to check everything with you first."

Sonny flings the pens at him furiously. "You idiots can't use the measly brains you have. How do ya know for sure they're gonna build here?"

Swanson recovers, and another slide appears. "Sonny, this is a copy of the federal zoning permit approving it." The slide changes. "And here's a list of three hundred other locations where new on-and-off ramps will be built in the next six months. If we buy up the land around them, I figure we can make five hundred thousand a month." Swanson smiles. "I guess it pays to have friends in Washington, doesn't it?"

Sonny replies caustically, "Friends, shit . . . it's those tapes I got on that bastard of a highway commissioner." He scowls at the men. "You guys seem to forget I got tapes on everyone. My tapes are my friends—I trust everyone else like a fence. O.K., get goin' on that immediately." He shouts, "Richie, gimme a bottle of wine," then turns his attention to Gregory. "What about our securities deals, Gregory?"

The distinguished bank executive stands next to his slide—a list of obscure company names. "Sonny, stock in these companies is selling right now for about a dollar a share. In two months they'll be thirty dollars a share."

Sonny raises his hand and stops him. "Hold on . . . hold on. How do ya know they're gonna go up that much?"

A list of blue-chip companies appears on the screen. "These corporations are in the market for additional companies. We can find out in advance which ones they've decided to purchase by wiring their executive offices and conference rooms. We buy stock in those small companies at a dollar, and as soon as the merger is announced, the price on the exchange will shoot sky high . . . then we sell. It's that simple. By my estimates we can make a million a month."

Sonny snaps his finger and points at Joe Anadaro, a sixty-year-old, ultra-conservative New York attorney sent by Don Giuseppe. He's counseled Mafia families all his life. Sonny likes him and trusts his judgment above the others. "Joe, what legal problems do we have here?"

The lawyer replies cautiously, "Well, we do have to watch out for the Securities and Exchange Commission . . . ."

Sonny challenges him. "Why? We're not workin' directly with any of these corporations, and we're not gonna have the same shell corporations purchase more than one company. They can't subpoena the records of an offshore corporation . . . Even if they could, before they even got wind of it, we'd have sold them already."

The Harvard graduate looks at his illiterate boss in admiration. "You're right, Sonny, you'd be perfectly safe with this scam."

Sonny growls at his other executives. "Then why the hell didn't any of you guys think of that? Goddam it . . . what the fuck am I paying you for? Shit, I gotta do everything around here." He pours a glass of wine and takes a sip, then spits it out. "This tastes like piss." He stands and hurls the glass against the wall. "A five-million-dollar hotel and I can't even get a decent bottle of wine. Richie, get me another bottle . . ."

Richie protests, "But, Boss, that Valpolicella's from your private stock."

The executives watching the incident cast apprehensive sideways glances at each other. Sonny becomes unglued and shouts at the top of his lungs, "But I don't give a shit . . . do what I tell you!" Richie hurries out. Sonny sits down again, his face reddened with anger, his schizophrenic frenzy apparently over. The personality of the Wall Street wizard now takes charge of the madman. Sonny touches his pen to his lips and looks to the men. "Hey, wake up . . . I didn't bring you guys here to stare at each other. Who's next?"

Allen Collins stands. He takes his place next to the screen, which is now illuminated by a slide of some swampland. "Sonny, we can buy this land in the Florida Everglades for about twenty dollars an acre. We can sell single lots for eight hundred and ninety-nine dollars. But first we have to build——"

Sonny leans forward and interrupts him. "You drunk this morning, Allen? What kind of fuckin' joke is this? How the hell you gonna build anything on a goddam swamp?"

Allen calls for the next slide; a beautiful ranch house with manicured landscaping appears. "We can build this house by putting in ten thousand dollars worth of landfill, then——"

Sonny flies off the handle. "Jesus, Allen, the Bahamas sun musta fried your brain. We're gonna put in ten grand and get eight hundred and ninety-nine back . . . I'm gonna lose over nine thousand dollars. Hell, Angelo's got better ideas than that!"

Allen tries to explain. "Hold on, Sonny, we only have to do that to two or three lots. We'll fix up the houses to look like a showplace and send brochures in the mail: 'Vacation is Sunny Florida . . . this beautiful land is yours for just eight hundred and ninety-nine dollars.' We'll make a fortune selling through these brochures. Most people will never even come down to see the land."

Again Sonny turns to his trusted attorney. "What are the risks, Joe?"

The lawyer thinks. "Well, the only real offense would be mail fraud, but as long as you don't mislead them in the circular, you're protected. If anyone should come down to inspect the property, you'd have to tell them the truth. . . . It sounds like a viable idea to me, Sonny."

Sonny takes a sip of wine. "Good, Allen . . . and make sure the brochures show pictures of people fishin', water-skiin', Mom, Dad, and the kids . . . all that shit. . . And be sure you have figures showing how much they'll save by buyin' the lot and spending their vacation in Florida instead of stayin' at some hotel for two weeks." He leans forward dramatically. "You gotta have bait for the people to bite on . . . you guys better remember that." He sits back again. "O.K., Jeff. What'd you find out about that insurance scam?"

"I came up with——"

Before he can answer, Sonny turns to R. B. Agnew, the other attorney in the room. "And what about my escrow agreements, Agnew? Shit, according to the statement there's only two hundred thousand in escrow. What the hell's wrong? . . your men jackin' off, too?" The lanky attorney says, "There are a lot of escrows pending that should come in next week. Writing insurance on that many people can increase a company's volume from two million to fifty million in just a few months. We'll sell these companies for twenty times what we paid for them. The corporation that purchases them will never know what kind of clients they have until a year later when it comes time to pay the premiums. I need about half a million dollars to buy two more companies . . . I can do it with a Bank of Sark check or a Telex guarantee . . ."

Sonny looks at Anadaro. "What do you think about that?"

"Sonny, as long as the offshore company makes the purchase, there's no problem." The attorney shakes his head in amazement. "Writing life insurance on dead people . . . that's one of the best scams I've ever heard of."

Sonny says, "Yeah, we get our money up front, and they can collect theirs from the ghosts." He gets up and stands before the men. "From now on I want you guys to stop sittin' on your brains. If you see a chance to make money . . . take it . . . I need all the cash I can get for my Big Scam. We're gonna continue with our monthly meetings here, but from now on I want a weekly phone report. We'll do it on Mondays. That'll give you guys the weekend to get your ass together. Linda will always know where I am. It'll be your responsibility to get a hold of *me*. I don't care if I'm in China." Sonny looks down at his watch and hollers at Angelo across the room, "What the hell's wrong with you, Angelo? I told you to tell me when it was twelve. I got a broad waitin'."

"Uh . . . I didn't think I should interrupt you, Boss."

Sonny turns abruptly and pokes him on the shoulder. "Shithead, you're not gettin' paid to think . . . you're gettin' paid to take orders. I want you to follow them . . . understand?"

Angelo shrugs, "Yeah . . . O.K., Boss."

Sonny is not more than twenty feet down the hall when Richie's beeper from Central Control goes off. The bodyguard picks up the nearest house phone. He listens, then tells Sonny, "Hold on, Boss,

Control reports those guys back there are talkin' about you."

Sonny heads back to the conference room. His blood is boiling by the time he reaches the door and flings it open violently. Sonny's madman surfaces again as he points an angry finger and warns loudly: "I thought I told you guys to stop sittin' on your asshole brains. You got better things to do than shoot the shit." He glares at the group. "Look, if you guys got something to say, say it to my face. . . . except for Joe. You all could take a lesson from him. He only talks when he's supposed to . . ." He looks at them in contempt. "But then, he's Italian."

Angelo says, "Boss, the broad's waitin'."

"What the hell are you botherin' me for, Angelo? Can't you see I'm talkin' to these knuckleheads?"

"Uh, Boss, I thought you . . ."

"Never mind, Angelo." Sonny slams the door shut, and the executives start packing their briefcases. Jeff whispers to Gregory, "You really have to be careful what you say around here."

Gregory agrees as they walk out. "Yeah, it wouldn't surprise me if he had the urinals bugged."

With the profits from 120 corporations and his scams, Sonny's operation is soon taking in six million dollars cash a month. Half of that goes to the Sicilian Mafia, but no one else knows how much money he's actually making. Because of Sonny's sophisticated accounting system and skillful manipulation of his executives, he's able to keep everyone in the dark. By this time Sonny has become a bona fide magnate in stocks, real estate, insurance, and banking; the financial press christens him "the Wall Street Wonder Man." It is an undisputed fact that every corporation Transcontinental Casualty purchases becomes a gold mine in a few months. Except for sex, the only letup Sonny has from all the pressure is on the golf course, but he even conducts some business there. An excellent player and con man, his clients usually lose the game and their money. One afternoon the boss is out practicing by himself for an upcoming match with an industrialist from Miami. The four bodyguards with him know better than to disturb Sonny, especially after a bad shot. All of their walkie-talkies are plugged into earphones so that the static doesn't distract him. Sonny is in the rough, figuring out his next shot, when Angelo approaches. "Uh . . . Boss . . . sorry to bother you, but Jeff Wolfman's comin' out to see ya."

Sonny looks up—even the sound of his executive's name is vexing. "What the fuck does he want?"

"I don't know, but he said he hadda talk to you. He'll be here in a couple a minutes." Sonny goes back to lining up his difficult shot. He starts his backswing just as Wolfman turns his golf cart onto the fairway between the tee and the green. Sonny sees him in his peripheral vision.

When he hits the ball, it rolls only thirty feet away. He throws down his club in disgust. Just then Jeff pulls up. "Having a good game today, Sonny?"

The boss explodes, "I was till you got here. What the fuck you want, Jeff? You're messin' up my game."

Wolfman gets out of the cart and follows Sonny to his. "I have to talk to you about something important. It couldn't wait."

Sonny opens a 7-Up, spraying it all over Jeff. "What the hell is it, Jeff?" He throws the executive a towel.

Wolfman brushes off his jacket, then explains, "Sonny, you know we're really doing well in our real estate and stock companies. You have a sensational reputation on Wall Street."

"Yeah . . . so what? You come out here to tell me somethin' I already know, idiot?"

"No . . . my point is that we have enough capital now to actually go into the casualty line. There are some charters available in the states we could pick up if we act by tomorrow. We could become a legitimate insurance conglomerate."

Sonny taps some dirt from his golf shoes. "Look, Jeff, the legitimate thing is fine for someone who's gonna be around ten or fifteen years, but I gotta get in and get out." He looks up and begins lecturing Jeff like a child. "I told you. We're in the paper business. We're sellin' nothin' but a piece of paper with a lotta promises, Jeff. It don't cost much to type up. To get legit takes all kinda permits, and then the government comes in and takes a big piece. Right now I don't have no partners . . . that's why we're staying like we are."

Jeff stands firm. "I still think it'd be a good idea."

"Stop thinkin' so much about that and start thinkin' about those tombstone policies you're supposed to be workin' on . . ." Sonny starts walking to the ball.

Jeff gives it one last try. "Well, I guess we're gonna blow this deal then . . . the companies are up for grabs now . . . "

Sonny turns around, exasperated. "Lemme ask ya somethin', Jeff. It's gonna cost me to buy these companies, right?"

"Well . . . sure, but . . ."

"O.K., for every dollar that I put in, can I get two back . . . tomorrow?"

"No, Sonny . . . there are regulations . . ."

Sonny stops him loudly. "THANK YOU, JEFF . . . now get back to work . . . And Jeff, next time ya have something to discuss, bring it up in the meeting . . . I don't ever wanna see your face out here again."

Jeff Wolfman leaves puzzled by his boss's reluctance to give up the con games. What the executive doesn't know is that Sonny has a master plan for the future and needs more than a king's ransom to pull it off. Equally important to the scheme, though, are the confidential papers and tapes Sonny personally files away in the Operation BS drawers in his cabinet. These are the most significant element in his Big Scam.

Soon after his conversation with Jeff, Sonny's ability as a con artist reaches new dimensions. He begins linking his name with Jimmy Hoffa's to clinch business deals. A close friend of the union boss, who was in prison at the time, Sonny tells developers that Hoffa is his father-in-law, leading them to believe that his proposals have the monetary backing of the union. With this sham, Sonny makes enough money to form 30 additional corporations, bringing the total to 150. His employees now number 6,000. Still, he continues to branch out into a wide variety of enterprises: the manufacture of dune buggies, a nationwide chain of used car lots, auto financing and repossession, and ski resorts. He never has trouble financing his purchases. Whenever Sonny has a problem with a banker or anyone else, Angelo uses the magic phrase that works every time: "Let's take 'em for a plane ride."

Sonny's business isn't the only one that's booming at this time. The American economy is also on the upswing as a result of the escalated war in Viet Nam. Sonny, who is constantly on the lookout for ways to finance his Big Scam, comes across one quite by accident. He is looking for someone to head his international security and asks Richie if he knows anyone who would fit the bill.

The bodyguard thinks a second. "There's one guy. He spent a lot of time in Nam as a Green Beret. He was decorated four times."

"Is he still there?"

"No, he's a mercenary now . . . he's in Africa someplace."

Angelo asks, "Uh . . . what the hell's a mercenary?"

Richie explains, "They're legal assassins. They get paid to kill."

Sonny thinks out loud. "A mercenary . . . good." He says to Richie, "Can you get a hold of this guy?"

"I think so . . . he should be in Chicago soon. He goes with a cousin of mine."

"Good. Get him down here as soon as you can. I wanna talk to him right away. If it's gonna be after next week, tell him to come to Miami." Sonny has just purchased a big hotel with a Bank of Sark check and is setting up plush offices there.

Not more than a month goes by before Tony Pettizini is in Miami, sitting in front of Sonny's desk. The mercenary's battle scars are not on his body but in his eyes. He is a man who's seen more than murder on the battlefield. Tony's face is hard and has been exposed to the sun too long, but the leather skin gives him an attractive, rugged look. He carries four guns with him at all times . . . two on his ankles, one at his side, and another behind his back. The last two have special upside-down holsters. With the side holster there is no telltale bulge of a weapon because the barrel of the gun, not the butt, is under the armpit. Sonny feels that this soldier's training must have been as thorough as his own. It had to be . . . Tony was still alive. Sonny offers him some wine as he pours some for himself.

Tony declines. "No, thanks . . . I don't drink. I like to keep sharp."

"That's good, I like that attitude." Sonny puts down his glass. "I'm gonna get right to the point, Tony. I want you to work in my organization. I need another chief bodyguard."

"Bodyguard? I've never done that before."

"You've done it for yourself and your troops. You can do the same thing for me . . . by the way, do you know the Sicilian dialect?"

Tony gives a slight laugh. "No . . . man, Sicilian's a bitch unless you're familiar with it. I speak Italian. Most of the other languages I speak are Far Eastern 'cause of my time in Nam."

"How many languages do ya speak?"

Tony enumerates them on his fingers. "Tagalog, Japanese—three dialects—French, Spanish, and Vietnamese . . ."

"You speak fluent Vietnamese?"

"Yeah."

"How'd ya like Nam?"

Tony's eyes brighten. "I loved it. I wasn't a mercenary there. I was a Green Beret."

"Richie told me . . . he said you were decorated four times. . . That's somethin', isn't it?"

Tony says scornfully, "What the fuck's a medal get you? That and a dime will buy you a cup of coffee."

Sonny studies Tony's face for his reaction to the next statement. "You came close to court-martial, too, didn't ya?"

Tony replies frankly, "I never followed orders blindly. When I came across a village with one Viet Cong, I blew everybody up . . . women and children, too."

"Is that why they threw you out?"

"No, sir . . . I wasn't really thrown out . . . I resigned. I shot one of my lieutenants in the back. Some gooks started to come at us and he ran, so I shot him. The Green Berets got a tough reputation. They didn't want anyone to know they had a yellow belly in their outfit, so instead of court-martialing me, they gave me the option to resign." Tony adds, "I was just as glad. I got tired of blowin' up a bridge one day and watchin' them rebuild it the next. Besides, that's a money war over there. I didn't see any point in gettin' my ass shot at for the guys makin' the big bucks."

"What was that in?"

"Narcotics."

"Ya mean it's cheaper over there?"

"Shit, yeah . . . it's half the price if you pay in dollars."

Sonny's genius begins to scheme. There was a fortune waiting for him in the battle zone. "Can you get the stuff outta the country?"

Tony teases him. "I could, but you couldn't."

"Why not?"

" 'Cause I know the bush. I know how to get it once it's hidden. The gooks would eat your Italian guys up like spaghetti."

Tony has made Sonny's decision for him. "How would you like to head up my international security operation?"

Tony says, "Sounds good."

Sonny stands and walks the room. "If you work for me, I got a very strict rule." Sonny stops. "All my men have prepaid contracts on 'em. Even if I die a natural death, they all get killed."

Tony smiles. "I've lived with death all my life, I'm not worried about that. What concerns me more is how much I'm gettin' paid."

"What'd you make last year?"

Tony says proudly, "Thirty-five grand . . . that's the top a mercenary gets."

"You're gonna start at forty. If this narcotics deal gets pulled off all right, you'll get a raise."

Tony stands and shakes Sonny's hand. "You've got yourself a new chief bodyguard, Mr. Gibson. I'd like to have some details on your operation and your men."

Sonny says to his personal bodyguards, "Angelo, you and Richie fill Tony in on our procedures. He's gonna be workin' with us." He turns back to Tony. "I want you to go to Nam right away and get your contacts together. I wanna know how much we can bring in on the first run."

"I can leave the day after tomorrow."

"Good." Sonny has a final instruction for his new employee. "And Tony, one more rule. When I give an order, you will follow it blindly . . . There's no options here."

Within a few weeks Tony has the operation running in high gear. The drugs are bought in Southeast Asia with black-market Vietnamese currency, picked up by Tony's hand-picked men and taken to the Philippines. There Sonny's contacts see that the drugs are shipped to the States and the Mafia families who handle distribution. For his part Sonny receives twenty percent of the $100 million profit.

At this time in his life, Sonny is riding high. His companies are operating in the black, and all of his scams are making money. Just when Sonny is at the pinnacle of his financial power, his political pawn in the Bahamas has some bad news for him. He breaks it one afternoon on *The Lucky Dolphin.* The Bahamian sips a rum and Coke leisurely; his host is already on his second glass of wine. Sonny is anxious about this meeting; he's always called the shots before. "What's up? . . . What'd ya wanna see me about?"

The official puts down his drink and takes a paper from his inside breast pocket. He hands it to Sonny. "I want you to have a copy of this. It's the new law just passed by Parliament."

Sonny takes it and tosses it toward the bar. "I told you I can't read. . . . What's it say?"

"It says, basically, that the government will soon be taking ninety percent of the gross of every casino down here; the operators will keep ten percent."

Sonny is livid. "What the hell you talkin' about?"

"I'm talking about keeping money in the Bahamas, Mr. Gibson. You and all of your Italian friends on Paradise Island have taken plenty of money out. Your heyday down here is over. You have six months left to operate under the present law."

Sonny's blood pressure starts to rise. "What about our fuckin' deals?"

"Indeed, what about them? I don't see any development going on down here."

Sonny glosses over this. "The contractors have been holdin' me up. Let me have an extension on the law, say a year . . ."

"I can't do it, Mr. Gibson. I've done enough favors for you already . . . I even kept Meyer Lansky out because you told me to. Now, since Sicily refused him admittance, he's making a lot of noise about the Mafia in the Bahamas."

Sonny is bitter. "That's why I had ya keep him out . . . he's no fuckin' good."

His contact continues, "You haven't helped the Bahamas, you've hurt us. . . . The American government will not give us any more money for new facilities unless we turn over our records about your operations."

Sonny grabs him by the lapels, "If you give one piece of paper to them about my business, you're a dead man . . . "

There is a frightened silence from the black. Sonny lets him go. Finally, he stands. "You're welcome to stay down here, Mr. Gibson. Truthfully, I hope you do . . . you bring in a lot of business. But if you stay, you'll have to abide by the new law. Either turn over ninety percent to the government, or our own people will run your casino."

Sonny laughs. "If you let your niggers run things, in ten years ya won't have a soul comin' down to the Bahamas. Gamblin's gonna be legalized soon in Philly, New York, or Atlantic City. We only need a few more years to get the right bills pushed."

"That's all speculation . . ." The Bahamian starts toward the launch, "There's nothing more to say, Mr. Gibson. You have the alternatives . . . you have six months to make your decision."

As soon as the black man leaves, Sonny starts thinking about selling the Lucky Ace. It has been a good scamming quarters, but Transcontinental Casualty and the Bank of Sark have given him far more profit with fewer headaches. Even with the sale he wasn't leaving himself "hotel-less." Sonny always believed people should have a pleasant place to stay while they're being conned, and his Hollywood hotel and his ski lodges around the country would serve that purpose well. There was one other fact to consider. Sonny was no philanthropist. He wasn't in the casino business to give ninety percent of his profits to the Bahamians. He began making plans to move the base of his operation from the Bahamas to California.

One night during dinner, while he's going over the financial statements of prospective buyers, Angelo comes over with the phone, "Uh . . . it's Vito, Boss. There's some kinda trouble in the casino. . . ."

Sonny takes the call, "Yeah, Vito . . . what's the problem?"

"Sonny, there's a guy down here from Austin, Texas . . . he's dropped about twenty-five grand. He wants another fifty, and he's causin' a stink."

"What's his credit look like?"

"Yesterday his bank showed he was good for it. We always check when someone's losin' big, just like you told us." The pit boss adds, "He's not a smart gambler, Sonny, he's just a dumb Texan . . . we didn't even have to use a mechanic on him."

"Give him twenty-five more, Vito . . . . That's it."

Sonny has not even finished his cannoli when Vito is on the line again. Sonny sighs impatiently, "What's wrong this time?"

"That same guy dropped the twenty-five grand before I finished puttin' in his marker. He wants a hundred now."

"A hundred! Nobody gets that kinda credit. Tell him no, but if his bank wires the money down here tomorrow, he can have it then."

"All right . . . but he says he's very close with a friend of yours and wants to meet you . . . Sonny Gibson."

"What's his name?"

"Bert Hodges."

"He's bullshittin' . . . who's he say he knows?"

"Your union man . . . Bill."

"Well, Linda's out . . . I can't get a hold of Bill now." Sonny pauses, he doesn't want to offend a friend of Bill's. "Awright, Vito, I'll be down to talk to this guy."

When Sonny gets to the craps table, the 250-pound loser swaggers over to him. He's dressed in a cowboy outfit with an oversized hat; a solid gold steer's head buckle accents a belt holding up his baggy pants. Hodges's thumbs in the two front loops point insolently at Sonny. "Listen, Gibson, I'm good for the hundred grand . . . I got the biggest cattle ranch in Texas." He blusters, "Hell, you'd think you'd wanna lend me money. What kinda business you runnin' down here anyway, boy?"

The gambler infuriates Sonny, but he says, covering nicely, "It's a casino business, Mr. Hodges, not a loan company. . . ." Sonny continues obligingly, "But if your bank can wire you the hundred grand, I'll be happy to give ya credit in the morning."

The fat man's loose cheeks puff out indignantly. "That's bullcrap . . . I need the money now. I may not be hot in the morning."

Sonny negotiates. "I'll tell ya what. Call Bill, and if he says you're good for it, I'll give ya the hundred grand tonight."

The man stammers, "Well, uh . . . I don't have his number on me . . . it's in my office in Austin. Oh hell, Bill and I went to college together."

"I'm sorry, Mr. Hodges, I can't do it."

The rancher lunges at Sonny, "You lily-livered son-of-a . . ."

Angelo pounces on the Texan and pins him against the wall. "Can I crush the cowshit outta him, Boss?"

Hodges is screamining, "Get this gorilla off me, Gibson . . . I'll sue you for assault, boy."

Sonny stands in front of him and says plainly, "I'm not your boy, Hodges. . . You're leavin' tonight. I expect my fifty grand tomorrow mornin'." He turns to Angelo. "Mr. Hodges is checkin' out. Have one of the guys make sure he gets outta his room."

Angelo pulls the Texan by his collar. "Come on, cowboy . . . you're goin' back home on the range."

The next night Sonny is hurrying to an important meeting with sheik who's contracting him to blow up an Iraqi pipeline. On the way to the penthouse with his bodyguards, Sonny notices something peculiar. "What the hell is that?" Two black waiters are wheeling room service carts toward them. "The kitchen's closed after nine o'clock . . . where the hell are they goin'?"

Angelo draws his .357. "Hey . . . you guys . . don't move."

When the blacks pull out guns, Sonny jumps away and hits the panic button. A piercing siren goes off alerting Central Control and the rest of his employees that he's in danger . . . instantly every door locks. Angelo shoots at the men, who are firing at him and the three bodyguards. One of the blacks gets hit. The other turns and runs; Angelo takes off after him. Sonny yells, "Don't kill him, Angelo. . . ." As part of the security system, doors hidden in the walls seal off all the hallways. One of them slides in front of the black man now. He claws at it like a trapped animal trying to escape. When Angelo reaches him, he hits the panicked man across the neck with his hand. The assassin slumps to the floor. By this time, all of the other bodyguards are at their emergency stations. Twenty have arrived at the trouble spot as back-up. Three men are on the roof with high powered, fluorescent-scoped rifles. Every twenty feet, floodlights illuminate the grounds brighter than a night game at Yankee Stadium. The rest of the men patrol the area with orders to shoot running suspects in the legs.

Back in the hall, when Sonny is out of danger, Angelo calls Control, "We've got the guys . . . send the doc with an ambulance."

The doctor and medics arrive in ten minutes and examines the two men. The one Angelo hit is dead . . . the blow broke his neck. Angelo apologizes, "Uh . . . I didn't mean to kill him, Boss."

"Don't worry, Angelo, the other nigger's still alive."

Meahwhile, Richie has been searching the bodies. He pulls out two wallets, "Hey, these guys have local IDs."

Sonny pounds the wall, "Only our fancy contact would be stupid enough to hire niggers."

The doctor says with concern, "Better get this one to the hospital."

Sonny pulls Angelo aside, "Go with the doc in the ambulance. Find out from this nigger who paid him. . . . After he talks, make sure he don't get to the hospital."

"You want me to shoot him, Boss?"

"He's already shot . . . just kill him with your bare hands."

The hallway doors slide into the walls again and the blacks are carried out on stretchers. Sonny and his men gather in the office to unravel the mystery of the hit. The boss is raising hell with the body-guards. "How the fuck did those niggers get that cart . . . two dumb fuckin' niggers got in my hotel . . . on my floor! What the hell do I pay you guys for . . . you're supposed to be my security." Sonny is in such an insane fit, none of the men even attempts an explanation

An hour later, Angelo rushes into the suite. "The nigger talked, Boss."

"Who the fuck paid him, Angelo?" Sonny is sure it's one of the dons he conned for Alfonso.

"Uh, the cowboy, Boss. Hodges."

"That fuckin' asshole! After I gave him credit."

"Uh . . . can I get rid of him Boss?"

"On one condition, Angelo . . . make it look like an accident."

Four days following the hit, Richie comes into the office at 9:30 A.M. Sonny looks up, "Where's Angelo? He was supposed to be back today."

"He's in bed . . . he got back late last night, but he has good news." Richie holds up an Austin paper.

Sonny asks, "What's that say?"

The bodyguard paraphrases as he reads, "It says: Wealthy cattle rancher, Bert Hodges, was found frozen to death in the meat locker of his slaughterhouse on Monday. Police investigators rule the death an accident. They believe Hodges was working there late one night and went into the freezer without his safety key."

Sonny smiles, "That is good news . . . good work on Angelo's part too. That was a smart way of doin' it." Sonny puts on his golf cap, "This will certainly improve my golf game. I won't have to be lookin' for any more niggers takin' pot shots at me." Linda stops him on his way out. "All the RSVP's are in for the closing-night party, Sonny. There'll be about a thousand coming down."

"Good . . . Call John and tell him I'm flyin' to the States tomorrow morning . . . I wanna leave by ten. We'll be turning right around and coming back with two passengers." Over the years Sonny had played host to billionaires and kings, but these are his most important VIPs to date. He's never flown to pick up any guest personally . . . until now.

Linda's surprised, "You're picking them up yourself?"

"Yep . . ."

"They must be special, you've never done that before."

"They are, Linda . . . they're very special."

The day Sonny lands at Indianapolis airport is atypical for the fall. Chilling winds whip spirals of snow over the huge banks that line the runways. Flurries of the season's first storm are already blanketing the ground as Sonny parks his plane near the commuter terminal where his passengers are waiting. Tony gets out to escort them on board. From the window of the cockpit Sonny can see his mother's thin, delicate frame approaching, followed by Pops in his familiar checked overcoat and pork-pie hat. This trip is an event for his parents. Pops' idea of a vacation is being off from work for two weeks, but his wife has finally talked him into a real holiday. Soon they leave the bleak Indiana weather behind for the warm, tropical Bahamas sunshine.

Immediately after takeoff Sonny goes back to the cabin to relax with his folks. His mother exclaims, "This is such a beautiful plane, Sonny. Is it yours?"

"Yep . . . I have another jet and two prop planes, too."

His mother enthuses admiringly, "And you're a pilot . . . You're so talented, Sonny."

Pops, a practical man, has a question for his son, too. "How can you afford the planes and the hotel and everything? You didn't buy them with your insurance commissions."

Sonny evades the question expertly. "In a way I did, Pops, I used my money and made a lot of smart investments . . . I have a few partners in the hotel business." He switches the focus back to his father.

"How's the agency in Indianapolis doin'?"

"Fine, fine . . . in fact I have to go back in a couple a days."

Mrs. Gibson scolds him, "Now, Pops, you really don't . . ." She complains to Sonny, "He's working himself to death in that job . . ."

"Now, Nina . . . they need me . . ."

Sonny intervenes. "You know what, Pops? I have a proposition for ya. I think you should leave the insurance business . . ."

"What? Why, you were the one who convinced me to go into it."

"I know, but I have another proposition for ya . . . I bought a used-car chain as an investment."

His father is amazed. "Are you the Sonny of 'Sonny's Auto Sales'?"

Sonny laughs. "Yeah, Pops, that's me."

"I saw that advertised when I went to Columbus last month. . . You must be be doing well . . . it was all over the TV."

Sonny says, "Yeah, we're branchin' out even more . . . I wanna open a lot in Indianapolis, and I want you to run it."

His father's first reaction, once again, is negative. "Oh, no . . . what do I know about used cars? I couldn't do that."

Nina's excited. "Pops, I think you'd be good. . . . You sell a lot of insurance . . . you could sell cars."

Sonny prods him. "You're a helluva salesman, Pops. . . . You don't have to give me an answer now."

His father sighs. "All right, you two . . . I'll think about it."

After they settle into their spacious suite, Sonny shows his folks around the Lucky Ace. They are impressed by their son's success; the hotel is booked solid, and the casino is jammed with people. The staff have all been alerted to be on their best behavior whenever Mr. and Mrs. Gibson are close by, but one of the hookers insists on meeting them. Rita thinks buttering up Sonny's parents can get her Donna's job. She comes up to the Gibsons and gushes, "I just wanted to tell ya what a great son ya got here . . . now I know where he gets his good looks."

Sonny doesn't give his parents time to respond. He glares at her sternly. "Don't you have some work to do, Rita?"

The hooker says meekly, "Uh . . . I have to be goin' now, but it was nice meetin' ya."

When Rita has gone, his mother says, "What a lovely girl." She turns to her son. "With all these pretty women down here, you'd think you could find one to settle down with. You're not traveling anymore. Don't you want to have a family someday?"

Sonny lies. "I do, Mom, but I'm looking for someone who's interested in having a home . . . these girls down here are only interested in their careers."

"Oh? They work for you?"

Sonny thinks fast. "Uh-huh . . . they're in public relations, Mom."

Sonny starts walking them toward the restaurant for dinner. His mother is curious. "What is that, public relations? What do they do?"

"Well, Mom . . . they talk to people . . . show 'em a good time . . . make sure they wanna come back to the Lucky Ace again."

His mother turns to her husband. "Pops, wouldn't that be a good part-time job for me? I love people . . ."

His father throws Sonny a sideways glance. "Yes, Nina . . . we'll check into public relations for you as soon as you get back to Indianapolis."

When Mr. Gibson goes home, his wife stays on, enjoying the sun, shopping, and indulging in a little gambling. Sonny's men fix the roulette wheel so that she always wins; the thrilled look on her face when it stops on her number is worth a million dollars to her son. He loves this simple woman and would do anything for her, but knows he can never do enough to repay her for the sacrifices she made in the days when they called him "Stinky." Today both of his parents are unaware of his underworld connections. He's done everything in his power to keep that from them. Mother's intuition is not that easily deceived, however. On the plane ride home Mrs. Gibson asks more questions than Sherlock Holmes.

Orion's starry belt twinkles in the crystal-clear sky the night Sonny takes off for Indiana. Fifteen minutes into the flight his mother comes up to the cockpit. Sonny tells his copilot, "Why don't you go on back and relax, John. We'll put it on automatic till we land."

"Roger, Sonny."

Mrs. Gibson sits in the vacant seat beside her son. Her eyes roam the instrument panel in awe. "This all looks so complicated . . . I would never in my born days be able to fly an airplane."

Sonny says, "It's like anything else, Mom. Once you learn, it's easy."

She points to the panel in front of her. "What are all those dials for?"

"They're like the instruments you have in your car—a speedometer, gas gauge, temperature—but there are more things to measure in a jet."

She looks up at the ceiling of circuit breakers. "My, what do these do?" Sonny patiently explains each one to her, but knows she hasn't come up to learn how to fly. At last she says casually, "Sonny, why do you always have that big man with you? By the way, he was very nice to me . . . "

Sonny replies quickly, "Was anybody not nice to you, Mom?"

"Oh, no. They were all wonderful, especially Rita. . . . But why do you have that big man with you all the time?"

Sonny answers honestly, "Well, I'm in the casino business,

Mom . . . some people get mad when they lose. He's my security man."

Mrs. Gibson continues tentatively, "Sonny, I've seen some articles in the paper about you. They say you're involved with the Mafia." Her brow creases in concern. "I hope you're not . . . those people are very treacherous . . . "

Sonny shrugs it off. "No, Mom. The papers always push that junk. You remember the Loganno kid?"

She nods. "He was such a quiet boy."

"Nick's a good friend of mine. His grandfather's very powerful, so I get a lotta heat." Sonny can see she needs more convincing. "Look, I'm in the insurance business, Mom. You really think I could be involved with somethin' like the Mafia?"

She's swept with relief. "No, Sonny, I don't, but I've been praying to St. Jude for you, like I did for your Uncle Pietro."

Sonny tries to control his anger. "Mom, I don't wanna hear about that crap . . . keep your saints. They belong to you, not me. I gotta be honest with you . . . the almighty dollar is my God . . . that's why I'm successful."

She says softly, "I'm still going to keep praying for you Sonny." There is a moment of silence, then she turns to him anxiously. "Son, look me in the eyes and tell me you're not involved with the Mafia."

He looks straight at her. "Mom . . . really . . . I'm not."

She hugs him. "I'm so glad . . . ," then breaks the embrace. "You know, when I was just a little girl in Sicily, your Uncle Pietro was involved. He believed in the violence. My brother thought he would be a great soldier." Tears fill her eyes, "He was only twenty-two when he died . . . shot in the back on our doorstep." She starts to cry. "I don't want anything like that to happen to you."

Sonny dabs her tears with his handkerchief. "Don't worry, Mom . . . nothin' like that's gonna happen to me." He lifts up her chin. "Who'd want to kill an insurance man?" His mother smiles, and Sonny turns his attention back to the controls. He thinks about his Uncle Pietro, who might have been a powerful don had he lived, and wonders why he was killed, then erases him from his mind. "Look, Mom . . . I know you're tired . . . why don't you go back and rest?"

"All right, but before I do, I'll bring you some coffee."

Sonny smiles. "You'll be the prettiest stewardess I ever had."

After Sonny drops his mother off in Indianapolis, he turns right around and heads back to the Bahamas for the final fling at the Lucky Ace. Four jets with full crews are chartered to shuttle his 1,000 guests, mostly union officials and insurance executives. The overflow 800 are put up at two neighboring hotels on the island. The party lasts for three days. All of the cocktail waitresses are outfitted in revealing red satin costumes. Special events during the day include fifteen minutes of free gambling at 2:00 P.M. No one has to pay if they lose, but the maximum bet is $100. In the evening the celebration starts at eight with dinner and a show in the main room at eleven. A different name headliner performs each night. Afterward, of course, the casino is jammed with gamblers until daybreak. The closing weekend is a resounding success, and Sonny is sure to let everyone know that they can have the same good time in the States at his new hotel on Hollywood's Sunset Strip.

After the bash one of the jets flies him back to New York. On the plane Sonny meets a pretty brunette stewardess named Vickie. He's attracted to her and tells Tony to set up a date as soon as they land. Vickie likes the idea of dating the boss . . . she accepts.

Before they go out, Vickie makes a stop at her apartment in Queens to change clothes. She asks Sonny to come up to meet her three stewardess roommates. One of them, Theresa, is standing on the third-floor balcony above, watching the long black car pull up in front of the building. Its arrival is an unusual event for the sleepy middle-class Queens neighborhood. The only time Theresa has ever seen a limousine is at a wedding or a funeral. She's surprised when Vickie gets out. Theresa calls to her, "Hey, whose car is that?"

Her roommate shouts back, "It's mine . . . I just bought it." This typical sarcastic remark annoys Theresa. If she had her way, Vickie would be thrown out, but they need her share of the rent. Theresa continues to look down with curiosity as four men get out of the car behind Vickie. Only one goes inside with her.

Upstairs Sonny is superficially polite to his date's two blonde stewardess friends. His attention is drawn to the shapely dark-haired girl on the balcony. A sun-worshipper, Theresa is enjoying the warm rays of the Indian summer in a bright yellow bikini that shows off her curvy figure to its best advantage. Vickie yells to her, "Theresa, come in here a minute, will you?" She puts a territorial arm around Sonny's waist. "I want you to meet my friend. Sonny, this is Theresa Ruggiero." When they're introduced, the Italian girl looks at him more with inquisitiveness than attraction. She wonders what kind of a man has a limousine. The brunette gets more than Sonny's interest . . . he's hot. Sonny would love to get that body in bed with him and Vickie. His date announces snootily to Theresa, "Sonny's taking me to the Plaza tonight . . . he has a suite there." She turns to him. "I have got to get out of this uniform . . . I won't be long. I'm just gonna put on something simple." Vickie leaves the two alone to make small talk.

Theresa starts awkwardly, "Are you staying at the Plaza, Sonny?"

"Yeah . . ."

"You're not from New York, then."

"No. I'm from Indiana."

"What were you doing on Vickie's flight from the Bahamas?"

"I was there on vacation."

"That's nice . . ."

Sonny takes a step closer to her. "You're a very beautiful woman, you know." Theresa is oddly excited. Her first reaction to this fat man, physically, was negative, but he has a sexual magnetism she can't deny. "How long have you and Vickie been friends?"

Theresa says quickly, "Oh, we're not friends . . . just roommates. We fly together sometimes."

Just then his date reappears in a purple satin pants suit with a rhinestone chain belt. As usual she has a matching bag. Vickie spins around. "How do I look?"

Sonny whistles. "Good enough to eat."

She says suggestively, "Mmm . . . I'm hungry, too." Vickie kisses him, then grabs his hand and waves to her friends on the way out. "Bye-bye girls . . . don't wait up for me."

Sonny and Vickie indulge in their private orgy all night, and when he drops her off the next day, he goes back upstairs hoping to see Theresa again. Sonny is disappointed that he won't be able to make any moves on her. She has left on a flight to Chicago, so he makes a date with Vickie for the following Thursday.

On the way to the airport Angelo cracks, "I've always wondered what those stewardesses look like without any clothes on."

Sonny says snidely, "Put the broad upside down and split her legs, they all look the same . . ."

"Uh . . . but Vickie musta been really good. You're seein' her again."

"A woman's only as good as the man she's with . . . I never had no bad pussy yet, Angelo." A few minutes go by. "Uh . . . I guess the plane's gonna be in the shop soon, huh? . . . We're gonna get free plane tickets now?"

"What the hell you talkin' about, Angelo?"

The bodyguard reminds him, "Well, you never fuck for nothin', Boss . . . why are you seein' Vickie twice?"

"I want somethin', Angelo . . . I wanna bang her girlfriend . . . that Theresa. Vickie'll be sure and tell her how good I am . . . . Next time I'll get 'em together."

That is Sonny's plan, but one week later, just before they land at Kennedy, he tells Angelo, "I got a funny feelin' this broad's not gonna be here tonight."

"Uh . . . no one would dare stand you up, Boss."

"It's not that, Angelo . . . I dunno . . . maybe I'm wrong."

Sure enough when Sonny gets to the apartment, Vickie's not there. Richie comes back to the limo. "The other broad said she wasn't home."

Sonny says anxiously, "Was she a blonde?"

"No . . . she had dark hair . . ."

Sonny shouts to Angelo up front, "Call Vickie."

The bodyguard turns questioningly. "Uh . . . she's not home, Boss."

"Just do what I tell ya."

Angelo turns in a minute. "It's ringin', Boss."

Sonny picks up the rear phone. Theresa answers. "This is Sonny Gibson, Theresa . . ."

Her heart jumps involuntarily. She's surprised at this reaction. "Hello, Sonny . . ."

"Where the hell is Vickie?"

Theresa says half-truthfully, "She had to leave on a flight."

"Did she say anything about our date?" Theresa holds back the other half of the truth. "Not really." Vickie had told her roommate to give Sonny her number in Chicago. She'd be waiting for his call at ten o'clock. "Where are you, Sonny . . . your chauffeur was up here a few minutes ago looking for Vickie."

"I'm downstairs."

"What?"

"Yeah . . . I'm talkin' to ya from the limousine phone. Go on the balcony, you'll see."

He says to Angelo, "Go outside and wave to Theresa."

When she comes out, the giant waves furiously at her. She laughs. "I never had anybody call me from a car."

"Well, why don't you come down? I have reservations at a place near here. Did you eat yet?"

"No . . ."

"Would you like to have dinner?"

Theresa accepts eagerly. "I'd love to have dinner . . . I'm starved to death. I'll be right down."

Within minutes Theresa is downstairs, dressed in a black miniskirt and a tight gold sweater. The thin knit stretches over her full breasts, hugging the erect nipples delectably . . . she has no bra on. Richie opens the door of the limo for her, then takes a seat right in front of them next to Willie. Angelo is sitting next to Georgie, the driver. Sonny introduces her to the men.

"I didn't know you had company."

Sonny says flatly, "I don't . . . they won't be joining us."

She asks, "Where are we going?"

"Villa Penza in Little Italy. The owner is a friend of mine."

"I've heard of that place . . . it's very expensive."

He pats her knee. "Don't you worry about it . . . order anything you want."

Theresa looks around the luxurious limo. She rubs her hand along the leather seats, then points at the TV. "Hey, does that work?"

"Yeah . . . but you can't get 'Bonanza' on it . . . it's a computer."

"Why do you have a computer in your car?"

"It prints out the financial reports of all my companies."

This gets her attention. "What kind of companies?"

"Mostly I'm in the insurance business, but I have a lot of other companies as investments."

"Oh . . ." She would never admit that Sonny's wealth impresses her, but it does . . . Theresa was raised in abject poverty.

When they get to the restaurant, Theresa skips through the menu like a kid in a candy store. "There are so many goods things here, I can't decide."

"I told ya . . . order whatever you want."

She looks up at the patient waiter. "O.K., I'll have a large pepperoni pizza, a plate of spaghetti with meat sauce, and a Tab."

Sonny looks at her. "You want all that?"

She says innocently, "You said I could. . . "

"I don't mean you can't . . . it's just . . . isn't that a lotta food?"

She shakes her head firmly. "Not for me."

He laughs and turns to the waiter, "Bring it to her . . . I'll have linguine and clams, and bring us a bottle of your best Sicilian wine."

While they wait for their order, Theresa asks, "Where do you live most of the time, Sonny?"

"I have a house in California and one in Florida."

She breaks off a piece of piping hot Italian bread.

"Which one is your wife in?"

Sonny looks at her evenly. "Neither . . . I don't have a wife."

"Are you pretty serious about Vickie?"

"Why do you ask?"

"Oh, I'm just curious." She says cagily, "Vickie thinks you'll probably marry her . . ." Theresa knows this will drive a man away fast.

Sonny replies without hesitation, "As a matter of fact I'm not gonna see Vickie anymore . . . I don't like bein' stood up . . ."

"I don't blame you." She sighs. "Poor Vickie . . . she told me what a great time you two had together." Theresa butters her bread and continues to fish. "Have you ever been married?"

"Nope. I'm not gettin' married either."

"Why not? You have something against marriage?"

Sonny says seriously, "No . . . I'm married to my business, Theresa . . . it's my wife, my woman, and my blood."

The waiter arrives with the wine just in time to end this discussion. He shows Sonny the label, and when it's approved, he pours some of the burgundy liquid for him to taste. Sonny swishes it into his mouth, swallows, then motions the waiter to fill their glasses. Sonny toasts, "To Vickie . . . without her we wouldn't be here."

She laughs. "To Vickie." As Theresa sips her wine across the table in the pale glow of the candlelight, he can see that she is uniquely beautiful. Dark, loose curls frame her long exotic face. Classical Roman features give Theresa the look of a graceful statue that could easily have adorned the Temple of Venus. During dinner Sonny watches incredulously as this beautiful girl devours the last piece of her pepperoni pizza. When the steaming plate of spaghetti is placed in front of her, he teases Theresa. "When you said you were starving, you weren't kiddin'. I bet it'd be cheaper to clothe ya than feed ya."

Theresa defends her appetite. "So . . . I like to eat." She twirls her spaghetti and smiles. "From the looks of things so do you."

Her remark hits home. At first Sonny is insulted by the reference to his weight, but then he laughs. "Yeah, I do . . . but you eat like ya never seen food before."

Theresa confesses, "To tell you the truth, except for what I get on the plane, I really don't eat very much. I can't afford to." She confides, "Sometimes it gets so bad, we have to steal food."

Sonny is amazed. "Ya mean you don't make enough money to buy food?"

"Nope . . . and it's either buy food or pay the rent."

He's curious. "You must make a pretty good living as a stewardess . . ."

"I'm afraid we're not exactly at the top of the pay scale, and Vickie borrows a lot of money from me. Her father's rich, but she's trying to make it on her own. I don't mind giving her the money . . . I'm used to not having any."

Sonny is intrigued by her honesty. "Where are you from?"

In between mouthfuls of pasta she tells him, "I'm from Queens. My father's a barber. We never had much money and things are really slow now. But, papa always said as long as you're honest, you're rich." She takes a swig of wine. "What's your father do?"

Sonny says soberly, "My Pops was a poor dirt farmer. He lost the farm when I was just a kid."

Theresa can tell by his voice this part of his childhood meant a lot to Sonny. "You liked that farm, didn't you?"

"I loved it there. I hated the people in the city." He sniggers. ". . . Still do."

"Why don't you buy a farm now if you liked it so much? You can afford it."

This is getting too personal for Sonny. No woman's ever asked him these questions. He picks at the thick layer of wax on the Chianti-bottle candleholder to avoid her eyes. "What's the point, Theresa, you can't ever go back. I don't think I'll ever have that kind of freedom again."

She philosophizes, "Papa always said freedom was a choice. Men make their own prisons . . ."

Sonny looks up and smiles, "I'll bet you were his little girl."

Theresa shakes her head. "Me? Hell, no. I didn't have time for that. I was the oldest girl. I hadda take care of all five kids. I joined the airline just to get away."

She laughs. "I guess I always liked being in uniform. It saves me the trouble of standing in front of my closet trying to decide what to wear."

Sonny smiles. He is enjoying the company of this witty, unassuming girl; she's a refreshing change of pace from the hookers he has to keep happy and the snooty women he romances for profit. Just as he is feeling comfortable with Theresa, Richie approaches the table. "Boss, you wanted to know when it was ten-thirty."

Sonny waves him away, annoyed. "O.K., so now I know . . . get the check."

The bodyguard pays the bill, and the waiter deposits a doggie bag in front of Theresa. She says sheepishly, "I hope you don't mind . . . I ordered leftovers."

On the way home in the limousine Sonny begins his play for Theresa, teasing her sexually. At first she is embarrassed in front of the bodyguards, even with their backs turned, but Sonny's expert advances soon obliterate all thoughts of them. Her nipples stiffen as his fingers flutter across them. His passionate kisses send a thrilling tingle down to her womanhood, which he's massaging sensuously through her wet panties. By the time they reach Theresa's building, she's on fire, but Sonny says to Richie, "Make sure Theresa gets upstairs okay."

She's stunned. "Uh . . . don't you want to come in? All of the girls are gone . . . we can be alone . . ."

Sonny is all business now. "Can't . . . I have a meeting at eleven-thirty tonight. I'll give you a call tomorrow." She's speechless and horny. Richie opens the door. Theresa gets out. Sonny calls the bodyguard back. "Hold on a minute, Richie. Georgie, gimme an envelope." The chauffeur hands one back to him. Sonny peels off five $100 bills from a large wad and puts them inside. He seals the envelope and hands it to Richie. "Give this to Theresa . . . she can use it."

The next morning Sonny gets an unusual delivery at the Plaza. The envelope he gave to Theresa is returned to him, with the bills torn up into tiny pieces. This really piques his curiosity. This girl may not have much money, but she has plenty of character. He calls Theresa to ask her out again. She gives him the cold shoulder. "Hello, Sonny. Are you calling to buy another date?"

"What the hell you talkin' about? I'm callin' to ask you out again and to find out what you sent the money back for."

Her reply is icy. "I go out with people 'cause I want to, not 'cause I get paid to . . . "

Sonny informs her just as coldly, "For your information I never gave a woman money in my life. I thought you could use the extra cash." She doesn't answer. Sonny keeps trying, "I'll tell you what . . . how about a nice dinner tonight? I won't give ya any money . . . O.K.? In fact, if it'll make ya feel better, you can pick up the tab."

Theresa says quickly, "Let's not get carried away . . ."

"Will you have dinner with me?"

To her chagrin she finds his charm irresistible and gives in. "O.K. . . ."

"Good . . . we'll try another place on Mulberry Street. The car'll be there at seven-thirty."

The first few minutes at dinner are slightly uncomfortable, but after the antipasto Theresa is herself again. Sonny is more relaxed, too. When she probes him further on his childhood, he is more tolerant. They have a relaxing evening afterward. The limo takes them back to the Plaza for a nightcap. Theresa points excitedly when they get out of the car. "Look at that man, Sonny . . . look at his outfit." Across the street a hansom cab driver dressed in an old English morning coat and top hat is standing next to his buggy adorned with garlands. The horse pulling it has a large white rose behind one ear. She tugs at his arm. "Let's take a ride around Central Park."

"Nah, let's go upstairs."

Theresa's lower lip pouts sadly. "O.K. . . ."

Sonny can't stand to see her so disappointed. He turns to Angelo. "We're goin' for a buggy ride . . ."

Theresa kisses Sonny. "Thank you." She leads him over to the buggy.

Angelo buzzes the other limo. "We're gettin' out here. The Boss is goin' for a ride." To accommodate the bodyguards Sonny has to hire three buggies, which form a caravan with them on their moonlight ride.

Theresa is like a little girl. "I always wanted to do this . . ." Just then one of the hansom cabs filled with his men pulls ahead. She asks naively, "Why do you need those men around you all the time, Sonny? Who are they?"

"They're professional security men."

"Security . . . why do you need security on a buggy ride?"

Sonny cuts her off. "I need 'em . . . O.K., Theresa? Let's not talk about it anymore." He puts his hand under the buggy blanket. "In fact, let's not talk at all. Let's go back to the hotel."

Her eyes glisten with longing. "Yes . . ."

Sonny calls to Angelo, who's sitting with the driver. "Tell the guys we're goin' back."

The bodyguard lifts the walkie-talkie. "Uh . . . the Boss is finished riding now. We're goin' back."

The bodyguards station themselves outside the door of the suite, and Sonny leads Theresa inside. They are alone for the first time. Their eyes meet, and it sparks a passion Sonny hasn't felt since Laura. His lips hungrily devour hers as he kneads her supple breasts. When he toys with the rock-hard nipples, Theresa feels a wanton excitement between her legs that makes her melt in his embrace. Sonny sweeps her up in his arms and carries her into the bedroom, their mouths still fastened. Laying her gently on the bed, he undresses Theresa slowly, savoring each part of her luscious body as it is revealed to him; then his hands travel down the rich nakedness to her silky mound. He parts the dark softness and teases the sensitive bud of her womanhood until she explodes. When her hips stop quivering, Theresa gently guides Sonny inside. Her beautiful face contorts in pleasure as she undulates sinuously beneath him. Sonny climaxes again and again . . . not since Laura has he found a woman so exciting. The lovers ravish each other for hours, until they finally fall asleep entwined in each others' arms. That night was a memorable one for Sonny. With Theresa he was making love instead of making money.

The next morning Sonny keeps the bodyguards out of the room while he and Theresa have a quiet breakfast together, just like any ordinary couple in America. In the light of day Theresa is even more beautiful to him. Her hazel eyes sparkle with the purity of an angel. Sonny sees a lot of his first love in Theresa. It's been a long time since he has sat across the table from someone who makes him feel like a human being. When Sonny is called to the phone, Theresa occupies herself with the *New York Times*. After he hangs up, she points to a front-page story. "This article is all about you, Sonny . . . it says you just sold a big casino in the Bahamas. It also says you work for Giuseppe Loganno." Her voice registers concern. "Do you?"

Sonny's tone is expressionless. "I don't work for nobody . . . I'm my own boss." He asks to see the paper. When she hands it to him, he pretends to read the article, then tosses the paper casually on the couch.

Theresa presses the issue. "Well, is it true? Do you work for Giuseppe Loganno?"

Sonny throws his hands up in disgust. "Hey, I get a lotta heat 'cause I'm half Sicilian. . . . They love to· print this crap . . . it sells papers." He sits down at the table. "So how'd ya like your breakfast? You have enough to eat?"

Theresa is on to his ploy. "I guess you don't want to talk about it, huh?"

Sonny looks straight into her eyes. "There's nothin' to talk about. And Theresa"—his eyes are stern—"don't believe everything ya read."

After that Sonny sees Theresa whenever he is in New York—about twice a month. They always have fun together, and one night at the West Castle, after having sex with four women, Sonny finds himself missing her. He calls and asks Theresa to meet him at his ski lodge in Michigan. She promises to be there in two days.

The night she's scheduled to arrive, Sonny lights a roaring fire in their suite and has a romantic supper laid out. When there is a knock, Sonny rushes over and opens the door with the eager expectation of a teenager. But it's not Theresa . . . it's Angelo. Sonny is irritated. "Whaddya need?"

"Uh . . . Theresa wasn't at the airport, Boss."

"She wasn't there?" Sonny can't believe it. "Maybe the guys met the wrong flight."

Angelo shakes his head. "The guys waited an extra hour, Boss, and they checked . . . there's no other flight comin' outta New York to Detroit."

Sonny wants to get to the bottom of this. "Somethin' musta happened to her . . . Get her on the phone. See where she is . . ." When Angelo dials, Vickie answers.

Sonny gets on the line. "Where's Theresa?"

"Oh . . . she had to go out on a special flight to Chicago." She is catty and cold to him. "By the way, I hope you had a good time with my roommate, Sonny. She told me she went out with you . . ."

"Yeah . . . I did, in fact, she's supposed to be here now."

Vickie laughs bitterly. "Getting back some of your medicine?"

"What the hell you talkin' about?"

"Well, you stood me up the night you first went out with Theresa."

"The hell I did . . . you never showed up or left a message."

Vickie is shocked. "What? You mean Theresa never told you? I left a message with her to make sure you knew I'd be in my room at ten that night."

Sonny's antenna comes up . . . why did Theresa deliberately lie? It was possible she just wanted a date, but Sonny is suspicious by nature and believes she had to have an ulterior motive.

Vickie is still seething. "Why, that little bitch. She said that to—"

Sonny breaks in. "When's Theresa gettin' back?"

Vickie huffs, "I don't know . . . you'll have to call her yourself. Good-bye, Sonny.

He hangs up, angry. "I'm bein' fucked around, Angelo. I dunno why, but I got a funny feelin' this girl's puttin' me on. Angelo . . . that airline she flies for . . . it's union, isn't it?"

"Uh . . . yeah, Boss."

"Get Bill on the line."

Ten minutes later Sonny is talking to Bill. "I want ya to find out if this gal, Theresa Ruggiero, is working tonight. Can ya do that?"

"Sure I can."

"All right. I'm gonna put Angelo back on. He'll give you all the information on her. Call me back if she's not on a flight."

Zabione calls back in twenty-five minutes. "Sonny, I gave them all the information on your friend . . ."

Sonny says anxiously, "She's not on a flight, is she . . ."

"No. As a matter of fact I just talked to her supervisor, and he said she has four days off."

Sonny plots his revenge on her for standing him up. "Well, tell him to give her thirty days off. Can you do that without gettin' her fired?"

"Yeah, I can do that . . . they'll just tell her a complaint came down from the top about her bad attitude and suspend her for a month." Bill pauses. "If we do that, it means her job will be in violation."

"So what's that mean?"

"It means she won't get her Christmas bonus."

This is a surprise extra for Sonny. "Good . . . that'll teach her. She'll really learn her lesson the hard way."

Two days later Sonny calls Theresa, and of course she is home. "What's wrong with you, Theresa? Why the hell didn't you show up? I thought we had somethin' going." It is obvious that she doesn't want to talk to him. A Mafia war over narcotics has broken out in New York, and Sonny's name is in the news again. He'd been accused of conspiracy in several hits for the Loganno family. Sonny's ties to the underworld were beginning to frighten her. Theresa admits, "I was scared. There are stories in the papers about you and Giuseppe Loganno, so I went to the library and read all about you. I know who you are." She continues, upset. "If you'd just told me the truth in the beginning, it wouldn't have mattered."

Sonny is irritated. "What I do is my business . . . but you're really somethin', talkin' about the truth. Just so you know how powerful I am, you won't be working for a month, and you won't be gettin' no Christmas bonus either. It's all over, Theresa. I don't like broads lyin' to me." He slams the receiver down and turns to Richie. "Have this broad checked out. Bug her. It bothers me . . . she's hot one day and cold the next." He says warily, "I smell a Fed."

Theresa slams her receiver down, too. She's sorry she made Sonny mad, but because of him she lost her job for thirty days and won't be able to send any Christmas presents home this year. Theresa, however, refuses to become a victim of circumstance. She picks up the *New York Times* classified section and opens it at random. A large ad catches her eye:

EARN EXTRA MONEY DURING THE HOLIDAY RUSH
APPLY NOW!
MACY'S DEPARTMENT STORE—HERALD SQUARE

Theresa sighs, then puts on her coat, folds the paper under her arm, and heads downtown.

Sonny wants to give Theresa some time to think about what happened. He has every intention of calling her the following week, but a visit from Nick alters his plans drastically. He comes to the West Castle with a message from Don Giuseppe. The two friends sit on a couch between two fluted columns in Sonny's Roman-style den. Nick says, "The don wants you to go to Sicily for a few months, Sonny."

"Why so long, Nick? I got a lotta business here. I don't like leavin'."

"I know, but it's the safest thing with all the subpoenas that are out for you. It'll take that long for our contacts in Washington to pull the strings on this investigation." He adds, "The don knows you didn't make those hits, but at the same time he doesn't want you to prove that. You're gonna take the heat off the other guys and take the rap for a while."

"How long does he want me to stay outta the country?"

"He says ninety days would probably do it . . . six months, the most."

Sonny says point-blank, "I don't agree that I have to go, but I'll do it for your grandfather. When does Don Giuseppe want me to leave?"

"As soon as possible, Sonny."

"O.K. Tell him I'll be on my way tonight." He says to Tony, "Call Linda. Tell her I want her over here in two hours with her bags packed . . . we're goin' to Sicily."

Tony replies, "She's not home, Boss . . . she had a date tonight."

Sonny insists. "Find her . . . beep her."

"She's not gonna be happy about that . . . she's been beeped on the last two dates with this guy."

This provokes the boss. "Well, she's gonna get beeped again . . . she won't have to worry about him, anyway . . . she's gonna be gone for the next ninety days."

"O.K., Boss."

Sonny gets up and pours some anisette. "Speakin' of dates, Nick . . . when's the wedding?"

His friend groans, "Aaa, that's off. Angelina reminded me too much of Maria."

Sonny stops the stream of liquor and turns. "It's off? Hold on, Nick . . . since I've been back from Sicily, you've been engaged six times. . . . I'm gonna grow a beard waitin' to be your best man . . ."

"You'll get your chance, Sonny." He takes the glass Sonny is offering. "This girl I'm going with now . . . she's different . . ." Nick explains excitedly, "This one's an Italian from Buffalo . . ."

Sonny laughs. "I've heard that before . . . Buffalo, Queens, Brooklyn . . . did your grandfather meet her yet?"

"Grandpa said he doesn't want to meet her until the wedding."

"I'm with your grandfather, Nick. I'll tell ya what"—Sonny puts an arm around him— "the day before the wedding, call me. I'll fly from anywhere in the world to be there." He stipulates, "But I'm not gettin' my tux cleaned until then."

Just three weeks later it's Christmas Eve, with no more shopping days till Christmas, and Theresa couldn't be happier. She must have wrapped over 200 packages in eight hours. Brushing a wisp of hair off her forehead, she promises herself that any gift she gives from now on will be in a brown paper bag. Theresa's mind wanders as she takes the scissors and scrapes the blade up the curling ribbon, sending it springing to the center of the bow. She wishes now she had the $500 Sonny gave her. Theresa chides herself, switching sides . . . she's glad she turned it down. He'd offended her with that offer. The next thought is of their passionate night at the Plaza. No lover has ever compared to Sonny. She curls the next strand angrily. Why did she have to be so attracted to him? Theresa sets the finished package aside. A voice on the intercom announces, "Cranston here for pickup." Sharon, the counter clerk, brings it out to the customer. Theresa looks at the next order routinely— a pile of sexy lingerie to be boxed and wrapped. She looks at the order slip . . . the name on it is Gibson. Her stomach tightens . . . could it be? Was Sonny here? Maybe he'd felt sorry for what he had done and this was his way of apologizing. Rich people did strange things like that. Theresa takes special care to wrap each item exquisitely, and when the intercom announces, "Gibson here for pick-up," she says to Sharon, "He's a friend of mine . . . let me surprise him and take it out. O.K.?"

The black girl shrugs. "It'd be a relief to my feet, chile . . . these babies are tired."

Theresa rushes to the small cracked mirror on the wall, primping in anticipation. Her heart pounds as she piles the boxes in her arms and brings them to the counter. "Mr. Gibson?"

Her heart sinks when a short man of about seventy replies, "I'm Mr. Gibson, young lady . . . is that my order?"

Theresa says, bewildered, "Why, er . . . yes, sir." She hands him the packages. "Here they are." She smiles wanly. "Merry Christmas, Mr. Gibson."

Theresa spends Christmas alone in New York; Sonny spends his holiday in Catania with Alfonso. It is a relaxing day off, but on the 26th

Sonny goes back to work. Even though he's based in Sicily, the Mafia Kingpin runs his business with an iron hand. Linda sees to it that his executives phone in their weekly reports and fly in once a month to update him on their activities. This exile is frustrating to Sonny. His staff is forced to take on more responsibility in his absence, and often their decisions are less than judicious. Finally, one day at breakfast, Alfonso gives him the good news. "You're going home, Santino . . . Don Giuseppe called and said it would be safe for you to go back to the States now. The heat's off. They're dropping the subpoenas against the East Coast families."

"Why, Alfonso?"

"One guy is taking the rap for all six hits."

"Who the hell'd they find to do that?"

"A guy by the name of Gino Loducci."

Angelo breaks in. "I know Gino . . . he used to work at the Fulton Fish Market."

This intrigues Sonny. "Why'd he do it, Alfonso?"

"He has cancer, Santino . . . he only has a year to live, but the cops don't know that. The Mafia set it up with Gino that his family would be taken care of for doing this . . . they're even sending his kids to college."

Angelo is still confused. "Uh . . . Gino's no hit man. He pays his parking tickets the next day. How'd he convince the cops he did it?"

Richie answers, "Simple. The Mafia fixed the police ballistics files so the bullets in the victim's bodies matched the ones in Gino's gun."

"Uh . . . why'd they go to all that trouble if he confessed?"

Sonny says, "They wanted to put a freeze on him in case he changed his mind. Our attorneys used the ballistics tests to get the subpoenas thrown out. . . . That's how come we're goin' back to the States. Right, Alfonso?"

"Yes, Santino. I've enjoyed having you here, but I know you want to get home . . . you can leave anytime."

Alfonso is right. Besides being anxious to get back to his business, in Sicily Sonny is reminded of Laura, which makes him think a lot about Theresa. Not that he hasn't been aware of her activities. Each week he received a complete rundown of her schedule and social calendar. He was relieved to know that she wasn't a federal agent as he suspected, but just an average American girl. As soon as he was settled in California again, he called Theresa and made plans to meet her in Phoenix for a reunion.

Before she arrives, Sonny checks himself one last time in the full-length mirror in the bedroom of the suite. He's pleased . . . the expensive new suit hides the extra twenty pounds well. Sonny is now a hefty 270, but his corpulence has in no way diminished his sex appeal. Women still flock to him for his services. No one has ever been turned off by his weight when they're in bed with Sonny. He brushes back his sideburns and goes into the living room. He checks that the champagne is chilled, then calls to Richie, "It's almost time. Light the candles."

The wicks have just started glowing when Theresa knocks on the door. Richie answers. Sonny's eyes brighten at the sight of her standing in the doorway, a portrait of a naughty angel in a dazzling white mini-dress. He waves the bodyguards away. "We're goin' to spend a quiet evening here tonight, Angelo."

"O.K., Boss. We'll be next door if you need us."

When they're finally alone, Theresa runs to Sonny's arms. They kiss feverishly, reviving all of the passion of their first night together. Sonny unzips Theresa's dress, and when it drops to the floor, he slowly slides her sheer lace panties down her firm thighs. The sight of her naked, voluptuous body inflames him so that they never make it to the bed, but satisfy their mutual desire on the floor.

By the time their lovemaking is finished, the candles have burned down to their holders. They eventually made it up from the rug to the closest couch. Theresa now sits there naked, curled up in Sonny's lap. He's opened a bottle of champagne and is in high spirits. He holds up his tulip glass, "To you, my love."

She smiles and clinks her glass against his. After a sip she raises her champagne. "To us . . ." Sonny hesitates. The last time he was part of an "us" was when he was married to Carolyn. Sonny never wanted to be half of a couple again. She frowns. "Aren't you going to toast to that?"

"Let's just toast to our gettin' together."

She shrugs. "O.K. To our reunion." Theresa takes a sip, then runs her fingers through the thick mat of dark hair on Sonny's chest. "Why didn't you call me all those months? I thought for sure you hated me." She adds indignantly, "I was pretty mad at you, too, for getting me suspended."

"I didn't call you because you lied to me, you never gave me Vickie's message, and you gave me back my money . . . I was leery about that. That's what government agents do to avoid entrapment."

Theresa laughs. "You thought I worked for the government? Why would I be a stewardess then?"

"Undercover agents do anything to get information, Theresa. They'd even shovel shit in Macy's window."

She snuggles up to him, dreaming. "If I worked for the government, I'd be a spy . . . I'd be the first female James Bond." Theresa looks up coolly. "Anyway, how can you be so sure I don't work for the government?"

Sonny says playfully, "Oh. . . .I read minds."

She mocks him, "You do not."

"Yeah, I do."

Theresa challenges him, "I don't believe you . . . prove it."

"You were born May 24, 1946 in Queens Hospital. You graduated high school in 1964 and went to work as a receptionist for a stock outfit on Wall Street. One of the bosses almost raped ya in the conference room so ya quit." Theresa's mouth opens in amazement. How could he know about that incident? Sonny continues. "You went to Washington, D.C., and worked in a law firm for two years before you went to stewardess school in 1967. Should I go on?"

Theresa challenges him. "That's all documented."

"I know every phone call you've had for the past year, too, Theresa, and where you went. I know you and your girlfriend dated a couple of attorneys one night. When she insulted them, they got pissed off and left you gals holding the check. . . . I also heard a coupla talks you and Vickie had about me." This embarrasses Theresa. Vickie was very explicit about Sonny's lovemaking in their conversations.

He smiles. "I can get anything and find out anything, Theresa."

She teases him, "Well, if you can find out anything . . . can you find out if room service is open? I'm starved to death."

Sonny laughs and tousles her hair. "It's open . . . it's only nine-thirty, and they close at eleven." He reaches for the menu on the end table. While she looks it over, he snaps his fingers in inspiration. "Hey . . . let's have dinner in Vegas. Then we can see a show later."

Theresa's hunger dampens her enthusiasm a little. "Well, do you think we'll make it? The last show is midnight, isn't it?"

"Don't worry, my love, we'll make it." He taps her nose affectionately. "I'm gonna fly us there myself." Theresa frowns; Sonny is quick to pick up her negative reaction. "What'sa matter? Don't ya trust me? I fly a hell of a lot better than any captain you got on your Mickey Mouse airline."

Theresa shakes her head. "That's not it . . . I just wanted to be alone with you tonight. I don't like all those guys around all the time. Can we go without them?"

Sonny has to give her request some serious thought . . . it's been five years since he's been anywhere without his bodyguards, but Theresa and the moment make him say yes. "Yeah . . . it'll be just us."

She jumps up and throws her arms around him. "Well, what are we waiting for?"

They get dressed quickly. Before they leave, Sonny opens the door. "Willie . . ."

"Yeah, Boss?"

"I'm gonna be in here all night. I don't wanna be bothered unless

I call you guys, understand?"

"O.K., Boss." Sonny turns to Theresa. "Let's go." She follows him through the suite to the bathroom.

"Why are we in here?"

"This is the only way we'll ever make it outta here without a crowd." He opens the window. Sonny always stays on the ground floor of hotels in case a quick exit is required in an emergency. The small opening accommodates Theresa easily, but Sonny just manages to squeeze through. They sneak across the street to the airport and the lovers head for Las Vegas in his jet.

As soon as they tie down at McCarran, Sonny calls a cab and sends Theresa on an errand. When she leaves, he paces the Falcon nervously, waiting for her return. Sonny has never been on the jet alone, and it makes him jumpy. All of his reflexes snap to attention when he hears someone outside. Sonny draws his gun, straining to distinguish the footsteps. He's satisfied that it's the click of Theresa's high heels coming up the steps of the plane, but he doesn't open the door or put his gun away until she gives the prearranged knock. She bursts in, flushed with excitement. "I got it." She hands a small package to Sonny, who takes it and disappears into the bathroom. A few minutes later he emerges in a false moustache and horn-rimmed glasses.

"You think this moustache makes me look mean? I don't wanna look mean."

Theresa laughs. "You could never look mean." She tugs his hand. "Come on . . . I'm hungry."

After dinner Sonny and Theresa hotel-hop on the Vegas strip like tourists from Kentucky. He enjoys her delighted reaction when she hits the ten-dollar jackpot on the nickel slots and comforts her when she discovers she's been fiercely holding on to twenty-two in a "twenty-one" game. Being with this naive girl is an eye-opener for Sonny. Only now, away from his sentinels, does he realize that wealth and power have made him their prisoner. The disturbing thought is quickly brushed aside. For these few hours at least he is a free man.

Eleven-forty-five P.M. finds them standing in the long line with everyone else waiting to see Frank Sinatra's show at Caesar's Palace. Crowds are a new experience for Sonny. He looks around the casino and sees Aldo, the pit boss at Caesar's and a good friend of his, rushing in their direction. Sonny lowers his head, but Aldo passes right by. When the casino man reaches his destination, a roulette wheel about twenty feet away, Aldo berates the operator loudly. "You're not taking another break now. What the hell's wrong with you? This is a Friday, the house is packed."

"But . . . let me explain . . ."

"I don't give a shit about your stories . . . get back to work."

Sonny is fascinated by the incident. His anonymity affords him a much different view of the world. He's never seen that tough side of his friend. Aldo has always been warm around Sonny, but then Sonny doesn't work for him. Most of Sonny's clients think he's a charmer, too, but his employees find him a hard-nosed and demanding boss. Sonny is still lost in these thoughts when Theresa nudges him, giggling. "I'd say that man won, wouldn't you?" She is pointing to an overalled farmer who's whooping and hollering at a nearby crap table. Sonny is about to make a cynical remark about greedy farmers when he stops . . . his stomach drops to the floor. Frank Manadeli is approaching with six bodyguards. The color drains from Sonny's face as he realizes the full impact of the stupid, dangerous thing he has done. In his business traveling without protection is like carrying an unloaded gun—both could cost you your life. Sonny grabs Theresa roughly by the arm and hurries her out of the casino. "Let's get outta here."

As they force their way through the crowd, she asks insistently, "What's wrong?"

Outside he snaps at her sharply, "Look, nothin's wrong . . . but this is the last time you'll ever see me away from my men. Don't ever ask me to do that again, Theresa." Sonny hails a cab, and their free-wheeling night on the town comes to an abrupt, realistic end.

During the plane ride home Sonny notices Theresa is ususually quiet. After he lands in Phoenix and taxis to the tie-down, Sonny goes back to the cabin to talk to her. "Look, Theresa, I didn't mean to yell at you. What happened wasn't your fault. I shouldn't have been so stupid."

She says sincerely, "It was my fault, and I'm sorry. I'll never ask you to do that again. It's too dangerous for someone in your position."

Sonny can tell by her wrinkled brow that something is still bothering Theresa. "O.K. You wanna tell me what's wrong?"

She looks at him innocently. "I was just thinking . . . with all your money and power, you could have any woman in the world. Why do you want to be with me?"

Sonny pulls her on his lap. "Oh, I don't know . . . I guess 'cause you're pretty and nice, you're fun to be with, you're smart . . ."

Theresa breaks in. "So . . . a lot of women are pretty and smart. Why is that special?"

Sonny gives Theresa the look that never fails to melt her. "Only one woman in five thousand is as passionate as you are. Most women can't keep up with me, they're asleep in a half-hour . . . but you . . . you can make love all night." He kisses her gently. "You're very special to me." Still kissing her, Sonny presses a lever on the arm of the seat and reclines it slowly for another session of beautiful, torrid love.

The next day Sonny has to go right back to work. Running his ever-expanding organization and continuing to stockpile money for his Big Scam is a twenty-four-hour job, but Sonny promises to try and arrange his schedule so that he can see Theresa a few times a month.

One afternoon Sam Scorzelli calls Sonny in California. Lou and Paolo Girardi, who run Sam's operation in Gary, Indiana, have been approached by wealthy Las Vegas land developer, Harry Wasserman, to put money into a hotel he's building on the Strip. The Girardis are hesitant about the deal. They don't trust Jews and know nothing about the casino business. Sam has suggested that the brothers talk to Sonny about being their partner. Sonny, who is always interested in making money, sets up a meeting to discuss the possibilities.

The three come in from Las Vegas to Sonny's penthouse office overlooking Beverly Hills. The Girardi brothers, hard-looking men in their late thirties, sit on either side of Harry Wasserman in front of Sonny's desk. The wiry, bespectacled Jewish man says amicably, "I'm happy we finally got to meet, Sonny. I've heard a lot about you. You're a very powerful man in Vegas."

Sonny smiles. "That's true, Wasserman. For your sake I hope you always remember that." He buzzes Linda. "Can we get some coffee in here?"

"Right away, Sonny." She comes in five minutes later with a tray. While the men fill their cups, she says to Sonny, "Are you going to keep that golf date this afternoon?"

"Who's it with?"

"Dr. Jenkins."

"Oh, yeah . . . definitely."

Harry interrupts, "He's a very important man in Nevada."

Sonny replies, "Yeah . . . and a very good friend of mine."

Linda continues, "I sent back the RSVP to the wine auction at the Waldorf saying you'd be there, Sonny."

"Good . . ."

Harry puts his spoon back on the tray. "Are you a wine expert?"

Sonny sets him straight. "I'm an expert on just about everything . . . that's why I'm successful."

Lou Girardi says, "Sonny came from the streets, Harry . . . that's a long way from Beverly Hills."

Sonny cracks sardonically, "Streets, shit . . . my neighborhood was the dumps." He buzzes Linda. "Hold all my calls. I don't wanna be interrupted."

"O.K., Sonny."

The springs groan loudly as Sonny leans back in his large leather armchair. "Now, what's the deal you guys have for me?"

Lou explains enthusiastically, "Sonny, Vegas is exploding like a firecracker . . . hotels are springing up overnight on both sides of the

Strip. . . . The town is becoming a gold mine. . . . We can make a mint there, but we've got to do it soon. Harry here wants us to go in on a new hotel he's building. It's called The Frontier."

Paolo takes over. "But we need you to go in with us, Sonny. Everybody knows the Lucky Ace was the smoothest run casino in the world . . . and the biggest moneymaker. You had the best mechanics in the business working for you."

Sonny smiles. "That's right, Paolo. More than anything, they were loyal. That's more than any crap game can bring ya." He takes a sip of coffee. "Ya know I couldn't get a dog license in the state of Nevada, let alone one to run a casino . . ."

Harry exclaims, "You don't need to . . . I got the land and I can get the license. I've never even had a speeding ticket. You guys would be my silent partners."

Sonny leans forward with his elbows on the desk. "Look, Wasserman, I don't like gettin' involved with anyone outside the Mafia . . . especially a Jew . . . but if I do, I demand a silent partner myself . . . understand?"

The developer nods. "Of course. You don't have anything to worry about there, Sonny. It's the best thing for both of us."

Sonny leans back in his chair again. "Now, what's it gonna cost me?"

Harry gives him the breakdown. "I need four million altogether. The Girardis are gonna give me two, and I'll need another two from you . . . a million to finish construction, plus a million for a deposit with the Nevada Gaming Commission."

Sonny considers Wasserman's request. He knows the desert town is developing rapidly, and he wants to get on the financial bandwagon. "O.K., Wasserman . . . I'll have my bank get a cashier's check over to your bank in the morning . . . with a few conditions."

"What are they? Just tell me."

Sonny spells them out. "I don't know what your procedure is, but I want a count twice a month. I want my own mechanics workin' the casino, and I want my own pit boss runnin' things."

Lou Girardi says, "Whatever Sonny says is fine with us."

His brother adds, "Yeah . . . we don't know about the gambling business, but I'll tell you one thing, Harry"—Paolo leans forward—"anyone fucks over my brother and I, we don't take it too kindly . . . ya know what I mean?"

Harry says hastily, "Hey . . . you're my partners. There's no danger of anything like that."

Sonny warns, "There'd better not be." He calls to Richie, Tony, and Angelo. "Hey, guys . . . open a bottle of Valpolicella . . . looks like I'm back in the casino business."

The grand opening of The Frontier is the most spectacular anyone has ever seen in Las Vegas. Sonny has his most beautiful girls working the junkets that bring heavy gamblers in from all over the country. With his mechanics from the Bahamas staffing the casino, The Frontier is soon making more money than any other hotel on the Strip. The Hughes Corporation comes to Harry with an offer to buy The Frontier for $12 million. Sonny recommends they sell and turn over a quick $8 million in profit, but Wasserman is against it. Since he owns the land and the license, the silent partners are powerless. Sonny distrusts Wasserman's motives, and one evening gets a call from his pit boss.

"Sonny, there's somethin' funny goin' on at The Frontier."

"What is it, Vito? Is it somethin' that can be talked about on the phone?"

Lomuscio says emphatically, "No . . . I gotta see ya, Sonny."

"All right, get up here right away. I'll have the guys pick you up. . . . Call Linda and let her know what flight you'll be comin' in on." When he hangs up, Sonny is disturbed. He's been getting his headaches, which tell him something's wrong . . . and he knows Harry Wasserman is at the bottom of it. Sonny finds out more when Vito gets to the West Castle. He hands Lomuscio a glass of wine. "All right, Vito, what's so important you can't tell me on the phone?"

The pit boss takes a gulp from his glass and says, "It's Wasserman . . ."

Sonny knew it. "What about him?"

"Well, I'm pretty sure he's cheatin' you. . . . He's goin' into the accounting room every week and——"

Sonny shouts, "Every week! What the fuck's he doin' every week?"

"He's comin' out with metal money cases, and they can't be empty . . . there's always four or five security men with him." Vito puts down his glass. "I assumed your procedure was a lot like it was in the Bahamas. . . . I know you had one big count twice a month, but I understand at The Frontier you're having one every thirty days."

"That's not true . . . we still have the same count twice a month." Sonny frowns. "You mean that's what everybody thinks? It's only once a month?"

Vito nods. "That's what they think. I don't know what your books show, but I know what we should be doin'. You should be makin' three million dollars a month there."

Sonny reels from this last statement. "WHAT!"

"Like I said . . . you should be doin' three million . . . you know I know the business, Sonny. I work the heavy shifts. Figure my shift takes in fifty percent, the other shifts gotta take in the other half."

"Whaddya think your shift takes in?"

Vito is prepared. "I know exactly what it took in . . . one point seven million dollars. I keep good records."

Sonny's blood is boiling. "We only showed around a million three hundred thousand last month . . ." He hurls his glass at the wall. "Goddam Jew. He's pocketin' fifty cents on every dollar. He must think I'm dumb." He turns to Vito. "Thanks for lettin' me know. . . . Angelo . . ."

The bodyguard rushes over. "Yeah, Boss?"

"Give Vito a nice envelope."

"How much?"

Sonny pats Vito's shoulder. "Put ten grand in it . . ."

When Vito goes, Sonny tells Angelo, "Have Linda get me the Girardi brothers on the line right now."

"They're gonna be mad, huh, Boss?"

"Yeah, and I want 'em to know I'm not in cahoots with that asshole Jew . . ." He pauses a second. "Wasserman's gonna pay for this."

For the next month Sonny has his electronics man bug Wasserman and keep him under twenty-four-hour surveillance. He learns that the developer has been skimming off the top, an easy thing to do for a hotel owner, one of the people who has free access to the cash. After the dealers send their money through a slot to a locked box under the table, the pit boss counts it. He signs three receipts; one for the accounting room, one for himself, and one for the owners. He gets another receipt when the money is turned over to the cashier's cage. There it is counted again, and the amount is registered with a computer. The owner can easily tamper with these tapes, erase any amount, and walk out with that money. Harry does this every Thursday.

Sonny calls Harry on Monday and tells him to fly right over to Monte Carlo. There is a big casino for sale, and because Harry is a developer, Sonny thinks he is the best one to look into the operation as a possible investment for them. Wasserman and one of the bodyguards leave twenty-four hours later. While he is away, Sonny and the Girardis take out four million in cash from the accounting room. Just three days later the Nevada Gaming Commission files a cease-and-desist order, closing down The Frontier's casino operation. Undercover men had taken pictures of Harry's silent partners. In the state of Nevada it is a violation for known Mafia figures to be seen entering the vault of a casino; Harry's license is revoked. He is forced to sell The Frontier to Hughes for just $200,000 above cost.

Not only has Wasserman lost his hotel and his money, he is about to lose his life. The Girardis have a contract out on him. The desperate developer goes to Sonny to try and make a deal. They make an appointment to meet at Sonny's office at nine P.M. Wasserman finds himself sitting across the desk from a cold, silent Sonny. Harry asks nervously, "I understand there's a contract out on me . . ."

Sonny interrupts him harshly. "Shouldn't there be, Harry?" He shakes an admonishing finger. "You did a very stupid thing. You didn't take me, you took the Sicilian Mafia."

Harry gets up and starts to pace, his bald head glistening with sweat. "Look, I got a deal where you can make back all your money."

"Harry, I don't wanna have nothin' to do with you . . ." He turns to his bodyguards. "Boys, whaddya think? Should I have anything to do with this Jew bastard?"

Angelo says eagerly, "Uh . . . no, Boss. Let's take him for a plane ride, huh?"

Wasserman wipes his head with a large handkerchief. Angelo's size alone tells Harry he's pleading for his life. "Wait a minute, wait a minute . . . listen, I've got an in with the Friars' Club. A big gin game goes on there every night. I'm one of the best players in the country . . . check it out."

Sonny's tone is expressionless. "I know." He leans back. "I know all about you, Harry . . . I know every time you take a shit."

The embezzler continues, his nerves frazzled. "Look, we can take in big money from that game. All we need is a good mechanic."

"I'm not that interested in anything you have to say, Harry. You don't know nothin' about gamblin'. All you know about is cheatin'."

"Well, cheating can bring in three or four hundred grand a week from this game."

Sonny is never one to turn his back on fast money. He looks at Wasserman as if he were a roach in a clean kitchen. "Harry, I think you're scum . . . I knew you were scum when you first came to me, but if you pay us back our money, we'll call it even."

Harry says frantically, "I can't pay you back . . . they took everything I own! If you do this thing with me at the Friars' Club, you'll make a lot more than I owe you."

Sonny finally agrees. "O.K., Harry, but I don't trust a fuckin' thing you say. I want my mechanic to check it out. I'll get back to ya in a week. I gotta get in touch with him." He warns the developer, "Get outta my sight."

Harry asks anxiously, "Can you call off the hit?"

"I'll tell ya what . . . I gotta make a call . . . I'll see if I can slow things down."

"You mean you can't call it off?" Sonny ignores Wasserman, but Angelo grabs the developer's arm. "Come on, Jew . . . the Boss told you to split."

One week later, in the back room of the Friars' Club in Beverly Hills. Harry reaches across the card table and pulls a pile of hundred dollar bills toward him. Al Connors, a notable Hollywood producer, remarks as he gets up from his chair, "Harry, you sure are hot this week, but you can't keep that up long. Your luck's bound to change . . . and I'm gonna be around when it does.''

Wasserman smiles at his friend. "Could be, Al." He adjusts the frame of his glasses and looks at the crowd gathered around the game. "Well, who wants to take me on next?"

High above Wasserman, Sonny's mechanic, Roy, sits in the ten-foot dropped ceiling of the room. His chair, which is on a steel track, can roll so that it is positioned over any table where Harry is seated. Roy's face is now buried in the wide mouth of a large megaphone. He can see both men's cards clearly magnified through a high-powered, wide-angle binocular lens in the narrow end of the cone. The lens itself, one-sixteenth of an inch in diameter, is lined up with a tiny hole in the acoustical ceiling tile. Even if a player should look up, the peephole is invisible to the naked eye. Roy tells Harry what cards his opponent has by means of a high-frequency communications system wired into Harry's glasses. Wasserman makes sure to lose a few hands at first, but when the heavy bets were on the table, he always won. In one night Wasserman could walk away with $150,000 or more.

Wasserman continues his incredible winning streak for the next six months. Ironically, it is not the FBI that exposes Wasserman's swindle, but a James Bond movie. Al Connors has just seen *Goldfinger*. He notices that 007's archenemy wins at gin as often as Harry; Goldfinger's girlfriend on a hotel balcony radios his opponent's hand to him. Al suspects Harry of cheating, too, and goes to the district attorney. A warrant is issued to search the Friars' Club, and the elaborate setup in the ceiling is uncovered. Fortunately Roy isn't there at the time. After the story breaks Sonny sends him back to Sicily. Harry is immediately indicted for fraud, and a prominent Beverly Hills lawyer, Grant Hopper, takes on his case.

A few weeks later the Friars' Club case is still in the news. Linda comes into the office to tell Sonny that Harry Wasserman is on the phone. "It's the third time he's called this morning."

"No way I'm talkin' to that son of a bitch Jew."

Richie looks up from a *Sports Illustrated* he's been leafing through. "Boss, you might want to . . . he could be giving information to the Feds."

Sonny thinks, "Yeah . . . his type would."

"Besides, it says in the papers he's goin' before the grand jury next week."

This makes Sonny reconsider. "You know what, Linda? I do wanna talk to him, but not on the phone. Tell Harry to be at Little Sicily tonight at one o'clock sharp." He calls to his personal bodyguard, "Angelo, when that fat Jew fucker comes in, I want ya to frisk him to make sure he's not carryin' any bugging equipment."

"Uh . . . we'll check him out good, Boss."

When Sonny gets to the restaurant, Joe, the plump and jovial owner, greets him warmly. "Sonny, how've you been, goombah? I got everything ready for you and the boys."

Sonny hugs him. "Great, Joe. The guys are starved."

"Wasserman is here already."

Sonny tells his bodyguards, "Go check him out before I sit down."

The men go to frisk the developer, while Joe hangs up Sonny's coat. "One of your friends was in last week . . . Lou, from Boston. He said to say hello."

"Does he still have that moustache?"

"Yeah, it looks good."

Sonny laughs affectionately. "You always say nice things about people, Joe. That guy couldn't look good if he had Gable's moustache." They both laugh. Sonny likes to come here whenever he eats out, usually after hours. While other restaurant owners intrude on Sonny's privacy, Joe guards it closely. Joe has no links to the underworld. His relationship with Sonny is strictly personal. Celebrities like coming to Little Sicily because Joe treats everyone the same—and of course the food is good. Underworld figures like it there because growing up on the streets of New York taught this proprietor to his mouth shut.

The developer is waiting for Sonny in a booth at the back of the restaurant, reading the LA *Times*. Sonny sits down and says sarcastically, "I see you're still making headlines, Harry."

Wasserman folds the paper. "It means nothing. I'm a cinch to win this case."

"Oh, yeah? What makes you so sure?"

Harry announces proudly, "Because Hopper stole the grand jury indictments from the DA's office this afternoon. You'll probably read tomorrow that my case was thrown out."

Sonny breaks off a huge hunk of Sicilian pizza bread and points it at Wasserman. "Your attorney is stupid, Harry. The DA did that just to catch you idiots." He shoots him an accusing look. "What was your attorney doing in the DA's office anyway, Harry?"

Wasserman stammers, "Well, he . . . uh . . . I suppose . . . he must have had some business."

Sonny cuts him off angrily. "Business, hell, I know why he was there. You were coppin' a plea, weren't you?" He pulls the developer across the table by his tie. "You know you were coppin' a plea, you stinkin' son of a bitch . . ."

Harry knows he's been caught red-handed. "All right, we were trying to make a deal . . . but it wasn't against you. They want to know who the mechanic was . . . I never mentioned your name . . . I swear."

Sonny is glad that Roy was using an alias. No one would ever be able to find him . . . even if they traced him to Sicily. He tells Wasserman with foreboding, "Remember, Harry, a lot of people would like to see ya dead." Sonny releases the developer and continues icily, "I trust ya like a fence, Jew. This conversation's over . . . I don't talk to rats." He snaps his fingers. "Boys, Wasserman is leaving."

The four bodyguards rush over to a table. Angelo says excitedly, "Where should we take him, Boss?"

"Just be sure this garbage gets to the street." With one hand Angelo lifts the frightened developer up from the booth and starts to push him roughly toward the door. Sonny shouts, "Hey, Angelo."

The husky bodyguard stops. "Uh . . . yeah, Boss."

Sonny opens his hands. "Be nice, huh . . . have respect for Joe." Angelo releases Wasserman and smooths out the wrinkled shoulders of Harry's jacket. Sonny watches as Wasserman is escorted outside. A large plate of linguine and clam sauce is placed in front of Sonny as Richie sits down in the booth.

"What's the problem, Boss?"

Sonny sprinkles a large helping of Parmesan cheese on his spaghetti. "Nothin'. I can't eat with rats around."

Joe comes over to Sonny's table. "Is everything all right, Sonny?"

Sonny glosses over the incident. "Great, Joe."

"Is the food O.K.?"

"*Molto bene,* as usual . . . sit down." Sonny slides over to make room in the booth.

Joe looks at him, concerned. "You look a little tired, Sonny . . . you're workin' too hard."

"Yeah . . . I am . . . I got a lotta businesses and too many idiots runnin' 'em for me."

Joe sympathizes. "I know what ya mean. If I leave the place for a night, the tables aren't even set up right."

Sonny philosophizes, "That's what comes with bein' the boss, Joe . . . ya almost gotta do everything yourself."

The very next morning Wasserman's case is in the papers, as he predicted. Grant Hopper has been indicted for stealing confidential grand jury documents. Soon afterwards both client and attorney are convicted of their respective crimes. While Harry is waiting to be sentenced, in a desperate attempt to save himself he goes to Aldo at Caesar's Palace for help. Aldo calls Sonny. "Look, we both know Wasserman's no good, but he's got a deal that's right up your alley." Because of Aldo's recommendation Sonny agrees to see Wasserman for five minutes to hear what he has to say.

When Harry gets to Sonny's office, the bodyguards frisk him. This time they strip him naked to be absolutely sure he isn't wired for bugging. As soon as he's dressed again, they usher him inside. Sonny sits back, his hand clasped over his large belly, as Wasserman explains his deal. "Sonny, I have a piece of land that's worth about two hundred fifty thousand. You can have it if you help me out." Sonny leans forward now, interested. That property would be worth double that to him. Dr. Jenkins and his partners have been looking for a good location for a jai alai stadium they want to build in Vegas. Sonny can sell that land for $500,000 to them right now. He gets up and paces slowly, probing for the ulterior motive of Wasserman's offer.

"All right, Harry. What the hell you want that you're gonna give me that property?"

Harry makes his pitch. "I've been doing some checking. They say you have the best electronics men in the country . . ."

Sonny urges him on, "Get to the point."

"I want you to tape a phone call between me and my contact in Washington."

"Who's that?"

Harry casts a worried look at the bodyguards. "I don't want anyone else to know." He scribbles on one of his business cards.

Sonny looks at the important name, then up at Harry dubiously. "This guy's gonna talk to you?" He passes the card to his men who nod to each other, impressed.

The developer stammers, disconcerted. "Well, no, he's gonna talk to his brother. A good friend of mine knows him. I told both of them that if they could get me out of this mess, they'd get twenty-five thousand each for setting up the call. If my case gets thrown out, I'll give them ten percent of my real estate holdings."

Sonny snaps, "And whaddya think the big shot's gonna ask for?"

Wasserman says, "Whatever it costs, I don't care." He grins sardonically. "When I get my hands on that tape, I can blackmail him and get off scot-free . . . without putting out a nickel." For once Sonny thinks Wasserman is making sense. A tape like that on such an important political figure would certainly be useful.

Sonny says cautiously, "Where's the call gonna be set up at?"

"That's just the problem. I don't know where it's gonna be . . . they won't tell me."

"Look, Wasserman, I don't wanna get involved . . . but I know someone who could. I'll call him."

Harry is worried. "We gotta do this soon, Sonny . . . my sentencing's coming up next month."

"I'll call the guy right now." When the developer leaves, Sonny tells Richie, "Get my electronics men over here right away; have 'em bring Jimmy. Tell him we need a scanning gun."

"This is a tough one, isn't it, Boss? You don't know if the call's coming from a pay phone or an office building or what . . ."

Sonny assures him, "No problem, Richie. Jimmy could bug two ghosts in a graveyard—as long as they're not talkin' on a sky phone."

Richie is still worried. "You think the guy's brother is smart enough to call from an airplane?"

"Nah . . . if he was that smart, he wouldn't be dealin' with Wasserman in the first place."

Angelo says, "That's how come you make a lotta your calls from the sky phone . . . huh, Boss?"

"You're gettin' smart, Angelo."

Richie adds, "The boss always has all the angles covered."

Sonny says to him, "That's why I'm successful, Richie. . . . Send Aldo ten thousand dollars for settin' this up . . . he just gave me an ace in the hole for my Big Scam."

Ten days later, Sonny watches the streetlights of Beverly Hills illuminate the city below his penthouse office. As the wheels of his tape machine turn slowly, the distinctive voice of the famous politician talking to his brother comes through the speaker, loud and clear: "If he's a draft-dodger or tax-evader, he won't get any help from me."

Another voice with similar inflections reassures him, "He's not. This is the guy that was just indicted in the Friars' Club scandal."

"Yes, I've heard about that. . . . Well, get me the details and I'll see what I can do."

At this point the developer jumps in excitedly. "This is Harry Wasserman."

The official is obviously upset. "What the hell is he doing on the line?"

The brother says, "He insisted on——"

Harry interrupts again. "I just wanna know how much this is gonna cost me."

There is a second of silence, then the steady reply: "Two hundred and fifty thousand dollars."

Harry answers belligerently, "No way . . . I'll give you a hundred grand—that's it."

The statesman's tone is firm. "The price is two hundred and fifty thousand." To his brother: "Call me tonight on the private line . . . alone . . . understand?" There is a loud click as he hangs up, then a dial tone.

Tony says, "Jeez, that tape's worth more than gold . . . you sure are smart, Boss."

Richie concurs. "He's a helluva lot smarter than Sam ever was."

Angelo adds his comments to the others. "That'll be a great tape for the families, huh, Boss? I'll bet Don Giuseppe is gonna be dyin' to get his hands on it."

Sonny says evenly, "I don't work for Don Giuseppe or anyone, Angelo . . . this is my tape . . . it's for *my* family."

Linda buzzes Sonny. "Harry Wasserman is here to pick up something."

Sonny presses his button on the intercom. "Tell him to wait a minute."

He turns to Richie and Angelo. "Go check him out." Sonny takes the tape from the recorder and hands it to Tony. "Put this in the safe . . ."

A few seconds later Harry enters Sonny's office. He plops himself down on the couch with his hands spread open behind him and says arrogantly, "That's some tape, huh, Sonny? I really got those guys by the balls now. They'll have to let me off." He laughs cockily. "And I'm scot-free." Wasserman pulls out some papers from his briefcase. "Here's the bill of sale. When I get the tape, I'll sign it over to you . . ."

Sonny, who is standing in front of the picture window, lights up a fragrant Cuban cigar. He walks over and blows smoke in Harry's face. "No deal, Harry . . . I'm keepin' that tape . . ."

Harry's eyes widen. "You can't . . . it's mine."

Sonny takes a long puff. "Ya made a big mistake, Harry . . . ya should've paid the two hundred and fifty grand . . . ya would've gotten probation . . . then ya wouldn't have to go to prison, and ya wouldn't get a record." He pours salt on Harry's open wound: "And I hear your friend Brother won't even talk to you now 'cause you cheated him out of the twenty-five grand you promised him." Sonny looks at the developer, who's now sitting upright on the edge of the couch. "You screwed up bad, Harry . . . real bad. But the tape is keepin' you alive . . . the Mafia wants it." He walks to Wasserman and stands over him, menacingly. "I wanna tell you something, Jew; next week, when you get sentenced, you'd better pray that the judge sends you to prison. With your money you'll go to a kindergarten prison . . . you won't get more than two years . . . but you'll be safe there." He pulls Wasserman off the couch by his lapels. " 'Cause if you don't go to prison, it means you ratted on somebody . . . It might be me, and I don't take any chances." He throws him back down on the couch. Sonny takes the bill of sale over to Harry. "You forgot to sign my bill of sale. I did my job . . . this is for trying to turn Roy in."

Wasserman says insolently, "What if I tell ya I'm not gonna sign? What're ya gonna do . . . kill me?"

Sonny pats his shoulder. "Harry, you just gave me a hell of an idea . . ." He motions to his bodyguard. "Angelo."

Harry smirks, "You're not gonna kill me here . . . it'll make too much noise . . . everybody will hear the shots."

Sonny says evenly, "Everybody's gone home, Harry. It's seven-thirty. Besides, my office is soundproofed." The developer's face drops as he does a frightened double-take over his shoulder. Angelo's .357 is pointed at him. The gun looks like a cannon. Sonny says coolly, "If Harry doesn't sign the paper when I get to ten, Angelo, blow his brains out." He starts counting, "One, two . . ."

Wasserman tries to protest. "But Sonny, be reasonable . . . I paid . . . it's my . . ." The count is up to four.

Angelo says, "Can I do it when we get to seven, Boss? A rat sent my brother up for twenty years."

Sonny just keeps counting slowly, ". . . five, six . . ." The bodyguard cocks his gun.

Harry screams, "WAIT . . . NO . . . hold it." He wipes his forehead. "I'll sign . . ."

Sonny hands him a pen, and watches the terrified man sign his name shakily—an event Sonny and the boys have seen many times before. He takes the paper from Harry. "Angelo, this garbage is beginning to stink up my office." Sonny turns his back as the huge man picks Wasserman up and carries him out.

Richie asks, "Are you gonna knock him off, Boss?"

"Yeah . . . when the time is right."

The next day Sonny reads in the paper that Harry Wasserman has been sentenced to three years in the federal penitentiary.

About a week later Vito Lomuscio comes into Sonny's office with an odd request. He wants the Mafia kingpin to try and get Elvis Presley back into Las Vegas. Some years before, Frank Manadeli had locked the singer out becuse he reneged on a benefit concert the underworld figure had arranged. Actually, one of Elvis's people had canceled the show in favor of another that paid a lot of money. Vito explains, "Elvis didn't do anything, but he bore the brunt of it. You have pull in Vegas, maybe you could talk them into letting him back in."

Sonny gives the problem serious consideration and finally agrees to help because the famous performer's indebtedness would be profitable for his Big Scam. Vito sets up a meeting for the two men to fly their private jets to a deserted airfield just outside Reno.

When Sonny lands at the airfield, Elvis's jet, "TCB," is already there. At the steps of Presley's plane his security man asks Sonny's bodyguards to surrender their weapons. Sonny informs him coldly, "My men don't go anywhere without guns. I guess we don't have a meeting."

He turns and starts to walk away, but the famous singer himself yells down from the doorway, "It's O.K. . . . they can come up." Sonny, Richie, and Angelo board; Eddie, Tony, and Willie stay outside to watch for federal agents. When they're inside, Elvis says, "Vito told me some nice things about you, Sonny."

Sonny is unimpressed by the star's stature . . . to him Elvis is just another person who needs a favor. "Let's face it, not too many people say too many nice things about me. . . . I'm here because Vito asked me to see ya. You understand I don't do things for nothin'."

Elvis replies quietly, "I understand." Sonny is struck by Presley's humility. He didn't expect it from this national hero.

As soon as they're seated, one of Presley's people launches into all the reasons why he wants Sonny to get Elvis into Vegas. "You know, Mr. Gibson, this is very crucial to Elvis's career. We really feel that it's hurt him to be away from the live performing so long. You know his record sales——"

Sonny snaps at him rudely, "You shut up a minute." He looks over at Presley, who has been silent during his man's pitch. "Elvis, do you wanna go to Vegas . . . or does *he* want ya to go? Don't lie to me . . . I'll know."

Elvis says quietly, "No, I want to go . . . I want to perform live again. All I wanted to do at one time was make movies in Hawaii, but I need to get back in touch with my audience—not for them, but for me. If I don't get back on stage, I'm gonna die."

Sonny says, "I can tell you're honest. That's more than I can say for some of the people that represent ya."

The man cuts in, oblivious to the insult. "What's this gonna cost us?"

Sonny snarls at him, "You don't have enough money to pay me to do this, but because Elvis wants to go, it's not gonna cost ya nothin'. Maybe I could bring a couple a clients into Vegas and Elvis could take some time to meet 'em backstage. I'm buildin' a hotel and casino in the Philippines." He turns to Elvis. "I'd like you to come down and open it up for me. . . . I'll pay you top dollar, of course."

Elvis says, "I'd be happy to do that, Sonny. Just let me know when." Then, with concern, "You think you can get me into Vegas?"

"I gotta make a few calls to some guys, but I'm pretty sure I can . . ."

Elvis shakes his head in amazement. "I don't understand. Why can't I play there? No one will give me the straight dope."

Sonny explains, "One of your people stepped on a few toes. You were supposed to do a benefit, but they pulled you out."

Elvis, known for giving his time to humanitarian causes, is outraged. "Who was it?"

"I'm not a rat . . . it's not my place to tell ya . . . but you did have some bad advice on the way up." The man is quiet now.

Elvis says seriously, "You really think you can get me back in . . ."

"Yeah, Vito wouldn't have come to me otherwise. It'll take me a couple a weeks."

"I appreciate that, Sonny."

Just then the man intrudes. "You mean this really won't cost us anything?"

Sonny turns on him. "I told ya it wouldn't, asshole, not because of you . . . you couldn't pay enough. I'm doin' this for Elvis." Sonny stands. "You'll be hearin' from me."

Elvis gives him a hug. "That's the way you do it, isn't it?"

"Yeah, that's the way we do it."

Elvis smiles. "You know, they used to call us the 'Memphis Mafia.' "

Sonny smiles back. "Elvis . . . there is no Mafia."

On the way out Angelo shakes the singer's hand in awe. "It's been a real pleasure meetin' you, Mr. Presley . . . you got a lotta fans in Brooklyn."

Elvis looks up at the six-eight bodyguard. "If they all look like you, I'm glad they like me . . . they sure do grow 'em big back there."

Sonny has a final parting word for him. "See you on opening night." He is halfway down the steps when Elvis comes to the door.

"Sonny . . ." When Sonny turns, Elvis gives him a little wave. "Thanks . . ."

Six months later Elvis Presley made his triumphant return to Las Vegas and broke all existing house records, and Sonny convinced several wealthy contacts that Presley would play at the grand opening of his hotel in the Philippines.

From Las Vegas, Sonny goes directly to New York. Elvis is no longer on his mind . . . Theresa is.

She's meeting him at the airport. Sonny can see her waiting for him at the executive hangar. As soon as the jet lands, Theresa runs up to him at the steps of the plane and hugs him. "I'm so happy you're here . . . I missed you."

They kiss, then he touches her face. Sonny really did miss Theresa, but he didn't want her to know that just yet. "I'm happy to see ya, too, baby." They walk arm in arm to the cars . . . there are three of them waiting. "Why are there so many limos today? Are you expecting somebody?"

"No . . . I gotta have more men with me now. I'm expanding my operation." When they get to the cars, Tony and Richie get into the other cars, and Angelo gets into the front seat of their limo.

Theresa is surprised. "I thought you said we'd be alone?"

"We are alone . . . there's no one back here with us."

"No, but Angelo is in the car."

He answers gravely, "Theresa, I told you before . . . there will never be a time when I won't have my men with me."

She says with resignation, "I understand." After a few seconds pass she says excitedly, "Where are you taking me tonight?"

"Someplace you've never been, my love, to a wine auction."

That night the Mafia kingpin mixes with society and enologists from all over the world. He buys the most expensive item up for bid that evening, a bottle of Chateau Lafite Rothschild '41 from the private stock of Winston Churchill. The price: $8500. To the horror of wine connoisseurs he breaks the rare bottle for the press, telling them, "The Mafia don't drink cheap wine." Sonny holds up a $2.99 Italian import. "We drink this Valpolicella." For his stunt, Sonny will make fifty cents on each bottle brought into the United States.

The next day, when Sonny has a meeting with Don Giuseppe, the old man teases him, "I got some Valpolicella for you, but if I owe you fifty cents . . ." He pulls a coin from his pocket. "Here . . ."

Sonny takes the half-dollar and flips it to Angelo, "Keep track of this . . . it all adds up." The two powerful men laugh as they sit on the couch. "Don Giuseppe, you didn't call me here just to drink wine. . . ."

No, Santino." He says more seriously, "We have some problems. There are two brothers in Nevada who got in debt to us. We went on the hooks for them on some property for a land development. The only way they can pay us is from the Crazy Q Ranch they run." This is the most famous legalized house of prostitution in Nevada. "But the brothers are having problems. Somebody put a bomb on their property the other night."

"Who did it?"

"We don't know . . . could be somebody from the mines nearby. Could be a religious group did it . . . they've been threatening the ranch. Law enforcement is looking into things, but we want you to handle this for the families."

"You want me to find out who did it?"

"No . . . more than that . . . we want you to straighten out the operation. You know broads, you know security, and you know marketing. If they get to where their profits go up, we get paid faster."

One thing is unclear to Sonny. "Why don't you just knock these guys off and take over the operation?"

The don shakes his head. "It's not their fault they're behind, Santino. With what happened, everybody's scared to go to the ranch now. Besides, they're not Mafia . . . we don't wanna do anything to hurt 'em, we just want our money." He makes an offer. "We'll give you half a million to start and a million when you finish if you'll do this, Santino."

Sonny hesitates. "I dunno, Don Giuseppe. I got my own business to think about, too."

The old man assures him, "It won't take that long . . . what, you go in one, two days to set things up, then once a week to keep it under control." He complains, "We could lose a lotta deals in Vegas if the Crazy Q goes broke. Since you're closed down, there's no place to bring clients anymore." No longer does Don Giuseppe give Sonny commands. He and the other dons have great respect for Sonny's power. "Santino . . . all the families will be grateful if you'd do this. Think before you say no . . ."

Sonny examines his request. It must be important to the Mafia to ask him. If they thought somebody else could have done the job, they would have gotten someone else . . . so they needed Sonny. He decides to take on the assignment of turning the Crazy Q operation around, not for the money, although he'd never refuse it, and not for the gratitude of the families, he doesn't give a damn about that. What Sonny wants out of this is their indebtedness. It will be an extremely valuable element when he gets ready to pull off his Big Scam. This is what finally persuades him. "O.K., Don Giuseppe, I'll stop in at the Crazy Q for a few days on my way back to LA."

The day after the meeting with Don Giuseppe Sonny flies to Nevada to confer with the two owners of the Crazy Q. After they tell him the details of their basic operation, Sonny tackles the make-over job like an efficiency expert for AT&T. He spends the first few days scrutinizing their system, observing and checking procedures. The Sunday morning after he arrives, all of the girls are assembled at eleven o'clock for an orientation meeting in the large front parlor. The majority of the hookers at the Crazy Q work for pimps. When a neighborhood would get too hot, they'd send a whole stable to the ranch until things cooled down. Sprinkled among the hardened prostitutes are aspiring actresses from all over the country—they came west to be stars but fell off the ladder of success near the first rung. Now the Crazy Q's eighty resident hookers cluster in small, sleepy groups gossiping about Sonny, waiting for him to arrive. A short redhead tells her circle, "One of my friends has been with this guy . . . he's hung like an elephant. She said she was out of commission for a whole week after they made it."

The girls' reactions to this remark vary from horror to eager anticipation. A brassy blonde confides to her clique, "I heard that sometimes the girls who worked for him disappeared mysteriously."

A sweet-looking brunette's eyes widen. "Really . . . what happened to them?"

The blonde gathers the group closer, her tone ominous. "No one knows. They never found the bodies." Before the others can react, their madam, a fiftyish former exotic dancer named Marie Le Tour, sweeps into the room, followed by Sonny, his bodyguards, and Donna, the head hooker from the Lucky Ace.

Marie claps her hands. "I want everyone's attention . . . girls!" The room quiets down instantly, as though someone had pulled a plug on all the conversation at once. "You all know there's been a little trouble lately, and it was lucky that no one was hurt. . . . There are going to be some changes around here to protect us. . . . Sonny is gonna tell you about them . . . Sonny."

Standing in the center of the room crowded with women, Sonny resembles a sultan surveying his harem. When he begins to speak, he clasps his hands behind his back and paces slowly. "I'm gonna be around here for a while and I'll be settin' up some new procedures. I expect all of you to follow them exactly." He stops and looks at the hookers. "Some of you girls got big mouths . . . the rest of ya got big ears . . . but no matter what ya hear, the Mafia is not taking over the Crazy Q. You're still gonna be workin' for the same people." Sonny begins pacing again. He now addresses the girls with the same businesslike tone he uses in his executive board meetings. "The first thing we're concerned about here is your physical safety . . . we wanna save your lives. If you listen to what I tell you, you won't get hurt." The hookers hang on his words. "The second thing we care about is your health, 'cause if you get venereal disease, you're out of whack . . . Even more important, when a guy comes here, he wants to know that he's not gonna bring anything back to his old lady and get into a beef. Donna here is gonna show you how to check a guy out to protect yourselves." All heads turn to look at Donna, an unlikely looking hooker in her Christian Dior tailored suit. Sonny continues, "The third thing, and a very important thing we're concerned with, is volume . . . Right now each girl turns about eight tricks a day . . . that's terrible! I been watching you girls . . . a lot of you don't even know how to fuck. If you stay here, you're gonna learn! Pretty soon you'll be makin' it with sixteen guys a day." The girls exchange surreptitious glances as he mentions this figure. Sonny spells out the new routine to them next. "You gals are not here for pleasure . . . you're here to work. From now on there's gonna be strict rules. You'll work eight-hour shifts . . . you can work two hours overtime if ya want. Nobody works more than ten hours. No more bullshit food like potato chips and Cokes. I'm puttin' you on high-protein, low-calorie diets. No booze and no pills. No visits from any-one—that means boyfriends and kids, too . . . no one. You'll work ninety days on and ninety days off. But when you walk outta here, you're gonna have some money in your pocket. Another thing," he says emphatically."There will be no climaxin' on the job. If you wanna get yourself off . . . do it with a vibrator on your own time . . . not ours. Your mind should be on gettin' the guy to come . . . and go. No trick over twenty minutes, unless he's payin' ya double. If he is, take ad-vantage of it and take your time . . . don't wear your ass out with him. And girls . . . make sure you keep your legs up when you're fuckin'. If your clit gets hit, you'll come and only be good for a few hours. Now if anybody has a problem, I wanna know about it." He adds sternly, "If you're smart, you won't try to cheat or relax on the job . . . I don't believe in second chances." He lets this warning register with them. "If you do what I tell you, we'll get along fine."

Sonny looks out at the girls, who have not uttered a single word during his discourse. He spots a few who look too young to be in such an old profession. Sonny walks over to one, a petite blonde in the front row. "What's your name?"

She says quietly, "Mona."

"Where ya from, Mona?"

She looks up at him. "Madison, Wisconsin."

"You been with a lotta guys?"

"Yeah."

"Do you like working here?"

"Yeah . . . it's really hip." Sonny is trying to get a reading on her speech pattern. Mona's responses to these basic questions will be immediate and natural because she's telling the truth, but if she's lying, her inflections will change . . . Mona will have to think about her answer. "How old are you?"

"Twenty-one." This is not true . . . her tone dropped. She continues, "That's what you have to be to work here."

Sonny informs her firmly, "Well, you can't work here, Mona . . . you're seventeen."

The blonde shifts uncomfortably. "I'm twenty-one."

"O.K., if you can show me a certified birth certificate, not some bullshit phony ID, you can stay." He looks at her steadily. "But you're not twenty-one, are you?"

Mona's head drops to her chest. "No . . ."

Sonny touches her hair. "Go on . . . get your stuff and go back home."

When she leaves, Sonny goes over to the other suspected minor. The brunette stands tall and looks at him defiantly. "I'm twenty-one."

Sonny asks, "What's your name?"

"Susie, and I'm twenty-one."

"How long have you worked here, Susie?"

"Six months." She adds haughtily, "I'm one of the best girls here . . . just ask Marie. I've already taken on sixteen tricks in a day . . . ask her."

Sonny looks at her evenly. "Susie, you're lyin' to me . . . you're eighteen." He twists her arm up roughly. "And you're a junkie." There are purple-blue marks in the crook of her arm. "You got more tracks than a bird walkin' in the snow." Sonny throws her arm back down. "You're not twenty-one, but you're old enough to kill yourself takin' dope." He pushes her toward the door. "You're gettin' outta here." The girl shoots him a hateful look and storms out of the room. Sonny looks at the others. "I won't have no addicts, heroin or otherwise, workin' here. I'm gonna interview each one of ya before the week's out. If ya got any habits, you can quit now, 'cause I won't stand for it. . . . Don't try and hide it, 'cause I'll find out . . . I'm a mind-reader." He warns, "And girls . . . when you see me . . . you're comin' to talk, not to fuck." Sonny turns to Marie, "What girls have been here five years or more?"

She points them out, "Doris, Lulu, Cindy, Pat, Clarissa, Sandy, and Nan."

"I wanna see them in my office right now." He strides out of the room, attendants behind him, leaving the prostitutes in a flurry of excited chatter.

The next day the new routine at the Crazy Q begins. Using a closed-circuit TV system the veteran hookers monitor every client who comes into the ranch. If the girls don't recognize him, the man is frisked and his ID is held until he leaves. If there is any chance that he might be a troublemaker, he is turned away. To tighten security outside, a steel drawbridge replaces the one that was destroyed and 'round-the-clock guards are posted at various points on the property.

Inside, Donna holds her sexual seminars. If there were such a degree, she would have a Ph.D. in hooking. The classy prostitute now shares the wealth of her knowledge with her colleagues. Donna sits on the edge of a desk in the large library where the class is being held and begins her lecture with the authority of a college professor addressing her students. "Our object is to get a man to climax quickly . . . it's easier on you, and it makes more money for us. Every man is different, girls, but if you know what you're doing, you'll see that the equipment basically works the same way." She holds up an illustration with various size penises. "These are average cocks. Of course, you will come across much bigger ones than these, but regardless of the size of the cock, to keep your client happy and to make him come fast, you've gotta make him think he's special . . . he's the best guy you've had today. If the man is average, tell him he has the hardest one you've ever seen. If he's big, tell him how much you love it. A guy who's really large could be self-conscious about it . . . treat him normally. If he's small, tell him how exciting he is. One important thing—every guy thinks he's a great lover, and most men will come if they think you're turned on. You have to make them believe it. Most guys will shoot faster if you tell 'em what they want to hear. If you're with a pimply-faced teenager, he wants to think he's a real man. If the trick's middle-aged and fat, tell him he's sexy. Old guys love to hear they fuck better than a twenty-year-old." Donna puts the graphic away. She lights up a cigarette and holds it up. "I'm gonna demand that for fifteen minutes each day you smoke a cigarette in your pussy. You can start out with a cigar first, and once you get that to puff, it means your muscles will be starting to contract.

Within two to three weeks of practice you'll be on cigarettes . . . then you'll be able to squeeze tight. This makes a man climax quickly . . . you won't have to work with him so long.''

A young redhead calls out, "What if you get a guy who turns you off completely? What do ya do then?"

Donna replies, "If you can't stand the guy, pass the trick. Don't waste your time and his money, 'cause he may not come back . . . plus he might tell other guys they've got assholes workin' here.'' She adds a word of advice. "However, I would recommend that you don't pass on more than one or two tricks a week, or else it'll look like you're trying to throw work on another girl . . . and we won't have that.''

A bleached blonde asks, "What if the guy wants us to get on top?"

"That's O.K. unless he's big—then there's more risk you'll get a bladder infection . . . . I'm going to show you a couple of other things to look out for to avoid infection.'' She brings up a pliable model of a penis, complete with foreskin, to demonstrate how to check for disease. "If a man is not circumcised and he doesn't wash, a substance called smegma gets trapped in the foreskin. Pull it back and wipe the guy with a damp washcloth before you fuck. Now, to check for VD—this is for a circumcised guy, too—squeeze his balls and milk the cock . . . like you were milking a cow's udder.'' She demonstrates the pumping motion. "If he's infected, you'll see pus or sometimes a white liquid come out of the head. Get rid of him . . . call security. You're going to have checks once a month for syphilis and gonorrhea anyway, but if you do do what I'm tellin' you, nobody should catch anything.'' She warns, "If you do, it means you got lazy . . . that'll get you fired.'' Donna opens the drawer of the big desk. She pulls out a stack of cards and passes them out. "Every time you're with a new trick, you have to fill out one of these when he leaves. It will tell us how a man likes to come. This information will then be fed into a computer. On his second visit, whoever gets the guy will also get a printout of his sexual preferences. This will guarantee the trick climaxes within twenty minutes. Keep a pile of these in your room. We expect them to be handed in every day.'' Donna wraps up the lesson. "If you have any questions, you can come to me anytime . . . . I'll be here with Sonny until the end of the week.''

Sonny's revamping of the Crazy Q operation works beautifully. Within a few months it is the only brothel in business in the area. Sonny has launched a massive promotional and marketing campaign; bellhops and cab drivers all over the state get kickbacks for sending them customers. Within six months over 300 hookers are working for the Crazy Q, and its profits increase from $80,000 to $300,000 a month. When the job is finished, Sonny collects the remaining million dollars of his fee for putting the house in order.

Commuting between Nevada and his own bases of operation has

been a tremendous strain on Sonny, but he's never too tired to make money. When Sam Scorzelli calls with a half-million-dollar job for him, Sonny agrees to meet him at the mansion in Boca Raton, Florida, to discuss the proposition.

Richie brings Sam and Sonny a bottle of Valpolicella as they sunbathe at poolside. Sam says proudly, "Sonny, all the guys are grateful for what ya did at the Crazy Q." He takes the glass of wine from Richie. "It'd be a sin if somethin' happened to that place."

Sonny stretches out on the chaise longue. He has on the dark sunglasses that he always wears in public now. They stop the press from printing pictures of him unless he wants them to. By law the newspapers are only allowed to show shots of a person's full face. Sonny basks in the blazing Florida sun. He says lazily, "Yeah, it's makin' a fuckin' fortune now."

Sam shifts in his chair. "Sonny, Don Giuseppe and Alfonso have a lot of confidence in you. They say you can do anything."

Sonny puts his hands behind his head and looks over at the Chicago boss. "O.K., Sam . . . whaddya want? You didn't come down here to play golf and get a suntan."

Sam gets right to the point. "Sonny, how many times can you come?"

Sonny sits up in his chair. "What the hell did you say?"

"I said, how many times do you think you can come?"

Sonny shrugs. "I dunno—why?"

"Think you could come fifty times in less than ten hours?"

Sonny laughs. "Hell, yes. What's this all about?"

Sam tells him, "You got half a million dollars if you can do it."

Sonny takes off his sunglasses. "Half a million dollars just for comin' fifty times?"

"Yep, Don Franco and I have some money riding on you with some guys from Vegas. Sonny, doctors will have to witness it . . . will that be a problem for you?"

Sonny answers confidently, "Shit no . . . for half a million dollars you can have the whole goddam U.S. Army watch . . . it don't matter."

Sam leans forward and touches Sonny's arm. "Sonny, be absolutely sure . . . don't say yes unless you know you can do this. It's one climax every twelve minutes."

"Shit, Sam, the first thirty minutes I can come twenty times . . . and I get ten hours, right?"

"Right, Sonny." Sam is astounded. "I heard about you, but how the hell can you do that in thirty minutes?"

"It's a long story, but I got a gland problem . . . I discharge a lot, Sam . . . I stay horny." Sonny lays back down on the chaise and drops his sunglasses again. "Don't worry about nothin', Sam . . . just tell me where you want me and when. But gimme a week's notice."

For a whole week before the bet Sonny gets plenty of rest and abstains from sex. Then he and his bodyguards fly to Vegas and drive to a small town twenty miles away, where the sexual bout is to be held. When Sonny arrives, Sam and three other people are already in the room—two doctors and a conservatively dressed, dour-faced executive. The executive will not be rooting for Sonny . . . he represents the people from Vegas.

A scholarly professor of gynecology at UCLA comes over to the subject. The doctor cleans his wire-rim glasses as he explains to Sonny, "Now, in order for this to be valid, we must actually see the discharge from your penis . . . is that clear, Mr. Gibson?"

Sonny grins and begins unbuttoning his shirt. "You wanna see me come, right, Doc?"

The doctor answers, slightly embarrassed, "Uh, yes, that's right."

Sonny takes off his shirt. "Okay, then let's get started." As he's taking off his pants, the door opens and Angelo brings in the first bed partner, a chunky, dark-haired hooker who's turned one too many tricks. She takes a look between Sonny's legs and heads back to the door. "Forget it . . . you couldn't pay me enough to put that up my pussy." The attorney is annoyed. "Who the hell picked these women?"

Sam says to the executive, "That's one of yours." He says to Richie, "Bring in one of my broads."

A *zaftig* black girl enters. She eyes Sonny's crotch, then the large jar of Vaseline, and starts rubbing it in on the lips of her vagina. "I can see why you need this, sugar . . . you are a big mother." When she drops her robe, Sonny grabs her passionately. He lays her down on the bed and pumps his hips into her fast. The doctors watch in astonishment as he pulls out, climaxing after only two minutes. Sonny rolls off the girl, and the gynecologist examines his discharge. The hooker puts on her robe, still recovering. "That was some wild fuckin' baby . . . I'd like to catch ya again when we got more time. I never met no black dude big as you." On her way out she asks, "Who should I send in next?"

Sonny leans back casually on the pillow. "It don't matter, just send in anyone, honey."

Angelo says, "Uh . . . and tell 'em not to worry, the boss is gonna get to all of 'em."

Sonny wins the bet for Sam in less than six hours. He collects his money and flies directly to Los Angeles. When he lands, the DA's men are there to greet him. An informant for the Vegas people has told them that Sonny took down millions for the Mafia. Sonny freely admits that he has $500,000 cash on the plane, which he got for committing an immoral act in the state of Nevada. Angelo confirms it. "Uh, yeah . . . I was there . . . the boss did an immoral act." They arrest Angelo for collusion and Sonny on a morals charge. The bodyguard is released the same day. The District Attorney tries to hold Sonny for seventy-two hours, but his attorney demands a preliminary hearing.

Sonny, Joe Anadaro, and his two assistant attorneys sit behind the defense table, listening to the gynecologist give his testimony to the judge. "I know it sounds impossible, Your Honor, but I saw it with my own eyes."

The judge asks incredulously, "Doctor, are you telling me that the obese man sitting over there actually climaxed with fifty different women in six hours?"

The elderly doctor pulls his glasses down and looks up at the judge sincerely. "That's correct, Your Honor. I believe it was done for a gambling wager. I was called in as part of a medical research team."

The judge inquires, "How much was the bet?"

"The rumor was that several large corporations lost fifteen million dollars."

Sonny's jaw drops. He had no idea so much money was at stake. No wonder Sam wanted him to be absolutely sure he could deliver. The judge looks over the frame of his tortoise-shell glasses at the other doctor sitting in the courtroom.

"Doctor, is your testimony essentially the same as your colleague's?"

The medical man nods his head in affirmation. "Yes, Your Honor."

The judge then looks over at the prosecuting attorney. "Mr. Masterson . . . you have wasted this court's valuable time." His voice rises in volume, and the judge's anger shakes him so that his glasses slide down his nose as he speaks. "What business is it of this court to rule on an immoral act in another state and another county where we don't have any jurisdiction?" As Donald Masterson starts to say, "But Your Honor . . ." the gavel slams down on the bench. *"Case dismissed!"* Sonny shakes his attorney's hand as the sheepish prosecutor gathers up his papers. Before he leaves, he walks over to Sonny. "This is not the last time we'll see each other in court, Gibson."

Sonny looks at him in surprise. "Masterson . . . you talkin' to me? If so . . . tell it to my mouthpiece . . ." Sonny turns his back on him rudely as Masterson storms out.

On the limousine ride home to Bel-Air Joe gives Sonny some advice. "You know we won a case today, but we made Masterson look like a fool. By the time the press gets through with him, he'll look like a wet-behind-the-ears law student."

This irritates Sonny. "What does that have to do with me? What the hell do I care about that son of a bitch or the press?"

Joe reaches over and pours himself some wine. "You'd better care, Sonny. You've been getting a lot of bad press lately, and it's causing heat in Washington. Masterson is out to get you, you know."

"Don't worry, huh, Joe, I can handle anything that comes my way."

The veteran lawyer tries to drive his point home in a language his client really understands. "Sonny, Masterson is going to make a vendetta out of this."

Sonny says hotly, "Hey Joe . . . I don't wanna hear about it. No one's gettin' in my way . . . no one can stop me or my Big Scam."

Anadaro has been burning with curiosity for months. "I've heard you talk a lot about that . . . what is this Big Scam of yours?"

"Never mind, Joe . . . you'll know in time . . . you'll be involved." Suddenly the men lurch forward as the driver brakes for a pedestrian. Sonny picks up the phone and shouts harshly, "What the fuck's wrong with you, Georgie . . . can't you drive?"

A short, uncomfortable silence follows, then Joe says quietly, "Sonny, you're gonna have trouble with Masterson."

"Maybe I should knock him off, huh, Joe?"

The lawyer panics. "No! Sonny . . . for God's sake don't do that. If he stubs his toe now, the press is gonna say you did it." He warns, "And by the way, don't you think you're getting too colorful with the press? . . . The jet planes, the broads, the bodyguards, that stunt you pulled at the wine auction. That stuff sells papers . . . they love it, but the press can bury you."

Sonny assures him, "I control my press. I wanna be colorful . . . it keeps the heat off the other families. Besides, the press don't know nothin' unless I want them to." The limo stops in front of the gates to Sonny's estate. A bodyguard waves at them as they drive through. Sonny pats his worried lawyer on the knee. "Relax, Joe . . . I'm gonna fix you up with a couple of broads tonight."

"I'm sixty years old, Sonny. Forget the broads . . . just listen to my wisdom."

"I have my own wisdom, Joe." The car winds up the long, private drive to the mansion. "Look at all this . . . I got an electrified fence around this place, twenty Dobermans, eighty bodyguards . . . and forty-two closed-circuit TV units all over the grounds. Nothin's gonna happen to me. I'm invincible . . . I got more power than all the dons put together."

The enormous West Castle looms into view. "Look, Sonny . . . I'm not stupid . . . I can see what you have . . . but I've worked with three men who thought they were invincible, too . . . Capone, Genovese, and your friend Hoffa. They all went to the slammer." When the car stops, Joe says solemnly, "You're more powerful than they ever were, Sonny, but you've got to be careful."

Tony opens the door for his boss; Sonny concludes the conversation with his concerned counselor firmly, "I don't wanna hear anymore about that shit, Joe . . . you gotta live for today."

Joe Anadaro has warned this Mafia Goliath that David is just around the corner, but Sonny continues to flaunt his kingpin image. It is rare to see him in public without his underworld apparel: black shirt, white tie, sunglasses, cigar, and black fedora. He gets his flash from Sam and his class from Don Giuseppe. The press follows Sonny like a yo-yo as he bounces from coast to coast, checking the progress of his operations. Once a month he stops in Indiana to see his folks. Sonny has now set his father up in a used-car business, and no one on the executive staff is allowed to interfere with this particular branch of Sonny's chain . . . he tends to it personally. This is the only lot costing him money, but it gives his dad a sense of accomplishment, running a place of his own, and it makes his mother happy.

Sonny also likes to see his own cash keep rolling in, so he keeps a tight check on the activities of his executive staff. At one special board meeting in Florida the subject is how his operation can make more money. The executives have barely finished their doughnuts and coffee when Sonny storms into the room. He calls them to order, anxious to start the meeting. "All right, gimme the bad news first. Where am I losin' money?"

Dr. Swanson, the CPA, opens his portfolio. "The dune buggy business is showing a loss of twenty thousand dollars a month."

Sonny demands, "Why? We're selling over a hundred cars a month."

"We can't get any more Volkswagen engines; the guys in Germany won't give us any deals on rebuilt ones, and we've bought every used VW engine from every junkyard in the country like you told us to. There just aren't any more."

Sonny waves his hand as if he's sweeping the company under the rug. "Get rid of it . . . sell it to one of the oil companies. Back the sale with a Transcontinental commitment, and make sure we make a profit. . . . What else?"

Swanson opens a second file. "One other business is losing money, the car lot in Indianapolis . . . "

Sonny cuts him off, annoyed, "I don't wanna hear about Indianapolis."

Swanson protests, "But Sonny, that lot is losing eighty thousand a month. Your father . . ."

Sonny flies into a rage. "Goddam it . . . I said I don't wanna hear about it. Forget it . . . it'll make money." As he's often said, Sonny doesn't have time to educate his men. This particular lot is being used for legal money transfers. Unbeknownst to his father, funds are floated into this branch of Sonny's Auto Sales from different sources and then floated out again. His outburst subsides, "Now, is that all the bad news you guys got?" The executives nod. Sonny says snidely, "Well, then, gentlemen, tell me some good news . . ."

Swanson continues, "Sonny, the on/off ramp idea is working exactly as planned. We're taking in five hundred thousand a month from those land deals around the country."

"Good, good . . ." Sonny turns to his real estate executive. "Allen, what about the Everglades land brochures . . . how much are we makin'?"

Collins looks at his figures. "We're taking in half a million dollars a month, too, just as we estimated."

"Fine, now we're talkin'." Wolfman's is the next head on the block. "Jeff . . . how are my tombstone policies workin' out?"

Wolfman says, "They're very profitable. We're building up a lot of companies . . . we're taking in a million a month . . . and I've also been able to get those stock lists you told me about. We'll be starting ten more companies with those names."

"Very good, Jeff." Sonny diverts for a moment. "You know, gentlemen, that's the first thing I learned in the insurance business in Oklahoma . . . those names are important." He points to his company picture on the wall. "Yessir, there's a real success story. Four years ago I was just an insurance agent . . . but in one year I became the top agent in the whole country." What Sonny neglects to tell them is that the Mafia put him in and gave him $60 million worth of union policies to write. That and screwing Cora Pitkin pushed him all the way to the top. "Those names, Jeff, are very important."

R. B. Agnew is still looking at the picture. "Gee, Sonny, you were pretty slim in those days. You've put on quite a few pounds since then."

Sonny snaps caustically, "What are you, Agnew . . . Mr. Universe or somethin'? Never mind about my weight . . . what the fuck are my escrows doin'? Are they increasin' or not?"

The lawyer hands him a report. "Yes, we now have two million a month in escrow. Transcontinental is doing just fine ... we're taking in a million cash a month there . . ."

Sonny pushes him. "We should be doin' even better than that. By the way, Agnew, we're puttin' the word out a little more about this nephew business with the Vice President." Sonny picks up a sheet of paper and hands it to the attorney. "Here's a copy of a letter the developers will be gettin'. It says how proud the Vice President is to have you as a nephew and what a good attorney you are."

The letter was forged, but no one except the Vice President himself would have known it.

Agnew looks at the signature, then up at Sonny. "This is signed by Spiro Agnew! We could get into legal problems doing this. What if one of the developers calls the White House?"

"Don't be an idiot, Agnew . . . he'd never get through. Besides, we don't leave the letter with 'em, we just show it to 'em."

Sonny stands. "Now, I got somethin' very important for you guys to listen to. Joe and I had a long talk last night. . . . You all know Joe's been practicing law for a long time. He says the only way the feds could get me is on a mail fraud beef. There's no problem yet 'cause we've been deliverin' everything by hand, and I wanna make it very clear that it's gotta stay that way . . . no one is to send a Transcontinental commitment or a Bank of Sark confirmation in the mail. Tell that to your men in the field, too. I'm holding you guys responsible if they fuck up. I know I've made myself clear." He turns to Wolfman. "By the way, Jeff, I want Transcontinental to be takin' in three million a month." Sonny looks at the escrow attorney again. "Anything else, Agnew?"

"Yes, Sonny. The Bank of Sark is picking up two million in properties every month."

"What kind of properties?"

Agnew checks his file, "Land, mostly."

Sonny yells at him, "Land! I don't want fuckin' land." Papers fly from Sonny's portfolio as he throws it at Agnew. "I want hotels, apartments, income . . . money coming in, so we can steal the cash flow before they find out the checks are no good." Gregory interrupts his rampage. "Sonny, I heard about some land I think you might be interested in.

Sonny glares at him. "What are you, dumb? Where the hell were you when I was just talkin' to Agnew—sleepin'?"

Gregory persists, "Sonny, I really think you should hear about this."

Sonny sighs, "Okay, Gregory, let's hear it."

"I know a guy who'll sell us old land grants in the Smoky Mountain National Park . . . we can buy them dirt cheap!"

Sonny leans forward, intrigued.

"Wait a minute . . . that's a resort area, right?"

"Right . . ."

He leans back in his chair. "I don't wanna buy them, but I'm interested." Sonny turns to his trusted lawyer. "Joe, find out all ya can about this Smoky Park thing . . ."

Just then Linda buzzes him. "Sonny, Richie is on his way in . . . he said it was urgent."

Sonny goes over to the door to meet him. "Boss, I gotta talk to you in private . . ."

Sonny steps outside. "What is it? You know I'm in my monthly meeting . . . I gotta spend a lotta time with these fuckin' dummies."

He can see Richie is worried. "Boss, I just found out from my contacts in Washington that the Organized Crime Strike Force has you and all the dons under surveillance. I wanna check out the room for bugs."

Sonny reprimands him. "I thought you did that this morning . . ."

"It was done, Boss, but I'd feel better if I double-checked it myself. I want to go in with a meter now."

Sonny reaches for the doorknob. "All right, wait a few minutes . . . I'm almost finished. It'll scare these assholes if they think the feds are after me." He goes back inside.

Sonny returns to his place at the head of the table and concludes the meeting. "All right, these figures I've been seein' . . . I'm not happy with 'em. You idiots are gettin' top dollar, and I expect top dollar in return. We're takin' in seven million a month now . . . I want ten . . . I need more money for my Big Scam."

Swanson asks, "How much more could you need? You're getting seventy percent of the profits now . . . ." Sonny shouts at the impertinence. "Swanson, when I want a fuckin' profit report, I'll get one! Sometimes your mouth is bigger than your salary." He looks at all the men. "Another thing, what the hell happened to the chain of command I set up? I can't go into an office without one of you executives botherin' me . . . the next nincompoop that does it gets fired." Sonny gets up to leave. "All right, I'll be talkin' to you on Monday . . . and use that scrambler when you call me. We gotta be more careful from now on . . ."

When Sonny's schedule takes him to New York the following morning, he manages to get his mind off business for a few days. The main purpose of his trip is to attend a birthday celebration for Don Giuseppe. Sonny never misses the annual event.

The first night he's in town, Sonny is planning to see a show with Theresa, but she has to cancel. Angelo takes her call at the Essex House and hands the phone to Sonny. Theresa is mad. "Hello, Sonny . . . I hate that lousy airline . . . I couldn't get off to be with you."

"That's O.K., baby . . . will you be back tomorrow?"

"No . . . that's just it. I have a layover in LA. I'll be leaving just when you're getting back. I feel like quitting this rotten job."

Sonny tries to soothe her. "I'll tell you what . . . when are you getting back to New York?"

"In three days."

"O.K., I'll stay over in New York an extra day so we can be together."

Theresa's mood brightens. "You will . . . really?"

"Sure, baby. Come right to the hotel from the airport. I can't wait to see you."

"Hey, Sonny"—Theresa pauses—"I love you."

Sonny is not ready to say that back to her. "I'll see you in a few days, baby. . ."

The afternoon of Don Giuseppe's birthday party a battery of bodyguards checks the room thoroughly for bugging devices and wire taps, since most of the dons are under surveillance by the FBI now, too. That night everyone gathers in the penthouse suite of the Essex House to honor the boss of bosses, Giuseppe Loganno. The room is crowded with familiar faces when Sonny and his bodyguards arrive. Nick spots his old friend first and rushes over to hug him. "Sonny! God, it's good to see you . . . I'm glad you could make it. I tried to call you earlier, but Angelo said you were tied up in meetings."

Sonny assures him, "I was, but you know I'd never be too busy to be at your grandfather's birthday."

They walk over to the bar together. "By the way, Sonny, that wine thing you did was great . . . it took a lotta heat off the families."

"That's what it was supposed to do, Nick." Sonny looks around the room. "Where is Don Giuseppe?"

"We're expectin' him any minute. We have a special surprise for him. The chef downstairs made the biggest goddam pizza you've ever seen . . . it's four and a half feet wide. Come on down with me . . . I was just going to check on it."

Angelo says, "Yeah, Boss . . . I'd really like to see that."

Nick, Sonny, and their respective bodyguards get down to the kitchen just as the chef, Luigi, is putting the finishing touches on the large pie. When he places two salamis on it, Angelo says, "Gee, Boss, your joint is bigger than both those things."

Everyone laughs, but Angelo's wisecrack inspires Nick. "Hey, what a joke. Why don't you put your joint on the pizza? When Don Giuseppe turns around, you back off and he'll wonder who took his salami."

Sonny looks at him in disbelief. "You gotta be crazy." But the men all egg him on: "Come on . . . it'll be fun." "Yeah, there's only guys up there."

Sonny persists. "Hey, that pizza's hot . . . I'll get fried."

Nick says, "Hey, can you fix it so Sonny can put his joint on the pizza?"

The old immigrant says in broken English, "I can fix it uppa real beautiful, Nicholas. I canna fix anything."

Nick turns to Sonny. "See . . . "

Sonny is still doubtful. "Are you sure I'm not gonna get burned? This is a valuable piece a property here . . . it's gotta follow me around for the rest of my life."

The old man pats his shoulder. "Donna you worry . . . I'ma gonna fixa you up nice." The chef takes a plastic pad and lays it on the steaming pie, then puts some cheese cloth over that. This lining makes it safe, so Sonny finally agrees to the harmless prank. He unzips his fly and puts his human salami where the real one was. The chef pours sauce on him and dresses it with olives, peppers, and a hefty sprinkling of mozzarella cheese. Sonny's salami looks just like the other ones.

Nick, Mario, and Angelo carry the oversized Sicilian pie at Sonny's crotch level to the service elevator. A note on the door informs them it is out of order. At that moment the hotel elevator next to it arrives, crowded with people. Sonny reacts instantly. "It's O.K., folks . . . we'll catch the next one."

Nick says impatiently, "No, man, we're late now. Come on, let's go . . . there's plenty of room." The men start to walk, and unless Sonny intends to expose himself to the hotel guests, wherever the pizza goes, so does he.

On the long ride to the top floor the other passengers admire the exquisitely prepared, aromatic pizza. At the eighth floor a middle-aged couple get off. On the way out the man says, "Didn't that salami look good, Harriet?"

The prim wife retorts, "Harold, you know I don't like salami."

As the door shuts, Angelo yells after her, "Hey, lady . . . I bet you'd like this one." The men laugh all the way up to the penthouse floor. When they get there, a special key opens the elevator door, and they march in ceremoniously to present the pizza to Don Giuseppe. He is moved.

"What a beautiful present. You guys couldn't have gotten me anything better." He takes a fork from one of the tables to sample the pie, but instead reaches over and gives Sonny a sharp stab. The "salami" jumps back two feet, and Sonny yells "Jesus Christ!" As the others scramble to keep the pizza balanced, he looks down in disgust at his sauce-drenched pants leg. "Goddam . . . this shit's all over me."

Don Giuseppe's eyes twinkle. "How many times have I warned you, Santino . . . if you weren't careful, that thing was gonna get you in a mess someday." The room breaks into hearty laughter.

Nick asks his grandfather, "How'd you know it was Sonny on the pizza?"

"Nothing goes on that I don't know about. Don Giuseppe knows everything." He wags a finger in the air, "I know everything." The don then holds his arms up and signals the festivities to begin. "Enough talk . . . everybody, *mange.*" Besides the pizza, a buffet table is laid out with a variety of pastas and Sicilian delicacies. After dinner a three-piece band provides music for the party. Soldiers and dons pair up, jackets off, guns bouncing in their shoulder holsters, as they link arms in an energetic tarantella. Sicilians believed that the deadly poison of this spider could be sweated out of the body by dancing. Nick partners up with Sonny, and when the music stops, the men all applaud each other.

Still panting, Nick says, "I'm not as young as I used to be. I couldn't keep that up for long . . . I'd die if the spider ever bit me."

Sonny laughs. "Me, too."

Nick puts his arm around his boyhood benefactor. "Indianapolis seems like a million years ago, doesn't it?"

Sonny wipes the sweat from his forehead. "Yeah, but I'll never forget it . . . or you, Nick. If it weren't for you, I wouldn't be here."

Mario calls Nick away. The men are now forming a line to pay their respects to Don Giuseppe. A peculiar feeling hits Sonny . . . this scene is uncomfortably similiar to those he has seen at the parties in Sicily. He gathers his bodyguards around him in a corner of the room and whispers to Tony, "Gimme one of your pieces." He hands Sonny a gun.

Richie says, "What's wrong, boss?"

"Nothin' yet, but keep a close watch on everybody. If anyone goes for Don Giuseppe, kill him."

Angelo says loyally, "Uh . . . I'll watch you, Boss." Sonny observes tensely as each man gives the don a hug and a kiss, but the line dwindles without incident until Nick is the last one to kiss his grandfather. It is now Sonny's turn to pay his respects. After they embrace, Don Giuseppe says, "Come with me, Santino, I want to talk to you about something. Let's go up on the roof and get some fresh air."

Sonny and Don Giuseppe stand on the edge of the hotel roof a few minutes later, their bodyguards silhouetted nearby. The old man makes a sweeping gesture over the awesome mosaic of the Manhattan skyline. "This is all mine, Santino. But sometimes, even I am powerless. You know, I'm getting old. I don't know how many more birthdays we'll be celebrating."

Sonny can see that the don has aged considerably in the years he's known him, and he's looking strained. "What's wrong, Don Giuseppe?"

"I have a problem I've been trying to solve. . . . I never thought of asking for your help." He laughs, "Until I saw you on the pizza tonight."

"What's the problem, Don Giuseppe?"

The don sighs. "The French government has just accepted a bid from an oil company executive to build offshore drilling rigs for them. Our people need to see a copy of his offer to undercut it. By law, the government has to give the job to the lowest bidder." He urges Sonny, "It won't take much time from your schedule if you help us with this problem, Santino."

"How much time do you think?"

Oh . . . no more than ten days." Sonny is about to ask another question, but the don is chuckling to himself. "That pizza thing tonight . . . that was really funny. I gotta tell Alfonso about that. . . ."

"Don Giuseppe, how the hell did you know it was me?"

"You know how, Santino," he waves a finger, "I know everything."

Sonny begins to understand., "Uh huh . . . Luigi called." The don nods. Sonny asks tentatively, "I hope you weren't offended, Don Giuseppe."

"I wasn't offended. In fact, I'll remember this as the highlight of all my birthday parties." He adds, "And by pulling that pizza stunt, Santino, you gave me the answer to my problem."

Sonny is confused, "I don't get it, Don Giuseppe. . . . How does all this fit in with the pizza?"

The old man hands Sonny some tapes and a picture. "This is his old lady. She's gonna get you that contract for us. You'll get a hundred grand to be with her and another hundred when the papers are delivered to the Mafia."

Sonny stares at the famous face in the photo. "Don Giuseppe, this broad's classy. She's not gonna go for me."

"She'll go for you salami, Santino."

Sonny is still doubtful. "I dunno, there are all kinds of stories about this broad. From what I hear, her legs are locked so tight, she walks pigeon-toed. Her old man can't even get 'em open."

The don pats Sonny's shoulder. "Don't worry, Santino. After a couple of days with you, she'll be walking bowlegged."

This has been true of women who have paid for his sexual talents in the past, but Sonny is uncertain about his mark.

"Don Giuseppe, just because I'm a little different from most guys isn't gonna get *her* to bed . . . not this broad."

"Santino . . . this plan has been in the works a long time; long before I brought you up here tonight. Listen to the tapes. You'll know what to do. You know how broads think."

Sonny is amazed that any surveillance was able to penetrate her tight security. "Don Guiseppe, how in the fuck did you get tapes on her?"

"How in the fuck do you get your tapes, Santino . . ." He holds up his characteristic finger, "No one is invisible from Don Giuseppe."

Sonny is finally convinced, "Okay, Don Giuseppe, how do I meet her?"

"She'll be a houseguest of Andrew Delacroix. He'll take care of everything. . . ."

"When's she gonna be there?"

"In about two weeks." The don emphasizes. "This assignment is very important to the Mafia. If we get that job, our people work. We're all counting on you, Santino."

"I'll do my best, Don Giuseppe."

Sonny spends the next ten days listening to cassettes. There were forty hours of conversations taped over a six-month period. The Mafia obtained them by using a system the CIA had developed called WMDM, Whistling Monitor Device Mechanism. This tiny piece of equipment could be installed on any phone simply be unscrewing the mouthpiece of the receiver to place the bug inside. The device is then activated by calling the telephone number and playing a high frequency whistle after one ring. If someone picks up, they'll get a dial tone, but whether the receiver is lifted or not, the mike is live. It will record any sound in the room. At the end of the day, an electronics man takes the twenty-four hours of tapes and edits out the pauses. Sonny's tapes have no dead time . . . they were pure conversation from beginning to end. He finds most of them boring. There were the routine doctor's appointments, visits to the hairdresser's, and family gossip. All this couldn't have been less interesting to Sonny. He was looking for references to sex; any signs that the woman might have fantasies, fetishes, or perversions, but the tapes droned on. He found several bedroom conversations between husband and wife. One bone of contention was that he dribbled urine on the toilet seat. Another heated issue many nights was sex. The oil mogul usually stayed on the telephone many nights talking business until bedtime, so he was always tired. She was always horny. Sonny heard more than a few tapes of the proper matron masturbating.

Her one close friend was a freewheeling, 35-year-old designer, Barbara Bronson. Most of their conversation revolved around sex. They giggled like teenagers about their ideal man. Barbara wanted a diplomat; the society woman wanted a rogue, someone like James Bond who would sweep her off her feet and make mad passionate love to her. She was tired of being on the proverbial pedestal. Barbara titillated her one night after she had been to a swap party. "It was fantastic . . . everybody just started changing partners. At one point, I had two men working on me at the same time." This excited the woman. She may have been a prisoner of propriety, but she did have fantasies.

"Two men . . . what did they do?"

"Well, one sucked my nipples while the other ate me out and I was playing with two cocks at the same time. I came like crazy . . . it was really wild." Her friend suggested she try it sometime. "I know people who would be discreet."

The woman bemoaned her situation. "I have my position to think of."

Barbara sighs, "I guess you're right. I keep forgetting you're famous, to me you're just my friend."

"But you know, Barb, if I ever found a man who could suck me and make love at the same time, I'd risk anything for him."

"If you find a guy like that, send him over to my house when you're through."

The woman laughs, "I'll check with my astrologer to see if it's in the stars for me to meet anyone like that. I have an appointment with him today."

Sonny clicks off the machine. This last exchange has given him the key he needs to unlock the legs of this famous female.

Sonny arrived in the Virgin Islands three weeks later. He briefed Delacroix for two hours and it was arranged for him to meet his mark the following Sunday.

A tea party was the last place anyone would expect to find a Mafia kingpin and his bodyguards, but on Sunday afternoon, that's exactly where they were. Angelo, Richie, Tony, Eddie, and Georgie were all decked out in three-piece suits and introduced as Mr. Gibson's business associates to the other guests. The men had been instructed to keep a low profile after the amenities. As soon as he arrived, Sonny spotted his target immediately . . . there were just a few people clustered around her. When they left, Sonny seized the opportunity to introduce himself. She was slightly taken aback by the vision of this fat stranger approaching. When Sonny reached her he said, "Excuse me . . . I hope you don't mind, but I've been watchin' you and I think you're the most beautiful woman in this room . . . you're even more beautiful than they say."

She is flattered, "Why thank you, Mr. . . ."

"Gibson . . . Sonny Gibson." He slips in his first con. "You know, I can tell by looking at you. You're very troubled . . . you have an awful lot of personal problems."

Her defenses come up. She says superciliously, "What are you . . . a reporter?"

"No . . . I'm just a businessman, trying to make money like every other businessman." Just then, Delacroix passes by on cue, Sonny calls to him, "Andrew . . . come here a minute, will ya?"

The black comes over, "Ah, I see that you two have already met. Sonny is a very good friend of mine and one of the young tycoons of the financial world."

She raises an eyebrow. This interests the slim, well-bred brunette. "Are you a Wall Street tycoon, Mr. Gibson?"

"In a way . . . and please . . . call me Sonny." He continues, "To answer your question, I work with a lot of banks on Wall Street, but I do business all over the world. My main office is in Los Angeles."

Delacroix fires the con. "Did you know Sonny was a psychic? He's extremely modest about it, but I've had several readings with him that have been absolutely uncanny. They've helped me make some important government decisions." He continues baiting her. "Sonny is known in investment circles as the psychic of the business world. Maybe he could give you a reading on some of your private investments."

Sonny asks her innocently, "Do you believe in the stars?"

She fibs, "Not really," afraid to let the press get wind of her interest in the occult. "Why . . . are you an astrologer too?"

"No, but I can tell just by looking at you that you're a Leo. . . ." He struggles for a minute, "Let's see . . . you were born on July . . . July . . . twenty . . . July twenty-eight."

At this point, Sonny gives Delacroix a look and the black man says, "That is incredible, he did that to me when we first met." Another look dismisses him. "If you'll excuse me, I have to circulate."

"Of course, Andrew." She says haughtily to Sonny, "I'm not impressed, you know . . . my birthday is public record."

Sonny forges ahead. "Is it public record that you have a birthmark below your navel?"

This stuns her; no stranger could know that. Sonny moves closer, "Leos are very regal, they were born to rule." He moves closer still, "They're also spoiled easily if the elements are right. You've been spoiled by men all your life, but there's one thing they haven't been able to give you."

"What's that?"

Sonny looks into her eyes, "No man's ever been able to give you what you need in the bedroom."

Her eyes flash at this suggestive remark, but she changes the subject quickly, "When do you think you could give me a reading, Sonny . . . could we do it now?"

He looks around, "I'm afraid not . . . it's too distracting here. Maybe you could join me on my yacht tomorrow night for dinner." She looks at him slightly askance; he says quickly, "I know what you're thinking . . . it's wrong . . . it's strictly for the reading . . . I like you . . . I think I can help you."

"Can I bring a friend with me?"

Sonny says without hesitation, "Sure, but I hope it's someone who believes in psychics, because if they don't, I'll pick up their negativity. . . . You'll really get a better reading by yourself. Why don't you come by around seven thirty?"

"I'll have to let you know. . . ."

The next day, Sonny was very perturbed . . . he wasn't sure his dinner invitation would be accepted. This was the first assignment the con man didn't feel completely confident that he could deliver. Trying to make love to the Queen of England before her court would have been easier for Sonny than getting this tough cookie to crumble. Finally at 3:00 P.M. her security man called to say that they would be there at

7:30.

That night, Sonny drinks a glass of wine out on the top deck while he waits for them to arrive. Lost in the lights glimmering on the distant shore, he recalls Don Giuseppe's words of wisdom: "The net is as effective as the sword, Santino." When the launch pulls up, Sonny starts spinning the web that will bring the mark into his lair and goes below to the living room of the yacht so that he can greet her alone. She comes in by herself; her security man, Charles, is instructed to wait right outside the door. She is dressed in a street-length black chiffon Halston, the décolleté neckline tastefully filled in with a single strand of pearls. Sonny kisses her hand, gently licking her fingers . . . he knows that this is something that arouses her. The woman's body stiffens at his boldness, but she doesn't pull her hand away. He runs his fingers lightly down her arms as he removes the diaphanous shawl. "You look even more sensational tonight, if that's possible. You hair is so beautiful . . . it has the luster of a precious onyx."

"Thank you." Sonny drops the wrap on the nearest chair.

"Would you like a glass of wine?"

"I'd love some."

He opens a bottle of Chateau Lafite Rothschild '59. She leans over the bar as he pours, and remarks, "That was a very good year." Sonny hands her a glass. "Like a good woman, wine gets better with age." He toasts, "To your beautiful vineyard." The compliment is acknowledged graciously with a slight bow of her head. Sonny says, "My chef has dinner ready now. I thought we'd do your reading after, if that's all right. I'll be more relaxed then. My psychic powers will be more open."

During the meal, Sonny is a charming, intellectual companion, something he rarely chooses to be, but it brings this fly closer to the spider. The conversation covers a broad range of topics, from people to politics. She remarks that Sonny sounds like a man with a great deal of knowledge, but doesn't sound like a man with a great deal of education. Sonny admits that he never finished high school, but reminds her that as a psychic and someone who can read the stars, he didn't need to get his wisdom from textbooks. Sonny refills their glasses several times. The woman is worried that the wine might dull Sonny's psychic powers. He tells her cagily that with most subjects that might be the case, but the force of both their ruling planets is so strong, his powers are immune to the effects of the alcohol. When they're finished eating, the pair sit on the couch in the living room with snifters of brandy. Sonny now launches into an analysis of her personal problems. "You know, Leo is the proudest of all the signs . . . because of that, people misunderstand you." He wraps one lacy strand of his web around her. "In spite of all your wealth, you're a very lonely woman. You have only one close friend . . . her name is . . . uh . . . Barbara . . . Barbara

Bronson." Her eyes widen. Noting the reaction, Sonny continues. "She likes you for who you are. Everyone else thinks you're a snob, but you're really very shy." She lowers her head, fingering her pearls.

"That's right . . . that's amazing. My sister was always the one who liked all the fancy parties and the attention."

Sonny recites from memory, "You were happiest when you were first married, weren't you?"

"Yes." Her eyes soften. "We were both excited then about raising a family . . . but it wasn't too long after that the spotlight hit." She looks up sadly, "It's been blinding me ever since."

Sonny adds another strand, "Your beauty would dim the brightest spotlight in the world." He shakes his head, "I have this crazy feeling." Sonny puts a hand on her leg and looks into her eyes, "I wanna lay you down on this couch and make passionate love to you, right here." He inches up her thigh. "You're a very exciting woman." Sonny leans over, pushing her back gently, his hard bulge pressing against her. His mouth finds hers, and although closed lips resist him at first, it is only seconds before the two tongues lash at each other. This man was arousing a deep primitive need in her. Last night as she masturbated, thinking of the things he said, lust overwhelmed her. Now the sensation was being rekindled as her hips ground urgently against his obvious excitement. Sonny's lips slide to the hollow of her neck and continue nibbling downward until they close around her large, stiff, ruby nipples, tickling them gently. She moans with pleasure. The seducer goes in for the kill. Sonny reaches under the hem of her dress and moves his hand lewdly up her thigh into her panties as they sink slowly to the floor. He teases her at first, kissing her all over. There is a feeble protest, but the flimsy barriers she has thrown up to resist him crumble as his tongue licks its way insinuatingly down her body. A wave of emotions sweeps over her—guilt, shame, longing. Her mind flashes to her husband, but all thoughts of him are driven away by desire when Sonny reaches the center of her femininity and buries his face in her moist loins. The famous head flails rhythmically from side to side in response to his flicks, her hands caressing his head. In a few minutes Sonny brings her to a thundering orgasm. Only then does he realize how badly she needs a man. She grips his shoulders violently, clawing them with her fingers, driving him deeper into her.

When Sonny gets up and takes off his pants, the matron gasps at the colossus jutting from his pelvis. "My God, you're not from this world. . . . It's too big. I can't take you. . . ."

He strokes her hair gently, "Relax . . . you're loose now . . . besides, you're woman enough to handle it." Sonny assures her, "It's in the stars for me to be in you." Still in the aftershock of her ecstasy, her mounts her. There is a groan as his massiveness fill her completely.

Jolts of pleasure shoot through her body with each thrust of his powerful organ. She clutches him desperately as they make love, like a drowning woman on a piece of driftwood, until another raging climax storms through her body. Sonny stops, but the continued rocking motion of her hips tells him she is famished for sex, so he starts again . . . this time satisfying his own desire with hers. Then, still inside her, he cups the fleshy globes of her buttocks and brings the swollen clitoris up to him. He licks it as he makes love, bringing her to two crashing orgasms at once. She lets out a long, loud scream when she comes. Sonny uses all of his sexual tricks that night and discovers that this refined, cultured woman is no different from any other he has conquered.

His affair with the famous society woman lasts ten days. At the end of that time, Sonny gets a copy of her husband's bid, and the Mafia gets the $42 million French drilling job and work for the families.

When Sonny returned to California, the country was in the throes of a four-month-old dockworker's strike that was immobilizing the American economy. Boats crammed with shipments from overseas and merchandise waiting for export were piggybacked in every harbor in the country.

The Port of San Francisco was the hardest hit by the strike. There was a great deal of shipping traffic in the Pacific at this time because trade with the Orient was booming. Thousands of cars, cameras, televisions, and other Japanese products sat in cargo holds of freighters waiting to be unloaded. Shipping lines and warehouse owners were refusing to give in to the workers' demands, leaving negotiations at an impasse.

The stakes were high for everyone, and Sonny became involved. During the strike he was a highly visible and controversial figure and there were several threats on his life, but it had always been standard procedure for his bodyguards to look for bugs, wiretaps, and bombs wherever he went. One Friday night Sonny was called back to Los Angeles for an important meeting with a potential investor in his Big Scam. His scheduled departure from San Francisco was nine P.M. At 8:45, as the men were sweeping his private jet with an explosives detector, the red warning light came on. They double-checked it; in the past gunpowder in bullets had triggered the signal. A third check proved conclusively that there were explosives on board. The police bomb squad was called in, and they combed the plane. At exactly 9:15, Butler Aviation got a call telling them that Sonny Gibson's jet had been blown up.

In the meantime three sticks of dynamite had been found under the fuselage. They were timed to blow fifteen minutes after the landing gear had retracted. Whoever set the charge knew that twelve minutes out of San Francisco would put the jet over the ocean, the High Sierras, or the desolate Monterey Belt. If the plane had blown up, it would never have been found.

Something tells Sonny that this was not the work of any organized criminal operation. If it were, the hit men would have known that the plane hadn't left the ground and Butler Aviation would never have gotten the call. This had to be an inside job.

In the next two weeks all of Sonny's employees from executives to office boys take a polygraph test, except for two—both are bodyguards. Larry Zumba has been out of town, and Billy Mendini says he just hasn't gotten around to it. Sonny tells them both not to worry; he's sure none of his men could have betrayed him.

Sonny throws his men a party at Little Sicily a few nights later. When all the bodyguards have arrived, Angelo gathers them together. "All right . . . listen up, you guys . . . the boss is gonna make a speech." The men form a group near the bar where Sonny is standing.

"There's a reason why I'm having this little party here tonight. I just wanted ya all to know the polygraph tests everybody took came out good. I'm happy to know my men had nothin' to do with the hit. Of course, I knew that'd be the case." Sonny points to two men waiting in the back of the restaurant. "We got a couple a mandolin players in. I want you guys to have fun tonight . . . Joe says you can do whatever you want, provided you don't tear the place apart. After dinner we're gonna pull out the tables, and Ricco and Georgie are gonna show you how they really dance in Sicily."

Georgie yells out, "You're gonna dance, too, aren't you, Boss? You know the tarantella."

The bodyguards all join in his request. Sonny calms them, "I dunno . . . we'll see. Maybe." He calls to Joe, "Hey . . . can we get some food out here for these gorillas?"

The plump man scurries to the front. "Right away, Sonny. It's all ready." The men sit down, and while they eat, the mandolin players strum Italian songs.

Afterward the tables are moved away so that the native Sicilian bodyguards can perform the tarantella. The men all shout for Sonny to dance, so finally he joins them, arms high in the air. In just a few minutes he quits, panting hard from the strenuous dance. Now 290 pounds, Sonny can barely make it up the stairs of the West Castle without huffing and puffing. When the music stops, Joe brings in a case of wine for a drinking contest. The man who can swallow the most in one breath wins. This is the first time Sonny has ever allowed his men to drink, but it's a special occasion, so even the boss enters into the fun. To no one's surprise Angelo wins. All the Chianti consumed heightens the spirits of the party, which finally breaks up about three in the morning. Angelo picks one man to ride in Sonny's car with him, Richie, and Tony . . . Billy Mendini. Richie and Angelo sit on either side of the bar across from Sonny and Billy. The seats of this new, more elaborate limousine face each other. Everyone is loose, and the conversation is casual. The men are laughing about past incidents they have shared. Richie kids Angelo, who has been noticeably sullen during the banter. "Hey, Angelo, do you have to win everything? You won the pizza bet, now the wine contest."

Sonny smiles. "Angelo . . . did you have a bet with the guys with a pizza?"

Angelo has to answer the boss. "Uh . . . yeah . . . I ate two whole pies."

Richie jokes, "You should've seen him, Boss . . . he was still hungry after."

Billy says, "I'm not bettin' against you anymore, Angelo . . . I lost a hundred dollars tonight. You almost drank a whole goddam bottle of Chianti in one shot!" He reaches over to pat Angelo's knee. "You drink like a big whale." Angelo pushes Billy's hands away. Mendini is offended, "Boy . . . you sure are touchy tonight."

Richie says, "Come on . . . Angelo's never touchy."

The big man gives Billy a hard stare, making him uncomfortable. "What are ya lookin' at me so funny for, Angelo? All I said was I'm not gonna bet with ya anymore. . . . It was nothin.'"

Angelo says expressionlessly, "Shut up, Billy. I'm tired of hearin' you talk." Richie looks over at Angelo in surprise . . . he's never heard that tone of voice from him before. Is it the wine that's made him this testy?

Sonny breaks the tension. "You know, I got a really great bunch a guys workin' for me . . ." He puts his arm around Billy. "You've only been with me a couple a years, but I really love ya, too."

Billy says sincerely, "I feel the same way about you, Sonny. You're like the brother I never had."

"I thought you felt that way, Billy," Sonny replies coolly. "That's why I don't understand how you could've set me up like that."

Every muscle in Billy's body tightens. Richie pulls his gun and points it at the bodyguard with a warning, "Don't go for your piece."

Angelo says flatly, "Don't worry . . . I took the shells out when he was dancin'."

Sonny asks coldly, "Angelo . . . you fix up the piece?"

"Just like you told me, Boss."

"Give it to me." Angelo passes him a .38 with a taped trigger and a silencer.

Billy eyes them nervously. "How'd you find out? I didn't take a polygraph test."

Sonny slowly screws the silencer on the gun. "Only someone who knew my flight plan would know that fifteen minutes outta San Francisco would put us over no-man's-land. Exactly fifteen minutes after we were supposed to take off, the phone call came in. . . . That was a stupid move . . . I thought you were smarter." Sonny turns to him. "But the thing that really tipped me off was you, Billy . . . you haven't been able to look me in the eye for the past two weeks." He puts his finger on the trigger and points the gun at the guilty man. "If you tell me who called the hit, I'll let you go."

Angelo protests violently, "No, Boss . . . he's gotta die. You promised me I could kill him!"

Sonny flares, "Hey . . . I make the rules around here. If I say he lives . . . he lives." Sonny puts his arm around Billy again. "I don't wanna see ya get hurt. You mean an awful lot to me, Billy . . . you're one a my favorites."

The traitor can feel the daggers of hate from Angelo's eyes. "Yeah, but how do I know Angelo won't come after me? He's crazy."

"Angelo, gimme your word that you won't go after Billy."

The husky man defies him. "I can't do that, Boss. You don't want me to do that."

Sonny shouts, "Angelo! I said *gimme your word.*"

The bodyguard grudgingly concedes, "All right, Boss, I won't kill him."

Sonny turns to Billy and smiles. "See . . . Angelo won't come after you . . . none of my guys will. If they do . . . I'll kill 'em myself."

Sonny has Billy convinced. "O.K. . . . I'll tell ya. I never really wanted to be involved, but I needed the money. My girl and I are gettin' married. She wanted a fancy house . . . you know how it is . . ."

Sonny nods sympathetically. "I knew there had to be a good reason, Billy . . . it figures a broad would be behind it." The bodyguard confesses, "Some politicians wanted to get rid of you because your involvement was holding up the negotiations. They said you were hurting the economy. They went to Vinnie Ponciello in Vancouver."

Sonny gives Billy a hug. "You did a good thing tellin' me, Billy . . . I'm gonna let you go." Just then the limo swings around the last curve on Sunset Boulevard, and the panorama of the Pacific appears. "Look at that, isn't it beautiful, Billy?"

The bodyguard turns to look at the view, then turns back in disbelief. "You're really not gonna do anything to me?"

Sonny squeezes his shoulder. "No, Billy, I really love ya." Angelo watches, unable to accept that this treacherous man is going to live. The vista of the Pacific fills the whole horizon now. Sonny says, "Look out there, Billy, isn't it peaceful?" This time, as soon as the bodyguard turns his head, Sonny puts the gun against Billy's chest and fires five shots into the unsuspecting man's heart. The traitor slumps against the window.

Angelo says excitedly, "Boss, you said you weren't gonna kill him."

Sonny's answer is plain. "I didn't kill him, Angelo . . . he killed himself." He unscrews the silencer. "But I'm still gonna keep my promise to you, Angelo. Call John . . . tell him to get the Lear ready. I'm gonna get some rest . . . you're gonna take Billy for a plane ride." Sonny hands him back the gun. "Throw this out with the garbage."

Richie is feeling slighted. "Hey, Angelo . . . how come you knew it was Billy?"

"Uh . . . the boss told me a coupla days ago."

Richie looks over at Sonny, hurt by the exclusion. Sonny answers his unspoken question. "You're my overall security man, Richie. Angelo's my personal bodyguard . . . he had to know." Sonny calls to the front, "Hey, Georgie."

The driver turns as the car stops for a red light. "Yeah, Boss?"

"Get a new seat back here tomorrow . . . this one has rat's blood on it."

Shortly afterward the politician who ordered the hit died in a mysterious car accident, and Ponciello was executed by the Sicilian Mafia.

As soon as the contracts were signed in San Francisco, Sonny left for Los Angeles. He couldn't wait to get back . . . Theresa was meeting him. He always looked forward to seeing her. When they were together, he could forget his problems—and there had been plenty of them lately. The Bank of Sark checks were coming in for collection, and Sonny had refused to pay one too many Transcontinental commitments. His victims were starting to file complaints with the Treasury Department. Half of his time now was spent dodging subpoenas.

The day after Theresa arrived, she wanted to go to Disneyland. Sonny was totally against it, dismissing the idea as kid stuff. He was really afraid the visit would bring back too many unpleasant memories for him. Sonny hadn't been near an amusement park since he was being exhibited as a freak and selling himself on the carny circuit. Unaware of his past, Theresa insisted on going and dragged him to Anaheim.

As soon as they entered the gates of the Magic Kingdom, Sonny was bewitched, mostly by Theresa. He was swept away by her enthusiasm as she pointed out her favorite cartoon characters come to life and had her picture taken with Mickey Mouse; she even introduced Angelo to Goofy. "You two have a lot in common." Eventually Sonny let himself go and really started having fun. It was an odd sight to see Sonny, Theresa, and the fleet of bodyguards sail through the Pirates of the Caribbean, form a long chain on the Matterhorn bobsled, and fill every car on the Wild Teacup ride. When they got to the Haunted House, Angelo was afraid to go in. "I'll stay out here, O.K., Boss? It's too spooky for me. Richie can take care of you inside." The group stayed at Disneyland until the park closed, and at the end of the day Sonny, the Mafia kingpin, has had another taste of what it's like to live like a real human being.

In Los Angeles Theresa has always stayed at Sonny's hotel, but one night on her way out to the airport Sonny stops to show her the West Castle. On their tour of the thirty-room mansion Theresa remarks casually, "I like this place . . . it has potential."

Sonny is highly insulted. "What? I just spent fifty grand to have some fancy decorator fix everything up! What's wrong with it?"

Her answer is blunt. "It doesn't look lived in."

"What the hell you talkin' about, Theresa? I got a lotta people livin' here."

She looks at him in surprise. "You do? I thought the bodyguards had their own place."

"They do."

"Then who lives here?"

Sonny avoids a direct answer. "You'll meet 'em . . . they're upstairs."

As they continue the walkthrough, Theresa indicates what changes she'd make. They stop in the enormous living room that is filled with heavy, dark Italian furniture . . . gold cherubs and red flocking abound. She looks around slowly, one finger on her chin. "You know what this place needs?"

Sonny is almost afraid to ask. "What?"

"Plants . . . living things . . . something to make this place alive." She picks up a fold of the maroon velvet drapes. "This material is so heavy . . . it makes everything dreary. You need light colors to brighten this room up."

Angelo encourages her. "Hey, Boss . . . Theresa really has some good ideas. I never liked the little fruit that put all this stuff in here anyway."

"That little fruit cost me fifty grand."

The amateur decorator volunteers, "I'd be happy to give you some more ideas."

Angelo adds, "Yeah, and Theresa wouldn't charge you fifty grand, Boss."

She laughs. "That's right, Angelo. I'll give them to Sonny for one kiss . . ."

Sonny says, "O.K., you two . . . I haven't done the upstairs yet. Lemme know what you think, Theresa."

"Let's go up now."

They climb the wide center staircase and stop at the first landing. There is an eight-foot oil painting of Sonny on the wall in a carved gold frame. Theresa comments, "That's good, Sonny. The artist has really captured you, except that you look a little older.''

Sonny jumps on her. ''That don't look like me. . . . In fact, if I ever find that son of a bitch, I'm gonna have him killed for paintin' me like that.'' The portrait shows Sonny in his kingpin apparel, a black suit and black fedora, holding a half-empty glass of wine; a bottle of Valpolicella and a map of Sicily are in the background. Richie says, ''That guy who painted it almost did get killed.''

Theresa turns. ''Why? Did he have an accident?''

Angelo answers, ''Tell her what happened to the little junkie, Boss.''

Sonny relates the story. ''See, we got this guy Rossi 'cause they said he was one of the best painters around. He started workin' on this thing two years ago. I paid him, then I don't hear nothin' for like six months. So Angelo and Richie go over to his place, and the picture's hardly worked on . . .'' Sonny complains, ''That guy made me sit for five fuckin' days so he could get his outline, too. When the boys told me about it, we brought Rossi here as my guest.''

''You kept him here against his will?''

''Damn right . . . I wanted to get my fuckin' painting done . . . but he got out.'' He shoots an accusing look at the bodyguards.

Angelo is still making excuses for that one. ''Uh . . . I dunno how he got out, Boss . . . we watched him every minute.''

''Yeah . . . well, ya couldn'ta been watching him that close 'cause he got all the way to Kansas City . . . it took us ten months to find him. I hadda send my jet to bring him back. This time he had a twenty-four-hour guard on his ass. When Rossi said he was finished, I was out of the country. The guys assigned to watch him said it looked great, so they let him go.'' Sonny says in disgust, ''After all that, look how in the fuck he painted me . . .'' The eyes of the portrait glint evilly from the canvas . . . it is this malevolence that disturbs him. ''I don't look that mean.''

Theresa tries to brush it off. ''Oh, nobody ever likes their own pictures.''

She turns to the huge bodyguard. ''Angelo, did you ever like a picture of yourself?''

Angelo says shyly, ''Uh . . . most pictures I take, they only get half my head. I always look good from the chin down.''

Theresa laughs and jokes Sonny out of his irritation. She takes his hand. ''Come on . . . I'm dying to see the upstairs.'' They take a right turn and continue their tour.

The second floor of the West Castle looks like a sorority house. Bras and panties hang from towel racks in the bathrooms of all eleven boudoirs, where women in negligees lounge on the beds, reading, eating, or talking. Sonny introduces Theresa to each of them as they pass by.

Her response to all is polite but frosty. She says jealously, "The upstairs needs a lot of work . . . it's so cluttered. For a start I'd throw out all those extra ornaments you have around." When they get to Sonny's door, she says coolly, "Is this the master bedroom?"

Angelo opens the door. "Uh . . . yeah, this is the Boss's room."

She looks around. "What are these big steel doors?"

Richie answers, "They're part of the security system. They slam shut and an alarm goes off if anybody breaks into the house." He points to a second set on the opposite wall. "That's an escape hatch . . . it leads to the outside of the property through a chute." The focal point of the room, naturally, is the enormous bed.

Theresa cracks, "That is the biggest bed I've ever seen."

Sonny retorts, "Yeah . . . well, I'm a big guy . . . I toss and turn a lot in my sleep." She shoots him a skeptical look.

Angelo says enthusiastically, "Come on, Theresa . . . you gotta see the boss's pool. It's really somethin'."

The grounds of the West Castle simulate those of a Roman villa. The Olympic-sized pool is surrounded by fountains and tall cypress trees. Statues of curly-haired men and women in togas are the swimmer's stone companions. Theresa hardly notices any of this, too preoccupied with the dull ache in the hollow of her stomach. She finally screws up her courage and asks, "Sonny, who are all those women?"

"They're close friends of mine."

"How close?"

He pauses. "Oh, two, maybe three sleep with me every night." Her eyes sadden, but she is silent. Sonny reminds her, "Hey . . . you should know how I am by now." She gives him a little nod but turns away. "Look, Theresa . . . I'm no angel . . . I told you that."

She looks at her watch, desperate for anything to say that will cover the hurt. "It's getting late . . . we'd better go if you want me to meet your friend Joe before I leave."

He puts his arms around her waist. "You know, you can stay here, baby, next time you come out instead of stayin' at the hotel."

Theresa's reply is quick and frank. "No, thanks . . . I don't like crowds." She wriggles away. "Come on, I'm hungry . . . let's go."

Sonny knows Theresa is hurt but feels it's her own fault. He never said he was any good for her. They have an uncomfortable dinner that night. She doesn't bring up the subject of his private stock again . . . and neither does he. On the way to LAX Theresa realizes that the incident so upset her that she forgot to change into her stewardess uniform. When she begins undressing, Sonny says, "Angelo, go up front." The bodyguard gets out, and Sonny slides over to fondle Theresa's breasts. In spite of her mood she moans; he is one man she can never resist. As they start making love, Angelo's voice comes over the speaker box. He tells the car behind them, "Uh . . . I'm up by Georgie now. The boss is gonna fuck the broad." He corrects himself. "Uh . . . no, that's not a broad . . . it's Theresa."

This breaks her mood. She laughs, but Sonny picks up the phone and yells at him. "How many times I gotta tell you guys, unless it's important, don't talk on the goddam box when I got a broad back here."

Theresa says, "Don't get mad at Angelo, Sonny. At least *he* knows I'm not a broad."

When they get to the airport, Sonny goes to the gate to see Theresa off. He says sincerely, "I mean it, Theresa, next time I want you to stay at the West Castle."

She looks at him sadly. "I'd like to, Sonny, but I can't share a house with all those other women."

"Just think about it, O.K.? I really want you to be with me." She vacillates a second. "Well, maybe, if . . . if . . ." Then she says firmly, "No . . . I can't. I just can't be second best."

Sonny proclaims firmly, "Well, I'm not giving up my fuckin' broads for any woman."

Theresa says without missing a beat, "O.K., then, we'll keep on seeing each other the way we have been."

Sonny had never expected her to give up without a fight. Her quick rejection of his magnanimous offer irritates him. "Theresa, what the fuck's wrong with you? Can't you hear? I said I want you to be with me."

Theresa stands her ground. "When all the bras and panties go, I'll stay."

Her stubbornness frustrates him. Sonny really prefers Theresa's company to all the women he has . . . she's a good sex partner and a stimulating companion, but he is not ready to make a commitment to her. Sonny likes the idea of his freedom. He warns her, "Even if I get rid of 'em, I can't promise I'll be faithful."

Theresa softens. "Sonny, I'm not asking you to change, I just don't want to be part of a harem, that's all . . ."

Sonny takes a beat, then says, "O.K., I'll get rid of all the broads." He points his finger at her. "But there's one thing I'm gonna demand as long as we're together, Theresa . . . you don't ask me any questions . . . ever. Where I go and what I do is my business. If someone asks ya somethin', ya don't know nothin' . . . is that clear?"

"If I say yes, does that mean you're asking me to live with you?"

Sonny says reluctantly, "Yeah . . . I'm askin' you to come live with me." She throws her arms around him excitedly. "I accept. I promise I'll never interfere. I just want to be with you."

They kiss until another stewardess on her flight interrupts their good-bye. "Hurry up, Theresa, Captain Connors is already on board."

They break their embrace, and Theresa runs to the plane. At the door she turns and shouts, "I love you," then disappears inside. On the way out of the terminal Sonny tells Richie, "Get all the broads outta the West Castle by Friday."

Angelo asks, "Uh . . . are you really gonna get rid of the broads, Boss?"

Sonny smiles. "Nope . . . they're going to Boca Raton . . . I'll use 'em down there."

Before they're out of the airport, Linda calls on the limo phone. "Sonny, you're half an hour late for your appointment with the sheik."

"What the hell's wrong with you, Linda? I told ya I didn't wanna meet that guy now. I wanna do it tomorrow night. Can't you get anything straight, or do I have to look for a new secretary?"

She tries defending herself. "Sonny, you told me yesterday——" He explodes, "Goddam it, Linda, don't argue with me. I'm payin' the fuckin' bills around here." The bodyguards are quiet during this conversation. Sonny has always treated Linda with respect.

She says calmly, "O.K., Sonny, what time tomorrow?" He shifts 180 degrees. "Jesus, you're a stupid broad, Linda. Why should I do it tomorrow when he's there now? Tell him I'm gonna be another twenty minutes." He hangs up on her, complaining loudly, "I got a bunch of idiots working for me . . . they're all fuckin' idiots." Sonny's men have noticed that he's been increasingly irascible in the past few months . . . except when Theresa is around. With her he is generally calmer and, in particular, not as short-tempered with them.

Two weeks before Christmas Theresa moves in with Sonny. He likes having her around; she makes his home a relaxing personal oasis from the pressures of business. By this time the holiday season is in full swing. In the past Sonny has been a Scrooge who saw the celebrations as an annoying slowdown in his work schedule, but Theresa changes all that—Christmas finally comes to the West Castle. It's Christmas Eve, and Sonny is on the phone when Theresa and the bodyguards come into the living room laughing, arms filled with boxes of glittering ornaments. Angelo is right behind them, carrying a fifteen-foot spruce tree. Sonny yells, "Hey . . . can ya keep it down? I'm tryin' to do business here."

Theresa whispers, "Put it in the corner, Angelo. I think it'll look nice over there."

Sonny hangs up a minute later. "What the hell's all this crap?"

The Italian girl bubbles, "Christmas decorations . . . we're trimming the tree tonight."

"Don't we have anyone to do that?"

She looks at him in exasperation, hands on her hips. "Sonny, you don't hire someone to decorate your Christmas tree . . . it's a family thing."

Tony reminisces, "Yeah . . . when I was a kid, I used to help my mother string popcorn."

Sonny recalls bitterly, "When I was a kid, we couldn't afford a branch, much less a tree."

Theresa enthuses, "It should be fun, then, if you've never done it before."

Sonny demurs. "You have a nice time . . . I can't be bothered with that shit."

She tugs at his hand. "Oh, come on, don't be so stuffy. It'll be fun."

Angelo pipes up, "Yeah, Boss, it'll be fun . . . we're all gonna help."

Theresa's big eyes beg him. "Please . . . please." She finally wins him over, and Sonny puts his papers away.

"O.K. . . . what do I do?"

Angelo reacts like a child whose father is taking him to the movies. "Oh, good . . . the boss is gonna help."

Theresa runs over to get Sonny a box of delicate crystal snowflakes. "Here, you hang these . . . and don't break them." Theresa climbs the ladder next to the tree; Angelo hands fragile, multicolored balls to her. Richie and Tony team up to spiral twinkle lights around the branches.

Sonny hasn't even put the second snowflake on when the phone rings. Linda is calling; Angelo tells her, "The boss is decoratin' the tree . . . can you hold on a minute?" He shouts, "Hey, Boss, it's Linda."

Sonny picks up. "Yeah, Linda . . ."

She says, surprised, "You're decorating a tree?"

"Yeah . . . a Christmas tree . . . it's Christmastime, ya know. All families do it."

"I know, Sonny, but you never celebrated before."

"Yeah, I always celebrate . . . I just do it inside. I think Christmas is too commercial."

She reminds him, "Your Christmas sale at Sonny's Auto made a lot of money."

He replies quickly, "That's different . . . that's business."

"Are your Mom and Dad coming to LA this year?"

Sonny complains, "Nah . . . now that Pops is in the used-car business, he never wants to leave the fuckin' lot . . . says he might miss a sale. I'll stop and see 'em on my way to New York next month." Sonny is confused, "Where the hell are you anyway, Linda? I thought you were gone."

"I am . . . I'm in D.C. with my folks . . . I go there every year, Sonny."

"Oh, yeah . . . yeah. Well, whaddya need? Why'd ya call?"

"Well, two reasons. First, I wanted to thank you for the Mercedes sports car."

"You deserve it . . . you've been a loyal secretary, Linda. What else?"

"I also wanted to let you know that Joanne is going to be delivering the papers you've been expecting from Mr. Cordone." Sonny's contact is sending him a detailed map for one of the Philippine islands.

He asks, "Who in the hell is Joanne?"

Linda sighs. "She's my assistant. She's been working for us two years, Sonny. The guys all know her. She'll be up on Thursday." She continues, "By the way, Joanne will be taking care of your appointments while I'm away."

"Oh, O.K."

"Have a Merry Christmas, Sonny. Thanks again for the car. I'll see you next year."

Sonny panics. "What the hell you mean . . . aren't you comin' back next week?"

"Yes, Sonny, but that's after New Year's . . . it'll be 1971. Have a nice Christmas, O.K.?"

"You, too, Linda." Sonny puts the phone back. "Angelo, you know some gal who works in the Sunset office . . . Joanne?"

The bodyguard says immediately, "Yeah . . . a pretty little blonde. She's been with ya about two years, Boss. She's——" Sonny cuts him off. "Yeah . . . I've already heard all that."

Theresa hands him his box of snowflakes with an accusing look. "You've only hung one of these . . . you have forty-nine to go." Sonny complains as he clumsily puts each snowflake on its branch, but Theresa's excitement is infectious. By the end of the night he is really in the spirit of things. With the exception of the bodyguards with their guns and holsters, scenes like this one are occurring all over the country.

When the last ball is hung, Theresa says excitedly, "It's time for the most important part." She hands him a box. "You get to put this on."

"Where's it go?"

Theresa points to the top of the large tree. "Up there."

Sonny says firmly, "Up there! You gotta be crazy . . . I'm not climbin' up that ladder. Give it to Angelo . . . he don't even need a fuckin' ladder."

Theresa insists, "Sonny, please . . . the head of the house has to do it . . . it's tradition."

Angelo backs her up. "Yeah . . . it's tradition, Boss."

"All right, all right." Sonny grudgingly climbs up the ladder and, when he gets to the top of the tree, places a beautiful golden angel on its spire. He climbs down, and Theresa plugs in the lights. When a rainbow illuminates the room, everyone applauds. Sonny puts his arms around her waist. "You really did somethin' special tonight . . . you gave me somethin' I never had in my life . . . a real home."

In the hall the grandfather clock begins to chime. She kisses him. "It's midnight . . . come on . . . let's open our presents." Angelo comes in with a big pitcher of eggnog as Theresa gets the gifts from under the tree. She sits on the couch and calls out the bodyguards' names.

Angelo comments on the exquisite packages. "These are really beautiful, did you wrap them yourself, Theresa?"

She laughs. "Yes, Angelo . . . I used to do that for a living." Theresa winks at Sonny.

The bodyguard exclaims, "Gee, Boss, we never got no real presents before . . . just money."

"Yeah, well, don't thank me . . . thank Theresa."

She says, "I hope you all like them."

Theresa has gotten sterling silver shoehorns for the rest of Sonny's men, but his three closest chief bodyguards get special gifts. Tony opens up his, a clock that tells time all over the world. "Man, I can sure use this . . . thanks a lot, Theresa." He hugs her.

Richie's present is a computer that calculates the distances from city to city in the United States. "Hey . . . look at this, Boss . . . this'll be great when we travel." He hugs her, too.

Angelo opens his package last. Inside is a solid gold Fortuna horn on a gold chain. Sicilians believe this good-luck charm keeps evil spirits away. The big man is moved. "This is what I always wanted, Theresa . . . I had one when I was a kid, but it was plastic."

She puts her arms around his waist. "I wanted to get something that would keep you safe. I love Sonny, Angelo. If you're protected, he's protected . . . you have a very important job."

Angelo says shyly, "Uh . . . I love the boss, too, Theresa." He gives her a peck on the cheek. "Thanks."

Sonny breaks in, "Where the hell's my present, huh?"

Theresa goes to the tree and gets a small box wrapped in gold foil. Sonny tears off the paper and takes out an expensive meerschaum pipe. "What the hell am I gonna do with this?"

Tony says, "Yeah, Boss, you don't even smoke a pipe."

Theresa replies calmly, "That's true, Tony, but I was hoping Sonny might like to use it when he's in the house instead of those cigars."

Sonny retorts, "I dunno about that. Pipes are for brains . . . the working man smokes cigars." He then opens the present from his men, a Gucci tobacco pouch.

Richie says, "It's good leather, Boss. It's Italian."

Angelo confesses, "Uh . . . Theresa said we should get you that . . . I think you put money in it or something." Theresa cringes at this last remark. That was supposed to be their little secret.

Sonny puts the pipe in his mouth and winks at her. "Well, what do you think? Do I look like Bing Crosby?"

She sits on his lap. "Much better, even if you can't sing."

Angelo hands him another box. "This is from Don Giuseppe and Nick, Boss. The don sent Luciano out here with it."

"When the hell was that?"

"Last week . . . "

"Why didn't you guys tell me?"

Angelo explains, "Uh . . . the don didn't want us to give it to you before Christmas."

Sonny opens the rectangular package. Inside is a Corum watch with a 1¾-inch solid gold wristband. A single word is engraved on the back SPARTACVS. Sonny asks, "Spartacus . . . wasn't he a soldier?"

Tony answers, "Yeah, he was the best gladiator in the Roman Empire."

There is a note enclosed with the gift. "To Santino: For your loyalty as a soldier. Corum told us they only made two watches like this. You have one, Elvis Presley has the other. Love, D.G. & Nick."

The bodyguards all examine the present. Tony says, "Boss, there must be six ounces of gold here. Maybe we should put it in the safe."

Angelo agrees, "Uh . . . yeah . . . this is kinda heavy to wear all the time, isn't it, Boss?"

Sonny takes the gift and slips it around his wrist. "You guys will never see me without this watch from now on . . . it's very special to me."

Theresa touches the gleaming gold. "It's very beautiful, Sonny."

Richie comes over now and places a large box with an enormous red bow at Theresa's feet. "We got you some presents, too, Theresa, but you should open this one first . . . it's from the Boss."

She looks at Sonny in anticipation. "What is it . . . what is it?"

He smiles. "I'm not tellin' ya . . . open it."

Theresa slides off his lap and lifts the lid of the gigantic box. Inside a tiny white poodle is whimpering softly. Her eyes light up. "Well, look at you!" When Theresa picks up the puppy, his soft pink tongue licks her face happily, the tiny tail wagging furiously. She cuddles the puppy to her face. "He's beautiful . . . he's so cute." Theresa looks at Sonny, "What should we call him?"

"That's up to you, my love . . . "

Theresa looks at Sonny puffing on his pipe, then at the puppy. "I think I'll call him Bing."

On Christmas Sonny and Theresa throw an open house on the

tennis court of the West Castle for his Los Angeles employees. When Tony came onto the staff, he suggested they carry ID's with pictures. Before anyone is admitted now, this identification card must be shown at the gate. People drift in and out until midnight, enjoying the boss's unexpected hospitality. Sonny has fun at the party, but the very next day a black cloud covers the happiness of his holiday season. There is an urgent call from Don Giuseppe. "Santino, Mario is on his way out to see you . . ."

Sonny doesn't like the tone of his voice. He senses real trouble. "What's the matter, Don Giuseppe?"

"Mario will tell you when he gets there . . . I don't wanna talk about it on the phone."

"You don't sound good, Don Giuseppe. Are you O.K.?"

"I'm fine."

"This must be important if you're sending Mario out here."

The don replies darkly, "It is, Santino . . . it is the most important thing you'll ever have to do for me."

Mario's flight from New York gets in at 11:30 that night. Sonny is so concerned about the purpose of this trip that he goes with the bodyguards to pick up Don Giuseppe's lieutenant at LAX. Mario is waiting for them outside the United terminal, his face drawn. Sonny thinks he is probably there to tell him Don Giuseppe is dying. After they hug and get in the limousine, Sonny asks, "What's up, Mario? Don Giuseppe wouldn't have sent you out here unless somethin' was wrong."

Mario looks at him grimly. "It's Nick."

"Nick . . . somethin' happened to Nick?"

The lieutenant says dully, "Nick's dead . . ."

Sonny replies quickly, as if stepping on Mario's statement could squash it. "Dead . . . whaddya mean, Nick's dead? He's too young to die."

"He's dead, Sonny. We think he was hit." Now there is a stunned silence. Mario is telling him his best friend is gone.

Angelo groans, "Oh, no . . . not Nick . . . no."

Sonny asks, "Who did it, Mario?"

"We don't know exactly. It could've been two people . . . Eddie is one of them."

"Shit, he was one of your own soldiers. What makes ya think he did it?"

"Eddie, Pete, and Nick were makin' a delivery up in Harlem. They were carryin' ten million in heroin to the Cassano brothers. The don gave the Cassanos control of the drug traffic up there if they'd dry up the market for ninety days and double the price. Don Giuseppe sold 'em this stuff for a million dollars for doin' it."

Sonny is confused. "Why would Nick be goin' with two carriers to

Harlem?"

"You know there are only three people Don Giuseppe would trust to pick up that kinda cash: you, me, and Nick. I couldn't go 'cause the feds are on my ass, and you're even hotter than I am."

"What's the Cassanos' story?"

"They say they never got the drugs"— Mario looks at Sonny—"but we know better."

"Whaddya mean, you know better?"

"Bernardo, one of the lieutenants for the brothers, came to Don Giuseppe . . . he was scared there'd be a vendetta when Pete surfaced."

"Where'd he surface?"

"In the East River . . . . with two slugs in him."

Sonny deduces, "So ya got a contract out on Eddie?"

Mario nods. "Him and Gino DiCola."

Sonny stops him. "Hold on, DiCola was one of the don's carriers, too."

"That's right, Sonny . . . but you know Don Giuseppe's not well . . . everybody's grabbin'. DiCola made a side deal with the Cassanos for a half a million dollars and a piece when they sold the narcotics." There had been rumors for two years that the don was dying. The power struggle had already started in New York, but it was most likely that Mario would get the don's territory.

Sonny tells him, "I heard DiCola was out here someplace."

"Yeah . . . he's settin' up a deal with the Matrano brothers."

This is bad news to Sonny. "Shit! Those guys are friends of mine . . . what if he double crosses 'em?"

Mario says seriously, "The Loganno family will be blamed . . . you know what that means."

Sonny nods. He knows only too well and finally understands how a Mafia war could break out over one carrier. He says, "From the sound of things I'd say the don wants me to find DiCola, right?"

"Yeah . . . whoever killed Pete and Nick probably killed Eddie, too."

Sonny asks hopefully, "Mario, are you sure Nick's dead? Maybe they're holdin' him for ransom."

The lieutenant shakes his head. "We thought of that, but it's been ten days . . . there would've been a note by this time." He says with conviction, "Nick's dead." Sonny stares out of the window for a few minutes, thinking of his quiet friend who never wanted any part of violence but was its victim. Mario says, "The don wants to know where his narcotics are, Sonny, but there's something more important to Don Giuseppe."

Sonny remembers the don's words, " . . . the most important thing you'll ever do for me, Santino . . ."

"What's that, Mario?"

"He wants to know where Nick's body is . . . he wants to bury him."

Sonny feels a wave of sympathy for the old man who had so much and lost the only thing that ever really meant anything to him . . . his grandson. Sonny knows that life is something power and money can't ever replace. He finally says, "I don't guarantee I'll find out where the narcotics are at, but tell Don Giuseppe one thing"—Sonny grips the armrest in determination—"I'll find out what happened to Nick if I have to cut DiCola's dick off to do it."

As soon as they get to the West Castle, Mario goes to bed, but Sonny wants to get started on his assignment. "Angelo . . . you're gonna go to San Diego and get DiCola and——"

The bodyguard clenches a huge fist. "I'm gonna kill him, Boss."

Sonny yells, "No, Angelo . . . haven't you learned anything from me yet? How the fuck you gonna get information from a dead man? Just bring him up here." He warns, "And Angelo, be nice to him."

"What should I tell him, Boss?"

Sonny thinks. "Tell him I want him to be my special carrier for a twenty-million-dollar heroin shipment comin' in from the Philippines . . . he's gonna stay with me till it comes into Manila."

"Uh . . . O.K., Boss."

"There's somethin' else you gotta do. Tell the Matrano brothers what's happening and that the Loganno family wants to warn 'em that any deal DiCola's workin' on is a setup. That's important, Angelo . . ."

"Uh . . . O.K., Boss . . . I'll tell 'em." The bodyguard starts to leave just as Theresa enters the den. Sonny has some final orders. "Tell John to get the Lear ready . . . we're gonna be goin' to Tahoe tomorrow night."

Theresa jumps into the conversation. "Ooo, can I go?"

Sonny is firm. "No . . . you can't."

She runs her finger along the edge of one of the Roman columns, sulking. "I'm tired of sitting in this house. I wanna go to the ranch and ride Palomino Joe."

"I said no, Theresa . . . you can go to Tahoe next week. I got business."

"Aw, come on, Sonny, I won't interfere in your stupid business . . . I'll be out riding a horse."

Sonny is getting aggravated. "I said no, Theresa. You can't go. That's final."

At the airport the following evening the guard crosses in front of Sonny's private jet in the hangar and peers out of the peephole to see who's ringing the bell so insistently. He recognizes Theresa and buzzes her in. "Hi, Gus, we're going to Tahoe in about a half-hour. I have to put some things on the plane for Sonny." Since the pilot has just called in his flight plan for the trip, Gus doesn't question her story and unlocks the plane. Once she's inside, Theresa relocks it, then hides in the shower.

Twenty minutes later Sonny arrives with DiCola and the bodyguards. Gino has had a pleasant, relaxing day with Sonny, but after takeoff there is no more casual conversation. As soon as they are safely away from the mountains, the pilot descends to 10,000 feet, and Sonny asks Angelo for his piece. He grabs DiCola by the collar and hits him repeatedly across the face with the butt of the gun. Bloody teeth fly. The stunned man clutches his bleeding mouth as Sonny pulls DiCola by his hair over to the door of the plane. "You stinkin' bastard. You set up Don Giuseppe's men . . . Nick was my best friend." He hits DiCola again, then gives Angelo back his gun. The bodyguard hands him a switchblade. Sonny clicks it open next to Gino's throat, grazing the Adam's apple with the sharp edge. He holds the frightened man's head back and presses the knife against it. "I'm gonna cut your nuts out . . . you had a man killed who never hurt nobody . . . He was the only friend I ever had. You're gonna die, DiCola."

Gino starts to beg, "I don't wanna die . . . please . . . I was just doin' my job. It was nothin' personal, Sonny . . . please."

Sonny yanks his hair. "Tell me where Don Giuseppe's drugs are at, and I'll let you live."

Gino starts to cry. "I don't know . . . I swear on my mother's soul."

"What happened to Nick?"

"I don't know. . . . Don't kill me, please . . . please. Look, I'll make it worthwhile."

Sonny knows Gino's lying. He says contemptuously, "You're not even worth cuttin' up Sicilian style . . . it's too much trouble." Sonny throws Angelo the knife. "Gino's ready to leave . . . toss him out."

"It'd be my pleasure, Boss. Nick was like my kid brother." Angelo yells, "O.K., John." The pilot pulls back power, and Richie cracks open the door. The force of the wind blows blood across DiCola's face. The immense bodyguard picks up the kicking, screaming man.

Sonny thinks of Nick and stops Angelo. "Hold on a minute, Angelo . . . I wanna throw this son of a bitch out myself."

When Richie opens the door all the way, Theresa bursts into the cabin. "*Sonny, no!* STOP . . ." She freezes as Sonny whips around.

"Get her the fuck outta here." Angelo goes over to Theresa, who is transfixed with fear; Sonny throws the whining man on the couch. "You're gonna live . . . for now. That girl just saved your life." He walks over to Theresa and grabs her roughly by the hair. For an instant he considers killing her, but for the first time in his life his emotion overcomes his duty. Sonny says calmly, "You did a very stupid thing," then releases her. "Angelo, get Theresa away from this scum." He turns, and Theresa starts to follow him.

"Please, Sonny, don't hurt him."

Angelo pulls her back gently, "Come on, honey. It's for your own good. You shouldn't see this." The bodyguard escorts the trembling girl to the back room. Before she goes through the door, she turns to Sonny. Their eyes meet for a second. She has never seen his look so cold.

Theresa starts to say something, but Angelo nudges her inside. "Let's go." After she's gone, Sonny spits at DiCola, "O.K., toss him out, Angelo. I don't wanna dirty my hands."

DiCola gets on his knees. He can barely speak through his throbbing, aching mouth. "Wait! Don't . . . I'll tell . . . I'll tell . . . but for God's sake, have mercy on me . . . I'm in pain." He sees his teeth on the floor. "Oh, my God . . . my teeth . . . my God . . ." He starts to weep.

Sonny says coldly, "Tony, get him a rag." DiCola lets out a low moan. Sonny stands over him and threatens, "You make one more sound and I'll cut your eyeballs out. Where are the narcotics hidden?"

Gino rasps weakly, "They're in the basement of a church on the corner of St. Nicholas and 168th Street."

Sonny gives him a kick in the ribs. "I'm gonna kill you for killin' Nick." Gino grovels before him. "Wait a minute . . . I didn't kill Nick . . . I got rid of Pete and Eddie."

"Is Nick still alive?"

"No . . . the brothers took him to the Firestone plant and shot him in the head."

"What'd they do with him?"

"The Cassanos threw him in the boilin' rubber. It was nothin' personal. The brothers hadda kill him. They didn't expect Nick to be there. It was nothin' personal."

Sonny is sick at the thought of his friend dying this way. He kicks DiCola hard. "You're scum, DiCola, but I keep my word. I'm gonna let you live." Sonny turns to Richie. "Tell John to drop Theresa off in Tahoe. . . . Eddie, you and Willie are gonna stay with her . . . don't let her outta you sight."

"O.K., Boss."

Sonny warns, "I'm holdin' you both responsible . . . if somethin' happens, you're dead . . . I gotta decide what to do about Theresa." Richie and Angelo look at each other apprehensively as Sonny adds, "I'm gonna talk it over with Don Giuseppe."

For the next two hours Sonny looks out at the clouds, thinking about Theresa. He really loves her, but knows his duty. This is one of the hardest decisions he's ever had to make in his life. Sonny is certain Don Giuseppe will have an answer to his problem. When he goes up to the cockpit to land the jet, the bodyguards are worried. Angelo asks, "What do you think the boss is gonna do about Theresa?"

Tony says matter-of-factly, "Don Giuseppe will tell him to kill her."

Richie says, "Yeah . . . why do you think the boss is so quiet?"

Angelo is furious. "Well, I'm takin' that fucker Gus. . . . He had his orders . . . Theresa shoulda never been on the plane."

Tony says, "Yeah, but she was, Angelo . . . I wouldn't wanna be in the boss's shoes now."

They land at LaGuardia at six A.M. DiCola is detained on the plane with four bodyguards until his story is checked out. Sonny goes directly to the Loganno estate. When he gets there, the don himself opens the door; Mario is by his side. "Santino . . . what did you find out? Nick . . . is he still alive?" Sonny would give his fortune if he didn't have to extinguish the old man's hope. He knows it will worsen the don's failing health.

Sonny says grimly, "Don Giuseppe . . . Nick's dead." This news devastates the don. The old man sways, and Sonny and Mario help him over to the couch. The lieutenant brings him some water. Don Giuseppe takes a sip, then asks, his tone emotionless, "Who did it?"

"The Cassano brothers."

"How?"

"They took Nick to the Firestone factory . . . there's no body."

Mario jumps up, insane with hate. "You've done nothing but help those two bastards, Don Giuseppe . . . . We'll put an open contract on them, but I'm gonna kill them both myself."

The don holds up his hand. "Not yet, Mario."

"Why, Don Giuseppe? . . . They're no good."

The don replies ominously, "I'm not finished with them." He turns to Sonny. "Did DiCola tell you where the narcotics are?"

"They're in a church basement . . . on the corner of St. Nicholas and 168th. DiCola made a side deal with the brothers just like that Cassano lieutenant said."

Don Giuseppe composes himself and takes charge again. "Mario . . . I want you, Lou, and Frank to check it out. We'll meet you in Manhattan."

The lieutenant implores, "Let me kill the Cassanos, Don Giuseppe."

The don says steadily, "I told you, I'm not finished with them. The wise man kills when the time is right . . . . I'm gonna use the Cassano brothers like a pair of two-bit whores."

After Mario leaves, the don turns to Sonny. "Come upstairs, Santino. I want to give you something." Sonny follows the old man to the second floor, helping him up the steps. They go into Nick's room. Don

Giuseppe walks over to the dresser and picks up a picture. The wide smiles of two young boys radiate from its gold frame . . . Nick and Sonny in Indianapolis. The don looks at it for a few minutes. His voice trembles as he says, "I know Nick would want you to have this." He hands Sonny the picture. "Nick loved you, Santino, and I know you loved him, but sometimes we don't always say it." Sonny can see the don's eyes brimming with tears through the thick glasses. "I love you, too, Santino."

"Don Giuseppe . . . let me revenge Nick's death . . ."

"No, Santino . . . I will do that personally. DiCola's dead, right?"

Sonny hedges. "No, Don Giuseppe . . . I didn't kill him. Theresa was on the plane. She hid there 'cause she wanted to go to the ranch. I didn't wanna to do it in front of her. Besides, I wouldn't kill him till you found your stuff."

The don commends him, "Very smart, Santino . . . very good." Then he says gravely, "But you let the girl interfere."

Sonny says evenly, "I know what the rules are, Don Giuseppe. She's very close to me, but if you want me to kill her . . . I will."

"I'm not going to tell you what to do, Santino . . . you have to make that decision. No one can do it for you."

Sonny is stopped at the door by a family portrait on the wall. "Nick really looked like his father, didn't he?"

"Yes, Santino." The don says bitterly, "I lost him, too. Right after they came home from Indianapolis. I sent them there for protection, and his parents get killed in a car accident." The old man sighs. "Remember, Santino, everything in life has its price. I've paid dearly in my seventy-three years." He takes a final, long look around Nick's boyhood room, then shuts off the light. On the way downstairs Don Giuseppe says, "We'll go have breakfast in the city, Santino . . . after, I want to take you someplace special, someplace Nick and I have been going ever since he was little."

"Where's that, Don Giuseppe?"

"You'll see when we get there, Santino . . ."

Before they leave, Sonny checks in with Eddie at the ranch. "How's Theresa doin'? Is she O.K.?"

The bodyguard says, "Seems to be, Boss. She went right to her room."

"Did she mention what happened?"

"Not to us . . . said she wanted to get to sleep so she could get up early and bake a cake for you." Sonny knows Theresa was badly shaken when they dropped her off in Lake Tahoe. She was either putting on a show for the bodyguards or the incident had her completely traumatized. "Boss, when are you comin' back?"

"We're leavin' tonight." Sonny repeats his previous warning,

At five Sonny enjoyed the same things other young boys did.

Left: *Sonny lost this pony and his freedom when he left the farm.*

Right: *Eight-year-old Sonny right after his move from the farm to the city.*

Below: *Sonny spent his happiest childhood days on the dirt farm where he was born in Indiana.*

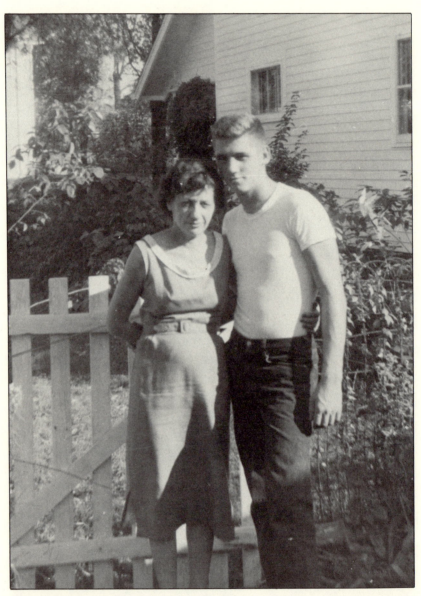

Sonny exhibited himself as a freak on the carny
circuit so that he could get his folks out of
Riverton. This picture of him and his mother
was taken in front of the new house he bought
for them.

Above: *Sonny earned a reputation as one of the Mafia's fiercest assassins. Here he is at twenty-three after fourteen hits.*

Left: *Sonny was a modern-day Scrooge before Theresa came into his life. Pictured here with him is Bing, his present to her on their first Christmas together.*

Above: *Sonny closed many deals on the golf course. His cart was specially equipped with a security system and full bar.*

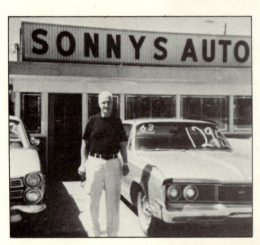

Left: *Sonny owned 150 corporations, including a used-car chain. Here Pops Gibson stands in front of his branch.*

Right: *Although he rarely had time for it—he was too busy planning scams and con games—fishing was the only relaxing activity the Mafia kingpin allowed himself.*

Most of Sonny's big catches were millionaires, but this sailfish he caught was mounted in his office at the Lucky Ace.

With 80 armed bodyguards on his payroll, Sonny rarely needed a gun. Here he holds a rifle he used when he hunted at his ranch in Lake Tahoe.

*Even though he couldn't read or write, Sonny flew his own jet.
Bankers who refused to cooperate would be "taken for a plane ride"
to change their minds.*

*A black fedora was
an integral part of
this Mafia kingpin's
apparel.*

Left: *Sonny conned a concert violinist out of his $250,000 Stradivarius violin in Las Vegas.*

Below: *Sonny and one of his attorneys celebrate his first day of probation in the $80,000 limousine equipped with computer and bullet-proof windows.*

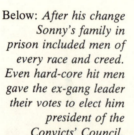

Below: *After his change
Sonny's family in
prison included men of
every race and creed.
Even hard-core hit men
gave the ex-gang leader
their votes to elect him
president of the
Convicts' Council.*

Sonny was nonviolent by now, but he fought this match to stop one group from persecuting another. He was told in a dream that he'd win in the first few minutes of the bout.

Sonny could bench-press 400 pounds and was the prison weight-lifting champion. In 1975 he received a presidential sports award from Gerald Ford.

Theresa snapped this photo the day Sonny was released. He is climbing a tree to talk to God.

"Remember what I told you guys . . . don't let her outta your sight."

"Don't worry, Boss, I'm in the living room watchin' TV. She can't get out without passing me. Willie's takin' the mornin' shift."

Sonny reminds him sternly, "If she gets out, I'm holdin' you guys responsible."

Sonny and Don Giuseppe ride into Manhattan and have breakfast at a small coffee shop near Columbus Circle. When they finish eating and are back in the car, Sonny asks, "Where is this place you're gonna take me, Don Giuseppe? Is it far?"

"No, Santino. Just a few minutes away . . . we'll go there and wait for Mario to come back." It is not more than a minute before the limousine turns into Central Park. As they pass the merry-go-round, the don tells the driver to slow down. "That's where Nick first learned about fear, Santino . . . he fell off one of the horses. I told him unless he got back on, he'd be afraid to fall his whole life. Nick was still crying, but he climbed back on . . . and rode again, too." The car winds through a stark corridor of barren trees on either side of the road, eventually crossing the park. They stop near 72nd Street on the West Side and get out. Don Giuseppe leads Sonny to a small wooded path. The two walk along, bodyguards close behind them, as the limousine follows slowly on the road beyond. Don Giuseppe looks over at some children frolicking in a playground nearby. "Nick used to ride on those swings. . . . He'd say, 'Look, Grandpa, I'm flying . . . I'm flying . . .' I can still hear him." The don smiles. "You know, we would take long walks on this path whenever Nick had a problem. I heard plenty about the girls . . . all Italians from someplace. Nick . . . he could never make up his mind. Just a few weeks ago we came here to talk about a problem. I didn't want him to go with Pete and Eddie, but Nick insisted. I think deep down in his heart he wanted to prove to me that he was a real soldier."

Sonny says gravely, "He died like a soldier, Don Giuseppe."

"I know, Santino . . . I know."

At that moment another limousine pulls up behind the don's. Mario gets out and hurries over to them. "Don Giuseppe, Sonny was right. We found the stuff hidden in that church basement."

The don pats Sonny's shoulder. "I knew I could trust you to get the information." He turns to his lieutenant. "No one knows you guys took out the narcotics this morning?"

"Not a soul saw us, Don Giuseppe."

"Good . . . that means the Cassano brothers still think they have the drugs."

"That's right."

The don starts plotting. "Put the word out that I'm looking for DiCola and I'm not doing business with anyone till he's found. I'm putting a freeze on all the narcotics. Go to the Cassano brothers. Tell them DiCola double-crossed me and their lieutenant, Bernardo, betrayed them. I know Nick's dead, and they have my stuff. I'll give them twenty-four hours to get it back to me." He has a second thought for his lieutenant. "By the way, Mario, get rid of Bernardo today, and drop his body off in Harlem . . . that'll tell the other dons I mean business."

"What about the Cassano brothers? When are we gonna hit them?"

"I told you, Mario . . . we're gonna use 'em."

Mario is puzzled. "How, Don Giuseppe?"

Sonny breaks in. He can see the clever con the don is pulling. "Don Giuseppe, that's one of the most brilliant plans I ever heard. You're not dealin' with anybody until you get DiCola."

The don says, "And you know what to do with him, Santino."

"Yeah . . . so no one'll ever find DiCola. Then the brothers have to get your narcotics back in twenty-four hours, but you got the drugs, right?"

"That's right, Santino."

Sonny continues, "So, for the brothers to get pure heroin, they're gonna have to steal it from the other dons. The dons are gonna come up short and put a contract on the Cassanos. Once the brothers are outta the picture, that opens up the nigger territory."

Mario says, finally comprehending, "Every don'll be fightin' for Harlem." This worries him. "Don Giuseppe, you have to be more careful now."

The old man smirks. "Why, Mario . . . no one's gonna come after me . . . they think I'm dying. Every day someone asks, 'Is the don dead yet?' We're still gonna be careful—that's how I got to be so old—but no one's gonna bother with me . . . they'll be too busy knocking each other off."

Sonny doesn't understand the don's sudden bellicose behavior . . . he's always been fair and just. "Don Giuseppe, why would you wanna to start a Mafia war among the families? Some of the dons are your close friends."

The don's face hardens. "I have no friends now, Santino. You see, they're responsible for what happened to Nick, too."

"How? DiCola worked for you."

"Santino, there's never just one rat . . . there could be two or three betrayers in my family working with the other dons. . . . I'm not taking any chances."

Sonny fits the last piece into the puzzle. "Jesus Christ! That means in about a year from now the whole East Coast territory will be open."

"Exactly, Santino . . . they'll all have to come deal with me." He puts an arm around Mario. "After I go, it'll be Mario's problem."

Sonny says in admiration, "That's the most brilliant plan I ever heard. I thought you were doin' it out of bitterness, ya know . . . 'cause you lost Nick, but the Loganno family will control everything.''

The don says flatly, "It is because I lost Nick, Santino, but I have no family now, except you and Mario.''

"You're gonna teach 'em all a lesson, Don Giuseppe.''

The old man says fiercely, "Once I get control, we're gonna go back to the old ways . . . when we didn't have rats and Mafia soldiers double-crossing their dons.'' He turns to his chief lieutenant. "Mario, Santino and I are gonna walk some more . . . tell Luigi to keep following us.''

"Yes, Don Giuseppe.''

When Mario leaves, Sonny and the don continue their walk. "Have you decided what to do about the girl yet, Santino?''

"No, Don Giuseppe.''

Just then a football lands at the don's feet. Memories of Nick's childhood flash before him. He picks up the ball and sees a young boy who's chasing after it. The old man throws it back to him. The boy yells, "Thanks, mister,'' and runs back to his friends. The don turns to Sonny. "Do you want children some day, Santino?''

"Yes, Don Giuseppe.''

"Do you love this girl?''

'Yes, but my loyalty and discipline as a soldier are more important to me.''

The don puts an arm around Sonny. "I was in love once, too, Santino, and I was in the same situation.''

"What did you do, Don Giuseppe?''

The old man says quickly, "What I did is not important, just know that I made the right decision. You've done a lot, Santino . . . you've earned the right to decide for yourself.'' Don Giuseppe looks at Sonny. "You don't need me to tell you what to do . . . I trust your judgment.'' He adds, "I trust that you will also take care of DiCola now.''

Sonny says resolutely, "I swear on Nick's name . . . I'll take care of him, Don Giuseppe.''

Sonny leaves for Lake Tahoe that evening. In the cabin of the plane, he sees DiCola hunched in his seat, still in pain, his cheeks badly swollen. The traitor asks anxiously, "What's gonna happen now? You gonna kill me?''

Sonny pats his shoulder. "I told you, Gino, I'm not gonna kill ya . . . but Don Giuseppe thinks you're dead. When we land, you gotta get outta the country. You'd better get some sleep.''

DiCola says effusively, "I wanna thank you for showin' me mercy. You know I really liked Nick. It was too bad he hadda be there. It was nothin' personal, Sonny, just bad luck. That's—''

Sonny shouts his hate at him, "SHUT UP, DICOLA!'' When

Gino's eyes reflect terror, he pats the traitor's arm. "Relax . . . I know you had nothin' to do with it, Gino . . . get some rest."

DiCola says quietly, "Thanks again, Sonny . . . I heard you keep your word."

Sonny motions for Angelo to follow him into the office in the rear of the plane. Once the door is closed, he tells the bodyguard, "Have Allen cut power when we're over the Grand Canyon."

"I knew you weren't gonna let that fucker live," Angelo says eagerly. "You gonna throw him out, Boss?"

Sonny gives his loyal soldier the long-awaited word. "No, Angelo . . . you are. I'm goin' to sleep."

About four hours into the flight the pilot pulls back the power. The six-foot-eight giant looms over the dozing DiCola and shakes him roughly. Gino looks up groggily. Angelo says, "Come on, creep, the boss don't want you clutterin' up his plane no more." He picks DiCola up in his arms.

Gino screams, "You can't do this . . . Sonny said he wasn't gonna kill me . . . he gave me his word." Angelo walks purposefully to the door. Gino tries to squirm out of the powerful arms. "Get Sonny. You can't do this, you guys are nuts! I wanna talk to Sonny. He said I was gonna live!" Richie opens the door, and DiCola shits when he feels the gale-force wind on his face. The traitor screams "Noooo" as Angelo tosses him out callously, head first. DiCola's screams pierce the air, decrescendoing slowly as he falls to the chasm below.

When the door is closed again, Angelo says, "That one's for Nick." He takes a seat across from Richie. "What do you think the boss is gonna do about Theresa?"

"I don't know, man . . . that's a cold scene there . . . I got to like that little broad."

Angelo is concerned. "Well, if he's gonna do something, I hope the boss don't make me do it."

Sonny tries to sleep on the plane but tosses and turns, thinking about his problem with Theresa. He loves her, but he loved another woman before . . . even then, loyalty to the Mafia overpowered love. It would be difficult, but Sonny knows Theresa could be replaced. Any woman could . . . except his mother. When they land, Theresa is waiting for him at the airport with Eddie. As soon as the steps of the plane are lowered, she races to Sonny and jumps on his hips, legs wrapped around his waist. She smothers him with kisses. "I missed you so much." She hugs him warmly, but Sonny is unresponsive. Theresa knows something is very wrong. She jumps down. "What's the matter?"

"I'm just tired, Theresa . . . there's nothin' wrong."

As they walk hand in hand across the field to the waiting limo, she confesses, "I thought a lot about what I did . . . I shouldn't have done it, Sonny. I just didn't understand . . . you treated Gino so nice at the house."

He replies coldly, "That was business, Theresa."

When they reach the car, she looks at him, her face grave, "I know that now, and I promise . . . I'll never interfere in your business again."

He looks down at her seriously. "In the old country Sicilian women keep their mouths closed and their eyes shut . . . they don't know nothin'. Over here it's different . . . women wanna know everything." He says harshly, "I can't have that, Theresa."

She says quietly, "I understand, Sonny." Theresa lowers her head, bundling her coat around her as a gust of wind chills the night air.

"I don't know if you really can understand." He looks at her sadly. Why did it have to be his duty as a soldier to kill this sweet, innocent girl? Sonny grabs her, hugging her fiercely. "I love you, Theresa."

She looks up, her big eyes filled with tears. "I love you . . . "

At that moment Sonny makes his decision. "Come on . . . let's go home."

When she gets in the limo, he gathers Richie, Angelo, and Tony around him. They shuffle over dejectedly. The bodyguards know he has decided about Theresa. Sonny tells them, "We're gonna be stayin' up here for a few days, but I got some jobs I want you guys to do. Tony . . ."

He answers glumly, afraid of his assignment. "Yeah, Boss?"

"Tell Cordone I'm comin' to the Philippines the first part of next year. I can see I gotta ride that guy's ass if anything's gonna get done. Richie . . . "

He replies tentatively, "Yeah, Boss?"

"I want buggin' devices in my attorney's cars . . . I trust 'em all like a fence. Don't use the WMDM system . . . it won't work on the car phones."

The trio look at each other in astonishment. Could Sonny be so cold that he could discuss routine business at a time like this? Angelo flinches when Sonny turns to him . . . he is sure it will be his job to kill Theresa. He says to Sonny, "Uh . . . you know Theresa really loves you, Boss."

"Yeah . . . she's a great girl." He looks at the sad faces. "Hey, what the hell's wrong with you guys?"

Angelo says, "You're not gonna kill Theresa, Boss?"

Sonny looks at his concerned men. "You guys should know me better than that. Would we be stayin' here if I was? I wouldn't wait to kill her . . . I'd do it right now." He adds, "But if I was gonna do something' like that, you can be sure of one thing . . . I wouldn't lay it on you guys. I'd do my own dirty work."

Angelo says cheerfully, "I'm glad she isn't gonna die, Boss, but can I kill that fucker Gus? He let Theresa on the plane."

"No, Angelo . . . you don't have to do that. Just fire him. I can't have anybody that stupid workin' for me. I got enough idiots around already." Sonny has one other instruction. "Angelo, from now on, I want two men on that shift. We all learned a lesson on this one. It's never gonna happen again."

Theresa and Sonny spend a relaxing two days in Lake Tahoe, then fly to LA to ring in 1971 by throwing a party for all of his executives. They fly in from all over the country to spend New Year's Eve with their boss at the West Castle. Sonny enjoys watching Theresa play hostess, chatting with each man. Later on that night, after their love-making, they are both starving. Theresa raids the icebox and brings them up some cold rigatoni. While they eat in bed, she talks about the party. "That Dr. Swanson, what kind of a doctor is he?"

"I dunno . . . he works in insurance now . . . he's a CPA, too, you know."

Theresa plays with the ribbed tubes of macaroni on her plate. "What about Gregory . . . what did he do before he worked for you?"

"Gregory was a bank president. . . . He and Jeff Wolfman both got four degrees in business."

"You know, you really have some smart men working for you. I've seen a lot of guys like that in first class, but believe me, Sonny . . . they're *not*."

This remark puzzles him. "What's that mean?"

She turns to him. "I don't trust them, Sonny. They'd all turn on you in a minute to save their own skins . . . except for the bodyguards and Joe."

"That's 'cause they're Italian."

"You know, I don't understand that. . . . Why is Joe the only Italian executive you have? Why aren't they all Italians?"

Sonny reaches across her to turn out the light. "You're not supposed to understand . . . I told ya, I don't want ya thinkin' about my business."

She grabs his arm. "You're my business . . . I don't want anything to happen to you."

Sonny throws off the covers and gets out of bed. "Look, Theresa, you worry about the house . . . I'll take care of myself. Believe me . . . I trust 'em all like a fence."

She doesn't understand his last remark. "What does that mean . . . trust them like a fence? You've used that before."

Sonny shouts impatiently, "Look, Theresa, I don't have time to educate you."

Theresa knows he's mad. "I'm sorry, I didn't mean to upset you."

Sonny puts on his robe and heads for the door, shouting, "I'm not upset . . . go to sleep."

"Where are you going?"

Without looking back he says, "I got work to do."

The door slams, but Theresa can't go to sleep. She is thinking about Sonny. Theresa has seen him yell at his men and his employees, but he's never been quarrelsome with her before. It must have something to do with his business, and she knows she can't ask anything about that. Theresa fluffs up her pillow in frustration. She loves Sonny but is uncertain about their future together. Could she live the rest of her life with him, unable to share the things most normal couples do? The submissive role she had to play was getting uncomfortable, too. After all, women began voicing their opinions when they got the vote. . . . Theresa wasn't a women's libber, but she considered herself a liberated woman. In spite of this she had always dreamed of marrying a rich man who'd take care of her. Poverty hung over Theresa's head like the sword of Damocles. She drifts off to sleep, dreaming of wedding gowns, wondering if the day will ever come when she becomes Mrs. Sonny Gibson.

Sonny has something quite different on his mind. When he gets to his office in the den, he calls Angelo on the intercom. The groggy bodyguard comes in a few seconds later. "Yeah, Boss?"

Sonny paces. "Angelo, get me the tapes of all the conversations we bugged on my executives last week."

"You gonna listen to 'em *now*, Boss?"

Sonny snaps back, "Just do what I tell you, huh?" Angelo brings in a pile of boxes a few minutes later. When he leaves, Sonny puts the first one on his machine . . . a conversation between Gregory and Jeff Wolfman. Sonny listens to all of the tapes until the last word is spoken . . . Theresa has opened up his Pandora's box. His executives are still talking about business, but Sonny wonders what they'd say if they knew the Justice Department, the FBI, the Organized Crime Strike Force, Interpol, CIA, and Scotland Yard were all watching him.

This close scrutiny doesn't worry Sonny. In spite of it, he continues to scam. Joe comes to the West Castle with his information about the Smoky Mountain National Park scheme. After listening to Joe's report, Sonny feels confident that he can engineer another successful land fraud. The Registry Office in the Macon County Courthouse has records of 6000 acres of land grants that have never been claimed. Sonny sends Gregory down to get them from the greedy Registrar, who sells them all to him for $1000. Sonny has the title papers forged so that each $100 grant is worth $10,000, then calls a company from Goshen, Indiana, to erect prefabricated houses on three of the lots. He tells the contractor the job must be completed in ten days. Some European investors are coming to look at the development in California, and Sonny wants them to see his first. Ground is broken for the project the next day.

When construction is complete, three beautiful, fully landscaped homes, complete with swimming pools, stand in the center of the Smoky Mountain National Park. The minisuburb comes equipped with sidewalks, streets, and electricity. The only things missing are the station wagons in the driveways and the kids playing on the lawns.

Now Sonny starts to scam. He throws cocktail parties for developers and hands out brochures with the champagne and hors d'oeuvres. They picture a typical family enjoying life in the model homes. "YOUR NEXT-DOOR NEIGHBOR CAN BE THE BEAUTIFUL SMOKY MOUNTAIN NATIONAL PARK. LIVE IN PEACE FOR A CHANGE." Sonny has formed a new company, Off Shore Ltd., to handle the deals, with Gregory as the president.

A total of four developers bite; each one puts up five million dollars. The money goes into escrow in the Bahamas, but through his contacts Sonny gets the cash released immediately. Eventually, it is a retired Tennessee tax collector on a fishing trip who exposes the fraud. Driving through the park, he spots the illegal housing and alerts the government. When his story checks out, it makes national headlines. The angry developers come to Sonny to get their money back because they can't find Gregory. Sonny says he can't help them. Off Shore has duped him too, but since he's Mafia, he's news. The government tries to indict Sonny . . . when they can't link him to Off Shore Ltd. in any way, the charges are dropped.

In the meantime, two different developers contact Joe Anadaro to see if Off Shore has any more land available. Joe is against selling them the grants, but Sonny disagrees, "The government couldn't touch me before . . . It'll work, Joe."

The lawyer expresses concern about Gregory, "What if he rats?"

Sonny's answer is definite: "We'll take him for a plane ride."

The greedy developers are wined and dined. Sonny has used Jimmy Hoffa's name around the country to close other deals. He tells these men that he is Hoffa's son-in-law and can get the unions to guarantee the financing for their home buyers. The developers bite, putting up $10 million each. Once again, the money is released from the Bahamas escrow immediately. Sonny has made a total of $40 million from this scam and has now sold the Smoky Mountain National Park twice.

5
Closing In

Every morning from this point on Sonny got tapes of his executives' phone calls daily. The biggest topic of conversation now was the heat they were starting to get. Most of them were scared. An article in London in the *Sunday Times* on January 31, 1971, had linked one of Sonny's executives to the problems at the Bank of Sark. Jeff Wolfman reassured an uneasy Dr. Swanson on one recording, "Don't worry . . . Sonny's powerful. Whatever happens in this country, he'll have enough pull to get us out." Sonny was getting a lot of heat himself. Often after an indictment he was unable to go to his office, which was teeming with federal agents waiting to arrest him; Sonny's average bail bonds were $200,000.

Although business pressures were closing in, his personal life was opening up. He and Theresa spent their winter weekends at the ranch in Lake Tahoe horseback riding, snowmobiling, and building an occasional snowman; theirs was the only "Frosty" in town with a black Fedora, sunglasses, and a cigar.

One night Theresa insisted that they all go to a country-and-western bar. Sonny would rather listen to a good mandolin player, but knows she likes this cowboy music, so he indulges her. As the steel guitar twangs, Theresa stares at the musician playing it, trying to figure out how she knows him. "Sonny, one of those guys looks so familiar to me . . ."

He sits up and looks at the band. "How can ya tell what any of 'em look like with those big hats they got on?"

Suddenly Theresa's eyes widen in recognition. "Holy cow . . . that's Hank Canfield!"

Sonny takes a swig from his beer bottle. "Who in the hell is Hank Canfield?"

She turns excitedly. "He's an old friend of mine." Theresa entreats him, "Can I ask Hank to come over to the table on his break, Sonny?"

"I dunno . . . how well do ya know this guy?"

"He practically lived at our house. He was my brother Tommy's best friend. Can he come over?"

Sonny shrugs. "O.K. . . . O.K., ask him to if you want to . . . long as I don't have to entertain him."

When the set is finally finished, Theresa goes up to the small stage to see her friend. There is some rejoicing at the reunion, then she brings Hank over to join them. After he's introduced to Sonny, Hank says to him, "Did you know this girl sings like an angel?" He puts his arm around her. "Yessiree, old Gabe himself would be proud to have this little lady in his choir."

That surprises Sonny. "I didn't know you could sing . . ."

Theresa corrects him. "Yes, you do . . . I sing around the house all the time."

"Yeah, but that's just hummin'. You never sing words. If you can sing . . . sing."

Hank suggests, "Why don't you sit in on our set? Do one of those songs you wrote when you sang with the band back home . . ."

She refuses modestly. "I don't know if I can remember any of those . . . besides, I haven't sung in years. I forget how to do it."

Hank coaxes her. "Come on, Terry . . . singing's just like ridin' a horse . . . you never forget how to do it . . ."

"But what about the rest of the band . . . they won't know the song."

"I'll lead 'em through it. . . . I'll make a rough chart right now."

When Hank leaves, everyone encourages her. "We wanna hear you sing, Theresa."

Angelo says, "Uh . . . can you do some Italian songs too, Theresa?"

Sonny jumps in, "Now that I'd really like to hear."

Theresa replies, "The band wouldn't know any."

Richie says, "Come on, Theresa, we all wanna hear you . . . the boss does, too."

She looks at Sonny. "Do you? Is it O.K. if I go up there?"

"It's up to you, baby."

Theresa's decision is made for her. Hank is announcing, "We have a very special treat at the Corral tonight . . . I'd like to bring up a lady who has more country soul than Loretta Lynn and Lynn Anderson put together. I'd like you all to give a warm welcome to my friend, Theresa . . ." She recognizes the first strains of her song, and the music in her soul draws Theresa to the stage. Hank hands her the mike, and from the first note she has the attention of every person in the room. The warmth of her voice captivates them . . . she brings sensitivity to even the simplest song. Theresa looks at Sonny as she sings. He watches her in admiration. Every day he discovers something that makes him love Theresa more. When she's finished, the audience goes crazy. They whistle and stomp their feet in response to her performance, yelling for an encore. Theresa just bows shyly. Back at the table all the men congratulate her, but she is only interested in one man's opinion. "Was I O.K., Sonny?"

He strokes her hair gently. "You were great, baby. That ol' boy Hank was right . . . you do sing like an angel."

They leave Lake Tahoe late that night, and Sonny is back at work the next morning at nine o'clock. He usually spent just a few hours a day in the office now, preferring to entertain prospective investors for his Big Scam on the golf course. Sonny is on his way out at 11:30 when Linda reminds him, "Did you forget you have a meeting with Henry Stevens this morning? He called Friday and you O.K.'d it."

Sonny turns at the door. "Shit, that's right." He leans his clubs against the wall.

"Linda, call the country club and get a message to Jimmy Taggert that I'm gonna be about a half-hour late . . ."

She is excited. Politicians never impress her, but show people do, even those behind the scenes. "Ooooo, are you playing with Jimmy Taggert? Can you get me a Jack Gaudio album? He produced Jack's records."

"I don't think he'll be carryin' any in his golf bag, but I'll get ya one." He turns to Richie. "Check out this guy Taggert . . . see who his connections are besides Gaudio . . . I wanna find out who else he knows." Sonny turns back to Linda. "Where the hell is Stevens?"

His answer comes in the form of the celebrated criminal lawyer himself, walking through the door. Henry Stevens' name alone often gets results in a trial, but Sonny didn't hire him because of his fame. He is a masterful lawyer known for his cool courtroom demeanor and his ability to manipulate juries. Sonny is not happy to hear what Stevens has to say this morning. The attorney's eyes are anxious. "Sonny, the government is very close to getting an indictment to stick."

"Who the hell told you that?"

"Some friends in Washington." Stevens sits and lays his attaché case on the coffee table. Sonny sits opposite him.

"What kinda indictment are they talkin' about?"

"I don't know, but my contacts say they're gathering some pretty solid evidence against you. I hear——"

Sonny stands and paces nervously. "I don't give a shit what you hear. You're not the only one with contacts in Washington." He reasons, "Besides, if they do indict me, who cares? An indictment can't get me sent to prison."

"A conviction can."

Sonny stops and confronts his lawyer menacingly. "That's what I'm payin' you for, Stevens, to make sure I don't get a conviction."

Angelo interrupts, "Uh . . . excuse me, Boss, but we gotta get to the airport now if we wanna take off before the air traffic gets too bad." Sonny grabs his briefcase and heads for the door.

"If you need me, Stevens, Linda knows how to getta hold of me . . . Remember what I told ya."

Sonny was leaving for Manila that night. Soon there wouldn't be any indictments for him to worry about. He was getting closer and closer to pulling off his Big Scam. The Mafia kingpin had been setting up for this deal with his political puppet in the Philippines, Pedro Cordone, who was going to obtain for him the gaming rights to one of the islands and ninety-nine-year leases on all the properties where his hotels and casinos were being erected. In effect Sonny would have his own country. For the past few years he had been convincing wealthy underworld figures, politicians, and corporate executives that under his guidance this spot would become the most successful resort paradise in the world. If his salesmanship failed to convince potential investors, his Operation BS file drawers were crammed with documents and tapes that would. Over the years Sonny had been accumulating evidence that his marks were engaged in illegal activities, and he intended to use that information to blackmail them into cooperating. In most cases that was unnecessary. His marketing package was so effective that many interested airlines had already agreed to schedule flights to his as-yet unpopulated island. The potential investors were putting their money into a forty-two-month escrow in Las Vegas. When construction started on the first hotel and casino, the cash would be delivered to Sonny in the Philippines . . . his goal was $500 million. Sonny figured he would need at least that much to live like a king for fifty years. Batista did it in 1958 with just $75 million, but nothing escapes inflation. Cordone had been promised half the money, but while it was being transferred to Manila, Sonny planned to take him for a plane ride. Once he had the cash in hand, the kingpin was going to stay on the island. He planned to build himself a fortress, surround it with a 300-man battalion of bodyguards, and live like an emperor for the rest of his life. Sonny's Big Scam would be the biggest con job the world had ever seen.

When Sonny returns to the States, he receives some distressing news. His father calls at six A.M. "Why are ya callin' so early, Pops . . . what's wrong?"

"I just wanted to let you know your mother's in the hospital."

Sonny frowns. "What's the matter with her . . . what happened?"

"She had a mild stroke. The doctors said her heart was beating too fast. They thought she should be under observation for a few days."

"Should I fly out there?"

Pops assures him, "No, no . . . it's not necessary . . . they just want to keep an eye on her."

Sonny knows how dangerous even a mild stroke can be. "Does she have any brain damage, Pops?"

"They don't think so, but she's slurring her speech a little."

"You sure I shouldn't come out there?"

"No, it's not that serious. . . . Just say a prayer for her."

"I don't do that crap, Pops. . . . Be sure and keep me informed."

"All right."

Sonny is very worried about his mother. He paces the room. Theresa sits up. "What's wrong?"

"My mom's in the hospital . . ."

She gets out of bed and puts on her robe as Sonny takes a suit from the closet. "Is it serious, Sonny?"

"No . . . but I gotta get the guys together." He buzzes Angelo, who is there in just a few seconds. Sonny buttons his shirt. "Find out where the nearest Catholic parish is . . . we gotta go to church."

Angelo and Theresa exchange surprised looks. The big man says blankly, "Uh . . . I didn't get ya, Boss."

Sonny pushes his tie through its knot. "I said we're goin' to church, find out where the nearest one is . . ."

"You're goin' to church, Boss?"

"Angelo . . . what's the matter . . . are you dumb? Find a fuckin' church. My Mom's sick . . . I wanna light a candle."

"I thought you didn't believe in that religious stuff, Boss."

Sonny yells, "Just do what I tell ya . . . go wake up the guys . . . I wanna leave right now."

Angelo knocks at each room, rousing the sleeping bodyguards. "Get up."

Richie flings his door open, gun in hand. He's angry when he sees who it is. "What the fuck's wrong with you, Angelo?"

"Uh . . . we gotta get up, the boss is gonna go to church."

By this time the racket has awakened most of the men. Doors open up and down the hallway. "What's happenin'?" "What's goin' on?"

Angelo makes the announcement. "The boss's mother is sick. We gotta go to church."

Tony exclaims, "Church! He's never been in a church."

"Uh . . . I know, but the boss wants to go right now . . . he's already dressed."

Sonny and the sleepy, uncomprehending men arrive at the Church of the Good Shepherd in Beverly Hills thirty minutes later. The soft rattle of rosary beads is the only sound that can be heard in the church as the parishioners wait for the seven o'clock Mass to begin. All heads turn when the noise of the bodyguards' heavy boots shatters the reverent silence . . . they are following Sonny to the statue of the Blessed Virgin. After he lights his candle, Angelo whispers loudly to the others, "All right, everybody's gotta light a candle for the boss's mother . . ." Just then the pastor comes out of the sacristy. He watches the line at the shrine with great satisfaction . . . it's rare to see so many men in church these days. When Tony reaches the rail, he drops the matches. Bending over to pick them up, his gun falls from his holster and spins like a bottle across the slick, marble floor. It stops one foot from the pastor's shoes. Unperturbed, Tony picks up the piece, then grins at the astonished priest. Both pastor and parishioners stare after them in amazement as Sonny and his men depart. A white-haired old woman comes up to the altar rail, clicking her tongue. "Isn't that awful, Father? A man carrying a gun in church."

The priest, not wanting to alarm her, quickly fabricates a story. "Don't worry, Mrs. O'Hara, they were just some of our fine detectives from the Beverly Hills Police Department."

"Oh, isn't that wonderful, those nice boys coming to church . . . I feel so much safer now."

The day after his visit to Good Shepherd, Sonny gets a call in the office from his father. "Pops, what's wrong? Is Mom worse?"

"No, no, that's why I'm calling . . . she's much better. Your mother's coming home tomorrow."

"What'd the doctors say?"

"She had a mild stroke, just like they thought, but there was no permanent damage. They gave her something to slow her heart down."

Sonny is relieved to hear she's out of danger. "Tell Mom I'll give her a call later. Did she get the flowers I sent?"

Mr. Gibson laughs. "She got them, all right . . . She said her room looks like a funeral parlor and to tell you she's not dead yet."

Sonny laughs with him. "That sounds like Mom. Next time I'll send her candy." He adds quickly, "But I know there isn't gonna be a next time."

"Are you coming to Indianapolis soon, Sonny?"

"I can't get away right now, Pops. I should be there in about a month."

"Oh . . . well, all right . . .we'll see you then."

"Kiss Mom for me."

Sonny hangs up and tells his men, "My mom's O.K. . . . she's goin' home tomorrow."

Tony says, "Hey . . . thank God."

Angelo says, "Yeah, he really answered your prayers fast, huh, Boss?"

Sonny snaps back, "You know I don't believe in that crap, Angelo . . . it was the doctors that cured her, not some God." He lights up a cigar. "Richie, what'd you find out about Jimmy Taggert? I'm supposed to have a golf game with him and Jack today."

The bodyguard says, "He checked out O.K., Boss. He's a big record producer . . . plays golf with Gaudio and Chet Bartlett a lot. He's also worked with Frank Sinatra."

Linda buzzes him. "Sonny, Jimmy Taggert's on the line . . . he says he can't meet you today. He has to go to New York to do some work in the studio with Chet Bartlett. He'll be gone for about four weeks. Do you want to talk to him?"

Sonny is peeved. "No, just get somethin' up for when he comes back." He clicks off. "That figures. Those fuckin' show people are so goddam unreliable." He buzzes his secretary. "Linda, I want Jeff, Gregory, Dr. Swanson, and Allen in for a meeting tomorrow."

"What should I tell them it's about?"

"Linda, that's not your job . . . I'll tell 'em what it's about. You just get 'em in here."

Richie is curious, too. "Boss, you just had the regular staff meeting last week."

"I know, but I gotta get to those fuckin' dummies and talk to 'em, there's a lotta heat comin' down. I gotta make sure they don't get scared an' rat . . . they're not Italian and they're not that smart."

Sonny is successfully juggling his executives, his attorneys, and his Big Scam investors when suddenly, three weeks later, his whole world is thrown off balance . . . his mother has a serious stroke. He gets the news on the golf course and goes straight to the airport. When he arrives at the hospital in Indianapolis, his mother is in a coma; Pops is in the crowded waiting room. He looks much older than the last time Sonny saw him, just two months ago. He rushes over to his father, bodyguards trailing behind him. "What happened, Pops?"

"I don't know . . . your mother was fixing breakfast. When I came downstairs, she was on the floor. I've been here seven hours, but she hasn't come out of the coma yet."

Sonny is frantic. "Where's the doctor? I wanna talk to him. Can I see Mom?"

"They won't even let me see her."

Sonny shouts, "What! Who the hell's in charge here?"

The other visitors in the waiting room now look up. Pops is uncomfortable. "Don't make a scene, Sonny. There's nothing we can do."

"That's bullshit, Pops. There's always somethin' you can do. . . . First of all, I wanna get her outta this rat trap and into UCLA Medical Center. They got the best doctors in the world out there."

A white-coated young man who looks more like an athlete than a physician comes over to them. "Mr. Gibson, can I see you outside?"

Sonny interrupts, "Are you the doctor?"

"Yes."

"I'm her son . . . I wanna see my mother."

"Can you both follow me, then? . . . Please." Sonny, the bodyguards, and his father leave the room; they are taken to a small cubicle just outside the admitting area. Sonny and Pops go in alone. "I'm afraid I have some bad news for you, Mr. Gibson . . . your wife just passed away."

Sonny goes crazy. "What the hell you talkin' about? My mother couldn't have passed away . . . she'd be dead!"

Pops nods grimly. "That's what he's talking about, Sonny. Your mother's dead . . . Nina's dead."

The doctor says routinely, "I'm sorry. Where would you like us to send the body?" Sonny's rage subsides. When the doctor says this, it finally hits him that his mother is no longer a living, breathing woman, but just "the body" to be disposed of in some way.

Pops is dazed. "Can we take her home?"

Sonny puts a hand on his father's shoulder. "No, Pops." He turns to the doctor. "Can we see her?"

The physician nods. "She's up in 202. Take the elevator to the second floor and turn right. It's at the end of the hall."

Sonny takes his father's elbow. "Come on, Pops, we're gonna see Mom . . ."

Nina Gibson is still warm when they get to the room. She looks like she's sleeping. Sonny kisses her forehead, wishing he had said "I love you" to her more often, knowing now it is too late. Pops bends over to his wife, then Sonny gently leads his father out of the room. He turns one more time to look at his mother before they go and realizes an important chapter of his life has ended. . . . She was his last real link to the carefree boy who grew up on a farm in Indiana.

Sonny's father bore up well under the strain of the three-day wake, during which family and friends expressed their condolences. He was composed during the Solemn Requiem Mass celebrated for his wife, and now looks on soberly outside as Father Francis blesses the casket before the pallbearers place it in the hearse. Mr. Gibson gets into the waiting limousine, but before Sonny does, Father Francis comes over to him. "Can I talk to you for a few minutes, Sonny?"

"Can't it wait? We're on our way to the cemetery."

"I know, but I may not see you afterward."

Sonny doesn't care to hear what any priest has to say, but he looks into the limo to tell Pops. "I'll be right there. I'm gonna talk to Father Francis a minute." Sonny closes the door and steps a few feet away from the car. "What's this all about, Father?"

The priest says, "I'm sorry about your mother. She was a good woman, Sonny . . . she loved you very much."

Sonny's tone is gruff. "Get to the point, Father."

The priest continues boldly. "Your mother lived in constant hope that you'd change. You're a very powerful man, Sonny, but there's more to life than money and power."

Sonny bristles. "My money and power got her out of a two-room shack. I know the kinda life she led when I was a kid . . . how she sacrificed for me. I would've done anything to make sure she never had to live like that again."

The priest shakes his head. "Don't use your mother as an excuse for your greed. She prayed to St. Jude every day in this chapel that you'd stop the life you're leading."

Sonny retorts sharply, "My mother never knew anything about my life, Father, except what I wanted her to know."

The priest looks straight at him. "You're wrong, Sonny . . . your mom could read newspapers, and she wasn't stupid. She knew you were in the Mafia, just like her brother. That talk you had on the plane ride back from the Bahamas didn't fool her."

Sonny looks at him, annoyed. "Are you finished?"

The priest nods sadly. "Yes, I am."

Sonny turns and gets into the limousine. His father asks, "What did Father Francis want?"

"Nothin', Pops . . . he just wanted to say again how sorry he was about Mom. He's gonna say an extra Mass for her."

Mr. Gibson nods. "That's good . . . Nina will like that."

The services at the graveside are brief. The Gibson family listens as Father Francis solemnly reads the prescribed prayers for the dead. Here, unlike in Sicily, the mourners are spared the agony of seeing the coffin lowered into the ground, but there is something equally disturbing . . . the gravediggers who sit on a large mound of dirt nearby, like birds of prey waiting for their next meal. After the ceremony Sonny sends his father home with the family. "I'll be there in a little while, Pops, there's somethin' I gotta do . . ." Sonny and the men get into the limo. He gives Georgie directions as they drive until they are in an industrial area next to a polluted river. The large, familiar smokestacks from three factories beyond send a shiver up Sonny's spine. The combined smell of wet sawdust, fish, and slaughtered hogs confirm that this is still the wrong side of the tracks.

Richie sniffs. "Boy . . . it really stinks around here. Where are we, Boss?"

Sonny replies flatly, "Nowhere . . ." He calls to Georgie, "Stop here. I'm gettin' out."

Tony asks, "What for, Boss?"

Sonny turns to him. "I said I'm gettin' out . . ." The bodyguards are surprised. Outside there is nothing but rubble where some houses have obviously been razed to make way for new construction, but they all follow Sonny. Only he knows, however, that they are standing in front of what used to be the two-room shack where Sonny grew up. The outhouse is the only thing left standing. The bodyguards also have no idea that Sonny is now in another dimension . . . the past. He closes his eyes and takes a deep breath—the stench from the factories fills his nostrils. Suddenly he is a schoolboy again, coming home with hate for the kids at school who called him "Stinky." Sonny opens his eyes. He takes a few steps and walks to the center of the shack's foundation. He stands in the ruins, remembering. To the right, in his mind's eye, he sees the converted pantry that was his bedroom. To the left is the cluttered, all-purpose, living room where the family spent most of their time. In one corner the old potbelly stove belches smoke through a cylinder to the roof. In another corner his mother is preparing breakfast in the "kitchen," an icebox, a hotplate, and a badly stained sink its only fixtures. In that tiny sink his mother washed out his clothes every night so that his smell wouldn't make him the object of scorn among his classmates. As he looks around, Sonny notices an object next to the outhouse. He walks over to it and recognizes the stove he once gave his mother. Sonny remembers how he got the money to buy it, working for Blackie, and how big his mother's heart was when she left it for the next poor family because she had a stove in the new house. He touches the clock on top. This was a new feature then, and his mother had reacted like a little girl when she saw it. Time stands still for Sonny until the bodyguards come over to him.

Angelo asks, "Uh . . . are you O.K., Boss?"

Sonny turns, in a trance. "What?"

"Uh . . . I said, are you O.K.? . . . You look kinda funny."

"I'm O.K. . . ."

Richie points to the stove. "Hey, look at this antique . . . I wonder if it's worth anything."

Sonny says quietly, "Thirty-six dollars . . . that's what it was worth when it was new."

Tony says, "This thing was old when it was new, but I'll bet it's still pretty solid." He gives the stove a hard kick.

Sonny shouts harshly, "DON'T DO THAT!"

The men look at him in amazement. Richie says, "What's the matter? Is somethin' wrong, Boss?"

Sonny returns to reality. "Nothin's wrong. . . . Come on, let's get outta here. I can't stand this smell anymore."

On the way back to the house Angelo says, "Uh . . . why did you wanna stop there, Boss?"

Sonny's voice is steady, "That's where I grew up, Angelo."

"It is? Gee, Boss, that's worse than the Brooklyn slums . . . at least they don't stink."

"My mother washed my clothes out so they wouldn't stink, but you can never get rid of that odor, Angelo. It'll be with me as long as I live."

Tony says, "It's a wonder you're successful, comin' from a place like that, Boss."

"That's why I am successful . . . I would've done anything to get outta there. I never wanted to be poor again." Sonny thinks about his mother's miserable existence in that two-room shack. For the first time in his life tears well up in his eyes. The bodyguards all feel his grief and are at a loss for what to do, except for Angelo. The giant puts a big, comforting arm around Sonny. "Don't feel bad, Boss. It's O.K. . . . I cried when my mother died, too."

"I'm not cryin', Angelo . . . I got somethin' in my eye."

Sonny spends the rest of that day with Pops, then flies back to Los Angeles. As if his mother's death hadn't been bad enough news for him, Sonny finds out the grand jury is scheduling hearings on his activities and has subpoenas out for everyone connected with him. He goes to Florida to dodge his; Theresa stays behind at the West Castle. In spite of his strong warning not to leave the house she insists on going shopping, and when she comes out of the store, the federal marshals hit her with a subpoena. When she gets home, she calls Sonny, hysterical, "I got a subpoena today. What does that mean? What do I have to do?"

Sonny is furious. "What the hell were you doin' out, Theresa? I told you not to move from the goddam house . . . they could never have touched you there."

She explains guiltily, "The sweaters I ordered for Bing came in, and I wanted to pick them up."

Sonny explodes. "You went outta the house to get that fuckin' dog a sweater!"

"Don't yell at me! You don't want to have any kids . . . that dog's all I have." She starts to cry. "I didn't know that would happen. Nobody saw me leave."

"Don't be stupid. They were waitin' at the gate . . . they tailed you, idiot. Who drove you?"

"Freddie . . ." She's sobbing now. "I didn't mean to do anything. I'm scared, Sonny, what's gonna happen?"

He is gentle with her now. "Don't worry about it . . . I'm gonna send Joe to court with ya . . . he'll tell you exactly what to do. Listen to him, O.K.?"

She sniffles. "All right. . . . I love you, Sonny."

"I love you, too . . ."

When they hang up, Sonny is mad. "Didn't I issue strict orders Theresa wasn't to leave that place?"

Richie answers, "Yeah . . . everybody knows."

"Well, she went shopping and got subpoenaed. Some idiot drove her into town."

Tony says, "She can be pretty demanding, Boss . . . no one wants to get her mad."

"Nobody should give a fuck if she's mad . . . only if I am, and I'm goddam mad now . . . Who's this Freddie?"

Richie says, "Freddie DiFrancia . . . he's been with us about a year."

"Where's he from?"

"The Matrano family in San Diego."

Sonny says brusquely, "Send him back . . . he's fired."

Angelo comes to Freddie's defense. "Uh . . . Theresa can be convincing when she wants something, Boss."

"You guys are workin' for me, not Theresa. Make sure everybody knows why Freddie's fired. I wanna make an example outta him."

When it is finally time for Theresa to testify, Joe Anadaro goes with her to the Federal Building, but attorneys are not allowed inside the grand jury room. He coaches her in the limousine. "Watch out for Martindale, the government attorney . . . he's sneaky. When you get up there, he'll try to trick you. He'll say all kinds of things about Sonny."

"Like what, Joe?"

"Well, he knows you're living with him, so he'll probably play on your jealousy."

"In what way?"

"I don't know. Maybe he'll tell you they have proof that Sonny is living with another woman . . . Who knows? But whatever he asks, you plead the Fifth Amendment."

"How do I do that?"

"Just say, 'On the advice of my attorney, I reserve the right to take the Fifth Amendment.' "

Theresa writes it down as he says it. "What does this mean?"

"Under the Fifth Amendment to the Constitution you can't be forced to testify against yourself if it might implicate you in a crime, even if you're no more than a link in the chain of evidence . . . and that's what you are." She looks confused, so he continues the explanation. "Let's say I do something wrong, and you're my friend. Even though you're innocent, just the fact that we know each other could start people thinking you were involved somehow, but if you don't ever admit that we're friends, that can't happen."

Theresa is beginning to understand. "Can I answer any questions at all, Joe?"

The attorney's answer is firm. "No . . . if you answer one, you waive your right to plead the Fifth again."

"Joe, I'm nervous." She studies the piece of paper. "I'd better memorize this."

Inside, after she is sworn in and has identified herself, William Martindale, the U.S. attorney, shows Theresa a picture of Sonny. "Do you know Sonny Gibson, the West Coast Mafia kingpin, also known as Crazy Sonny?"

Theresa's voice is steady. "On the advice of my attorney, I reserve the right to take the Fifth Amendment."

He continues to bombard her with questions. "Did Sonny Gibson buy you those rings you're wearing? . . . Have you seen Sonny Gibson threaten anyone's life on his jet plane? . . . Do you live with Sonny Gibson?" Theresa pleads the Fifth Amendment on everything he asks. Gaudiodale can see he's not making any progress this way, so he hits her below the belt. "Are you aware that Sonny Gibson controls over six hundred women and has twenty women of his own right now?"

Theresa doesn't bat an eye. "On the advice of my attorney, I take the Fifth Amendment."

He continues badgering her. "Did you know that just last night Sonny Gibson had an orgy at his mansion in Florida, and we know that he slept with at least ten women." For a second Theresa sees red, but she thinks about what Joe said. Martindale is trying to trick her. The night before she had tried to call Sonny in Boca Raton, but he wasn't home. She finally tracked him down at Fazzio's pool hall, where he was playing with the bodyguards after hours.

Theresa looks at her inquisitor and says clearly, "On the advice of my attorney, I take the Fifth Amendment."

Martindale is not beaten. He keeps up his harrying interrogation for a half an hour. Finally the jury foreman intervenes. "I see no reason to question this witness any further." Theresa is excused.

When Theresa gets outside the courtroom, she's trembling. Joe helps her down the long hallway to the limo. As their footsteps echo off the marble, she says, "Joe, it was really awful in there."

"Did you take the Fifth on everything?"

"Uh-huh . . . and just like you told me, Martindale said terrible things about Sonny." She asks innocently, "Why does he hate him so much, Joe?"

Anadaro gives her a lesson in political ambition. "Sonny's a very powerful man. If Martindale can get a conviction, it would get him elected senator."

Theresa observes, "The scales of justice are tipped, then, aren't they? I mean, look what they put me through, and I didn't even do anything."

Joe shakes his head. "Martindale's a barracuda, all right . . . he'd do anything to put Sonny behind bars."

This stops Theresa at the revolving door. "Joe . . . do you think there's a chance Sonny will go to prison?"

Anadaro comes back quickly, "No way . . . there's not a prison big enough to hold him. Besides, he's too smart. I wouldn't worry about it, Theresa. Sonny will get through this just fine."

She hugs him, relieved. "I'm so glad to hear you say that." Theresa heads out to the car. Joe follows her, happy to see that she believes him. Anadaro only wishes he could be as certain that what he said was true, but he knows that the heat on Sonny is dangerously close to igniting any day.

The day after, Martindale puts Linda through a grueling forty-five-minute interrogation. Alleged details of Sonny's operation are hurled at her like javelins, but the loyal secretary never flinches. She looks the attorney straight in the eye and pleads the Fifth Amendment every time. Joe had her well briefed, but Linda isn't scared . . . she would do anything to save Sonny. On the way back to the office in the limo they discuss the proceedings. "Joe, in all my years in Washington I've never seen an attorney who went after his witness with such vengeance. I hate to think what he's going to do to Sonny when he gets him on the stand."

Anadaro assures her, "Sonny can take care of himself. That guy won't be any problem for him."

Linda looks at Joe. "I hope not, but I'm still worried about Sonny."

"We all are, Linda."

She hesitates a second. "I love him, Joe . . . I always have." Linda says quickly, "Please don't tell Sonny what I said . . . it'd probably cost me my job, I just had to let it out to somebody." She sighs. "I don't know how to handle unrequited love."

Joe puts a fatherly arm around her. "You mean an awful lot to Sonny, Linda. He'd never let you go . . . but he could never love you, either. I doubt he really loves any woman."

She looks at him questioningly. "What about Theresa?"

"Oh, Sonny has a great deal of affection for her, but you know there has only been one woman he's ever really loved . . ."

"Laura?"

Joe nods. "I doubt if a hundred Theresas could ever take her place, but even with Laura he had another love."

Linda looks at him. "He did?"

"Power is his love . . . and money is his mistress."

Eventually everyone on Sonny's western staff was called in to testify. They all took the Fifth Amendment, and the closing question was always the same: "Do you know where Sonny Gibson is right now?" No one ever did. It was Theresa who accidentally revealed his whereabouts. She received a phone call from Sonny's father in Indianapolis. The FBI had been to his house looking for Sonny. He'd read in the newspaper that his son was under indictment and was worried about him. Theresa assured Pops that Sonny was all right; in fact he was coming into Burbank airport that night to dodge a subpoena issued for him in Florida.

As soon as she hung up, Theresa realized that she had put Sonny in jeopardy. She was right. The minute he stepped off the plane, a U.S. marshal served him with a subpoena to appear before the grand jury at nine A.M. the following day.

The next morning, reporters jam the hallways of the Federal Building waiting for the Mafia kingpin to arrive. When he finally does, cameras click furiously, and a barrage of questions are fired at him. All the hungry journalists get from his attorneys is a repeated "No comment," as a phalanx of bodyguards escorts Sonny to the courtroom. One of the photographers bumps into Angelo. The imposing giant grabs the man's camera and squashes it with one hand, warning, "Go take your mother's fuckin' picture."

Before he goes inside, Sonny shouts at Henry Stevens, "Get a court order to keep those damn reporters away from me." Sonny disappears into the grand jury room before the lawyer has a chance to answer him.

The men and women on the grand jury have been waiting a long time for this day. Most of the jurors are ordinary working people, some with nine-to-five jobs, some of the women are housewives, so when the notorious underworld figure finally gets on the witness stand, they are spellbound. They listen intently as he swears to tell the truth and nothing but the truth. As soon as Sonny sits down, Martindale begins his machine-gun style questioning. "Is your name Ronald Gene Gibson, also known as Sonny Gibson, Crazy Sonny, Big Boy, Sonny the Stallion, and Santino Gino Genetti?"

Sonny takes the Fifth Amendment on each of his seven identities, adding, "I refuse to answer on the grounds that it might tend to incriminate me."

The court clerk than brings out a picture board with eight-by-ten glossies of all the Mafia dons and known underworld figures. "Is it true that every one of these men has been in your company at some time in the past ten years?" He points to Don Giuseppe. "Is it true that you work for his man?"

Sonny answers dully, "On the advice of my attorney I reserve the right to take the Fifth Amendment."

"Is it true that you have homes in California and Florida worth over fifteen million dollars?"

Sonny says flippantly, "The Fifth . . ."

The jury foreman, a woman in her forties, interrupts. "Mr. Gibson . . . what does that mean? Are you saying that you're taking the Fifth Amendment?"

"That's what I said . . . the Fifth."

The foreman tells the court stenographer, "Let it be recorded that the defendant's last answer refers to the Fifth Amendment of the Constitution." He says to Martindale, "You may continue with this witness."

"Is it true that you have eighty bodyguards, ten full-time?"

"The Fifth . . ."

"Is it true that you have several jet planes?"

Sonny's answer is still the same. "I plead the Fifth Amendment . . ."

Martindale is livid, but he doesn't stop until he's asked a total of 240 questions. Sonny has been on the stand for an hour and a half when the federal attorney finally says, "Mr. Gibson, is this jury going to hear you take the Fifth Amendment on every question asked today?"

Sonny looks straight at him. "On the advice of my attorney, I reserve the right to take the Fifth Amendment."

Martindale throws his hands up in exasperation. The foreman puts an end to the questioning. "It is obvious that this witness is going to continue to take the Fifth Amendment."

Martindale makes a request. "Before Mr. Gibson is excused from the witness stand, I would like to ask him one more question." The foreman nods her consent. The attorney turns to Sonny and says plainly, "Have you at any time ever told anyone that you were related to Jimmy Hoffa?"

This is a loaded question. Sonny turns to the jury foreman. "I wanna have a consultation with my counsel before I answer."

She nods again. "You may do so, Mr. Gibson, but remember, you'll still be under oath when you come back in."

Sonny leaves to confer with his lawyers in the corridor. Joe says, "What happened . . . did they excuse you?"

"No . . . I came out 'cause they asked me about Hoffa."

Stevens asks, "What about him?"

"They wanna know if I ever told anybody I was related to Jimmy." Sonny is worried. "If I take the Fifth, they'll think I have a lot to hide. It'll put heat on Jimmy. I don't wanna do that . . . he's up for parole. That guy's done enough time. What happens if I say no, Joe?"

"You could get a ten-thousand-dollar fine and five years in prison for perjury." The lawyer thinks a second. "I think we should leave, Sonny. That's the safest thing."

Stevens jumps in hotly. "I don't think so. It'll cause too many problems. I think you should go back in there."

Sonny looks at his trusted attorney, "Should I, Joe?"

"No, Sonny . . . I think you should leave."

Stevens disagrees vehemently. "The press will eat that up. When you do come back, they'll murder you. I know this district."

Joe says steadily, "I know you've dealt with this district, Henry, and if it were any client other than Sonny, I'd agree with you, but he can go to Sicily . . . it would take another year to resubpoena him there." He turns to Sonny. "I think we should leave."

Stevens says, "You're making a big mistake, Joe, believe me . . . I know."

As the attorneys argue back and forth, Sonny thinks. He can't go to Sicily because he wouldn't be able to continue working on his Big Scam. Sonny puts an end to the lawyers' bickering, "Look, I can't spend my time in Sicily. I have to be here even if it means dodging more subpoenas. Besides, they already asked me the question about Jimmy. If I split now, it'll look like I'm tryin' to avoid answerin' it, and that could put heat on him, too. I'm gonna go back in there and get it over with, Joe."

Anadaro says reluctantly, "O.K., Sonny, you know what you're doing."

When Sonny returns to the stand, Martindale asks him again, "Have you ever told anyone at any time that you were a relative of Jimmy Hoffa's?"

Sonny takes a chance on beating the perjury charges. "No, I never told nobody I was related to Hoffa."

Martindale is astonished. He thought Sonny would surely plead the Fifth. He replies, "Thank you, Mr. Gibson . . . there are no further questions."

Sonny was positive that an indictment would be handed down after the grand jury investigation, but it happened sooner than he expected. On Monday morning, May 17, 1971, federal agents surrounded his office building. The bodyguards weren't sure what was happening and suspected it was a hit. They had spotted a car following the limo from the West Castle that morning. The two men inside were grabbed and spread-eagled on the hood, their ID's and guns confiscated. They were then handcuffed and brought to the bodyguards' office. When their identities checked out, Tony told Sonny, "They're FBI guys, Boss. What should we do with them?"

"Give 'em back their guns and ID's . . . Richie made a few phone calls. I've just been indicted for perjury. I'm goin' downtown with the attorneys to surrender myself."

The loyal bodyguards waited all night outside the jail where Sonny was being booked. Bail had been set at $500,000. Richie and Tony went to Las Vegas to get the bail bond. Sonny would never use his own money for this directly, because there was a chance the government could nail him for tax evasion or retain the money if he were convicted. It was cheaper to pay a ten percent fee for the bond.

The headline of the Los Angeles *Times* on May 17, 1971, read, "THREE INDICTED ON PERJURY CHARGES IN LOAN FRAUD PROBE." Gregory and Jeff had also been caught. They thought they could get by without taking the Fifth Amendment, but the crafty U.S. attorney managed to trick them. Sonny was sure his two executives would rat. The grand jury had already heard testimony from other bankers who'd been involved with Sonny. Even though they themselves were scared to testify against him, other witnesses confirmed allegations that the bankers were a party to Sonny's scams. Some said they had overheard them talking about the threat of being thrown out of his plane. Martindale had these men in a corner. He warned them that they faced a forty-count indictment for perjury and twenty years in prison if they didn't become government witnesses. Every man talked, and the Justice Department gathered enough evidence to indict Sonny again. On July 27, the New York *Post* headlines proclaimed, "MAFIA KINGPIN INDICTED ON 34 COUNTS OF VIOLENT EXTORTION."

Sonny now had fourteen indictments pending in courts around the country, but his lawyers managed to keep postponing his trial dates. For the next two months there was at least one major headline daily about Sonny in newspapers all over the world. On July 10, 1971, *Business Week* ran the longest article on crime in its history with details about Sonny and his operation. The names of the executives with Transcontinental Casualty in the Bahamas and the Bank of Sark in St. Petersport, Guernsey Islands, were linked with "known Mafia figure, Sonny Gibson." A photo of the Bank of Sark's main branch over a hairdresser's shop in a rundown building accompanied the story. There was also a cartoon that showed Interpol, the CIA, the FBI, and Scotland Yard as law-enforcement caricatures searching the globe for the brains behind the operation . . . Sonny Gibson.

In spite of all the publicity Sonny continued accumulating money for his Big Scam. There was now $250 million in a three-and-a-half-year escrow in Nevada. Forty-two months was the length of time Sonny felt he needed to reach his $500 million goal and make final arrangements with Cordone in the Philippines. Sonny knew it wouldn't be long before he left the country and all of his problems behind, but he still spent five to six hours a day listening to bugging tapes of his executives and his attorneys. Fighting his indictments was expensive, so Sonny started to liquidate almost everything he owned. He sold *The Lucky Dolphin* and all of his planes except for the Lear. The Miami Hotel note was due, so he drained the rest of the cash flow from it and got rid of that, too.

His Hollywood hotel and his ski lodges around the country were disposed of the same way. Sonny knew he only had two more months to live at the West Castle because the Bank of Sark check in escrow was due for collection. Theresa was now looking for a place for them to live, which was not an easy job since Sonny had given her a long list of requirements; the most difficult was finding six apartments next to each other on the ground floor. Apartment hunting can strain even the best relationships, and the enormous pressure on both of them was beginning to affect their formerly tranquil home life.

Fortunately for Theresa, Sonny went to Manila at this time to firm up arrangements for his gaming license and land leases. A letter of intent is ready for Sonny when he arrives. Cordone has coffee brought in while they discuss the details of Sonny's proposed Philippines operation. Stirring in three teaspoons of sugar, he says to Sonny, "I was reading the bank statement yesterday. It shows you have two hundred fifty million dollars in escrow already. . . . Why don't you come over right now?"

Sonny refuses coffee and asks for a glass of wine instead. "No, once I get the letter of intent from you, I can raise six or seven hundred million . . . I know I can get at least another two."

Cordone lowers the cup to his lap. "We've still got the same arrangement?"

"Yep, fifty-fifty, right down the middle." He takes a sip of wine. "But there's a problem. My escrow money won't be released until my hotel and casino are built. You won't give me my gaming license until then either."

"I'll give you your license if you transfer the money here now."

Sonny is adamant. "No way. In the first place, according to the escrow agreement, the money can't be transferred for forty-two months . . . even then they won't release it till I break ground. In the second place, I have no protection under international law until you give me citizenship. I gotta protect my own ass. How do I know you won't kick me off the island after my hotel is built? Then you've got my money and a thirty-million-dollar complex." Sonny adds sternly, "I'm not goin' around beggin' every fuckin' country to let me in like Meyer Lansky."

"I assure you, Mr. Gibson, that won't happen."

"Damn right it won't . . . you're gonna put up half my costs . . . fifteen million dollars cash plus my citizenship papers right now."

Cordone smiles. "I can get you citizenship but I can't give you that kind of money. This is a poor country, Mr. Gibson."

Sonny cons him. "O.K., Cordone . . . I was prepared for this . . . you either find a way to get it or I'm takin' the whole fuckin' deal over to

Fiji. Some people over there are real interested in it."

Cordone leans forward, concerned. He makes Sonny an offer. "Mr. Gibson . . . I can't give you the fifteen million in cash, but I can put up a piece of collateral that is worth much more than that. You can have it with one stipulation . . ."

"What's that?"

"It must be placed in a British, Swiss, or American bank."

Sonny replies quickly, "Great . . . I'll give you a note from the Bank of Sark . . . that's a British bank."

Cordone smiles. "Where are you going to put my collateral at the Bank of Sark . . . in the closet? You insult me, Mr. Gibson. Just like you, I did my homework, too."

Sonny says cautiously, "You didn't have to study very hard, Cordone. My name's in the papers every day with pictures of the Bank of Sark." He adds, "But I'm glad you checked me out . . . I like to know I got smart partners." Sonny is curious. "What is this collateral you're talkin' about anyway?"

The Filipino motions his guards to follow them. "Come, I'll show you . . ."

Cordone takes Sonny and his men to a bank across the street. The bank manager opens the vault; inside, a red globe the size of a bowling ball sits on a wooden stand. The bodyguards surround the sphere, studying it like an object from outer space. Sonny asks, "What the hell is this?"

Cordone beams proudly, "It's the largest blood-red ruby in the world."

Size doesn't impress Sonny. He's much more practical. "What's it worth?"

Cordone touches the ruby. "At least fifteen million dollars . . . if you had to put a price on it."

Angelo remarks, "Boss, that's a lot of money for a piece a rock, isn't it?"

"Yeah, it sure is. I wanna check this out, Cordone. We'll see what it's really worth."

That afternoon Sonny makes a phone call to his bond company. An expert there says that the ruby's value exceeds $15 million, and Sonny returns to Cordone's office that evening. "O.K., the stone checks out . . . I'll put it in a U.S. bank with a couple a conditions. First, neither one of us can take the stone unless we both sign the withdrawal papers."

"I don't see any problems there."

"Second, it's gotta stay in the vault for the first ten years of my operation here."

The Filipino objects strongly to this. "You mean I won't have my ruby back for ten years? It can't be out of the country that long."

Sonny reminds him, "I'm gonna be bringin' in over two-hundred-fifty million dollars. With that kind of money you can afford to let that rock rot in the bank." His partner scolds him, "I thought you said you checked me out, Cordone. If you'd really done a good job, you'd know I started out in the insurance business . . . I'm still in it. That ruby's my insurance you're gonna sign all the papers I need to stay on this island."

The Filipino is confused. "But why ten years? Why not five?"

" 'Cause if I'm gonna live here the rest of my life, I gotta make sure my operation is totally secure." Sonny reasons, "With as much money as I'm gonna be takin' down outta that escrow, I won't have no friends." He says firmly, "That's the deal, Cordone. If you don't take it, I'll bring my business over to the Fiji Islands." This is another con . . . Sonny knows it would be foolish to bring the deal to Fiji since tourists have easier access to the Philippines.

The Cordone finally gives in. "All right, Mr. Gibson, but I get to pick the bank."

"O.K., as long as it's on the West Coast of the United States. I'm leavin' tomorrow on a ten o'clock flight. I wanna bring the ruby with me."

"I'll be going with you to put it in the vault. It's not that I don't trust you, Mr. Gibson, it's just that a wise man has to think like a soldier. That's why I like doing business with you . . . you're a soldier first."

Sonny smiles. "That's the way I was trained, Cordone."

The Filipino official takes two men with him to guard his collateral on the commercial flight to Los Angeles. He has decided to deposit the ruby in Nevada because the escrow money is there. When they land at LAX, Sonny himself will fly the entire party to Las Vegas.

Richie has arranged for a Brink's truck to take the stone to Air Research, where Sonny keeps his Lear.

After they finally get the ruby safely on board and take off, Angelo comes back to the cockpit. He closes the door. "Uh . . . what're we gonna do with those guys, Boss? Are we gonna toss 'em out? You got the rock now."

Sonny says impatiently, "Don't be stupid, Angelo, that's all I got . . . I don't have my fuckin' papers, and you wanna toss out the guy that's gonna give 'em to me?"

"Uh . . I remember you said you were gonna get rid of him, Boss."

Sonny pats the bodyguard's arm. "Don't worry, Angelo, you'll get your chance to take Cordone for a plane ride, and when you do, you can tie that fuckin' rock around his neck." He smiles. "But if I never get that ruby outta escrow or not, it don't matter. . . . We're takin' five-hundred million dollars to the Philippines . . . fifteen million'll be chicken feed to me then.''

With the Filipino on the hook and his papers secure, Sonny is able to raise another hundred million dollars within sixty days. He gets eight million from Sam Scorzelli, who is so excited about the idea that the Chicago boss brings in five other Mafia families, including Don Giuseppe. (Sonny, however, plans to give Don Giuseppe his money back before leaving for the Philippines. . . . He would never con his benefactor.) With Cordone's letter of intent in hand, three more airlines agree to schedule flights to Sonny's as-yet unpopulated island. It is Sonny's marketing package that really sells them, though. He has detailed sketches of his hotel: One wing is called the "Bachelors," a place for businessmen to swing; the "Stud Lounge" is where women can meet men. About a mile from the hotel is the proposed site of an amusement park. What impresses Las Vegas investors the most is Sonny's idea for a gambling area on the roof—the world's first and only nude casino. This tropical paradise will definitely have something for everyone.

Sonny is staying at Caesar's Palace in Vegas, and before he returns to Los Angeles he gets a call from Aldo. The casino operator has been keeping him apprised of high rollers who might be good prospects for Sonny's investment. He is phoning about something quite different this time. "Sonny, a guy just left my office . . . Jacques Delon. He's a string player in the showroom orchestra. He's got something he wants to sell. I think you oughtta take a look at it.''

"What's he got?''

"An original Stradivarius violin . . . ''

"A violin . . . what the hell am I gonna do with that? How much could that be worth, huh, Aldo?''

Aldo drops six figures on him: "$250,000.''

Sonny is astounded, "What! You tellin' me a fuckin' fiddle is worth a quarter of a million dollars?''

Aldo assures him, "This one is . . . it's the only one of its kind in the world. He's got papers to prove it.''

"How much is this guy askin'?''

"A hundred grand.''

The deal is sounding better and better. "Why's he sellin' it so cheap?''

Aldo explains. "I think he's sick and wants to leave something for his family.''

"I'll give him a Bank of Sark check.''

"He won't take a check from anybody. He needs cash.''

"I'm interested, Aldo . . . I think I got a guy in the Bahamas who'd buy it right now. Tell this fiddler to meet me in the dining room tonight between shows.''

Sonny drinks three espressos while he waits for Jacques Delon to arrive. Richie asks, "How the hell can you stand that stuff, Boss? It's too strong for me."

Tony asks, "Yeah, whoever came up with the idea of that anyway . . . they must have been drunk."

Sonny holds up the small cup, "You're half right, Tony. Don't you guys know where espresso started?"

Angelo says, "Uh . . . didn't they bring it over from Italy around 1905, Boss?"

Sonny says, shaming them, "You guys don't even know your own heritage. What kinda Italians are ya? I guess I gotta take time to educate ya. Espresso goes way back to the Roman days. Centurions on sentry watches used to drink a lotta wine on duty, which of course they weren't supposed to do, so to cover up the smell of alcohol, they'd suck on a coffee bean, what espresso's made from. In those days, if you got caught sleepin' on the job, they didn't fire ya . . . they killed ya. The coffee kept the guys awake and also cured their hangovers the next morning."

Eddie says, "Yeah . . . that stuff keeps me up all night, Boss."

"Well, now ya know you're not the first."

At that moment, Angelo sees a man approaching their table. The giant is up in an instant, blocking his path. "Can I help ya?"

"I'm Jacques Delon. I have an appointment with Sonny Gibson. The maitre d' said he was over here."

"You the guy with the violin?"

Delon holds up the case, "That's right."

"Yeah, the boss is expectin' you." The bodyguard brings him to the table "Boss, the fiddle guy is here."

Sonny says, "All right, get these cups outta here. Have the waiter bring us over a couple a bottles of wine." Sonny shakes hands with Jacques. "I hear you got a pretty valuable instrument you wanna sell."

Delon sits and smiles sadly. "I don't want to sell it, but I have to."

Sonny is anxious to get to the crux of the meeting. "Let's see this thing."

Jacques puts the violin case on the table and carefully removes the instrument. He touches it gently, like a mother would her newborn child. "I played a command performance for the Queen of England on a Stradivarius when I was twenty-five."

Sonny takes the violin to examine it. "What's the big deal? This looks like any other violin to me."

Delon is not surprised at his ignorance. "Mr. Gibson, do you know anything at all about a Stradivarius?"

"Yeah . . . I know a guy who's gonna pay a lotta money to get it."

"Did you know the man who made that violin was Italian?"

Sonny looks up. "He was . . . Yeah, well, no wonder it's worth so much then. What part of Italy did he come from?"

Jacques tells him. "Antonio Stradivari came from Cremona, Italy. In the eighteenth century he had the most famous violin shop in all of Europe. In his lifetime he made 1500 of these instruments." The bodyguards listen with interest as the old man continues extolling the virtues of Stradivarius. "The master himself worked on each one. They were made from the finest spruce and maple wood. The violin you're holding is called the Lady Blunt . . . it was made in 1721 and handfinished by the Antonio Stradivari himself. The tones are pure gold, Mr. Gibson." Delon extends his hand. "May I show you?"

When Sonny gives him the Stradivarius, the musician plays a section from a Bach violin concerto. All the men applaud at the end; Angelo is touched. "That's really beautiful . . . isn't it, Boss?"

Sonny is unimpressed. "Violins all sound the same to me."

The man slowly lowers the instrument from his chin. "A Stradivarius can make an artist out of an amateur."

"I don't give a shit about that. I just wanna know if this is the real thing, Delon."

The violinist is offended. "Any serious musician would know it is, Mr. Gibson, but I do have papers to prove its authenticity and my ownership." Jacques takes an envelope from his inside coat pocket and hands it to him.

As Sonny is studying the papers, Tony says, "I always thought Stradivarius violins came from Germany."

Delon looks over hopefully, "Are you a music lover?"

The bodyguard smiles, "Not really. I travel a lot . . . I pick up a lot of information."

Jacques tells him, "There are a lot of these instruments in Germany because the Nazis plundered art objects from Italy during the war." He says wistfully, "When they started looting, they destroyed a lot of things too. There are only seven hundred Stradivarius violins left in the world today."

Sonny breaks into the man's explanation, "There's a guy I know in Phoenix I wanna have check this out for me . . . Why don't ya sign the papers over to me now and I'll turn over the cash to you as soon as I get back."

Delon say adamantly, "Mr. Gibson . . . I know who you are . . . I'm not turning over my instrument to you unless I get my money. You might not come back."

"Come with me to Phoenix then . . . it's your choice Delon."

"I think I'll do that, Mr. Gibson . . . it would be the safest thing."

"O.K., we'll fly over there around ten tomorrow."

According to plan, they leave for Phoenix the next morning. As soon as the Lear is in the air, Sonny sits back casually in his swivel chair. "Here's what's gonna happen Delon . . . I'm gonna take your violin, but you're not gettin' your money. If you don't wanna sign the papers over to me, I'll have Angelo here throw ya outta the plane."

Delon looks over at the immense bodyguard, but oddly enough, there is no strong protest from the Frenchman. "I was warned not to get involved with you Mr. Gibson, but I don't understand . . . you're not even a music lover. Why do you want a Stradivarius violin?

Sonny snaps back, "Same reason you wanted a hundred grand for it . . . money."

Delon surrenders without a fight. "I'm human, Mr. Gibson. I don't want to die. I have a handicapped granddaughter who depends on me . . . I'll sign." Richie hands him the ownership papers. Jacques takes a gold pen from his pocket. "Before I do this, make me a promise that you'll sell it to someone who will appreciate it. I want to know it's going to be taken good care of."

Sonny replies obligingly. "Sure, it'll go to someone like yourself . . . a musician." He'd say anything to get legal ownership of the violin . . . it wouldn't bring as much on the streets. After Delon's signature is on all three copies, Sonny says to Tony, "Tell the pilot we can land now."

Jacques is teary-eyed. "By taking this from me, you've taken my whole life."

Sonny smirks. "You think life means anything to me?"

The musician looks at him bitterly. "I guess not, Mr. Gibson."

"I still don't see what's so special about a fuckin' piece of wood."

Delon barks at him angrily, "You have no right to call that instrument a piece of wood!"

Sonny is taken aback by this audacity. His instinct is to kill Delon for it, but something stops him. This violin player has a great deal of loyalty to his instrument . . . loyalty is something Sonny understands. Jacques resumes his praise of the instrument, "This is one of the . . . "

But he gets silenced quickly. "Shut up, Delon . . . Save it for somebody who gives a fuck."

After they drop the violinist in Las Vegas sans violin, the jet heads down to the Bahamas. There Sonny sells the Stradivarius to a private dealer for $250,000. The next stop is LA. On the way from the airport, Linda buzzes him on the limousine phone, "Sonny, Aldo has been trying to reach you for the last hour. He wants you to call him right away."

"Did he say what it was about?"

"No, but it must have been important. Aldo usually waits for you to get back to him."

"Okay, I'll give him a call."

When Aldo gets on the line he is upset. "Sonny, Delon's sitting in my office . . . we got a problem. He says unless he gets the hundred grand for the Stradivarius, he's going to the police. The problem is,

Sonny, that'll involve not only me, but the casino."

"Look Aldo, don't worry about it, okay? Delon's sittin' there now?"

"He's right across my desk."

Sonny says confidently, "Lemme speak to him."

Jacques gets on and says smugly, "Well, Mr. Gibson, I guess I'll get my money after all. You can tell Aldo to give me the cash and charge it to your marker."

Sonny replies just as smugly, "Delon, I'm not gonna authorize that . . . "

"What do you mean . . . I'll call the police. I told Aldo. . . "

He gets cut off sharply. "I don't give a fuck what you told anybody. I'm tellin' you somethin' now . . . if you go to the police, you'll upset me and you'll upset some of my partners in Sicily. They'll come over here and get that little granddaughter of yours that lives on Bacon Street. . . . I think it's a second floor apartment. . . and we'll put her in the same seat in my airplane you sat in, but she'll have a one-way ticket." There is silence on the other end. "Ya understand what I'm sayin', Delon?

"That's the coldest thing I've ever heard."

"Why . . . she's handicapped, isn't she? I'd be doin' you and her a favor."

There is a loud clank as Jacques throws the phone down. Aldo picks it up a few seconds later. "I dunno what you said to him, Sonny, but he left . . . and he really wanted that violin back when he walked in here."

"Aldo, Delon's got a more valuable piece of property than a fiddle . . . he won't be botherin' you no more." Sonny hangs up and gets Linda on the intercom. "Did Jimmy Taggert confirm our golf game today?"

"Yep, he called yesterday and said everything is set up for you to meet Chet Bartlett at the Riviera Country Club at noon." She pauses. "Oo, I love him. Can you get me an album, Sonny?"

"What the hell's wrong with you, Linda? I pay ya enough . . . buy your own albums."

"O.K. Will you get Chet to autograph it?"

"Hell, no. The only autograph you should care about is mine . . . on your paycheck."

There is a good reason why Linda is so excited about Chet Bartlett—the singer is one of the hottest artists on the charts. Sonny only likes Sicilian music, however, so that doesn't interest him. What does is Chet's $12 million in royalties from his record sales. Bartlett would be a perfect investor for his Big Scam. Sonny is surprised to find the celebrity unassuming, despite his skyrocketing fame. The two hit it off very well, and after that game they play golf a few times a week whenever Chet is in town. At this time Bartlett made it a point to be in LA as often as he could. He was meeting with architects to discuss plans for a $6-million home he wanted to build in Bel-Air for his wife, Julia, and their three children. She had struggled with him in the days when the singer was just another guitar picker trying to make a living. This mansion was her thank-you present. Even though Bartlett himself was a multimillionaire, in many ways he was still just a country boy. He impressed easily, so Sonny took him around town in his limousine, and when the singer played a show in Indianapolis, the Mafia kingpin flew him there in the Lear. Once they were in town, it only took one phone call to supply Bartlett with girls every night of his stay. Sonny and Chet were now close friends.

One week while the country singer was away on tour, Jimmy Taggert set up a golf game with another one of his famous friends . . . Jack Gaudio. Sonny is curious about meeting this veteran performer. The whole underworld loved Gaudio because he gave his time generously to their charities and, of course, because Gaudio is Italian. They are introduced by Taggert at the Bel Air Country Club. Jack greets him. "I've heard a lot about you from Jimmy and Chet."

Sonny shakes his hand, "I've heard a lot about you, too, Jack."

As they walk to the first tee, Gaudio says "You know, Sonny . . . we probably know a lot of the same people." Sonny lets this remark drop until after the game. They go to the bar for a drink, and when everyone has left the table, Sonny tells him, "I don't know what you've told other people to impress them, but you and I both know that you're not connected . . . neither is Frank. So from now on, when you're around me, don't tell anyone we know the same people." Jack is startled by his comment but doesn't say anything. Sonny continues, "I'm not sayin' you don't know who some of the guys are. All Italians respect you and Frank . . . includin' myself. But don't bullshit me that you're connected . . . because I am, and you're not." Sonny leans in closer to him. "I don't ever wanna hear you say that again. O.K., Jack?"

Gaudio stammers, "Well, uh . . . I never said I was connected." He takes a sip of his drink, then looks at Sonny. "You know what, Gibson? I like you. You wanna play golf tomorrow?"

"Maybe . . ."

Gaudio puts down his glass. "You shoot in the low seventies all the time?"

Sonny smiles. "I shoot what I have to shoot to win, Jack."

"How'd you like to be my partner . . . I usually shoot in the low eighties. We can clean up in the matches here and over at the Riviera. We could play over there tomorrow."

"What time do you play?"

"Oh . . . games usually start around noon."

"I'll meet ya there at noon . . ."

In just a short time Sonny and Jack became good friends too. The popular entertainer liked Sonny because he treated him like just another guy who played a good game of golf. Chet often joined them on the course, and Sonny always had an elaborate Italian lunch from Fazzi's Delicatessen catered for them. A long table with wine, cheese, stuffed artichokes, cold cuts, peppers, bread, and fruit was laid out on the tenth tee, and during these leisurely breaks the trio would discuss their personal problems. Sonny genuinely enjoyed the company of these two unpretentious men . . . they were changing his image of show people.

Whenever Sonny and Jack played together, they'd win the match, but Gaudio wasn't so lucky alone. It was the talk of the Riviera that a garment manufacturer named Sy Cohen was hustling Jack. Sonny sent Angelo to warn Cohen that Gaudio was a friend of his and that it wouldn't be a good idea to keep taking his money. A few days later, however, Sonny found out that Sy took Jack for $20,000 in one game, making the singer the laughingstock at the country club.

Sonny decided to take the matter into his own hands, and he set up a game of his own with Sy.

As soon as they're ready to tee off, Sonny says coolly, "By the way, Sy, you're gonna give me a stroke a hole this round."

The Jewish manufacturer looks at him with disdain. "You've got to be joking! I wouldn't give my mother that kind of handicap . . . and she's seventy-five. Why should I give it to you?"

Sonny pulls a cassette recorder from his golf bag and pats the seat of his cart. "Sy, come here. I got somethin' you're gonna find very interestin'." As soon as the manufacturer sits, Sonny presses "play." The tape rolls. On it is a conversation between Cohen and his partner. Sy's face whitens as he hears them scheming to fix the weight of their imports; tax on foreign goods is paid by the pound. Through Sy's contact at customs their declarations were forged to drop the weight, conveniently losing a zero . . . 100,000 pounds became 10,000.

Sonny clicks off the machine. "We'll play for a hundred grand today."

Cohen objects. "Those stakes are awfully high, don't you think?"

"You're bein' punished, Sy . . . you were warned not to play with Jack." Sonny ejects the tape and holds it up. "Your suppliers in Japan would pay a lot more for this. If what you did ever got out, their license would be pulled, too. If they have to buy the tape, they're gonna stop dealin' with you, Sy, and you'll go broke. A hundred grand is a drop in the bucket, considering."

The manufacturer cannot object when Sonny tells his bodyguard, "Angelo . . . put Sy down for a hundred grand at a stroke a hole."

Word spreads like wildfire about this game, and by the third hole the course is crowded with regulars eagerly watching the outcome. Even an amateur could win with that handicap, so naturally Sy loses. Cohen is the new object of derision at the Riviera.

The next day Sonny plays golf with Jack. As they walk to the tee, Sonny says, "I think you should know, Sy's been cheatin' ya all along, Jack. I had a little golf game with him myself yesterday."

Gaudio says smoothly, "I heard about it."

"Yeah . . . I got twice as much money from him as he took from you. After all, you're my partner." Gaudio is puzzled by this remark. Sonny goes to hit the ball and gives Angelo the high sign. The bodyguard walks over to the singer. "Uh . . . Mr. Gaudio, there's a gift for you in your golf bag. I can't say who put it there." When Jack looks inside there is an envelope with $50,000 cash . . . half of Sonny's winnings from his match with Cohen. Sonny does not see Gaudio's reaction when he opens it—he is too busy watching his ball land on the green and stop about ten feet from the first hole. "Hey, Jack . . . looks like I'm hot again today." Neither of them ever mentions the money.

Later on Sonny and Jack sit at the bar, relaxing over a glass of wine and talking. Because they've become good friends and Gaudio knows he can trust Sonny to keep things to himself, Jack often asks for advice. His smooth voice oozes with worry now. "Sonny, I got two million dollars to do my TV show. They just offered me three million if I sign with them next year. I don't know what to do."

Sonny exclaims, "What the hell you mean, you don't know what to do! Don't you like bein' on TV?"

Jack sighs. "Yeah, but I'm tired of TV . . . and it'll take two days a week away from my golf game."

Sonny reacts with astonishment. "You're thinkin' of turnin' down three million dollars a year 'cause it'll fuck up your golf game?"

Jack says seriously, "Sonny, this is the only relaxation I have . . . I need it, my life's so damn hectic as it is."

Sonny leans back. "Then I wouldn't do it if I were you. Hell, Jack"—Sonny grins—"money isn't worth that much . . . golf is more important."

Gaudio slaps Sonny on the back. "I knew you'd have the answer."

The trade papers announce the week after this conversation that Jack Gaudio has signed with the TV network for another year of shows. Richie is reading the news to Sonny when an emergency call comes in from Chet Bartlett in Las Vegas. The singer is frantic. "Sonny, can you meet me here in Vegas tonight? . . .It's important."

"What's the matter, Chet?"

"I can't talk about it on the phone. I'd really appreciate it if you could get over here to see me somehow. I can't leave. I'm working at the Hilton."

"O.K., Chet . . . I'll be there in a couple of hours."

When Sonny gets to the dressing room, the singer's boyish face is contorted in worry. He jumps up and rushes over to Sonny. "Thanks for coming so fast. I don't even know if you can help me, but I had to talk to you about it." Chet pours himself a bourbon. His hands shake nervously as he raises the glass to drink.

"What's the problem, Chet? You know if there's anything I can do to help, I will."

Sonny sits on the couch as Chet paces. "I got a call the other day . . . some assholes are trying to blackmail me. They got some film on me naked as a jaybird with a broad."

"Are you sure it's you? Have you seen the film?"

Bartlett sits down. "It's me, all right. They told me the time, the place, and the girl's name."

Sonny reasons, "That don't always mean they have film . . ."

Chet sighs. "They do . . . they sent me a piece of it." He picks up a cocktail napkin and shreds it methodically. "If this gets out, it'll kill me with my record company. They don't want that kind of publicity. I'm getting ready to record some religious albums for them. It'll kill me with the networks, too." He looks at Sonny. "And it'll get me divorced from Julia. You know I can't afford that right now."

Sonny says impatiently, "I told you not to build that fuckin' castle."

"It's too late to back out. Besides, I want her to have it . . . I love Julia."

Sonny dismisses that. "Love, shit, what the hell's it ever get ya?"

Bartlett throws the pieces of his shredded napkin aside. "What should I do, Sonny?"

"How much do these guys want?"

"Three hundred thousand dollars. . . . What do you want to handle this for me?"

Sonny assures him, "I don't want any money from you, Chet . . . we're friends. After this is all over, we'll talk about this hotel I'm building . . . maybe you could play down there a couple a weeks a year."

Bartlett looks at him desperately. "Sonny, get me that film and I'll do anything you want."

"All right, Chet. You relax and let me handle it. When are these guys gonna be in touch with you again?"

"They said they would call my assistant, Tom, on Friday night after the midnight show. They're gonna tell him where to bring the money."

Sonny starts to scheme. "I got a plan. There's a guy I know in New York who looks just like Tom. I'm gonna fly him in here, and he'll be Tom on Friday. Tell your assistant he's gonna have to talk to those guys

when they call because they know his voice. I'll take care of the rest."
Sonny pats the singer's arm. "Don't look so worried, Chet, I'll get that
film for ya."

The phone call from the blackmailers comes in at 1:40 A.M. on
Friday. The real Tom takes the call, but the impersonator drives to the
designated drop-off point near Boulder Dam. Almost as soon as the car
stops, a truck pulls up. Two Arabs get out with their guns drawn and
warn "Tom" not to move. "You got the money?"

"Yep." He opens the case to show them the cash. "You got the
film?" The blackmailers hold up the can of evidence. They slide into
the front seat to count the money, when suddenly two of Sonny's men
who had been hidden under a canvas in the back seat surprise the Arabs.
They hold machine guns at their heads.

"Tell your man in the truck, if he fires, you're dead."

One of the Arabs sticks his head out and shouts, "Goby, don't
shoot. It's a set up. Don't shoot." At this warning the driver peels off,
leaving burning rubber and his two partners behind him. Sonny's men
grab the film from the blackmailers and hold it against the headlight.
When they're sure it's Chet, the blackmailers are shot through the head.
The bodies are then taken out to the desert and blown up with dynamite.

The next day on the golf course Sonny has good news for his friend.
"I got the film, Chet."

The singer is swept with relief. "Can I see it?"

Sonny takes the can from his golf bag and hands it to Chet, who
holds the celluloid up to the sun. "That's it all right." He turns to Sonny.
"How do you think they got this, Sonny?"

"Somebody at the Hilton set you up. Did ya meet this broad at the
hotel?"

"Yeah, through the p.r. department. I can't believe Fred Roberts
would set me up like that." Chet is angry, "What should I do, Sonny?
Should I tell the Hilton about it?"

"Hell, no . . . don't tell nobody. As far as you're concerned, this
never happened."

Bartlett starts to put the film away in his golf bag, but Sonny grabs
the can. "Uh-uh . . . we're gonna burn this." Sonny walks over to a
metal trash bin. He unwinds the film from its reel, puts it in the middle
of a newspaper, then lights it. They both watch the evidence go up in
smoke. Even though Sonny had hired special hit men from New York
for this job, he was making sure that there was not one frame of film
left to link him to the blackmail scheme.

Chet says gratefully, "You have no idea what you've done for me."

Sonny pats his arm. "It was nothin'. I was glad I could help ya out,
Chet." He picks up his club. "Let's tee off. After the game I wanna
show you some sketches of this new place I'm buildin' in the Philippines.

You know, I'm still lookin' for investors."

"I told you before, I got eight million in royalties to play around with."

Sonny smiles. "Chet, believe me . . . this would be a perfect investment for you. You'll thank me someday."

Bartlett says seriously, "I already have a lot to thank you for, Sonny."

Sonny flies back to LA that afternoon. He's just gotten the latest batch of wiretap tapes in on his executives and is listening to them when Linda comes in. "I have some bad news, Sonny." This is just what Sonny doesn't need. Linda takes a deep breath, "The Riviera Country Club turned you down for membership."

"What! How in the hell'd they do that?"

She paraphrases from the rejection letter. "The LA police commissioner is on the board. He knows who you are, and they classified you 'undesirable'. They won't accept your application unless two honorary members sponsor you."

"Shit. Call Chet Bartlett."

When the singer comes on the line, Sonny explains his problem. Chet is glad to help. "Hell, I'm an honorary member . . . so's Jack. I'll sign your papers. I'm sure he will, too."

On the golf course that afternoon Sonny tells Jack about his rejection. Gaudio is livid. "Damn right I'll sign for you. Those assholes try to keep everybody outta that place, especially Italians. Hell, they probably wouldn't have accepted me . . . but I'm Jack Gaudio!" He says with determination, "Just get me the papers, my friend. I'll sponsor you."

Sonny replies, "That's great, Jack. I'll have Angelo get them over to you later."

The next morning Sonny puts in a call to the head of the membership department, Clyde Franklin. "I'm havin' my man bring my money and the membership papers out to you this afternoon. I had 'em signed by two honorary members."

Franklin says frostily, "They really have to be honorary members, Mr. Gibson . . . not just some celebrities you run with."

Sonny says smugly, "Are Jack Gaudio and Chet Bartlett honorary members?"

"Yes, but don't tell me you have their signatures."

"Damn right, Franklin . . . they're good friends of mine."

Franklin is doubtful. "I don't believe it." Then reconsiders, "Well, I might believe it of Jack Gaudio . . . he's Mafia, too."

Sonny retorts, "I don't give a shit what you believe. I've got the papers and I expect my fuckin' card today."

When Angelo gets back from the country club, he is perturbed.

"Uh, Boss . . . they wouldn't give you a card."

Sonny goes nuts, "What! What the fuck you mean, they wouldn't give me a card?"

"They said that even with the two signatures they wouldn't accept you as a member, but you could play golf there anytime you want."

Sonny seethes. "Those idiots . . . who in the fuck needs 'em anyway? In a few years I could buy the whole goddam place and turn it into an Italian country club." He turns to Angelo. "But I'll be in the Philippines by then, livin' like a king."

"Uh . . . you'll have your own golf course there, Boss."

Sonny grins. "Angelo . . . I'll have my own fuckin' country."

At this time the Justice Department was putting together a strong case against Sonny from the grand jury testimony of witnesses all over the country. One day, on the golf course, he got a call from a Washington contact who said that an indictment was imminent. That evening Sonny flew to Catalina to hide out.

On January 25, 1972, the Miami *News* and the *Wall Street Journal* broke the story: U.S. JURY INDICTS 22; BIGGEST MAIL FRAUD PLOT. Greg and Jeff had slipped up. They'd gotten lazy, started sending commitment letters through the mail. The article stated that after forty-two months of intensive investigation, the Postal Inspectors Office, the Treasury Department, and the FBI were issuing warrants for the arrest of twenty-two men in the biggest mail fraud conspiracy in history. All defendants were charged with seventy-eight counts, and Sonny Gibson was named as the key figure in the case. His bond was 5 million dollars; total bail for the twenty-two men was $20 million.

On January 26, the L.A. *Times* reported that "Transcontinental Casualty is a shell company without assets whose address is a post office box in Nassau and whose name is written on a shingle attached to a garage of a house there." The story behind the Chicago *Tribune* headline of January 28, "STRONGARM HOODLUM INDICTED," talked of Sonny's alleged involvement with several gangland murders and his part in the scams of the indictment.

Sonny kept track of the progress of the case by having newspapers from all over the United States flown into Catalina. Through Richie's contacts in the police department Sonny was able to find out which of his executives had been arrested. So far they were all in custody except Joe Anadaro.

Angelo came into the living room in Avalon one afternoon to tell Sonny that the fugitive attorney was on his way in to see him. "Shit . . . there's a warrant out for Joe, right?"

Richie answers, "Yeah, Boss, but he's coming in on one of those little private planes . . . he'll be dressed like a tourist. We're picking him up about four-thirty.

Sonny replies, "No, no . . . I don't want you guys pickin' him up."

"Uh . . . why not, Boss?"

"Angelo . . . nobody knows I'm here right now, but the feds might be lookin' for me. They all know you guys . . . they'll tail ya back here."

Tony remarks, "It's a good thing your friend is lettin' you stay in his house, huh, Boss?"

Richie says, "That's the least he could do after the boss financed his car dealership."

Angelo's mind is still on Anadaro. "Uh . . . who's gonna pick up Joe, Boss?"

Sonny thinks a minute. "Have the housekeeper do it . . . give her twenty bucks. Call Joe and tell him what she looks like."

When Anadaro arrives a few hours later, they sit in front of a big picture window to talk. Joe tells Sonny, "I finally decided what I'm going to do . . . I'm going to escape to Sicily."

Sonny is not surprised to hear it. "I figured you might, Joe."

Anadaro says gravely, "I'm sixty-four years old. If I go to prison, I'll die . . . it'd kill me. Why don't you come over, too, Sonny?"

"No way, Joe. I only need another two hundred million in escrow for my Big Scam. I've been workin' on that for years. I can't take off and leave now." Sonny adds, "Besides, I got a way to beat the indictment."

Joe raises his eyebrows. "You do? . . . . How? This is a big case, Sonny. The U.S. attorney is on your ass, and Masterson is right behind him waitin' his turn."

"Don't worry, Joe. I got a tape that'll get me off if I have to use it."

"That must be a helluva tape."

"It is . . ."

The attorney concedes, "Well, I've learned to respect your decisions, Sonny . . . they're always sound."

Sonny puts a hand on his loyal attorney's shoulder. "We've come a long way together, Joe. I've always paid ya good every year, but I want you to have some extra cash. When you get over there, Alfonso will see to it that you get two hundred grand. I'm also one step ahead of you." Sonny pulls a passport from his jacket. "I got this in case you decided to leave the country. My jet can't fly you over, but I chartered a plane from Mexico City to take you to Sicily."

Joe is close to tears. "You know, all my life I wanted to go to live in Sicily . . . half my family was there. Now that I'm going, most of them are dead." He looks up in concern. "I hope you don't think I'm runnin' out on you . . ."

"There's nothin' else you could do, Joe." Sonny pats Anadaro's arm. "You advised me better than any attorney I've ever had. If I'd have listened to you, I wouldn't have this indictment to start with . . . you never did want me to go back into the grand jury room."

Joe is still fuming. "I knew we shouldn't have . . . it was that goddam Stevens's fault."

"No, Joe . . . I made the decision to go back in, but I had no choice . . . I knew things you and Stevens didn't."

Joe asks soberly, "What are you gonna do now? You can't hide out forever . . . how are you going to operate?"

"I've made plans, but I wanted to talk to you about them. I'm gonna go with Liebowitz next week and surrender myself."

Joe shakes his head firmly. "I don't like it . . . why don't you just come to Sicily?"

"I told you before . . . I got my Big Scam workin', I can't leave." He tries to allay Joe's fears. "What the hell . . . what's the bail? Two, three million dollars? Shit, the trial won't be for another six months to a year, a year and a half. I have a forty-two-month escrow. I only need another two and a half years. After the escrow clears, I'll be outta the country before they even know it." Sonny assures him, "I'll be all right, Joe."

The attorney sighs. "I hope so. If you ever need anything, you know where to get me."

"Thanks, Joe . . . I may call you. Say hello to Alfonso. Tell him everything's O.K."

On January 28, 1972, Sonny surrendered himself to the U.S. marshals. His booking time downtown was inordinately lengthy. As soon as bail was posted for one charge, they hit him with another indictment and he was required to go through the tedious, ten-hour booking procedure all over again. After three days Sonny was finally released; his bail bonds totaled $5 million.

While he was in jail, Sonny instructed his attorneys to bail out his executives, too. The day he was set free, Sonny found out all of them had been released on their own recognizance, which can mean only one thing . . . they had turned rat. Every one of the defendants was now in protective custody except Joe; the government assumed he was dead.

Since the indictment had been handed down in Miami, the case would go to trial there. Sonny flew to Florida with his lawyers to begin a tug-of-war with the U.S. attorney over the jurors. Several candidates asked to be relieved of jury duty because they had heard of Sonny's involvement with the Mafia and were scared. The presiding judge excused them, and the rest were sworn in collectively.

The jury selection process drags on for four weeks. Finally, after seeing 300 candidates, five men and seven women were chosen for the jury. The attorneys are finally ready to go to trial.

The night before the court battle Sonny's lawyers have a conference with him at his mansion in Boca Raton. Theresa sits in one corner of the den, listening quietly. Sonny's second-string attorney, Harold Liebowitz, tells him, "We have to be careful. If we win every count but one and you get a conviction, you can still get a lot of time. They'd probably want you to do twenty-five or thirty years. He's a hanging judge." Theresa's brow wrinkles when she hears this ominous label.

Sonny assures the attorneys, "Don't worry, we're not gonna get a conviction . . . even if we do, we can't lose this case."

Stevens joins in, "I don't know what you're talking about, Sonny . . . if you get a conviction, you go to prison."

"Not with what I got planned."

Liebowitz is annoyed. "Can you tell us what it is you have planned? After all, we're representing you . . . we might be able to use it."

Sonny looks directly at Stevens. "Lawyers got me in this fuckin' mess to start with . . . I'll use it myself when I have to."

The attorneys gather up their briefs. "All right, we'll see you in court tomorrow morning then." Stevens reminds him, "Don't forget to dress like an all-American boy—leave the sunglasses and cigar at home."

"Can you believe I actually had to dress like that one time."

Liebowitz says, "Why?"

Sonny laughs. "I was an insurance agent in Oklahoma. I've had to pull that all-American crap a lot for them."

Stevens assures him, "It'll be a big help to the case, Sonny."

"I don't see how, but I'll do it."

When they leave, Theresa comes over, fretting. "What's this about twenty-five years? What do you think your chances are of getting off . . . really?"

He puts an arm around her on the couch. "Good, Theresa."

"What makes you so sure . . . they're not—"

"Lawyers never see the good side of nothin' . . . if they did, they'd all be outta work."

"But how can you be so positive you're going to win?"

"I don't know about winnin' the case, but I'm not goin' to prison . . . not off these trials."

She's still worried. "Martindale and Masterson want you real bad, Sonny."

He strokes her hair lightly. "Don't worry, baby, I'm not goin' anywhere . . . how could I ever leave you?" Sonny kisses her. "Let's not talk about it anymore." He lifts her skirt playfully, "What are those pretty panties you got under there? Take those off . . . let me see them."

Theresa protests, "I'm still worried . . . "

He lays her down gently. "Don't be . . . nothin's gonna happen,

Theresa . . . I promise."

Ever since the indictment, there had always been cars outside the West Castle and the Florida mansion waiting to tail Sonny. Reporters wait for Sonny wherever he goes—and a crush of them are outside the Federal Building when he arrives on the first day of his trial. Theresa and the bodyguards are at his side as he enters the courtroom. Richie points to Gregory, who is surrounded by U.S. marshals in plainclothes. "The rat's here, Boss."

Sonny says without emotion, "I smell him."

Angelo shouts, *"Va fungool . . . Baccala!"* then turns to Sonny. "Boss, I'll kill him right here if you want."

Sonny reminds him sharply, "Angelo not now . . . we're in a federal building. We'll get those guys in time." Just then the judge enters the courtroom as the bailiff announces, "All rise. The United States District Court is now in session. 'The People versus Ronald Gene Gibson, alias Sonny Gibson.' " A severe-looking, scowling man sweeps onto the bench, black robes trailing behind him. He looks over at Martindale and Stevens. "Are counsel ready to go to trial?" When they both confirm that they are, the judge asks, "Does the government have an opening statement?"

Martindale stands. "Yes I do, Your Honor." He crosses to the jury box. "Ladies and gentlemen of the jury, the United States government will prove beyond a reasonable doubt that Sonny Gibson, being of sane mind, willfully committed eighty-six acts of mail fraud, conspiracy, perjury, and acts of extortion. There is nothing good to say about this man. Ladies and gentlemen, you will see the power Sonny Gibson had as a leader of the underworld and the violent methods he used to maintain his control."

Henry Stevens replaces Martindale in front of the jury box. He leans on the rail. "Ladies and gentlemen of the jury, if the government can prove these things, I recommend we get on with the trial. I suggest we don't waste any more of your valuable time." Stevens walks coolly back to the defense table. The judge thanks the attorneys and asks the prosecution to call its first witness to the stand. Gregory Stanford is sworn in. Martindale asks if he knows the defendant and if he's ever worked with Sonny Gibson. Gregory says yes to both questions. The prosecutor continues, "How many years did you work for Sonny Gibson?"

"Five years."

"In that time did you ever see Mr. Gibson perform violent acts against anyone?"

"Yes."

"Against you, Mr. Stanford?"

"Yes."

"Did he ever hit you, Mr. Stanford?"

"Yes, he did."

"Did you fear for your life?"

Gregory's eyes fill with fright. "Yes . . ."

"When did you start fearing for your life?"

Stanford looks over at Sonny. "Since the day I started working for him."

The prosecutor asks, "Why were you afraid of Sonny Gibson?"

"Because he was the head of the Mafia."

A low murmur breaks out in the courtroom. Stevens leaps up. "I object to that word being used, Your Honor. Mr. Gibson is a U.S. citizen, not the head of some Mafia. We don't even know what 'Mafia' is. If the word is used, we should define it. If that's the case, is this a trial to educate the jury about the Mafia?"

"Objection sustained."

Martindale resumes pacing in front of the witness box. "Mr. Stanford, you've admitted that you were afraid of Mr. Gibson . . . would you say that you were afraid he might kill you?"

Stevens jumps up again. "I object, Your Honor . . . the U.S. attorney is leading the witness."

"Objection sustained. The prosecution will rephrase the question."

Martindale is unruffled. "All right, Your Honor, I will put the question to the witness another way. Mr. Stanford, how was your safety in danger while you worked for Mr. Gibson?"

Gregory replies with a slight crack in his voice, "He took me for a plane ride and threatened to throw me, my wife, and our little girl out."

Sonny bristles at this blatant lie. He whispers to his attorney angrily, "He's lyin' . . . that goddam fucker's lyin'."

"So, Mr. Stanford, is this court to understand that you remained in Sonny Gibson's employ as one of his top executives because you were afraid he'd harm your family?"

"Yes, that's true."

"Right now, even though you are in protective custody, are you afraid to be in the same courtroom with Sonny Gibson?"

"Yes, I am." Gregory points to Angelo and Tony. "His bodyguards are carrying guns right now."

Stevens objects again. "Your Honor, it is a law that no one is allowed inside a federal courtroom with firearms. Even though these men have a license to carry weapons, Mr. Gibson's men surrendered them to the bailiff."

The judge asks the bailiff, "Is this true?"

"Yes, Your Honor."

"Is it true that these men have permits?"

The bailiff nods. "Yes, Your Honor, and they're all bonded."

"It is the court's understanding, then, that none of these men is carrying any weapons."

"Yes, that's right, the guns will be returned to them after the hearing."

"Objection sustained. The jury will disregard the last statement made by the witness."

Martindale turns back to Gregory. "You're protected from Mr. Gibson. You don't have to be afraid of him *here*." He leans on the rail in front of the stand. "Mr. Stanford, have you ever been in any kind of trouble before?"

"No, sir."

"Has the federal government made any kind of promises to you to get you to come forward to tell the truth?"

Gregory says flatly, "No, no promises whatsoever."

Sonny yells from the defense table, "Bullshit!"

The judge says harshly, "Mr. Stevens, please calm your client." Stevens whispers an admonition to Sonny, but it is ignored. He glares at the traitor as the U.S. attorney asks his next question.

"Mr. Stanford, can you look the defendant right in the eye and say that you are telling this court the truth about your involvement with him?"

"Yes, I can . . ."

When Gregory looks over at him, Sonny jumps up and leans across the table, shouting, "You're a stinkin', fuckin' rat."

The judge pounds his gavel. "This is a federal courtroom. We don't use that kind of language. Where you come from it might be acceptable . . . here it is not. I want to warn you now, Mr. Gibson, if there is another outburst like that, I'll have to cite you for contempt." He turns to Martindale. "You may continue."

Martindale says, "I have no further questions. The prosecution is finished with this witness, Your Honor."

The judge turns to Stevens. "Does the defense wish to cross-examine?"

Stevens stands. "Yes, Your Honor."

Henry Stevens gets up and paces in front of the witness stand slowly, one hand behind his back, one hand under his chin. "Isn't it true, Mr. Stanford, that when you came to work for Mr. Gibson you had a thirty-five-thousand dollar house?"

"Yes, it is."

"And will you tell the court what kind of a house you live in today . . ."

Gregory balks. "Well, uh . . . it's a little better."

Stevens looks at him. "A little better? Would you please tell the court how much better? In dollars and cents, how much is your house worth?"

Gregory defends himself. "I'm not an appraiser. I have no idea . . ."

"I see." Stevens walks to the defense table and picks up some papers. "Your Honor, I'd like to present this to the court as Exhibit A. This is the latest bank appraisal on Mr. Stanford's home. It lists the value as four hundred thirty five thousand dollars." There is a buzz in the jury box. The court reporter records the statement as Exhibit A. Stevens continues, "Mr. Stanford, before you worked for Mr. Gibson, your average salary was in the neighborhood of thirty thousand dollars a year, was it not?"

"Yes, I think that's correct."

"Would you please tell the court what your yearly salary was working for Mr. Gibson?"

Gregory hesitates. "Well, it's hard to say . . . I did a lot for him."

Stevens says coolly, "Just answer the question, Mr. Stanford. Wasn't your salary much, much larger than it was at your bank? Aren't we talking about five hundred thousand dollars? Isn't it true that you were earning over five hundred thousand dollars a year and that most of this money was paid to you in cash in the Bahamas?"

"Yes."

"Isn't it true that you conducted the meetings with Mr. Gibson's other executives?" Gregory says quickly, "Yes . . . but Sonny always told us what to do."

Henry looks at Gregory in surprise. "Mr. Stanford, why would a man like you, with a degree in finance, economics, and accounting, take orders from a man like Mr. Gibson, who can't even read or write?" His point made, Henry moves on. "Do you have any witnesses to the violent acts with which you were allegedly threatened by Mr. Gibson?"

"I certainly do . . . the other guys are gonna tell . . . they're all gonna tell all about the airplane . . ."

Sonny stands up and shouts, "Yeah! They're all goddam fuckin' rats like you!!"

The judge slams the gavel down. "If that man over there says one more word, I'll have no choice but to cite him for contempt. Will counsel please approach the bench?" When the two attorneys are before him, the judge whispers harshly, "Mr. Stevens, you're going to have to control your client. I will not allow that man to talk this way in my courtroom. You must understand that." He scolds them both, "Now, what's wrong with you two men? This trial is beginning to look like a circus, and I will not tolerate it. This is a court of justice."

The judge pounds the gavel. "We are calling a recess. Court will reconvene at ten o'clock tomorrow morning." He looks at Sonny. "I would recommend to all parties that they hold their temper in this courtroom.''

After the judge sweeps out of the room, Stevens warns Sonny to calm down. "With your bond it would be hard to get contempt to stick, but your outbursts don't help us with the jury.''

Sonny replies sharply, "If you'd do your fuckin' job, I'd have nothin' to say.''

The next day Sonny has a breakfast meeting with his attorneys and issues an order to them. "When you get that fuckin' Gregory on the stand today, you make him tell the truth.''

Stevens tries to calm his client. "Look, Sonny, I've already accomplished my objective with Gregory. The jury knows he's lying. They know he was involved . . . they can see he wasn't a lily-white observer. Martindale's finished with Stanford, and so are we. We're not gonna ask him anything else.''

Sonny goes berserk. "What! Why not? Gregory said he's afraid I'm gonna kill him. I never did nothin' to hurt that guy. . . . Those jurors'll think I'm mean.''

Liebowitz argues, "Sonny, if we call Gregory back to the stand, he's going to do more harm than good. What do you think he'll tell the jury . . . you're a nice guy? Believe me, Stanford's already said enough.''

Stevens supports him. "The less he says now, the better it'll be for us. The U.S. attorney expects me to do his dirty work. He released Gregory because he thinks I'm going to question him all afternoon. All Martindale wants to do is get the facts out. Now that the prosecution has dismissed Gregory, they can't call him back without a good reason . . . Martindale loses this round.'' Stevens assures him, "I know how to handle these trials. I've been doing this as long as you've been in crime. I'm playing chess with him.''

Sonny is unconvinced but gives in. "All right, but you guys better know what the fuck you're doin'. It's my ass on the line, not yours.''

When the court reconvenes and the legal formalities are dispensed with, Gregory returns to the stand. Stevens turns to the judge. "To refresh my memory, can the court please read the transcript of my last question in yesterday's proceedings?'' The judge nods consent to the court reporter who checks the record, then says loudly, "They're all goddam fuckin' rats like . . .'' The judge stops him as the courtroom breaks into laughter. He calls for order and says with irritation, "I don't want to hear that again. Please read Mr. Stevens's last question to Mr. Stanford.''

The reporter checks back further. "Mr. Stevens asked, 'Do you have any witnesses to the violent acts with which you were allegedly threatened by Mr. Gibson?' ''

Henry turns to Gregory, "Well, do you have any witnesses to the violence, Mr. Stanford?"

Gregory squirms in his seat. "Well, uh, no, not actually."

Stevens turns to the judge. "I have no further questions for this witness, Your Honor."

Martindale is flabbergasted as the attorney walks back to the defense table. His reaction time is cut short when the judge says, "Will the prosecution kindly call its next witness?"

The prosecution calls Jeff Wolfman to the witness stand. Martindale begins with some basic questions. "Mr. Wolfman, do you know Sonny Gibson?"

"Yes, I do."

"Did you ever work for him?"

"Yes."

"In what capacity?"

"I was one of the executives in his operation. I was also the co-founder of several companies with Mr. Gibson."

"Can you tell the court the names of those companies?"

"Certainly." Wolfman does so.

"When you were founding these companies with Mr. Gibson, did you come across anything that was legitimate in his operation?"

"No."

"You mean not one of the one-hundred-fifty corporations that he had was legitimate? The used-car lots, the hotels, weren't they legitimate?"

"No. They were purchased with fraudulent cashier's checks from the Bank of Sark. I told Sonny"—Jeff looks over at his ex-boss—"You remember that day, out on the golf course?" Sonny doesn't react. Wolfman continues anyway. "I told him we could make just as much money in legitimate businesses."

"I see, and what was Mr. Gibson's comment to that statement?"

"Sonny said he wasn't going to be here that long . . . he didn't have much time. He was going to leave."

"You mean he was going to leave you holding the bag?"

"That's right . . . that's why he deserves whatever he gets. A hundred years wouldn't be enough for him!"

At this point Sonny stands, but Stevens puts a warning hand on his arm to calm him. Sonny sits down without comment as Stevens objects. The judge rules, "Objection sustained." Martindale continues, as he did with Gregory. "Mr. Wolfman, were you ever afraid of Sonny Gibson?"

Jeff says bravely, "No . . . but I was afraid of some of his associates."

"Would you please tell the court why you were afraid of them, Mr.

Wolfman?"

Jeff starts to ramble incoherently. "They had him like a puppet, they pulled his strings. Anything they said, he did. Some of the things were vicious. It was a horror, a horror . . . and the way things happened . . . people just disappeared. It was a nightmare, all those years for me." He points to the bodyguards. "And the men that work for him, they're crazy . . . they're killers!"

Stevens leaps from his seat. "I object, Your Honor. This is not a murder trial. Mr. Gibson's men are not defendants here."

"Objection sustained."

Martindale explains. "Your Honor, what I'm trying to do is illustrate the kind of element Mr. Gibson has around him to show the jury why Mr. Wolfman is afraid."

Stevens goes crazy. "I object! I object, Your Honor. Counsel is not only leading the witness, he is now leading the jury."

"Objection sustained. Would you please ask your witness to answer the questions directly?"

The prosecutor proceeds. "You say you were afraid of Mr. Gibson's associates? Which ones were you afraid of in particular?"

"Definitely Joe Loganno . . . he's Mafia."

Stevens is on his feet again. "I object, Your Honor."

"What is it, counselor?"

"For the jury's information, Your Honor, no court of law has proven that a Mafia exists in this country."

The judge looks over at him. "Mr. Stevens, I'm sure the jury appreciates the information, but it doesn't need a law lesson right now. Your objection is sustained." He now looks at Martindale. "The witness will have to refrain from using the word 'Mafia' in his testimony. The court stenographer will strike the word 'Mafia' from the record. The jury will disregard the last statement made by the witness."

When the judge has finished with the instructions, Martindale continues. "So, Mr. Wolfman, you were afraid of Mr. Gibson's connection with the underworld. Then——"

Stevens jumps up again. "I object."

The judge looks at him wearily. "What are you objecting to now, counselor?"

"Your Honor, it has not been proven that Mr. Gibson is connected with the underworld."

"Objection overruled."

Martindale's line of questioning is an attempt to convince the jury that Sonny is heavily involved with organized crime. He also repeatedly emphasizes the personal fear Sonny's executives had of him.

Stevens manipulates this to his own advantage when he begins cross-examining Wolfman. He walks slowly in front of the witness stand.

"Jeff, don't you think it's strange that Gregory Stanford is scared of Sonny and you're not? Gregory is a much bigger man than you are, and he's afraid of Sonny."

Jeff gets flustered. "Well, I'm not saying I'm not scared of him . . ."

Stevens nails him. "Then you're actually lying on the witness stand. You just told us you weren't scared of him, and now you're telling me you are . . ."

Wolfman tries to save himself. "No, I told you I'm scared of his contacts more than I am afraid of him."

Stevens toys with him. "I see . . . who are the contacts you're afraid of?"

"Joe Loganno."

"Have you ever met Mr. Loganno or spoken to him?"

"No."

Stevens zeroes in. "You're telling me you're scared of a man you've never met?" He has tricked Wolfman.

"You don't know . . . you don't know how they are . . . they're ruthless."

Stevens keeps cool. "But you don't know how they are, either . . . you said you've never met them." Stevens goes back to the defense table. He picks up some papers, but pauses and tilts his head questioningly at Jeff. "Hmmm . . . you know what?" He looks at the jury, then at the judge. "I have no further questions for this man. I can't cross-examine a man who lies." Henry has cleverly slipped in a doubt about the veracity of Wolfman's testimony.

This time Martindale jumps up. "I object, Your Honor. My witness is not lying under oath."

The judge tells the court reporter, "Objection sustained. Strike that last statement from the record. We have no proof that Mr. Wolfman is a liar."

Stevens says, "Your Honor, there is definite proof that this man has no idea what he's afraid of. He doesn't even know what he's saying half the time. I'm trying to get at the truth." Stevens turns to the jury with his arms outstretched. "Ladies and gentlemen, how can we believe the testimony of a man who can't make up his mind?"

The judge replies sternly, "I think you've made your point very clear to this court."

Henry says, "I have no further questions for this witness, Your Honor."

When R. B. Agnew takes the stand, it is obvious that he is truly frightened of Sonny. He testifies for the prosecution that he handled over seventy-five million dollars in escrow for Transcontinental Casualty. "Are you afraid of Mr. Gibson?"

Agnew looks over at Sonny. "Yes, I am . . . he has powerful contacts in Washington, and we used my name to make deals . . . we told people I was the Vice President's nephew. He even had a letter signed by Spiro Agnew."

"Did you use that letter?"

"Yes, but Mr. Gibson's security man always came along as my associate. He would take it back after the people read it."

"You said you were frightened. Why was that, Mr. Agnew?"

"One of my colleagues has disappeared"

"Which one?"

"Joe Anadaro. He was the chief advisor to Mr. Gibson."

"When was the last time you saw Mr. Anadaro?"

Agnew thinks. "Oh . . . about two . . . no, three months ago at Mr. Gibson's mansion in Los Angeles."

"And you haven't seen or heard from him since?"

Agnew says, "He's dead. I know he's dead."

The defense objects. "Sustained."

The U.S. attorney continues. "Just so the court understands, we do have an open indictment for Mr. Anadaro and we have not been able to locate him." Then Martindale returns to his old tricks. "Mr. Agnew, were you afraid of Mr. Gibson when you worked for him?"

"Yes, I was."

"Why?"

"He was very powerful with the Mafia . . ."

Stevens objects again. "Your Honor, prosecution witnesses were instructed to refrain from using the word 'Mafia'."

"Sustained. Strike 'Mafia' from the testimony. The jury will disregard the last statement made by the witness."

Martindale proceeds. "Are you afraid of Sonny Gibson right now?"

He answers, "Yes, I am . . . you don't know this man . . . I do. I don't care how many U.S. marshals you have protecting me . . . I'm scared to death."

"The prosecution is finished with this witness, Your Honor."

Stevens picks up the questioning. The first thing he does is give the witness a tissue to blow his nose. He pats the man's arm. "It's O.K., Mr. Agnew. There's nothing to be afraid of . . ." This solicitousness is intended to lower Agnew's guard. "Mr. Agnew, you said you used a copy of a letter signed by the Vice President to close deals. Can you show the court this letter?"

"No, no . . . no one had a copy, only Mr. Gibson."

"Uh-huh, so what you're saying is that these fine men and women of the jury or the judge or anyone else cannot see a copy of the letter."

"No . . ."

"So there is no proof that this letter actually exists then?"

Agnew protests. "It did . . . we used it many times."

Stevens says quickly, "Would you swear that it was signed by the Vice President?"

"Yes, I know the signature . . . no question about it." Agnew was never told the letter was forged.

Stevens stands and paces now. "Let me understand this, Mr. Agnew. You want this court to believe that Mr. Gibson, whom you are so afraid of because of his alleged underworld dealings, had a letter signed by the Vice President of the United States. Do you expect the men and women of the jury to believe this?"

Agnew says nervously, "Well, I don't know . . . I mean yes . . ."

Stevens continues, "Now . . . if he did have such a letter, then Mr. Gibson would have to be either a friend of the Vice President or a legitimate businessman." Stevens turns to the jury once again. "Ladies and gentlemen, I don't think the Vice President of the United States, Spiro Agnew, would associate with a man of alleged questionable character." He turns to the judge, "I have no further questions for this witness, Your Honor."

The judge calls for the witness to step down. Dr. Swanson is then called. He tells the prosecutor that he thought he was working for a legitimate insurance company. Martindale asks, "When did you find out it was not legitimate?"

"Two months after I started."

"And why didn't you leave then?"

Swanson confesses, "I didn't want to go back to a boring accounting department. I enjoyed Mr. Gibson's flashy lifestyle."

"Dr. Swanson, you have heard other witnesses in this courtroom testify that they were afraid of Mr. Gibson. Do you know why?"

The CPA says with certainty, "Oh, yes. After a few years with him I saw how ruthless Mr. Gibson was . . ."

"In what way?"

"Well, he threatened to throw people out of his jet plane. I knew one of them . . . a banker from Las Vegas." Swanson continues seriously, "I have a degree in psychology, Mr. Martindale. I can tell you that Sonny Gibson is the most vicious man alive today." The prosecutor dismisses him. "I have no further questions, Your Honor."

Stevens starts his cross-examination by asking, "Dr. Swanson, did Mr. Gibson ever threaten you directly?"

"No."

"Have you ever seen him inflict bodily harm on anyone?"

Swanson says excitedly, "Yes, I did . . . in the Bahamas once, in the conference room, I saw him slap Gregory Stanford."

Stevens pauses for an instant. "Dr. Swanson, do you have any children?"

The witness says proudly, "Yes . . . I have three children and five grandchildren."

"When your children were growing up, did you ever slap them?"

"Oh, no . . . we never did that."

"Did you ever spank them, then?"

"Sometimes . . . when they deserved it."

The attorney paces. "I see . . . you did take your open hand to them?"

"Yes."

"Mmm-hmm . . . did Mr. Gibson take his open hand or his fist to Mr. Stanford?"

Swanson says positively, "It was his open hand . . . he slapped him."

"I see . . . and you have also used your open hand on your children. Do you consider yourself a vicious man, Dr. Swanson?"

The doctor stammers, "Well, no . . . I see what you're doing, you can't compare the two."

Stevens retorts, "Well, I am comparing them. If you say you're not a vicious man, how can you say Mr. Gibson is?"

The doctor continues to stutter, "Well, I . . . it's all over the papers. Everybody's said it."

Stevens raises his finger. "Ah . . . now I see." He turns to the jury box. "Ladies and gentlemen, this man's testimony comes from hearsay and the newspapers, then. I have no further questions, Your Honor." Another government witness has been tricked.

During the course of the trial Sonny's attorney continues to make his executive staff look foolish—but Sonny wasn't worried about them. What was beginning to concern him were the victims the prosecution was starting to question, including one of his most terrified airplane passengers, banker Sid Dillman. A parade of seventy witnesses testified against Sonny, accusing him of defaulting on loan commitments, passing phony cashier's checks, pushing swampland in the Everglades, selling nonexistent houses in a national park, and a host of other offenses. Almost 300 more people were scheduled to testify in the next four months of the trial. The case against Sonny was getting stronger each day, and it looked very likely that the Justice Department would get a conviction.

When the court took a three-day recess for a holiday weekend, Sonny flew to New York. He could see that he was fighting a losing battle, so he devised a way to be free long enough for him to pull off his Big Scam. There was one important factor in the scheme . . . he needed the permission of the Mafia's top six family heads—Don Giuseppe, Sam Scorzelli, Don Franco from New Orleans, St. Louis' Tony Tedesco, Migel Steffalino from Miami, and the Matrano brothers of San Diego. Sonny asked Don Giuseppe to set up a meeting for him, and they all met in the elegant study of the Loganno estate.

The six powerful family heads sit in Don Giuseppe's mansion, waiting to hear what Sonny has to say. He addresses them solemnly. "You guys know what I'm tryin' to put together in the Philippines, and you're part a my action . . . always." He monitors their faces for reactions as he speaks, "You know what kind of heat I have on me now. If I split to Sicily, we can kiss this deal good-bye. Cordone won't work with you . . . he won't deal with anyone but me. I've got him on the hook." Sonny has half of the $15-million ruby. The men listen attentively as Sonny goes on. "I got a way to buy myself some time." The dons look at him doubtfully, but he continues. "Here's what I need from you guys. I want an O.K. from the families that I'm gonna rat on 'em."

There is a stony silence in the room; Sam breaks it. "Santino, what the hell are you talking about?"

Sonny says flatly, "I'm talkin' about connin' the government."

Don Franco says, "Santino, you're a helluva con man, but you'll never get away with it."

Sonny assures him, "Yeah, I can. I got a tape that's gonna get me probation."

Don Giuseppe asks, "What kind of a tape, Santino?"

"I'll let ya hear for yourself."

He plays the conversation between the high-ranking Washington politician and Harry Wasserman. When it's over Don Giuseppe marvels, "Santino, I thought I was smart, but getting that tape was brilliant."

Sonny replies, "It's better than that. This tape is gonna get me probation . . . but even my guy can't push Hoover to give it to me unless I make a deal."

Sam asks, "How the hell are you gonna get Hoover to go along with you?"

Sonny primes the dons. "He wants to nail every one of you guys. We'll be each other's bait."

Tedesco cracks, "I'd like to use that fuckin' fag for fish bait . . ."

Sonny outlines his plan. "I'm gonna make up stories about the Mafia . . . you guys . . . that will make the government a laughingstock."

Don Franco smiles. "I like the idea already, Santino."

Sam's cigar hangs from his mouth. "How are you gonna do that, Sonny?"

Sonny digresses to make his point. "Let me ask you something . . . are any of you guys involved with stag films or protection rackets for sex shops and porno houses?" Before they can answer, Sonny says, "No. But if I tell them that we're gonna take over a massive operation in pornography in this country, they're gonna believe it."

Don Migel asks, "Why will they believe it, Santino?"

"Because the feds eat up all that Hollywood bullshit about the Mafia. They love to believe we're corrupting the morals of the country." He clarifies further. "But I guarantee they're gonna buy it after you guys put the word out on the streets that I'm heading up the operation for you."

Don Giuseppe is puzzled. "How will that do anything?"

Sonny explains, "The government informants on the street will go runnin' to the feds. All the rats will be givin' 'em the same story . . . it'll check out all over the country."

Sam says, "Sonny's right . . . they'd believe it then."

"I want you guys to give me an O.K. to do this . . . Afterward you're gonna love me for it."

Don Franco is confused. "But Santino, we'll all be indicted . . . how's that gonna help us?"

Sonny explains, "When I get on the witness stand after I'm given immunity, I'm gonna tell those assholes I don't know what the fuck they're talkin' about."

Sam reminds him, "Even with total immunity they can get you for perjury . . . can't they?"

"So what? All I can get for that is five years. Right now, with a seventy-eight-count indictment, I'm facin' five hundred." Sonny continues enthusiastically, "I'm connin' 'em . . . They'll have to throw out your cases, and your attorneys will be able to get a restraining order against the government to get off your backs . . . *and* you can get them for false charges."

Don Giuseppe says, "What's gonna happen to you when they find out? They could set you up and kill you. They've done it before, Santino."

Sonny says confidently, "A lotta people have tried to kill me. The feds are idiots, they can't do anything to me. Anyway, by that time I'll be in the Philippines, and we'll all be rich." The dons are still skeptical. "Don't you guys see? This'll be the greatest con ever pulled!"

Don Giuseppe says, "I believe Santino can do this con, or else he wouldn't be here wasting time . . . he'd be in Sicily now. Besides, we can all use a gimmick to keep the feds off our back, using their own men to do it."

Sam agrees. "I'm gonna go for it to protect my own interest in Sonny's Big Scam . . . I got eight million invested."

Tony Tedesco says, "I got five . . . I'm in too, Sonny."

The rest of the dons all follow suit. They surround Sonny, hug him, and wish him luck. Don Giuseppe announces, "We're all gonna go eat at Vinnie's place tonight . . . it's on me."

Sonny says, "No . . . it's on me this time, Don Giuseppe. I wanna have the pleasure of taking you guys out to celebrate how we're gonna fuck the government. Everybody on Mulberry Street can join the party.''

The next day Sonny calls his contacts in Washington to tell them he has a tape that "could put a big politician in the slammer." A government official meets with him on a yacht Sonny has rented in Miami to listen to the tape. He is spellbound as he hears a familiar voice say, "The price is two hundred and fifty thousand dollars. Call me tonight on the private line—alone—understand?" After hearing it, the man says quietly, "O.K., what do you want?"

"I want probation."

"No way we'll do that. The Attorney General and Hoover want your ass in jail."

Sonny silences him. "You shut up for a minute. I'm tellin' you what *I* want. Probation and a lotta cash. Half now and half twelve months from now. Then you can have the tape . . . there are no copies. If I don't get probation, I'm gonna give it to AP and UPI. You tell your bosses that I'll be deliverin' the top six Mafia heads on a silver platter."

"How? What do you mean?"

"I mean, with two years to operate, I can get you the evidence you need against the Mafia. In return I want a free run on the streets . . . no buggin', no FBI shit. I also want a guarantee that I won't have to testify against 'em. To keep the U.S. attorneys happy, I'll plead guilty to one count of everything . . . all to be run concurrent."

"We want the Matrano brothers. Can you get them for us?"

Sonny says confidently, "Sure I can. You guys already know the brothers are my best friends."

"Are you saying you're going to be another Valachi for us?"

"A lot better than Valachi. He could only give ya New York . . . I'm giving ya the whole fuckin' country. I'm gonna be the boss of the new pornography protection racket."

"Yeah, we know you're getting into that. We already have confirmation from our informants . . . it's a big deal."

Sonny eggs him on. "Yeah, we'll be takin' in fifty to a hundred million in the first ninety days."

By the end of the meeting Sonny had the government man convinced he was going to betray the Mafia. He gave him a copy of the tape for his superiors to hear, and just ten days later the arrangements were in the works for his probation. Sonny got the first installment of his money in crisp new bills with a warning, "If you ever mention this to your attorneys, it will be your word against ours!"

When they get to the Federal Building the next day, Sonny and his lawyers go directly to the judge's chambers. After the defense and prosecution attorneys are seated, Stevens tells the judge "My client is changing his plea to guilty."

The judge asks, "Do you have the papers drawn up?" Martindale hands him a file. The judge is curious, "What prompted all this? We're already ten weeks into this trial."

Martindale explains, "Mr. Gibson is going to help us go after the top Mafia figures in the country with the understanding he will not have to testify against them. According to our agreement Mr. Gibson will plead guilty to one count of mail fraud and one count of conspiracy . . . both sentences will run concurrently. Our recommendation is five-year probation."

That morning Courtroom A in the Federal Building is jammed with public and press anxiously waiting for the day's proceedings to begin. The hour delay tells them something special is happening. The buzz in the courtroom is silenced by the bailiff's introduction of the judge. After the court technicalities are over, the judge turns to the jury. "Ladies and gentlemen, there has been a change of plea. Thank you all for your cooperation and patience on this case. You are excused." There is an excited murmur in the courtroom. The judge says, "Mr. Gibson, it is the court's understanding that you wish to change your plea."

Sonny and his attorney rise. Stevens says, "Yes, Your Honor. That's right."

The judge looks at Sonny. "You understand that if you plead guilty to one count of mail fraud and one count of conspiracy, you could get up to ten years' imprisonment and a ten-thousand-dollar fine or both?"

Sonny replies, "Yes, Your Honor."

"Mr. Gibson, has anyone made any promises or threats which would cause you to change your plea?"

"No, Your Honor."

"It is the court's understanding then that you are changing your plea freely and of your own accord."

"Yes, Your Honor."

"In that case the court will accept your new plea. How do you wish to plead at this time?"

Sonny says steadily, "Guilty, Your Honor."

The press stampedes out of the courtroom like a herd of cattle to phone their editors with the news. The judge says, "The court will accept your new plea and orders you back for sentencing in thirty days. Until then you will be allowed to remain free on the same bond." The gavel slams. When the judge leaves the courtroom, pandemonium breaks loose.

Theresa comes over to Sonny, concerned. "Are you sure you did the right thing, honey?"

"Don't worry—I'm not goin' to jail . . . all of this will be over soon." The bodyguards surround Sonny and Theresa and rush them out of the courtroom through the mob, which is starting to close in on them.

The next day, Sonny went to Sicily. His lawyers had gotten him special permission to leave the country because of his numerous businesses abroad. On this trip he was planning to consolidate the moneys from all of his foreign bank accounts. The cash he had set aside to build his $30-million Philippines operation was slowly being eroded by bail bonds and costly attorneys' fees.

While he was in Catania, Sonny checked on Joe Anadaro's situation there. Alfonso had taken good care of him. The lawyer had citizenship papers to prevent his deportation and was an advisor to the Sicilian Mafia on the American legal system. Of course, Sonny was happy to see his godfather again. He and Alfonso took a walk through the countryside to discuss all that had happened in the past few months.

The bodyguards follow the men to one of their favorite spots. As they stroll, Alfonso tells him, "Santino, the deal you made with the government was fantastic. Some of the dons over here are planning to use the same type of procedure to con the Italian government. Only you could have thought of that."

"It'll be a real pleasure to see our people get restraining orders to keep 'em from bein' harrassed, Alfonso."

The old man shakes his head sadly. "The government makes whores out of men. Did all of your men rat, Santino?"

"Yeah, but the two biggest I'm gonna kill personally."

"Do you know where they are?"

Sonny recalls bitterly the two men testifying against him. "Yeah . . . Jeff Wolfman split to Canada, and Gregory Stanford'll be goin' to prison soon."

"Why not just kill Stanford there? It would be easy to cover up. . . ."

Sonny's jaw tightens. "I don't want it covered up. I want every rat to know exactly who did it so they can worry the rest of their lives, they're gonna be next."

"Won't that put extra heat on you with the feds?"

"I got the feds sewn up and I got plenty of witnesses to where I'm gonna be when it happens." Sonny smiles sardonically. "Besides, the feds could care less about those rats. They want the Mafia and they think I'm another Valachi. I got a two-year free run in the States."

Alfonso sits on a low wooden fence. The walk is a strain for him. "Santino, I'm a sick man. I'm tired of the hate and violence." His eyes turn cold. "But these men should not live." Alfonso looks at Sonny. "I'm going to hit them for you; I owe you that much . . . you took care of the Nazi pig for me, I'll take care of these rats for you."

Richie protests, "Wait a minute, we wanna kill those bastards."

Angelo agrees, "Uh . . . yeah, Boss, we've been waiting a long time to get them . . . the Boss always treated 'em good, a lot better than they treated him.''

Sonny chastises his men. ''Angelo, Richie . . . have respect for Alfonso.'' He puts a hand on the old man's arm. ''You don't have to do this, Alfonso.''

''Santino, it would be an honor to get rid of that garbage. When are you going back to the States?''

''I'll be leaving as soon as I finish up my business, probably tomorrow night.''

''Santino, are you sure you'll have enough time to do your Big Scam?''

''Don't worry, Alfonso, you'll live to see me finish that job. I guarantee it.''

When Sonny returned to the West Coast, the Gibson entourage moved into a luxury high-rise apartment building on Doheny Drive in Beverly Hills. Sonny finally compromised with Theresa and was living in several suites on the second floor. He had now liquidated everything, including his house in Bel-Air. As soon as he got any cash, it went into a marker in Las Vegas. Ordinarily a marker indicated a debt, but through Aldo at Caesar's Palace Sonny was able to buy plus markers, which were lines of credit. Using this system the government was unable to trace the $35 million Sonny had in twenty casinos all over town.

Without the pressures of running his 150 corporations Sonny now had even more time and energy to concentrate on his Big Scam. He needed to build up his own bank account, too, as well as the escrow, so he continued to con. One of the groups he swindled was an organization of black ministers. He promised to finance the construction of all their churches for the next ten years if they put $2 million up front to guarantee the $20 million in financing, which they had been unable to get anywhere. The executives of the foundation were courted until they were convinced that Sonny had enough money to back them. The jet plane and his penthouse office impressed them, but what really closed the deal was the fact that Sonny was ''Jimmy Hoffa's son-in-law.'' The clergymen thought their project was being backed by union money.

Sonny's freedom also allowed him more time to socialize. He played golf at least three times a week with Chet and Jack, and of course he was still entertaining potential investors. To impress them Sonny kept up the flamboyant image of a Mafia kingpin. Whenever he went to Little Sicily, everyone from the dishwasher to the maître d' got a $100 bill. His tips were $2000 before the check was paid.

Sonny had almost reached his $500-million escrow goal when he was called in to testify in a trial against the Matrano brothers in San Diego. He was surprised by the subpoena, which was served to him while he was playing golf with Jack Gaudio at the Bel-Air Country Club.

The process server, posing as a golfer, comes up to Sonny at the ninth hole. "Sonny Gibson?" The bodyguards can tell by the tone of his voice this is not a friendly visitor. They form a barrier between him and their boss.

Sonny barks, "Whaddya want?"

The clerk throws the papers on the ground. "Here, you've been served, Gibson."

As he walks away, Angelo says, "Should I throw him on the ground, Boss?"

"No . . . no violence, you guys. What's the big deal? So I got served a subpoena. I get 'em every day. Eddie, take it over to Linda so she can give it to Stevens. Let him find out what it's all about." Sonny picks up his clubs. He looks at his golf partner and says in a loud voice that belies his calm, "All right, we need to make this to win the three grand, right, Jack?"

Gaudio pats his shoulder. "Hey, Sonny, slow down a little. There's a lot of money on this putt. Don't let him get ya all excited." He complains, "I don't know how that guy got on the course."

"How do they get anywhere, Jack? They're snakes, those guys. He slithered on." Sonny walks to the ball. "Come on, let's play. My mind's on the game . . . fuck that subpoena."

About six hours later Sonny gets a call at his apartment from Stevens. "Did Linda tell you what the subpoena meant?"

"No . . . I pay you to tell me what it means. What does it mean?"

"It means they want you on the witness stand in San Diego next week."

"What! I'm not supposed to testify. It's in the plea-bargaining agreement."

"I know, and we're gonna try to fight the subpoena. I don't think the judge understands that you don't have to testify."

Sonny is crazed. "Goddam right! I'm not gonna testify. Besides, they're supposed to wait another year before I give 'em anything. How come they're comin' this early?"

Stevens reasons, "Well, they want the guys who did those warehouse fires." Sonny is worried. He knows that if he testifies now, he'll have to expose his con when he still needs another $100 million for his Big Scam. The government, however, is planning ahead: There is a presidential election in 1976, and they want the current administration wants to reap the glory of convicting the top six Mafia dons. The Attorney General knows that it would take at least three years to conclude the trials.

Sonny tried to fight the subpoena for several weeks. His attorneys showed the judge his federal plea-bargaining agreement which exempted him from testifying, but they were told it carried no weight in the San Diego Court. The lawyers even told him that if Sonny came forward now, he'd be killed by the Mafia. The judge was unsympathetic. He assured the attorneys, "Gibson will be all right . . . nobody kills witnesses today." Sonny had no choice in the matter. He would have to appear.

Coincidentally, before he left for San Diego, Sonny heard that Gregory Stanford had been killed in a suspicious fire in his office in Atlanta. The authorities questioned Sonny about Gregory's death, but a call to Washington stopped the investigation promptly. A few weeks later Sonny took the stand for the first time as a witness for the prosecution. This was the first in a series of trials scheduled against the dons in major cities around the country.

On the opening day of the proceedings the courtroom is packed to fire-violation capacity. Donald Masterson, the DA from LA, has kept his promise to see Sonny in court again, but the last thing he expected was for them to be on the same side. Masterson is now a state attorney, and Sonny is the chief witness. The prosecutor is on edge about his testimony and requests a brief pretrial conference with Stevens. "Your client's going to stick to the story he told the government about the pornography protection operation, right?"

Stevens replies, "My client will live up to his plea-bargaining agreement, but you know, Masterson, it says that he's not supposed to be called to the stand."

The prosecutor is a bundle of nerves. "I don't care about that . . . that was the U.S. attorney's deal, not mine. We're using Gibson right now because we have to get these Matranos and put them in prison . . . where they belong!"

Stevens's cool equals Masterson's agitation. "I'd think you wouldn't want Sonny to testify. He'd do more for you if he was out getting evidence to make the conviction stick." Stevens is also trying to buy time.

Masterson says emphatically, "We have enough already. We're going after the Mafia now. The judge ordered Sonny to be here, and I'm asking you as a fellow officer of the court to be sure that your client will be a cooperative witness."

Stevens says cagily, "He will live up to his plea bargaining."

"All right . . . that's what I wanna hear."

When he returns to the defense table, Henry tells Sonny, "I just had a little talk with Masterson. He's very concerned about your living up to the plea-bargaining agreement."

Sonny smiles. "Don't worry, Stevens. I'm gonna live up to my end the same way they lived up to theirs."

After Sonny is called to the stand and sworn in as a government witness, Masterson looks at him confidently and asks, "Mr. Gibson, is it true that you are one of the kingpins of the Mafia?"

Sonny replies, "On the advice of my attorney I reserve the right to take the Fifth Amendment."

The lawyer is stunned; Masterson rushes up to the bench for a conference with the judge. "Your Honor, Mr. Gibson had promised to be a cooperative witness. However, it appears that the only way to accomplish that would be to grant him immunity."

"I don't see that as a problem. I'll talk it over with my colleagues." Masterson goes back to the prosecution table to discuss the situation with the other government attorneys. He then returns to the bench. "Your Honor, the prosecution has no objection to immunity."

"All right, I will grant Mr. Gibson total immunity at this time." Masterson returns to his place in front of the witness box, and the judge tells Sonny, "Mr. Gibson, you cannot plead the Fifth Amendment. You will be required to answer Mr. Masterson's questions because the court is prepared to give you total immunity from prosecution . . . the only thing that you can be charged with in this court would be perjury."

"May I have a conference with my attorneys?"

The judge's decision is firm. "No . . . we've spent many weeks trying to get you to the stand, Mr. Gibson . . . I said I'm giving you total immunity."

Sonny looks at him. "Let me understand this. . . . Whatever I say, I can't be prosecuted except if I lie . . . that'd be perjury." The judge nods. Sonny asks cagily, "Your Honor, what is the worst punishment for perjury in this state?"

"A perjury charge carries five years in prison, a five-thousand-dollar fine, or both." The consequences are now court record. Sonny leans back comfortably in his chair. This is the opportunity he's been waiting for. The judge continues, "Mr. Gibson, you understand now that if you don't answer Mr. Masterson's questions, I'll have to hold you in contempt."

Sonny smiles. "Hell, lookin' at the fact that the most I can get is five years and five thousand dollars, I'll tell ya anything ya want."

Masterson continues his questioning, sure that Sonny will cooperate now. "Mr. Gibson, did you tell the Postal Inspector's Office and the Organized Crime Strike Force that you would be running a pornography racket for the Mafia and that the Matrano brothers would furnish you protection in San Diego?"

"Yeah, I told 'em that." Masterson looks over at the defense table smugly, but neither the Matranos nor any of their attorneys react negatively to Sonny's statement. The prosecutor thinks this odd. He continues, slightly disconcerted. "Is it true, Mr. Gibson, that you told the government that the Matrano family was involved with the destruction by fire of warehouses in San Diego and that they were responsible for several murders in connection with these conflagrations?"

"Yeah, I told the government that, too"—Sonny looks at Masterson evenly—"but it's not true."

The prosecutor is shocked. "What do you mean, it's not true? That's what you told them."

Sonny agrees. "Yeah . . . that's what I told 'em, but these men never did any of it. I did all the killings and burnt up the warehouses." Sonny shouts over to the jury, "I'll take a polygraph test on that. I conned the United States government . . . I conned 'em 'cause they wanted to send me to prison." Everyone is astounded by his revelation. "They wanted the Mafia so bad they let me go free. These people on trial today aren't even part of the Mafia."

Chaos erupts in the courtroom. The defense attorney jumps up excitedly. "The defense demands that this case be dismissed." The eager pack of journalists rushes out the door as the judge futilely pounds his gavel for order in the court.

Masterson is at the bench during the disruption. "Your Honor, Gibson is a hostile witness."

The judge cuts him off angrily. "Look, Masterson, you're the one who fought to get him on the witness stand . . . not me." He pounds the gavel, shouting, *"Order in the court! Order in the court!"*

When everything finally settles down, the DA says, "Your Honor, this man is lying, and I want a perjury charge."

The judge looks over at Sonny. "I don't believe this man is lying. He just got probation on the largest mail fraud case in United States history. I believe he did con the government."

The defense attorney now has his opportunity to take advantage of Sonny's con. "Your Honor, we request that the case be dismissed on the grounds that the government witness just confessed to the crimes with which our clients have been accused."

The judge slams the gavel down for the last time, proclaiming, "Case #350674, the State of California against the Matrano brothers, is dismissed." The acquitted men leap up, hugging each other, shaking their attorney's hands. Then they all come over to do the same to Sonny.

Liebowitz panics. "You shouldn't be doing that . . . you shouldn't be so friendly to them." Sonny whirls around with a sharp retort, "Fuck you, Liebowitz . . . I can do anything I want . . . I have immunity."

Masterson is beside himself. He comes over and rants at Sonny, an index finger aimed at him, "I'll see you in prison, Gibson, even if I have to go with you. I'm gonna get you someday . . . you mark my words, I'll get you." He storms out of the courtroom, leaving some very happy men behind him.

That night Sonny throws an acquittal party for the Matrano brothers at his apartment. Food is catered in from Little Sicily, and the men ridicule the irate DA, imitating him as he raced out of the court. Even Angelo mimics the reserved Harvard attorney flying off the handle at Sonny. But what happens just one week later is no laughing matter.

Liebowitz comes to Sonny's apartment, and he's scared. Sonny pours the nervous attorney a straight brandy. He downs it in one gulp. "Sonny, we got a call from the U.S. attorney's office about an hour ago. Martindale said the Organized Crime Strike Force told them there's a Mafia contract out on you. The dons are very unhappy about your deal with the government."

Sonny comes back quickly, "I have no deal with the government. I thought I made that clear in the courtroom in San Diego. How come the feds don't know that? It's all over the fuckin' papers . . . can't they read?"

This is a clever con the government is trying to pull on Sonny. They think they can frighten him into testifying. Martindale can't outcon a con man, but Liebowitz is worried. "Sonny, what if they subpoena you to New York?"

Sonny laughs. "Let 'em. The DA there knows he's gonna look as stupid as Masterson if he puts me on the stand."

The lawyer asks hesitantly, "Are you sure you don't want to reconsider and testify? You might get killed."

Sonny stops laughing and snarls, "You fuckin' Jews are all goddam chickens. I gotta get an attorney with some balls, Liebowitz . . . Don't you ever tell me to become a fuckin' rat again."

Because Sonny refused to testify, the government has lost its key witness, and all of the charges against the six Mafia dons are dropped. He gets a call from each one, congratulating him on the triumph of his scheme. The night before the New York hearing is scheduled to convene, Sonny takes his chief bodyguards to dinner at Little Sicily . . . after hours, as usual. Sonny's brilliant con was still the topic of conversation when the cannolis were served. Eddie shakes his head. "I dunno, Boss, I still can't believe the feds would think you'd rat."

Richie pats him on the back. "Didn't I tell you they were stupid? Those guys are like the Keystone Kops."

Tony cracks, "And everybody's laughing at 'em, too."

Sonny says, "That comedy show's gonna play all over the country, Tony."

Angelo asks, "Uh . . . what'd Don Giuseppe say when you talked to him, Boss?"

"I didn't talk to him . . . Mario called. He said the don couldn't come to the phone but to tell me the don enjoyed watching my sideshow on the news." Sonny frowns. "Don Giuseppe's gettin' worse . . . he

can hardly get outta bed now." He looks down at his watch and remembers Nick, then covers his feelings by snapping, "Georgie, did ya
bring the car around yet?"

"No, Boss. I thought since we're all leavin' now, we'd go together."

Sonny admonishes him, "I don't like that. I dunno what's wrong
with you, Georgie . . . you've been pullin' this shit a lot lately."

The driver stands. "I'll get it, Boss."

"No, no . . . but from now on have the car ready when I come out
the door."

As they walk out, Joe hugs him. "Take care of yourself, goombah . . . see ya soon."

"Joe, that pepper steak was perfect . . . not too rare."

The proprietor unlocks the door for them. "Good, I'm glad you
enjoyed it. Don't be such a stranger. See you soon, huh?"

"Yeah, Joe."

On the way to the parking lot Angelo says, "Theresa is gonna be
mad that you didn't have dinner with her, Boss."

Sonny snaps guiltily, "Look, Angelo, I'll handle Theresa . . . your
job is to watch my ass. I can't stand sittin' in the apartment, I'm too
cramped in that fuckin' thing." They are almost at the limo when a
black Lincoln Continental slows down in the alley beyond them. A man
inside shouts a warning, "SONNY . . . STAY OUT OF SAN DIEGO!"
Richie throws Sonny to the ground, and Angelo lies on top of him to
act as a shield. Tony, Eddie, and Georgie start firing. As the first shot
rings out, Angelo rolls Sonny under the limousine for protection. The
gunfire continues until a direct hit shatters the would-be assassin's windshield, sending the car screeching away.

Angelo helps Sonny out from under the limousine. The boss is
mad. "Look at my suit . . . there's fuckin' grease all over my five-
hundred-dollar suit!"

Tony brushes Sonny off. "Are you all right, Boss?"

Sonny ignores the question. He's just seen the roof of his limousine . . . a bullet has ripped right through it. Sonny starts raising hell.
"Look what those motherfuckers did to my car!"

Richie rushes over. "I think I hit one of 'em."

Tony says, "No, they kept going. The window broke, that's all."

Sonny is still ranting. "I'll kill 'em. I'll kill the cocksuckers for
fuckin' up my car."

The sound of a police siren wails in the distance. Eddie says,
"Maybe we should get outta here, Boss."

"Fuck no, Eddie. We haven't done nothin' wrong." A squad car
pulls up, and two rookies jump out. One of them looks at Tony's gun.
"Have you got a permit for that?"

Sonny answers him, "All of my men got permits. Richie, take care of this.''

Two more police cars arrive at the scene. A lieutenant gets out of one. He recognizes Sonny. "Hey, you're that Mafia guy, huh? What happened here? We got a report that there was an exchange of gunfire and a possible robbery.''

"Damn right, there was gunfire. Some assholes were shootin' at me.''

The officer needles him, "Isn't that what you mobsters usually do to each other?''

Sonny is boiling but controls his temper. "These were no mobsters . . . if they were, it would've been a more professional job.''

"Was anybody hurt?''

"Just my fuckin' car.'' Sonny points, releasing his anger. "Look what those assholes did to my car!''

An officer yells from across the street, "Somebody was hit . . . there's blood here.''

The lieutenant turns back to Sonny. "I guess you'll sign a complaint and be a witness.''

"Hell, no . . . I'm not gonna be no witness. I'll take care of this my own way.'' He says to Richie, "I'm not talkin' to these cops no more . . you talk to 'em.''

"Gibson, you'll have to go down to the Western station and fill out a police report.''

Sonny opens the limo door. "Nope, I'm goin' home to bed.'' He calls his men, "Come on, let's get outta here.''

The lieutenant tells Richie, "I'll have to take all of the guns for ballistics tests. You'll get them back when you come down to the station and file your report.''

"Yeah, O.K.''

On the way home to Beverly Hills Sonny is still bent out of shape about the bullet hole. He examines the damaged ceiling and makes it the target of his pent-up nervousnous from the close call. "Look at this shit . . . will ya just look at it! A fuckin' eighty-thousand-dollar car shot to hell . . . Georgie, I want this car perfect by tomorrow night. And another thing, from now on I'm not goin' nowhere until the fuckin' car is outside, understand?''

"Yeah, Boss.''

Tony asks, "Who'dya think those guys were, Boss?''

Eddie assures him, "Whoever they were, they sure were dumb. No Mafia guys would yell, 'Sonny, stay outta San Diego.' ''

Sonny says, "Exactly right. The Mafia don't warn and kill; they kill and then they warn.''

Angelo can attest to that. "Yeah, in Brooklyn you never tell nobody you're gonna kill 'em. You just shoot . . . and you don't miss neither.''

Richie deduces, "It hadda be the feds. They called to tell you the Mafia had a contract out and then probably hired some local guys to do it."

Eddie says, "Ya know, I bet they do that a lot. That's how come the Mafia gets blamed for everything."

Tony agrees, "Yeah . . . it hadda be the government, Boss. You're a hero with all the dons since they got their restraining orders."

Sonny agrees, "It was the feds, all right, but they didn't hire nobody . . . They couldn't take a chance with local yokels . . . a dead witness won't do 'em no good." Something dawns on him. "Those guys musta *aimed* at my fuckin' car. They knew it would piss me off."

Angelo is curious. "Uh . . . how would they know somethin' like that, Boss?"

"Come on, Angelo . . . we bug people to find out stuff, so do the feds. They know how much pride I have in my car."

Tony breaks in. "I think one of us hit one of 'em, Boss."

"Good. I hope you hit 'em in the fuckin' head for shootin' up my car."

Richie says, "You know, if one of those guys got hit, they probably went to a hospital. I'm gonna make a call and find out if anybody was treated for gunshot wounds in any of the hospitals around here."

Sonny says, "You can do that if you want, but I know it was the feds . . . they were tryin' to scare me into testifyin'."

"Uh . . . nothin' could make you rat, Boss."

"I know, Angelo, but they don't . . . they're assholes."

The suspicion that the government ordered the hit as a scare tactic was confirmed when Richie discovered that a federal agent from New York had been admitted to Santa Monica Hospital with a .45 bullet in his left arm. Medical records showed that the man was injured while cleaning his gun. In addition, all of the dons called the next day to assure Sonny that they had nothing to do with the shooting. The news of the unsuccessful assassination attempt hit the headlines the following day: "GIBSON ATTACK LINKED TO MAFIA TESTIMONY." Donald Masterson read the story with great satisfaction . . . he'd like to see Sonny's name in the papers again soon. The state attorney is out for blood and is doing everything in his power to indict Sonny on charges for anything that will stick; he would make a federal case out of a bar fight. It isn't long before Sonny himself gives Masterson the chance to do just that. The incident occurs at the Los Robles Inn in Los Angeles.

Sonny has just finished playing a very satisfying round of golf and is now relaxing in the lounge with his bodyguards. Three unkempt men in their early thirties sit at one corner of the bar, downing their fifth bottle of beer. The trio has been staring at Sonny, trying to figure out where they've seen him before. The most inebriated is Frederick Stern, a six-foot-two construction worker. He finally snaps his fingers, pointing at Sonny. "Hey, now I know who you are . . . you're that Mafia guy in the papers." Sonny ignores the man, but the bodyguards are immediately on the alert. The drunk turns to his friends, who are trying to quiet him down. "Yeah . . . that's who he is . . . I know all about those big shots . . . they think they can get away with anything. Can you believe it? People are actually scared of that fat slob!"

Angelo says, "You want me to get rid of him, Boss?" The drunk is beginning to irritate Sonny, but he replies, "No, Angelo, we've got enough heat already . . . that's all Masterson needs."

The smartaleck keeps on rambling. He stands on the rungs of his stool and brazenly leans across the bar, slurring, "You know what, Mr. Big Shot . . . I'm not afraid of you. Whaddya think about that?"

Sonny walks over to him, for once controlling his anger. "Look, you've been drinking . . . why don't ya just go home, O.K.? I don't want any trouble."

The man shouts to the others, "Hey, whaddya know! The big man doesn't want any trouble. He can't be such a *big* man . . ." He looks at Sonny through heavy-lidded eyes and proclaims, "You know what I think about all Italians and members of the Mafia? Their mothers are cunts!"

Sonny says calmly, "What'd you say?" When the man starts to repeat himself, Sonny smashes him across the face with an empty wine bottle, knocking him off his stool. Then Sonny goes completely berserk. He breaks the bottle on the edge of the bar and holds the jagged glass inches from the drunk's face. "Crawl like a dog, motherfucker . . ." Stern sobers up and whines, "Please don't kill me . . . don't kill me . . . I don't wanna die."

Sonny walks around the barroom floor, menacing him with the broken bottle. "Come on, boy . . . come on . . . you wanna say somethin' bad about my mother? Go ahead, say something bad about my mother now . . ."

Everyone is the room is mesmerized by the scene except for the bodyguards. Tony tries to reason with him. "Boss, everybody's watchin' . . . let's go."

Sonny is crazed. "I don't give a shit . . . stay outta this." Sonny then "walks" the pleading man outside. "Come on, boy . . . this way . . . that's a good dog. Bark for me, boy, come on . . . bark for me . . . bark!"

The terrified man starts to yelp like a mongrel, still pleading, "Please, let me up . . . I didn't mean anything. Don't kill me. Please."

As soon as they get past the door, Sonny grabs Tony's gun. The bodyguard panics when he sees Sonny getting ready to pull the trigger. Tony holds his hand over the cylinder. "Not here, Boss, not here."

Angelo says, "Come on, Boss, we'll get him later. I'll pull his head off."

At that moment Sonny comes to his senses and sees the crowd of witnesses gathered around him. He straightens up and looks down at the quaking man. "You're gonna live, motherfucker . . . there's too many people here. Don't ever get in my way again!"

On the way out Angelo kicks the man in the ribs. "That's for my mother."

Naturally the press had a field day, some even describing the event as a "wine-bottle slashing" by the vicious Mafia kingpin Sonny Gibson. Sonny surrendered himself, and his bail was set at $200,000, an excessively high amount for the offense. Money was not a problem for Sonny; Masterson, however, was. When Sonny started to buy off witnesses to the attack, one of them reported it. The vengeful state attorney hit him with a bribery charge. Bail for this indictment was $250,000.

There were now so many newspaper stories about the case that Sonny's attorneys claimed it was impossible for him to get a fair trial in the state of California. They asked the court for a change of venue. Sonny was desperately trying to buy time . . . his escrow wouldn't be released for a year. His lawyers requested that the case be heard in an out-of-state court . . . "Request denied." They requested that the trial be held in a smaller county in California . . . "Denied." In the meantime Masterson was busy preparing his case against Sonny for the preliminary hearings concerning the barroom brawl.

The bodyguards are doing some preparation of their own. They pay a visit to Frederick Stern before he takes the stand. The instigator had been staked out for a week before Sonny's men finally confront him carrying packages from a grocery store. They know he wouldn't be wired up just to go marketing. Stern's heart stops when he sees Angelo and the others surrounding him. Richie says calmly, "Just be cool. Get in your car and you won't get hurt." Stern gets in the front seat. Angelo and Richie slide in one either side of him; Tony is in the back. Richie warns, "Tomorrow in the hearing you're not gonna press charges against Sonny, understand? You're gonna tell 'em the truth, motherfucker . . . you were drunk."

Tony says, "Sonny isn't goin' to prison over you, asshole, but no matter what happens to him, your life isn't worth a shit unless you keep your mouth shut."

Angelo puts a mammoth paw on Stern's puny shoulder. "Uh . . . if you say anything against the boss tomorrow, I'm gonna tear your fuckin' head off and stick it up your ass." The giant presses his gun against Stern's nose. "You were wrong at the club that night, and now you're gonna tell the truth, right?" The frightened man quakes but manages a nod against the barrel.

The men get out of the car and go directly to Sonny's apartment to tell him the good news. Tony says, "Don't worry about Stern, Boss . . . everything's taken care of. He's gonna tell the truth on the stand tomorrow."

Sonny sneers, "I doubt it. Masterson's gonna make him testify against me."

Richie shakes his head. "No, he won't. He won't say a word, Boss. Angelo put a piece up his nose."

"WHAT! Are you guys nuts? You know the cops are watchin' him all the time now."

Richie says, "Nobody saw us . . . we've had him under surveillance. We got him at just the right time . . . Stern's not gonna say shit."

Richie was right. The next day the drunk admitted in court that he had started the fight and refused to press charges against Sonny. In spite of that Stevens can't get the case thrown out or a change of venue. Masterson had won this round; Sonny was up against the wall. So he bribed a Congressman and a California state judge to help him. The DA then slapped him with another indictment and $500,000 bail. In addition to assault and bribery, Sonny got indicted for "grand theft money." Churches had filed charges against him for taking a total of $40 million from religious institutions around the country. Sonny's attorneys now had eight counts to fight.

While Sonny was going through all of these problems, Theresa was living her own nightmare. When they spent time together, Sonny was often distracted, but that was a welcome relief from his usually churlish mood. The only place they still seemed able to communicate was in bed, and even there, though they made love more often, sex was just a release for Sonny's fury and frustration. His adversities were truly her adversary. Through it all Theresa was a loving, understanding mate, and when Linda's assistant Joanne had to be laid off, Theresa offered to help out. Sonny assigned her the job of handling the sale of some instructional golf films one of Sonny's companies had produced for Jack Nicklaus. In the middle of all the heat he had kept his operation humming with ways to make money. Theresa was a hard worker, but it was a touchy situation for Sonny's lady and his loyal secretary to be sharing the same space . . . there was quite a bit of friction between them.

One morning Linda came into his office, obviously upset. "What the hell's wrong with you today?"

Linda puts one hand on her hip. "Sonny, do you like the way I've handled things for you for the past eight years?"

"What kind of stupid question is that? You wouldn't be here if I didn't."

"I know, but it's just that I feel like I can't do anything right anymore . . . Theresa is constantly criticizing me."

Sonny is surprised. "Theresa . . . she has nothin' to do with my business affairs—that's your job."

"That's what I thought. I don't want to insult her, Sonny, but she's getting on my nerves. She thinks she's in charge out there."

"You just keep on doing your job, I'll handle Theresa."

"I appreciate it." On the way out Linda turns, "Oh . . . I almost forget why I came in here. Henry Stevens is coming by in a few minutes."

"Why? . . . We don't have an appointment today."

"I know, but he said he had good news for you."

Sonny scowls. "Impossible . . . that guy's been nothin' but bad news from the start."

"I'll buzz as soon as he's here."

When the secretary is gone, Sonny calls Theresa. She answers cheerfully, "Hi, sweetheart. The golf film sales are really doing well."

"That's good . . . listen, honey. You keep on taking care of the paperwork you're doin', that's your job, and you let Linda do her job." He says sharply, "Don't interfere with her."

She pouts. "What's the matter? Don't you love me anymore?"

Sonny is annoyed. "I don't have time to hear all that shit, Theresa. I do love you, but let Linda handle the job she's been handling for me for eight years, O.K.? I can't afford to lose her right now."

There is a pause, then Theresa says, "O.K., Sonny. I love you."

A few minutes later Linda buzzes to say that the attorney had arrived. "Tell him to come in." The lawyer enters, wearing a broad grin. "What the hell are you so happy about, Stevens?"

"I have some good news . . . I talked to the my man at the state capital yesterday."

"What about?"

Henry sits on the couch and leans back. "About getting you a pardon."

"A pardon? What'd he say?"

"He figures things are too hot right now . . . there's too much press on you. But when things quiet down again, it could be arranged . . . you have to plead guilty first."

Sonny knows there is a catch. "Plead guilty! Un-uh, no way I'm pleadin' guilty."

Stevens reasons, "Look, Sonny, they're not just going to let you go. But if you surrender yourself, my man will make sure you get to a special board in six months and you'll be paroled."

"How can you be so sure?"

Henry grins. "I guaranteed him a half a million dollars."

Sonny has his own ideas about this. "Why can't we just pay the money now . . . get the case thrown out?"

The attorney explains. "Nothing can be done until you're in state

custody. My contact can get you out of prison, but you have to be there
for him to do it. He asks the parole board to be lenient, and it's a nice,
neat release."

Sonny warns, "If I'm stuck behind bars, you're a dead man."

Stevens says with certainty, "It'll happen."

Sonny now had a difficult decision to make—surrender himself or
escape to Sicily. If he left the country, he could forget about his Big
Scam and the $500 million. He would be able to take his own money
with him, but he'd need that to live. Going to Sicily could also be
dangerous. As long as Alfonso and the old dons stayed alive, Sonny
was protected, but when the old regime was gone, he could be the target
of their vendettas. If he went to prison for six months, the time he spent
wouldn't hurt him financially . . . the escrow money would still be earning interest, and since he wouldn't have operating costs to worry about,
the dividends would help to replenish his own ailing bank account.

All of Sonny's calamities were compounded when the news of Jeff
Wolfman's murder made front-page headlines. About a week before
the hit on his former executive a man in a dark car stopped alongside
Sonny's limo with a message from Sicily. "Alfonso has taken care of
the rat." Sonny assumed Jeff would be found soon after, but he was
not prepared for the furor it created. Wolfman's body was discovered
tied to a chair with his eyes gouged out, genitals cut off, and a pigeon
stuffed in his mouth. Vancouver police reported the killing as the most
brutal on record. The death made such an impact on the other witnesses
that even those in prison got scared and asked for protective custody.
The government was so worried about their safety, all of them were
transferred to a high-security military compound. Two of the witnesses,
however, never even showed up for their surrender date . . . Allen
Collins and Danny DiMarco had dropped out of sight. The government
assumed Sonny was responsible and stepped up their efforts to get him
indicted for conspiracy to murder. In fact Sonny hadn't had anything
to do with these disappearances, but because Mafia families around the
country liked him, they were taking it upon themselves to rid the country
of his rats, thinking they were doing him a favor.

Sonny finally decided to plead guilty to bribery and assault to commit murder. His lawyers could not get an extension on his trial date for
the barroom fight. He was sure he'd be convicted on the testimony of
witnesses to the brawl, but couldn't be sure the prison terms for both
counts would run concurrently. If Sonny didn't plead guilty, he could
get two years instead of one. That wasn't his main concern . . . he knew
he would be out in six months. This change of plea was a stopgap
measure to buy him some more time since he'd be free on his own
recognizance until sentencing. When Sonny went to the court, he had
to bring papers proving that his Lear was up for sale, and he was forced

to surrender his passport. Neither of these preventive measures would have stopped Sonny from escaping, but he did plead guilty . . . and the judge ordered him to return in thirty days.

The Mafia kingpin was really wrestling with his decision now. Sicily or prison. Although he still played golf with Chet and Jack, he never discussed his personal problems with them. But on the way home from dinner one night Sonny asked Bartlett for a favor.

The limousine stops in front of the mansion the singer has had built on top of his mountain. Sonny grabs Chet's arm before they get out. "Hey, ya know I may have to go outta the country for a while . . . or go to prison . . . I don't know which yet. But whichever it is, I want ya to keep an eye on Theresa for me . . . maybe get her a job in your office or somethin'."

Chet pats his arm. "Don't worry, Sonny, I'll take good care of her."

"If I go to prison, I won't be there that long, and Angelo's gonna give you twenty-five thousand dollars to make sure she's O.K."

Bartlett protests, "You don't have to do that . . ."

"Yeah, I do . . . Theresa's a helluva a good worker, and proud of it. I don't want her to know I'm buyin' her a job."

"Hey, Sonny . . . I told you, don't worry. Isn't that what you told me once? You have my word, Theresa won't be left out in the cold as long as I'm around, O.K.?"

Sonny puts an arm around him. "Thanks, Chet . . . if you do this for me, we'll call it even."

In spite of the fact that Sonny pleaded guilty, Masterson was still obsessed with his personal vendetta against him. One day, as they left the apartment on Doheny, Georgie spots a car following them. "We're bein' tailed, Boss."

Angelo gets on the walkie-talkie to the Cadillac behind them. "Keep an eye on the car behind the boss's limousine . . . it's a tail."

Eddie's voice comes crackling through. "We noticed . . . we got him."

Georgie heads north, and before they make the right turn onto Sunset Boulevard, the first car turns left; another one replaces it. The underworld men are not fooled. Richie says, "It's a hide-and-seek tail, Boss." Sonny nods. This is an old trick that might throw a civilian off the track because the same car would not be behind him all the way.

Angelo looks out the rear window. "Uh . . . those guys don't look like cops."

Richie answers, "The first two didn't either . . . they're cops."

Sonny has an idea. "This is what we're gonna do. Tell the guys in the back to park on Hammond Street. Georgie, you drive into our building. When you turn the first corner in the garage, Richie, Angelo, and I will get out. Tony, you stay in the back seat and put on my Fedora and my sunglasses. Now, Georgie, you wait enough time for the tail to catch up, then go to the third level. Stop there, and the guys'll sneak up behind and put a piece on 'em." He turns to Richie, "Don't hurt 'em, just get their ID's and see who they are. If they're process servers or cops, you know you can't hold 'em, but if they're not, beat the shit outta them until you find out who sent 'em." Richie gets on the walkie-talkie and gives Sonny's instructions to the bodyguards in the Cadillac behind them.

Once the limousine is inside the building, the plan is executed. Sonny, Richie, and Angelo get out; Georgie waits a few minutes, then drives on with Tony in the back seat. Sonny and Angelo go straight to the stairway. Richie and some of the men from the second car head up to the third floor. In a few minutes the tail pulls into the garage and stops behind the limousine. The bodyguards descend on it. Richie puts his gun against the driver's window. "Don't move. . . . Keep your hands where I can see 'em or you're dead." The two men get out of the car and are made to straddle the hood while they're being frisked. Eddie empties the shells from their weapons. Richie checks their ID's . . . they are investigators from the district attorney's office. He confronts one of them. "What's this all about?"

The lawman shrugs. "I'm just doin' my job. We got orders to follow Gibson . . . there are a lot of plainclothes guys around here this morning."

This alerts Richie that there is real trouble. He calls Sonny from the limo phone. "Boss, there's somethin' big comin' down . . . this place is crawling with DA investigators. . . . Masterson sent this guy to follow you."

"What the fuck . . . it's only eight o'clock."

Sonny has some idea what this is all about. He knows he has to get out of there immediately. "All right, I'm not gettin' back in the limousine. Tell Eddie to switch places with Tony. As a matter of fact I'm gonna take off my coat and I'm gonna walk to the Cadillac on Hammond by myself. If Angelo comes with me, he'll stick out like a sore thumb and they'll nab us for sure. Tell the guys to pick me up on the corner. We'll all meet up at Air Research later on tonight."

Sonny leaves the 9000 Sunset Building through the side exit, and for the second time in his Mafia career he is totally alone. He feels naked as he walks down the street without bodyguards . . . the short block seems like a mile. When he gets in the Cadillac, Richie, Tony, and Eddie are already there. "Are you all right, Boss?"

"Yeah . . . it felt weird bein' without you guys."

Tony asks anxiously, "Why's the DA tailin' ya, Boss?"

Sonny laughs. "Masterson thinks I'm gonna skip bail and go to

Sicily. He's probably tryin' to get my bond revoked. The judge don't get to court till nine A.M. He wanted to grab me as soon as he got the order."

Richie asks, "Are you gonna go to Sicily, Boss?"

Sonny says more seriously, "I dunno . . . I'm gonna make that decision soon. Get word to Linda I'm closin' up the office."

That morning Masterson had convinced the judge to revoke Sonny's bail. The call came through to pick him up, and the police stopped the limousine near the Beverly Hilton Hotel. When they saw how they'd been duped, the cops surrounded the 9000 Building. Flashing search warrants, they burst into Sonny's office. Angelo and Theresa had guns held to their heads while the office was ransacked. A few tapes Sonny had in his desk were confiscated. When Angelo told them that as far as he knew the boss was still in the building, every office for two blocks was searched, but of course Sonny had escaped.

That evening, when Richie got to his house, the police were there. They arrested him and the bodyguard was booked for assault on the DA's investigators in the garage that morning. His bond was set at $50,000. Normally a person charged with this crime would be free on $5,000 bail, but a spokesman for the DA's office stated in the LA *Times* that such a high figure was justified because the security man works for Mafia kingpin Sonny Gibson.

Sonny himself is safely in Newport Beach, on board a yacht owned by his friend the car dealer. When he calls Liebowitz, the lawyer is concerned. "Sonny, where are you?"

"I can't tell ya where I'm at, but ya gotta post bail for Richie. Eddie'll bring ya the money. When can ya get him out?"

"Ten hours after the bond is posted. What about you? They're going to list you as a fugitive."

"How many days do I have before they do that?"

"About ten days."

Sonny thinks a minute. If he doesn't surrender within ten days, his five-million-dollar bail is forfeited. If he decides to go to prison later, the government could conveniently get rid of him there, claiming the bond company hit him because they lost their money. Sonny needs time to plan. "All right, you tell the court you know where I am and that I'm finishin' up my business. I'll surrender in ten days. I'll get back with ya tomorrow to find out what's goin' on."

As soon as Richie is out on bail, he takes a roundabout route to Newport Beach making sure no one follows him. The bodyguard is on the yacht the next day when Sonny calls Liebowitz. The attorney has good news and bad news for him. He delivers the optimistic tidings first. "Tell Richie they dropped the charges against him."

"How'd ya get 'em to do that?"

"I told them he was a professional security man acting in the line of duty. If he pleads guilty, they'll give him a misdemeanor so they can take away his firearm permit. What does he want me to do?"

Sonny covers the mouthpiece of the phone and asks Richie, "If you plead guilty to the misdemeanor, they'll just take away your permit— there won't be no trial or case over this."

Richie is concerned, "If I do that, I won't have a gun."

Sonny brushes the worry aside. "You won't need one where we're goin' . . . I'm gonna own the country." In spite of that, when he gets back to Liebowitz, he says, "Look, prolong the case, I don't like the idea of Richie pleadin' guilty to anything. What about the fugitive thing?"

This is the bad news. "They'll only give you a week, Sonny . . . Masterson wants you in jail."

"Well, they'll have to come get me in a week, then. I'm goin' away for a few days."

"Can you tell me where you're going?"

"Nope . . . the less people know where I'm at, the better."

Sonny and Theresa take refuge at the Ojai Country Club, where they can be away from all the pressures. In recent weeks they have gotten close again. Sonny has come to appreciate her patience and devotion through all of his tribulations. They make love often, escaping to the inner sanctum of the bedroom as though this were the only place in the world they could be safe. Theresa now sits on the edge of the bed, while Sonny weighs his options for the last time. The surrender date is just a few days away. Sonny is pacing and thinking out loud. "If I go to Sicily, I'll be a fugitive . . . if I stay here, I'll go to prison . . . but I've been guaranteed that I'll be out in six months."

"How do you know for sure you'll get out then?"

"My attorneys made a deal with the guys at the state capitol. It cost me half a million. But I dunno, Theresa . . . I trust 'em all like a fence." He turns to her. "What do you think, baby?"

She gets up from the bed and puts her arms around his waist. "Honey, you know you're the only one who can make that decision."

He then tells Theresa something no other woman has ever heard from him, "If I go to Sicily, I wanna have a family. I want kids, Theresa." Her reaction is unexpected . . . she frowns.

"What's the matter?"

Theresa hesitates. "Sonny, you know I'll go with you to Sicily . . . but I won't have any kids. I'd be afraid to raise a family there—you have too many enemies. It'd be too dangerous for the children, and I couldn't live with that."

He can see genuine fear in her eyes. "I understand, but goin' to prison . . . "

She says quickly, "You said you fixed everything so that it would only be six months."

Sonny puts his hands on her shoulders. "I did, but what if somethin' happens once I'm locked up . . . what if it's more than six months?"

"What's the longest you think you'd be in for?"

"I dunno, what if it's ten months, a year?"

Theresa gasps inside. How could she be away from Sonny that long? When he was gone now, even for a few hours, the ache of missing him was agony. Tears roll down her cheeks. "I'd wait . . . I'd wait for you, six months, sixty years . . . whenever you get out, we can start our life again. I love you, Sonny, I'll always love you."

He wipes the teardrops gently from her face. "I'm gonna go in, Theresa."

She tries valiantly to suppress the sobs that are building up as Sonny says softly, "Let's go out and tell the guys . . . Are you O.K.? Are you gonna be a big girl about this?"

Theresa nods, but she gives herself away when she throws her arms around Sonny, clinging desperately to him. "I'm gonna miss you—oh, God, how I'm gonna miss you."

He strokes her hair. "I'm gonna miss you, too, baby . . . but six months isn't so long."

She looks up at him. "An hour without you seems like an eternity."

He smiles and takes her hand. "Come on . . ."

Sonny's chief bodyguards are assembled in the living room of the suite, anxious to hear his decision. Richie rushes over as soon as Sonny comes out of the bedroom. "What'd you decide, Boss?"

Sonny looks at his loyal solidiers who have served him so well. "I'm gonna go in."

Angelo argues, "Boss, no. You can't go to prison, they'll hurt you. I know. I had friends at Attica." The giant begs, "Let me go in, Boss . . . I'm strong— no one's gonna fuck with me."

Sonny is touched by the innocent offer. "Angelo, you can't go, they won't let you take another man's place." He tells his men. "The contracts on you and your families have been canceled. Until I get out, you'll be working for other dons . . . pick up any one you want."

Angelo says, "I guess I'll go back to Don Giuseppe."

Sonny's next order is strict. "No . . . I don't want anybody goin' to the Loganno family. Don Giuseppe is a sick man, and when he dies, there's gonna be a war over his territory. I don't want any of you guys in the middle of it. Decide who you wanna work for and let me know . . . I'll make the arrangements." His statements are met with a glum silence. "Hey, relax . . . I'm only goin' in for six months . . . I'll be out before you know it. Tony, open some wine. Richie, get out those tapes we bought on Mulberry Street." The strains of the Sicilian tarantella play too loudly, and Sonny dances, clapping his hands in the air. When the boss quits, Georgie takes over, and the men form a circle around him. Tony is handing out glasses of wine to everyone. Theresa is on the couch, tears flowing, silently watching the forced festivities. Angelo sits next to her and implores, "Can't you talk him out of it, Theresa? Us guys . . . we need him."

Her heart goes out to the gentle giant. "No, Angelo, I won't do that. You know whatever Sonny has done is for the best . . . we all have to be strong for him." She sees his eyes start to water and hugs him, sharing his grief. "It's O.K., Angelo . . . it's O.K."

A few days before he goes in, Sonny flies to Lake Tahoe to meet with Aldo and Al Vigiano, a long-time friend of Alfonso's. These two men are being appointed as trustees to oversee Sonny's thirty-two million in cash. At a meeting in the rustic but luxurious den of the Vigiano estate, Al says, "Alfonso ordered me to get involved in whatever this is. You know we're still close, but since Tahoe's been built up, I've broken my ties with the American families."

Aldo observes, "That could be dangerous."

Al continues casually, "They threaten me a lot for not cuttin' 'em in on my casino action, but I can take care of myself . . . the Sicilian Mafia's behind me." He turns to Sonny. "What is it you want me and Aldo here to do?"

"Right now I've got about thirty-two million dollars in plus markers in Vegas. I want you to oversee my cash. I'm gonna switch the accounts around so the money can only be pulled out with all three signatures. For doin' this I'm gonna give you each five hundred grand now, and when I get out, you'll get another million. Then, when I set up my casino operation in the Philippines, I want you guys to come over for a million dollars a year to run it." Sonny was conning to the end. He only dangled the high wages in front of them to ensure their total cooperation. It was never his intention to pay anyone a million-dollar salary. Sonny continues laying out his plan, "If one of you guys dies, Alfonso will appoint a new administrator and tell him the numbers of my markers . . . I don't wanna know 'em myself."

Aldo is amazed. "You're gonna turn over thirty-two million dollars to me and Al, and you don't wanna know where it is?"

Sonny looks at him. "Aldo . . . where could you and Al go that the Sicilian Mafia couldn't find you? Al's got a business here, and where are you gonna go? You guys know how the game plays . . . you're not goin' anywhere."

Al is still confounded. "But why don't you wanna know the numbers, Sonny? I don't understand . . ."

"I don't know what's gonna happen in prison. I've been a good soldier for many years. One of the reasons I stayed alive so long is 'cause I know all the answers. They could give me truth serum and make me talk . . . I trust 'em like a fence."

Al agrees. "I know what you're talkin' about. The feds could set you up in the joint and have you knocked off. Papa Mike will get the word out on the prison yard that the government hates your ass. Nobody'll touch you then."

Sonny is confused. "How's that gonna stop anybody?"

"The guys'll think whoever did it works for the government. One thing cons hate worse than child molesters and rats is authority. I'll get word to Papa Mike that you're goin' in . . . he won't talk to anybody unless he's told about it first."

Aldo asks, "How much time you think you're gonna get, Sonny?"

"I don't care what they give me. I'll be out in six months."

"Everybody on the street thought for sure you'd go to Sicily."

Sonny explains, "Look . . . I got an obligation to the families. I got almost five hundred million in escrow for my hotel in the Philippines . . . they'll get their money back if somethin' happens, but they're in with me 'cause they wanna make a fortune. If I go to Sicily, the whole thing's down the drain."

Tony asks, "Are you sure you're doin' the right thing?"

Sonny assures him, "I always do the right thing, Tony . . . I'm gettin' out in six months. I'll be back up to see you guys then."

6
Prison

October 8, 1973, is the day Sonny surrenders himself. He and Theresa spend the whole day in the bedroom at Ojai. In between making love, they sit talking, snuggling, and reminiscing about their life together. At one point she asks, "What'd you really think when you first saw me?"

He looks down at her, wrapped in his arms. "Oh, I thought you were sexy . . . I wanted to get you and that Vickie in bed together."

Theresa is offended. "What? You wanted to make love to both of us!"

Sonny's eyes flash devilishly. "Uh-huh."

"It's a good thing you never told me that when you called. I never would've spoken to you." She nuzzles against his naked chest. "But then, I'd never be here now."

Sonny sighs. "Maybe here isn't such a good place to be, Theresa. Life with me's been pretty rough this past year."

"I know, but I've been doing a lot of thinking. I decided that when you really love someone, you can go through anything. You know the old saying, 'Love conquers all. . .' " She laughs. "I used to think that was the corniest thing I ever heard . . . until I found someone I really loved." Theresa looks up at him. "I'd do anything for you, Sonny." Her voice is beginning to crack. "I'm gonna visit you every week. Do you know when I can go yet?"

"No, Richie'll find out all that stuff when he comes up the first time."

"The guys are pretty broken up about this . . . especially Angelo."

"Yeah, but they'll be all right. I fixed it so they'd be able to work wherever they wanted to while I'm in. That's the least I could do."

Theresa studies Sonny's face. Under the dark circles and lines, a product of the stress, was a loyal man who had deep feelings she could only catch glimpses of, even at a time like this. It must have been hard being boss . . . always having to make the right decision, always having to be the one with the answers when nobody else could figure out the question. She felt sorry for Sonny at that moment. He'd been to hell and back and was about to make the trip again. The emotions of these trying months suddenly overwhelm her; she can no longer be brave about his leaving. Theresa clings to him. "Please don't leave me . . . I don't know how to live without you."

He holds her close, stroking her, calming her. "Shhh. It's O.K. . . . it's O.K. You'll be fine. I have to do this, Theresa."

She looks at him, vision blurred by her tears. "Promise me you're coming back . . . promise."

"I promise, Theresa. I love you. We won't have to live without each other that long."

The hours fly by all too quickly that day, and midnight is almost upon them. Sonny starts dressing, but looks at Theresa and has to make love to her just once more. It would be six long months before he felt her softness beneath him again. This last time is almost like a dream as he floats through his orgasms on some kind of erotic cloud. Finally he can put it off no longer . . . he has to go. Theresa walks him to the limo for their final good-bye. They kiss, then hug for a long time. "No prison bars can ever keep me away from you, Theresa."

She breaks the embrace and touches his cheek gently. "I'll be waiting for you. I love you."

"I love you, baby." The men inside the limousine all have long faces. "Whatsa matter with you guys? You look like you're goin' to a funeral."

Angelo says glumly, "Uh . . . it feels like it, Boss."

"Well, cheer up . . . I'm not dead yet." Sonny rolls down the window to wave at Theresa as they drive away. She blows him a kiss. After the car is gone, Theresa stands there alone, missing him already and wondering what life will be like without her love.

There is not much conversation on the ride to the jail. When they get there, Harold Liebowitz is waiting. The attorney stays on the sidelines as Sonny's men surround him to say good-bye. Angelo says sullenly, "Boss, I don't know why you're doin' this."

Sonny tries to make light of the dire situation. "Angelo, six months is nothin'. Look, I need the rest. I've been working too hard . . . you guys know that. Ya know how I've been yellin' at everybody lately." He's not getting through. Angelo's still morose. "Hey . . . it'll be good for me . . . I'll lose some weight . . . there's no linguine and clams or antipasto trays here."

"Uh . . . Boss, I don't wanna go work for that little squat in Chicago."

"Angelo, I gave you a choice, you don't have to work for Sam . . . who do you wanna work for?"

The bodyguard is emphatic. "I don't wanna work for nobody . . . I'm gonna pull a robbery, Boss, and go to prison with you."

Sonny tries to reason with him. "Look, Angelo, if you rob somebody, we probably wouldn't end up together anyway. I don't know where I'm gonna be. I want ya to stay out of trouble, Angelo. I'm gonna need ya when I get out. Promise me you'll do a good job for Sam while I'm gone."

Angelo says obediently, "O.K., Boss."

Sonny gives his men some final instructions. "I don't want any of you guys writin' to me . . . it'll put heat on your bosses. Richie's gonna stay out here and keep eye on Theresa. It's O.K. if you wanna give her a call and find out how she is."

Georgie worries. "I don't know if I'm gonna like New Orleans. Drivin' for you's been fun. I don't know how the Castino family's gonna be."

"You'll like Frank, Georgie . . . he's a good man."

Tony speaks up now. "I'm with Angelo. I don't wanna work for that flashy asshole in Chicago. I'd rather go back to mercenary work."

Sonny is firm. "I don't want ya killin' yourself in some jungle. I need ya. You're gonna have plenty of action in the Philippines when I get back."

Eddie asks, "How will we know when you're out, Boss?"

"Richie will be visitin' every week. You guys can check with him if ya wanna know anything."

Angelo complains, "Why couldn't I visit you, too, Boss?"

"Richie's an ex-cop. If those asshole guards get nasty on the visiting yard, he knows how to deal with 'em."

Angelo shakes his huge fist. "Uh . . . I'd like to see one of 'em get nasty with you, Boss. I'd bust 'em right in the head."

"That's why you're not comin', Angelo, then I wouldn't have nobody visitin' me."

Richie pats Angelo's arm. "You know the boss always makes the right decision." There are tears in the giant's eyes. When Sonny sees them, he realizes for the first time how much he loves Angelo. Sonny puts a hand on his face.

"A big man like you, Angelo, don't need to have no tears."

"Uh . . . O.K., Boss. I'm sorry."

Sonny gives his cheek a pat. "You should be. I wanna hear good reports from Sam now, ya understand?"

"Uh . . . O.K., Boss, I'll do a good job for you."

Liebowitz interrupts the farewell scene. "We'd better go in now." Sonny hugs each of his chief bodyguards and then waits for the steel gates of the jail to slide open. Once he's through them, Sonny turns to wave one more time. When the gates roll closed, he can barely see his men through the bars as they all wave back.

Inside the administration building Liebowitz presents his papers to the deputies seated behind the desk. "I'm delivering Mr. Gibson. Under the court's order he's to be sentenced next week and sent to the state penitentiary."

The two officers are pleasant enough. "Do you have any firearms, Mr. Gibson?"

"No."

"Any narcotics or tobacco?" Sonny takes two Cuban cigars from his pocket. "We'll have to take those."

"What? You mean I can't keep my cigars?"

The deputy says, "Nope . . . why don't you give them to Officer Rooney over there . . . he likes cigars."

Sonny looks at the old man standing in the corner. "Hell, no . . . I'm not givin, nothin' to the cops." He turns to his attorney. "Here, Liebowitz, enjoy yourself."

When the paperwork is complete, the deputy shouts, "O'Dowd," and a young, blond officer comes over. The clerk hands him a file. "Get Gibson downstairs, then book him on through." Sonny is escorted down a long corridor by the cocky guard, who looks at the booking papers. "So, I get to take Mr. Big Shot to the tank. Well, at least I'm gonna be able to go out for a beer tonight . . . you won't."

Sonny's impulse is to kill the smartaleck, but he holds his tongue. One thing is certain: If the guard had said that on the street, Angelo would've killed him before he got the first word out. They stop in front of a control booth. The officer inside presses a button, and the iron door slides open. Sonny is pushed into a twenty-by-ten-foot holding tank. Even though there are very few prisoners in the room, the odor of perspiration is strong . . . the stink of men's sweat has saturated the porous cement walls. Sonny lies down on the cold, concrete floor, littered with cigarette butts and ashes, the only place to rest. He drifts off to sleep, dreaming of Theresa, but is rudely awakened four hours later by loud voices and the rattle of chains. Peterson, a sloppy guard with a pot belly over his belt, is barking orders to the prisoners.

"All right, listen up, you dummies. When I call your name, repeat your number so we know we got the right guy, then keep your mouth shut till I'm finished. Garcia . . ."

A Mexican kid answers, "Four-two-six-nine-eight-seven." He enters the holding tank after he's checked out. One by one eighty men are sent in. By the time Sonny leaves, the room is so crowded that everyone has to stand; the scene reminds him of cattle waiting for slaughter.

They are brought to another, larger room for a skin search and contraband check. Peterson shouts, "All right . . . you're gonna take your socks and shoes off and put 'em in front of you; put your jewelry and anything in your pockets in front of that. Then strip and roll up your clothes in a ball." He disappears outside while the men follow his instructions.

When Sonny takes off his pants, the other men make comments about his size. One black, Curtis Jones, eyes him. "I can see you got some black blood in you, brother." Sonny flies into a blind rage. He attacks the man and knocks him down, pressing his foot against Jones's throat, "I'm not your brother, nigger."

Another black warns, "Hey, man . . . break it up, break it up, the guards are coming."

Sonny lets Curtis go, and as soon as he hears the key in the lock, Jones gets brave. "You'd better get your shit together, white boy, 'cause the next time I see you, I'm gonna cut ya a new asshole."

Sonny threatens back, "You're a big man with the cops here, aren't ya, nigger, but you're not talkin' to some punk white boy . . . 'cause while you're cuttin' on my ass, I'm gonna be cuttin' off your dick,"

Peterson barks, "All right, you clowns, cut the racket . . . listen up. I'm gonna say it once and once only . . . I don't wanna repeat myself." Ten guards plus Peterson are in the room now, ready to search the men. "Pound your shoes on the floor, turn your socks inside out and shake 'em." As 160 socks flap in the air, the stench of sweat now mixed with foot odor creates an overpowering aroma. "O.K., hold out your arms and wiggle your fingers and toes." The officers check the armpits, hands, and feet to be sure nothing is hidden there. "Now, bend over and brush out your hair and pull back your ears." These are two more places narcotics could be concealed. The whole procedure is frustrating for Sonny, who is not used to being told what to do. "O.K., now hold up your balls and pull back your skin." The foreskin is an easy place to hide cocaine. "All right, bend over, spread your cheeks, and cough."

Sonny asks the man next to him, "What's the cough for?" The obvious ex-convict says, "You got anything up your ass, man, it's gotta come out."

The officers inspect each man's anus, and after this humiliating check, Peterson says, "Everybody can get dressed except Gibson."

As the rest of the men put their clothes on, the guards come over one at a time to gawk at Sonny. He shouts to Peterson, "Hey, cop, I'm not standin' here much longer. In a minute I'm gonna start bustin' heads."

A hulking guard, with his fingers in his belt loops, walks over to Sonny. "Who you gonna bust, big boy? We know who you are . . . you're nothin' in here, Gibson." He stomps down hard on Sonny's toe with the heel of his heavy shoe, crushing the toenail. The pain is excruciating, but Sonny doesn't even wince. He remembers Alfonso's words, "Pain is a simple case of mind over matter, Santino."

Another guard comes over to harass him. Sonny can feel the man's foul breath on his face. "You Mafia guys are inhuman, aren't ya?" He jams his nightstick into Sonny's balls and steps on his injured foot. "Yell a little bit for us, Gibson." Sonny looks straight at the obnoxious man and spits in his face. The incensed guards throw him against the wall. One cracks his nightstick across Sonny's right temple, splitting it wide open. Now Sonny slumps to the floor, but the guard pulls him up by the hair. "Come on, asshole, pick up your shit and get outta here."

As he shoves Sonny toward the door, another guard says anxiously, "Man, how we gonna explain this to the sergeant? We better get this guy to the medics."

"Fuck, no. I'm bookin' him in . . . that's my job."

Sonny is bleeding badly and can hardly walk, but he is hustled out of the room. Still naked, he goes with the other men down to the booking room. There he is photographed, fingerprinted, and red-tagged. This is a special band that labels a man as a murderer or a member of organized crime. As far as the government is concerned, Sonny is both. After booking he is finally allowed to dress, then all the men are taken to a room where they turn over their personal effects. The clerk behind the cage hands them a receipt, six dollars in cash, and a dime for a phone call.

The next holding tank the men are taken to has cement benches, but Sonny isn't fast enough to get a seat. He's too fat to squat, so he stands miserably in a corner, surveying the filthy, smoke-filled room which reeks of urine. Since naked bulbs supply the only light, he can only guess what time it is. Sonny has received no medical attention; by now his foot is swollen and his head throbs with pain. The blood from his wound has dried and matted his hair. A skinny guard comes in and tells the men to strip again. This time they are herded into a room where they're sprayed with a disinfectant to kill lice and crabs, then each man is given a towel the size of a dishrag and told to shower. Their civilian clothes are stamped and put on a hanger, and new ones are issued: a blue shirt and bluejeans—the men keep their own shoes. When the new clerk sees Sonny's bloody face, he orders him to the medics, who sew up his head with ten stitches. Afterward he is returned to the dirty holding tank. A guard comes in to announce the names of the men who are going to court that day. Gibson is first.

A riled Sonny goes up to him. "Hey, man, I'm not goin' to court. I'm goin' to the state pen . . . I'm through with the fuckin' courts."

The guard looks up blankly. "Wrong, Gibson . . . they wanna see you in court.''

Sonny is mad now. "What? Who the hell wants to see me in court?''

The guard checks his papers. "State Attorney Donald A. Masterson, that's who.'' Sonny's nemesis strikes again.

"What the hell's he want me for now? I gotta call my attorney right away.''

The guard goes back to his list, "Relax, Gibson, you'll get a call later like everybody else . . . when I'm finished.''

About a half-hour passes and the men are taken to an area with four pay phones. The guard announces they will each be allowed one call. The ex-cons and more violent men push to the front of the line; the old and the weak often get the receiver jerked from their hand in the middle of a word . . . if they've been lucky enough to get to the phone at all. Sonny has no trouble elbowing his way to the head of the line. He calls Theresa. When she answers, her voice seems unreal in this world. "Hi, baby . . . are you O.K.?''

"Yeah . . . I don't have much time to talk, I gotta go to court.''

She's concerned. "What for?''

"I don't know . . . somethin' to do with that fuckin' Masterson. Tell Liebowitz to get his ass down here by nine A.M.''

"Well, what do you——'' He interrupts agitatedly. "Don't ya understand, Theresa? Get him on the fuckin' line and get him down here.''

"O.K., I'll try.''

Sonny shouts, "Don't just try . . . do it! I don't know what the fuck's goin' on, they don't tell ya nothin' around here. You can't believe——'' Just then a black man tries to grab the phone out of Sonny's hand. Sonny growls, "Get outta here, nigger . . . don't fuck with me.'' The black backs down, afraid that if a fight breaks out, he'll lose his call. Sonny puts the receiver back to his ear, but there is a dial tone . . . somebody down the line had hung up the phone. Sonny is trying to borrow another dime when Peterson shouts, "All right, clowns, you're through. Let's go!''

The men are returned to the holding tank, and another loud-mouthed guard calls out names for the court line. He shouts to a man in the corner, "Hey, Blue! Stand up straight or I'll throw ya in the hole.'' All of the men straighten up immediately. "Blue'' is the name the guards call the convicts because they're all dressed in the same color. Sonny asks the man next to him, "What the hell they talkin' about . . . a hole?''

The weathered, middle-aged convict says, "The hole's someplace you don't wanna go, man . . . you lose all your privileges, and some men lose their minds there. It's dangerous, too . . . the guards got a good excuse to beat your ass. They're real brave when you're handcuffed.''

Just then the guard comes over to them. "All right, Blue, no talking . . . get in line." Sonny is pulled aside as the other men are handcuffed together; he is shackled separately. The guard puts a chain around his waist and cuffs his hands to it.

Sonny says hotly, "What the hell's this for!"

"Shut up, Gibson . . . you're red-tagged." The guard then shackles his ankles together.

"What the fuck do I need those things for?" The guard doesn't answer but pushes him out the door. Because of the chains Sonny can only take one step at a time. His pain is agonizing now, and if he didn't know he was going to see Theresa in court, he'd beat up the guard just to get himself into the hospital for some rest.

Once they arrive at City Hall the men are put into a holding tank that is twice as crowded as any of the others he's been in. Prisoners from all over the county are waiting for trial here. Once inside even the illiterate men scramble to grab the few newspapers in the room to fold them into makeshift sleeping masks and seat cushions for the concrete floor. The close quarters cause fights to erupt sporadically, but Sonny keeps to himself . . . he's in too much pain to care.

When Sonny is finally taken up to the courtroom, the first person he sees is Masterson, grinning like a Cheshire cat. Theresa rushes over. She looks at Sonny's bandaged face and black eyes and starts to cry. "My God . . . what happened . . . what'd they do to you?"

"It's nothin'." Something more important is on his mind. "Where the hell is Liebowitz?"

She shakes her head. "I couldn't get a hold of him."

Masterson whispers to the deputy, who then shouts, "Get that girl away from Gibson . . . he's not allowed to talk to anybody . . . he's a state commitment."

The bailiff takes Sonny to the custody booth where the other convicts are seated. When his case comes up, the judge asks Sonny, "Do you have an attorney, or would you like the court to appoint one?"

"I have an attorney, but he wasn't notified in time to be here."

Masterson volunteers to speed things up. He wants to get the new charges slapped on Sonny so that a trial date can be set. "I'll get in touch with his attorney and see that he's here, Your Honor."

The judge turns to the bailiff. "Bring this defendant back tomorrow." Sonny is so tired by this time, all he cares about is getting to his cell. He's had no sleep and nothing to eat since he surrendered himself at midnight, and he hurts.

When Sonny gets back the jail at nine P.M., Richie and Harold Liebowitz are waiting to see him. He meets them in the attorney's room. Richie's jaw drops, "Boss, what the hell happened to you? Theresa's goin' crazy."

Sonny says wearily, "I had a run-in with the cops . . . it's nothin'. Tell her I'm O.K. . . . I fell down some steps. Did all the guys leave?"

Richie nods. "Everybody's gone. Angelo called three times today."

"Tell him I'm O.K., too." Sonny turns to Liebowitz. "When the hell am I gonna get sentenced? We can't file the appeal bond till I get sentenced." Sonny wasn't taking any chances. He was filing for an appeal despite the deal his attorneys had promised. But Liebowitz says, "We need more money."

Sonny never liked this skinny lawyer, and now lashes out: "I told you there's no more money till I get out."

Liebowitz shrugs. "Remember, *you* pleaded guilty . . . that's gonna make it hard to get a bond."

Sonny grabs Liebowitz by the tie. "Listen, Jew, you guys got paid good, I'm sick and tired of this fuckin' jail . . . I wanna get outta here."

The guard pries Sonny away from his lawyer. "That's enough outta you, Gibson, get back to your cell."

Richie yells as the guard pushes Sonny out of the room, "Boss, you want me to do something to him?"

Sonny shouts over his shoulder, "No, Richie, just make sure Liebowitz is in court tomorrow!"

The guard threatens, "Let's go, Blue—you're askin' for the hole."

After their meeting Sonny is brought to a room where he is issued a mattress and one blanket. Because he is on a court run, he goes to the late chow line. Dinner that night consists of a bologna sandwich on white bread, two cookies, and an orange. Sonny's face is so swollen that he can't eat, but all he really wants to do is sleep. It seems like he's just hit the bunk when it's time to get up again. At five o'clock the guard shouts at his door, "Gibson 356789-R . . . roll it up for court." The grinding of the steel bars sliding open is deafening to Sonny. He drags himself from the bunk, still in pain, but remembering Vincenzo's torture at Ponza helps him forget about it. By now all the men have poured out of their cells, the majority of them going to breakfast.

The most prominent sound on each tier is the distinctive shuffle of hundreds of feet as the prisoners walk down the halls. The men for the court line are singled out and brought down to the holding tank. On the way a Mexican kid who's behind Sonny, says to him casually, "I'm Bobby . . . I'm on the tier above ya, man. Why don't ya sell my drugs for me? . . . I can't get down there."

Sonny answers dully, "No, Bobby . . . I'm not gonna be here that long."

"You must have a lotta connections, man. I read about your case. How come you took the beef for all those guys? You could've ratted 'em off and never been here at all."

Sonny glares at Bobby. "Don't you talk to me no more." He turns his back on the Mexican for the rest of the walk, sure that this inmate was a federal agent planted to get information.

In the holding tank Sonny is shackled separately, as he was the day before. When he gets to court, this time, however, Liebowitz is there, with Richie by his side. Masterson has hit Sonny with a wiretapping charge based on the tapes that were confiscated at the office as evidence. Sonny pleads not guilty, and a trial date is set. He finally gets back to his cell at 9:30 that night and crashes; in the past two days, he's had about four hours sleep. At five A.M. the guard stops at his door again. "Cell 5C, Gibson . . . court line."

Sonny argues groggily through the bars, "No, no . . . you've got the wrong guy . . . I've already been to court twice."

The automatic door slides open. "You're goin' to court, Gibson." Sonny would rather sleep in his cell all day, but he gets dressed immediately and steps outside. Yesterday a convict who missed the court line had to stand on his tier the whole day.

Sonny sits on the rail, waiting with the other men, listening to the harsh orders of the guards bounce off the walls. "No talkin' in chow line, Blue." "All right, Blue, up against the wall . . ." "Let's go, Blue." There is a commotion on the tier above, but Sonny takes no real notice of it . . . he has learned already that noise is a fundamental part of prison life. All of a sudden what seems like a bucket of water comes pouring down on him. He jumps off the railing and looks up at a grisly sight. A man's head, eyes still open, is dangling by a small piece of skin over the edge of the tier above. Blood is gushing out of his neck as fast as water from an open fireplug. The sound of running punctuates the shouts ringing out in the halls. "Man down! Man down!" One cynical inmate yells, "Man down, hell! Man's dead." In spite of the brutal murders he's seen in his life, Sonny is unnerved by the incident; he knows now there is no protection here . . . it's every man for himself. Sonny looks down at his damp clothes and, to his horror, sees that he is drenched with blood. He asks a guard passing by, "Hey, man . . . can I get some dry clothes?"

The officer keeps walking past as he replies, "Speak to the officer in the holding tank."

By this time guards have spread out on the tiers. Everyone who may be a witness to the hit is taken to a special room for interrogation. Sonny and the four convicts closest to the murdered man's cell are questioned first. Peterson is on duty. He swaggers over to them. He starts with Sonny. "We know you were talkin' to Bobby . . . what'd he tell ya?"

Sonny says flatly, "I dunno nothin'."

Another guard comes over. "That's Gibson . . . he isn't gonna talk."

Sonny says, "They told me I could get a clean shirt down here."

The officer says dully, "They told ya wrong . . . get back in line, Blue."

Sonny persists, "Hey, the guy upstairs said I . . ."

The officer snaps, "I don't give a shit . . . let him give it to you . . . now get in line and get chained up." The blood on his clothes is dry and putrid by the time Sonny is shackled for the long bus ride to the court. When he gets there, his name is not even called out. He goes up to the officer in charge. "I'm Gibson, when do I go up?"

The guard looks at Sonny's wristband and checks the papers. "We don't have you on the list."

"Whaddya mean . . . what the hell am I here for?"

The officer snarls, "Shut up, Gibson, there's been a mistake . . . you have to stay." The nasty guard refuses to process Sonny back to jail on the afternoon run, forcing him to stay in the filthy concrete holding tank all day wearing his smelly, bloody clothes.

When Sonny gets back to his cell at 8:30 that night, the tiers are still buzzing about the hit. The cells of the jail are crowded; often six men are squeezed into a six-by-eight cell. Sonny is sharing his with a white and a Mexican who are now playing pinochle and two blacks playing dominoes . . . all he wants to do is get out of his bloody clothes and to sleep. Since he was never issued a clean one, Sonny has to wash his shirt out in the toilet bowl. He is squatting in front of it while the inmates discuss the murder that morning.

One of the blacks says, "Those Mexican Mafia guys cut up Bobby bad, man . . ."

Sonny starts listening. The Mexican replies coldly, "He deserved to get his throat sliced, man . . . he was a fuckin' rat." Bobby was the kid who spoke to him the other day. At least Sonny knows now Bobby wasn't a federal agent. He thinks to himself that death was just punishment for the rat. A voice comes over the loudspeaker, "Owens, 893661. Roll it up . . . you made bail." Announcements in the jail are made anytime, night or day.

The white inmate in Sonny's cell snaps at him, "Hurry up, will ya! I gotta use the shitter." There is no peace *or* privacy in jail.

Sonny snaps back, "I gotta wash my fuckin' shirt. You're gonna have to wait." He looks at the white man's eyes . . . the two sunken hollows tell Sonny he's a junkie.

The hillbilly asks, "You use, man? Peabody's the dope connection around here . . . the big musclebound guy on the third tier."

The Mexican laughs. "Don't you know nothin', hick? That's Sonny Gibson . . . he's a hero with the Mafia."

One of the blacks looks up. "Hey, brother, I bet they fixed you up fine in here . . . you must got a lotta bread, man."

Sonny retorts, "Look, nigger . . . what I got is my business."

The black starts to lunge at Sonny, but the second black pulls him back. "Don't fuck with him . . . he's a hit man."

At that moment a clean-cut official in a suit comes up to the bars, smiling. He looks over the group and finally sees who he's looking for. "You're Sonny Gibson . . ."

Sonny stands and wrings out his shirt. "Yeah . . . who in the fuck are you?"

"My name is John Rawls. I'm your probation officer."

Sonny hangs his shirt on the corner of his bunk and walks over to the bars. "Probation officer, that's a joke. I'm goin' to the state pen."

Rawls is still smiling aggressively, "I've been assigned to do your presentencing report. Would you like to go to a private room and talk?"

Sonny knows this would be a bad move. Prisoners are suspicious of authority, and the other men may think if he leaves he has something to hide. Sonny says firmly, "Hell, no. I'm not goin' to no private room. In fact, there's no use in our talkin' at all." Sonny turns his back on him. "Get lost."

Rawls says, less friendly now, "I'm just doin' my job."

"Well, go do it somewhere else."

Rawls says, "You just had your interview, Gibson." He strides off angrily.

The Mexican says, "Man, you're tough . . . that guy could make it hard on you in the courtroom."

Sonny replies arrogantly, "Fuck him. He can't make it hard on me. He's just another government asshole."

The next day Sonny begins the routine of his life in jail. Up at 5:30 A.M. for an hour wait on the tier for chow. Seven minutes to eat breakfast, then back to the cell. Lunchtime is the same procedure. Dinner is a more leisurely meal . . . ten minutes to eat. TVs and radios in the cell are out of the question here, and newspapers are the only thing you're allowed to read. The men have three other contacts with the outside world: attorneys, visitors, and the store man. He comes every Wednesday, selling gum, toothbrushes, toothpaste, soap, razors, blades, pencils, writing pads, newspapers, and candy. The "canteen" is set up at the end of the tier; for the store man's safety all items are passed to the men through the bars. There is always a long line for the canteen, and by the time Sonny gets to the head of it, all the candy is gone. The man in front of him bought the remaining twenty-five Snickers. Sonny figures out that there is a sugar monopoly here. Junkies need the sweets and men who come in after a ten-hour booking would pay anything for some food. The first night Sonny was in his cell, he saw an inmate buy a fifteen-cent Baby Ruth for a dollar. This was a big moneymaker in jail.

When Sonny gets up to the window, he picks up a razor, blades, a toothbrush, and some toothpaste.

"How much?"

"One seventy-five." Sonny hands him two dollars. The store man checks a list of names and hands his money back. "You'll have to get these next week."

"What the hell you talkin' about?"

The store man says blankly, "I said, you'll have to get these next week."

"What the fuck's wrong with you . . . I need 'em now!"

The guard senses trouble. "Those are the rules, Blue . . . get back to your cage."

Sonny looks at him defiantly. "What'd you say?"

The officer saunters over. "You lookin' for trouble?"

"I'm not afraid of you . . ."

The guard presses his nightstick into Sonny's chest. "I'm only gonna tell ya one more time . . . get back to your cage."

Sonny starts to say something else, but an old convict stops him. "It ain't worth it, man, they'll just throw ya in the hole. Rules are ya gotta sign up Tuesday to buy stuff."

Sonny gives the guard a hateful last look and turns to walk down the tier with the old man. "Thanks . . ."

The seasoned convict smiles. "That's O.K. I've been in the joint fifteen years, but I remember what it was like when I first came in."

"How come they don't tell ya nothin' in this place?"

"They don't wanna make things easy . . . you're supposed to be here to suffer." He apologizes to Sonny, "I would've bought that stuff for ya, but I owed a guy a carton of cigarettes."

"That's O.K." Sonny stops. "This is my cell."

The convict finally says, "My name's Zabinini . . . I know who you are. I'm goin' to the state pen tomorrow—look me up when ya get there."

"How do ya know that's where I'm goin'?"

Zabinini smiles. "That's where they send all the Mafia guys. There's somebody you should meet."

A guard passes and shouts harshly, "All right, Zabinini, break it up . . . you're not a good-will ambassador. Get movin'."

Zabinini shakes his head. "Those hacks never quit."

Sonny is annoyed he missed the canteen because Theresa is coming to visit him. He hasn't brushed his teeth or shaved for a week, but on Saturday he tries to fix himself up in the small, dented piece of aluminum that is his mirror. His name is finally called on the loudspeaker: "Gibson, 356789-R, roll it up for visit." The tier guard gives Sonny a pass, and he's taken down to the visiting room, where he stands in line with the other convicts waiting for a visiting stool to be assigned. All of the men must be seated before the visitors are allowed in. When he sits down, Sonny cranes his neck, trying to catch a glimpse of Theresa in the crowd. It is hard to see past the walls of the cubicle on the other side of the wired glass that separates the convicts from their friends and loved ones. The moment he sees Theresa, the world brightens for him again. Her eyes fill with tears. She now has a chance to take a good look at Sonny; his face is still bandaged, and his eyes are black. Theresa presses her lips to the thick window, and they kiss. When she sits down, they pick up the phone to talk, but it's dead; just seconds later the guard turns on all of the phones in that section. A large sign warning that calls are monitored prevents them from talking about any significant details of his business or his case. Fighting her tears, Theresa says, "Oh, my God . . . what have they done to you, honey?"

Sonny tries to ease her mind. "Hey, there's nothing wrong . . . I . . . I was just clumsy . . . I fell down some steps."

She shakes her head. "I know that's what you want me to believe, but Richie told me about jails. He said jails in LA are as bad as in Chicago."

"We don't have much time, Theresa. Are you gonna waste our visit talkin' about what Richie says? I fell down some steps. O.K.?"

She wipes her eyes and holds up a bag. "I brought you some things today . . . I called the jail, and they told me what I could bring. I got your toothbrush and shaving kit, a pair of socks, and a tee shirt. I brought some long boxer shorts, too, so you could be comfortable without your clothes. . . I couldn't bring toothpaste . . . they said you could buy that."

"That's great, honey, I'm dyin' to brush my teeth." There is a second of silence.

"Have you gotten word when you'll be going to the state penitentiary?"

"I won't know until after they sentence me . . ."

"How much time do you think they'll give you?"

Sonny says impatiently, "How many times do I have to tell you, it don't matter what they give me . . . I'm gettin' out in six months."

Theresa's eyes question him. "I hope so . . . that Masterson hates you so much . . . he wouldn't even let me talk to you in court the other day."

Sonny complains, "They made me go back to court again the next day . . . after I saw you."

This upsets her. "You mean you had to go through that again? What did Masterson charge you with this time?"

"Nothin'. It was a stupid mistake."

Theresa holds up a note in Sicilian, which Sonny can read. "RICHIE

SAYS ALFONSO IS COMING TO SEE YOU NEXT WEEK." This is very uplifting for him. "Really, he's comin' to see me?"

She nods. "I can't wait to meet your godfather. I'm sorry it has to be under these conditions." Sonny can't believe Alfonso will be there. More than anything else, prison makes you feel abandoned by the world. Theresa puts her hand on the glass; he puts his up, too. Sonny can feel the warmth of her skin through the cold pane. "I miss you, Sonny."

"I miss you, too, baby."

She starts crying again. "I love you so much."

Sonny is frustrated by his helplessness; he wants to cradle her in his arms. "Don't cry, baby . . . I'll be home in six months . . . I . . ." His time is up, the phone goes dead. Sonny didn't have a chance to say "I love you," so he mouths it to Theresa. She indicates that she doesn't understand him, so he mouths it again.

From the reflection in the window the guard sees that he is talking and taps Sonny on the shoulder. "All right, Blue, follow me." He pushes Sonny out the door.

Theresa is frantic. She can't hear what the guard is saying, but knows Sonny is in some kind of trouble. Visiting time is up, and the guard chases her from the section. "All right, lady, visiting's over. We got strict rules around here . . . if you don't leave now, your old man's gonna lose his visit next week."

Theresa says anxiously, "They just took my husband away . . . Why did they take him away? What's happening?"

The guard shakes his head ominously. "Looks like your old man's in trouble today."

"Please . . . I have these things. How can I get them to him?"

He looks at her coldly. "I wouldn't worry about those. If your old man goes to the hole, he won't be needin' 'em."

Theresa panics. "What hole? What's the hole?"

"You'll know when he gets out . . ."

"I want to know what's gonna happen to him."

"Well . . . you can find out what the disciplinary action is on him if you wanna wait, but it might be three or four hours."

She sits down resolutely. "My husband needs these things . . . I'll wait."

Sonny was taken to a small room down the hall. An hour later he is still standing in the corner, being punished for his "crime" . . . speaking after the cut-off time. He wonders if he'll be sent to the hole he's heard so many stories about. A crusty, cranky officer comes over to him and picks up Sonny's wrist. He says snidely, "Red tag, huh? How many people'd you kill?"

Sonny's tone of voice echoes his. "I don't have a conviction for murder."

"When do you go to trial?"

Sonny sighs. "I'm not. I'm ready to go to the state pen."

The guard sneers, "Good, the sooner we get rid of ya, the better."

A sergeant and two other officers stop in front of him. "What's your name, Blue?"

"Gibson."

"That's not your name . . . what's your name?"

Sonny insists, "Gibson," but the sergeant persists, "No, no . . . that's not your name . . . look at your band."

Sonny holds it up to his tormentor. "See . . . Gibson . . . my name is Gibson . . . look. What's wrong, can't ya read?"

The vile officer smiles smugly. "Your name's not Gibson." He reads the tag, "In here your name is 356789-R. . . . That's your name . . . that's who you are." The three men circle Sonny slowly; the sergeant says, "What are you waiting here for, anyway?"

"The visiting sergeant told me to wait on the line."

"Ah, you did something wrong then . . ."

Sonny says, "Yeah, I told my old lady I loved her."

"Well, you're not on the line . . . your foot's off by an inch . . . I can see it." He turns to another guard. "Hey, Ed, isn't that a violation of the jail code?"

The other man nods. "Yep, Blue's violatin' the rules again."

The sergeant turns back to Sonny. "Get your clothes off. Let's check you out, clown . . . see if ya got any contraband."

They force Sonny to go through a humiliating skin search, and after he's dressed, one of the guards asks the sergeant, "We sendin' Gibson to the hole?"

"Nope . . . can't be bothered writin' him up. The hole wouldn't teach him nothin'."

An officer sticks his head in the door. "You guys finished with Gibson? His visitor's got somethin' for him."

The sergeant says, "All right, Gibson . . . get up to the window." Sonny is taken down the hall to another part of the visiting room. The guard motions him over to a nine-inch square of heavy glass with a slot underneath it. He can't see Theresa head on, but has to look around the windows, which are at right angles to each other.

The officer barks at Theresa, "Hurry up, lady, whaddya have for Gibson?"

Sonny wants to flatten the guard for being so nasty to her, but he knows it would put his visiting privileges in jeopardy. She shows the guard the contents of her package. Everything is approved except the tee shirt. When the guard dunks it in water, she says, "What are you doing that for?"

"Rules, lady . . . all garments gotta be wrung out to check for heroin or narcotics."

During this procedure Theresa says, "I love you, honey."

"I love you, too, baby."

The guard snaps his head around. "You're not supposed to talk, Gibson . . . you know that." He shoves Theresa's package with the dripping tee shirt at Sonny, "Let's go, Gibson . . . get back to your cage." Theresa and Sonny look at each other until he finally disappears from view.

Sonny hates the jail and curses his lawyers every day that goes by without sentencing . . . he's anxious to get his appeal bond in the works. On Monday he hears his name over the PA. "Gibson, you have a visitor in the attorney's room." Sonny's cell door slides open, and he goes to the end of the tier to get a pass from the module officer. He's expecting to see Harold Liebowitz when he gets to the attorney's room, but instead two FBI agents are waiting for him. They are Robert Cooper and Lloyd Andrews. They look like government bookends, identically clothed in blue suits, white shirts, and an arrogance only J. Edgar Hoover could breed into a man. Sonny flops in a seat across the table from them.

"You know who we are, Gibson?"

"No . . . but you gotta be cops . . . you look like 'em and smell like 'em."

Cooper says, "Those kind of remarks are probably what got you in here."

"Nope . . . I surrendered to do my time."

Andrews says cagily, "You don't know how much time you're gonna get, do you?"

Sonny sits back. "Why don't ya let me worry about that, huh?"

Cooper suggests, "You know, Gibson, we could be very helpful to you and you could be helpful to us. We know for a fact that you have a lot of information, not only on the Mafia but on some political people you've worked with."

Andrews picks up. "We also know that you have to be very careful. Those guys in Washington who made your deal were nuts. Callin' you in to testify like that was a stupid move. They had no way to protect you." He continues accommodatingly, "We could . . . we'd like to get your testimony, and in exchange we'll fix you up with a new identity later." Sonny tips his chair on its back legs and stares silently at the agents pitching hard to get him to be their stool pigeon.

Cooper's tone is foreboding. "You know you won't live long in the state pen. So . . . you can either die in prison or work for us."

Andrews adds, with pseudo-sincerity, "We'd really like to help you, Gibson."

Sonny finally speaks. He leans across the table at them. "Look . . . you tell those idiots in Washington I'm not as stupid as they are . . . I already conned 'em once." He points a finger at Cooper. "You don't come from the streets, you're an Ivy League attorney. I know about death. I can smell it around the corner, and I can tell ya right now . . . no one's gonna fuck with me." Sonny gets up. "Guard, I'm ready to go back to my cell . . . it stinks in here."

The next day Sonny finds it peculiar that his name was not called out for the court line . . . he thought he was scheduled for sentencing. A guard finally stops at his cell at ten o'clock. "All right, Gibson, roll it up for court." He is escorted to the holding tank and given his own suit of clothes for his appearance before the judge. Four marshals will be bringing him by private car to the LA Superior Court. As usual he is shackled, but before he is allowed to get in the back seat, Sonny has to be chained to two of the men. When he arrives in court, Theresa, Richie, and Henry Stevens are waiting for him. She waves from the back of the room; Sonny smiles at her, then takes a seat at the defense table. The bailiff announces the entrance of the judge, and everyone rises. When they sit again, the judge looks through some papers. He takes off his glasses to rub the indentation they've made on the bridge of his nose, and when he puts them back on he says, "This is a very difficult case . . . I would like to hear what the prosecution and the defense have to say. Mr. Masterson, does the state have any comments to make before sentencing?"

"Yes, Your Honor." Masterson goes before the bench. "Your Honor, in your consideration of a sentence for Sonny Gibson, I would like to bring several points to your attention. As you have read in the brief, he is a known kingpin of organized crime and head of the West Coast Mafia. He was also indicted by the federal government in the largest mail fraud case in history. Right now he faces charges of grand theft money and wiretapping."

Sonny bristles when he hears this. The evidence they will submit for the latter crime are tapes of daily phone calls made to the DA's office. As part of his bail agreement after he pleaded guilty to assault, Sonny had to check in with Masterson every twenty-four hours. Sonny wanted proof that he had complied, but since it is illegal to tape a phone conversation without prior consent, they charged him with wiretapping. In his long crime career Sonny had never left tapes lying around, but he felt these particular cassettes were harmless records.

Masterson continues, "Our office has received word that there are other indictments about to be filed against Mr. Gibson. There are also many crimes that intelligence agencies have revealed to me for which we cannot get indictments due to lack of witnesses. Records show that Mr. Gibson was a known supplier of narcotics for the underworld, smuggling large amounts of heroin and cocaine into this country. We know for a fact that he's committed murder both in and out of the

United States. Two witnesses in the government's case against him were killed, and two disappeared. We feel Mr. Gibson had a direct hand in these murders or ordered them to be committed. Sonny Gibson is also a person of the lowest moral caliber, having engaged in licentious acts for money on numerous occasions. Your Honor, I would now like to read excerpts from a report made by Sonny Gibson's probation officer, John Rawls. It was filed after Mr. Rawls had an extensive presentencing interview with Mr. Gibson."

While Masterson walks to the prosecution table to get the papers, Sonny whispers angrily to Stevens, "Extensive! I saw that guy for two minutes."

Henry checks the report. "It says here you two spoke for forty-eight minutes."

"That's bullshit . . . I told him to get lost as soon as he got there."

Stevens nods. "I figured that. His report looks like it was taken from newspaper articles."

The DA reads gleefully. "Mr. Rawls says, and I quote, 'Sonny Gibson is a leech on society who has repeatedly conned innocent people out of large sums of money while on federal probation. He made a vicious and unprovoked attack on a helpless man, then bribed witnesses to the assault. My recommendation is that Sonny Gibson remain in prison where he can no longer feed on society as he has done in the past.' " Masterson looks at the judge. "Your Honor, the state has one demand for this court. That Sonny Gibson go to the state penitentiary and serve the maximum penalty for his crimes. I have no further comments, Your Honor." Masterson walks back to the prosecution table and sits down.

The judge looks at Stevens. "Does the defense have any comments?"

The attorney stands. "Yes, Your Honor." He walks to the bench and paces for a few seconds. When he finally speaks, his words are forceful. "First, Your Honor, I would like to comment on John Rawls' presentencing report. Mr. Rawls visited Mr. Gibson in the county jail and spoke to him in front of four other prisoners. He didn't ask Mr. Gibson one question about his past, nor was he interested in his psychological outlook for the future. Your Honor, Mr. Rawls didn't spend more than two minutes interviewing Mr. Gibson." Henry continues to pace, collecting thoughts. "Now, as for the attack on Frederick Stern, the crime for which Mr. Gibson is being sentenced today. Mr. Stern could hardly be classified as a 'helpless man.' He was drunk, and Mr. Gibson attacked him only after Stern used a four-letter word in reference to Mr. Gibson's mother, who has recently passed away. Any other person who defended his mother's memory would not be sent to prison . . . he wouldn't even be charged with a crime. Your Honor,

John Rawls is about as objective about Sonny Gibson as a fox terrier perched over a mousehole. As for the charges leveled at Mr. Gibson by the district attorney, most of them are unfounded. There is no evidence that Mr. Gibson committed murder or ordered anyone killed. The state cannot show that Mr. Gibson smuggled drugs into this country. Your Honor, under our system of justice, isn't a man innocent until he's proven guilty? Mr. Gibson realizes that he has made mistakes and he's willing to rectify them. He surrendered himself to do his time, and he and his fiancée have intentions of settling down in California to begin a new life. Your Honor, we strongly recommend that he be given probation."

The judge says emotionlessly, "Thank you, Mr. Stevens." He looks over the papers again, and after a few minutes he says to Sonny, "Is the defendant ready to receive his sentence?"

"Yes, I am."

"Will you please approach the bench?"

Theresa squeezes Richie's hand hopefully, "Do you think he'll get probation now?"

"No . . . Sonny knows that, too."

The accused stands before the bench as the judge looks down at him sternly. "Mr. Gibson, I have been reviewing your case for over thirty days. The court has no choice but to deny you probation." Theresa's heart sinks as he goes on. "Furthermore, it is the judgment of this court that you be remanded to the state penitentiary for no less than eight years and up to the duration of your natural life." Theresa is horrified. If Sonny didn't get out in six months, he never would. The defendant himself is surprised at the stiff sentence handed down for assault and bribery, but his six-month deal keeps him from panicking.

Stevens has one major concern. He rises. "With due respect to the court, Your Honor, may I make one last request on behalf of the defendant?"

"Yes."

"I would deeply appreciate it if the unfounded statements about Mr. Gibson's alleged smuggling, wiretapping, and murders, made by the district attorney, be stricken from his summation. They are charges which will follow Mr. Gibson to the parole board and could be damaging."

"The request is denied. They are official court records and cannot be deleted." The judge slams down his gavel, proclaiming, "Case #100070, The People versus Ronald Gene Gibson, alias Sonny Gibson, is now closed."

Everyone in the courtroom rises as the judge leaves the room. Theresa rushes over to Sonny. "Honey, they said life . . . the judge said you could get life." She turns to Stevens frantically. "When would he be eligible for parole?''

The attorney thinks. "Probably seven years . . . maybe sooner."

Sonny pats her arm, "It's O.K., honey. I told you . . . I'll be out in six months."

The marshals with Sonny laugh. "Six months. Gibson, you're dreamin'. You're gonna rot in the pen . . . . Masterson's ordered you a special cell with no key." One of them grabs Sonny's elbow to lead him away before Richie has a chance to talk to him.

"I'll tell the guys what happened, Boss."

Sonny shouts back, "Tell 'em not to worry."

Theresa blows him a kiss, and then he's gone. She breaks down. Richie comforts her. "Come on, Theresa . . . there's nothin' we can do. I'll take you home."

She looks up at him. "Richie . . . they said they were giving him life." The bodyguard sighs. "I know . . . but the boss know's what he's doin'."

Theresa says hopefully, "You really think so?"

Richie nods. "That's the only thing I can figure. There's no way the boss is gonna be locked up in prison for long. One way or another . . . he'll get out."

The following morning Sonny hears his name called over the loudspeaker. "Gibson, report to the visiting room." He says out loud to himself, "Who the fuck . . . Theresa's not comin' today." Only one twenty-minute visit is allowed per week. He wants to save it for her, but he gets a pass anyway and goes down to the visiting room to see who's there. Since the name he has been given is not on Sonny's approved list, the guard asks, "Will you accept a visit from Joe Lee Miller?"

This sounds like another agent to Sonny. "Hell no! I'm not accepting any visit from a damn fed." He turns to go when it suddenly dawns on him that Joe Lee Miller was the name on his passport when Don Giuseppe sent him to Sicily . . . Joe Lee Miller must be Alfonso! Sonny goes back to the guard. "Yeah, I'll take my visit." He's assigned a stool, and when the crowd starts to come in, he scans it, looking for the short old man with his beat-up straw hat. He finally sees Alfonso and is startled by his appearance. His once chubby cheeks are gaunt, his eyes are sunken in, but the fire is still there. They pick up the phones. "Hey, Santino, remember me? . . . Joe Miller . . . it's been a long time since I saw you at that UCLA game . . . that was some home run they threw, wasn't it?" Sonny laughs. Alfonso knows as much about football as he does about ballet. The old man continues his small talk. "Across the ocean our church members are all praying for you." During this chitchat Alfonso holds up a note in Sicilian: "FOUR GUARDS WILL TAKE YOU TO THE PEN ON THURS. AT 10:00 A.M. WE CAN HIT THAT VAN.

CALL THE ESCAPE 'THE BAIL BOND.' "

Sonny looks at Alfonso and points to the note against the window. "No, Joe, I only got six months to do . . ."

Alfonso says grimly, "I don't know, Santino . . . I don't trust them. My feelings say you'd better get your bail bond and go back to church. You'll be protected there. Our people all respect you. The only condition is that you'll have to wait one year before Theresa can join the congregation. . . . You heard about Mario?"

"No . . . what about him?"

"They locked him up this morning without bail. He made four hits, they say. You know the old man is like a vegetable now. Two days ago I sat with him. I told him I was coming to see you . . . he didn't know who you were. He doesn't even remember Nick."

"Oh, no . . . the old man's dyin'?"

"Yes, Santino . . ." Sonny can hardly believe that Don Giuseppe, who was so strong and who knew everything, was a bedridden invalid who had forgotten the joy of his life, his grandson. Alfonso says gravely, "Santino, this is the best chance we have to get you a bail bond."

Sonny asks, "How do you know that is the day I'll make bail?"

Alfonso smiles. "Certain members of our church have a direct line to God. They know . . . believe me, Santino, they're never wrong."

Sonny is surprised to hear he's leaving on Thursday. He had been told it would be at least six weeks before he would go to the state pen. "Joe, tell the other church members I appreciate their prayers, but I'll be out in six months. I'll see them then. We'll have a big party."

Alfonso frowns. "I don't like it . . . something smells about it. Getting a bond would be easier here, but wherever they put you, we can always bail you out. When you get to the state pen, I'll get word to the guy Al Vigiano told you about."

"I think I know who it is . . ."

Alfonso advises, "Listen to him, Santino . . . I taught you the things you needed to stay alive on the outside, he will teach you how to survive inside prison. It's a different world." The phones are cut off; the twenty minutes with his godfather are over. Alfonso gets up and gives a little wave good-bye. When he is about twenty feet away, the old Sicilian turns and waves again, then gets swallowed up by the crowd.

Early Thursday morning Sonny asks the guard if he's scheduled to leave on the Gray Goose that day. This is the bus that transports prisoners from the jail to the penitentiary. His name is not on the list, but Sonny packs his things anyway . . . Alfonso's never been wrong. Sure enough, at eight A.M. another guard stops at his cell. "All right, Gibson. Roll it up. You're goin' to the state pen." With his personal belongings in one hand and his mattress under his arm, Sonny walks along the tier to the sound of men yelling out their good-byes to him. "Good luck in the pen, Sonny. See ya there, man.''

"So long, hope I don't see ya there."

"Hey, look up Larry, he'll get ya all the dope ya need."

Their voices have faded by the time Sonny gets to the mattress bin at the end of the hall. He deposits his, and is brought down to releasing and receiving. Seventy men are already there waiting to be chained up, but Sonny is segregated from them in a special holding tank. The guard shouts to another officer, "Here's your high-powered prisoner . . . Gibson."

"O.K., bring him over here . . . let's get his prints. We wanna make sure Transportation's got the right guy." As soon as Sonny is fingerprinted, he is turned over to two state correctional officers. They shackle Sonny and cuff him to a waist chain. The rest of the prisoners get on the Gray Goose, but Sonny is escorted to a van with two more officers inside. He gets in the back seat with his two escorts, who chain themselves to his waist. Everything is just as Alfonso predicted. Sonny leaves for the state pen at exactly ten A.M. in a van with four men.

The five-hour ride to the penitentiary is uneventful. Most of the conversation between the guards revolves around fishing, sports, and women, but at one point Sonny is asked, "When do you figure you'll be gettin' out, Gibson?"

His answer is confident. "About six months."

All four men laugh. "Six months? You'll be lucky if you get out in ten years . . . be more like twenty, probably." Alfonso's words echo uneasily in his mind under their laughter—"I don't trust them . . . I don't trust them . . . I don't trust them."

The first entrance to the prison is deceptively pretty. The grounds look like a pleasant place to stop for a leisurely lunch. About a mile beyond is the main entrance, and what is behind those iron gates is no picnic. The driver communicates with the control booth by radio. "Correctional Unit Two-seven-four, one and a half miles west of the prison gates . . . we have Gibson." A few minutes later the van stops. Coiled wire with razor-sharp hooks stretches across the top of the thirty-foot wall that surrounds the prison compound. The guard comes out of his shack to take Sonny's papers from the driver. "How're you doin' today? High power, huh? Good . . . Gibson's finally here. The warden will rest easy now." Sonny is surprised that they seem to be waiting for him. After the papers are checked, the officer calls on his walkie-talkie to open the gate. When it closes behind them, a second set opens and they drive through. The first thing Sonny notices are the hexagonal guntowers crowned with enormous searchlights. The men inside are armed with high-powered rifles with telescopes.

The Gray Goose has already arrived, and Sonny joins the rest of the men in R & R. The guard on duty, Lieutenant Jefferson, a Georgia redneck, drawls to another officer, "You know, Ed, I don't know why in the hell they ever called this releasin' and receivin' . . . They never do release anybody outta here. It's all receivin' . . . yessir, all receivin'."

When Sonny is finally brought into the room with the other convicts, the men call out, "Hey, that's Sonny Gibson, head of the Mafia."

"Yo, Sonny, how ya doin'?"

"Hey man, they givin' you a rough time?"

The guard observes that Sonny already has a certain stature with the other inmates. "Well, Gibson, looks like you're a big man in here, you got a lotta friends. Good thing . . . you're gonna be here for about the next fifty years." He jerks Sonny hard by his chains. "Come on." After the long ride, listening to the inane chatter of the guards, and the two weeks of harassment at the jail, Sonny is not about to be pushed around. He plants his feet firmly. The guard jerks his chains again. Sonny still resists. The guard's face turns purple with anger, "I thought I told you to come on . . . you dumb guineas are all alike." This time Sonny steps forward of his own accord and spits in the belligerent officer's face. The convicts cheer for the kingpin—he's living up to his reputation. They root for him, "Way to go, Mafia man."

"Stick it to the pig . . ."

"You show him, Sonny."

The guard hits Sonny hard and knocks him to the ground. The men boo and get rowdy. "Hey, bull, why don't you hit him when he's not chained up?"

"Yeah, let's see how big ya are then."

Conway, the sergeant in charge, starts to panic. It's against the rules to hit a cuffed man. If this causes a riot, the higher-ups in Sacramento will give the warden hell and Conway's job will be on the line. He reprimands the guard sharply. "This man is shackled—you have no right to hit him." As Sonny is getting up, he thinks there may be a decent officer in the system . . . until he hears the next remark. "This man is my responsibility. This is my area . . . I'll do the ass-whipping around here." He looks at Sonny. "With this guy, I can see there'll be plenty of it." Sonny knows now that the sergeant is not really a nice guy, he just wants a piece of the disciplinary action. Conway yells, "All right, empty your pockets and put everything in front of you."

The guards check each item, discarding anything that might contain drugs or be considered a weapon. When they get to Sonny, his toothbrush, razor blades, and comb are tossed in the garbage. He objects, "Hey, what's the matter with them? . . . I bought that stuff at the canteen in the jail."

The guard says routinely, "Don't matter, ya didn't get 'em here, they go in the shitcan." He holds up Theresa's letters. "You got money on the books you can send these back, otherwise we dump 'em." Sonny doesn't know it, but heroin is often smuggled in under the stamps. He turns over $6.00 in cash to the guard, who then records it. Convicts are not allowed to carry money in the penitentiary; the amount on the books is applied to all prison purchases. Sonny's shackles are then removed for the skin search, which is more detailed than the one at the county jail. His fingernails, toenails, lips, ears, nose, mouth, and anus are all inspected with a light. Sonny receives special attention because he is red-tagged . . . this time, however, there are no wisecracks about Sonny's nudity. The officers at the jail can afford to be brave—they know the men are transients. But the guards here know they're going to be on the yard with these convicts, and life means nothing to a man who's destined to spend the rest of his behind bars. Any excuse is a good excuse to kill a guard.

After the contraband check Sonny is given a crew cut, then goes with the others to be sprayed, showered, and clothed. The state is more generous . . . issue here is two pairs of jeans, two blue shirts, two tee shirts, two pairs of shorts, one pair of thick-soled shoes, and two blue handkerchiefs (used by most convicts as headbands). After they've gotten dressed, the men are brought to another room to be fingerprinted, photographed, and given their prison ID. Sonny's red tag is removed, and he's issued a red card with a large OC for Organized Crime . . . his equivalent of a scarlet letter. Because he is classified as a dangerous criminal, Sonny is the last one to be processed.

It is 8:30 P.M. when Sonny finally picks up two blankets and a canvas sheet for his mattress. The last thing he receives is a pass to his cellblock, an area of three tiers with 240 cells each. The guard tells him, "Your block's all the way down the end, Gibson . . . B Block." The gears grind shrilly as the metal door from R & R slides open. It rumbles closed with a low, sepulchral boom. Sonny stands motionless for a few minutes; only now does he realize how vulnerable and alone he really is. The nauseating stench of Pine Sol and sweat follows him as he starts his long, solitary journey down the dimly lit hallway, his steady footsteps echoing off the walls. The walk down the corridor is like tuning a a giant radio, with each cell a different ethnic station. Soul music blasts from the first he passes; two blacks are inside. When they see him, one man, Big Monty, presses his mouth to the bars and yells, "Hey, bloods . . . here comes some new white meat." Monty taunts him, "Hey, white boy, what you in for? Speedin'?" The blacks both laugh and continue to jeer, but Sonny ignores them.

As the sound of their music fades out, the trumpet and guitars of a mariachi band fade in. Ramon Juarez, a Mexican with a headband, drums the beat on the bars of his cell with two wooden rulers. He stops and shouts rhythmically as Sonny goes by, "Hey, Pedro, fish comin' down, new fish comin' down. . . . Dope sale, dope sale." The new arrival shoots a disgusted look at the Mexican hanging out of the bars.

This walk is a rude awakening. Sonny suddenly realizes that he has to live every day of his life with these minorities he has hated so much on the outside. Already he finds himself beginning to hate them even more on the inside. About halfway to his block Sonny hears Johnny Cash wailing out a song. A strapping hillbilly with just a few teeth yells at him, "Hey, brother, join our gang, man. It's the toughest in the yard . . . you're gonna need protectin'. We white boys stick together in this pen."

Sonny just keeps on walking, wondering if there's an Italian gang here, too. Johnny Cash is soon overpowered by Jimi Hendrix, and a junkie reaches out to touch Sonny. A swastika is tattooed on the convict's arm; he can hardly get his words out, he's so high. "Hey, man, Hitler's gonna save us . . . he's alive." Sonny looks over at him, repulsed. How could a man have such little respect for his own life? The junkie's insignia magnifies the hate Sonny has for the animals in this stinking, concrete cage. He is relieved that the half-mile walk down the hall is almost over when a burly black man yells, "Hey, white boy, I'm gonna butt-fuck you good 'less you can pay for protection. They call me MoJo."

This time Sonny stops and turns to the cell. "Listen, nigger, my name's Gibson. Come near me and I'll cut your heart out."

A voice in the next cell mocks, "Hey, man, we got a brave one here . . . he's tough."

By this time Sonny has been infected by their insanity. He shouts down the hall like a crazy man, "Yeah, I'm tough . . . you bet your goddam ass I'm tough."

Now a symphony of comments rings out. "You tell 'em, Mafia man. We take no shit off no niggers."

"White boy's lookin' to get cut up, man."

"Say that in the yard, nigger."

During the ruckus Sonny goes over to MoJo's cell and shouts angrily, "You just look at me, nigger, and I'll kill your black ass . . . don't fuck with me." With his words a tense silence settles over the hallway. Every man can feel the hatred in the air as the white and black stare each other down through the bars. A few seconds later all that can be heard is the steady sound of Sonny's footsteps on the concrete again.

When he reaches his cellblock, Sonny buzzes the guard to let him know he's there. The steel gate squeaks open, and he presents his pass to the module officer, Buchanan, who's reading behind a beat-up wooden desk. Without even looking up the guard takes the pass and throws it in a drawer. "You're in cell 38C." Still buried in his *Hustler* magazine, he says to Sonny, "I'm gonna say this one time, Gibson, listen up. I got better things to do than repeat myself." He looks up at him now. "You're not a boss in here . . . I'm gonna tell you what *my* rules are. You wanna know anything, write it down. If you can't write, draw a picture. Put it in the box on the way to chow, the next night you'll get your answer . . . maybe." He pushes himself up from his chair. "Follow me, Gibson, I'll take ya to your mansion." They go up to the third tier, and the guard opens a cell, the sixth steel door Sonny's been through since he arrived. It slams shut with a loud clang.

Sonny's cellmate, a man who bears a slight resemblance to Bogart, looks up from his book, "Name's Spider . . . rules are the one here longest gets the bottom bunk. You can help yourself to the books." Spider returns to Emily Dickinson.

"My name's Sonny." He's glad to see Spider can read. It means he can help Sonny write his letters to Theresa.

Sonny throws his gear on the top bunk and sits at the edge of the bed. The gauntlet he's just passed through has been unsettling. The men here have no fear, and he can understand why. Most of them have a lot of years behind them and a lot more to go. Unlike Sonny, who was a loyal soldier following orders, killing to some of these convicts means nothing more than breaking the monotonous routine. Through the bars Sonny stares out of the window on the far wall across from the tier. Most of the four-inch-square panes are broken or dirty, but he can still see the sky through the bars. He wonders that Theresa is doing. The vivid memory of their nights of love make him long for the touch of her silky skin on his, but harsh shouts down the hall jar him out of his fantasy.

"Hey! What do you guys do when the shitter don't flush?"

"Stick your head in it, asshole."

A black voice warns from the other end of the tier, "Hey mother-fuckers, I'm tryin' to sleep. I'll stick both your heads in the shitter if ya don't shut up!"

As Sonny listens to the crude exchange, the full impact of prison life hits him. This is no game . . . this is a human jungle. The gates of the tier slide open again. This is followed by more random shouts from the men: "Hey, Big Jim's back." . . . "How'd it go, Big Jim?" . . . "Yeah, what happened, man?"

A deep voice answers, "Nothin' . . . they hadda drop the charges."

There is whistling and shouts of approval now. A black shouts, "Right on, man."

A Mexican yells, "Damn right they dropped the fuckin' charges. We ain't got no rats on this block, man."

Sonny can hear heavy footsteps getting closer. The convicts continue shouting their welcomes. "Hey, Jim. It's good to have ya back."

"Yeah, man, it hasn't been the same without ya these four days."

The deep voice agrees, "It's good to be outta that fuckin' place, I tell ya . . ."

The footsteps are passing his cell. When he sees Big Jim, Sonny lets out a mental whistle. He comments to Spider, "Shit, will ya look at the fuckin' muscles on that guy? . . ." Jim is a brawny six-foot-one Italian with the physique of Mr. World. "Where the hell'd he come back from? Where was he for four days?"

Spider answers without looking up, "Court . . . Big Jim's a hit man. They tried to get him on a murder beef. He hit two guys in the showers in this block, but you know . . . nobody saw nothin'."

The guard is approaching now. His footsteps are quicker and lighter than Jim's; the rattle of keys also identifies him. Sonny's awareness training from Sicily is always in action. As the key turns, Sonny says, "Is that guy Big Jim . . . is he right next to us?"

"Yeah . . . he's a weird dude, man . . . I just keep to my books." Spider finally looks up. "I didn't tell ya nothin' either . . ." He puts his head down again.

Sonny can hear the conversation next door. "It's good to have ya back."

The baritone voice replies, "It's good to be back. I can't wait to get back on the weight pile . . . those four days I felt like I got soft." Sonny wonders if the weight pile is some kind of job. He knows he'll find out soon enough. He has a lot to learn.

At six o'clock the next morning the cell door slides open. Spider leaps out of bed and nudges Sonny. "Get up. Ya got five minutes to get dressed and outta here for breakfast."

Sonny rolls over. "I'm skippin' breakfast. I don't wanna wait on that fuckin' tier."

Spider pulls on his jeans. "No, man, they don't make ya wait here, ya just go. Come on." Sonny swings his feet over the edge of the bunk. He jumps down, splashes some water on his face, and gets dressed. About ten seconds after he leaves, the door of the cell grinds closed.

The line is long when he gets to the chow hall. Unlike the setup in jail, men can sit wherever they want in the large room. But here the blacks always sit together, and the whites and Mexicans mix. The breakfast menu that day is bread, gravy, fried potatoes, cereal, instant coffee, and one pat of butter. The men are given twenty minutes to eat.

As soon as Sonny gets back to his cell, Officer Buchanan gives him a pass for orientation in the gym. An officer hands out books to the men as they arrive. When all of them are seated, the sergeant in charge comes in. "For those of you who can't read my name tag, I'm Sergeant Conway. Some of you might remember me from R & R. Once a week the warden picks an officer to give orientation . . ." He cracks, "I got lucky this week. Now, listen up." Conway slaps the manual in his hand

and paces as he speaks. "I want everyone to read this . . . these are some of the rules we're gonna go through this morning. Number one, and a very important rule, when you approach an officer, you call him Sir or Officer and his name. If his tag says 'Johnson,' it's Officer Johnson. Not hack, not pig, not bull. If you refuse to address him the right way, you can get a writeup. Now, a writeup can do two things. It can take away your privileges for visiting, mail, and canteen . . . or it can get you in segregation." He stops and smiles. "I don't have to explain this to you old-timers . . . but for you first-timers that's what we call the hole . . . and it is just that." Conway surveys the sea of faces in the gym. "I don't know where else you've been, but our hole isn't very pretty. A man gets put in there without clothes. He gets one blanket to sleep on the concrete floor. You get one piece of bread a day . . . which meal it's eaten with is up to you. You get a warm bowl of soup in the morning and a bowl at night. You get two paper buckets . . . one's for your water, the other one's for your shitter . . . . there's no plumbing in the hole. When you get out of the hole, you'll go in front of a disciplinary committee. In this penitentiary the lieutenants are gods . . . they determine how your case will be handled." The sergeant stares directly at Sonny. "The hole's for a purpose—to keep the guys who don't wanna listen, or the guys who think they're tough, in line. The hole'll break a man's spirit . . . we have no tough guys in here." Conway pauses a second to let Sonny digest his words. Pacing again, the sergeant continues, "If you wanna know something, it's best to ask one of the convicts who's been here a long time, 'cause we're not an information booth. The officers here are one thing . . . baby-sitters. Our job is custody . . . to keep ya locked up and safe." Conway stops and faces them again—he wants to make sure this next message gets across loud and clear. "I'm accessible. You can approach me anytime, especially if you wanna give me information which could save a man's life."

A voice in back yells out, "You mean rat?"

Conway continues, ignoring the remark, "If somebody wants to 'rat,' or whatever you call it, we'll put you in protective custody, and then maybe we'll send you to a nicer prison."

Sonny has been sitting stonefaced during the speech, arms folded on his chest. Now he sits up. Sonny can't believe they play the same game with the men inside that the feds tried with him. He shouts, "Don't matter where you send him . . . no rat's safe in prison."

The sergeant silences him. "Shut up, Gibson . . . you're askin' for the hole." Sonny leans back in his chair defiantly as Conway lists the rest of the rules. "If you're gonna be in here a long time, it's best ya get a job. You'll get paid seven dollars a month, and it'll make the time go faster. Otherwise you can sit in your cell and grow old." Sonny is onto this. He knows they want the men to work because it saves the prison money for salaries. "For the next ninety days you'll have a cellmate till you go through classification and we figure out what to do with ya. You'll be given IQ tests . . . if you score high, we'll give ya a chance to get an education. The rest of you will learn a trade, so you can be a man when you get out. You're gonna be tested by a psychiatrist. Be very honest with him . . . he can help you with your problems." Conway opens the rulebook. "You'll see on page fifteen that there's cell inspection once a week, and on page eighteen are the rules for the chow hall. If you get caught taking a spoon outta there, you get hole time. The rest of the rules are in the book . . . learn 'em 'cause you're all gonna be livin' by them." The sergeant wraps up the orientation. "One more thing, you'll all be assigned to a counselor . . . he'll be glad to help you out with any problem you have here or at home. Remember, your counselor is like your father. You can depend on him . . . he'll do everything for you."

When Sonny gets back to his cell, Spider is reading again. He puts a bookmark in his place and closes the book. "How'd ya like orientation?"

Sonny unties his shoes. "That's a real crock a shit they give the guys, huh?"

"That's what the hacks get paid to do." Spider points to the toilet. "Pull up a chair." The latrine is the only thing besides the bunk and two tiny shelves in the five-by-eight cell.

Sonny sits on the edge of the bowl. "Don't they have no toilet seats in this fuckin' place?"

"Some guys make 'em, but the guards just take 'em away. You'll get used to the feel of cold porcelain on your ass. It's a lot better than the hole." Spider reminds him, "And it could be worse. Our shitter could be stopped up for two days like Johnson's. I'm glad we're not next to that stink!" Spider gets up and puts his book away under the bunk. "Some guys told me about ya today. It's a pleasure havin' ya in my cell. I didn't know who you were last night when ya came in . . . anything ya need, just let me know. If you want some stuff, I'll get it for ya till you get your canteen ducats to draw on." Spider sits back down on the bunk.

Sonny says, "Thanks. When do ya sign up for the canteen?"

"They don't do that around here, that's the system at the jail. Here ya put in for your canteen draw. In about ten days ya get a card that's good for twenty-five dollars a month."

"That don't buy much . . ."

Spider says matter-of-factly, "You don't need much here."

Sonny is curious about his cellmate. "Spider, you remind me of a brain, but ya don't look the type."

The convict laughs. "A brain . . . why? 'Cause I'm a bookworm? Shit, there's nothin' else to do in here."

"How come ya don't have a job? They said we should get one."

Spider smirks. "That's another crock a crap. Jobs are for suckers. Whaddya get out of it . . . seven bucks a month? That won't buy shit at the canteen. I'd rather stay in my cell and read."

"If ya don't work, how'dya get money on the books?"

"From my brother. Everybody gets money from the outside unless they're hit men, dope dealers, or pimps. They make enough money inside."

Sonny files that away mentally for future reference. He studies Spider's rugged face and wonders what brought him to the state pen. "Where ya from, Spider?"

"Texas."

"How'd ya end up here?"

"Same way you did . . . I got caught. I was busted in LA pullin' an armed robbery."

Sonny flashes back to the days when he and Johnny were doing the same thing, but they were smart . . . or lucky enough not to get caught.

"How'd they get ya, Spider?"

"My partner didn't watch my back. We were robbin' a drugstore, and he took off. If I ever catch that son of a bitch, I'll kill him."

"I started out pullin' armed robberies with a guy in Indiana."

"Yeah? Ever get busted?"

Sonny thinks of Johnny again. As thick as he was, Johnny always protected him. "Nah . . . I had a good pair of eyes."

"Where's your partner now?"

"Michigan State Penitentiary."

Spider says sardonically, "He couldn't have been too good a pair of eyes . . ."

"Yeah, he watched me all right . . . he just got into somethin' he didn't know nothin' about."

Spider philosophizes, "That's why most guys are here. We get caught 'cause we get in over our head. If I'd stayed pushin' drugs, I'd a been all right, but I decided hittin' this drugstore we'd get a lotta narcotics. How the hell was I supposed to know the owner would be one of those greedy-ass son of a bitches who had the first dime he ever made and fight to hell and back for it? He shot me."

Sonny observes, "Guess you're lucky ya aren't dead then, aren't ya, Spider?"

The convict rubs his back. "Yeah, but my shoulder gives me a lotta pain. In the wintertime it's freezin' here. In the summer it's hotter'n blazes and the humidity's somethin' bad."

Sonny is surprised. "In California? There's not much humidity here."

Spider corrects him. "Not outside these prison walls there ain't, but inside it's a fuckin' steambath. There's a lotta things you'll find out about this place . . . none good." Spider gets up and crosses to his shelf. "I gotta get back to my books. By the way, you can borrow 'em if ya want, Gibson."

"Thanks, but I can't read or write."

Spider is shocked. "What! How the hell'd you take down so much money and get so powerful with the Mafia?"

Sonny smiles. "You don't have to read to be with the Mafia . . . the only thing ya need is loyalty. As for takin' down money . . . if you can talk, you can con . . . Hey, Spider, I was thinkin' . . . maybe you could help me write some letters to my old lady."

"Sure . . . long as it don't take too much time."

"Thanks . . ." Sonny moves from the toilet seat to the edge of his bunk and jumps up on it. "How long you been in, Spider?"

"Ten years."

"Ten years?"

"Yep . . . the parole board keeps denyin' me, but I'm close to gettin' home soon. In the meantime I'm tryin' to get to a camp center."

Sonny is curious. The only camp he's ever heard of is run by the Boy Scouts, and nobody in the pen would qualify for that. "What the hell's a camp center?"

"It's where they fight fires. You work your ass off for the state, but you're outside all the time. The food's better, too, and if you're careful, you can sneak off into the woods with your old lady."

That idea appeals to Sonny. "How'dya get to this camp center?"

Spider says pessimistically, "I doubt they'd let you go there . . . you're OC . . . unless you got a way of connin' your counselor."

That was encouraging to Sonny. He'd try to get to a camp center himself. Sonny lies down on the bunk now, one hand under his head, and is startled by what he sees. There are full-color pornographic drawings on the ceiling. "Hey, Spider, whoever drew this stuff was good . . . a guy could jack off to this."

"Yeah, Pedro was a real fine artist."

Sonny looks closer. "Jesus, I musta been tired not to see that last night. . . those broads got good-sized tits, don't they . . . "

"Yeah . . . he was a tit man . . . you a tit man?"

"Nah . . . I like 'em with a hairy snatch." Sonny is fascinated by the detail in the sketches. There are scenes of women in different settings and erotic positions. "Ya know, this guy was really talented. He's even got scenery."

"Yeah . . . he'd been in over thirty years."

"Well, he didn't need no *Hustler* magazine to jack off." Seeing these pictures reminds Sonny that he is horny. He takes off his pants and gets under the blanket to start fondling himself. Theresa and the thousands of other women he's had bring him to a stiff erection immediately. Just about the time he is ready to climax, a guard shouts, "Gibson!"

Sonny jumps nearly two feet in the air and sits up. "Yeah . . ."

"I got a pass for your physical tomorrow." Sonny gets down from the bunk and walks to the bars, still hard. The guard looks at his naked crotch. "Sorry to bother ya, Gibson, but you'll have plenty of time for that." He hands Sonny the pass and walks down the hall.

Sonny turns to Spider. "Shit, a guy can't even jack off in peace around here . . ."

"Nope, the bulls think just 'cause you're like a monkey in a cage, they got a right to look in anytime. You'll get used to it. If you're gonna stay sane, you gotta." Just then the cell door slides open. Spider closes his book. "Let's go, Gibson . . . lunch is served."

At chow Sonny spots Zabinini, the old man who saved him from getting into trouble at the canteen line in the county jail. He motions for Sonny to join him at his table. Sonny gets his daily ration of the same kind of starchy food he had for breakfast and, when he sits down, says, "Tell me somethin', Zabinini . . . they ever hear of eggs in this place?"

The old convict smiles. "Yeah, the chickens here work once a week . . . you'll get your eggs on Sunday."

Sonny watches the old man picking at his food. "Hey, what're ya doin' that for? Why you takin' so much time. We only got twenty minutes."

"Got to, Santino . . . the guards in the kitchen put dead flies and roaches in the food." Zabinini finally dunks his bread in the greasy gravy. "Have you gone through orientation?"

"Yeah."

The old man stops mid-mouthful. "Don't believe anything they tell you, Santino . . . you'll find out for yourself in time what really goes on around here." He keeps on eating but slips something into Sonny's hand under the table.

When the guard's not watching, Sonny looks at it. "This is an officer's pass!" Zabinini nods coolly. Sonny is amazed. "How the hell'd you get this?"

Zabinini lowers his voice. "Mike Matullo gave it to me . . . he wants to see you."

"I heard Papa Mike was here." The old man was still a legend in the Mafia. Matullo went to prison in the fifties because he wouldn't testify against the family in a big drug bust. Sonny says, "I felt bad when he got sent up again. Didn't he do ten years?"

Zabinini says sadly, "Yeah . . . and ya know what got him back in the joint? One of his bodyguards left a piece in the car while Papa Mike was making a donation at his grandson's school. The cops got him on a beef as an ex-con carrying a firearm because the car was registered in his name . . . Papa Mike's never carried a gun." Zabinini says gravely, "He's dying now, Santino, it's good he's got an easy job. He works in the legal library, that's what the pass is for. Men fighting their own cases can spend a lotta time there."

Just then a guard shouts, "All right, back to your block, chow's over."

At the garbage can, as they dump their trays, Zabinini urges Sonny, "Go see Papa Mike today . . . If ya need anything in this place, he'll set ya up."

That afternoon Sonny goes over to the library. The guard at the door looks at his pass and remarks snidely, "Another Perry Mason, huh? I never seen any of you clowns win a case yet, but go on in." Sonny enters. This small room with its low shelves barely qualifies as a library. It does have one thing in common with its larger counterpart . . . a musty smell. Here the odor comes from antiquated volumes donated to the prison by law firms; it is Papa Mike's job to see that the legal books are up to date. He is hunched over a book when Sonny first sees him. The first impression he has is how much he looks like Alfonso. Physically they are similar—short, fat, and balding. A long scar down his right cheek tells Sonny that Papa Mike, like Alfonso, is also a survivor. When the old man sees Sonny, he hugs him warmly and says in Sicilian, "I got a message from your godfather to make sure you're taken care of." Then, in English, "It's been five or six years since I've seen you, Santino." He sweeps his hand around the room. "This place is not as nice as the Lucky Ace."

"That's for sure . . ."

Papa Mike picks up some books and hands them to Sonny. "Go through these like you're looking up a case number." He heads for the shelves. "I was surprised to see you come in here, Santino. We read in the paper you surrendered. You must have a good reason . . . I hear you could live like a king in Sicily."

Sonny looks at him. "There's a very good reason, Papa Mike." The old man walks slowly, carefully putting the books back in their places. "Did Alfonso tell you about Don Giuseppe?"

Matullo nods, "Yes . . . the don was never the same after Nick died. I heard you avenged his death, Santino."

"He was the only real friend I ever had . . . we grew up together." They walk a few more steps, and Sonny asks, "Papa Mike, who's the muscle around here?"

"I am."

"Then the Mafia runs this place?"

"No, Santino, reputation runs a prison. People know who I was on the outside. That got me on top. I stayed there 'cause I made sure every gang got a piece of the action." He says gravely, "You were powerful on the outside, too, Santino, but you've never been in before. I'm gonna talk to you like you were my own son. Listen carefully to what I tell you . . . it's the only way you're gonna survive this hell." He takes a large book from Sonny. "When you go to chow, don't stare at anybody—some men are looking for trouble. You could look like a cop he knows or some witness who sent him up. Never reach over another man's plate . . . ask the guy at the table to pass what you want. I saw a man get killed 'cause he wanted some salt. Never go behind someone's back without telling them. If someone goes behind you, turn around fast . . . it could save your life. Be aware of everyone, Santino . . . be as sharp as if you were committing a hit." They walk to the other side of the room. "Don't let anyone get close to you who's wearing a jacket . . . chances are there's a shank up his sleeve."

Sonny's curious. "Where do the shanks come from, Papa Mike? There's none in the chow hall . . . I've been eatin' with a spoon so long I almost forget what a knife looks like."

"Most of 'em are snuck outta the butcher shop, Santino. When the blades get too dull, they're thrown out. The handles are taken off so the guys can't use 'em, but you can make a sturdy handle with shank tape."

"What's that?"

Papa Mike explains, "Bandage tape from the hospital. To make a handle, take a ruler and break it in half. Put the blade on, and wrap up the whole thing. The tape doesn't fingerprint either." Papa Mike stoops to file another book. When he gets up, he continues. "In the hall walk close to the walls, but when you get to a corner, take it wide . . . if a riot's starting, the blacks could kill you just 'cause you're the first white guy they see." The guard at the door looks at them suspiciously. They pretend to be looking something up. When the officer turns away, Papa Mike continues with Sonny's prison education. "Don't ever talk to the cops. If you wanna know somethin', ask me or Zabinini . . . we've been around a long time." He stops and says with concern, "Zabinini told me how he helped you out at the county jail . . . you were gonna take on all the pigs single-handed." The old man puts a hand on Sonny's shoulder. "Santino, you can't do that here . . . you just won't win." They start walking again. "Don't say anything to your old lady on the visiting phone. This place is bugged, and you're OC. Everything you say is sent to Washington."

Sonny says out of the blue, "Hey, Papa Mike, they said in orientation they'd throw you in the hole for takin' a lousy spoon out of chow hall . . . what's that shit about?"

"They're afraid you'll make a shank out of it."

The guard on duty who noticed them before now shouts, "Hey, this is not a social club . . . get to your business, Gibson."

Papa Mike hands Sonny a book and tells him one more thing. "Meet me in the yard tomorrow at nine . . . wear a long jacket." He goes on in a loud voice, "I think you'll be able to handle that case. Just be sure you send the papers to the original court that sentenced you."

Sonny hands Papa Mike the books. "Thanks . . . I'll remember what you told me."

On the way out the old man says again, "Don't forget . . . it's the court that sentenced you . . . I'll be on the yard tomorrow if you have any questions."

The convicts are allowed four hours yard time a day—nine to eleven in the morning, and one to three in the afternoon. The cells open automatically to let the men out; five minutes later they close, and unless a guard unlocks the door, you're trapped for those two hours. At nine the following morning Sonny hurries down to the yard. It is his first day outside. The rays of the sun are blinding. When his eyes adjust, Sonny sees that the yard is already crowded. Even though the air is fresh, it is impossible to escape the stink of prison that permeates the convicts' clothes. Some men are clustered in small ethnic groups and gangs, while others play softball, basketball, or dominoes. Despite these seemingly harmless activities there is an undercurrent of antagonism between the races that could erupt into violence any second. The guards in the guntowers above stare coldly at the prisoners below. The sun reflects off the telescopic sights of the high-powered rifles they carry, and the officers stand with their feet apart, scanning the yard like hawks for any hint of trouble. Sonny remarks uncomfortably, "Are those guys always that alert?"

"Yeah, and they'd love to use any one of us for target practice."

Sonny points to the barbed wire on the high wall as they walk. "What kind of wire is that? I've never seen it before."

"They used it in Viet Nam . . . the government sent the surplus to the prisons."

"Anybody ever make it over that?"

Papa Mike says bitterly, "Just a week before you got here, a guy went crazy and tried to climb the fence. A guard told him his old lady was fuckin' somebody else. They didn't even have to shoot . . . that wire made mincemeat outta him." Sonny and Papa Mike walk in slow circles around the yard. The old man says without expression, "I've got two shanks for you. Keep one in your cell, one in somebody else's. There's an Italian guy on your block—you can't miss him—Cigar Eddie."

"Yeah, his cell stinks like hell."

"He's the boss of B Block, and he's looking for an enforcer. Eddie will be a big help to you. He'll keep one of your shanks and tell you where to hide the other one . . . Eddie does the plumbing for your block." When he's sure no one can see, Papa Mike slips the shanks up Sonny's sleeves. "Carry these with the points down . . . It might cut your hands, but it'll save you from getting stuck someday."

They keep circling the yard. Sonny says, "Ya know, I don't know how the hell they did it, but at the jail some guy got his head cut off with a razor blade. I'd like to get my hands on a weapon that small and that deadly."

Papa Mike says, "It's easy, but it takes some time to make. Buy two toothbrushes and some blades at the canteen. Cut the bristles off, put the two handles back to back, and line up the blades inside them. Then heat the plastic till the blades are melted between them. Get some shank tape. Wrap a pencil with it to extend your handle. When you're finished, you'll have a ten-inch switchblade that'll slice a man's throat like a tomato." Papa Mike turns to Sonny. "It's a good weapon if you're gonna make a hit, but for protection you need a long knife. You might have to fight off four or five guys."

At that moment Sonny sees MoJo in a crowd of blacks. They glare at each other across the yard. "Yeah, I might have some niggers fuckin' with me."

Sonny and Papa Mike sit on the bleachers to watch the softball game. "Don't worry, Santino, niggers only hit you when they're in a gang . . . or they stick you in the back." He warns, "If you hear anything that sounds like a dull thump, turn around fast . . . that's a shank going into somebody. If a guard asks what happened, you never see or hear nothin' . . . that's your life insurance in this place."

Sonny reminds him, "That's our life insurance outside, too."

Papa Mike laughs. "Santino, I forgot . . . for your young years, you're a veteran." His voice gets serious. "But be careful, Santino . . . you have a reputation . . . anything you get involved in's gonna bring you heat."

"Look, Papa Mike, I'm goin' crazy . . . I gotta do somethin'. Who's the competition for runnin' things around here?"

They get up and start walking again. "You won't have any . . . you're tough. Two things you could do . . . collect money for narcotics and run the homosexuals. Enforcing and pimping is right up your alley. I know a couple of guys on your block who'd pay for your services. Let's go over to the weight pile, Santino. I want you to meet somebody." When they get there, Sonny can see that the weight pile is just that . . . a pile of weights where men work out. Papa Mike says, "You know, Santino, one thing the niggers are afraid of is a white boy with muscles."

"I can see why . . . some of these guys are bigger than my body-guards."

"Some of them have been working out for fifteen years." Papa Mike suggests, "Why don't you lose that fat while you're here, Santino? Come on, I'll introduce you to Big Jim . . . he's Italian. Matter of fact, you guys have some friends in common . . . he was a hit man for the Cleveland families."

Sonny hesitates. "Papa Mike, I can't shake hands—I got these shanks up my sleeves."

"Don't worry about it, Santino, there's no hand shaking in here."

When Sonny finally meets Big Jim, he reminds him of Angelo. The body builder says, "I know your cellie, Spider."

Sonny nods. "Yeah, you're in the cell next to us."

Jim picks up a fifty-pound barbell and holds his arm out. He lifts effortlessly. "Was . . . but they changed me over to C block."

"Why?"

"They think you're startin' to get too much action, they'll move ya . . . especially if a crime happens where you're at. A coupla guys got killed in the showers, and they tried to pin it on me."

Papa Mike says, "I told Sonny he ought to get in shape while he's here. We could use another strong Italian."

Jim puts down his weight. "O.K., Papa Mike, I'll work with him." The brawny man turns to Sonny. "You're flabby, you need a good workout. Meet me on the yard this afternoon and I'll help you with your weight-lifting routine."

"I can't. I have my physical."

"O.K., see you in the morning then."

A shrill whistle blasts, disquieting Sonny. "What's that, Papa Mike?"

"Yard recall . . . it's time to go back."

"It sounds like the whistle that called pigs to slaughter at one of the factories near where I grew up."

The three men start walking back to the compound. "This is no different from a slaughterhouse, Santino . . . they treat men like pigs here, too." Before he does back to the library, Papa Mike says, "Don't forget . . . look up Cigar Eddie as soon as you can."

On his way back from the yard Sonny hears screams from MoJo's cell. Four blacks have a twenty-two-year-old named Tommy pinned to the floor, and the enormous MoJo is standing naked over the pleading boy. "Take this black dick, white boy. Take this black dick."

Tommy begs him, "Don't do this . . . oh, God, no! Please . . . help me, somebody help me!" Ignoring his cries for mercy, MoJo rapes Tommy viciously while the others wait their turn. Sonny is incensed by the violence. He wants to kill the black men but remembers Papa Mike's warning: "Don't get involved in someone else's fight." Sonny forces himself to turn away. Tommy's desperate pleas get fainter and fainter as Sonny continues walking down the hall. Finally he can't hear them anymore.

That afternoon, when Sonny gets back from his physical, he stops at the module desk. "Officer Buchanan, is it O.K. if I stop at Cigar Eddie's before I go back to my cell?"

The guard looks over his feet propped up on the desk. "You can do what ya want, Gibson. I don't open the doors till three o'clock."

As Sonny heads down the corridor, the smell of cigar smoke soon tells him he's close to Eddie's cell. When he gets there, the door is open. There are old butts on the floor and a lit one in the scrawny man's mouth. "I'm Sonny Gibson."

Eddie squints at him through thick glasses. "Yeah . . . Papa Mike told me about you at chow today. Come on in." Sonny goes to sit on the edge of the toilet, but Eddie hasn't flushed it in a while. "Somethin' wrong with your shitter?"

"Nah . . ."

Eddie gives him a quizzical look when Sonny hits flush. Now he sits down on the bowl. "You must have juice around here. How come your door's open?"

"It's gotta stay open . . . I'm the plumber, might be an emergency somewhere." Eddie peers at Sonny through a cloud of cigar smoke. "Papa Mike tells me you're a tough guy. A lotta tough guys come and go here. I don't do my own enforcin' . . . that's why I need 'em. Losin' Big Jim cost me, but if ya want, you can take his place. You're gonna be workin' out with Jim, right?"

"Yeah."

"Good. Most guys are scared of ya already, but that'll give ya even more juice on the yard."

"Why are guys scared of me?"

"They know the kinda power you had on the outside. What they don't know is ya don't have that kinda power here . . . no one does, except what a shank gets ya."

Sonny looks at the puny man in amazement. "How'd you get to run this block?"

Eddie takes a few short puffs. "Havin' guys like you and Jim workin' for me. You got the job if ya want it. Here's the deal . . . you get twenty percent to pick up money, twenty-five percent if ya gotta enforce it. If you handle any drugs, that's twenty percent, and ya get another twenty-five percent to pimp out my broads—I got four on this block."

"Broads? What broads?"

"Fags . . . we call 'em broads here."

"Where do they work at? There's guards crawlin' all over."

"During yard time a guy can go anywhere he wants. The showers is a good place, and in the yard there's a shack with a shitter. Nobody says nothin' if you put a broad in a guy's cell, but they'll be locked up, so make sure the con's payin' to get his dick sucked for two hours, or else get three or four guys in there to bang him at one time." A huge ash drops off Eddie's cigar onto his shirt. He doesn't brush it away but goes right on talking. "The R & R clerk told me there's a couple of real pretty boys comin' in next week. Those young asses can bring a lotta money . . . I want you to turn 'em out."

Sonny stops him. "Hold on, Eddie. I'll pimp the guys that are already fuckin', but you gotta turn new ones out yourself."

"Big Jim always got a hold of 'em and made 'em fuck."

"That's Big Jim. I never turned out a broad in my life, I'm not gonna start now."

"All right, have it your way." Eddie holds out his hand to shake. "Deal?"

Sonny refuses. "I don't shake nobody's hand, but yeah . . . we got a deal."

"You trust me, then?"

Sonny smiles. "Yeah . . . like a fence." He slips a shank he's been carrying up his sleeve to Eddie. "Papa Mike said you'd hide this."

"Sure . . . no problem." He slips the knife under his bed.

"Don't they shake ya down, Eddie?"

The foul-smelling man lights another Panatella. "Nah . . ." He takes a long puff. "The warden likes me. I fix all the shitters around here. Nobody else's smart enough to do the job."

"When do I start workin', Eddie?"

"Now. There's a guy named Billy Travers . . . he owes me a twenty-dollar narcotics debt . . . I want you to get the money. If he don't pay, kill him."

"What do I get for knockin' him off?"

Eddie says coolly, "Nothin', that's part of the job. I'll get ya a pack a cigarettes."

"I don't smoke . . ."

"All right, I'll get ya some Tang, then. All the workout guys drink that." Eddie picks up his plumber's case and gets ready to leave. "Remember, Sonny, if they don't pay, kill 'em. The only thing they know around here is violence . . . that teaches the welchers."

The next morning at nine o'clock Sonny meets Big Jim at the weight pile in the yard. The musclebound convict is lying down on the bench press, lifting a bar high in the air. When he finishes, Sonny goes up to him. "That looks like a lotta fuckin' weight, Big Jim. How much is on there?"

The strapping convict wipes his hands with a towel. "Four hundred pounds . . . you'll be able to lift that some day."

"Four hundred pounds? Forget it. I'll never be able to lift that much."

"You will, but you'll go slow." Jim removes some of the weights and puts the bar back. "Lie down, Sonny, we'll start with a hundred pounds. Grab the bar, take a deep breath, and lift it over your head, up and down. That's one rep . . . short for repetition."

Sonny takes his place at the bench press and manages three reps before he quits, breathing hard. "Man, that's heavy, and I'm pretty strong, too."

"Yeah, but you're not built up . . . you gotta develop your arms first. Here." Jim hands Sonny a long iron rod with two humps where the hands fit. "That's a curl bar . . . it's good for your biceps."

This is easier for Sonny. As he lifts, he notices that the pile is segregated. "Are the weights different over there, Big Jim?"

"Nope, that's the blacks' side. You don't borrow anything from 'em 'less you want trouble. Most cons here are serious about body building, but you still gotta be careful. We'll get another guy, and the three of us will be partners to make sure nobody sticks ya while you're workin' out."

Sonny drops the curl bar, panting. "Shit . . . how long you think it'll take before I'll be in shape?"

"Get some honey and protein to build up your strength, and it won't be that long . . . with the routine I'm puttin' ya on, it shouldn't be more than a coupla years."

"A coupla years! That's a long time."

Jim smiles. "That's no time at all. I've been workin' out for twelve."

"Yeah, well I'm only gonna be in six months . . . what can I do in that time?"

"Six months! Where you goin' . . . on vacation? I read you got life."

Sonny assures him, "I got connections, I'll be out in six months."

"I'll put ya on the same routine anyway, but lemme set ya straight." Jim's face darkens. "I don't teach nobody. I'm doin' this as a favor because Papa Mike saved my ass once. If you start with me, you don't quit."

Sonny can see the viciousness in Jim now. "Hey, I wanna come out here. It's better than stayin' in that fuckin' cell."

"Long as ya understand where I'm comin' from."

The yard recall whistle blows, and they start back to the compound. "Big Jim, whaddya do in the wintertime or when it rains?"

"Work out as usual. You gotta keep it up, or your muscles get soft. You'll get used to it."

Sonny sighs. "Yeah . . . I'm gettin' used to a lotta things around here."

By the end of the week Sonny is settling into his routine at the penitentiary. He meets Big Jim on the yard every morning to work out and spends his afternoons taking care of things for Cigar Eddie. Sonny still hasn't collected the narcotics debt for him because Billy Travers has been in the jail and is not due back for a few days. Sometimes life here has a surrealistic quality for Sonny. It's as though the women, the bodyguards, the jet planes, the power, and the money never existed . . . even Theresa seems phantasmal most times. There are moments when he misses her, but most of the time he doesn't think about her at all. She has no place inside these prison walls. In some ways she represents everything he's lost. Her letters are his only link to what was, but Sonny can no longer relate to the things she talks about or the problems in her world. However, on Sunday, when Theresa is scheduled to visit for the first time, Sonny is excited about seeing her.

The visiting procedure at the state pen is similar to that in the jail. A convict must be seated before his visitor is allowed in. As soon as Theresa sees Sonny, she waves wildly. When she gets to the cubicle, they kiss through the window . . . this one is even smaller and thicker than the one in the jail. Holding their hands to the glass, they pick up the phones to talk. "I love you, Sonny . . . I miss you."

"I miss ya, too, baby. How'd ya get up here?"

Theresa grins. "I bought a car. It's a Chevy Capri." She holds up a brochure to the glass. "Here's what it looks like, only the one I got is fire-engine red."

"That's great, baby." Sonny thinks a second. "You know what, I'll bet I could see you drive up in that little car of yours. There's a tiny window way across the tier I can see out of a little. Why don't ya put somethin' on the antenna so I know it's you . . . like a pair of panties."

Theresa laughs. "I don't think I'd better do that . . . they wouldn't make it past the gate anyway." She studies Sonny's face as he smiles. He looks much better here than at the jail. "Honey, you look like you're getting a little color."

"Yeah, we get two hours' yard time in the morning and two in the afternoon . . . and guess what. See that guy over there?" He points to Big Jim. "I'm gonna look just like him."

She admires his muscles. "He's got really big arms. They're bigger than Angelo's."

"Jim's my workout partner . . . we lift weights together. I'm gonna be a regular Charles Atlas by the time I get out."

There is a brief silence, then Theresa's eyes fill with tears. "Do they beat you up here too, Sonny?"

"No . . . this place is better than the jail. Ya get more food . . . I have a nice cell . . . a pretty good cell partner . . . his name is Spider.

Hey, are you gettin' my letters? He writes 'em for me."

Theresa composes herself for him and smiles. "Yes, and I got something from a Mr. Barker the other day . . . he sent me a form. What should I do?"

"That's my counselor. . . . Is it a personality form?"

"I think so."

He instructs her excitedly, "Fill it out. If you do it right, I might get to go to a camp center."

"What's that?"

"I can't tell ya anything about it except you're allowed contact visits." He lowers his voice. "And sometimes you can sneak out in the woods and fuck. Fill out that form good . . . maybe Barker'll recommend I go there." Sonny is thinking ahead. If things don't turn out as planned, it will be easier for Alfonso to break him out at the less secure camp center. Now he notices that Theresa is quiet. "What's wrong, honey?"

"Sonny, I'm looking for a job."

Sonny cuts her off, upset. "NO . . . I don't want ya workin'."

She pauses for a second. "It's lonely in that big apartment without you there, and I'm bored. Besides, the money you left isn't going to last forever." Suddenly Sonny realizes that his being in prison is hard on Theresa, too. "The rent is only paid for two more months. I can't afford two thousand a month. I've gotta look for a place to live soon."

"No, ya don't. Go see Chet. Tell him I said to lend ya twenty-five thousand . . . he'll do it. He might be able to help ya get a job too."

"I think I already have one singing in a club downtown."

"That's no kind of work to be doin'."

She says quietly, "The man at the club said I had a very good voice."

"I know ya do, baby . . . if that's what ya want, do it."

"At least I'll get twenty-five dollars a night singing."

"O.K., just be careful when ya come home late . . . lock your doors." Before they can say anything else, the phones go dead. They mouth "I love you" and kiss good-bye through the glass.

During this half-hour Theresa has made Sonny feel human again, but as soon as he gets back to his cell, his personality changes. Sonny cloaks himself in the mantle of hate that transforms him into a pimp and an enforcer. The next morning, with a shank up his sleeve, Sonny goes to the yard to enforce the narcotics debt for Cigar Eddie. The mark, Billy Travers, is sitting near the weight pile where Big Jim is working out. Sonny walks over and picks up a ten-pound dumbbell. "Hey, Santino . . . you ready for a hundred fifty pounds today?"

"Yeah, come 'ere and check out my arms." Sonny pulls Jim aside and points to Travers. "Do me a favor . . . go stand in front of that guy and block the guntower."

"Why?"

Sonny answers impatiently "Just do that for me, O.K.?" As soon as Jim is in position, Sonny hits his victim in the back of the head, knocking him out. While Sonny pretends to be putting some weights together, he props the unconscious Travers into a sitting position, then he motions for Jim to leave with him. They walk casually across the yard together.

Jim, says angrily, "Hey, man, I get the hit jobs around here . . . you're buttin' into my business. I hope we don't have to kill each other over this shit."

Sonny calms him, "Don't worry, this is my own business. I'm takin' care of things over in B Block now."

Jim argues, "That man's not even in B."

"No, but he owes Cigar Eddie a narcotics debt."

"Then he's lucky you just bashed his head in. I would've killed the son of a bitch."

Sonny stops and turns. "What good would that have done me, Big Jim? You can't get money from a dead man."

By the time he reaches his cell, the news of "man down" is all over the block. While the convicts wait on the tiers for the cell doors to slide open, they talk about what happened. The man next door to Sonny says to his cellie, "I told ya it was dangeous workin' out with those fuckin' weights . . . one drops on ya, you're dead."

Someone shouts to Cigar Eddie as he passes by with his plumber's kit, "Hey, Eddie, you lost one of your best customers on the yard today, huh?" There is no comment from the boss of B Block as he stops next to Sonny. The guard following him unlocks the door. "Lemme know when you want out, Eddie."

"That's O.K., just leave it unlocked." As soon as Sonny gets inside, he hides his shank, wedging it in back of the pipe behind his toilet. Eddie squats in front of the bowl, pretending to be fixing something. He is riled up, "What the fuck did ya bust Travers in the head for? . . . .I didn't tell ya to make a hit."

Sonny leans against the sink. "No, Eddie, I hadda to make him an example. Now everyone in the fuckin' yard will pay me when I go talk to 'em. It should be the last time I'll have to do somethin' like that."

Eddie takes a wrench to tighten the washers. He's calmer now. "Since ya put it that way, it's a helluva good idea . . . I wonder why Big Jim never thought of it."

" 'Cause I work the Mafia way. I know about enforcin', Eddie, I get results . . . you just stick to cleanin' shitters."

The plumber stands menacing Sonny with his tool. "Watch your mouth . . . that wasn't called for, Gibson."

Sonny grabs Eddie's wrist and twists the wrench from him. "Don't you ever lift somethin' to me again, asshole."

The plumber backs down. "O.K., forget it . . . this is a bad day, everyone's uptight. Do whatever ya want as long as I get my money." He flushes the toilet and announces loudly, "This shitter's workin' O.K. now, Gibson. Lemme know if it fucks up again." Eddie picks up the wrench and puts it back into his kit.

Sonny stops him on the way out. "Hey . . . Papa Mike said ya had two more shanks for me."

"Yeah . . . one's in the hallway behind some loose bricks near the plumbing pumps, the other one's in some broken concrete in the yard. I'll show 'em to ya tomorrow."

Sonny reminds him, "Remember, Eddie, I do things my way. You don't get to say shit about it, but I'll get your bread, all right."

Because the guards reported seeing Sonny near the weight pile, he is suspected of making the hit. Two guards come to his cell and bring him before the warden for questioning. George C. Hacksworth is a stone-cold veteran of the penal system. A former police captain, he has found his niche of power and flexes the muscles of his authority frequently. Warden Hacksworth believes prisoners are guilty of everything and capable of anything. To him a convict is a convict is a convict. Sonny stands in front of his desk while the warden looks over his file. He finally closes it and looks up. Hacksworth blusters officiously, "Gibson, your jacket's not a very good one . . . it shows that you've been involved in almost every kind of criminal act, including several murders."

Sonny sets him straight. "I've never been convicted for murder, Warden."

"That may be true, but you see, we go by what we read in your jacket, not by your convictions." He leans forward. "There's a rumor that you attacked this young man, Billy Travers. Fortunately Travers is gonna be all right, but if you would like to come forward and tell the truth about what happened, we'll be very lenient in our disciplinary action."

Sonny has his alibi all set. "Man, I don't know what the hell you're talkin' about. I wasn't even near the weight pile. Me and Big Jim were playin' basketball . . . ask him."

Sergeant Conway speaks up. "No sense askin' him, Warden . . . those Italians stick together like cold spaghetti."

He turns to Sonny. "Gibson, you gave me problems when I was in R & R . . . I was the yard officer today. I'm gettin' the feelin' that you like to cause trouble when I'm around."

Sonny looks at him plainly. "I'm doin' my time. I guess you gotta do yours."

Conway blows up. "We'd better not have another run-in, Gibson, if ya know what's good for you."

He turns to the warden. "No sense talkin' to him anymore. He's Mafia . . . he won't say anything."

Hacksworth says, "Go back to your cell, Gibson, and stay clean from now on."

On the way out Conway warns, "I'm gonna be watchin' for you, Gibson . . . I'm gonna be watchin'."

Since there are no witnesses to the hit, Sonny is released without disciplinary action, but the hit served its purpose . . . the men all fear him. It is only violence that helps Sonny survive the long days, which drag by slowly. When he's in his cell, Spider reads and writes his letters to Theresa, but when he's not doing that Sonny is planning new ways to collect money or pimp out the "broads." It seems like a year before the store man finally arrives. Sonny's ducats to draw on have not come through yet, so instead of getting paid in cash from Eddie, the boss has gotten some of the men to use their money on the books to buy things for Sonny. When he gets to the canteen, the line is long. In the penitentiary you're only allowed to make purchases twice a month. While they wait, the convicts talk about their cases, their girlfriends, and home, but Sonny is absorbed in checking his list, which is a long one. The line is moving slower than usual that day, when Sonny suddenly hears four quick thumps . . . the sound Papa Mike warned him about. He whirls around and sees a man with four shanks stuck in him. The convicts scatter, and the storekeeper slams his window shut, afraid of a riot. Sonny knows the guards will be everywhere in minutes. He hesitates for a few seconds as the dying man staggers toward him, hands reaching desperately for help, blood spurting from his wounds. But Papa Mike has taught him well. Sonny turns his back heartlessly and hurries to his cell.

As callous as Sonny was before he came to prison, he becomes more cold-blooded after this incident. Soon he is known as the most violent enforcer in the prison. Eddie has told him that a black named Leroy Cooper is threatening to take his broads from him. Sonny takes care of the problem in the yard. He spots Cooper standing near the bleachers by the softball field. When Sonny gets over to him, he puts a friendly arm around Leroy, turning him away from the guntower. "Hey, Leroy, how're you doin', man?" With his other hand Sonny holds the deadly point of his shank against the startled black man's throat. He whispers fiercely, "I'm gonna have to kill your black ass if don't stop fuckin' with Eddie's broads." He presses the knife harder. "And ya owe him ten bucks for gettin' your dick sucked last night . . . I'm collectin', now, nigger, understand?"

Leroy's eyes widen. "Hey, don't kill me, man . . . I don't got no money. I don't got it."

"Call one of your nigger buddies over."

The black shouts frantically, "Hey! Hey Tyrone! Tyrone, come 'ere man . . . come 'ere."

His friend runs over to see what Leroy wants. He sees the shank and panics. "Hey, what you doin', white man? You crazy?"

Sonny tightens his grip. "I'm gonna kill your buddy."

Cooper is getting more excited by the minute. "Give him ten bucks, man . . . give it to him . . . give him the ten."

Tyrone says, "What kinda shit's goin' down, man?"Sonny stretches Leroy's throat and punctures his skin with the blade. "Just give him the money, Tyrone . . . give it to him, motherfucker." Tyrone takes a ten from his pocket and hands the enforcer the money. Sonny grabs the bill and whispers in Leroy's ear, "Stay away from Eddie's broads . . . next time I won't be Mr. Nice Guy."

When Sonny gets back to Cigar Eddie's cell, he holds up the $10. "This is mine, Eddie."

"What the hell're you——" Sonny cuts him off. "We're fifty-fifty partners, now . . . don't fuck with me."

Eddie squints at him, chewing his cigar. "Yeah . . . what makes you think you're worth fifty percent? I could replace you easy . . . there's plenty a guys with muscle around."

Sonny puts the ten in his pocket. "Maybe some guys have more muscles, but nobody's got more guts. There won't be nobody takin' this job once the word gets out I'm gonna kill 'em if they do." Eddie stops puffing now as Sonny continues, walking closer to Eddie's bunk. "You gonna get off your skinny ass and collect your debts? Huh, Eddie?" Sonny is standing over him now; the con is frightened. "You're lucky I'm makin' you a partner, Eddie. I'd just as soon knock ya off and take over, but I need ya . . . you know who supplies the drugs."

Eddie looks up at him. "O.K., Sonny . . . listen, you won't have no beef from me . . . fifty-fifty's fair for what you do."

"Eddie, if you really knew what I could do, you'd have shit in your stinkin' pants by now . . . don't make me have to show ya." Sonny uses the same strong-arm tactics in prison that he used when he was working on the streets of Chicago, and everyone is just as terrified of him now as they were then.

Despite his power in prison Sonny wants out. He still wants to get to a camp center. There has been no word about when his counselor will see him until one day Officer Buchanan comes to his cell with a pass. "Barker's gonna see ya at ten tomorrow."

Sonny takes the pass. "Man, that's right in the middle of my workout time."

"Too bad . . . ya gotta be there, and be there on time."

Sonny jumps up on the bed. "Man, why the fuck couldn't they call me now?"

Spider answers from the bottom bunk, "That's the way they do things. They never call ya when you're in the cell . . ." He adds, "And you'd better be on time. If you're five minutes late, he takes five minutes off your visiting time. If you're a half-hour late, your lose your visit altogether."

Sonny lies back and looks at the ceiling. "Man, this place is fucked up."

The next day Sonny arrives at his counselor's office at ten A.M. exactly. A Mexican who is just leaving shuts the glass door behind him. When Sonny goes to turn the knob, it's locked. Barker is going through some papers, so he knocks to get the counselor's attention. The official looks up, then picks up the phone and dials. Sonny knocks again. This time Barker swivels his chair around so he can't see Sonny. The other convict has waited to see what would happen. He now says cynically, "Forget it, man. He's not gonna open up till he's good and ready."

"Man, I've been waitin' two weeks to see this guy."

The Mexican laughs. "You're lucky, man. Some prisons make ya wait thirty to sixty days to see your counselor." Sonny knocks again, harder this time, but Barker still has his back to him. The convict shakes his head. "I told ya so, man, he ain't gonna see ya."

"How the fuck long do I have to wait here?"

The Mexican shrugs. "Who knows?" He turns to go but comes back. "Hey, man . . . I liked what ya did when ya came in the joint, how ya told MoJo you'd fuck him up good. The guys all respect ya for it . . . nobody around here likes that black ass. My name's Ramon Juarez. If ya need any stuff, I got a good connection."

Sonny informs him, "I don't use, Juarez."

"Yeah . . . none of you Mafia guys do. Well, I gotta go. Good luck in gettin' to see Barker."

Two hours later Sonny is still sitting there. Finally the door opens, and he stands to go inside. Barker locks it behind him. "I gotta go to lunch, Gibson. It'll be yard recall pretty soon . . . I'll see ya this afternoon. Give me your pass." Sonny hands it to him, and he scrawls his initials approving Sonny's return.

Sonny looks at it. "One o'clock! That's yard time."

"That's when I get back from lunch, Gibson . . . be here then."

When Sonny gets back to the office, the door is closed again, but this time it is only thirty minutes before it opens and he is summoned inside. Barker, in his fifties, has a chalky complexion that makes him look like he's suffering from constipation. He indicates a chair next to his desk for Sonny and pulls out a file. Barker flips through it for a few seconds, then speaks bombastically. "I've been studying your jacket,

Gibson. The reason you had to wait so long this morning was it took me quite some time to read it."

Sonny doubts that. "It took you two hours just to read my file?"

Barker says sternly, "You're a wise guy, Gibson . . . that's what probably got you in here."

"No . . . I got sent up for assault and bribery."

"Don't tell me what you're here for . . . I know exactly what you're here for." He closes the folder. "Gibson, you're going to be under observation for ninety days, and I have the job of determining where you will be placed."

"What are the chances of gettin' transferred to a camp center?"

Barker leans back in his chair and laughs. "You . . . go to a camp center! You're on a life sentence, Gibson. You're 'max-max'—organized crime and Mafia. The President of the United States couldn't get you sent to a camp center if he was your counselor. You'll be lucky if you get a contact visit, Gibson." He leans across the desk vindictively. "I doubt if I'd even recommend you for that." It's obvious now that the father figure mentioned in orientation is a myth. Barker continues sarcastically, "I got a letter from your common-law wife . . . Tell her to quit bothering me, she calls every day."

Sonny says hotly, "That's 'cause you never write back and tell her nothin'."

The counselor snaps, "I'm gonna give you disciplinary if you're disrespectful to me again, Gibson."

Sonny shouts, "I don't give a shit."

"You yell at me one more time and I'll pull your visiting privileges . . . I have the power to do that." This is Barker's ace. Theresa's visits are important to Sonny. "You owe me an apology, Gibson."

Sonny says quietly, "All right, Barker . . . I'm sorry." The counselor shakes an index finger at him. "Uh-uh-uh . . . *Mr.* Barker."

Sonny holds his temper. "I'm sorry . . . *Mr.* Barker. Can I go now?"

Barker smiles. "Sure. Come back anytime you have a problem, Gibson . . . my door's always open."

That Sunday, when Theresa visits, she gives him an update on the outside world. "I quit singing at the club last night."

"Why?"

She hesitates. "I just didn't like it, that's all . . ."

"But you were so excited."

"I know, but it turned out the guy wanted me to do more than sing for him."

"What guy wanted more . . . who was it?" Sonny is burning. "I wanna know, Theresa!"

She says reluctantly, "The owner."

"That son of a bitch."

Theresa tries to cool him off. "It's O.K. . . . . I didn't like that smoky club, anyway. I applied for a job at a medical firm . . . I think I'm gonna get it."

"Did you go see Chet?"

"Yes . . ."

"What'd he say?"

"He told me things were slow and there weren't any openings right now."

Sonny is suspicious. "What'd he say about lending you the money?"

"He said he'd do that, but I'd have to wait a couple a weeks."

"Make sure he gives it to ya, so ya can stay in that apartment."

"I will." She says, perking up, "Did you get my poetry?"

Sonny smiles. "Yeah, baby . . . Spider says it's real good . . . he reads a lotta that stuff."

"I'm going to write music around the words . . . I have some of the melodies in my head, and I bought one of those portable cassette players so I could sing in the car on the way up here. I'll play you the songs when I'm finished." Theresa continues filling him in on the news. "Pops is coming to live with me . . . he'll be looking for a job, too."

"What happened?"

She explains sadly, "They took away the lot and the house you bought."

Sonny bangs his fist on the table. "Damn, I told Pops to sell out months ago. Why the hell'd he wait so long?"

"He thought you'd pull through somehow . . . everything would be okay."

"Goddam it."

Theresa says gently, "Don't be too rough on him, honey. He's taking all this pretty hard. He wants to come up and see you when he gets here. Is that O.K. with you?"

"Yeah . . . it's O.K."

"Linda wants to come up, too. She won't be able to come up with me 'cause she's not family and I'm not giving up my visit for *her,* Sonny."

He thinks a second. "Tell Linda there's no point in comin' all the way up here anyway. I'll be out soon. How does she like Tahoe?"

"Not much . . . she said to tell you she's anxious to work for you again. Hospital work is boring."

Sonny smiles. "Tell her it's not too excitin' here either . . . and thank her for the card. She knows why I'm not writin' back. I don't think Spider would like the idea of bein' my new secretary."

Theresa jumps subjects. "You know, I never did get to meet Alfonso. How come?"

"He was too busy. You'll meet him when I get out . . . we'll take a vacation in Sicily." Sonny presses his hand harder on the glass against hers. "Baby, I miss touchin' you. I wanna kiss your body all over. I miss makin' love . . ."

She asks anxiously, "Did you talk to your counselor about going to that camp center?"

Sonny lies, "Yeah . . . he said he'd see what he could do."

"Have you gotten a date for your hearing yet?"

He says confidently, "No, but I've only been in a month. They don't let ya know till it gets closer to the time for the parole board." She frowns. Sonny says quickly, "Don't worry, baby. It'll be all right . . . I know it." She smiles. Sonny has convinced her, but in the back of his mind Alfonso's words still haunt him—"I don't trust them . . ."

Just one week after the run-in with his counselor Sonny meets with another prison official for the first time . . . his psychiatrist. As usual he is called to see him during yard time. This time he doesn't have to wait two hours, but is called into the office as soon as he arrives. Seated behind the desk is a Dr. Gerhardt, a Freudian zealot who resembles the father of psychiatry himself. The doctor's bushy eyebrows knit in a frown as he studies Sonny's file. "Mmm . . . mmm . . ." He turns a page and shakes his head. "Mmm . . . mmm . . . mmm." He looks up at Sonny. "You certainly got around, didn't you, Gibson? It's a wonder they didn't give you the gas chamber instead of life." Sonny knows this is not going to be an easy interview and is glad Gerhardt wasn't the judge on his case. The doctor continues, "It says here you made money peddling your own flesh and that of innocent women." Gerhardt looks at him sympathetically, "Gibson, you really didn't have a normal childhood, did you? Your mother and father quarreled, maybe he beat your mother a lot, eventually they got divorced. Perhaps your mother ended up a prostitute."

"She was a saint, and my father never raised a hand to her. I didn't have no problems when I was a kid."

The Freudian rubs his eyes and looks at him. "Then how do you account for your obvious maladjustment to society? This report is staggering. Perhaps you indulged in excessive masturbation as a child."

This is too much for Sonny. "What the fuck does that have to do with my crimes? I jack off in my cell now . . . five, six times an hour when the guards aren't starin' at me."

Gerhardt's eyes widen. "Mmm." He makes a note on his report. "Gibson, tell me, what were your feelings when you killed a man?"

"Wait a minute .. . . who said I killed anybody? I'm not in here for murder . . . I'm in here for assault."

"Mmm-hmm . . . you can't tell the truth, can you, Gibson . . . you're a pathological liar. I mean, you can't be honest with a professional psychiatrist who can help you." He leans back in the chair, tapping his fingertips together in front of him. "And you conned the government. Don't you feel bad that you didn't testify? Those men in the Mafia are selling narcotics to our kids on the streets. They're filling our prisons with junkies and murderers." He looks at Sonny over the rim of his glasses. "Don't you think, as a sensible man . . . you should testify? Don't you have any feelings at all, Gibson?"

Sonny looks at him. "Yes, sir, I do." He stands. "Suck my dick."

Gerhardt's nervous hands come to a dead stop, and his face reddens. "What? Gibson, I'm making out your report for the board . . . this will follow you the rest of your prison days . . . do you know what you're doing? Are you crazy?"

Sonny says snidely, "You get paid to figure that out . . . not me. You're bustin' into my workout time!" With that he turns and walks out, leaving a flustered Gerhardt to finish his report.

From the psychiatrist's office Sonny hurries to the yard. He's backing up Big Jim today. The two enforcers follow Jim's target and two friends into the tunnel, a four-foot-long covered passageway connecting the yard and the prison compound. There is no guard stationed in the short hallway. Jim says, "I'm gonna talk to this guy for a minute." When they get into the tunnel, to Sonny's surprise, Jim grabs one of the men, covers his mouth, and stabs him in the heart five times.

Sonny pulls his shank on the other two. "Freeze, man."

Jim then turns to them. "You say one word and you're next . . . now beat it." The frightened men run back to their cells.

Sonny asks, "How come ya didn't kill 'em? Now ya got witnesses."

Jim says flatly as they hurry back out into the yard, "No witness is safe inside." The rest of his answer is chilling. "Besides, I'm on a life sentence. The hole means nothin' to me, and it'll take a miracle to get me paroled, so I take care of the child molesters and the rats . . . that guy raped a six-year-old."

Sonny shakes his head. They're walking leisurely to avoid suspicion. "Man, rapin' a little kid . . . there's a lotta sick fuckin' people in this world. You were merciful to that son of a bitch . . . I would've cut his dick off."

Jim assures him, "I would've, too, but I didn't have that much time."

"Papa Mike told me you worked for the Patrones in Cleveland."

"I did . . . for seven years."

"What'd you get sent up for? You get caught makin' a hit?"

Jim smiles. "Fuck, no. The family had a place in San Francisco . . . I was workin' as a bouncer. Some guy got rowdy, so I tossed him out. He hit his head on the curb and died on the way to the way to the hospital. The Patrones told me to surrender myself and they'd make my bail. They didn't know there's no bond for murder here. I was supposed to get off with manslaughter, two to ten, but they slapped murder one on me . . . I got life."

Jim takes off his shirt. Sonny asks, "What the hell you doin'? It's fuckin' freezin' out."

"Could be some blood splashed on me, gotta ditch it so they can't match it to the dead guy."

Just then the yard recall whistle blows. The "man down" has been discovered in the tunnel. All of the convicts go back to the cell, where their fingernails and clothes are checked for bloodstains. Jim and Sonny both pass inspection . . . another successful hit.

A few days later, while Spider is reading one of Theresa's poems to Sonny, Officer Buchanan stops at their cell. "I got a pass for ya to go see Barker, Gibson . . . he wants to see ya right now."

Spider looks up, surprised. "That's somethin'. Ya never get a call from a counselor unless they change your classification."

Sonny buttons his shirt excitedly. "Maybe he got Theresa's form back and he's gonna tranfer me to camp center after all."

Spider unzips his fly and stands in front of the toilet. "Maybe, but I wouldn't get my hopes up . . ."

When Sonny gets to the counselor's office, Barker has his feet up on his desk, reading Sonny's psych report. He closes the folder. "I'm very ashamed of you, Gibson . . . you're uncooperative." He sits up. "In light of this report I can't possibly recommend you for a camp center."

"You weren't sending me there anyway, remember?"

Barker points a finger at Sonny. "As a matter of fact, Gibson, if we had a cell under the ground, that's where I'd send you."

Sonny stands. "Ya know what I said to the psychiatrist?"

"You mean that filthy thing you suggested— yes, I just read that."

"Same goes for you, Barker."

He walks out. Barker calls after him, "I'll write you up for this, Gibson . . . I'll write you up." Sonny stops and turns. "If I'm gonna get a writeup. I wanna be sure you understand what I said to the doc." He shouts, "Suck my dick!"

The counselor flies into a rage. "That's it, Gibson . . . don't you come back here again . . . you're finished!"

When Sonny gets to the visiting room on Sunday, he finds out that Barker has filed disciplinary action and pulled his visit. Through the control booth window he can see Theresa waiting in line with the others. She looks tired after the five-hour drive. Sonny makes a mental note to be careful not to lose his visiting privileges. The guard chases him. "All right, Gibson, get back to your cell . . . you're not seein' your old lady today."

When Theresa finally gets to the desk and signs in, the guard shakes his head as he checks his sheet. "Sorry, Mrs. Gibson. You're not on the list . . . your husband's visit's been pulled."

Theresa gets nervous. "Why? What's wrong?"

"I dunno, you gotta call his counselor."

"I've been tryin' to reach him, but he won't return my calls."

"Your husband should've written to tell ya he lost his visit."

Theresa reasons, "But mail takes two or three days."

The guard looks at her apathetically. "I can't help that. Your husband musta done somethin' bad for the counselor to pull his visit. They don't like doing that. We give these men a lotta respect, and we demand the same from them." Then he says, rudely, "Can you step outta the way, lady . . . there's a lotta people behind you."

Bewildered, Theresa moves aside, but in a minute she's back at the desk again. "I wanna see the visiting sergeant."

"Look, lady . . . I have all these people to process through . . . I'll get him for ya when I'm finished. Now, please . . . go stand someplace else."

Theresa waits in the corner of the room for nearly forty minutes before the visiting sergeant, Tom Quinn, finally comes out. He comes up to her and says politely, "What seems to be the problem, Mrs. Gibson?"

She looks at him anxiously. "My husband's visit was pulled. I'm trying to find out if he's in some kind of trouble."

He can see she's distraught. "Look, I'll go back and check. Just wait here."

Only five minutes later Quinn returns. "Don't worry. It couldn't have been that serious, he's back on the list for next week."

"What'd he do?"

"Oh, maybe he got into an argument with a guard, maybe he was late for his job . . . who knows? There are a lotta little things he could've done wrong."

"I wanna thank you for being so nice." Theresa opens her wallet and takes out a $20 bill. "Do you think you could have this put on the books for my husband? He said you had to do that."

Quinn apologizes, "I'm sorry, but we only accept checks or money orders. Mail it in to Accounting and put his name and booking number on it. We can't take cash . . . sometimes the guards forget to turn it in."

Theresa smiles. "I understand."

He says gently, "I'm afraid you'll have to leave now."

"That's O.K. Thanks for all your help." Theresa puts her coat on and walks dejectedly out the door. She looks forward to these visits as much as Sonny and feels the loss of him as acutely now as the day he left . . . Theresa has not yet been able to adjust to life without him.

That week, because he wasn't with Theresa on Sunday, Sonny is especially fierce on the yard. One morning Jim backs him up while Sonny threatens a Mexican who owes $15 for marijuana. "Look, pea-picker . . . I'm not givin' ya another chance."

The mark begs, "Hey, man, don't kill me, just don't kill me. I'll get ya the bread this afternoon."

"No good, greaseball." Sonny starts to drag him away. "We're goin' for a walk in the tunnel now . . ."

In the middle of all this a small skinny man approaches them; he's the prison priest, Father Molinari. "Sonny, I'd like to talk to you."

Sonny stares at him. "Are you crazy, man? Can't you see I'm busy?" The white-haired priest insists, "It will only take a minute of your time."

Sonny knows he can't do anything with a witness around, so he releases the terrified convict with a warning, "I'll see ya in the yard after count . . . I want that money, mop-slinger."

When the Mexican is gone, Father Molinari continues. "I understand that you're half Sicilian, so you must be a Catholic . . ."

Sonny is short with him. "My mother was Catholic . . . I'm not."

"You were never baptized?"

"Yeah, I was baptized, but I don't believe in all that shit, Father . . . you're hittin' on the wrong guy."

Father Molinari says calmly, "O.K., O.K. . . . well, anytime you have a problem, please come see me."

Sonny gets friendlier now. "Hey, Father, I'm having a problem gettin' to the camp center. If I get sent there, I'll tell everybody you helped me and how good the Catholic Church is . . ."

The street-wise priest says evenly, "I didn't say come con me, I said come see me. I'll pray for you, Sonny."

Sonny calls after the gutsy little man who walks away, cassock flapping in the wind, "Don't waste your prayers on me."

Jim yells after him, "Hey, pray for me, Father. I'll take the prayers, O.K.?"

Father Molinari turns. "I will . . . I'll pray for you, too, Big Jim." For a few minutes the hit men watch him circulate among the convicts on the yard. Jim says, "He's goin' up to Juarez . . . that guy's got a lotta guts. Ramon's a hard son of a bitch." As they walk back to the weight pile, he says, "Ya know, you oughtta be nice to Father Molinari . . . priests have a lotta pull in here."

Sonny picks up a twenty-five-pound dumbbell and starts pumping. "Fuck that, Jim, I don't believe in all that religious shit . . . I don't have to be nice to no one."

Sonny's daily pattern at the penitentiary hardly varies from one day to the next: workout, enforce, eat, sleep, and masturbate. Laura, Theresa, Vickie, Hot Pasta, Juanita, and scores of other women all take their turn in his fantasies.

Six months pass and Sonny still has not been called before a parole board. He pesters Barker daily about getting a date for his hearing. One day, after another fruitless visit to his counselor, Sonny returns to find his cellie packing. "Hey, what's this? You gettin' moved?"

Spider says ecstatically, "No, man, I made the camp center . . . fresh air, good food, touch my old lady . . ." He holds up an enormous wooden cross. "This is what did it."

"What the hell is that? Where'd ya get that fuckin' thing?"

Spider beams. "My friend made it." He taps it on the bars. "Solid oak . . . it's my ticket outta here."

"Spider, what the hell you talkin' about?"

"I'm a born-again Christian, man . . . I've been goin' to my counselor all week long, praisin' the Lord." He waves the giant cross in the air. "This is what did it, Sonny."

Sonny leans on the bars. "Come on, Spider, what kind of crap is this?"

His cellmate insists, "They know religious guys don't cause no trouble." Spider is trying to stuff the cross into the cardboard box he's packing. It won't fit, so he shoves it at Sonny. "Here, this served its purpose, I don't need it anymore."

Sonny knocks it to the floor. "That fuckin' thing won't do me no good."

Spider picks it up and hands the cross back. "If you don't wanna use it, give it to a friend a mine in Cell Block G. Tell him about the con I pulled. He can do the same thing."

"Maybe he could, but that goddam cross would never get me outta this place . . . I can't even get to the parole board."

Spider rolls up his mattress. "Religion's it, Sonny . . . that's it. I'm a Jesus freak for the rest of my days."

Sonny says skeptically, "You tellin' me you believe that religion shit?"

Spider straightens up. "Fuck, no . . . but it got me to the camp center."

On the way out he says, "Make sure George Forest in Cell Block G gets that cross, O.K.?"

Sonny watches in amazement as Spider walks down the long hall. "O.K."

The morning after Spider leaves, Sonny goes to look for George in Cell Block G. He says to the module officer, "I wanna take this cross to George Forest."

The guard says, "He's cleanin' up the showers now . . ."

"Can I go back and give this to him?"

"Yeah, O.K." The guard calls after Sonny, "But don't stay more than a couple of minutes . . . this is yard time. You're not supposed to be in this block." When he gets to the humid showers, Sonny searches for George. His voice echoes off the tile as he shouts for him, but Spider's friend is nowhere in sight. Suddenly Sonny hears footsteps behind him. He spins around fast and is confronted by MoJo with two of his friends. The huge black flashes him a malevolent grin. "Time to get your pants down, white boy . . . we gonna butt-fuck you good . . ."

Sonny snarls, "Don't you come a fuckin' step closer, nigger."

MoJo pulls a shank from his sleeve, the biggest knife Sonny has ever seen. The other two blacks pull out their shanks now and start closing in. "We gonna butt-fuck you after MoJo tears up your white ass." Sonny has no shank, but when they come toward him, his Sicilian defense training goes into action. He assumes a karate stance and slices the air in front of him with the giant cross, knocking the shank from MoJo's hand. It lands behind Sonny. When one of the blacks comes close, Sonny swings the hard edge of the cross under the man's chin, breaking his jaw and knocking him out. Then Sonny pretends to be going after MoJo. As soon as the third black lunges Sonny turns the giant cross and smashes it into the aggressor's throat. With the wind knocked out of the man, Sonny kicks him in the balls, sending him sliding across the slick tile to the other end of the showers. Sonny grabs the nearest shank, but MoJo is now so scared of that cross, he reaches up to shield his face, leaving his body open for attack. Sonny sticks the shank through the black man's chest, forcing it out his back. The impaled giant doubles over, and with all his strength Sonny crashes the cross down hard on MoJo's head, splitting the skull wide open. The black reels back, blinded by the blood pouring into his eyes. He staggers for a few seconds, finally slumping to the concrete. Sonny hurries out of the showers, but when he gets out on the tier, he walks casually back to B Block. On the way he takes off his jacket and shirt to wipe the blood from the cross, then throws his clothes in the hallway.

In the meantime one of the blacks limps out onto the tier for help, telling the module officer that he fell in the showers. The guard takes him to the infirmary, and when he leaves, the black tells the medics that two men are hurt badly in the G Block showers. Three of them race to the scene. The convict practitioners know that if they can get a wounded man mobile enough to go back to his cell, the guards may never find out there's been trouble. When disciplinary action is the consequence—black, white, or Mexican—the men stick together . . . convicts have more hatred for the system then they have for each other.

They arrive to find both blacks bleeding badly. MoJo is unconscious, the other is moaning in pain. Two of the medics rush over to begin administering aid, but one of them hangs back . . . Tommy is paralyzed with fear. He watches his partners carry the one dazed black back to the infirmary. As though in a trance, Tommy walks over to MoJo just as he's coming round. The black can barely see the outline of a man, but starts begging him for help. "Get me to hospital. I'm hurt bad . . . can't breathe." Tommy kneels down beside him. MoJo clutches at the knife desperately. "Don't pull the shank out . . . don't pull it out." Even in his delirium he knows once it's removed, blood will gush from the wound.

Tommy assures him in an eerie monotone, "Don't worry, man . . . I'm not gonna pull it out for long . . ." He starts shaking with rage. "I'm gonna put it right back in." He grabs the knife, which slices the black man's palms as it comes out of his chest. Tommy raises the shank over his head and with both hands plunges it into MoJo's crotch, then starts stabbing him insanely. The big man writhes and tries to get away, but he can't escape the blows. Unearthly death screams reverberate through the showers. Soon the huge body is motionless, the torso a bloody mass. Tommy has cut MoJo from his balls to his throat . . . in one minute he has stabbed MoJo forty times. The young boy has finally gotten revenge for his vicious rape.

When the other medics return, the knife is still in Tommy's hands. MoJo's nearly severed head is rolled to the side, eyes frozen open in fear. One of the medics takes the knife. "I'm glad you killed that motherfucker." He sticks the shank back into MoJo's chest, then helps Tommy out of his bloody jacket and throws it over MoJo.

The module officer arrives a minute later . . . he'd seen the medics heading for the showers. All three convicts are around MoJo, pretending to save him. The guard hovers over them. "Is he breathing?"

Tommy looks up emotionlessly. "Nope . . . this one's dead."

The officer radios the security control booth. "Man down in G Block showers . . . he's dead. Should we call a lockdown?"

The voice on the other end crackles impatiently, "Of course, you dumb ass . . . we got a riot on our hands." Guards know if they label any trouble "a riot," they'll get double pay for hazardous duty.

The yard whistle blows, and the men are called in for count. By this time Sonny is near his cell. The doors slide open and slam shut almost immediately. The guards call out, "Lockdown, lockdown. This is a lockdown."

Sonny asks the con in the next cell, "What the hell's a lockdown?"

The veteran says, annoyed, "It's a fuckin' pain in the ass. No goin' to chow, no visits, no yard time, no nothin' except a bologna sandwich, a cookie, and an orange at night."

"How long you think we'll be locked up?"

"Twenty-four hours a day till they figure it's safe or when they feel like lettin' ya out . . . but they're gonna be around soon to harass everybody."

Within fifteen minutes after lockdown guards are crawling over every tier, emptying out the cells for inspection. Sonny is smelling the perfume on Theresa's letters when they drag him out of his cell and start tearing it apart. "You've been accused of making that hit, Gibson."

Sonny says innocently, "What hit?"

The guard growls, "All right, Gibson . . . STRIP!" They inspect his fingernails for blood and skin-search him. One of the officers in the cells yells, "Where's your other shirt, Gibson, you only have one here."

"Somebody stole it in the yard."

He finds Sonny's cross. "We'll take this."

Sonny argues, "Hey wait a minute . . . I'm religious, you can't take my cross, man."

"It's evidence, Gibson. It's gotta be examined in the lab." Sonny knows he's cleaned off the blood, but he's sure it's been nicked in the fight. The guards shove him down the hall. "Come on, Gibson . . . you're going to the hole."

Sonny is held in segregation for two days, but because he hasn't been found guilty, is allowed to keep his clothes on and go out to the bathroom. In spite of these "conveniences" the hole is not a place Sonny would like to see again soon. On the third morning of solitary Sonny is called up for his disciplinary hearing. He remembers what Conway said in orientation about lieutenants being gods there; he can only hope his will be a merciful one. When he is brought into the hearing room, Sonny recognizes Lieutenant Jefferson, the Southerner from R & R. Seated next to him is Sergeant Conway and the first officer who was on the scene of the hit. Jefferson drawls, "You a religious man, Gibson?"

Sonny says solemnly, "Yes I am. My cellmate, Spider, read me the Scriptures, and I've been saved . . . I'm born again."

Conway shouts, "Don't believe him . . . Gibson is a hit man in the yard."

The lieutenant holds up the cross. "Is this yours, son?"

After a slight hesitation Sonny says, "Yes, sir, it is."

"Did you use it on those three niggers?"

The lieutenant's bigotry is showing, so Sonny quickly says, "No, sir, I didn't use it on no niggers. That would be sacrilegious."

Jefferson points the cross at Sonny. "I believe you, boy, 'cause this cross came back from the lab clean." He sits back and proclaims, "If he used a cross, it wasn't this one." For an instant Sonny believes there's a God, but what he believes in even more is the incompetence of the prison lab technicians.

Conway protests, "But the two blacks saw him use that cross."

"Look, Conway, don't insult my intelligence. First place, I don't believe no niggers. I know how niggers lie, especially if they're not Christian niggers. Second place, that nigger boy was stabbed forty times. Now, no cross is gonna do that." Jefferson hands the religious symbol over the desk to Sonny. "You can have this back, Gibson."

The officer on the scene protests, "But Gibson was in that area looking for someone just before the hit."

Sonny agrees. "Yeah, I went in lookin' for someone, but I came out when he wasn't there."

The lieutenant checks the report. "That's right, it says here the module officer recalls letting him back into the cell block before yard recall." Jefferson says effusively, "You know, I'm a Christian, too, Gibson. I'm glad to see you found religion, boy, 'cause you got a lot of days to spend in here. You'll find it's a comfort, son . . . yessir, a real comfort." He hands the files to an annoyed Sergeant Conway. "Gibson didn't do this . . . I know killers . . . and he doesn't look like a killer to me." The lieutenant looks at Sonny. "You didn't kill those damn niggers, did you, boy?"

"No sir."

Jefferson stands. *"Case dismissed!"*

When Theresa comes to visit the next Sunday, she is sick with worry. "Sonny, what happened? I called the counselor to see about the letters for the parole board and they said you were in the hole. Are you all right?"

Sonny calms her, "I'm O.K. It was just a misunderstanding."

"What's the hole . . . what is that? It sounds awful."

Sonny doesn't want to scare her by telling Theresa what it really is, so he says, simply, "The hole is segregation . . . like solitary confinement. You can't see nobody."

Theresa is still concerned. "Barker said they might prosecute you for this killing."

Sonny tries to dismiss it casually. "Oh, those counselors . . . they'll tell you anything. Besides, the lieutenant already dismissed the case. There's nothin' to prosecute me for."

She looks at him gravely. "Sonny, did you kill that man?"

"No . . . I wouldn't do anything like that, Theresa . . . especially not before my parole hearing."

She asks hopefully, "Have you heard anything about when that will be?"

"Yeah, I'm supposed to go any day now, but Barker won't tell me shit."

"I called him the other day to get the right wording on the character reference letters you need for the board. I sent one out to Chet and Jack."

"Did Chet lend you any money yet?"

"No, he won't even return my calls."

Sonny covers his anger. "O.K. You have Richie come see me next week . . . I wanna talk to him."

She pauses before she brings up the next item. "Sonny, you're not gonna like this, but the best offer I had on the limousine was thirteen thousand."

"What! That's a fuckin' eighty-thousand-dollar car."

"I know, but nobody cares about the options . . . the computer equipment, the alarms, the bulletproof glass. The dealers only care about what the car itself is worth."

"Don't sell it yet. Chet'll give ya the twenty-five grand. Try to hang on till then." He changes the subject. "How's your job?"

"O.K. I like the people there . . . and I got a promotion already. I'm a secretary, but it's a good thing there's not much typing—I'm so slow. Pops has a job now, too . . . he's parking cars. it's not much money, but it keeps him busy." She smiles, "He runs that lot like a real tyrant. The other day he chased a guy halfway to Beverly Hills when he didn't pay." They both laugh. As usual, the phone cuts off too early, and another thirty minutes with his love is over all too soon.

The next Sunday Richie comes to visit instead of Theresa. It's been over seven months since he's seen Sonny. They pick up the phones. "Hey, Boss, you look good! You look like you're losin' some weight."

"Yeah, I am . . . ya know they don't feed in here like Joe does. How're ya doin' Richie?"

"I'm O.K. The assholes took away my gun permit . . . I hope I can get it back someday."

Sonny tells him with certainty, "Don't worry about it. When I get out, you won't be needin' one."

Richie is worried. "When are ya gettin' out, Boss? . . . It's way past six months now."

"I know, but I never thought it'd be six months exactly . . . things move slow in here." Sonny asks anxiously, "How are the guys doin'?"

"Fine . . ." Richie frowns, "Well, not fine, really . . . Georgie hates workin' for Frank."

"Why? He wanted to go to New Orleans."

"I know, but Frank always makes him get out and open the door. Georgie's gotta wear a cap and gloves, too, like a fuckin' chauffeur."

Sonny is amazed at this pretension for a Mafia don. "What! Why's he have to do that?"

"Frank hangs around with a lotta bankers and high-society people."

Sonny nods. "Then it's for a good reason."

"Yeah . . . well, you hung out with fancy people, but you never did that, Boss."

"I'm not Frank." Sonny switches the phone to his other ear. "How are Angelo and Tony?"

"Angelo doesn't like Sam . . . he thinks he's a little con, and Tony . . . Tony hates him. I'm afraid he might kill him, Boss. He said Sam makes the bodyguards eat at a separate table . . . you always let us eat with you, when it wasn't business."

Sonny explains, "He's old . . . Sam comes from the old school . . . he treats bodyguards like servants."

"Angelo wants to come see ya, Boss . . . he calls me every day. When I told him about Chet, he wanted to wrap the guitar around Chet's neck . . . He said he gave him the twenty-five G's. He said he'd go get it if you want, Boss."

"No . . . tell Angelo to keep cool. He'd kill Chet, and that's all I need. You go see Chet."

Richie sighs. "I'll try Boss, but I don't think he'll see me."

"Why not?"

" 'Cause the FBI came down hard on him . . . and Jack and Jimmy Taggert. The feds gave 'em a lotta hassle. They think because these guys ran with you, they know where a lotta money's at. The cops also told Chet and Jack you were gonna take 'em for millions of dollars."

"What! Those cocksuckers!"

"I'll go see Chet if ya want."

Sonny reconsiders. "No, don't, Richie . . . it might cause ya some heat. The feds'll think you're tryin' to extort money or you're threatenin' him. I got a letter in to Chet and Jack . . . I'm waiting to hear from 'em for a parole reference."

Richie says confidently, "I know one of 'em will come through, Boss. You did a lot for those guys."

The afternoon Richie leaves, Sonny goes into the yard to work out with Big Jim. At 1:30 the yard recall whistle blows. Sonny puts down the curl bar. "Shit . . . what the fuck's happenin' now?"

Ramon Juarez says as he passes the weight pile, "Two blacks and three white guys got stabbed."

Sonny picks up the oak cross he now carries with him wherever he goes. The tension between the races builds as they walk back to the compound. "What's it about?"

Juarez explains, "It's over the kid that got raped yesterday."

Jim says, "Did ya hear how he got raped?"

"No . . . I just heard he did."

Juarez tells him. "The blacks stuck a broom handle up his ass and broke it inside him . . . they expect him to die. Some of the whites got tired of that shit."

Sonny sighs. "Well, you can forget workin' out for a few days."

Jim says, "Yeah, ya might even forget visits if they don't open up by the weekend.''

Someone shouts from across the yard, "Hey, Mafia-and-the-Cross man. Where were you when the shit hit the fan?"

"I was on the weight pile with Big Jim . . ."

Someone else shouts, "Hey, Gibson, how come you carry that cross?"

Another con jokes, "Sonny's religious, man."

Jim yells back, "Yeah, he religious just like me . . . we pray while we're workin' out together."

A Mexican shouts, "You better get on your knees and start prayin' if Sonny comes after ya with that cross. I'd rather face the barrel of a shotgun than that fuckin' thing." Because it's a symbol of Christianity, Sonny is allowed to carry the giant cross on the yard, but he uses it as effectively as any knife or gun to enforce. Sonny is just about at the door when the con going in next to him says, "Hey, Mafia-and-the-Cross man. I'm in the cell below ya. How 'bout tradin' your cookies for my oranges?"

"All right, you got a deal. Give 'em to the tier jerker, O.K.?" This is the con that mops off the tiers.

"Sure . . . talk to ya later."

The yard didn't open up until the next Monday, so Sonny lost his visit with Theresa. He did, however, see one person that week . . . Harold Liebowitz. When Sonny gets to the attorney's room, he remembers how much he dislikes this skinny, hirsute lawyer. "What the fuck's goin' on, Liebowitz? It's two months, almost three past my board! By the way, where the hell is Stevens? How come he never comes with you?"

The counselor hedges. "Well, he's on another case right now that's taking up a lot of his time . . . it's that big murder trial. He's defending that guy who killed his whole family."

"Oh, one a those glamor things where he can get a lotta press, huh? You ask that asshole what the fuck happened to his friend's deal . . . he'll know what I mean. I'm supposed to be out by now—when the hell am I gettin' to the board?"

"Any day, any day."

Sonny flares, "You're no better than those fuckin' counselors." He leans across the table and whispers fiercely at Liebowitz, "I wanna hear I'm gettin' parole next time I see you, understand?"

The attorney closes his attaché case. "I'll do my best . . . I can't make any promises."

"If you wanna stay healthy, you'll do more than your best. You'll get me to the fuckin' board."

Liebowitz stands. "Good-bye Sonny. I'll see what I can do."

By the time Sunday rolls around, Sonny is so excited about seeing Theresa that he paces in his cell for two hours, straining to see the red

Capri through the dirty window across the tier. When he sees the car, Sonny goes to the mirror to comb his hair. The guard comes by forty minutes later with his pass, but it is almost an hour after that before Theresa is finally in the seat across from him in the visiting room. As usual they kiss through the glass and put their hands up to the window while they talk. "Honey, are you okay? When I came last week, they told me there was a riot in the prison. What happened?"

"Nah, it was nothin'. The guards say there's a riot whenever there's any trouble . . . they get more money that way. A coupla guys got into a fight is all." Sonny smiles, "Have you been gettin' my letters? Since Spider left, I got this Mexican guy who cleans the tiers up to write for me. I can't tell if his handwriting's good enough to read, though."

"It's fine. I got one yesterday. Something else came, too . . . a letter from Chet Bartlett."

Sonny says anxiously, "Did ya make copies? I wanna give it to my counselor . . . he told me the board might be comin' in this week."

Theresa shakes her head. "I don't think you'll wanna show it to them."

"Why not? What's it say?"

She pulls an envelope from her purse. "It was sent by his secretary." Theresa reads, "I am sorry for the delay in answering you, but Chet has been out of town for the past two months. In reply to your letters, due to circumstances which have arisen concerning Mr. Gibson, it is Chet's request that he no longer be considered involved with Mr. Gibson or his affairs. Consequently, he regrets that he cannot be of help to you." Theresa folds up the paper angrily. "I can't believe this, Sonny. You two were so close . . . you played golf practically every day. When he was in town, you treated him like a king." She puts the letter away. "How about Jack? Do you think you'll hear from him?"

Sonny's reply is pessimistic. "I doubt if I'll hear anything from Jack."

"Well, how important do you think these letters really are?"

Now Sonny explodes at her. "They're important. They're goddam important . . . everything's important. Guys say if you have letters, it'll help ya."

"Richie told me in the courtroom you had some kind of a deal. Do you have a deal?"

"What the hell's wrong with you, Theresa? We're on the phones at the state penitentiary."

She sighs. "I'm sorry, I forgot . . ."

Theresa looks at him, eyes pleading. "Sonny, if there's any way you can come back home, please . . . do it . . . I need you. I miss you." She starts to cry.

Sonny wishes he could kiss away her tears. "It's all right,

baby . . . I'd like to have the letters, but I'll get my parole without 'em. Don't you worry about it. How's Pops doin'?"

She sniffles. "He's O.K." Theresa smiles. "He's a character. Pops has a little side business going now. He sells tool kits to the customers. It brings in a little extra for the rent."

"That's good, baby . . . you can bring him up with ya next time. Have ya hea——" The phones cut off. There is never enough time for Sonny to catch up on everything in thirty minutes. They kiss through the glass and say "I love you" before Theresa has to vacate the hard stool for the next poor wife or relative of a man behind bars.

On Monday Sonny goes through the battery of psychological tests needed to complete his classification. The IQ test is administered orally; his score is 162. If he could read or write, Sonny would have a good chance of getting an education, but school is the furthest thing from his mind. He knows the parole board is coming in that week, and Sonny wants his hearing.

On Tuesday the word is out all over the prison compound that the board will be there on Friday. Thursday afternoon a list is posted in each block with the names of the men who are scheduled to appear. The crowd is four deep around it. Sonny yells to Juarez in front, "Hey, Ramon, is my name there?"

"I dunno, Mafia-and-the-Cross man. I don't got no time to look."

Most of the men turn away cursing their exclusion. When Sonny finally gets to the list, he checks the numbers anxiously, but his is not there. He leafs through the papers scanning every sheet for his name. Sonny kicks the wall. "That fuckin' Liebowitz. I'm gonna cut off those measly balls of his." He walks back to the tier with Ramon.

"Bad luck, man, you're not on."

"You on it, Juarez?"

"Yeah . . . but I've been waitin' a year, man. It's about time."

The yard recall whistle blows, and the cells open. Sonny goes into his. "So long, Juarez . . . good luck, man."

Sonny can't believe that he's been overlooked. He's so sure there's been a mistake, when Buchanan comes by with the night mail, Sonny asks, "Hey, ya got my ducat for the board tomorrow?"

The officer checks his list. "Your name's not down here Gibson . . . I'm tired of this shit." He shouts across the tier, "All right you guys, listen up . . . I told ya once, I'm not tellin' ya again. If you're not on the list, you're not goin' to the board tomorrow. I have no ducats except for the men on the list." He turns back to Sonny. "Ya understand now, Gibson?"

"Yeah, yeah, bullshit to that. I should've been to the board three months ago."

"Gibson, that's your problem . . . take it up with your counselor."

He turns and walks down the hall.

Sonny calls after him, "I'd have better luck talkin' to the shitter!"

The next day Sonny goes out to the yard at nine o'clock. He's taking his anger out on the bench press when his name comes on the PA. "Gibson, report to the control booth."

Sonny drops the bar. "What the fuck do they want?"

At the booth inside the guard says, "You're supposed to be over at the board, Gibson."

Sonny is flabbergasted. "What? My name wasn't on the list."

The guard checks. "Well, it's in my book. You're supposed to be there now. You're already late. You'll probably have to wait till this afternoon, but go on over to the board room now in case they get finished with the first group early." Sonny hurries to the small office where the parole board is meeting and waits for two hours.

When the yard recall whistle finally blows, the guard outside the door says, "All right, Gibson. Get back to your cell for count."

"What if the board's ready to see me?"

"If they wanna see ya, we'll send an officer to come get ya, but ya gotta go back for count now."

Regulations require that the prison physically count heads six times a day to ensure that no man has escaped. Counts are at two, five, and eleven-thirty in the morning, four-thirty in the afternoon, and nine and midnight in the evening. The module officer assigns two guards to check that each convict is in his cell. At night they shine a flashlight in the sleeping man's face. After each count the number of "live bodies," men in their cells, is called into control. Industry, the department that records the men on work detail, phones in their "dead count," convicts out of their cells. Control then adds the two figures. The sum must match the total number of men in the prison population. If they match, a buzzer sounds, releasing the men. If they don't, a recount is called; the men are required to stand at the bars where the guard can see them. This time when the dead count is called in by Industry, the names and IDs must be checked against one another. Any recount before a meal cuts into chow time.

Fortunately the 11:30 A.M. count comes back all clear, and the convicts move on to the chow hall. Sonny gets his lunch ration— a bowl of beans, a slice of bread, one pat of margarine, and some Kool-Aid— then sits down next to Zabinini. As they eat, Sonny watches the guards pacing the catwalks like panthers ready to pounce on their prey. Sonny puts some beans on the bread. "Man, I still can't get used to those guys up there."

Zabinini nods. "I know what you mean, Santino. In fifteen years I haven't gotten used to them either."

"Ya know, Zabinini, I never asked you what ya got sent up for."

The old man says, "I wrote a bad check for some groceries."

"What! How'd ya get fifteen years for that?"

"I didn't . . . I only got a year for that, but they gave me an extra year 'cause I was Italian. We all get labeled Mafia." He smiles. "Only some of us deserve it."

"So how'd ya get the fifteen?"

"I was on the canteen line when a guy came up to me with a pipe to steal my stuff. I was strong, then, so I grabbed it and used it on him . . . that got me assault, and fifteen more years. . . . I'll be goin' home in nineteen months, Santino."

"Zabinini, what'd ya do on the outside?"

"I was a musician . . . I never made a name for myself, but I played pretty damn good guitar in my day."

"Yeah . . . I've heard ya playin' those Italian songs on the yard. It's too bad ya don't have a mandolin . . ." Zabinini lights up, "As a matter of fact my sister's sending my father's mandolin from Sicily. You're gonna love it, Sonny. In the old days the Mafia soldiers used to carve their names in the wood."

"I'll bet it's really beautiful, huh?"

"A real work of art, Santino . . ."

"When's it comin'?"

"It should be here next week. The warden's already approved it. He likes me . . . I play country music for him."

Sonny looks up at the huge clock in the chow hall. The conversation hasn't taken his mind off the board. He goes back to his cell and waits for another hour before an officer finally comes to unlock it. "The board's ready for ya now, Gibson." Sonny follows the guard closely, annoyed at the man's slow pace. He knows that every step is bringing him closer to his release from the fetid, concrete pit.

When they get to the board room, Barker is outside. "I wish most men luck, Gibson, but you won't need it." He grins, "All the luck in the world's not gonna get you out." He opens the door. Sonny starts to go in, but Barker stops him. "You're gonna have to wait till you're called, Gibson. The board has to review your file."

Forty-five minutes later Barker sticks his head out. "Come on in, Gibson. They're ready to see ya now." Sonny enters the room and stands before the two board members and a special prison counselor, all of whom are seated behind an old wooden table. Sonny has been waiting a long time, so he thinks they must have given his case special attention because of the his deal. One of the board members is Italian, Joe Vitone. This is an encouraging sign to Sonny, but Vitone looks at him sternly. "Gibson, it looks like you've been in more trouble since you came in than before you got here." He closes the folder. "In light of this I have no alternative but to deny you parole. As a matter of fact,

Gibson, we considered giving you a ten-year review date, but since three years is our policy, I'm going to put you down for a three-year review."

Sonny is confused. "Lemme ask ya somethin'. Does that mean that I'm gettin paroled and I'll be reviewed in three years?"

Vitone laughs. "*No,* Gibson, it means you'll be in for three years before we even consider you for another hearing." He emphasizes, "Not parole . . . it will be May, 1977, before you can even come to the board for a parole review hearing. I told you we could make it ten years. If we wanted to, we could make it fifty . . . you're on a life sentence."

The rancor in Vitone's voice makes Sonny uneasy, but he still thinks Vitone is the plant who's putting on an act for the other members of the board. "Don't you have any record, say from Sacramento, that I'm supposed to get paroled now?"

Vitone laughs again. "Are you kidding, Gibson? Your psych report says you're mentally unbalanced, violent, and potentially dangerous. With that kind of a report I wouldn't let you out if the governor himself gave you a pardon."

Sonny starts yelling, "That can't be! . . . I'm supposed to get a date . . . I'm supposed to released."

Vitone says firmly, "That's enough outta you, Gibson." When Sonny quiets down, Vitone continues, "You're not being released anywhere. I doubt if you'll ever be . . . this hearing is over."

Barker approaches. "That's it, Gibson."

Sonny pushes him away. "That's it, shit." He leans across the table, into Vitone's face. "Look, motherfucker, I'm supposed to get released . . . you're supposed to know about it."

Barker pushes a buzzer. "Get in here and remove Gibson . . . if he gives ya any trouble, let me know. I'll send him to the hole."

Sonny shouts, "Fuck you, fuck the hole." The guards come in and drag a yelling Sonny from the room. "You're all a bunch of cocksucking assholes!"

As soon as Sonny is gone, Vitone looks at the other two men. "Gerhardt was right . . . he does have a filthy mouth."

On the way back to his cell the guard warns, "Ya know you should be cool, Gibson. If Barker says put ya in the hole, ya go to the hole . . . so just calm down."

Sonny spits at him verbally, "Fuck the hole and fuck the system. I don't give a shit about anything anymore."

The day after his hearing, Sonny goes to see Papa Mike; the old man is being released. When Sonny gets to the cell, Matullo is bent over, packing his few things in a small cardboard box. Sonny says, "Papa Mike . . . can I come in your house?"

The old man straightens up. "Come in, Santino . . . sit down. I was going to come see you to say good-bye before I left."

Sonny sits on the edge of the bottom bunk. Directly across from it is a perfect rendering of a colorful Sicilian cart. "Papa Mike, that's a beautiful picture. I wish I had that in my cell insteada those fuckin' nudes."

Papa Mike says seriously, "I would never allow them in my house." Sonny gets up to examine the intricate detail. "This is just like the carts they have in Catania . . . who did this?"

"A young white kid . . . a very fine artist."

"Yeah, there's a lotta talented guys in here. How'd he know what it looked like?"

"I showed him a picture, Santino." Papa Mike pulls out a faded photograph from the box. "This is me and Alfonso standing next to that same cart."

Sonny smiles. "That's Alfonso? He was really handsome, Papa Mike. How old were you then?"

"Twenty-two, Santino, but it seems like two hundred years ago."

Sonny is fascinated by the picture. It had been hard for him to imagine what his godfather looked like this as a youth. "Hey, how'd that painter get those colors so good? . . . this is a black-and-white photo."

"I described them to him, Santino."

"Where'd he get the oils from?"

Papa Mike explains, "He used to take felt tip pens and drain the color from them. If you mix that with a little soap, you'll get an oil that will stick to cement."

Sonny takes a last look at the photo, then hands it back. "You know, Papa Mike, I came to see you because of Alfonso . . . I want you to get a message to Richie for me if ya can."

"Of course, Santino, what is it?"

"Tell Richie to tell Alfonso . . . I'm ready for my bail bond . . . I've been conned by my attorneys."

Papa Mike shakes his head. "Never trust your attorneys, Santino— you of all people should know that."

"You're right, Papa Mike . . . I should've listened to Alfonso and gone to Sicily. They denied my parole yesterday. My next review won't be for three years."

"I heard, but if you remember the things I told you, you'll stay alive to see your next board. Remember, Santino, you can't win in here." He closes the box. "If you get out on bail, look me up . . . we'll have dinner at Little Sicily." The rattle of keys ends the talk. They hug.

"Good-bye, Santino."

"Good-bye, Papa Mike . . . and thanks."

A guard calls through the cell door, "O.K., Matullo, let's

go . . . looks like you're gonna get to die in your own bed." The old man picks up his meager belongings. Head held high, he walks down the long hallway once more, this time to freedom. Sonny watches as he goes and wonders when, if ever, he will be taking that walk. Without parole, Alfonso is his only hope.

For the first time since he's been in prison, Sonny is dreading Theresa's visit . . . he has to break the news about being denied parole to her. As soon as they kiss through the glass and pick up the phones, she asks, "What happened? What'd the board say?"

Sonny evades the question. "Hey, why're you so late today? I've been waitin' over two hours."

She fumes. "I was so mad. I brought my tape recorder to play you some songs, and they told me I couldn't bring it in . . . I had to leave it at the desk. Naturally I didn't want to do that, so I went back to the car. When I got to the desk again, they made me go all the way to the end of the line and sign in again."

"Sergeant Quinn made ya do that?"

"No, no . . . Sergeant Quinn wasn't there."

Sonny comments cynically, "Yeah, they probably transferred him for bein' too nice. I wonder why they wouldn't let ya bring a recorder in here."

"They said there might be a bomb in it."

"A bomb! Those fuckin' guys are crazy. What do they think . . . I'm gonna blow up this window and crawl through? Man, they're really assholes."

Theresa is on to his diversion, "Sonny, what happened at the board?"

"Nothin'."

Her heart stops for an instant, "You didn't get a parole, did you . . ."

Sonny dismisses it. "No . . . I didn't get one. I think I got conned by my attorneys." She looks down sadly. "But don't worry about it. I've got some people workin' on a bail bond for me." He says assuredly, "I'll be home in a month."

"You said you'd only be in for six months . . . it's been eight already."

Sonny snaps, "What the hell can I tell ya, Theresa? The damn board fucked up . . . somebody didn't get the right message. That's why we lost our visit last week. I cussed 'em out . . . the cocksuckers. I told them."

She says quietly, "Do you really think you can get out?"

"Yeah, I'm gettin' out."

"Who's helping you . . . who are those people?" Sonny shakes his head, miming that they shouldn't talk about it. For the rest of the visit they talk about other things . . . the promotion she just got, Pops, his job. But it's hard to keep her real feelings pent up. Theresa doesn't want to break down in front of Sonny, so she finally says, "I think I should go now . . . it's almost time."

"Why? It's not time till they——" The phones cut off. Theresa hangs up and puts her lips to the glass for the good-bye kiss. On the way out she turns and waves. The pathetic image of Sonny behind the tiny window tears her apart. Theresa runs to the car, no longer able to hold back the tears. She puts her head down on the steering wheel and lets the sobs wrack her body. Never in her life has she felt so lonely and alone. When she is cried out, Theresa reaches into the glove compartment for a tissue, recalling what she once told Angelo: "We must be strong . . . for him." She wipes her eyes and starts the car. As soon as Theresa gets home, she'll call Harold Liebowitz. Together they can start working to get an appeal.

Two days later Sonny is taken to the LA court to fight the additional charges the ministers filed on him after he surrendered. While he's waiting in the county jail, Theresa visits him. She is very disturbed.

"What's the matter, baby?"

"Sonny, Liebowitz won't be there tomorrow."

"What?"

"He said he wouldn't represent you unless he got some more money."

"That little asshole Jew . . ."

She goes on, "He won't even return my calls now. The secretary just said he wouldn't be in court."

"That's all right . . . I don't need him anymore anyway, believe me."

After a minute she says, "Sonny . . ."

The tone of her voice telegraphs death. He's never wrong about it. "Who died, Theresa?"

"Angelo."

Sonny is shocked. The big bodyguard had never been sick a day in his life. "How'd it happen?"

"Richie said he was making a hit and he went crazy. Angelo went in and just started shooting at everybody. He didn't even protect himself. Richie says it's like he committed suicide." She pauses, "You know, he was never the same after you went to prison. But what really did it was when he found out you weren't getting out. Angelo started crying like a baby. Sam even called Richie to find out what was wrong, but Richie told him to mind his own business. Angelo wanted to fly out here to kill Stevens. Richie had to go to Chicago to tell him if he did anything, you'd never get outta prison." She continues sadly, "But Angelo called me a couple of nights ago and asked if it was true that you weren't getting out. I didn't know what Richie told him, so I said you were denied parole. Angelo's last words were that he'd be out in California next week to straighten things out. He would've killed Stevens, Sonny."

"It wouldn't have been a bad idea."

Theresa looks at him guiltily. "I feel like I'm responsible for Angelo's death. I wouldn't have told him the truth if I knew he was gonna go crazy like that . . ." She looks at him. "He really missed you."

Sonny sighs. "I know . . . poor Angelo."

"I got the name of the mortuary he's in. We can't afford much, but we'll send some flowers, O.K.?"

"Sure, baby."

When Theresa leaves, Sonny thinks about Angelo. He remembers the bodyguard's innocent offer—"Let me go in, Boss, I'm strong . . . no one's gonna fuck with me." Sonny didn't know it then, but he knows now . . . Angelo was volunteering to condemn himself to hell. Never has he had such a loyal friend . . . Sonny will never forget him.

Sonny is so positive Alfonso is going to break him out that the next day, in court, he asks to see the state attorney. "Look, Masterson, this court shit isn't gonna do me any good . . . what do I have to do to plead guilty?"

The attorney looks at him in amazement. "You know, Gibson, I'm not the government. If you plead guilty, I won't ask for any five-year probation . . . I won't be that lenient."

Sonny interrupts him, "Look, I'm on a life sentence . . . what the hell more do ya want?"

Masterson smiles. "Plead guilty on all counts."

Sonny thinks a second, then says, "You got it, but I want them to run concurrent with all my other beefs or I'll go ahead and fight it, and I wanna get back to the state pen today—I don't wanna wait six weeks in the goddam jail." Masterson hesitates. Sonny says impatiently, "What more do ya want, Masterson? I got life, and it'll be three years before I even get a review for parole."

The vindictive attorney concedes. "O.K., Gibson, I got a heavy case coming up, and I really don't have time for this. When the court convenes, plead guilty . . . you're already in custody, so we'll waive probation reports . . . you can be sentenced at the same time."

Sonny asks, "Can I go back to the pen today?"

"Well, I don't know."

Sonny fights him. "That's the deal . . . I go back today."

"O.K., I'll see to it that the court orders you back today."

Sonny returns to the penitentiary and some more bad news. Richie comes to visit him on Saturday. "Mike Matullo called and told me you wanted Alfonso to get your bail bond."

Sonny asks anxiously, "How soon will he be here?"

Richie looks at him grimly. "Alfonso's dead."

Sonny's heart sinks. "He's what?"

"He's dead, Boss. Your godfather died a week ago. I tried to tell you when you were in the county jail, but you were already on your way back here."

Sonny sits in stunned silence as he thinks about the dire consequences of Alfonso's death. Finally he says solemnly, "Richie, I'm gonna be in prison a long time."

Richie shakes his head. "Boss, I wish you'd never done this . . . Angelo didn't want you to go in."

Sonny thinks back to the day Angelo begged him at the gates not to surrender, then he hears Alfonso's words, "I don't trust them." Sonny says sadly, "I lost a hell of a lot, Richie, a hell of a lot. Get a hold of Aldo in Vegas right away. Tell him what happened . . . tell him to come see me . . . I need to talk to him."

While he's waiting for Richie to get in touch with Aldo, Sonny keeps himself occupied enforcing and working out four hours a day. One morning Big Jim comes over to the weight pile. He tosses his newspaper on the ground. "Hey, Santino . . . you're bench-pressing three hundred pounds . . . you'll be passing me pretty soon."

Sonny gets out from under the bar. "I'm gonna bust some pig heads." As he grabs a towel next to the paper, his eye is caught by a picture of Al Vigiano, Alfonso's friend in Lake Tahoe and one of Sonny's trustees. Sonny hands the paper to Jim excitedly. "Here, read this . . . I know this guy . . . what's it say?"

Jim lies down on the bench press. "I'll read it this afternoon at chow . . . we only got two hours to work out."

Sonny insists, "It's important, Jim . . . read this for me, will ya?"

Jim sits up. He's never heard this urgent tone of voice from Sonny. He scans the article and summarizes: "They blew this guy up in Lake Tahoe. His car was blown to smithereens in his driveway. Police think it's probably revenge . . . a jealous girlfriend or a guy who lost some money in the casino. FBI says it's definitely not linked to the Mafia."

"What? We're always the first ones blamed for everything . . . there's somethin' funny here, Jim . . . I don't like it."

"How do you know this guy, Sonny?"

Sonny says quietly, "He's got half my fortune . . ."

"Half your what?"

Sonny turns away. "Nothin', Jim . . . nothin'."

"The board really made you cold, didn't it man?"

Sonny's jaw tightens. "I was cold when I came through those gates, Big Jim, but not half as cold as I am now . . ."

That Saturday Richie visits him again. Sonny picks up the phone to talk, tapping on the receiver nervously before its turned on. "Hello . . . hello . . . what the hell!" Sonny knows there must be something wrong for Richie to blow a visit for Theresa. As soon as the phone is live, Sonny says anxiously, "What is it, Richie?"

"Aldo died of a heart attack yesterday."

This floors Sonny. "What! Everybody's fuckin' dyin' on me. How do you know? Are you sure it's him?"

"Yeah, I'm sure. I called to find out if he could come up to see you today, and his wife told me he was playing golf in Phoenix. When I called the hotel there, they told me he had a heart attack. He died on the golf course that afternoon."

Sonny doesn't know what to say to Richie, who's not aware of the plus markers in Vegas. Even if Richie knew, Sonny couldn't mention them on the phone. Sonny says numbly, "Tell Maria I'm sorry to hear about Tony, and have Theresa send some flowers . . ."

"O.K., Boss." Richie fills him in on some news. "You know they gave Mario ten years . . . and Don Giuseppe's really sick now. Already everyone's fightin' over his territory. Who do you think's gonna get it, Boss?"

Sonny says expressionlessly, "I don't give a fuck about those people." He looks straight at him. "And Richie . . . I'm not a boss no more."

Sonny is really at a loss. He's been in prison almost a year. His surefire escape died with Alfonso, and now his money is gone, too. Mounting frustration and hate turn Sonny into a vicious animal. His methods of enforcing become more violent and establish his reputation as the "Mafia-and-the-Cross man." Even the guards are scared of him and the cross.

A month passes. It is December, when crowds bustle in department stores buying gifts for loved ones and undernourished sidewalk Santas ring their bells on street corners. The only signs of the holiday season for Sonny are the carols sung on the convicts' radios, and cheery disc jockeys announcing the number of shopping days till Christmas. There is no colder place to be during this time than a penitentiary. The state plays Santa Claus on Christmas Eve by giving the men a sack with an apple, one cookie, and twenty pieces, exactly, of hard candy. Theresa has sent Sonny a package filled with presents, but most of the items are ruled unacceptable. Rather than spend $8 to send them back or throw them in the "shitcan," Sonny donates everything to the chapel. On Christmas Day he and Theresa are allowed to visit through the glass for one hour. They talk about the past mostly, and their first Christmas together—how Angelo carried their enormous tree into the house with one hand, and how they all helped decorate it that night. These are painful memories for Sonny. Angelo is dead, and so are most of the other things he remembers from that time . . . except Theresa. She keeps the small part of him that's still human alive.

On the way back to his cell after she leaves, Sonny sees two men get stabbed, one in the yard, one in the hall. So much for Christmas spirit in the penitentiary. That day Big Jim also knifes two men. One of them dies, and the prison goes into lockdown for a week. Sonny spends his New Year's Eve confined to a cell. Not that there would be much cause for celebrating. Jim is thrown in the hole while they try to get a murder conviction. The warden wants Big Jim on death row.

Before Jim was sent to the hole, he told Sonny about a mile-long sewer pipe that fills with water every hour and washes everything out to the canal. If it's timed properly, and a man is a strong swimmer, he has a good chance of escaping. When Sonny is not enforcing, he spends his time poring over blueprints of the sewage system, which Cigar Eddie has gotten for him. Sonny is obsessed with finding a way to break out.

Through the gravevine Sonny finds out that Big Jim has been sent to the jail. With him and Papa Mike both gone, Sonny spends more time with Zabinini. They now have cells on the same block. One morning on the way to breakfast Zabinini says excitedly, "I'm pickin' up my mandolin today . . . it's here."

"Hey, that's really fantastic . . . now we can have some real Italian music out in the yard."

"I can't wait wait till you see it, Santino . . . it's really beautiful."

Buchanan overhears them talking. "Zabinini, I won't allow a mandolin on my block. I can't allow a man to have an instrument and play in his cell—it's too much noise. As long as I'm unit officer, it won't be approved."

The old man protests, "But the warden already approved it."

Buchanan rants, "I don't care what the warden says, I run this unit . . . I'm the one that has to approve it."

Juarez chimes in from behind them. "Aaa, don't argue with him, you know he's an asshole."

Buchanan threatens the Mexican, "If you don't watch your mouth, Juarez, I'll write ya up for bein' disrespectful to an officer." The guard looks down the hall. "Hey, Montez . . . straighten up . . ." He takes off to harass another victim.

As the convicts walk to the chow hall, Juarez reminds the old man, "Zabinini, if you got a letter from the warden, Buchanan can't say shit about it."

Sonny agrees, "Yeah, the warden runs things around here. If you've got his O.K., Buchanan's gotta eat shit. As a matter of fact you should play louder on his shifts."

Two days later the instrument arrives, and Zabinini skips lunch to get his mandolin from the warden's office. On the way back to "B" his fingers slide lightly over the frets, strumming a plaintive "O Sole Mio" When he gets to the block, one of the guards says to Buchanan, "What's that thing Zabinini's playin'?"

The module officer shouts, "ZABININI!" The old man walks over to him, and the guard says accusingly, "I thought I told you about that. Lemme have it." Buchanan grabs the mandolin. "You're gonna have to keep this instrument in the gym with the others."

Zabinini grabs it back. "No, that's mine."

Just then Sonny comes running in, huffing. "I'm sorry I'm late, Buchanan. I got sick over at chow today. I hadda to throw up, man. I couldn't make it back."

The guard says unsympathetically, "Gibson, I told you I don't like people bein' late in my module."

Sonny gets indignant. "I told ya, I got sick from the fuckin' food here."

"All right, Gibson, get up on your tier . . . I'll let you in when I let Zabinini back in." Before he goes, Sonny spots the instrument. "Hey, you got your mandolin." He fingers the signatures of the Mafia soldiers carved on the deep, rounded body. "I can't wait to hear ya play it."

"GIBSON! Get up to your cell."

"All right, all right . . ."

Sonny turns to Zabinini. "I'll see ya this afternoon on the yard."

He leaves, and Buchanan comes over to the old man. "Lemme have that thing, Zabinini."

"No . . . it's mine. The warden says it's O.K. for me to have it."

"Well, I gotta check with him myself." He tugs at the mandolin. "Lemme have it."

Zabinini resists. The struggle until it finally falls on the floor. The neck of the guitar breaks in two. Zabinini stares down in disbelief at his shattered family heirloom. He stoops to pick up the pieces. Buchanan shouts, "Leave it there . . . get back to your cell. The tier jerker can sweep that junk up with the trash." The guard kicks him in the ass, and the old man stumbles. Sonny is watching the action from above. As Zabinini lifts his head, Sonny sees his chin is bleeding badly where he'd hit it on the concrete. One of the other guards says, "The guy's cut . . ."

Buchanan bellows, "Aaaa, he can take care of himself. Get your ass on up there, Zabinini." The old man takes his mandolin and starts up. Halfway up, Buchanan shoves him with his nightstick, but Zabinini loses his balance and falls back down the flight of steel steps.

Sonny shouts down from the tier, "Hey, man, leave that guy alone, he's old . . . and keep your fuckin' hands off his mandolin." The other convicts have been craning their necks to watch the incident from their cells. They start yelling, too.

"Hey, pig, pick on somebody your own age."

"Yeah . . . lay off grandpops."

"Hey, Mafia-and-the-Cross man . . . help him." Zabinini is lying at the bottom of the steps. Buchanan comes over and kicks him hard in the ribs. "Get up, old man." By this time Sonny is wild. He jumps twenty feet down from the tier, grabs Buchanan, and rams his head into the cellblock door. The men cheer. The other guard is on him by now, but Sonny picks up the 250-pound man and hurls him effortlessly against the bars. Another guard down the hall hits the panic button. Sonny picks up the mandolin and tries to help Zabinini, but the old man is unconscious. The cons on the third tier yell a warning down to him, "Watch out, Sonny, the guards are comin'." Sonny knows he has no escape. He drops the mandolin and leaps up to the second tier again. A year and a half of working out and bench-pressing 300 pounds have made him as strong as Superman. Eight guards come running into B Block. They shout up to Sonny, "Maybe you can take two guards and an old man, but you're not gonna be able to whip us." They're blaming Sonny for what happened to Zabinini.

He yells back, "I didn't touch the old man. That's what this is all about . . . Buchanan and his partner were beatin' him up."

The convicts shout in support, "Yeah, he didn't touch Zabinini."

"The fuckin' pigs did it, man."

The guards yell, "Gibson, we're comin' up."

Sonny leans over the railing, his feet firmly planted. "No, ya aren't . . . you're not comin' to get me, motherfuckers. Don't crowd me . . . I'm warnin' ya."

Buchanan is back in the picture now. "That son of a bitch . . . he's goin' to the hole. GET HIM!"

One of the guards says, "Come on, Gibson, Officer Buchanan wants to talk to ya."

"Talk, shit . . ." Sonny shouts, "You have him come up here and see me." Buchanan starts up the steps. As soon as he gets close enough, Sonny picks him up over his head. The officers below watch in horror as the musclebound convict throws the screaming guard off the tier. More reinforcements arrive. There are now fifteen guards on the block. When they start to converge on Sonny from both sides, he tosses each one over the railing like King Kong swatting flies. After the ninth man hits the cement below, a gun with beanbag pellets is fired at Sonny's legs. It takes five shots to knock him down. As soon as he falls, the guards are on him. They cuff his hands behind his back and knock him out with a nightstick, then drag him by the hair down two flights of metal steps to a small room. There he is forced onto on a wooden bench and stripped. Sonny is just coming to when they put a black hood on him so he can't see who's in the room. The guards beat him savagely.

One kicks Sonny repeatedly in the balls with his heavy boots, while another cracks his nightstick ferociously across Sonny's back. Two others use their sticks on his head. A vindictive remark accompanies each of their blows. "This'll teach you to fuck with us."

"Let's kill the son of a bitch."

"You can't throw our friends off the tier and get away with it . . ."

"You're dead, punk." Even after Sonny has slipped into unconsciousness, the guards continue to pummel his body mercilessly. They are out for blood, and they get it.

Sonny wakes up four hours later, shivering. He has no clothes on. His eyes are badly swollen, but through the slits he can see a bright light overhead. All of his back teeth are knocked out, his body is black and blue . . . he hurts everywhere. Sonny can't walk because the beanbags have cramped his muscles, so he drags himself to the door and pounds on it with what little strength he has left. After about ten minutes a guard comes over. Sonny begs, "Hey, man, I'm cold . . . I need a blanket."

The guard says callously, "You're goin' to the hole, Gibson. You'll get one then, not before . . . but we're watching ya right now . . . just to make sure ya don't cause any more trouble."

Only then does Sonny realize he's in a room that is all windows . . . a glass cage. He says to the guard, "I'm hurtin' bad . . . when am I goin' to the hospital?"

The cruel officer spews hate, "You're not, Gibson . . . you're gonna die." The peephole slams shut. Fatigue overtakes him again, and Sonny slides back down to the icy concrete floor.

Theresa is denied her visit that Sunday. By now she is used to the minor scrapes Sonny gets into from time to time and calls Barker. "When will I be able to see him again?"

The counselor is evasive. "I dunno . . . probably not for a long time . . . he's being detained indefinitely."

She asks anxiously, "Why's that? What's wrong?"

"He's locked up for his own good. He got into a fight with some guards."

Theresa panics. "Is he hurt?"

Barker says casually, "Nah, they didn't hurt him. I saw him this morning . . . he's O.K."

Theresa is unconvinced by Barker that Sonny is unharmed. She goes up to the prison on Sunday to find out for herself. Theresa waits on the long visiting line, and when she gets up to the desk, asks, "Is Sonny Gibson on the list this week?"

The sergeant doesn't even have to check. "Gibson's visiting privileges have been pulled. No one's allowed to see him till there's been a disciplinary hearing." He looks at her cruelly, "Your man did something real bad . . . he beat up on some officers.''

She asks quickly, "Did any of them die?''

"No, but one's in critical condition . . . he has three kids, too . . .'' He says firmly, "Look, lady, you'll have to get off the prison grounds. Warden Hacksworth made it clear you can't see Gibson. You have to leave . . . now.'' He takes her arms and pushes her toward the door.

On the long ride back to LA Theresa stops the car and is sick on the side of the road from the worry. She knows there is nothing at all she can do except call the prison . . . and wait.

Sonny is held in the glass observation cage for three days. The guards come over to torment him, crowding around to watch him defecate in a small cup or ripping up letters from Theresa before his eyes. They want to teach him a lesson for beating up their friends. Sonny is already dropping weight. His only food is some oats in the morning and a bowl of soup at night.

On the third morning the door of the cage opens. "It's time, Gibson.''

Sonny looks up, semiconscious. "I'm goin' back to my cell?''

The guard sniggers. "No such luck . . . you're goin' to the gas chamber.''

"The gas chamber?''

The guard kicks him in the back. "All right, Gibson, get up.'' The room spins as Sonny stands and is shoved out the door. Five guards walk him through an underground corridor, finally surfacing on a prison tier. As they walk down the dark hallway past a long line of cells, the convicts inside all stare but are uncannily silent . . . the eighty-seven men on death row don't have much to say. Even in his stupor Sonny can feel their sands of life running out around him. At the end of the tier the guards stop at a large set of iron doors and push Sonny through. One warns the others, "Make sure it's closed so they don't see us turn right.''

Sonny is still confused. "Where am I goin'?''

"We told ya, Gibson . . . you're goin' to the gas chamber. It's time for your execution.'' The door slams behind them, and they push him along.

As bewildered as Sonny is, he knows something is very wrong. "Wait a minute, where's the priest? Isn't he supposed to be here?''

"Father Molinari wouldn't have nothin' to do with you, Gibson. He said you're worse than the devil himself, and he hopes you burn in hell forever.'' Sonny flashes back to Chicago, when the blacks there called him "The White Devil.'' Is this what they mean? The men now stop at a smaller iron door. They go inside and lead Sonny over to a metal armchair in the center of a five-by-six room. Forcing him down, they start to strap him in. One officer puts a large steel band around his chest to keep him from struggling, but Sonny is so sore that he can barely move. Once the guards fasten his leg and arm clamps securely, they leave. The last one turns. "It's the end of the line for you, Gibson . . . you've beaten up your last guard." He slams the door and takes his place with the rest in the observation booth. Sonny can only see five grinning faces in the small rectangular window . . . one man is waving good-bye. Sonny breaks out in a cold sweat. This must be it, he's going to die. He wonders, after all his denials, if there really is a God after all. Sonny heaves a deep sigh . . . what will death be like? He has killed many men, but Sonny always thought he himself would come to a more violent end, maybe being blown up or shot. Never did he think five men would strap his body into a chair and gas him . . . it was such a passive way for one of the Mafia's finest soldiers to die. Sonny's life does not flash before him, nor does he think of his loved ones. Neither Laura, nor Theresa, or anyone else is on his mind. What he's thinking is that perhaps death will be a relief from life . . . he's still in agonizing pain. Sonny closes his eyes but opens them as the gas starts pouring in . . . or is it? He remembers what Alfonso said, "They can play games with a man's mind, Santino."

Sonny has just closed his eyes again when the door scrapes open. The guards come in, chuckling. He opens his eyes. "Whatsa matter? It's not workin' right?"

One cracks, "Ya know, I lost money on you, Gibson . . . you're the coldest son of a bitch I ever met. I never saw a man in here who didn't beg."

Sonny says groggily, "Can I see a doctor now?"

The guards undo the clamps and pull him up out of the chair. "You're not gonna see anybody for a long time, Gibson . . . let's go." They take the long grim walk past death row, then throw Sonny back into the glass cage. At that moment it looks better to him than any mansion he ever owned. Lying down on his concrete bed, he drifts into sleepy oblivion . . . his only escape from the world.

A few hours later a guard comes to the door. "Hey, Gibson . . . GIBSON." Sonny wakes with a start and in his daze sees a smiling picture of Theresa before him. He drags himself over to the bars to grab it. "Gimme that, you fuckin' pig. You're not good enough to touch her."

The guard laughs. "Yeah, but I'm good enough to fuck her. Your old lady came up here and slept with all the guards." Sonny stands weakly. "You're a godamm liar."

A guard behind him says, "It's true, Gibson. We all had her . . . she was a pretty hot little broad, too." They put a match to the photograph. "You won't be needin' this anymore. Your old lady's dead . . . committed suicide the next day." Sonny watches as Theresa's face disappears in a cloud of black smoke. The guard keeps taunting him. "Ya know you killed her, Gibson . . . if she hadn't come up to see you, she'd be alive."

Sonny lets out a piercing wail. "NOOOO . . ." He goes berserk, pounding the walls of the glass cage with his fist, insane with rage. "FUCKIN' PIGS . . . COCKSUCKIN' PIGS!" He shakes the bars. "Theresa . . . where's Theresa? What'd you do to her, you bastards! The strenuous fit exhausts him, and in just thirty seconds he sinks back down to the sound of their cruel laughter.

On the fourth day of observation Sonny is taken out of the cage. A short walk down a damp corridor leads him to a solid steel door. He is given two paper pails, each about as big as motel ice buckets. One is for his water, the other is for his toilet. The guard hands him five pieces of rough towel to wipe himself. The tumblers of the lock click open, and Sonny is thrown inside the six-by-six metal cage. The door slams shut with a resounding boom. Sonny lies on the cement floor, naked and in pain . . . he still has not received any medical attention. A dim glow from the hall outside seeps under the door, giving enough light for Sonny to make out the faint outline of his hand. He sits against the cold wall and starts to worry about Theresa, but soon drifts off into an aching, troubled sleep.

About an hour later Sonny finds out that there is light in the hole when the brightest light he's ever seen flicks on and off the entire night . . . another game the guards play to harass him. It is the sound of knocking, though, that wakes Sonny up. He thinks he's dreaming, but the raps are real . . . and insistent. It is hard to tell which direction they are coming from until he hears a familiar voice: "Hey, Sonny . . . hey, Sonny."

"Is that you, Big Jim? Where are ya?"

"Right next to ya, man. Go to the wall. We can talk through the air duct."

Sonny crawls to a ten-inch-square grating. "Big Jim, how'd ya know I was in here?"

"I just got back from the jail . . . they dropped my case. Jesus saved me, man."

"Fuckin' A, they dropped it. Those assholes had nothin' on ya . . . they couldn't put ya on death row." Jim's remark about who saved him had gone right over Sonny's head. "Get a Bible, man. Jesus loves you . . . he loves ya."

"A Bible . . . what for? What the hell're you talkin' about, Jim?"

"A Bible . . . it's the only thing you're allowed to have in here."

Sonny thinks. "Hey, you're smart, Jim . . . the pages are soft. I can use 'em for crap paper."

"No, man . . . you don't understand. The Bible is the greatest high you'll ever get . . . just ask 'em to give you a Bible. You'll get high,

Sonny . . . trust me."

When the guard comes by to bring his evening meal, a bowl of cold broth, Sonny says to him, "I wanna get a Bible in here."

"What the hell you gonna do with that, Gibson . . . sit on it?"

"Hey . . . I'm a Christian man . . . I gotta have my Bible with me. You sayin' I can't have it?"

The guard backs down. "All right, I'll get ya a Bible . . . beats me why."

While Sonny is in the hole, the penitentiary is trying to file charges against him for the assault on the officers. Masterson would love to see Sonny on death row, but the guards in the prison are trying to quash it. Their egos would be crushed if it got out that one convict beat up nine of them.

One morning a week later, when the guard comes to deliver Sonny's breakfast broth, he has a Bible with him. "Here, Gibson, you can have this, but nothin's gonna save your kind . . . you're rotten to the core."

As the guard leaves, Sonny shouts, "Hey, it stinks like hell in here . . . when do ya empty the shitter?"

"We don't, Gibson . . . you'll have to eat it." Fortunately the light is on at this time, so Sonny starts looking through the Bible, frantically flipping the pages and shaking it. He's in pain and needs whatever Jim said would get him high. When he doesn't find a joint or any pills, Sonny knocks on the air duct angrily. "Hey, Jim, you really fucked up! There's not a goddam thing in this Bible. How the hell am I gonna get high? I'm hurtin', man."

"No, Sonny, you get high just readin' it."

Sonny shouts, madder now, "Shit, Jim, you know damn well I can't read."

Jim says calmly, "Just look at the Bible, man, Jesus loves you . . . it'll come to you. . . ."

"What the fuck'll come to me?"

"Sonny, you'll be saved. You'll find out that killing's not right."

"What kinda crap is this?"

Another voice down the line whispers loudly, "It's not crap. It's true. I saw him readin' the Bible every night in the jail. Maybe you can talk some sense into him, man."

Sonny still can't believe this is his friend. "Shit, Jim, what'd they do, beat you stupid?"

"No, . . . I'm born again, Sonny. I've found——"

Sonny shouts, "I'm onto that shit, Jim. I know what you're doin', you're playing the same game Spider did."

Jim insists, "Sonny . . . I found God." Sonny starts to rant, "I don't wanna hear that religious shit." He takes the Bible and heaves it against the wall. "There's no fuckin' God . . . ." He kicks the Bible all over the cell, then tries to rip it apart with his bare hands. "If there was a God, he wouldn't make a place like this." Sonny collapses from the frenzy, but unconsciousness is a welcome deliverance from his desolation.

Time stands still in the cold, dark abyss that is the hole. Sonny has no idea how many days have passed. He has finally become numb to the hurt even though he's had no medicine. Alfonso is with him always: "Pain is a case of mind over matter, Santino . . ." Sonny hears a knock. "Yeah?"

Big Jim says, "Pull out the air duct screen, something's comin' by . . . reach up and pass it down."

Sonny removes the panel and feels a hand give him a string. When Sonny pulls on it, he jumps back, repulsed by a dead mouse on the other end. "What the fuck is this?"

Jim says, "It's food, Sonny, the only meat we got . . . the guy in here the longest gets it."

"Where the hell'd it come from? There's not a fuckin' living thing in here."

"Early in the morning . . . you smell the bakery?"

"Yeah . . . I get starved to death."

"O.K. You'll find the mice runnin' up and down this duct . . . it's the only way they can get to the kitchen. Put your blanket out, and when you feel one, grab it. Bring the mouse into your cell and smash it in the blanket. Pass this one down to Johnny . . . he's been in here four weeks."

Sonny looks at the mouse in disgust and passes it down. "Man, I'll never get that hungry."

Hate is the only thing keeping Sonny alive now. He spends his long days planning hits on everyone who has betrayed him. He's already killed Stevens, Hoover, the governor, the warden, Barker, and Vitone. The next targets are the Mafia dons. Sonny feels his own have abandoned him. In between ruthless murders he has wild sex fantasies, and even Cora Pitkin surfaces again. Sonny remembers the figure but tries to forget the face as he ravishes Cora over and over again. The one person who escapes this hate is Theresa.

One day Big Jim knocks on the duct. "Hey, Sonny . . . I'm passin' somethin' to ya." When the mouse comes down, Sonny says, "I thought you're supposed to get it, Jim . . . don't you want it?"

"Yeah, Sonny, I'm starving, too, but Jesus Christ says to share your wealth with others, so I'm givin' it to you."

Sonny is still nauseated by the thought of eating a dead mouse. "Well, give it to somebody else . . . I don't want this shit."

"O.K., Sonny, pass it down to Mike."

A few days later Sonny pounds on the wall for Jim. A voice tells him, "Jim's not here, man . . . he got out."

Another voice calls down, "Jim said he's gonna get to the priest and let him know what's goin' on." Sonny has been in the hole for 57 days, even though prison regulations state that a man cannot be kept longer than thirty days without a disciplinary hearing. In the yard there is a rumor that the guards have killed Sonny.

Meanwhile Theresa is going crazy. The prison officials have told her that Sonny has been transferred but will not tell her where. Since she cannot afford an attorney, she has no way to force her hand with the state department of correction. She writes letters to everyone from the governor to Sergeant Quinn trying to find out what has happened to Sonny. Barker eventually tells her that he is being detained until Officer Buchanan is off the critical list.

The guard's injuries are serious, and even if he pulls through he'll probably be paralyzed for life. The counselor tells Theresa coldly that everyone there is hoping Sonny will be sent to the gas chamber . . . the world would be better off without him.

Big Jim went to see Father Molinari as soon as he got out and told the priest about Sonny's situation. When Father Molinari looked into it, he was told that Sonny was being held because of his violence. The veteran priest refused to take the prison officials at their word and started his own investigation.

Back in the hole Sonny was making a new hit every day. To date he'd killed all of his executives, Masterson, Conway, all of the guards, every banker he'd ever dealt with, and his hated diving instructor, Robert Sanders. This was the most fun. A knock on the wall interrupts one of his most violent killings . . . a mouse is coming down. Sonny opens the air duct to pass it back, but he has now been without solid food for two months and he's lost eighty pounds. Sonny hesitates an instant, then removes the animal from the string. The smell of rotting flesh is overwhelming, but it is not as strong as his hunger pangs. Sonny breaks the body in half . . . a stinking fluid oozes out over his fingers. He put the mouse to his lips, but the touch of fur on his tongue makes him heave . . . the animal drops to the floor. Sonny throws up water, the only thing he's had all day. (The guards cut off his soup long ago.) As if to obliterate the experience, Sonny buries the dead mouse in his shitter and crawls to a corner of his cage. He sits in a fetal position for a whole day until his godfather comes to visit him.

Sonny uncurls slowly. "Hey, Alfonso . . . it's good to see ya." He smiles. "How come Gino and Carlo aren't here? Listen, next time you see 'em, tell 'em I finally got Sanders . . ." He laughs maniacally. "I put a bomb in his air tanks. I blew that grinning son of a bitch to kingdom come." Sonny addresses the apparition seriously now. "I found that dirty rotten bastard for you, Alfonso . . . I killed Hitler the worst.

I saw your face smilin' when I started in on him. First I chopped off his toes and his heels, then his legs . . . slowly, all the way up to the hips. I packed the wounds real good like ya told me so he wouldn't die right away. I chopped off his hands and his arms. You should've seen him, Alfonso . . . that bloody body was squirmin' around like some kinda worm. Finally I cut off his dick and stuffed it in his mouth with that rotten heart. It was an honor to do this for you, Alfonso." Sonny pauses. "Hey, Alfonso . . . tell Laura I miss her, O.K.? Yeah . . . I . . . I love her too." He frowns. "You're right . . . I know I didn't treat Laura so nice, but I'm gonna fix everything. I'm gonna marry her as soon as I get back to Sicily next week." Sonny stretches his legs. "I remembered what ya taught me, Alfonso, and what Vincenzo went through. I can bear the pain. Are you proud of me, Alfonso?" Sonny nods. "Yeah, I remember that, too. You told me I'd have to eat shit like that, but Alfonso, it smells bad . . . I know . . . I have to keep up my strength." Sonny listens intently. "Yeah, I remember . . . it's just hard to believe that fuckin' thing's a plate of lasagna . . . I know . . I know . . . mind over matter."

There is a knock on the air duct. A voice whispers, "Mouse down, mouse down." Sonny stands. "I gotta get somethin', Alfonso, don't go away." Sonny reaches up and pulls in a mouse. He puts it on the concrete in front of him. "Can ya stay and have somethin' to eat?" Sonny's face saddens. "Oh . . . too bad. Ya gotta get back. Joe will be disappointed you didn't stay for dinner. If it's all right, I'm gonna start." Sonny picks up the dead animal. This time, when he tears the mouse apart and raises it to his mouth, he *is* at Little Sicily. Sonny pictures linguine and clams and takes a bite of the bloody mouse. "*Molto bene.*" The next mouthful is a juicy pepper steak. Sonny smacks his lips. "Great, this is cooked just right." He continues his imaginary feast down to cannoli for dessert, until the mouse is completely devoured. As he puts the bones in his shitter, Sonny yells, "Joe, the food was great tonight. Angelo . . . give the chef a thousand bucks." Sonny gets excited. "I said do it, Angelo, do it . . . now . . . now, right now, Angelo." He calms down. "Good, Angelo, good." He turns around fast. "Georgie, where the hell's the car? I told ya to bring the limo around back. We gotta go pick up Theresa. Hey, Angelo, where's Theresa?" Sonny stops. "Angelo . . . who in the hell *is* Theresa?"

Meanwhile, through contacts in the yard and his own digging, Father Molinari learned that Sonny had been in the hole sixty-five days without clothes, solid food, or medical attention. When he asked the hospital for their record of Sonny's injuries after his beating, he was told that the file had been misplaced. The enraged priest went to the warden and threatened to go the state capital with the story of Sonny's mistreatment in the hole unless there was an immediate hearing. Hacksworth said he didn't know anything about Sonny's lengthy detention . . . and acted immediately. The same afternoon that Father Molinari saw the warden, Sonny was released from the hole.

On the sixty-sixth day of Sonny's solitary confinement, the tumbler of the lock to his hole clicks for the last time. The guards open the door . . . it's now pitch-black inside. Sonny is delirious. He's just hit Chet Bartlett and Jack Gaudio and is now in the middle of choking Father Molinari. "That'll teach you to bother me in the yard when I'm collectin' money, you skinny little bastard." The guard interrupts the brutal murder, shouting through the darkness, "All right, Gibson, you lucky son-of-a-bitch, you're gettin' outta here." He flips on the light. Sonny throws his hand up to shield his eyes from the glare.

Father Molinari helps him. "Come on, Sonny. It's O.K. now . . . let's go." Sonny is so weak he can hardly stand, but the priest puts an arm around his shoulder and helps him walk to the infirmary down the hall. A doctor is called in. After a brief examination he says, "This man has to go to the hospital immediately. He's in serious condition." Sonny is vaguely aware of a man in a black robe walking beside him as he is carried on a stretcher from his dungeon. Father Molinari grabs his hand . . . then everything goes black.

When Sonny wakes up twenty-four hours later, he is sore. Perhaps the softness of the bed after sleeping on the concrete has been a shock to his muscles. His mind is still in the hole, and he starts planning another hit when Father Molinari comes in. Sonny lashes out at him. "Look, I don't wanna hear any of your shit." When the priest gets close to the bed, Sonny grabs his arm, but his grip isn't strong enough to hold the skinny man. "Look, I don't wanna see you anymore . . . I killed you, priest." The strain of this outburst causes Sonny to fall back on the bed.

Father Molinari looks at him and says gently, "You're not going to kill anybody, Sonny . . . it's O.K. now. Rest."

A few days later the priest comes to see him again. He pats Sonny's foot cheerfully. "How are you doing today, Sonny?"

The patient shouts, "Get your fuckin' hands off me, I don't wanna know anything about you." To Sonny, Molinari is just another prison official who inflicted 65 days of torture upon him. He planned to kill every guard, the warden, and the priest, too, as soon as he got his strength back.

"Did you get the book I left for you?"

Sonny says scornfully, "Goddam it, I can't read. Quit botherin' me. What are you botherin' me for?"

The guard stationed to watch Sonny comes over. "Your old lady's downstairs, Gibson. You got approved for a ten-minute phone visit thanks to the priest here." Sonny tries to get out of bed, but his knees collapse under him. Father Molinari helps him to the phone and calls for a nurse to get Sonny back to bed after the call. When Sonny picks up the receiver, he barely recognizes Theresa's voice on the other end. "Honey, how do you feel? Are you O.K.?"

He says dully, "Yeah, I'm O.K.." Sonny has lost touch with reality and has totally forgotten about the important part Theresa played in his life. "Listen, Theresa, don't bother comin' up here no more . . . it's too long a drive."

She is alarmed by his zombielike state and starts to cry. "My God, what have they done to you?"

"Nothin', I'm fine . . . just don't come up here anymore, okay?" He hangs up abruptly. His survival instinct tells him it's dangerous to talk to her. Sonny considers Theresa a threat to his existence now. He knows she represents love, and hate has been keeping him alive. He's afraid that if he sees Theresa, he'll die.

One week later, when Sonny has finally put on a few pounds and is beginning to feel stronger, Father Molinari comes to see him again. The priest picks up some books by the side of the bed. "Did you read your books?"

Sonny knocks them violently out of the priest's hands. "Goddam it . . . I told ya, I can't read."

"I can teach you, Sonny."

"You can't teach me shit. I controlled millions of dollars at one time, and I got along great without any Mickey Mouse books. I used my brain, Father."

The wise old priest picks up on this. He stoops to gather his books on the floor. "You know, Sonny, that's true. You were one of the smartest and most powerful men in the Mafia." Father Molinari straightens up. "That's why it's unbelievable that a man like you needs a Mexican janitor to write letters for him." There is an angry silence. "Wouldn't you like to be able to write your own letters to Theresa? Wouldn't it be nice to be able to read hers instead of just smelling the perfume on the envelopes?"

Silence from Sonny. Finally he answers, "Why don't you get the hell out of here, Father? Leave me alone."

Father Molinari does leave but comes back the next day to check on Sonny. He sits down. "How do you feel today?"

"How the hell would you feel? I feel lousy."

The priest says optimistically, "I think I'd be happy to be alive."

"Why . . . so I can go back to that hell . . . you call that bein' alive, Father?"

"There are a lot of people worse off than you . . . at least you can see, and hear, and walk. You have a lot to be thankful for." Sonny has no answer for this. Father Molinari goes on, "Big Jim asks every day about you. He wanted me to give you some books, but I told him he'd have to wait until you learned to read. He's glad to hear you're gonna learn."

Sonny erupts. "Who in the fuck said I was gonna learn to read, Father?"

The priest stands. "Nobody, but I left some more books . . . they're very simple. I'll be glad to go through them with you when you feel up to it, but I'm not gonna sit here now if you don't want to learn." Sonny sweeps the books off the night table angrily. Father Molinari bends to pick them up. He stands and says firmly, "I'm not ever gonna do that again, Sonny." The priest strides out of the room.

When he's gone, the sight of the books in Sonny's peripheral vision keeps distracting him. There's nothing else to do anyway, so he takes one of the volumes and opens it. Sonny recognizes a few of the most common words like "and," "is," "it's." He struggles to read a whole sentence, but after a minute throws the book across the room. "That's too fuckin' hard."

The next day Sonny waits for his daily pestering from the priest, but the morning passes without the usual visit. When a nurse comes in to give him his shot, Sonny asks, "Have you seen Father Molinari today?"

"Yes . . . he's always here on the floor by twelve."

"Well, it's four o'clock in the afternoon. I wonder what happened to him."

"I guess he went back to the chapel."

Father Molinari stays away for the next two days after that. Finally, on the fourth day, he pays Sonny another visit. "I heard that you've been asking for me . . ."

"Yeah . . . what happened? Where the hell were you?"

"I had other things to do, Sonny. How do you feel today?"

"I'm gettin' a little better, Father." He pauses. "I looked at a couple of those books . . . the words are hard . . . "

"No . . . that's because you don't have anybody teaching you."

Sonny says hesitantly, "Well, I guess you wouldn't have the time, would ya, Father? . . . You got the whole compound to take care of."

Father Molinari says, "Oh . . . I'd probably have an hour a day to start with."

"That'd be O.K. with me." Sonny qualifies his statement: "I'm not sayin' I wanna read, Father, but you know, if you wanna show me some of your teaching techniques, I think I could learn . . . maybe . . . I dunno."

The priest smiles. "You can learn, Sonny . . . we'll start our lessons tomorrow."

The next day Father Molinari comes into the room carrying a large box. He puts it down on the table and pulls out two first-grade readers. He hands one to Sonny. "This is yours, open it." Sonny turns to the first page. On it is a picture of that all-American trio: Dick, Jane, and Spot. The priest starts, "Look, Spot, see Jane? Look, look, look."

Sonny is bored already. "What the fuck is this? I don't wanna hear that baby shit . . . I thought we were gonna read books."

The old man says wisely, "We are, Sonny, but first we have to read words. You try it."

Sonny looks at his copy as the priest coaches him. Sonny says haltingly, "L-l-look, Sp-Spot . . . See J-Jane . . . " After his incredible rise and fall from money and power, this thirty-three-year-old man is finally learning how to read.

Sonny progresses quickly. Working with tapes all his life has trained his ears to listen and his mind to retain. Father Molinari is surprised by his pupil's aptitude. Within a week he is on the fourth-grade level. "That's very good, Sonny . . . if you keep going like this, we can get you a GED in no time."

"GED—what's that?"

"A high school diploma . . . according to your records you never graduated from high school."

"Nah, I got kicked out." Sonny laughs. "I was the football hero, too."

Father Molinari assures him, "Well, you'll get your diploma for sure this time, Sonny."

"You think that's so important, Father?"

"Yes, I think it's important if you want to go on to college."

Sonny laughs harder now. "College! Just because you got me readin' these idiot books don't mean I'm goin' to college. Boy, you gotta be nuts, Father."

"You should go to college." He says seriously, "It'll be very important how you conduct yourself from here on in . . . you're an example, Sonny."

"An example . . . I don't get ya, Father. Whaddya mean?"

The priest says plainly, "If you continue being violent, it will convince the prison staff that no matter what they put a man through, a convict can never be anything but bad."

"Come on, Father, I could become a priest and they'd still think I was bad."

Father Molinari observes, "That's the first time I've ever heard you talk about reality, Sonny."

"Well, let's talk about it some more then . . . reality is, the warden's tryin' to put me on death row right now."

Molinari shakes his head, "No, he isn't. Conway's the only one trying to get you there . . . and if I have anything to say about it, that's not going to happen. To get the death penalty they have to prosecute you. Believe me, they're not interested in opening up this case . . . ."

Sonny is silent for a second. "Do ya know what happened to Zabinini's mandolin, Father?"

"What?"

Sonny sighs. "Never mind . . . they probably shitcanned it."

Father Molinari encourages him. "You know, Sonny, you're a born leader. You're the first convict I've seen who has gotten so much respect from the other men. You represent hope to them now. After all, you endured . . . you survived. When you walk out of this hospital, you'll see . . . they'll be looking up to you."

Sonny says scornfully, "No one's ever looked up to me in my life, Father, except a few Sicilians, but that's family."

"This whole prison is your family. Every man here is related . . . it's like a beautiful vine of Christ."

"I don't wanna hear that Christ shit, Father. I told you that . . . let's get back to the lesson, huh?"

The priest backs off. "O.K., Sonny, let's open to page seventy-three."

In their remaining five weeks together Father Molinari never mentions religion again—until the day Sonny is released from the hospital. The priest suggests, "You know, we have a rosary hour before Mass every day—you should come. It'll give you a chance to get out of your cell before lunch."

"I told you, I don't believe in that crap, Father. I don't even believe in God . . . God wouldn't let men go to the hole."

Molinari doesn't push.

"That's all right. You don't have to believe in God, but come to the Rosary hour . . . come to Mass . . . at least you'll be out of the cell." This is as clever a con as any Sonny has pulled.

"Don't hold up the works for me Father, O.K.? I won't be there."

The guard comes to pick him up. "Your clothes are in the cell, Gibson. You'll have to wear those whites for now."

It's quite a way to B Block, and Sonny is shaky by the time he starts the walk down that long, concrete hallway to his cell . . . the same trip he took just eighteen months ago when he came in. This time the comments from the convicts as he passes are very different:

"Hey, look . . . Sonny's out."

"Hey, Mafia-and-the-Cross man, see ya in the yard . . ."

"Sonny, we want you to be the president of our council."

A black voice agrees, "Yeah, Gibson'll tell the warden to kiss off!"

A Mexican shouts, "Hey, we want longer visits, tell that to Hacksworth, O.K.?"

"We need better food, tell the Ax that too, Sonny."

The men are asking him to be the head of the Convicts' Council. Maybe Father Molinari was right . . . maybe he was a leader. A voice shouts, "Everybody in favor of Sonny for president, say 'Aye.' " The bars of B Block reverberate with a resounding "aye" from the men.

Sonny has become a prison hero for his courage and fortitude, but this popularity makes the guards hate him more than ever. When he gets to his cell, he's told, "You won't have a cell partner, Gibson . . . warden's orders. You're OC . . . we like to keep the dangerous animals alone."

That afternoon Sonny goes out into the yard; it's the first time he's seen daylight in months. After all the weeks inside his eyes are sensitive to the sun's blinding glare. As Sonny squints, he scans the grounds, trying to find Big Jim. Juarez calls out, "Hey, you showed everybody in this fuckin' place us guys in B Block are tough . . . huh, Sonny?"

Another man shouts, "Better watch out, Mafia-and-the-Cross man is back on the scene."

Cigar Eddie approaches; Sonny opens his eyes wide now. Can this be? Eddie hasn't been out of his cell in ten years . . . in his business somebody's liable to stick him. Cigar in hand, he pats Sonny's shoulder. "As soon as you get all your strength back, we'll be in business again, eh, Sonny?"

The convicts around them all listen for the answer. Sonny hears Father Molinari's words, "You're an example, Sonny." He hedges. "I dunno what I'm gonna do yet, Eddie . . . I'm not thinkin' straight right now. Look, I wanna get over to the weight pile to see Big Jim."

He turns to go but is confronted by another recluse, "Shitty Freddy." This palefaced convict earned his name by throwing balls of feces at the guards. The veterans all stay away from Freddy on the tier, but new recruits invariably get a smelly pat on the back to welcome them aboard. He's been in and out of solitary countless times for his bizarre behavior, but now everyone just leaves Freddy alone. He says to Sonny, "I wouldn't come outta my cell for nobody else, man . . . I just hadda tell ya . . . I've been in that fuckin' hole myself. It was bad . . . but I heard ya hadda eat mice to stay alive. I wanted ya to know, if I ever gotta go there, it'll make it easier thinkin' what you went through, Sonny."

"Freddy, I hope there'll be a day when no con gets sent to that fuckin' place." He pats Freddy's arm, "See ya later, man, I gotta go over to the weight pile."

When Sonny gets there, he can't believe his eyes. Big Jim has his arm around a black reading the Bible to him. The hit man spots Sonny, and rushes over. "Hey, it's good to see ya . . . I heard you got out. See . . . Jesus loves ya. We Christian brothers prayed for ya every night."

"Come on, Jim . . . cut the crap. It's me . . . Sonny."

"I know, Jesus loves you too, man."

A Mexican comes up to them. "I'm here, Big Jim . . ."

Jim apologizes to Sonny. "Sorry, man, I gotta go, but we'll work out tomorrow morning, O.K.? You lost a lotta weight, and we gotta build those muscles back up."

Sonny watches in disbelief as the born-again ex-hit man takes his Bible and starts walking around the yard, reading Scripture to the Mexican. Sonny is sure Jim has something up his sleeve. He stares after them as Father Molinari comes over.

"It's good to see you out, Sonny."

"What's wrong with Big Jim? He's actin' funny."

"He's found a new life in our Lord."

Sonny disagrees. "Nah, not Jim . . . he's connin'. I'll bet he's tryin' to get to a camp center."

"It's no con, it's real, Sonny. Jim's changed." Father Molinari asks optimistically, "Well, will I see you at Mass tomorrow?"

"Hell, no, Father."

The priest persists. "Look, Sonny, after Mass we'll spend some time reading. I have some new books."

"I dunno . . . I'll see."

Father Molinari shrugs. "It's up to you, Sonny. I thought you wanted to continue with your reading . . . that's the only time I have. It won't interfere with your workout." Molinari knows his student is eager to learn.

Sonny concedes somewhat, "O.K., I'll be there . . . but it don't mean anything . . . I just wanna get outta that cell." A guard passes behind Sonny, keychain rattling. Sonny turns around fast and flinches when he sees it's a guard. He's afraid he's going to be hit.

Father Molinari puts a quieting hand on Sonny's shoulder. "When you open your heart to your enemies, like Jim did, you won't have to be scared."

Sonny snaps, "I'm not scared a no one, Father."

The old priest smiles. "I'll see you at Mass tomorrow then."

From that point on Sonny goes to the chapel daily. Mass still doesn't mean anything to him, but reading does. He stays on afterward for his lesson in Father Molinari's office. Now up to seventh-grade books, Sonny can't wait to tell Theresa he can read. On Sunday she's coming to visit him for the first time since his release from the hole. When she gets to the visiting stool, Theresa tries to hide her shock at his frail appearance. After a long kiss through the glass, she sits. Theresa is like a stranger to Sonny too; he has to reacquaint himself with every feature of her face. Finally, when it is all comfortable again, he says,

"Baby . . . I'm sorry I talked to ya so bad on the telephone the other day . . . I love ya, ya know that."

"I love you . . . it's O.K. You sounded like you were on some kind of medication."

"Yeah, man, that was some kind of medication all right."

Theresa studies Sonny's gaunt face. It's been heavy ever since she's known him; his new thinness makes him more handsome. "How much weight did you lose?"

"Oh, a hundred and thirty some pounds. I lost a lotta muscle, though. Jim's gonna help me build back up." He says, still increduluous, "You know what? Jim's changed . . . he's a Christian now."

"Weren't they trying to get him convicted for murder?"

"Yeah, but they dropped that . . . Jim's readin' the Bible to everybody."

"Is that what got his case dropped?"

Sonny laughs. "Hell, no . . . they didn't have any evidence." He changes the subject, excited. "Hey, guess what . . . I'm learnin' to read."

"You are? That's great, honey, how'd that happen?"

"When I was in the hospital, the Catholic priest taught me. He's teachin' me how to write, too. You should be gettin' my letters soon."

Theresa says proudly, "I'm going to keep every one in a scrapbook for you."

"Ya know, Father thinks I could probably get a high school diploma and go to college. I'm readin' political science books now."

She laughs. "If I know you, you'll run for office some day."

"Yeah . . . the guys want me to run for president of the Convicts' Council. I think I might get it, though. I'm really liked now . . . I never was before. Father Molinari says I'm a leader."

"You are . . . look what you did when you were with the Mafia."

"Yeah but nobody liked me then, except for Sicilians. By the way, how's Angelo?"

Theresa is taken aback by this strange question. "Angelo's dead, Sonny . . . don't you remember?"

"Yeah, yeah . . . I meant Richie . . . how's Richie? What's he doin?"

"He opened up a detective agency."

"How'd he do that without a gun permit?"

"Richie didn't say, but he's hopin' someday he can fight that case and carry a gun again. He wanted to see you, but I didn't want to give up my visit."

Sonny nods. "I'm glad you didn't. I'll see Richie later on . . . how come Pops didn't come with ya?"

She laughs. "He said he was too busy at the lot. Tomorrow's a holiday, and he can make a lot of money today."

"How's your job?"

"O.K., I'm getting more responsibility. They made me a sales rep. I'm still writing songs, though . . . that'll never stop."

Sonny wishes that their visit could last forever, but, as usual, in thirty minutes the phones are dead. They kiss and wave good-bye till next Sunday. Theresa has made him begin to feel alive again.

When Sonny gets out on the yard that afternoon, he sees the other presidential candidates campaigning. He is running against a black and a Mexican. They're out canvassing votes by praising their platforms like any other politician, but penitentiary politics is a dangerous business . . . broken promises might get you killed.

The editor of the prison paper comes up to Sonny on the weight pile. "Could I talk to ya a few minutes?"

Sonny puts down his dumbbell. "Sure, Hooper, what can I do for ya?"

"If you win, will you use your cross on the guards if they're doin' something wrong?"

"Nope. . . That cross is not used for violence anymore."

The reporter says, "Yeah, well, what are you gonna do for the convicts if you're elected president of the council?"

Sonny thinks a second. "I'm gonna do exactly what I can do . . . nothin' more or nothin' less. How can I make any promises? I'm just one of you guys, but I'll do my best."

A day before voting the statements of the candidates are released. The other two proclaim they'll get longer visits, better chow, and go directly to the warden's office on any problems, but Sonny's words, "I'm just one of you guys," makes a powerful impact on the prisoners. The article goes on to say that Sonny's philosophy comes from the Mafia, which doesn't waste time with promises . . . they act and they get results. That editorial statement has a powerful impact on the warden. He announces over the PA, "I've seen some of the comments of the men running for president of the council in the paper today. I feel one of those men would be detrimental to this institution if he holds that office. He has no respect for this system. I would suggest that you do not vote for Sonny Gibson."

If some of the men weren't for Sonny before that speech, they were behind him after it. He is elected by a landslide 90 percent of the vote and is the new president of the Convicts' Council. Before his first meeting with the prison officials, Sonny starts talking to the men about some of their problems. In the meantime he continues his education with Father Molinari.

In just four months Sonny has reached high school level. The priest thinks his student is finally ready to take the GED. If he passes, Molinari is going to recommend that Sonny be transferred to a penitentiary where there is a college program. Sonny is enthusiastic about this idea because he wants to study law. He's seen money-hungry attorneys take advantage of too many men and wants to help convicts fight their cases from the inside . . . free of charge. Sonny goes to daily Mass and doesn't fight with Father Molinari about religion anymore. The cross he carries on the yard is slowly taking on a new meaning for Sonny, but to most of the men it is still a symbol of his viciousness. In fact, some of them are even more afraid of him now, convinced that his time in the hole must have made him even more violent.

One day two whites approach Sonny in the yard. "Hey, Mafia-and-the-Cross man, we got a problem. We wanna get Montez . . . Big Jim's the hit man for our block, but he won't do that no more. Can ya take the job? . . . you're the only one we trust."

Sonny reasons, "If Jim don't wanna hit the guy, maybe he didn't really do nothin' wrong."

One of them heats up, "Nothin' wrong! He's a fuckin' rat."

Sonny shakes his head. "I'm still not takin' the job, man. If Jim won't do it, there must be somethin' else he knows."

The convicts argue "No, man . . . Jim's a Jesus freak is all . . he's gone crazy."

"Well, I don't believe Jim's a Jesus freak either . . . get somebody else." Sonny knows that Jim has really changed, but he is still afraid to admit, even to himself, that he may be changing, too. As hard as he tries to fight it, Sonny is undergoing a metamorphosis. In time, instead of being filled with violence and hate, he works to stop it. It is not the words of Papa Mike that he remembers now . . . it is the words of Father Molinari, "Open your heart to your enemies."

One afternoon Sonny has passed up his workout to write to Theresa. It takes him a long time to form the letters, and he wants to make sure they look good. All of the cells are closed except for those of the men who work maintenance on the ground floor. Sonny is locked inside his when he hears screams coming from the tier below. He jumps up and puts his face to the bars. He can barely make out what's happening—four whites have grabbed a Mexican in what looks like a rape. Sonny shouts down to them, "Hey, man, don't do that . . . leave the guy alone."

The Mexican is begging, "Please don't . . . no, no . . . please. I'll pay, I'll pay." Sonny knows the man owes the others $25 for heroin.

"You got the shit, Hernandez, but Cigar Eddie didn't get no money."

The condemned man says desperately, "I don't have the bread man, but Rudy's got it. Get him, man, get him. He'll pay."

"It's too late for that motherfucker." Two of the men pin the

Mexican's arms back and drag him into the cell. Sonny calls down frantically, "Hey, man, don't do that . . . this is me, Mafia-and-the-Cross."

A guard comes over to him. "What are you yellin' about, Gibson?"

"You know what the hell I'm yellin' about . . . lemme out so I can get down there and stop that."

The guard shakes his head. "Sorry, Gibson, rules are that doors don't open till yard recall."

"You're crazy, man. If you lemme out, I can stop them." He watches in horror as the hit men stretch the Mexican's genitals across the cell's entrance. When the door closes, it will be as deadly as a guillotine.

"This'll teach all you fuckin greaseballs a lesson."

Hernandez's eyes bulge in terror. "No, man . . NO . . NO . . PLEASE DON'T . . . PLEEEEZE."

By this time Sonny is beside himself. "You asshole, don't try to act like you don't see what's goin' on!" The guard has to raise his voice over the man's pleas. "I don't see or hear nothin', Gibson. It's best you do the same." He turns and walks coldly down the hall.

Sonny shakes the bars of his cell, shouting after him, "Lemme out, man. I can stop it . . . I CAN STOP IT!" Just then, one last horrifying scream reverberates through the prison. The whites have slammed the cell door shut on the Mexican's crotch, slicing off his cock and balls. The enforcers run off down the corridor, leaving the castrated man bleeding to death. Hernandez lost his life for a $25 fix.

The prison goes into lockdown for three days while the hit is investigated. When the yard finally opens up again, Sonny tries to talk to two of the murderers. When they see his cross, the men run, certain that he is going to kill them. They have no idea that Sonny now uses this cross to help other convicts, not hurt them. He puts his arm around one of the enforcers, who looks at him in fear. "Am I gonna get hit, man?"

Sonny smiles. "Yeah, I'm gonna hit you . . . I'm gonna hit you with love and understandin'."

The man is still terrified. "I don't believe ya, man . . . you're Mafia-and-the-Cross . . . everyone knows you're deadly. You know Hernandez hadda get hit. We're enforcin' for the whole prison, man. Cigar Eddie needed to make an example outta him."

Sonny remembers when he suggested that to Eddie. "I know where you're comin' from, brother . . . but it don't have to be that way . . . you could've talked to the guy."

The white is still shaking. "Don't kill me, man, don't kill me!" Sonny pats his shoulder. "Relax . . . I'm not gonna kill you . . . I changed when I was in the hole. Look, why don't you come to Mass?

You'll get outta your cell for an hour."

The frightened man breaks away from Sonny. "Man, you're crazy." He runs to the guard, begging, "Lock me up . . . lock me up . . . put me in PC. . . . They're gonna kill me!" The man is asking for protective custody, where Sonny can't get at him.

Sonny turns to the other hit man. "You'll be at Mass tomorrow, right?"

"Yeah. I'll be there, man, I can't afford to go to lock up. I'd lose a lotta bread."

Sonny smiles. "That's good, brother. I'll see ya at eight A.M. then."

From then on Sonny has the chapel packed with men, but the convicts don't really believe he's changed. Like the prison officials, they think he's still conning. It's Sonny's reputation with the cross in his hand that scares them to the chapel doors.

After Mass Father Molinari gives Sonny a St. Joseph's Bible to read. "What the hell's this for, Father?"

"Well, I think you've improved enough, you could be reading some Scripture."

Sonny hands it back to him. "I don't think I wanna do that. I like to read stories."

Father Molinari smiles. "The Bible has some of the most exciting stories in the world . . . they're filled with sex, murder, greed . . ."

"They got that in the Bible?" Sonny takes the book back. "Where's it at, Father?"

The priest suggests, "Why don't you start with the gospels? Read St. John first."

When Sonny gets back to his cell, he puts the Holy Book on a shelf with his other readers. It sits there for a week until one night, as he's sitting on the bunk writing, he is drawn to it. Sonny takes the Bible and flips the pages until he comes to the Gospel of St. John. He reads in chapter 19, verse 1, "Pilate took Jesus and had him scourged." Sonny stops for a minute to look up the word "scourged." Among the meanings he recognizes "whip and punish." Sonny can empathize with that definition and compares the cruel lashing the Roman soldiers gave Christ to the brutal beatings the convicts get from the guards. Sonny reads further, and in John 19:17—"And bearing the Cross himself, he went forth to a place called, the Skull, Golgotha"—he thinks of the men in prison who carry the cross of inhumane treatment regardless of their color or faith. Sonny draws a parallel between Golgotha, where corpses rot away, and the hole, where men rot away without pity, eating the flesh of dead mice to stay alive. Leafing through the book he picks a page at random and reads in the gospel of St. Luke that Christ was tortured for over nine hours. A tear falls on the book. Of all the men Sonny has seen beaten in prison, including himself, none has ever undergone such barbaric punishment. He can relate to the pain inflicted on this innocent prisoner, for even a pagan Roman centurion, who dealt with criminals all of his life, said of Jesus, "This was truly a *just* man." Sonny remembers just men like Zabinini, who went to prison for a $10 crime. He commiserates with Jesus, who suffered to save his fellow men, and the convicts in prisons, who suffer injustices at the hands of their fellow men. Sonny closes the Bible and tosses it aside. He walks over to the bars and stares out the broken window across the tier, confused by his feelings. Why would he have such compassion for a man who lived nearly 2,000 years ago? Sonny wonders if this newfound emotion is enough to conquer the power of the hate and violence he still has inside of him.

A loud voice breaks his thought. "Here's a pass for your council meeting tomorrow, Gibson. You gonna ask the warden for minimum wage?"

"I hadn't thought of that, Officer Gallagher . . . I think I will. Got any mail?"

The guard says sarcastically, "You know mail call isn't for an hour yet, Gibson."

"O.K., well, thank you, Officer Gallagher."

As president of the inmate council Sonny has already had four meetings with prison officials. He badgers them to get improved visiting conditions, humane treatment in the hole, better food in chow hall, cross-checking by neutral officers to avoid collusion by the guards, and a list of other reforms. Sonny can see he's not getting anywhere. So he uses a tactic that worked effectively in union negotiations . . . Sonny calls a strike. Everything in prison shuts down. On the third day of the work stoppage Sonny is finally called into the warden's office.

As he is escorted along the hallway to the end of the tier, someone shouts, "Hey, look, Sonny's goin' to the bargaining table. Stick to our demands, man . . . don't give in."

The convict leader shouts back, "Don't worry about that, I'm not givin' in."

The guard says harshly, "Come on, Gibson . . . let's keep goin'. The warden's waitin'. You don't need to talk to everybody."

Sonny protests, "I didn't talk to nobody . . . I'm followin' you."

The men continue to shout support. "Hey, Sonny, I'm losin' weight in this cell, but if you took the hole, I can stand this, man."

"Yeah, Sonny, we'd all go to the hole for ya."

"Hey, Sonny, tell the warden we wanna see a movie once a month."

"Yeah, man . . . not some Walt Disney crap . . . we wanna see some tits and ass."

The guard says, "That's disgusting, Gibson. You've caused a lotta problems in this prison. You're the biggest goddam troublemaker I've seen in my twenty years here." Sonny ignores the insult, more concerned with the men's problems right now and what he's going to say to the warden.

When Sonny finally goes into Hacksworth's office, the official jumps from his seat. The dislike the two men have for each other is obvious.

"Gibson . . . aren't you guys tired of bologna sandwiches by now?"

"It tastes better than the baloney we get from the counselors."

The warden warns, "Look, Gibson, we can't afford this anymore. I'm gonna have you transferred to another prison."

Sonny smiles. "Good . . . I want outta this pit anyway . . . but that's not gonna end the strike." He reasons, "Another guy'll just take my place, Hacksworth. The damage is already done . . . the men are sittin' in their cells."

"O.K., Gibson, what can we do to end it . . . to get the guys back to work? We can't fill all of their demands. If we did, we might as well just hand them the keys to this joint."

"Well, you can start by extendin' the visits to one hour and lettin' 'em see an R-rated movie once a month. That's only two minor things the men want. If you give 'em those, it'll show good faith, and they'll go back to work." Sonny looks at the warden steadily, "But if some of the other demands aren't met, you'll have a riot on your hands, and you're gonna lose some lives . . . not all of them will be convicts', Hacksworth."

The warden points his finger at Sonny. "I could throw you in the hole for that, Gibson . . . you're threatening state employees with bodily harm."

"Nope, I'm just warnin' ya a couple a guards could get killed."

Lieutenant Jefferson drawls, "Gibson here has a point. Besides, if you put him back in the hole, that'll be the fastest way to cause a riot."

Hacksworth finally concedes. "O.K., Gibson, you win. Tell them they can have an hour visit and a movie."

"No, Hacksworth, you announce it, the men want to hear it from you."

The warden picks up the microphone of the PA. "Gibson's in my office going over the demands." He clears his throat. "You men know me, I'm a sincere warden. We're still discussing many of your demands, but to show you my good faith, visits will be extended to one hour, and an R-rated movie will be shown once a month." He looks over at Sonny. "Should I repeat it?"

"No, Hacksworth, just listen." The cheers of the men are deafening. "They heard you the first time."

The reputation of the Mafia-and-the-Cross man is spreading to other prisons. Sonny is a powerful leader and continues to carry his cross on the yard, not as a weapon, but as a symbol to show men they don't need a weapon. However, he never preaches to them. One afternoon Juarez comes over to Sonny while he's working out with Big Jim. Ramon is still a member of the Mexican Mafia. He sits at the weight pile, watching in admiration as Sonny bench-presses 400 pounds. "Man, you sure got muscles. I'll bet you can really bust heads now when you swing that cross."

Sonny puts down the bar. "I don't use it to hurt no more . . . it wouldn't be right."

Juarez shakes his head. "Man, I still can't believe it. The two best hit men on the yard turn religious on us."

Jim quotes from Scripture. "The Bible says the man who lives by the sword dies by the sword."

The Mexican says cynically, "Man, in here if ya don't live by your shank, ya just die by somebody else's."

Sonny tells him, "That's what I used to think, but ya get a lot more with peace and love than ya do with violence and hate."

The Mexican argues, "You're crazy, man. Try collectin' a narcotics debt with love, and it'll get ya shipped outta here in a box." He gets up. "I'll stick to my methods of enforcin' . . . I know they work."

When he leaves, Sonny says, "Think Ramon could ever change?"

The big convict smiles. "Oh, I think so . . . the Lord and I had a talk about him just last night . . . we're workin' on Juarez right now." He says with concern, "I've been talkin' to the Lord about you, too, Sonny. You don't praise him enough."

Sonny looks at him. "I'm not a preacher, Big Jim . . . you can turn off a lotta guys with the Jesus stuff . . . I'd rather be a doer. They can see how I've changed."

Sonny goes to eight-o'clock Mass every morning and is now one of Father Molinari's altar boys. One day after services the priest asks, "Where do you rush off to every day?"

"Well, I like to be the first one on the yard, Father, so I can set the weights up for Jim and I."

Molinari says, "Can you come into my office for a few minutes? I wanna talk to you."

"Sure, Father . . ." As soon as they're seated, the old priest pulls some papers from his drawer. "I'm very proud of you . . . These are the results of your GED."

Sonny says anxiously, "I passed, right?"

"Yep, and I'm talking to the classification committee now. It looks like they're going to transfer you, so you'll be able to take your law courses."

Sonny is amazed. "You're kiddin' me . . . you mean I'm finally gettin' outta here?"

"That's right, but if anything happens up there, they could send you back, and you'll have wasted all the time you spent getting educated. I don't have to tell you how serious that is."

Sonny says confidently, "Nothin's gonna happen, Father . . . I wanna be a lawyer."

The priest reminds him, "You might not be the cause of the trouble . . . you have a reputation that will follow you. Some men might want to push you 'cause they've heard you're tough. You've really gotta think hard to control the urge to push back. Remember what I told you, Sonny . . . you're an example."

"I'll remember, Father . . . I remember everything you taught me. Without you I'd have died in the hole." Sonny has tremendous respect for this dedicated priest. He asks Father Molinari what his counterpart will be like at the next penitentiary.

"His name is Father Schmidt . . . he's a good guy, but like you, Sonny, he's tough."

"Hey, I've been meanin' to ask ya somethin'."

"What is it, Sonny?"

"Well, the guys who take communion . . . they're different. They don't cuss, they're more polite . . . I dunno . . . there's somethin' special about 'em."

Father Molinari nods. "You're right, Sonny." He was wondering when his pupil would get around to asking about this. "Those men are special . . . they've broken bread with Our Lord. During Mass, when I consecrate the bread and wine, it's a reenactment of the Last Supper. Communion is sacred, Sonny. The body and blood of Our Lord Jesus Christ comes alive on the altar in the host."

"Is it important to take communion?"

"Tell me something . . . is it important to exercise and keep your body strong?"

"Yeah."

"You read to build up your mind, don't you?"

"Yeah, but I don't see what you're gettin' at, Father."

"The soul needs development, too . . . and when you take communion, you're strengthening your spiritual life."

What Father Molinari says makes sense to Sonny. "Well, could I take communion tomorrow?"

"I don't think so . . . I read in your file that you were married . . . was that in the Catholic Church?"

Sonny hedges. "Well, I was married a lot, Father, but the first one was in a Catholic church."

"Are you in love with Theresa?"

"Yes, Father . . ."

"In that case the first marriage will have to be annulled. We'll have to take your request to the Bishop."

Sonny is worried. "That's sounds pretty complicated."

"It's not simple, but we'll start the paperwork now, and I'll send everything to Father Schmidt."

Sonny's transfer comes through in just two weeks. The Friday Sonny leaves, a group of men are waiting in R & R to wish him luck. The exception is Sergeant Conway. "It's a good thing you're gettin' outta here, Gibson . . . you wouldn't live much longer." He looks at Sonny's cross. "You gonna use that thing on the guys over there?"

Sonny smiles. "Yes, I am, Sergeant, I'm gonna use it to help guys and maybe save some lives."

The last people he sees before he gets on the bus are Father Molinari and Big Jim. The priest hands Sonny a rosary and a pamphlet. "The little booklet will tell you how to say the rosary . . . do it every day, and remember the men here in your prayers."

"I will, Father." They hug. "Thanks for everything."

Big Jim hugs him next. "Jesus loves you, Sonny."

Sonny looks around. "Hey, have ya seen Juarez lately? I thought he'd be here to say good-bye."

"He's in the hole."

"Damn, what'd he do?"

"He got mad and spit in a guard's coffee. I'm sendin' Juarez a Bible today."

Sonny smiles. "Keep handin' those Bibles out in the hole, Jim . . . someday maybe a man won't have to read it there."

The ride is relaxing. This prison is in the mountains, a beautiful but isolated setting that earns it the title, "No-Man's-Land." Sonny is excited about going to college, but the thing on his mind most is seeing Theresa. Here they are allowed to have contact visits . . . it's been two and a half years since they've touched each other. Sonny stays inside his cell until Sunday, afraid that if he gets into any kind of scrap, they might pull his visit.

Theresa is excited, too. On Saturday she spends the whole afternoon and evening cooking. She called the prison to find out what the visiting regulations were and was told about the small yard with its outdoor grill where food could be heated. Anything brought up must be in plastic containers. At nine-thirty that night she packs the picnic hamper and loads it in the car, then showers, and picks out a pretty flowered dress to wear . . . Theresa wants to look beautiful for Sonny. By ten o'clock she's on the road to start the eight-hour ride to the penitentiary. When she gets there at six A.M., Theresa is the first one on line. She changes from slacks to her dress in the car, then unloads the hamper from the truck, and sits down against the concrete wall outside the gates for the three-hour wait until visiting time.

About fifteen minutes later a hefty black woman arrives. She takes out a seat cushion and sits down next to her. "You new around here, ain't ya? What's your name?"

"Theresa." The black flashes her a wide, white grin. "I'm Big Sally. This your first time?"

"Uh-huh . . . my husband just got transferred from the state penitentiary."

"Oh Lordy, chile, it's a good thing he be outta there. That's where my man did his first stretch . . . five years. His second stretch wasn't much time . . . two years. I'm glad the third one's up here now. At least a few of the guards are decent folk."

"How long has your husband been in?"

Sally thinks. "On and off, 'bout fifteen years." Theresa swallows hard. Sonny's thirty months have seemed like three hundred. Sally must have real dedication to come up for fifteen years. The matriarch takes out a sweater she's knitting. "You got any children, honey?"

"No . . ."

"Well, that's a blessin' anyway. It's hard on young'uns to have a daddy that's in prison."

Theresa is curious. "What do you tell people who ask about your husband? I never know what to say."

"Oh . . . I just tell 'em the truth. I'm proud of my man, honey. It don't matter what people thinks. Course, I don't go 'round announcin' he's in either . . . I don't need nobody's pity."

"Do you ever go out . . . you know, on dates?"

Sally laughs. "Funny you askin' that . . . you wouldn't know to look at me, but I do have a few people after my fat butt. I don't pay 'em no mind, though . . . can't be a man good as what I got." She drops a stitch. "Damn, now that's gonna be a nice hole."

"When's your man gettin' out Sally?"

"He's in for life, but we're workin' on an appeal right now . . . it's hard to say." A few more cars pull into the lot. A white and a Mexican woman come over and sit down next to Sally. "How you doin', mamas?"

"Fine."

"Good."

The black introduces the others. "Doris, Conchita . . . this is Theresa. She's gonna be with us for a while. You gonna come up every week, aren't ya, honey?"

Theresa nods. "If my strength holds up. I didn't get any sleep last night."

Doris assures her, "You'll get used to it. You're a prison wife now . . . we're a special breed."

By eight o'clock the line is in the hundreds. At nine o'clock the guard finally starts processing everyone through. When Theresa gets to the desk, the sergeant asks flatly, "Are you Molly Pratt?"

"No, Theresa Gibson . . . who's Molly Pratt?"

"Dunno lady, why don't cha ask your husband? She's on your old man's list."

"Well, take her off . . ."

"Can't do that, lady, convict's the only one that can . . . he has to write and do it through his counselor. I guess that's one broad he didn't tell ya about, huh?" Theresa is furious. She doesn't know whether to be mad at Sonny or the obnoxious guard, but she holds her temper. "I'll have to check that hamper, lady." Theresa opens it for him. The guard opens up all of the containers, poking through the food with one of her plastic forks, then stabs her cake repeatedly to check for narcotics inside. Theresa's heart sinks. She had decorated it with rosettes and flowers. "I love you, Sonny." was written across the top in pink gel . . . all that was left now was a mass of crumbs. The guard informs her, "You can't take these plastic containers out to the visiting yard, lady. You'll have to put the food on your plates and carry it that way."

Theresa protests. "But I called this week and they said plastic containers were okay."

"I dunno who you talked to, lady. Get to the end of the line, and I'll check it out."

Theresa takes a look at the blur of faces in back of her. "Can't you check it out now? I've been waiting for three hours, and I drove for eight . . ."

The sergeant says cold-heartedly, "Look, lady, you wanna see your old man or not? I'll pull your visit if you don't quiet down."

Sally whispers. "Don't give 'em no lip, honey . . . they love to hassle ya. Just do what he says."

Theresa trudges to the end of the long line. An hour later she's back at the desk again. A different guard signs her in. He looks through the hamper. "O.K., go on through."

"You mean the plastic containers are all right?"

"Yep, always have been since I've been here."

Theresa seethes at the cruel guard who made her wait and considers telling him off, but remembers what Sally told her. "Where do I go now?"

"The visiting yard is straight through that door . . . there are tables out there." Theresa closes her basket, heart pounding. In just a few minutes she'd be holding her love again.

In the meantime Sonny has been pacing his cell. Theresa has always been the first one in line. Today, she's over an hour late . . . he can't imagine what's happened. Finally his name is called, and the guard comes by with his pass. When Sonny gets down to the visiting room, he has his own problems. The guard pats him down, then says, "All right, Gibson, get your clothes off."

"My clothes . . . what for?"

"Ya gotta strip before ya go out on the visiting yard . . . ya might be tryin' to take somethin' out to your old lady."

"What the hell would I be takin' out? Ya gotta watch for stuff comin' in, don't ya?"

The guard snaps, "Gibson . . . you want your visit, take off your clothes." Sonny takes off his pants, shirt, and underwear. The guard hardly looks at him. "Get your shoes and socks off." When Sonny has done that, the guard says with his back turned, "All right, Gibson, put your clothes back on."

Sonny is mad . . . this is just a game they play with the men. He dresses quickly and hurries to the visitng room. Sonny scans the crowd but doesn't see Theresa. "Where's my visitor, Sergeant?"

"How should I know?" Just then there is a tap on Sonny's shoulder. Theresa is standing behind him, crying. They kiss, and instead of the cold, hard glass, Sonny can feel the warmth of Theresa's lips. As they hug, he rubs his hand over her back. "God, you feel so good, baby."

The guard barks, "All right, Gibson . . . do that someplace else."

Theresa takes his hand. "Come outside . . . I have a surprise for you."

When they get to the tiny yard, Sonny sees an Italian feast laid out on the table before him. "I cooked all of your favorite things . . . the ones I was allowed to bring in. They check everything when you get here anyway . . . I'm sorry about the cake." She points to the grill. "Look, we can heat everything up, too . . . I know it's a little early for linguine and clams . . ."

Sonny hugs her. "I don't wanna eat right now . . . I wanna talk. Will anybody touch this?"

"Uh-uh, I have somebody watchin' it for me." She brings him over to the next table. "Sally, this is Sonny."

"My, my . . . he's a handsome dude. You sure are a lucky girl. You two go ahead . . . ain't nobody gonna mess with your stuff while Big Sally's here."

Arm in arm, Sonny and Theresa stroll around the yard. Every few feet they stop and hug. After thirty minutes they lean against the hurricane fence to talk . . . visits here are five hours. "How's your job, baby?"

"Great . . . they made me head of the whole sales department."

Sonny asks, "Does anybody at work know about me?"

"My friends do, but I don't think it's anybody else's business. If they ask, I'll tell 'em . . . I'm not ashamed of you."

"Have you started school yet?"

"No . . . the professors will be here in a few weeks. I'm already on the list for the law program."

"That's great, honey."

Theresa pauses, then says hesitantly, "Sonny, Dr. Turner asked me to go out to dinner with him."

Sonny expected this day to come. "What'd you tell him?"

"I said no . . ."

"Is that what you wanted to do?" She nods. He sighs. "I dunno . . . maybe you should go out, Theresa. It's bad enough I'm in prison . . . you don't have to be."

"If I can't have you, I don't want anybody."

Sonny turns to her, "Theresa, I've wanted to ask you this for a long time, but things just weren't right. The way things are, now's as good a time as any, I guess." He takes her by the shoulders. "Will you marry me?"

She goes into shock. Theresa never thought she'd be *Mrs.* Gibson, and when Sonny went to prison, she'd really given up hope. "You wanna get married? I've wanted that for a long time, but why now?"

"Well, I found out talkin' to some of the guys. It works in your favor with the parole board if you're married." Sonny says excitedly, "And we can have a ten-hour family visit and make love." He pulls her closer to him. "But Theresa . . . I wanna marry you 'cause I love ya, baby."

Her eyes well up. "I love you, too. Sonny, I've waited for years to hear you say those words." She throws her arms around him. "Yes, I'll marry you . . . yes, yes, yes." Theresa breaks away excited, "When should we do it?"

"Well, it has to be approved first. I have a lotta things to find out about around here. I'm gonna go see the prison priest tomorrow and get a rundown on the way things work." Sonny can smell the aroma of different ethnic cuisines floating over from the grill. "Are you hungry?"

She looks at him. "When am I not hungry?"

"Well, come on then, let's eat."

They go back to the picnic table, and Sally says, "Everything's still fine . . . nobody came near."

"Thanks, Sally. How do you use the grill?"

"Just put your food in the pots and lay it on. There's a spot between Doris and Conchita." Sally yells across the yard. "Hey, Doris . . . hold the space for Theresa, will ya, baby?" The girl nods. Sonny and Theresa dump the plastic containers and bring the pots over to the grill. She introduces Sonny to the other prison wives.

As the food warms, Theresa says, "Who's Molly Pratt?"

Sonny shrugs. "I dunno . . . why?"

"She's approved for visits on your card. Who is she?"

"I dunno . . ."

"Well, how'd she get on the list if you didn't put her there?"

"Beats me . . . I never heard of the broad."

She persists, still skeptical. "Are you sure you didn't make love to her somewhere along the line?"

Sonny gets annoyed. "Look, Theresa, I'm not tellin' ya again . . . I don't know this broad."

Doris interrupts, "Excuse me, I don't mean to butt into your business, but I think you should know that the guards sometimes put girls names down to make the wives jealous. They used to do it to me at Nevada State . . . it nearly broke up my marriage."

Theresa is amazed. "Why do they do that?"

"Just to cause problems."

Sonny says, "I'm not surprised. They do the same thing on the inside. Guards don't change their personalities just 'cause they get assigned to visitin'. They love to hassle ya." The smell of linguine and clams is wafting up from the grill. He sniffs. "I could swear we were in Little Sicily." He twirls a plastic fork in the pot and takes a sample. "Man . . . this is great."

Sonny devours everything Theresa has brought up for him. They finish with coffee, and he unbuckles his belt, stuffed. "Baby, I can't believe you went to all that trouble cookin' . . . it was so good."

"I told you once before, I'd do anything for you."

Sonny grins lecherously. "Man, there's one thing I wish you could do right now." He puts his hand up her dress.

Theresa melts when she feels his fingers in her panties, but says nervously, "Maybe we shouldn't be doing this . . ."

He tickles her lewdly. "Why? Nobody can see . . . this tablecloth hangs down to the ground almost . . . that was smart, baby."

"It wasn't what I had in mind when I got it, but I'm glad I did." Sonny unzips his fly. Theresa reaches in and pulls out his beautiful manhood. He gets an instant hard-on at her touch, but tries to look casual and keep the conversation animated. For fifteen minutes they continue to talk, all the while playing with each other. Theresa finds it hard not to moan and yell when she comes. Sonny closes his eyes as Theresa keeps stroking his long shaft. "Ooo, baby, you're hands are so exciting."

He's just about ready to climax when a guard comes up behind them. "How'dya like your first contact visit, Gibson?"

Sonny snaps his head around quickly, afraid of detection. "It's very nice, sir . . . really good." Sonny and Theresa both hold their breath, waiting for the next word from the guard.

"Well, enjoy what's left of it."

The officer walks away, and Sonny slumps in relief . . . there's no telling what the disciplinary action would have been for exposing himself. "I gotta keep my eyes open next time. Where were we, baby?"

Theresa starts pumping him again. He's just getting stiff when the whistle blows . . . visiting is over. Sonny struggles to jam his erection into his pants and zip up.

"Are you ready?" Sonny nods, and they fold up the tablecloth. This time, kissing good-bye, Theresa is happier than she's been in years. Soon she'll be Mrs. Sonny Gibson.

" 'Bye, baby . . . see ya next week."

" 'Bye, honey . . . I'll be counting the hours."

The next day Sonny goes to the chapel office to meet the prison priest. Sonny approaches a clerk sitting behind a desk. "My name's Sonny Gibson. I'd like to see Father Schmidt."

The convict looks up. "I'm Chuck . . . take a seat . . . Father will be right with you."

The men have told Sonny that "Father Schmidt don't take shit from no convicts or no prison staff." When Sonny meets the priest, he sees why he gets respect. Father Schmidt is an imposing six-foot-three, 250-pound man, and while his size probably gives him his tough reputation, his real strength is in his eyes; they are as penetrating as an X ray. What Sonny sees behind them, though, is a gentleness and a sensitivity he has only recently learned to admire.

Father is very businesslike on their first meeting. "Gibson, I like to see a man's file before I talk to him, and I don't have much time to go into your background now. I'll call you back when I get your file."

"O.K., Father . . . I'll be waitin' to hear from you."

Sonny leaves. He closes the door and goes over to Chuck's desk. "Hey, on the way up here one of the guys was tellin' a story about this priest knockin' some guy named the Choker across two tables . . . what was that all about?"

Chuck smiles. "Yeah, I remember that . . . served the fuckin' Choker right."

"Who is he?"

"Sergeant Parker . . . used to work in the infirmary. It was Parker's game to go up to the patients and blow smoke up their nose till they choked. Then he'd put his hands around their throat and say he was gonna kill 'em. He got caught once . . . nothin' happened. They just transferred him to the kitchen. All the guys would love to kill him, but the Choker knows better than to be by himself."

"So why'd the priest have a run-in with him?"

"Father was called to the infirmary 'cause a guy got stuck. I guess he was dyin' . . . he asked for the Last Rites. When Father Schmidt got there, Choker wouldn't let him in . . . said prison policy was nobody could see the guy till they got a statement from him. You know how it is . . . they don't want nobody to know nothin'."

"Yeah, Chuck, I know how it is."

The clerk continues, "Anyway, Father said he was goin' in, and when the Choker tried to grab his arm, Father back-handed him . . . knocked him clear across the room."

"So the man did get the Last Rites?"

"Yep . . . he died a few minutes later, too."

Sonny observes, "Father Schmidt's a tough priest."

Chuck nods. "But he's a good man, Sonny. He works for the convicts, not for the prison system. Father's not one of their puppets."

"I like him already." Sonny turns to go but remembers something. "Hey, Chuck, where's the chapel?"

"Right around the corner."

"Is it locked?"

"Nah . . . it's never locked. Father Schmidt wouldn't allow that."

When Sonny walks inside the chapel, the first thing he sees is a beautiful white statue of the Blessed Virgin. She is a marble vision, arms outstretched, waiting for him. Sonny remembers Father Molinari's rosary and goes back to his block to get it. The cells are roomier than those at the state pen. They're not locked during the day, so each man has a tiny footlocker for his belongings to prevent theft.

Sonny takes his beads and pamphlet out, then hurries back to the chapel. As he reads the booklet to say the rosary, he feels a special closeness to the Mother of God . . . she will be his protector. Sonny prays that he can be an example here and help men realize they don't need shanks to be strong.

When he comes out of the chapel, Chuck says, "Ya know we got Mass here every morning at eight?"

"Is that right? Do I need a pass to get outta my cell?"

"No . . . it's not like the state pen. You can go to breakfast between six and six-thirty and go into the yard anytime from six in the morning to nine at night."

"You mean I can work out at six A.M. if I want?"

"Yep, except for when the fog rolls in . . . then there's no movement . . . somebody could escape, but I dunno where they'd go around here."

"Thanks a lot, Chuck . . . I'll see ya at Mass tomorrow."

The next day, shortly after dawn, Sonny goes out to the weight pile. To his surprise there are other convicts there already. One big man is under the bench press lifting 400 pounds. When he finishes, Sonny goes over to him. "That's pretty good, man . . . I lift about that."

"Where at? . . . I never seen you on the yard before."

"No, I just got transferred from the state pen. My name's Sonny Gibson."

The musclebound con sees the cross in Sonny's hand. "I heard you were comin' up here. You're that Mafia-and-the-Cross man, huh?"

"That's what everybody calls me."

The con smiles, "Everybody calls me Bear . . ." Sonny can see why . . . his body is covered with hair. "Real name's Al Marzullo. I know who you are, Sonny . . . it's good to meet ya." He extends his hand for the convict shake, a regular handshake followed by interlocking fingers and thumbs. "You got a workout partner yet?"

"No, that's what I came here to check out."

"Well, stop lookin'. Mine just got paroled . . . I need one. You wanna work out now?"

"Sure . . ." Sonny puts on his headband and takes off his shirt. He picks up a curl bar. "You got a job, Bear?"

"Yeah . . . I'm in the bakery . . . I can get us a lotta eggs and milk in the mornings if you can get the Tang for us to mix our protein drinks."

"O.K."

"What kinda job you gonna get in this joint?"

"I'm goin' to college. I'm gonna be a lawyer . . ."

Bear gets excited. "Hey, maybe you can help me file an appeal . . . they don't pay ya much in the bakery."

Sonny smiles. "Soon as I get my degree, that's what I wanna do . . . help guys just like you."

Two weeks pass, and Sonny still has not been called in to see Father Schmidt again. One morning the priest comes up to him on the weight pile. "I've seen your file, Gibson, I'd like to talk to you." Sonny slides off the bench and puts on his shirt. They circle the yard. "Sonny, you come to Mass every day. Why don't you take communion? Don't you think it's important?"

Sonny nods. "I got married in the Catholic Church, Father . . . my past is against me, too. If you saw my jacket, you know that. Father Molinari filed some papers about it . . ."

"He probably asked the diocese for a tribunal hearing."

"How long will that take, Father?"

The priest tells him honestly, "It could take years, Sonny. We have to get your first marriage annulled. I noticed in your file you came here to take a college program. What are you going to study?"

"I was thinking about law, Father."

"Why?"

Sonny explains, "A lot of guys get taken by their attorneys . . . their old ladies spend thousands tryin' to file appeals that never come . . . those guys live in that hope, and the money they spend is takin' food outta their kids' mouths. I wanna to help them."

Father Schmidt nods as Sonny is speaking, then says, "Sonny, that's a very laudable idea, but it would be years before you could actually help anybody, and it's sad to admit, but convicts hardly ever win a case. You know, Gibson, with your background, I think you'd do a lot better in drama."

Sonny interrupts. "Drama? How's that gonna help anybody?"

"Well, eventually you could put on plays . . . maybe describe some of your experiences, show the men how you've changed."

"Wait a minute, Father. Let's get somethin' straight right now . . . I don't preach to nobody."

Schmidt calms him. "I didn't say you had to . . . but once you get out of prison, you'd have more influence as an actor than if you became a lawyer. Movies and television are the quickest ways to reach people. You could help change some things inside and help men if you were a star."

Sonny says cynically, "You think the prison officials are really gonna do anything?"

"They'll have to if enough people hear about things like the hole."

Sonny vacillates now. Father Schmidt is making a lot of sense, but Sonny remembers the stars he'd met and how empty most of them were. "I hate show business people, Father . . . they're no good. They're a bunch a phonies."

Schmidt admonishes him, "Wait a minute, Sonny, you told me you were trying to be a Christian."

"That's right, Father, I am."

The priest smiles. "If you're a Christian, you're not supposed to judge." His wisdom makes a strong impression on Sonny. The men in prison are quick to judge each other, and some of them get killed because of it. Before Father Schmidt leaves him, he says again, "You should think about drama, Gibson. After all, the FBI said you were the most vicious con man for the Mafia. You even conned the government. There was a lot more at stake in your acting then than a few lousy reviews. I don't know much about the arts, but I think you'd be a natural actor."

Sonny considers what the priest has suggested but still leans more toward law than acting. One day, when he goes to chapel to say his daily rosary before the statue of the Blessed Virgin, Sonny hears the lush sound of a Bach concerto. Father Schmidt is seated at the organ in back, eyes closed, playing the difficult piece from memory. The rapture of the priest's face moves Sonny. He waits till Father Schmidt is finished, then goes up to him. "That's really beautiful. You play pretty good, Father"—he smiles—"for someone who doesn't know anything about the arts."

The priest has been caught in his own harmless con. "Well, I guess I know a little something, Sonny."

"Where'd ya learn to play like that?"

"In Salzburg. That's where I'm from."

"Why didn't you become a professional piano player?"

Schmidt gets up from the organ. "My love for God was greater than my love for music . . . Besides, I'm good, but I don't have the talent to be a concert pianist. You can help more people from the stage than I ever could . . . my work is right here."

"I've been thinkin' a lot about actin', Father." Sonny smiles. "You just helped me decide . . . I'm gonna do it. Are there any drama courses in the program now?"

"I don't think so, but if you can get ten men to sign up, they'll assign a teacher."

"That shouldn't be a problem, there's fifteen hundred men here."

"You get the signatures, Sonny, and I'll turn them in to the education department."

"When's the deadline, Father?"

"Next week."

Sonny says with confidence, "I'll probably have 'em for ya tomorrow."

That afternoon Sonny goes out into the yard and talks to one of the men on the weight pile he knows is enrolled in college already. "Hey, Murphy, you're goin' to school, right?"

The hulking Irishman is doing pushups. "Yeah . . ."

"How'd ya like to take a drama course this term?" The convict stops. "Drama . . . shit no . . . I'm studyin' business."

"So what . . . this'll help ya sell."

"Listen, Gibson . . . if drama was the last course, or the only one to study, I wouldn't take it . . . that's for fags. That's why there's no drama course here now."

Sonny is disappointed but not discouraged by his reaction. This was, after all, only one man's opinion. He walks through the yard, talking to other men, trying to find nine convicts who'll sign up with him. This goes on for five days . . . nobody wants to enroll. Finally there is just one day left. Sonny has to resort to drastic measures. He strides over to the toughest hit man on the yard, brandishing the cross. The Mexican says nervously, "Whaddya want from me, Mafia-and-the-Cross? I didn't do nothin', man."

He taps the top of the cross lightly on the man's chest. "I know, Chico . . . I want you to sign this list, is all."

"What's it say?"

"It says you're gonna take drama this year."

"Drama! I don't wanna take no fuckin' drama, man. That's for fuckin' sissies. Besides, I can't sit in no classroom, man."

Sonny moves a little closer, tapping harder. "Listen, ya only gotta be there the first two days, till they O.K. the course. After the professor's started comin' up here, you can fall out."

"I dunno, man." Sonny puts an arm around Chico's shoulder and squeezes. "Sign the fuckin' paper, O.K.? I'm not a violent man no more, but don't push me. I need this course to get outta here."

The Mexican can see in Sonny's eyes he's serious about drama, but more than that, Chico's afraid of him . . . he knew Sonny at the state pen. "O.K., O.K., don't get so mad about it. Where do I sign?"

Sonny points to the top line. "Right here."

Sonny leaves, and Chico's friend comes up to him. "What the hell you so scared of him for? . . . he's religious, man."

Chico shakes his head, "You can believe that if you want, but I was with him at the state pen. I saw him bust a guy's nose in three places with that cross. That was over five dollars' worth of shit. Mafia-and-the-Cross wants to get outta here bad. Whaddya think he'd do if somebody stopped him?"

"I dunno . . ."

"Well, I ain't findin' out . . . I'd sign my old lady away . . . if he wants me to."

By five o'clock that day Sonny had the additional eight signatures he needed. Not only will the drama course be given, but the meanest, toughest men in the prison were enrolled. A few weeks later the college courses began. That semester he was studying law, theology, and, of course, drama. This was the start of a new routine for Sonny. He'd go to Mass and work out in the morning and attend classes in the afternoon, skipping lunch to do his homework on the yard. He enjoyed all of his subjects, but the one he looked forward to the most was drama. The professor, Mr. Harper, an ex-actor and English teacher, was not too disturbed when the rest of the men dropped out . . . it had unnerved him on his first day to see the hardened convicts who were to be his new students of the arts. Harper came up three nights a week for their three-hour sessions. They read Shakespeare, Dickens, and many other great writers. Harper glowed as he talked about them, infecting Sonny with his zeal. The fiery man was also an innovative acting coach. Every time they met, Harper would take an article from the paper, pick a character from it, and assign one to Sonny. Then they both improvised a dramatic scene around the news event. These were taped, so of course Sonny learned to spot his mistakes quickly using this method. Soon he was outacting the teacher.

Because of Sonny's busy schedule he keeps to himself at this prison, but when Chuck asks him to attend a Christian Fellowship meeting, he agrees to go. When he gets to the library, where it's held, five men are sitting around a table. One of the convicts is reading the Bible haltingly in a dull monotone. Chuck comes over to Sonny and introduces him to the other members. The reader says, "I'm glad you could make it, Sonny."

"Yeah, me, too, but how come ya don't have more men here? A

lotta guys go to Mass."

One middle-aged con replies, "Many of them don't know how to praise the Lord, Sonny . . . going to Mass isn't everything."

Another says, "Yeah, and a lotta the Christians don't know the Scripture like we do."

Sonny reminds him, "Christ said in the Bible he didn't come on the earth to save the righteous. He came to save all sinners. You should open this fellowship up to everybody."

Chuck asks, "How would it work, Sonny? There's too many religions on the yard."

"Simple, insteada just readin' Scripture, we'll get a reading on each other. We'll have a talk session with the guys . . . there's other ways to spread Christian love besides the Bible. Why don't you plan on havin' a lot more people here next week?"

Chuck shakes his head. "We've tried. We can't get anybody else to come, Sonny. They wouldn't go anywhere for us."

Sonny smiles. "You let me take care of it."

The following Wednesday night the library is packed to the rafters. Sonny has taken his cross around the yard "requesting" that men attend the meeting . . . forty have shown up. One of them shouts, "Hey, man, before we start, we gotta offer an apple and an orange to Buddha."

A born-again Mexican shouts, "No, man, we gotta say a prayer in Jesus' name. We'll open up that way."

A Jewish convict disagrees, "Hold on . . . I don't believe in Jesus Christ."

The Mexican yells back, "That's awful. You don't believe in Christ, man, what's the matter with you?"

Sonny puts his hand up over his head. "Wait a minute, you guys . . . just calm down. We're not here to argue about our religions . . . we're here to help each other. That's love." He looks around the room. "Anybody here gonna argue with me that love's not part of their religion?" No one protests. "All right . . . then what we'll do is this, we'll talk about our problems . . . what's botherin' ya, whatever's on your mind. Then we'll let everyone give suggestions to help solve 'em, okay? Anybody wanna start?" There is a silence from the room. In prison, admitting something is troubling you could be read as a sign of weakness. Sonny is ready for this. "Hey, that's great . . . you guys must be livin' like kings in here . . . nobody's got problems."

One country convict on the side speaks up. "I got one . . . I don't think y'all can help me, though."

"What is it, Skeeter?"

"Well, my mom's havin' a hard time gittin' up here. They took away our car. Now she can't see me no more."

"Where's she live?"

"East LA."

Chico shouts from across the room, "Hey, man, my old lady comes up here every week from East LA. She can pick her up . . . if she'll pay half the gas."

Skeeter gets excited. "Hey, man, that'd be all right . . . I'd get to see her then."

Sonny smiles. "You guys can get the information later, but see . . . that's a start. Skeeter thought he'd never solve that problem and we did." He looks around. "What else?"

A burly black with a gravelly voice calls out, "Man, that's easy compared to the fuckin' trouble I got."

Sonny frowns. "Hey, Reggie, let's see if just for a couple a hours we can stay away from that kinda language, huh? When we get out on the street with the civilians, it'll turn 'em off."

Reggie agrees, "Yeah, O.K. My old lady says I cuss too much anyway . . . but what about Lou Jack?"

"Is he your problem?"

"Yeah . . . he's been hasslin' me about somethin' that happened over some narcotics when I was in three years ago. Looks like I'm gonna have to take a shank and kill his white butt."

Sonny bargains, "I'll tell ya what . . . tomorrow I'll go with ya and talk to Lou Jack . . . see what his problem is. Maybe a few words could solve it. God forgives. I'm sure you and Lou Jack could forgive each other."

One of the most hardened cons in the yard, Rattler, yells out from the back of the room, "Look, Sonny, I don't know what you did to get in here, but I killed two men. Is God gonna forgive me for that? I came tonight 'cause Reggie said I should, but it's easy for you to stand there and talk about religion . . . what'd you ever do, man?"

Most of the men just stare at him, surprised by his ignorance. Reggie says, "Lemme tell ya somethin' about Sonny, Rattler. About a year ago I saw him beat up four dudes bad with that cross. Put 'em in the hospital. A lot of us down from the pen know Sonny was the toughest hit man on the yard and one of the best for the Mafia . . . I dunno how many people he killed."

Chico yells, "Hey, Sonny, how many people have ya killed, man?" Sonny hesitates. The Mexican says, "It's O.K. if ya don't wanna say in here. You don't gotta admit to nothin'."

Sonny can see this is a crucial turning point. Showing them he has changed will be an example to the others. "I'm not praisin' this, Chico— it's wrong to murder—but I've killed more than two men . . . I've killed more than twenty . . . but I've done worse things than kill. I know God has forgiven me, and if He can forgive me, He can forgive you guys for what you've done."

Rattler says, "O.K., so maybe God forgives me . . . but I got a problem even God's not gonna be able to solve."

"What is it?"

"My old lady needs eighty bucks to fix the car so she can go to work . . . there's no bus to her job, and she'll lose it. Who the hell's gonna give *me* money . . . none a you guys got it."

Sonny thinks. "No, but I think I can get my old lady to kick in five bucks."

Chuck says, "Yeah, I can get mine to give ya ten . . . she makes a good livin'."

Sonny smiles as everyone starts to call out amounts. Within minutes Rattler has the eighty dollars he needs. It was working. For the first time these men, some of whom were deadly enemies, were beginning to help each other. "You see what we've done here already. Just think what'll happen with even more guys comin'. There's one thing everybody should understand, though . . . we gotta leave the gang problems on the yard. If there's some trouble, step away from it. When I was with the Mafia, everyone knew it was better to talk than to start a war, but at least there one side would win. Here our side has no chance . . . the prison system always wins, and in the end all the convicts lose if there's a lockdown."

Reggie says, "Yeah . . . my friend's been eatin' bologna sandwiches for two weeks at Michigan State. I'm gonna write and tell him about this fellowship thing, Sonny. Maybe they can get one goin' up there."

Sonny agrees. "That's a good idea . . . anybody else got friends inside, tell 'em about it, too, but right now you can start spreading the word about our group. We'll start by takin' care of our own."

The popularity of Sonny's fellowship grew. It comforted the convicts to know there were some people in prison who cared about them. Soon they were meeting twice a week. One afternoon Sonny was approached by Rattler and his friends to run for president of the Convicts' Council. A black was already in office, doing a good job, but Sonny knew the whites wanted him in so the black will be out. At one time he'd have felt the same way, but he had no prejudice anymore, so Sonny declined the candidacy but agreed to be a special advisor to the council.

Time passed quickly for Sonny because he was kept occupied with his fellowship and his studies. Soon it was Christmas . . . this time he was able to celebrate with Theresa. One weekend the wives and children were allowed to bring in ornaments, and everyone decorated a tree in the tiny yard. All gifts, however, had to be exchanged through the mail. Sonny made a jewelry box for Theresa, and he got the complete works of Shakespeare from her. On Christmas day, Pops came with Theresa to visit. She brought up a turkey dinner with all the trimmings to heat up on the big outdoor grill. Afterward the family strolled around the yard together. They were in high spirits, like most people on that day, but the guntower overshadowing the Christmas tree was a painful reminder that Sonny was not a free man. He squeezes Theresa's hand. "I know someday I'll be home for Christmas again."

"Yeah, I know . . . but when?" His answer is cut off as a black man rushing past bumps into Sonny, nearly knocking him over. The convict stops in fear at the sight of the huge, muscular man before him. "Hey, man, I'm really sorry."

Sonny puts a hand on the black's shoulder. "That's O.K. Have a good Christmas visit."

Theresa is amazed as she watches the man go. If that had happened on the outside, he wouldn't have gotten away so easily. She cracks, "It's a good thing it's Christmas and I'm here, or that guy would've been in big trouble, huh?"

Sonny turns to her. "No . . . you're wrong, Theresa. Even if we were alone, I would've done the same thing, and it's not because it's a special day either . . . we should have Christmas spirit every day of the year."

This astonishes her. "You mean you really would have let him get away with that?"

"He didn't do anything to me . . ."

"Are you O.K., honey?"

He says seriously, "I've never been better, Theresa. I don't have the hate and violence you once knew. I'm different."

She laughs. "Come on, Sonny . . . you don't have to play that game with me. Nobody's around. I mean, if anybody asks, I'll tell them you've changed and everything."

His tone is more serious now. "Theresa, I really have changed. Father Schmidt says I might even get to take communion soon."

"You mentioned that before . . ."

"Yeah, we filed papers to get my first marriage annulled. If I didn't love you, I could take communion now."

"What? That sounds stupid. I don't understand . . ."

"Well, I had to be honest on the forms. According to the Church laws I'm still married, but since I love you and wanna live with you when I get out, they consider that wrong."

"Well, I think that's dumb."

Pops interrupts now. "I think it's good that Sonny wants to take communion. His mother would have liked to see that . . ."

Theresa is still skeptical about Sonny's change. She remembers the look in his eyes the day on the plane when he was about to kill a man. How could anything overcome such coldness? The visiting sergeant's grating voice breaks into her thoughts. "Awright . . . visitin's over. Time for everybody to go home."

Sonny hugs Pops and kisses Theresa. Before they leave, she says, "I worry about you so much. Every time I hear the news I hold my breath, hoping I won't hear anything about a riot up here."

Sonny puts an arm around her. "Don't worry, Theresa . . . even if there was one, God's watching over me."

"I hope you're right, Sonny . . ." As Sonny watches her leave the visiting yard, he hopes that someday Theresa will know in her heart that he is not the same man who lived outside those prison walls.

The next year flew by for Sonny. Between his schoolwork and his fellowship, which kept expanding, he was occupied almost twenty-four hours a day. His courses now included anthropology, journalism, and creative writing. Sonny conned the university into sending Professor Harper back up again by getting ten different "ghost" students to enroll that year. Harper was not surprised when everyone but Sonny dropped out, and he didn't mind either. This pupil stimulated him unlike any other he'd had. They both enjoyed this class. Sonny spent hours with William Shakespeare every night. When the energy crisis hit, the prison did not escape its effects. Lights-out was moved up to nine P.M., but that didn't stop Sonny from studying. He read his books, not with a candle like Abraham Lincoln, but with light from toilet paper burning in its own cardboard tube.

Sonny's second Christmas was very different from the first. He'd been working for months trying to get permission for Theresa to give a miniconcert in the yard. With Father Schmidt's help the performance was finally approved. Theresa brought her guitar and sang the songs she'd written for the convict families. Everyone was touched by the moving lyrics she'd written over the years, which told of the trials of men in prison and the loneliness of the loved ones who waited for them. Theresa wrote the music to a special love song as a present to Sonny. The words told about their life together and what he meant to her:

We've been together a long time,
We've seen the bottom of the cup,
But somehow it never seemed empty
'Cause we had our dreams to fill it up.

There were times I thought of leavin',
But deep down inside me I knew
No one could ever be better
And I was lucky to have you.

Baby, sometimes it's not easy
Temptation weighs heavy on my mind
But I'd be a fool to ever let you go
'Cause a good love is hard to find.*

*Lyrics by Robert Jason. Reprinted with permission.

When Theresa finishes singing, they all applaud, and Sonny puts an arm around her waist. He kisses her. "That's the best present anyone's ever given me, baby . . . and somethin' no money could ever buy. I love you."

Sonny hopes that they can celebrate the next Christmas at Central as man and wife. His request to be married went to the state capital, but because he's listed OC, it is taking a long time to be approved. In June the papers finally come through. Sonny would like to have a nuptial Mass and take communion, but Father Schmidt tells him there has been no word yet from the diocese about the annulment of his first marriage. The Protestant minister would have to marry them.

The whole yard knows that Sonny's getting married, and the night before everyone stays out of trouble, afraid of what Mafia-and-the-Cross will do if someone interferes with the wedding. They know if there's a lockdown Sonny could lose his ten-hour family visit.

The morning of the big day the men on the weight pile all have their comments about it. Bear pats his back. "Man, you're finally gettin' some pussy . . . I'll bet you're really lookin' forward to that, huh, Sonny?"

Chico says, "Come a few times for me, will ya? I forgot what it's like . . . I haven't been with no broads in six years, man."

Rattler adds, "Yeah, get a blow job for me . . . that was always my favorite . . . oowhee!!"

Skeeter comes over, "Hey, Sonny, you think I should get married so I can fuck? Theresa got any sisters?"

Reggie teases him, "Skeeter, who the hell'd marry you with those big ol' ears stickin' a mile outta your head?" Sonny is quiet through all of their joking, slightly uncomfortable to be getting special privileges when he's just like them. However, his excitement about being with Theresa soon overcomes these emotions.

They are married at eleven A.M. that day in the Protestant chapel. There are no white flowers or fancy trappings during the brief service, but there is a celebration afterward in the yard outside the chapel. Bear had smuggled real milk and butter out of the warden's refrigerator to bake a special wedding cake for them. It is exquisitely decorated, complete with a bridal couple on top, hand-carved by Chuck. There are no guests from the bride's side at the reception, but Sonny's whole family is present. The yard is jammed with men of all races, colors and creeds, including the toughest hit men from every gang. Sonny's wedding probably saved some lives.

The groom's present to Theresa is a pencil portrait of her, copied from a photograph. Though he'd never drawn before, this one, the result of thirty-five attempts, is a perfect likeness. Theresa gives him a gold band, but of course the best gift comes from the warden . . . their ten-hour conjugal visit. The men all wink at him now as they leave but refrain from any crude remarks out of respect for Theresa. Sonny's heart races like a virgin's as he and his wife are escorted to the small trailer. There are no guards posted outside . . . the ones in the gun-towers are their prison chaperones. When they get inside, Sonny watches Theresa put away the things she brought for their ten-hour stay: juices, soda, and fresh fruit, all things the men are not allowed to have. He takes off his shirt and tests out the tiny bed, sinking down into it. "Man, this is the first soft mattress I've been on in a long time." He pats a place for her. "Come on over, baby."

Theresa's teary eyes are filled with longing. She lies down and wraps her arms around him as they kiss. Sonny gets erect at the first touch of her firm breasts, crushing her against his chest, the pent-up passion ready to burst from his groin. Still clothed, they roll on the bed, fondling each other, bodies straining with tempestuous desire. Finally Sonny can wait no more. He starts tearing at Theresa's clothes, ex-ploding with the urgency to be inside her. She pulls off his jeans, and the sight of that gigantic nakedness again nearly makes her swoon. Sonny lays his new bride back and climbs on top of her velvety body. The passionate juices flowing from Theresa's aching loins help him slip easily into her musky wetness. It's been four long years since he's felt the warm, soft walls of her vagina pulsing around him, sucking the need from his body. His first climax is shattering and comes with hers. Theresa screams beneath him, her thirst for a man seemingly insatiable.

She says over and over, "It's been so long, God, it's been so long. I love you. I love you . . ." Their lovemaking is like a dream, gentle at times, while at other times animal passion overtakes Sonny. He pounds her furiously, releasing his frustration in her, coming again and again, as if to make up for all the days of deprivation and store up sex for the many days of abstinence yet to come. In a while Sonny pulls out, anxious to bring Theresa a different kind of pleasure. He licks her silky skin all over, finally reaching her beautiful dark mound. She clutches him desperately as he devours it and, in one minute, brings her to a gushing orgasm. She is still throbbing when he mounts her again.

Three hours later the newlyweds finally take their first break. They lie back, sipping canned tomato juice and talking. "You're beautiful, baby. You know, you make me feel special . . . I've said that before, but never meant it, Theresa. I love you."

She touches his cheek gently. "I love you because you are special." Theresa frowns. "Do you think they'll ever come a day when we can touch each other again in our own bed, in our own home? Being here is like being in a fishbowl."

"I dunno . . . I wish I had a more comforting answer, but I just don't know.''

"God, Sonny, why does it have to be like this?"

"Baby, we're lucky . . . what if we didn't have this time at all?"

She nods, managing a smile. "You're right . . . at least we're together for ten hours, and I have love in my life. Some people never have that at all.'' Sonny thinks of Skeeter, who probably never would get married and most likely be in prison for the next fifteen years.

Theresa wipes her brow. They're both sweating in the steamy trailer. "You think the shower works in this thing?"

He takes her hand. "Well, let's find out . . .'' They go into the tiny stall together, and Theresa unwraps a bar of Dial. Sonny makes a rich foam in his hands. "Hey, look at that . . . this is great. Wish they'd let us use real soap here.'' He takes his slippery hands and runs them over her full breasts, playing with the hard nipples. Theresa lathers up and toys with him. Soon she's holding a lot more than she can handle. They try to make love, but it's too cramped. After a few minutes Sonny says, "I wanna go back to the bed where I can see every part of you." She hands him a soft bath towel. Sonny rubs it over his body, luxuriating in the plush folds . . . he'd forgotten what that felt like, too. He took so many things for granted on the outside, including his freedom. Theresa leads him back to bed and opens herself seductively to him. They begin to make love in a steady, erotic rhythm, and then the count horn blows. Sonny jumps off her, frantic. "What time is it?"

Theresa yells, "Goddam, that hurt! Why'd you have to pull out so fast?"

"What time is it?"

She's confused. "I don't know . . . we haven't been here that long, we have time."

He persists, "Theresa, just find out what time it is, O.K.?" She goes over to the small table and looks at her watch. "It's four-thirty.'' Sonny sighs with relief. "Thank God . . . it's only the four-thirty count."

"What are you talking about?"

He sits down on the edge of the bed. "They have to count the men six times a day . . . a horn goes off after, but the same horn goes off if there's any kind of trouble."

Now she's concerned. "You think there's trouble?"

"No, no . . . but if there was, the prison would be locked down, and that'd be the end of our visit."

Theresa doesn't know what to do . . . she's never seen Sonny this upset. Now she puts a gentle hand on his shoulder. "It's O.K., honey, you can relax. You're with me." Theresa sits on his lap. "Come on . . . where were we?" They start making love again, but this time Sonny just goes through the motions. All he can think of are the men inside. In only a few short hours he will be one of them again. Guilt overwhelms him. Many of the convicts would never be able to take advantage of a ten-hour visit with a woman, and he knows how the men in the yard sacrificed for him. That makes Sonny love the hit men even more than the others. They have to be hard-core to enforce, but even they stopped their operations for a whole day so Sonny could have sex. Theresa can never understand the feelings he has, and he doesn't attempt to explain them. For the rest of the visit he tells her how wonderful it is for them to be together, but he almost wishes it would end. It is cruel to give a starving man just one bite of food if he has already forgotten about his hunger.

Soon there is only one more hour left together. They make love, each keeping an eye on the clock for the countdown. At fifteen minutes Theresa says, "I guess we'd better get dressed . . . I don't want you to get into trouble." She gathers up her things. "How soon do you think we could get another visit?"

Sonny pulls on his socks. "It's hard to say . . . ten months, a year. I'm goin' to my counselor first thing tomorrow morning to put in for another one."

Theresa is trying to ease into her jeans. "OW!"

"What's the matter honey?"

"Nothing, I'm just real sore. Next time you can bet I'll remember to bring the Vaseline."

Sonny agrees. "Yeah . . . I feel like I got caught in a vice." He smiles. "But it was worth it."

Their last kiss is interrupted by a knock. "Time's up, Gibson . . . come on." They sneak in one more kiss, then he opens the door. "I'm ready, officer."

In September Sonny starts the final semester of course for his fine arts degree. He and his usual list of friends enroll in drama, but this year the university is on to his con. They refuse to send an instructor just to be his private tutor. When Harper finds out about it, he's concerned—Sonny needs that course to complete his requirements for graduation. The dedicated teacher has so much belief in his student's acting abilities that he comes up to the prison three nights a week in his free time, without pay, to work with him. Sonny studies arduously, preparing for all his finals, but he knows the university staff will be particularly demanding in drama. After all, he was the only member of the class. For part of his final exam they will drill him on Shakespeare. Sonny must learn five plays.

Sonny passes all of his exams with flying colors, but there is no graduation ceremony in the penitentiary. Two weeks later Sonny's diploma comes in the mail. Theresa brings a cake to the prison that Sunday, and they celebrate quietly.

The morning after, as Sonny is working out at the weight pile, a guy comes up and shouts to the men, "Hey, if anybody wants to see a show, two Jews are gonna get stuck unless they give up their canteen to some niggers . . . They're bein' harassed on the line right now." This news doesn't interfere with any of the convicts' workout routines except Sonny's. He puts down his weights.

Bear looks up. "Where ya goin'?"

"I'm goin' over there."

"Stay outta that . . . it's trouble."

"I've dealt with trouble before . . . this is nothin'." Sonny picks up his cross and heads for the canteen. The blacks are still razzing the Jews when he arrives. Sonny recognizes one of them, Big Monty, who was with him in the other pen.

When they see Sonny, the black yells, "Hey, here comes Mafia-and-the-Cross."

Sonny approaches calmly, "Hey brothers, how ya doin' today? Don't you have anything better to do than pick on two men twice your age?"

They laugh. "These are Jews, man . . . Jews don't fight for themselves . . . it's fun. Besides, they always buy more than they can eat."

Sonny looks at the group. "Ya know, you guys are actin' like niggers. You're not . . . you're black men . . . ya don't wanna get yourself in trouble in here . . . so quit harassin' 'em."

Big Monty hates whites but especially despises Sonny. However, he's afraid of him with that cross in his hand. "Are you gonna cause trouble, man?"

Sonny pauses. "Well, Monty, the Bible says I should turn my cheek. If you hit me . . . I will. If you hit me a second time, I'll turn my cheek . . ." Sonny thinks. "But if you hit me a third time, I'm gonna bust your head with this cross. The Bible don't say nothin' about a third time."

One black shouts, "You're pretty brave with that cross. I seen ya clobber guys with that. How brave would ya be, white boy, if you got in the ring with Big Monty?"

"He ain't gettin in no ring . . . everybody knows Christians are chicken."

"Yeah, Christ was a fag, man . . . he never had a broad in his life."

Sonny offers them a proposition. "If you promise not to hassle any of the guys in the prison, not just Jews . . . I'll fight Big Monty."

The men stare at him in amazement . . . the odds against Sonny are tremendous. Monty is a professional boxer, and Sonny has never fought before. "You're really crazy, man . . . Monty's gonna wipe your white ass all over the ring."

Another black says, "That's why they call him Crazy Sonny, man."

Sonny insists, "I'll fight him if I have that promise."

Monty interrupts. "I don't trust him with the cross . . . that thing's gotta stay outta the ring."

Sonny assures him, "Don't worry, I'll be fightin' ya with gloves."

"Hey, Mafia-and-the-Cross, if you lose, you don't carry that cross in the yard no more, O.K.?"

"O.K., I won't carry this cross in the yard unless I see you harassin' people."

The black grins. "Hey, that's all right, man, we won't have to harass nobody. We're gonna make so much money off this fight, we gonna buy the whole canteen. Come on, let's go make our bets." As they leave, Monty says, "You really think you're gonna beat me, white boy?"

Sonny smiles. "It won't be me fightin' ya, Monty . . . it'll be the Lord."

When the blacks are gone, the Jews come over to Sonny. "What's it gonna cost for you to protect us?"

Sonny looks at them. "Nothin', man . . . just come to the fellowship. We meet twice a week in the yard."

They both hesitate, "We can't come to a Christian fellowship . . . we're Jews."

"We're still all men, and you have problems . . . that's what we talk about. It's not religious.

"O.K., we'll be there, Sonny. Thanks."

A whole week before the fight an undercurrent of excitement runs through the prison. There is more at stake than just black against white. It is the classic callegory of good against evil. The men like Sonny, but even most of the whites bet on Monty . . . he holds the prison boxing title. Before Monty was imprisoned for killing a man in a barroom brawl, his fight record was perfect, mostly knockouts. Father Schmidt comes to Sonny's rescue. He's worried; the priest knows Sonny has a slim chance of winning. "Go see Rick, Sonny, he can help you."

"Rick the altar boy?"

"Yeah . . . just like Sonny the altar boy. Rick was a professional fighter. He's willing to train you."

In just seven days Rick tries to give Sonny all of his expertise about the fight game and shows him tricks so that Sonny can use his southpaw to the best advantage. Unlike Father Schmidt, Sonny's not worried about winning, but goes to the statue of the Blessed Virgin daily to pray for a different outcome. "Please let this fight be a message to the other guys. Help them understand that a religious man is not a weak man." One day he looks up and sees the statue smiling at him. That night Sonny has a dream that he'll knock Monty out in the first round. He goes to tell Father Schmidt. The priest has read in Sonny's file that he was called a psychic for the Mafia, but this time the clergyman has to trust his own intuition.

"Look, Sonny, let's be realistic . . . Rick's been helping you box, and he's a good fighter, but let's not get carried away—even the Blessed Mother may not be ready to work a miracle."

Sonny insists, "I'm gonna knock him out in the first round, Father . . . and it'll bring a lot of guys to the Lord."

The priest is still doubtful. "I don't know, Sonny . . . Monty's good."

"Are you gonna be there, Father?"

"I don't go to prison fights. They're usually no more than a bloody vendettas."

"This one will be different. Will you bless my hands, Father?" The priest hesitates. Sonny assures him, "I'm not gonna use 'em to hurt . . . I just wanna make an example." Father Schmidt makes the sign of the cross over him. Sonny asks anxiously, "Well, Father . . . will you come?"

The priest sighs. "I'll be there . . . somebody has to say a prayer for you."

That Friday night the convicts are crammed into the prison gymnasium, waiting for the fight to begin. Tension is thick as they talk about the odds. Most of them have bet on Monty, but when Sonny comes in, they all stand and cheer. When both fighters are in the center of the ring, the referee reads the rules. "Awright, I want a clean fight. No spittin' in the face, no kickin' in the balls, no callin' each other honky or nigger. If one convict goes down, the other one goes to the corner . . . understand?" Both fighters nod. "Tap your gloves and come out fighting."

In parting Monty warns Sonny, "I'm gonna knock your white ass all over the ring before I put the lights out on ya."

In the corner, as Rick puts in the mouthpiece, he says, "Remember, Sonny . . . surprise him. Use that left cross God gave you." Sonny nods. He is apprehensive about the whole thing. This is the first violent act he's been involved in since he was released from the hole, but it will be worth it if Monty's crowd stops picking on the guys in the yard. The bell rings. In the first five seconds of the round Monty gets a few good punches in, one almost knocking the wind out of Sonny . . . the crowd boos. Sonny gives Monty a right jab, and the black man falls. The crowd cheers; they've never seen Monty knocked down. The referee gets him up on his feet again, but the champ is dazed. Sonny hits Monty just one more time with a left cross, knocking him to the canvas. Monty is motionless. The men jump to their feet even before the referee starts the count. There is more pandemonium in the gym at that moment then there is at midnight on New Year's Eve in Times Square. Men are leaping up, throwing their headbands in the air, hollering, and hugging each other. Father Schmidt gives Sonny the O.K. sign as the convicts lift the winner on their shoulders and carry him out of the gym. Yet it is also a sad victory—Sonny can see Monty being carried out of the gym, too . . . on a stretcher.

The next day it's all over the yard that Sonny has broken Monty's jaw in two places. He feels genuinely sorry that he's hurt Monty and visits him in the hospital. Through his wired mouth the big man cracks, "The Lord sure packs a powerful punch, Sonny."

"He always will, if you have Him on your side, Monty." From that time on Sonny and Monty are fast friends. The black fighter even joins Sonny's fellowship when he's well. Another convict from the state pen is also in the group now, too—Ramon Juarez. One day a familiar voice had called to him from across the yard: "Hey, Mafia-and-the-Cross man, give the Ax hell."

Sonny turned, surprised to see Ramon. "Hey, Juarez, last I heard you were still in the hole for spittin' in some guard's coffee."

"Yeah . . . they couldn't keep me there that long. By the way, Jim sent me a Bible in the hole . . . I'm not the same guy I used to be."

"That's great . . . I told Jim to keep on handin' out those Bibles."

Juarez smiled. "That's what turned me around, brother . . ."

"Hey, Juarez, we got an interesting fellowship going here . . . the guys talk about their problems, it's like a rap session."

Juarez said snidely, "You mean like what the counselors are supposed to do?"

"Yeah . . ."

"Sounds good, Sonny, when is it?"

"There's one Wednesday night at eight in the library."

Ramon agreed, "I'll be there . . . I gotta go get my physical now . . . see ya then."

It is through Juarez that an important problem in the prison comes to light. Ramon is hospitalized with food poisoning, the first of many convicts to be stricken. They come to Sonny for help, and he goes to Superintendent Garcia, who is unsympathetic to his request for a food investigation. "If you want one, Gibson, you'll have to do it yourself . . . I'm not wasting any prison staff on something as useless as that." So Sonny starts his own investigation. Bear sneaks out the Department of Corrections guidelines, which specify that each day the convicts must be served seven ounces of meat, one ounce of eggs, and sixteen ounces of milk—the essential protein foods needed to stay healthy. He gets a scale from the kitchen and for ninety days weighs his portions at every meal. The men were getting only six ounces of milk in the morning, two ounces of meat a day, and one ounce of eggs a week. His investigation reveals that the convicts were being shorted

778.9 pounds of food daily.

Under Sonny's direction the report is smuggled out under Theresa's dress. She mails it to two state senators and the governor, registered, return receipt requested. Sonny asks Father Schmidt to hold the scale for him. When the story breaks, he wants to show it to the investigators. "They'll say I cheated, Father. I have a perjury conviction . . . they'll never trust me."

The priest hesitates at first. "Well, I shouldn't really get involved because I'm a prison staff member." He smiles. "But the safest place for that scale is in the chapel . . . I think you'd better hide it here."

It is one month before Sonny finally hears from Superintendent Garcia about the report of his food investigation. Sonny is called into the warden's office; Sergeant Parker, who's in charge of the kitchen, is already there. Sonny assumes the Choker has been called on the carpet for this. Garcia gets right to the point. "We found out where the shortage was, Gibson."

Sonny is surprised to hear them even admit to one. "Where was it?" He had been told by the outside kitchen staff that the guards were stealing the meat, and the guards told Sonny that the kitchen staff had done it. It really didn't matter who stole the food—gone was gone—but Sonny is anxious to hear the official explanation.

Garcia sits back. "The shortage is in the delivery trucks. It seems the meat shrinks on the trucks before it even gets here . . . something to do with the freezing process . . . so we're not even getting what we're supposed to." He looks at Sonny for a reaction. There is none, so Garcia continues officiously, "I'm sure you understand, and we commend you for bringing this to our attention. By the way, Senator Nejedly and Governor Brown received a report of your investigation . . . they did look into it."

Sonny is now sure he knows what happened. The shortage cost the taxpayers $220,000 a year for food they thought the convicts were getting. Any official would want that hushed up.

The warden quizzes Sonny. "By the way, Gibson, the mailroom has no record of that report being mailed. How did it get out?"

Sonny smiles. "Well, Superintendent, I guess it got out the same way the food did."

Parker snaps, "You're wasting your time talking to Gibson, Superintendent. He won't spill anything . . . that's why he went to prison. He refused to testify against the Mafia."

Garcia says, "I'm sure he'll tell the men what happened . . ."

Sonny says coldly, "I'm sure I will . . . I'm gonna tell 'em exactly what happened."

One afternoon Sonny is called from a fellowship meeting to Garcia's office. There are two men in the waiting room, Sonny knows immediately they're feds. He goes inside, and before the warden can even open his mouth, Sonny tells him, "I won't see anyone without Father Schmidt being present."

"Is that necessary, Gibson?"

Sonny folds his arms and sits back. "Yep." The superintendent grudgingly agrees. "O.K. . . . we'll try and find him for you."

Twenty minutes later they still have not been successful in locating the priest. Garcia reasons, "Look, Sonny, Agent Young and Agent Scott just wanna ask you a few questions about a guy you knew in Lake Tahoe."

Sonny's psychic powers tell him the warden is lying, but with the help of the Lord he plans to get rid of all the federal pests once and for all. "O.K., I'll see 'em."

The two FBI men are shown into the office. As soon as they sit down at the table, Young starts asking Sonny about Don Giuseppe. "You know, Sonny, Giuseppe Loganno is very sick. Who do you think will be taking over as head of the New York family when he dies?"

Sonny catches them in their con. "Hey, come on, you guys . . . you lied to me. You said you wanted to ask me about a friend of mine in Tahoe . . . Don't you know lyin' is a sin?"

The men are taken aback by this statement. "What did you say, Gibson?"

"Lying, gentlemen, is a sin against the seventh commandment of God." Sonny stands and walks slowly around the table. ". . . but I know that God will forgive you. After all, He gave His only Son to save men like you . . . and me."

The agents exchange puzzled looks. Young says, "What is this, Gibson, are you crazy?"

Scott joins in heatedly, "Gibson, if you don't cooperate with the United States government, when you go to the board next week, they're gonna deny you parole . . . then you'll have no chance of being saved."

Sonny really starts laying it on thick, "In the Scriptures it says that Peter denied Christ three times and he was saved. Do you know about the love of Jesus Christ?" He smiles. "Jesus loves you men."

The agents get up simultaneously, but Scott makes one last attempt. "If you change your mind, Gibson, call us . . . here's my card." As they walk down the hall, Sonny continues shouting after them, "Praise the Lord, Praise God . . . safe trip home."

After they're gone, Sonny tosses the card in the wastepaper basket. Garcia retrieves it. "You should keep this . . . it's important." He hands it to Sonny, who rips it up, saying, "Nothing is important enough to make me tell lies on the witness stand about other men." Sonny throws the pieces in the waste basket and strides out.

Sonny is due for his three-year parole review soon. When the list of convicts scheduled to appear before the board is posted, Sonny's number is on it. The following morning at ten o'clock he is called to the hearing room. Sonny is summoned inside right away; unfortunately, Joe Vitone has returned to haunt him. Vitone says sternly, "Well, Gibson . . . have you learned your lesson? Have you decided to become a good American?"

Sonny replies seriously, "Yes, sir. I feel I am becoming a good American. I love my fellow man and I love my country. Because this is a democracy, I was able to get an education."

Vitone looks at his file. "Yes, I see that you have a degree in fine arts now." He says coldly, ". . . but that's not good enough, Gibson. This report shows that you have continued your life of crime even while you've been in the penitentiary. You killed Danny DeMarco."

Sonny is astounded. "What? How could I kill DeMarco? Danny's still alive . . . he runs a bar in Ventura County."

Vitone checks again. "It says right here that DeMarco was murdered and that you did it . . . of course there was no conviction." He leans back and folds his hands. "Let me ask you something, Gibson. You refused to testify against the Mafia five years ago. Agent Scott informs us that you would be a very good witness for the government. Are you ready to fulfill your responsibility as a citizen of this country and testify against those men so that we can put them behind bars where they belong? If you do this, we'll put you where you belong . . . out on the streets with the good people."

"If you think I'm that good, then I guess I'll get a parole then, huh?"

Vitone leans forward, gesturing with his pencil. "Gibson, Father Schmidt recommends you for parole. He says you've really changed. If that's true, then you'll cooperate with the United States government. If you do, there's a very good chance that you'll be paroled." He sits back again. "If you don't, I can't guarantee what will happen."

Sonny looks him straight in the eyes. "If you're askin' me to rat . . . that's out . . . as a Christian it's not right to judge others, Mr. Vitone."

The board member goes berserk. "You're no more a Christian than Satan is, Gibson! I'll release you tomorrow if you get on your knees and say you've been conning everyone—including God. I'll parole you now . . . I'll . . ."

The counselor tries to restrain him. "Mr. Vitone, I think——"

He gets pushed away. "You shut the hell up, I'm running this board."

Sonny says calmly, "Mr. Vitone, if I got on my knees and did what you asked, you still wouldn't let me out. You can't con me . . . I've been there. I won't rat or renounce God, sir, but I do think you should calm down, or you'll get a stroke."

Vitone pounds his fist violently on the table. "Gibson, you're gonna stay in here till you rot! You're a disgrace to the Italian people. You're an insult to humanity." He slams the folder down. "Your hearing is over."

This time, when the guards lead Sonny away, he is relieved, but he turns at the door. "Ya know, Mr. Vitone . . . it's too bad you have so much hate. The Scriptures say we should love our enemies."

Vitone raves, "Get him outta here . . . I never want to see his face again."

The following week Sonny got word that his next parole review would be September 8, 1986. He brought the report to Father Schmidt, who told Sonny that he could appeal. Since Sonny had some law in college, they decided to file themselves. Father Schmidt obtained the necessary forms, and they worked around the clock to make sure the papers were properly prepared. Just three weeks later the answer came back in bold letters: "DENIED." Father Schmidt was called before the superintendent because prison regulations forbid any official to take part in a convict's appeal action. The priest told Garcia he believed what he did for Sonny was right. This was not going to stop him from helping convicts in the future.

That afternoon, when Sonny works out at the weight pile, Bear is the unwitting carrier of bad news. "Sonny, you knew all the Mafia guys in New York . . . right?"

Sonny is doing leg squats. "Yeah . . . why?"

"Did you know a guy named . . . Giuseppe Loganno?"

Sonny stands up straight now. "Yeah . . . what about him?"

"He died yesterday . . . it says in the paper there's a war goin' on over his territory."

Sonny reaches for the paper. "Lemme see that article."

As he scans it, Bear says, "Did you know him?"

"Yeah . . . I've heard of him." Bear puts down the bar. "It says he died a natural death and he was in his late seventies. That's sayin' somethin', isn't it, for a guy in that kinda racket."

Sonny nods sadly. "Yep . . . it certainly is." He drops the paper and puts on his shirt.

"Where ya goin', Sonny?"

"Bear . . . I don't really feel like workin' out today . . . I think I'm gonna go over to the chapel and say a couple of prayers."

When Sonny gets there, he prays for the old man who was such an important influence on him. In his own way the don had taught Sonny about love and honor among men. He says a rosary to the Blessed Virgin that she intercede for the repose of the soul of Giuseppe Loganno.

Six months after the don's death and Sonny's unsuccessful appeal attempt, Skeeter comes over to him in the chow hall at breakfast. He sits down next to him, and for the first few minutes watches a large pat of margarine melt on his oatmeal. "Ya hear what happened to the Choker?"

"No . . . what?"

"Well, ya know, after your food investigation he got transferred to the state pen. The guys here had been tryin to get the Choker for a long time, but he always had a lotta other guards around him in the kitchen. At the pen he went to work in the infirmary again and pulled the same shit on the sick guys . . . blowing smoke up their noses, the whole kaboodle. Well, Choker was finally kicked out and sent to the gym. Since there's only a couple of guards on duty there, everybody figured it'd be a perfect place to get him. They started about six different fights, hopin' the guards would go break it up and Choker'd be there alone . . . ya know he never gave a shit if two guys killed each other."

Sonny says, "Yeah . . . he's not the only guard like that."

"I know . . . anyway, every time there was trouble, Choker always went with the other pigs . . . until the last time. He got stuck on the gym phone talkin' to the warden. As soon as his buddies left, the guys locked the door. Seven of 'em raped the Choker . . . then they broke a bottle up his ass." Skeeter laughs. "Hot damn . . . he'll probably have to shit outta his mouth for a year. I can't wait to see who they try and blame this one on."

Sonny shakes his head. "You can't really blame the Choker or the guys for what happened . . . the system created the hate between 'em."

Skeeter mushes his oatmeal around in the bowl. "Well, you're lucky to be gettin' outta here . . . I saw an authorization in the office for your transfer." The country convict works for the superintendent, and tells Sonny his destination.

Sonny laughs. "Now I really know you're crazy. Even if they did send me someplace, it wouldn't be there . . . that's where I wanna go. But I can't even request a transfer till 1986. You better get your eyes checked, Skeeter."

"Sonny, I'm tellin' ya, it's true. There were some fancy newspaper people nosyin' around up here about two weeks ago askin' about that there food investigation y'all did. Well, ya know, the other three guys on the food committee got paroled or transferred." This makes more sense to Sonny than any benevolence on the part of the superintendent.

"Yeah, but it's a miracle if they're sending me there . . . they could send me anywhere."

Skeeter shakes his head. "Nope, they'd never take ya back at the state pen, and what other warden wants a guy who's listed as an instigator and OC?"

"Who's the warden over there?"

"His name's Larry Carpenter. Stories are he's a pretty good guy."

Sonny is still puzzled. "I wonder why they accepted me?"

Skeeter observes, "You must have one hell of a guardian angel watchin' over you Sonny."

"Yeah . . ."

Sheeter's information turns out to be correct. A transfer has come through.

In a way Sonny will be sorry to leave. One of his best friends must stay behind . . . the Blessed Virgin statue. She was with him through the fight with Big Monty, his schooling, the food investigation, and all of the trials he had to endure during his time there. There was, however, one problem even she had not yet been able to solve. On his last night Sonny goes to pray, asking that someday he will be allowed to take communion. When he's finished, Sonny sticks his head into Father Schmidt's office. "Did you hear anything from the diocese yet?"

The priest sighs. "Not yet, Sonny, it may take longer than we figured. I'll let you know what's happening through Monsignor O'Leary at Southern. You'll like him."

"I can't wait to meet him."

Father Schmidt points to the chair next to his desk. "Sit down a minute . . . I don't think I'll be here when you leave tomorrow. I wanna talk to you for a few minutes."

Sonny takes a seat. "You know, Father, I still don't know how I got transferred . . . that's exactly where I wanted to go . . . it's only an hour from LA."

"Maybe you could put on some plays while you're there, have some people from Hollywood come to see them."

"I was hopin' to do that, Father. I know I'd never get any of those big-shot producers and agents to drive all the way up here. I'm gonna send out letters as soon as I have somethin' going."

"That's good . . . very good. Are you still going to continue with your rosary?"

"Sure I am."

"Good. I'd also suggest you start your fellowship there. We've only had one man killed since you started the group . . . that's amazing, Sonny. I hope Juarez can keep it going."

"I'm sure Ramon will do a good job."

Father Schmidt leans forward. "We both know how much you've changed, Sonny, but your file hasn't, and a reputation is a hard thing to lose. You have several to contend with now. There'll be the guy who wants to knock you down 'cause he thinks you're tough, and the one who wants to push you around because he thinks you'll turn the other cheek." The priest pulls a manila envelope from his drawer and hands it to him. "This should help you in your time of temptation."

Sonny pulls out an eight-by-ten glossy photograph of the Blessed Virgin statue. "This is beautiful, Father . . . I was afraid I'd have to leave her here."

The priest shakes his head. "Even without the picture, Sonny, she is always with you . . . remember that."

Sonny gets up and hugs him. "Thank you, Father . . . maybe you can come down and see one of my plays. I wouldn't be doin' them if it weren't for you."

"I'll try . . . but I hope you get some people in the industry down there. They can really help you toward your goals. You're good, Sonny. . . . they'll come see you."

Just then Skeeter sticks his head in the door. "Sorry to interrupt, Father Schmidt."

"That's O.K . . . what can I do for you?"

"I just wanted to tell Sonny to meet me on the weight pile this afternoon."

Sonny laughs. "Don't tell me you're gonna be a body builder now!

Skeeter replies seriously, "Nope . . . I got somethin' for ya I know you'll wanna see."

"What is it?"

"It's important, believe me . . . just meet me, O.K.?"

Sonny shrugs. "O.K." When Skeeter leaves, Sonny gives Father Schmidt another hug. "Thanks for everything, Father. Are you sure Monsignor O'Leary will get my communion papers?"

The priest laughs. "I think that's what I like about you most . . . your persistence. Don't worry . . . he'll get them." He smiles. "Good-bye, Sonny, and God bless you."

As Sonny walks out to the yard, he thinks about what a good friend Father Schmidt has been. He will certainly miss this priest. When Sonny gets to the weight pile, Skeeter is already there. The country con hands him a folded newspaper. "What the hell's this, Skeeter? Is this what's so important?"

"Open it . . ." Inside is a manila folder with Sonny's name and number on the top. The file is stamped CONFIDENTIAL. "Holy shit, Skeeter. How'd you get this?"

"Your dumb counselor left a whole pile of 'em on the warden's desk. They forgot to lock the door. I was lookin' for my file, but it wasn't there. When I saw yours, I took it . . figured you'd be interested in seein' it."

"Won't you get in trouble when they find out it's gone?" Skeeter grins.

"Nope . . . I locked the door when I left. They'll just think records have been misplaced."

Sonny starts looking through the papers. "Man, I can't believe this! The state is tellin' the feds I should never be paroled. My parole hearing's even in here." He thinks a second. "Why would the feds wanna know about me for parole? I don't even have a date yet . . ."

"You got a federal beef?"

"Yeah . . .I got indicted in the biggest mail fraud case in history. I conned the government and got probation, but they revoked it when I went to prison."

"Well, then, that's normal. Washington always writes to Sacramento to find out the status of a federal prisoner in state custody."

"Is that what this is? Boy, they sure don't give me a good recommendation, do they."

Skeeter leafs through the papers. He looks up. "You're never gonna get paroled by the feds when they see this report. You'll have to do all your time for sure."

Sonny grabs back the paper. "Maybe they won't see this if I got it."

"I dunno . . . they must have copies in Sacramento.

Sonny pats Skeeter's shoulder. "I appreciate you gettin' this for me. I know you'll keep it quiet."

The country boy smiles. "I don't even know what you're talkin' about."

"Skeeter, I'll never forget ya for this. What can I do for you? There must be somethin', huh?"

Skeeter's reply is sincere. "You already did a lot for me, Sonny, with your fellowship. I have a lot more confidence in myself now . . . especially with girls. I'm writin' to one in Bakersfield." He breaks into a toothy grin. "Gettin' that file for ya' was my little goin'-away present. We're all gonna miss you Sonny."

Two days later Sonny leaves for his new prison. When he gets there, he finds that his reputation has preceded him. Although he hasn't been in any trouble for over four years, Sonny is classified "Organized Crime/Dangerous." Soon after he arrives, he is told the superintendent wants to see him.

This is the third warden Sonny has known in his five-year prison life. Larry Carpenter is surprisingly cordial to Sonny. He looks more like a Midwestern insurance salesman than a prison official. Word has it that the men respect him because he is more liberal and innovative than most superintendents. There is an experimental program at this prison that mixes minimum-security with maximum-security convicts. So far there have been no repercussions, proving that men, even those considered dangerous, don't have to be caged like animals. Carpenter asks Sonny to have a seat and gets right down to business. "Father Schmidt sent me a very nice letter about you, Gibson." Sonny nods.

Now he knows who his guardian angel is. The priest knew this would be the best place for Sonny to continue his acting. "Gibson, I'm going to take personal responsibility for you while you're here—otherwise you never would have been transferred to this prison. You know, Gibson, this is the first time a superintendent has ever done this for a convict. There's a lot at stake here."

"I appreciate what you and Father Schmidt have done, sir."

The superintendent continues, "Monsignor O'Leary also recommended you . . . he's a good friend of Father Molinari's. I understand you were one tough character at the state pen."

He smiles. "We need a character like you around here . . . that's why I want you to give orientations for me. I want to set a precedent for the prison system. I think convicts should talk to the men when they come in."

Sonny is suspicious. "There'll be guards in there, too, right?"

"Yes, but—"

Sonny says sharply, "Then I won't do it . . . 'cause the men might think I'm a correction officer, and I'm not."

The superintendent thinks a moment. "O.K., then there won't be any guards."

This astounds Sonny. "You mean I can tell the men anything I want?"

"Yep, whatever you want." Carpenter adds, "Of course you have to tell them the rules, but the rest is up to you."

"O.K., Carpenter, you've got a deal."

"I'm glad you're going to do this for us, Gibson . . . the guys need one of their own to preach to them."

Sonny corrects him. "Wait a minute, I won't tell anybody to stop what they're doing, but I will tell them what will happen if they don't. If you want a preacher, I'm the wrong guy."

Carpenter concedes, "O.K., I told you to say whatever you want. I still want you to do it."

They shake hands. "Fine, Superintendent . . . I'm looking forward to it."

On the way out Carpenter stops him. "By the way, Gibson, I usually don't allow anything to be carried in the yard, but I'm gonna let you carry that cross. I've heard about you and that cross. Reports are, though, that you haven't used it in years to commit violence."

Sonny says solemnly, "Superintendent, that violent man you once heard about died in the hole in 1974."

Sonny's orientations are a mixture of Papa Mike's street smarts and Father Molinari's wisdom. The first day about thirty new commitments wait expectantly for him to speak. The second- and third-timers are especially curious about what a convict would have to say about the prison system. Sonny stands and paces in front of them as he had many times before the powerful Mafia dons and his executives, but this time he is helping men instead of talking about cheating them. Sonny tells the convicts, "If you have any problems, come to me . . . but I won't fight your fights for ya. If you guys have it in for each other, the best thing to do is stay away from each other. If ya can't do that, go duke it out in the gym . . . don't involve your buddies . . . somebody's bound to get killed. Don't judge other men. Innocent guys have been called rats and gotten stuck. One thing I would suggest strongly is that you get educated. There's a lotta dead time here. I learned to read and got a degree. If ya don't want that, then get a trade." Sonny doesn't tell them not to kill or take narcotics but he warns, "If ya get caught in here for a lousy dope charge, you're adding five more years. If ya stick a guy, it'll be ten or fifteen more years. If he dies, they'll try to put ya on death row. It just doesn't pay. I'm not tellin' ya not to carry a shank— you guys have to make that decision."

One smartaleck says, "My cell partner says ya use that cross like a shank. Rumors are you fucked up some guys pretty bad with it."

Sonny stops and sits on the edge of the old desk in front of the men. He speaks honestly. "Those rumors are true. I was even more violent than that, but there's a different man you're looking at today . . . that's why I'm talkin' to ya now, like a friend."

A voice on the side says, "I got somethin' to ask ya." Sonny looks over and recognizes the convict as a man who's served time with him at the state pen. Paul Wilkins had been paroled after eight years in-side . . . Sonny was sorry to see him back in prison. "What's your question, Paul?"

The sandy-haired man replies skeptically, "What's the scoop here, huh? Are you really a Christian, Gibson?"

Sonny pauses a second. His answer will be critical . . . proselytizing turns many men off. "Yes, I believe in Christianity, but I'm not a preacher. I leave that to the priests, ministers, and rabbis . . . I'm just a convict, same as you guys." This seems to satisfy Paul, so Sonny stands. "Unless there's more questions, that about wraps it up." He scans the group, but no one speaks. "O.K., then orientation's over. Remember . . . I'm not tellin' you guys what to do, I'm just makin ya aware of what can happen in here." As the men start shuffling out, Sonny calls to his friend, "Hey, Paul, ya got a minute?"

"Yeah, sure . . ."

He ambles over, and Sonny says seriously, "I remember talkin' to ya the day before ya got out . . . what happened?"

Paul waves his hand in disgust. "Aaaa, you know, Sonny. Just 'cause you're back on the streets, it don't mean nothin'. Ya can't get a job . . . nobody hires ex-cons. The PO officer fucks up anythin' ya got goin', tellin everybody how dangerous ya are. Then the old lady starts in with the naggin', and the kids, and the hassles. I hadda go back to sellin' dope . . . it's all I knew how to do."

Sonny shakes his head. "The years I been in, I've known about a hundred and fifty guys like you come back . . . some of 'em two, three times. Seven outta ten cons that get paroled end up in the joint again. All the guys I know that came back never tried to change. They sit in their cells playin' dominoes, poker, or pinochle, sellin' dope, or plannin' how to do their crime better when they got out. When they did hit the streets, they just bounced right back behind these prison walls."

Paul implores, "So what're ya supposed to do, huh, Sonny?"

"Like I said . . . learn a trade or get educated. Join the fellowship . . . the Scriptures made me think. I'm not sayin' to become a Christian or a Jesus freak, ya understand, but there's a lotta things you can learn from the Bible."

"Like what? How's that shit gonna help me find a job?"

"It can help. It'll change your attitude. A lotta cons go out bitter . . . fightin' the world. Nobody wants to hire a guy like that."

Paul sighs. "I don't believe in all that God stuff, but I'm ready to try anything. I'm tired a comin' through this prison system."

"How long ya in for this time?"

"If I'm lucky, I'll get out in a year and a half . . . "

Sonny puts a hand on Paul's shoulder. "Come to the Fellowship. We meet on Tuesday nights right here. One thing you'll learn for sure, Paul . . . you're not alone."

The superintendent is pleased with the success of Sonny's orientations. The men respect Mafia-and-the-Cross. When he talks about life in prison, they listen. After about two months, Sonny asks to see Carpenter.

The warden is finishing up a phone call when Sonny comes in. "Well, Gibson, what can I do for you?"

"Superintendent, I'd like to put on a play."

Carpenter is enthusiastic. "You mean an outside play would come in . . . real actors and actresses? Yes, I'd welcome that."

Sonny says tentatively, "No . . . I wanna put on my own play . . . I think I have enough guys to start a drama workshop."

Carpenter says firmly, "No, Gibson, that's out of the question."

"Why?"

The superintendent explains. "About a year ago one of the guys thought he could sing like Johnny Cash . . . he put on a concert for the other men. If you take a convict from his cell, when he could be making his dope or homosexual connection, you'd better be good, especially if you're a guy they see all day. Another thing—if there's a show, the movie is taken away that week. We can't have both . . . you'd better be great for the men to miss that. Anyway, this guy was terrible. The guys warned him not to put on another performance, but he was planning another one . . . so they killed him."

Sonny feels sorry for the poor impersonator but objects to the comparison. "This is different . . . I feel I'm professional enough to do this . . . it's what I've been training for . . . it's what I'd do if I get out. Acting is in my blood. I love taking a script and bringing the author's words to life on stage. Even when I do your orientations, I'm exchanging energy with the men. The exchange with an audience is even more powerful." Sonny looks at Carpenter. "You see, Superintendent, the difference between me and that poor guy who tried to imitate Johnny Cash is that I know how to control that energy . . . that's the art."

The superintendent is silent for a few seconds. He's never heard such sensitive words from a convict before. Finally he makes a concession. "O.K., Gibson. If you can get four other men, I'll let you do it . . . but you'll all have to sign a statement that we won't be responsible for what happens to you. If you agree to that, you can put on your play."

Sonny smiles. "Superintendent . . . you won't regret it."

Sonny combs the prison looking for four men who would want to be involved with his project, but he strikes out. The men here also think acting is for punks and sissies. Sonny does not take the cross on the yard, "requesting" the cons to sign up for the play as he had done with the drama course. Sonny would never force a man onstage knowing it could get him killed. The only convict who is interested is a homosexual writer, Eric Westerfield, who's been the prison newspaper editor for twenty-five years. Eric comes to their first meeting armed with ideas about plays he thinks the men would relate to. "Let's do 'The Odd Couple,' Sonny. It's about two men, and we could both be in it."

"Hold on, Eric, I'll tell you what these men can relate to . . . and it isn't 'The Odd Couple' or Shakespeare or 'The Glass Menagerie' or 'Man of LaMancha.' "

Eric huffs, "What's wrong with those? They're great plays."

"Yeah . . . they're great, but not for in here. They could get me killed. You're gonna write me a play where I can be five characters. I'll do them all myself."

"What? Even Richard Burton or Rock Hudson couldn't do that . . ."

Sonny smiles. "Nope, but I can . . . you just write, Eric. I'll act. We're gonna put on a helluva show."

The end result is "Poor Boy." When Sonny brings a copy of the finished play to the superintendent, he asks for a date he can start rehearsals. Carpenter thumbs through the script in front of Sonny. "I'm impressed, Gibson . . . it sounds like a good play . . . you got five char acters." He laughs. "Hey . . . I'll be interested to see who you got in this prison to play the priest."

Sonny smiles. "He's a very fine actor . . . we were lucky to get him."

"O.K., Gibson, you can start rehearsals tomorrow if you want . . . but don't forget, I'll need all the guys to sign that release." Sonny is still smiling, "No problem at all there. Thanks"

In the midst of all this preparation Sonny is sending letters to producers and agents asking them to attend the play. In the visiting yard one day he has some special instructions for Theresa. "I've been reading Uta Hagen's book, *Respect for Acting*. She says that the biggest agency is William Morris. I want you to write a letter and tell 'em what's happening. I want 'em to come see me."

Theresa is hesitant. "Sonny you're in for life . . . how are they going to help you?"

"They can help . . . if I get some interest from the biggest agency in the country, when I go to the board, they may let me out to do some movies."

She laughs. "What makes you think you could be in the movies?"

"I'm better than any actor I've seen on television . . . If I can perform for an audience of tough convicts, I can certainly work in front of a camera . . . Theresa, do you understand that's what I want to do when I get out?"

"I thought you'd start some kind of a company or maybe get a real job."

Sonny insists, "Acting is a real job . . . it's hard work, too."

"Oh, come on . . . anybody can act."

"That's not true . . . it takes a lotta skill and talent."

"Well, I don't know about that. Do you think you'll be getting out soon?"

Sonny is frustrated. "I dunno, but I wanna be prepared when I go to the board. I hope to have fifty plays under my belt by that time."

She sighs. "All right, who's this person I have to call, William what?"

"It's not a person, it's the William Morris Agency." He hands her a slip of paper. "Here's the address and the name of the person in charge."

"How do you know they'll talk to me?"

"They will . . . they don't have any convict actors on their client list, so that'll get their interest." Theresa sighs.

"O.K., I'll get in touch with them . . . especially if you think it'll help you with the board. Did you put in for a family visit here?"

"Yeah . . . I can't believe we blew that last one . . . I wish I had gotten transferred two weeks later. Now we'll have to wait another ten months."

She kisses him. "Remember what I said when you went in—I'll wait. . . . I'll always wait for you, Sonny, no matter how long it is. I love you." The horn blows, signaling the end of visiting time. As Theresa goes, she waves. "I'll tell you what these William Morris people say as soon as I know anything."

Theresa's calls to William Morris are successful, but the prison authorities refuse permission for the agent to attend. In spite of that Sonny is excited about his opening night. He is a smash. The men give him a standing ovation for his outstanding performance as the five characters: poor boy, his crooked attorney, a hard-core convict, a prison guard, and a priest. The convicts all congratulate him, saying that if he were eligible for an Academy Award, they'd give him *five* Oscars for Best Actor. Each characterization was unique and flawless.

The next day Sonny is somewhat surprised to be called into the superintendent's office at six A.M. Carpenter paces angrily in front of him. "You conned me, you tricked me, and you lied. I could have new charges slapped on you for forgery. You didn't have four guys, but you had their signatures . . . I didn't think those names rang a bell."

Sonny tries to reason. "Look, Superintendent, it'll be 1986 before I even go to the board again, so I don't care what you do . . . but you were there . . . you saw for yourself . . . the men loved it! Some of them have already asked if they can be in the next one."

Carpenter doesn't believe him. "You really got other guys, Gibson? Is this another con?"

Sonny holds up his right hand. "I swear I do, I'll introduce them to you."

Carpenter smiles. "I don't know why I should trust a Mafia con man with a perjury conviction but . . . O.K., Gibson . . . you can put on your plays. But those guys better be real."

This time Sonny wasn't conning the warden. A lot of men had expressed interest in being involved in drama now, so Sonny started a workshop. Using theater games, the men would improvise scenes with each other, and the best ones were taken as premises for Eric to work with. In four months Sonny put on eighteen plays. Theresa was proud to read in the prison newspaper about the acceptance he was receiving as an actor, but she couldn't possibly know that Sonny's love for the arts was greater than any he'd ever had for a woman . . . even her. His performances were always packed—the men loved seeing their own problems brought to light on stage.

Sonny was in the middle of rehearsing a new play when his eyes began to give him trouble. He thought he'd gotten dirt in them from the weight pile, so he went to the prison doctor . . . who found nothing wrong. But each day Sonny's vision got a little worse, until one morning he woke up almost totally blind. Now the prison doctor recommended that he see a specialist. Since there was no ophthalmologist at the penitentiary, Sonny was taken to a private hospital for treatment.

Dr. Haber turns out the light after just a brief examination of Sonny's eyes. He says with concern to the guard, "I want to talk to the superintendent right away . . . this man needs surgery immediately or he'll never see again."

Sonny asks anxiously, "It's that bad, Doc?"

"I'm afraid so, Mr. Gibson. You know what you see right now?"

Sonny panics. "I can't see hardly anything."

"Well, that's the best you're going to see if we don't get you on the operating table within twenty-four hours. Both of your retinas are detaching."

"How does something like that happen . . . are you born with it?"

"No, Mr. Gibson, the most common cause is a blow on the head . . . can you recall anything like that?"

Sonny remembers the brutal beatings the guards gave him, but he won't rat . . . even on them. "I can't recall anything like that. What's the success of this operation you're gonna do?"

The doctor says honestly, "Well, you might see twenty percent from your right eye, but you won't see anything out of your left one."

This is one of the few times in Sonny's life that's he's ever been scared. The doctor is telling him he'll be blind for the rest of his life. Sonny calls Theresa from the doctor's office and tells her the bad news. The doctor patiently explains the whole problem and the complicated operation to her on the phone. Sonny goes back to prison with the marshals to pick up some of his things, but he is brought back the same night . . . he'll be in surgery the next morning.

Two guards are posted at the door to his room when he's admitted, and they shackle him to the bed. As Sonny lies there, barely able to see the ceiling, he makes a deal with God. "If I ever get my sight back, and get outta prison, and can work as an actor, and be as successful as John Wayne or Clark Gable, I'll put my money to good use. I'll give half of it to help kids and convicts find themselves. I'm gonna build a vocational center for 'em. It'll help get guys jobs when they get out of prison, and it'll help keep kids from going there. I'll talk to kids, too, tell them what it's really like inside. That's my promise to you, God."

The operation the next morning takes two hours. The doctor finally comes out to tell Theresa and Pops the prognosis. "Mrs. Gibson, there is almost no hope at all that your husband will ever see again." Pops puts a comforting hand on her shoulder. They wait at the hospital until Sonny comes out of the anesthesia to be sure he is all right, but it's two days before he's well enough for a visit.

When they finally get in to see him, Theresa says anxiously, "What did the doctor say today?"

Sonny says frankly, "Not much. He can't really know anything for sure, but it doesn't look good. In a few days he'll take the patches off and look at my eyes."

"Did you know that Father Schmidt, Father Molinari, and Monsignor O'Leary are all saying special masses for you?"

"They are? . . . That's great. With that kind of prayer power I'm sure to be O.K."

"And I'm going to St. Jude services at St. Victor's for you."

Sonny knows about St. Jude . . . this saint has been haunting him for a long time. "What kind of service?"

"It's benediction, and the priest puts out petition forms for your requests. He says the seven-thirty Mass on Sunday for the intentions of the people who attend."

"You know what, if anybody could help me get my sight back, St. Jude could. He's the patron saint of hopeless cases. My mother used to pray to him that I'd change . . . look what he did for her." He reaches over to the night table next to his bed and gropes for his beads. "Come on . . . let's say the rosary together, O.K.?"

"O.K." They pray together. Soon visiting hours are over, and it's time for Theresa and Pops to leave.

Sonny says, "Don't worry, I have strong faith—between St. Jude and the Blessed Virgin, my sight's gotta come back . . . "

When they leave, and Sonny is alone, suddenly despite the patches on his eyes, he can see everything in the room. An intern in a white coat appears at the foot of his bed. He is in his early thirties and handsome, but his face has no real distinguishable features. The intern starts to speak, "God has heard the prayers of many." Sonny assumes he means the people who have been praying for him at the St. Jude services Theresa has been attending and at the daily masses the three priests have all been saying for him. The intern continues. "You will see better than ever. You will get out of prison and work as an actor. In the first year you will do at least two feature films."

Sonny argues, "Now, hold on, the doctors tell me I'm never gonna see again . . . I'm on a life sentence and won't even have a hearing till 1986, and you're tellin' me I'm gonna get out of prison and work as an actor? When? When I'm a hundred years old?"

The intern insists, "You'll be getting out of prison soon. Write your life story. The book will become a bestseller, and the film will take in one hundred million dollars the first year of its release. Half the money you make must go to help kids and ex-convicts. As soon as your sight comes back, start writing your story." He turns and passes one of the guards, Frank Jones, who is coming over to Sonny.

"What's wrong with you, Gibson, are you delirious? You're talking to yourself.''

Sonny points. "No, I'm not, I'm talkin to the intern that just left. What's his name?"

The guard looks behind him. "What intern?"

"The one who just left."

"There wasn't any intern here."

Sonny cracks, "Man, you guards are really alert . . . Hey, ask Anderson, he just came on duty." The blind man has clearly seen the name tag of the man approaching the bed.

Anderson asks in surprise, "Hey, how'd you know it's me?" Before Sonny can answer, he says, "I know, Gibson, you heard my footsteps."

"No, Officer Anderson, I can see your name tag." Sonny adds, "And you shouldn't carry those ballpoint pens like that, there's ink all over your pocket."

The guard looks down at his stained shirt. "Hey, how the hell'd you know that?"

Jones jumps in. "Yeah, how in the hell did you see it—you got patches over your eyes."

Sonny says in amazement, "I can see."

"Yeah, sure, Gibson." He turns to Jones. "He's always connin', isn't he?"

On the way out Anderson accuses Jones, "You told him, didn't you?"

The other guard is genuinely puzzled. "No, I didn't . . . really."

Anderson laughs. "Sure, sure."

Jones turns around to look at Sonny, but Sonny can't see the guard anymore . . . everything has gone black again.

The next day Dr. Haber tells Sonny that he has to go back into surgery. "We thought we repaired the damage the first time, but you need another operation. I'm calling in a specialist from Jules Stein Research Center. Your left retina is still torn. To get to the spot we have to go through the muscle. You should be aware of the risks. Even if we repair the damage, there is the possibility we may not be able to repair the muscle." Dr. Haber says gravely, "Your eyeball could float, and your eyelid may never work again."

Sonny's voice is calm, "Go ahead, doc, it doesn't matter what you do . . . I'm gonna see better than ever." Sonny tells both doctors about his vision—naturally they are skeptical about it.

Every day Monsignor O'Leary comes in from the prison to visit Sonny. He puts his hand on Sonny's patches, and together they say the rosary and the prayer to St. Jude. The priest also believes Sonny will get his sight back. After the second operation, however, the doctors still have no hope that he'll ever see again. For the next few days Sonny thinks about the mysterious intern. Sonny prays to the Blessed Virgin everyday for guidance. He moves his finger along each bead, saying, "Hail Mary full of grace, the Lord is with thee. Blessed art thou among women and blessed is the Fruit of thy Womb, Jesus. Holy Mary Mother of God pray for us sinners now and at the hour of our death. Amen." He moves on to the next one. "Hail Mary . . . " Sonny stops. The intern has materialized again. This time Sonny can see him even more clearly.

"Let everyone know, prophesy these things I say. You will see better than ever."

Sonny interrupts. "Are you from God? If you are, tell him I'm no saint, but I wanna take communion. Ask him when I can do that . ..." The intern repeats his message. "God has heard the prayers of many. Keep your promise . . . write your story . . . pull no punches, tell everything. You don't have to mention anyone else's name but your own, but tell everything. The book will be a bestseller, and the film will gross one hundred million dollars the first year. Practice looking at large letters in your cell to exercise your eyes. You will get your sight back."

Sonny is still skeptical. "If a miracle happens, maybe I could get my sight back and work as an actor. Maybe I could even out of prison and write my story, but a movie that'll make a hundred million dollars? I was a good businessman, and I've never seen a return like that for a film."

The intern insists, "Keep your promise to God, help convicts and kids on the street, and it will happen." The man vanishes as suddenly as he appeared. Sonny drifts off to sleep, knowing that only time will tell if this prophecy will ever come to pass.

A week later Sonny is released from the hospital, his eyes still bandaged—the doctors have classified him as officially blind. Just six days after his return to the state penitentiary he is called before the parole board for review. A new law has been passed requiring the Department of Correction to give all convicts release dates regardless of the length of their sentences. When Sonny is called into the hearing room, he is relieved to hear that Joe Vitone will not be reviewing his case this time. A woman, Mrs. Jane Michaelson, is in charge of this board. Two other members, a counselor, and Monsignor O'Leary are also present. Sonny cannot see Mrs. Michaelson's face through his patches, but her words come across loud and clear. "Mr. Gibson, because the superintendent has taken responsibility for you, and because of your outstanding academic record and contributions to this prison, the state is taking you off your life sentence. You'll be turned over to the federal authorities to finish out the rest of your sentence for mail fraud."

Sonny is dumbfounded at this news. Even though he expected it, he never thought it would come so soon. God must be as anxious for him to leave as Sonny is. "How soon will I be released to federal custody?"

Mrs. Michaelson tells him, "As soon as the federal marshals get here . . . most likely in thirty days. There is one stipulation however . . . we need you to sign a release."

"What's it for?"

Mrs. Michaelson explains, "It simply says that you will not hold the state responsible for losing your eyesight."

"Sure, I'll sign that . . . you couldn't have had anything to do with it . . . it was an act of God . . . where do I sign?" The counselor brings him the paper and guides Sonny's hand to the dotted line.

When Sonny calls Theresa to tell her the good news, she starts to cry, "I can't believe you're off your life sentence."

Sonny assures her, "I can, Theresa . . . God told me it would happen." She disregards his comment, "I know what God told you . . . what else did the board say? Why did they do this?"

"They didn't say why, Theresa, and I wasn't gonna stand there arguing with them. I guess it's just God's will." Sonny is unable to sleep that night. He is lying in bed, thinking, when he hears the rattle of a guard's keychain down the hall. He strains to identify the officer. It only takes a few times for Sonny to recognize any man's walk. Sonny knows every guard and convict on his block this way, but even when the footsteps come close, he still can't tell who it is.

A voice whispers urgently, "Gibson . . . Gibson . . . come over to the bars." The spicy smell wafting toward him confirms that this is a guard; convicts are not allowed to buy or wear aftershave. The voice says, "I want you to listen carefully, I haven't got much time. Everybody knows you went before the board today and that you're getting released, but do you know why you're getting released?"

Sonny says positively, "Yeah . . . God did it so I could get off my life sentence."

"No, Gibson, that's bullshit." The guard lowers his voice further. "I'll tell you why you're getting released. The doctor that worked on your eyes . . . he wasn't a prison doctor. He put down on his report that your retina was so badly torn, it must have come from the beatings you got in the pen. He got your confidential records, and they showed you had no medical attention for sixty-five days. The prison officials were so upset by his report, some calls were made to Sacramento . . . they decided to parole you to the feds. They were afraid your family might sue for prison brutality. A seven-million-dollar suit was just paid at a state pen to the families of two guys who died from their beatings."

Sonny thinks back to the parole board; no wonder they wanted him to sign a release clause. The prison was afraid he'd do the same thing because his injuries were sustained the same way. Sonny asks, "Why are you telling me this?"

The mystery voice replies, "Let's just say I'd like to see some changes made around here . . . men don't have to be treated like animals. Good luck in your suit, Gibson . . . sue their asses off."

Sonny wants to know the identity of his source. "Hey, who is this?" His only answer is the jangling of keys as the guard walks away. This nocturnal visit gave him the final piece to his parole puzzle.

Sonny didn't have to wait a month to be transferred to the federal penitentiary, he left just eight days after his hearing. The U.S. marshals had told Theresa that he would probably go to the more secure prisons like Leavenworth or Marion because he was still listed as a dangerous criminal Mafia/OC. Sonny went to four prisons around the country before he was finally sent to a federal penitentiary just forty-five minutes from LA. Because of his past record, when Sonny got there, he was sent to Cell Block D, maximum security. Eight weeks after his eye operation he went back to Dr. Haber for a checkup. The patches were removed, and the doctor was baffled by Sonny's improvement. He had regained half of his eyesight in one eye and was seeing bright light in the other, but the doctor was still dubious about a complete recovery. Sonny struck a bargain with Haber. "If I get my sight back and pass an eye test saying I don't need glasses to drive a car, will you read one book I give you?"

"Absolutely."

"Read it all the way through, doctor?"

"Absolutely." He planned to give Dr. Haber the same book that had changed his own life.

Most of his time was now spent in his cell, looking at cards with large letters to exercise his eye muscles, as the intern had instructed. Six months after his operation Sonny had 20-20 vision in his right eye, 20-30 in his left. He saw better than ever and decided it was time to write his life story. He went to the warden to get permission to start work on it, but was turned down flat. Prison officials were afraid he would be too candid about his years in the penitentiary. Sonny was forced to write late at night by the light of his makeshift, toilet-paper candle. As each chapter was finished, Theresa smuggled it out. Once a month a guest was allowed to attend Mass in the chapel. Sonny would conceal the manuscript in his pants leg and pass it surreptitiously to Theresa, who had sewn a hidden pocket into her skirt. Sonny still carried his cross with him to chapel and his fellowship meetings because they were religious functions, but the warden had forbidden him to carry it in the yard, in spite of the fact that other convicts were openly armed with sickles, tin snippers, and hacksaws. He knew what these men could do, but the warden has heard too many stories about the Mafia-and-the-Cross man's viciousness.

Sonny began another drama workshop. The men were eager to join, and before long the reputation of this group of convict actors— especially their leader—had spread. A producer from the Mark Taper Forum in LA approached Sonny about being in one of their productions, "The Far Other Side." Sonny was cast in the role of Terry, an ex-convict who has two personalities. He went to the warden to ask permission to appear at the Mark Taper, but Hanly refused to let a maximum-security prisoner, labeled Mafia, off the prison compound—especially not before the convict has a parole date.

Sonny goes to his counselor, Jack Beasley, for help, and to his surprise he gets it.

Beasley tells Sonny, "I like what you're doing in your workshop, Sonny, especially with Willy. You're the first person that's really tried to help him."

Sonny smiles. "That's because I look at him as a person, Beasley." The counselor arranges a special hearing with the federal board two days later.

The federal authorities are more lenient than the state, and Theresa is allowed to be present at this review. The official in charge, George Brock, is very polite, praising the things Sonny has done and the con- tributions he's made to his fellow convicts. After a few minutes Theresa is asked to step out of the room. As soon as she leaves, Brock says coldly, "Look Gibson, you're listed Mafia and you wouldn't testify for the feds. You'll have to do all of your time for us . . . we're not giving you one day extra. Your parole date will be December 19, 1979.

When Theresa sees Sonny, she knows. "They're going to make you do all of your time, aren't they?"

"Look, it's only another eight months. After what we've been through, that's nothin' "

She's puzzled. "I don't understand . . . they were so nice to you in there. I thought they were going to release you today."

Sonny thinks a second. "The parole board only sees me as Mafia, Theresa, they don't see the cross."

Sonny did accomplish his main objective of the review. He now has a parole date, and so he goes to the warden to get permission to do his play. However, this warden is not as liberal or as cordial as Carpenter was. A gruff, hardened man in his fifties, Al Hanly is waiting for his federal pension and doesn't want to do anything that might sink his financial boat now. Sonny shows him the parole papers. "Look, Warden, I have my release date, can I do the Mark Taper?"

"I changed my mind, Gibson . . . that's not good enough. This whole thing's too risky. The press would eat me up alive for letting a Mafia figure out to do a play."

Sonny knows this play could be the start of his professional acting career. With only eight months to go before release, if he could get some good coverage; Hollywood doors would open up for him. He cons Hanly. "On the contrary, the press will praise you for being the first federal warden to allow a convict actor out to do a play, and I'll talk about how nice you were to let me do it." Sonny assures him, "I'm not gonna say anything bad about this prison. This place is Disneyland compared to the state penitentiary system."

It works. Hanly says pompously, "You know, Gibson, I think you're right. It would be a very good thing for the men, too. It would show them that I'm on their side. O.K. . . . you can do it."

Sonny receives a script and goes over his part alone in his cell; the warden was not about to go overboard and allow him out for rehearsals. The week before the play opens, a TV reporter came into the prison to interview Sonny. Beasley was present to monitor what Sonny said and reported to the warden that Sonny's remarks were not uncomplimentary to federal penitentiaries—all of the unflattering comments were about the state penal system.

A few days later Sonny is on the six o'clock news. The men cheer when he talks about how the guards beat the convicts, the cruelty of the hole, the bad food. Big Monty and Ramon Juarez, who have also been transferred, come over to congratulate Sonny. They reminisce about the hard times the three of them endured at the state pen. The warden watches the news that night, too, and he is irate about the interview. Through the magic of editing it sounds like these things were all happening at his prison. Both counselor and convict are called on the carpet. As soon as the door is closed, the warden storms around the office shouting, "You son of a bitch . . . you're lucky you're getting out of here, Gibson, I'd love to transfer you to Leavenworth or Marion, I'd love to."

Sonny tries to explain. "Warden, before you go any further let me—"

"Gibson! Shut up! You listen to me, I'm through listening to you. If there was any way to get you out of that play, I would, but now I'm already on the hook."

Sonny tries again. "Warden, I didn't say anything bad about this place. I don't know what happened . . . I said those things about the state pen."

"Oh, don't hand me that, Gibson."

Beasley breaks in to support Sonny. "It's true, Warden, I was there . . . I heard everything Gibson said."

Hanly warns, "I don't care how it happened . . . no more interviews . . . that's final." He turns to Sonny. "And if you do one thing wrong, Gibson, I'm going to appear personally at the disciplinary hearing and recommend you do your year of parole inside. Forget about being home for Christmas . . . I'll keep you in prison for another holiday season."

Sonny knows the warden will write him up for the slightest offense to keep him from doing the play, so he is extra-cautious that week. Finally the cast comes into prison for the dress rehearsal . . . it is the first time the entire ensemble has been together. On opening night two federal marshals escort a handcuffed Sonny to the theater and station themselves outside his dressing room door. Everything goes smoothly that first night, and some reporters and critics are allowed backstage afterward. One of them asks, "How do you think Hollywood will compare with the Mafia, Sonny?"

He thinks for a second. "Well, a lot of it is run the same way, but with Hollywood at least there are retakes. When you're with the Mafia and conning a corporation out of millions of dollars, you have to give an Academy Award performance every time . . . there are no second chances."

The marshals interrupt the small press conference. "Awright, Gibson . . . it's time to go." When everyone leaves, the guards cuff him for the ride back to prison.

The next night, about twenty minutes before curtain, Sonny hears someone out talking to the marshals outside his dressing room. "Got a report there's a broken light bulb in there. They sent me to fix it."

The guards take a look at the man's theater ID and wave him in, "Awright, go ahead, but make it quick."

The convict actor is seated at the makeup table when the short Italian enters the room. Sonny discovers immediately that this is not a licensed electrician. As the man unscrews the broken bulb, he says, "The guys from the East Coast got a job for ya. They'll pay real good 'cause they know you're the best. You gotta get rid of the Weasel."

Sonny knows this name. "You mean Jimmy Fratianno?"

"Yeah, he worked with Frank the Bump. The guys back there know they should've listened to ya and had 'em both knocked off years ago." These two men worked as enforcers at one time for the Matrano family. It was always Sonny's belief that Bompensiero (Frank the Bump) was giving information to the government about the San Diego family's operations. The mystery technician continues, "Did ya hear what happened?"

"No . . ."

"The Weasel's rattin' on some of the guys, he's gonna rat all around the country." He hands Sonny a slip of paper. "Here's the number of a pay phone in the Century Plaza Hotel. Be there at three P.M. the day after you get out. There'll be a note behind the phone tellin' ya where your money's at for the job. Ya get half then and half when the Weasel's hit. When ya pick up the bread, you'll get all the details on Fratianno.

One of the FBI guys is workin' with us."

Sonny says gravely, "Listen carefully, so you understand, and tell this to all the guys, O.K.? I don't do that anymore . . . I've changed." He tears up the paper and hands him back the pieces. "It's time to put on a show, man. If ya wanna watch my acting, you can stay . . . that's my job now."

The man protests. "Gettin' rid of the Weasel would do a lot for the families . . . he's the biggest rat since Valachi."

Sonny stands. "I can do a lot more for the families by praying for 'em. Tell the guys I'll remember 'em in my rosary." The man takes his broken bulb and leaves. That night Sonny gives one of the best performances of the run.

On the fourth night Rory Calhoun comes back to see him. After congratulating Sonny on a fine performance he says, to Sonny's surprise, "I met you years ago when you had the Lucky Ace, in the Bahamas. You were a little heavier then."

Sonny laughs. "I guess I was . . . I feel a lot better now."

The actor enthuses, "I was just interviewed by *Casting Call*—that's an industry paper. I gave you a very nice review. I think you're a hell of an actor." He pulls something from his wallet. "I believe in your acting so much I'd like to try and help you. Here's my card. Give me a call when you get out."

The guard breaks in rudely. "We gotta get back, Gibson . . . let's go."

Sonny is annoyed; he really wanted advice from a veteran actor who knows the ropes. "I have to leave, Mr. Calhoun, but maybe you could come up to the prison sometime." Sonny frowns. "I guess you wouldn't wanna do that."

Rory says quickly, "No, I'd like to. How about Sunday? Can I come up on Sunday?"

"Well, I have to get permission from the warden."

A star-struck guard calls out, "We'll get the approval for Mr. Calhoun to come in. When you come up, can you bring a picture, Mr. Calhoun, so I can give it to my kid? His name is Bobby."

Rory smiles. "Sure." He turns to Sonny. "See you Sunday."

When Theresa comes up that week she has a copy of *Casting Call* with her. Sonny reads Rory's comments as he and Theresa wait for the famous actor to arrive. "Listen to this, baby. 'Sonny brings out the honesty in the characters he portrays. I said it before and I'll say it again, this young actor is going places in Hollywood.' "

Sonny is thrilled by the review. "Theresa, this man has been around a long time . . . he's a fine actor himself and he has confidence in me." This is the first judgment Sonny has had from one of those he now considers his peers.

Suddenly there is a burst of excitement on the yard . . . Rory has arrived. One man calls out, "Hey, Mr. Calhoun, you were great in *Marco Polo*, that's my favorite movie." Rory has to sign a few autographs on his way across the yard. After Sonny introduces the actor to Theresa, he says, "I read *Casting Call* . . . I appreciate the nice things you said about me, Mr. Calhoun."

"I meant everything I said, Sonny. I do think you're good enough to make it."

Theresa excuses herself to let Sonny be alone with his new mentor. "I'm gonna go across the yard and talk to Big Sally. She's up here now."

"O.K., baby."

As soon as she's gone, Rory asks, "Sonny, how much money do you have? They say you've got millions."

The convict laughs. "Nope. All I'll have when I get out is the two hundred dollars they give you."

"You'll need more than that. You'll have to get your union card and some clothes. I'll help you get an agent, too."

Sonny is curious about his generosity. It is the rare actor who will take the time to help someone just starting out. "Why are you doing this? You really believe in my acting ability that much?"

Rory's eyes soften. "Yes, I believe in the actor I saw at the Mark Taper Forum, but it's more than that. I can sympathize with your situation. I did time at Springfield Federal Prison. When I came out, I worked as stable boy at Griffith Park. Alan Ladd gave me my break, and now I have a chance to repay it. I'd like to help you if you need it."

Sonny is grateful. "I certainly do need it . . . and I appreciate it, believe me."

As they walk around the visiting yard, Rory gives Sonny a few tips. "First you have to get an agent. Most of them won't do anything for you until you're on top . . . then they want to do everything for you. Don't depend on them, Sonny. You need one, those are the rules, but get out there and push yourself. Another thing, with your background you'll be getting a lot of offers to be a consultant on films . . . never work as a technical advisor unless you have a good role. Otherwise they'll just use you, and you'll never work as an actor." As they talk, Sonny thinks how lucky he is to have someone like Rory guiding him. He remembers with affection all of his teachers from the past and the wisdom they gave to him: Alfonso, who taught him awareness and discipline; Papa Mike, who taught him how to stay alive; Father Molinari, who taught him to read and write; Father Schmidt, who taught him how to love people; and now Rory, who is giving him the tools to be successful in the profession Sonny loves so much . . . the arts.

Rory stops near a guntower. He looks at it, then at Sonny. "You know, in my day they didn't even have a visiting yard, and the only drama we had was when we went before the parole board." He laughs. "Boy, you had to put on a hell of an act then."

Sonny assures him, "You still do."

Rory looks at Sonny. "One thing I know will never change . . . the cruelty inside. It still happens, doesn't it?"

"Yes, it does, Rory . . . and maybe I can help change that when I get out."

"I hope you can, Sonny." They hug. "Be sure and call me when you get out, O.K.?"

"I will, Mr. Calhoun, thanks again for comin' to see me."

Sonny's drama workshop at keeps growing. Soon he starts a classical masque theater, where all of the actors wear masks to indicate their emotions. This method provides the men with an outlet for their violence. Here it's all right to express your feelings and call somebody Nigger, Honky, Hebe, Greaser, or Wop—you're hidden behind the safety of the mask—but if you did that in the yard, it could get you killed. The theater also helps men open up and talk about themselves more freely. Sonny teaches them that to understand a character, you must be honest with yourself. He knows he is getting through to the men and that this is working faster than any group therapy session. Sonny has also convinced the warden to allow him to start an experimental program with some of the men in the forensic-psychiatry unit— those prisoners classified as mildly disordered. He feels that with a little patience and understanding he can reach these convicts too.

So far the program has been a resounding success. The first subject, Willy, a mulatto who's been ostracized by both blacks and whites, is responding well. Willy was a voluntary mute for three years before he joined the workshop. He had been raped the day after he was sent to prison, refusing to speak again. Now he is an active participant in the drama program and wants to be an actor when he gets out.

One day, when Willy is working with two other men, his guard, Officer Pearson, comes to escort him back to Forensic. Pearson is impatient because he has to wait until the scene is over before they can leave. Sonny goes over to pacify him. "Willy's progress is really amazing." They both watch his performance. After a few minutes Sonny turns to the guard. "Do you like the arts, Officer Pearson?"

The guard slaps his night stick in his palm as he speaks. "Yeah, I like 'em, but who said that's the arts?" He looks at Sonny. "Ya know Gibson, you give me a headache. I'm glad you're gettin' out next week. Everyday I gotta bring Willy all the way over here. It's a long walk from Forensic to the gym."

"Officer Pearson, if these guys can find themselves, even guys like Willy, isn't is worth the walk?"

The guard says cynically, "No, it isn't worth it. I've been here for eighteen years . . . five in Forensic . . . you can't never help them."

Sonny points to Willy. "But look at Willy, just look at him. He's talking . . . after three years."

Pearson says scornfully, "Yeah, he was probably faking it all the time. I wouldn't believe a convict if my life depended on it." He points to the actors in their masks, "And that . . . that's just fairy tales."

Sonny watches Willy for a minute. "No, it isn't . . . that's real . . . and it's a beginning. Maybe that's the trouble with prison . . . it's the end for too many men."

Pearson laughs. "Gibson, you're as crazy as he is."

Sonny looks at him hard. "Officer Pearson, that's exactly the kind of attitude I'm trying to overcome."

Sonny has taught Willy well. He's not afraid to speak up for himself anymore. That afternoon Willy goes up to the guard desk in the Forensic Unit dayroom. "Officer Pearson, can I change the TV to channel two? I wanna watch the soap opera so I can learn about acting."

Pearson looks up in surprise. "Willy, you never talked to me before. Sure, go ahead, change it if you want to . . . you know I have no say-so in there, the TV room is for you guys."

Willy goes back inside and turns on "The Edge of Night." As he watches the actors talk about problems that couldn't be more foreign to him, Charley Bates comes into the room. The white man stands right in front of the TV and switches the dial. Willy protests timidly, "Hey, I'm watching the soap operas . . . I'm gonna be an actor."

Charley laughs. "Willy, soap operas are for women. I'm watching 'Road Runner'—beep, beep."

Willy gets up purposefully and changes the channel back to two. When the actors come on the screen again, Charley's eyes glaze over. He gets up in a daze and walks to the corner of the room where Hank, another convict, is busy working on the plumbing. When Hank isn't looking, Charley picks up a small wood saw from the toolcase. Then he sneaks up behind Willy, raises the saw sideways, and with one powerful swipe chops off Willy's head. A shower of blood spurts from the jugular vein as the head rolls in front of the TV. Charley picks it up by the hair and walks over to the toilet. Without pausing, he drops it in the bowl. When Hank hears the splash he turns around, and is horrified at the grisly sight. The hardened convict runs from the room, screaming and choking on his vomit. Charley walks casually over to the TV splashed with blood, turns the channel, and sits down to watch "Road Runner."

When Pearson sees Hank running from the room, he goes in to investigate but stops short at the gruesome scene in the dayroom. Pearson starts yelling, "Oh, my God . . . my God . . . no!" Before he can even call security, the nausea churning inside him gives way, and he too rushes out, vomiting. In all of his eighteen years as a prison guard he has never seen such a gruesome hit.

At this time Sonny is in his cell, struggling with the job of putting his story down on paper. He's now convinced he needs a professional writer to help him. When the steam whistle blows for yard recall, Sonny looks up. It's too early for count. The cells open to let the men in, and as one of the convicts passes, he says, "Hey, Sonny, did ya hear what happened to Crazy Willy?"

Sonny sighs. "Man, don't call him crazy . . . he's not crazy."

The convict replies coldly, "Don't matter if he is or not anymore. Charley Bates just whacked his head off and stuck it in the shitter."

Sonny is stunned. "What?"

Another convict confirms it. "Yep, Hank was in Forensic workin' on the pipes. He said it was the worst thing he's ever seen . . . worse than anything that ever happened in Nam." The guard shouts, "Awright, awright, you guys, get in your cells for emergency count."

When the cell door closes. Sonny sits on his bunk in frustration. He was getting through to Willy. Willy wasn't crazy . . . how many other guys in Forensic were sane, too, but could end up like Willy, with their heads stuffed in a toilet bowl. In the excitement of his release Sonny had almost forgotten that he was still behind the walls of hell, and Satan's ax could fall anytime.

That evening Officer Pearson stops by Sonny's cell. "Hey, Gibson."

Sonny looks up. "What are you doin' here, Pearson? This is a long walk from Forensic, isn't it?"

The guard says humbly, "I wanna tell you somethin'. Willy talked to me today. I just wanted ya to know . . . I think what you're doing is good . . . the art shop . . . the mask shop . . . whatever you call it. First thing in the morning I'm going to the warden to ask him if he'll let some more of the guys in Forensic out to join that thing."

Sonny coaches him. "It's called a drama workshop, Officer Pearson."

"Yeah, well . . . I saw what it did for Willy. I hope I have a lot of walks over from Forensic from now on."

The only time Sonny leaves his cell that next week was for chow and chapel. Sonny knows that if a shank is pulled or a fight starts and he is anywhere near it, the warden could detain him for months. Sonny doesn't want anything to jeopardize his release.

Finally it is time for Sonny to leave the prison compound. He knows that the vision has predicted this day, but he can hardly believe it's actually happening. The night before he's released, Sonny doesn't sleep at all. He lies on the bunk, thinking about his life—the power he had with the Mafia before he came into prison, the first few violent years inside, his miraculous transformation. Sonny has made many different vows in his life, but none is more important than the one he has made to God . . . he will give half of the money he makes as an actor to build centers to keep kids from going to prison and keep men from going back. At eight o'clock the next morning Sonny goes to get his "dress out"—two shirts, one pair of pants, one jacket, one pair of socks and shoes—but before he goes to R & R, the warden wants to see him one more time.

In the office Hanly looks at Sonny solemnly, "You know, Gibson, some people say you're gonna end up back here . . . I hope you don't. I wish you a lotta luck in your career. You push . . . that's why you get things done." He stands and walks with his hands behind his back. "But I don't like those methods in my prison . . . that's why I cut off the reporters who wanted to interview you. I'm not a press agent for any convict." He stops and looks at Sonny. "Gibson, when you go to the window to get your money, you won't be getting two hundred dollars."

"O.K."

The warden pushes. "Don't you wanna know why?"

Sonny looks right back at Hanly. "No, if I don't get it, I don't get it."

Hanly paces again. "Well, I'm gonna tell you why. You're listed as Mafia and organized crime, Gibson. We don't believe your kind needs money, so we're giving you the exact cab fare to the parole office downtown—ten dollars and ninety-one cents. I wanted to let you know so you wouldn't cause a scene at the window."

Sonny smiles. "I wouldn't do that, Warden, but if you need that ten ninety-one, maybe you should keep it."

Hanly slaps his hand on the desk. "Gibson, that's the trouble with you, you're too independent and you're a smartass. Get outta here."

Sonny turns at the door before he leaves. "Warden Hanly, I'm gonna say a prayer for you at Mass next Sunday, so you can find some love in your heart for men, then maybe you could look at them for themselves instead of their numbers."

When Sonny gets to the releasing desk, a weathered lieutenant with white hair puts $10.91 in an envelope. "Here's your money, Sonny. I'm really sorry they didn't give you the two hundred. I don't think it's right."

Sonny looks at the brown envelope, then at the lieutenant, and smiles. "That's O.K. Can I have a pen, Lieutenant?"

"What for?"

"I wanna write somethin'."

The guard hands him a ball point. Sonny takes the money out. "What are you doing, Gibson?"

Sonny replies, engrossed. "I'm writing that my book will be a bestseller and I'm gonna win an Academy Award for my film. I won't open up this envelope until I'm on stage the night I receive the Academy Award . . . . And when I get it, that Oscar is not gonna sit in my house. It's gonna go around to all the prisons in this country and let men know what they can do if they really want to." Sonny puts the bills back in the envelope. After it's sealed, he says, "And ya know what this money's gonna do?"

"Not much these days." Sonny shakes his head.

"You're wrong . . . this money is gonna do a lot, Lieutenant. It will show men behind bars that they can be a success without pickin' up a gun or sellin' dope. If Sonny Gibson can get out of prison with ten dollars and ninety-one cents in his pocket and make it, they can make it, too."

The lieutenant shakes his hand. "Good-bye, Gibson. When you get that Academy Award, you can autograph your mug shot for me."

Sonny smiles. "I'll do that for you, Lieutenant."

At nine A.M. Sonny goes to the releasing window, where he's given his parole papers, is fingerprinted, and surrenders his ID card. The room is crowded with men waiting to say good-bye. Sonny shakes hands with all of them. The last two are Big Monty and Ramon Juarez. Both men have a hint of a tear in their eyes. They were the first two convicts Sonny saw as he walked down that long hall in the state penitentiary over six years ago. All of them have come a long way. Monty is getting out in a month and wants to work with boys' clubs, and Ramon will be released soon after. He's a minister now, and is going to go back to Mexico to work in the prisons there. Monty says, "I never will forget that left cross you and God gave me, Sonny."

Sonny smiles. "God smacked me with a left cross, too, Monty, only mine was given to me by a skinny little priest when I came out of the hole."

Ramon remembers. "Ya know, Sonny, when you came out of the hole, I was really afraid of you. I thought no one could ever be a human being after going through that."

Sonny tells him seriously, "I hope my experience can be an example that no matter how bad a person is, anyone can change. Sonny hugs his two friends good-bye, then picks up his box of books and his cross to start his walk to freedom.

Theresa has been waiting on the other side of the iron gates for over four hours. She watches the penitentiary compound, and every time the door opens, her stomach flutters. Several men have already come out to be reunited with their loved ones, but where is Sonny? Theresa paces nervously, afraid that something unforeseen has happened at the last minute to keep him from her. She would not believe Sonny was really free until she held him in her arms . . . outside those prison walls. Now the door is opening again. Her anxious frown quickly becomes a beaming smile as he walks down the steps. She starts waving furiously. Sonny quickens his pace, and when he's on the other side of the gates, she smothers his face with kisses. "I can't believe it, I can't believe you're out . . . I love you . . . God . . . I can't believe you're here." They hug for a long time. When they break apart she says, "I was so afraid something would happen. I couldn't sleep at all. I paced all night and thanked God you wouldn't have to be around these animals anymore."

Sonny looks into her eyes. "They're not animals, Theresa, they're men. I love them just as much as I love you. Someone has to care about them."

"Why does it have to to be you, Sonny?"

He looks back at the guntowers and the high prison wall with its coiled barbed wire, "Because I was an animal once, too." They walk to the car in silence. Sonny puts his box of books in the trunk. Theresa is crying, and Sonny's eyes are watering, too. They kiss passionately, then he says, "Hey, what are we doin' this for? . . . We've done a lot of that here."

Theresa nods. "You're right." She takes his hand. "There's a present for you in the car." She hands him a heavy jacket from the front seat.

Sonny is puzzled. "What's this for . . . it's seventy-five degrees today." "You're gonna need it . . . we're taking off for a few days by ourselves."

This idea is totally alien to Sonny. "We are? Where are we goin'?"

"Big Bear . . . I got a cabin with a fireplace . . . and it's snowing up there now. I borrowed some money so we could have some time alone together. We'll be able to get to know each other again."

Sonny smiles. "Well, let's go. I'm a free man . . . I can do anything I want . . . but I wanna call Rory Calhoun and I wanna stop at Little Sicily and see Joe."

She hugs his neck. "Why don't you make your phone call at Little Sicily?" She smiles devilishly. "We don't want to waste any time, do we?"

After six years of near abstinence Sonny's passions are exploding. "We sure don't . . . we've got better things to do."

On the way into LA Theresa chatters about Pops and their apartment and her job, but Sonny cannot keep his mind on conversation. His head is swiveling, looking at the scenery, thinking how incredible it is that just minutes ago he was in a cage, and now he's free. It saddens him to realize how many men are still there and in other prisons all around the world. Sonny would do something to help them now that he was out.

When they get to the restaurant, Theresa hides while Sonny goes over to Joe, who is seated at a table in the empty room going over the dinner checks from the night before. "Say, I used to work for Sonny Gibson . . . I wonder if my credit's still good around here."

Joe looks up blankly. "What's your name?" Then the shock of recognition hits him. "Oh, my God . . . Sonny . . . it's you! You've changed so much. You lost so much weight."

Sonny smiles. "Yeah, that's not the only thing that's changed. I'm not the same guy, Joe."

"Yeah, I heard. I think it's great." He pats Sonny's shoulder, "I heard you're gonna be an actor now . . . you're a natural for that. I remember when you did some pretty good scenes in here." They both laugh, then Joe says, "Do you have any money, Sonny?"

"No, that's all in the past. Rory Calhoun is going to lend me some . . . I'm supposed to call him now."

Joe smiles. "Listen, goombah, whenever you wanna come in here, I'll be happy to feed you . . . and if you have to take any big shots out to dinner, that'll be free of charge, too—he points a teasing finger at Sonny—"until you make it."

Sonny hugs him. "Thanks, Joe."

Sonny calls Rory to tell him he's out and that he and Theresa are taking off for a few days.

"Call me as soon as you get back. If you're gonna be in town for Christmas, come over to the house for a drink. Do you need some money?"

"Well, Rory, they gave me ten dollars and ninety-one cents."

Rory laughs. "When I got out, they gave me two-fifty . . . the feds must be getting generous."

This really makes Sonny laugh. "No, Rory, it's just inflation."

"Sonny, when you get back, I'll set up an appointment with my agent for you."

"God bless you, Rory. I'll never forget this."

After they say good-bye to Joe, Sonnny and Theresa take off for Big Bear but he's very nervous on the freeway. The ex-convict hasn't been in a car for over six years, and the traffic scares him. Sonny makes Theresa slow down, even though she's only doing forty-five. When they get into the mountains, he has a different problem. It's snowing heavily, and a warning sign has been posted that all cars must have chains. Theresa gets out and takes them from the trunk. Sonny breaks into a cold sweat when he hears the familiar rattle of steel. He won't have anything to do with them, but when he sees her struggling, he takes over. As Sonny puts on the chains, he realizes that he is truly free . . . these are chains for tires, not shackles for men.

They continue driving and are almost at the top of the mountain when Sonny says, "Hey, stop the car for a minute."

"What's wrong, honey . . . we're almost there."

Sonny stares out of the front windshield. "Nothin's wrong . . . we just have to stop." Before them is the biggest pine tree Sonny has ever seen. He gets out of the car and starts walking toward it. Theresa watches as he crosses the road. Sonny stands before the giant tree and looks up in awe at God's glorious creation. He swings himself up and starts to climb.

Theresa shouts, "Hey, what are you doing?"

Sonny calls back, "I've gotta talk to God." Theresa grabs a camera from the trunk and snaps him as he works his way up. The ascent is hard at first, but Sonny's strength coupled with his determination, helps him reach the top effortlessly. He straddles the fragrant branches and takes long, deep breaths of fresh, mountain air. It starts to snow. The flakes melt as they drop on his cheeks. Sonny revels in the beautiful panorama this lofty vantage point affords. There are no guntowers or barbed-wire walls to block his view of the forest around him. He looks up to the sky above and says with reverence:

"Thanks God, for giving me back my sight and allowing me
to be a free man. I know the time I spent in prison doesn't pay
back my debt to society. I can't take back the wrong I've done,
but I know that you have forgiven me. Thank you for helping
me find the arts . . . I'll keep my promises to you, Heavenly
Father. Please accept my prayer of thanksgiving."

Sonny's voice floats across the snowcapped mountain: "Our Father who art in Heaven, hallowed be Thy name. Thy Kingdom come, Thy will be done, on earth as it is in Heaven. Give us this day our daily bread and forgive us our trespasses as we forgive those who trespass against us. And lead us not into temptation but deliver us from evil. Amen."